Learning to Read across Languages and Writing Systems

Around the world, children embark on learning to read in their home language or writing system. But does their specific language, and how it is written, make a difference to how they learn? How is learning to read English similar to or different from learning in other languages? Is reading alphabetic writing a different challenge from reading syllabic or logographic writing? *Learning to Read across Languages and Writing Systems* examines these questions across seventeen languages representing the world's different major writing systems. Each chapter highlights the key features of a specific language, exploring research on learning to read, spell, and comprehend it, and on implications for education. The editors' introduction describes the global spread of reading and provides a theoretical framework, including operating principles for learning to read. The editors' final chapter draws conclusions about cross-linguistic universal trends, and the challenges posed by specific languages and writing systems.

LUDO VERHOEVEN is Professor in Communication, Language and Literacy in the Behavioural Science Institute at Radboud University Nijmegen and the University of Curaçao.

CHARLES PERFETTI is Distinguished University Professor of Psychology and director of the Learning Research and Development Center at the University of Pittsburgh.

Learning to Read across Languages and Writing Systems

Edited by

Ludo Verhoeven

Radboud University Nijmegen and University of Curaçao

Charles Perfetti

University of Pittsburgh

CAMBRIDGE
UNIVERSITY PRESS

CAMBRIDGE
UNIVERSITY PRESS

University Printing House, Cambridge CB2 8BS, United Kingdom

Cambridge University Press is part of the University of Cambridge.

It furthers the University's mission by disseminating knowledge in the pursuit of education, learning, and research at the highest international levels of excellence.

www.cambridge.org
Information on this title: www.cambridge.org/9781107095885

First published 2017

Printed in the United Kingdom by Clays, St Ives plc

A catalogue record for this publication is available from the British Library.

Library of Congress Cataloging-in-Publication Data
Verhoeven, Ludo Th., editor. | Perfetti, Charles A., editor.
Learning to read across languages and writing systems / edited by Ludo Verhoeven, Charles Perfetti.
New York : Cambridge University Press, [2017] | Includes bibliographical references and index.
LCCN 2017012403 | ISBN 9781107095885 (hardcover : acid-free paper)
LCSH: Language and languages – Study and teaching – Foreign speakers. | Comprehension. | Reading. | Reading – Social aspects. | Written communication – Social aspects. | Reading comprehension – Study and teaching – Cross-cultural studies. | Linguistic universals. | BISAC: LANGUAGE ARTS & DISCIPLINES / Linguistics / Psycholinguistics.
LCC P53.26 .L427 2017 | DDC 411–dc23
LC record available at https://lccn.loc.gov/2017012403

ISBN 978-1-107-09588-5 Hardback

Contents

Figures

Tables

Contributors

MIKKO ARO, *University of Jyväskylä*

CRISTINA BURANI, *ISTC Institute for Cognitive Sciences and Technologies, Rome*

MARKÉTA CARAVOLAS, *Bangor University*

XI CHEN, *University of Toronto*

JEUNG-RYEUL CHO, *Kyungnam University*

S. HÉLÈNE DEACON, *Dalhousie University*

SYLVIA DEFIOR, *University of Granada*

ALAIN DESROCHERS, *University of Ottawa*

AYDIN YÜCESAN DURGUNOĞLU, *University of Minnesota Duluthaa*

LINDSAY HARRIS, *Northern Illinois University*

ELENA L. GRIGORENKO, *University of Connecticut*

KEIKO KODA, *Carnegie Mellon University*

SERGEY A. KORNILOV, *Yale University*

KARIN LANDERL, *University of Graz*

KYLE LEVESQUE, *Dalhousie University*

CHUCHU LI, *University of Maryland*

SONALI NAG, *University of Oxford*

ADRIAN PASQUARELLA, *University of Delaware*

CHARLES PERFETTI, *University of Pittsburgh*

ATHANASSIOS PROTOPAPAS, *University of Oslo*

NATALIA RAKHLIN, *Yale University*

ELINOR SAIEGH-HADDAD, *Bar-Ilan University*

FRANCISCA SERRANO, *University of Granada*

DAVID L. SHARE, *Haifa University*

ANNA M. THORNTON, *University of L'Aquila*

LUDO VERHOEVEN, *Radboud University Nijmegen*

MIN WANG, *University of Maryland*

PIERLUIGI ZOCCOLOTTI, *Sapienza University & ISTC Institute for Cognitive Sciences and Technologies, Rome*

Classification of Written Languages

Asian Syllabic and Morphosyllabic Languages

1. Chinese
2. Japanese
3. Korean
4. South Asian alphasyllabaries

West Semitic Abjad Languages

5. Arabic
6. Hebrew

Indo-European Alphabetic Languages

7. Greek
8. Italian
9. French
10. Spanish
11. German
12. Dutch
13. English
14. Czech and Slovak
15. Russian

Non-Indo-European Alphabetic Languages

16. Finnish
17. Turkish

1 Introduction

Operating Principles in Learning to Read

*Ludo Verhoeven and Charles Perfetti**

For school success and participation in society, learning to read is obviously of utmost importance. In learning to read, children are confronted with the task of acquiring implicit knowledge of how a writing system works – how the written word reveals meaning through a layer of graphic forms. This layer of graphic forms has different properties across the world, classifiable typologically according to the levels of language the graphs represent: morphemes, syllables, and phonemes. All of these writing systems encode language in one way or another, often mixing levels. This volume considers this variability in written language and its impact on learning to read. Across seventeen written languages, the chapters address the relation between the spoken word and the written word, offering insight into how learning to read is affected by specific language and writing systems. In addition to revealing differences, core commonalities that center on the fundamental requirement of mapping graphic form to language are revealed. In this introductory chapter, we set the stage for seventeen language comparisons by providing diachronic and synchronic perspectives on written language, highlighting possible universals in learning to read – including operating principles on the part of the learner – and introducing the different orthographies to be reviewed.

1.1 Diachronic and Synchronic Perspectives on Learning to Read

1.1.1 Diachronic Perspective

Historically, the invention of written language – and thus reading – occurred in the fourth millennium BCE. Independently, but also as a consequence of cultural contacts, written language appeared in China (Yangshao culture), ancient Sumer in Mesopotamia, India (Indus valley), and Mesoamerica

* The editors would like to thank the Netherlands Institute for Advanced Studies (NIAS) for funding a workshop, "Learning to Read across Languages and Writing Systems," which formed the basis for the present volume. They also heartily thank the authors for their cooperation, and Lucy Wang and Lee Ann Weeks for their assistance during the editing process.

1

(Mexico region). Of those early writing systems, only Chinese evolved into a system that is still widely used today (albeit greatly changed).

Semitic alphabets were the first to map single graphemes to phonemes around 1800 BCE and set the stage for the emergence of Arabic and Hebrew *abjads*. (*ABJAD* refers to the first consonantal letter names: *a*leph, *b*eth, *g*amel, *d*aleth.) These abjads, which initially represented only consonants, gave birth to the Proto-Canaanite, or Phoenician, alphabet, which in turn gave birth to Greek with the addition of vowels (see Gelb, 1952). The Greek alphabet, the first to fully specify words into graphemes for both consonants and vowels, gave rise to the Latin, Cyrillic, and Gothic alphabets all over Europe, starting in the sixth century. With the fall of the Roman Empire, Greek stayed on to become the most prominent literary language. Starting in the seventh century, the spread of the Islamic religion allowed Arabic and Persian to become more prominent scripts and also led to the spread of the Arabic numerical system throughout Europe. The later renaissance in Europe initiated the revival of written Greek and Latin, with the latter giving rise to many language-specific adaptations of the Roman alphabet.

Up until the late Middle Ages, the act of reading was reserved for the elite (i.e., priests and scholars), with reading aloud the most common practice. Only during the last two centuries did literacy become more widespread, fueled by the industrial revolution and the spread of religion. The worldwide introduction of new technologies has produced personalized digital devices connected to the Internet with the further spread of reading and increased knowledge access for all citizens as a result.

1.1.2   *Synchronic Perspective*

Literacy rates vary greatly across the globe, as can be seen in Figure 1.1. Increased recognition of the personal, social, and economic value of literacy has fueled broader awareness of the need for increased literacy in areas of the world where literacy rates are low. Initiatives to develop and implement regional literacy have resulted in substantial gains in literacy levels for new generations. Recent worldwide census data show, moreover, that the adult literacy rate has increased from 83 percent in 1990 to 89 percent in 2012. In the population aged 15–24, 87 percent of females and 92 percent of males now have basic reading skills. Despite these gains, more than 700 million adults throughout the world are still unable to read, with almost two-thirds being female (United Nations, 2014). The illiteracy numbers and gender disparities are greatest in the so-called developing societies of the sub-Saharan and central regions of Africa and Southern Asia.

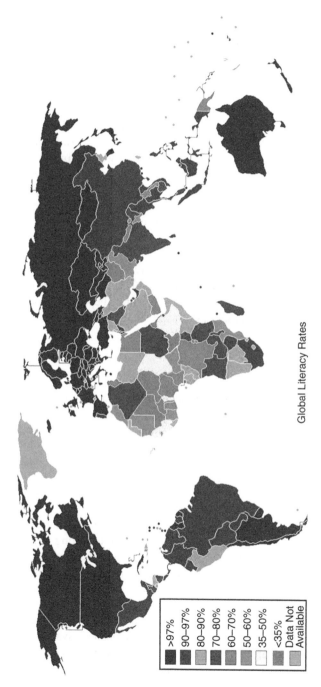

Global Literacy Rates

>97%
90–97%
80–90%
70–80%
60–70%
50–60%
35–50%
<35%
Data Not
Available

Figure 1.1 Distribution of literacy throughout the world.

1.2   Universals in Reading across Languages and Writing Systems

Writing systems can be typologically classified on the basis of the language constituents they represent: morphemes, syllables, and phonemes. Writing practices can intermix the different types of language constituents, as when Japanese is written using both syllable-based Kana and morpheme-based Kanji. Given the nature of writing and particularly the language constraints on writing, reading is universally grounded in both language and writing systems (cf. Sampson, 1985; Perfetti, 2003; Perfetti & Harris, 2013). Defined narrowly, reading is the decoding of language forms from written forms, and spelling is the encoding of linguistic forms into written forms. Learning to decode print into spoken language marks the transition from language to literacy and the literate use of language as a window for thinking. Indeed, beyond decoding, written language can also affect cognitive processes (see Olson, 1977). Given the diversity of languages and writing systems, we can expect the universal aspects of reading to manifest themselves at only very broad levels of consideration. And claims about universals of reading may constitute a universal grammar of reading (Perfetti, 2003). These claims cut across languages and writing systems, and they are elaborated upon in the next sections in which we consider the processes of word identification and reading comprehension.

1.2.1   *Universals in Word Reading and Spelling*

Universal 1: Reading Depends on Learning How a Writing System Encodes a Language   Figure 1.2 illustrates how language units are related to graphic units across writing systems. The basic assumption is that both reading and spelling draw upon a lexical representation containing both orthographic and phonological constituents (see Perfetti, 1997). It is useful to distinguish orthography from the writing system itself, although – like many conceptually clear distinctions – reality sometimes blurs the lines. The writing system reflects the level of writing-to-language mapping that is most prevalent in a written language; the orthography is the specific implementation of the writing system for that language. Thus, at the broad level of operating principles, writing systems can reflect a dominance of mapping at the morphemic level (with graphs corresponding to the basic units of meaning or morphemes), syllabic level (with graphs corresponding to spoken syllables), or phonemic level (with graphs corresponding to the minimal units of speech or phonemes). At the orthographic level, written languages show minor but significant variation in the rules for relating graphs to linguistic units. An alphabetic system, for example, can be almost purely alphabetic with one graph mapping to one phoneme, as in Finnish or Korean, or more mixed with graphs mapping to

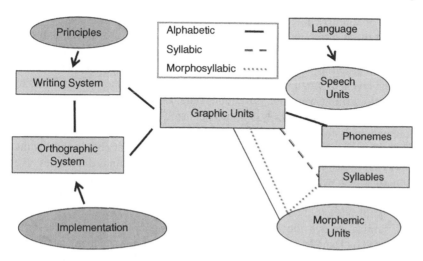

Figure 1.2 How writing systems map to languages.

both morphemes and phonemes, as in English, French, and Danish. Accordingly, Chinese, Japanese Kana, Japanese Kanji, and Spanish belong to three different writing systems, whereas Finnish, Italian, and English belong to the same writing system but have nevertheless different orthographies. A final and important aspect of written language is the script, which is closely related to the orthography of the language but defined more narrowly in terms of visual appearance and determined primarily by the written inventory of graphs and secondarily by font variations. Thus the scripts for Russian and Czech, which are both alphabetic Slovak languages, differ, with Russian calling upon a Cyrillic script and Czech calling upon a Roman script.

The reality of writing, however, blends writing system, orthography, and script. It is not as if writing developed via the random assignment of visual forms to different writing systems. The reality is that neither Roman nor Greek letters would do for the Chinese morpheme-syllable based system. Because there are thousands of morphemes to be written in Chinese, a set of 26 or even 200 letter graphs simply would not do. We thus tend to see the writing system in the script: Chinese morpheme-syllable based writing is adapted to its system of characters; alphabetic writing is only suited for abstract graphs, which give no clues to meaning.

Figure 1.2 reveals another simplification at odds with the reality of writing. It follows a tradition of tri-partite division (Gelb, 1952) to provide a view of the broad mapping choices available for writing. It is, indeed, fundamental to note these three well-defined levels of language (morpheme, syllable, phoneme) that provide mapping choices. However, writing systems have clearly intermingled these different levels of mapping, sometimes to a trivial extent – which thus allows English to be called alphabetic despite its low level of consistent graph-to-phoneme mapping – and sometimes to a deeper extent – with the levels of language systematically intertwined. The earliest forms of alphabetic writing were not fully alphabetic; they represented only consonants with graphs; and this system has persisted through modern Arabic and Hebrew which, following Daniels and Bright (1996), we refer to as an *abjad*. It is correct to refer to these as consonantal alphabets, but abjad captures the unique position that this system has in writing. That is, abjads did not devolve from alphabets with the removal of vowels but represent, instead, an earlier phase of writing that moved from syllabic graphs to more informative phoneme graphs.

A similar case is the *alphasyllabary*, or *abugida* (to use another term introduced by Daniels & Bright, 1996), which is used to write many languages of South and Southeast Asia. Here, the consonant plus vowel is written as a single unit, determined by the consonant graph with variations representing the vowel. These two systems must thus be added to the fundamental triad of morpheme, syllable, and phoneme systems to reflect the richness of the actual development of writing systems.

Finally, an additional type of mixing that has caused some confusion should be noted. Korean is an invented alphabet with very clear graph-to-phoneme mappings. However, it displays its letters in spatially segmented units that correspond to syllables, which has led some scholars to regard Korean as syllabic or alphasyllabic. The fundamental mapping principle underlying the writing of Korean, however, is alphabetic.

Universal 2: Word Reading and Spelling Engage Phonology and Morphology The Universal Phonological Principle (Perfetti, Zhang & Berent, 1992) claims that both word reading and spelling activate phonology at the lowest linguistic level encoded by the relevant writing system: the phoneme, syllable, morpheme, or word (Perfetti, Liu & Tan, 2005). This claim follows from the general language constraint that all writing systems encode spoken language. For alphabetic writing, this phonological activation is driven by letter-to-phoneme mappings that converge on letters to allow the identification of a written word. In systems that represent syllables, graphic forms activate syllable-level phonology, both as pure syllabaries and morphosyllabaries. Alphasyllabaries have the potential to activate both phoneme and syllable mappings. Ignoring the details of the extent to which phonemic and syllabic mappings produce identification, all writing systems can be assumed to support the immediate activation of *word* pronunciations from printed word forms.

Reading Chinese differs in some ways from reading alphabetic orthographies and this fact has implications for general theories of reading. The lexical constituency model of Perfetti, Liu and Tan (2005) provides a general framework for word reading across writing systems. In this model, the interplay between the three essential constituents of a written word's identity is clearly recognized. The model suggests, as found in priming studies in a variety of languages, a distinctive time course for the activation of the graphic, phonological, and semantic constituents during the reading of Chinese but with activation of the phonological occurring only when a threshold of orthographic recognition for a character has been reached. This activation process stands in marked contrast to the cascaded activation of phonology during alphabetic reading and suggests both a universal activation of phonology during reading and specific procedural variation imposed by the specific writing system.

Within the family of alphabetic writings, variations in orthographic depth have also been found to affect word identification procedures (Frost, Katz & Bentin, 1987). Grapheme–phoneme consistency (high for shallow orthographies, low for deep orthographies) and morpheme recovery (higher for deep orthographies) can produce corresponding variations in reading procedures, as shown by comparison of reading in English with its deeper orthography to reading in languages with shallower orthographies such as German (Frith, Wimmer & Landerl, 1998), Spanish, French (Goswami, Gombert & de Barrera, 1998), Greek (Goswami, Porpodas & Wheelwright, 1997), Dutch (Patel, Snowling & de Jong, 2004), and Welsh (Ellis & Hooper, 2001).

The basic units of meaning and grammar are what is retrieved from word identification. In principle, these meaningful units can be retrieved via phonological recoding of the orthography or directly from the orthographic form. Some writing systems, such as those of Chinese and Japanese Kanji, may encourage direct activation of morphology from orthographic form while also directly activating syllable-level phonology (Perfetti, Liu & Tan, 2005). Although the parallel activation of phonemes and morphemes is possible and likely in Chinese, the more general situation is one of ongoing trade-offs. Alphabetic systems of writing have developed spellings that activate only phonology and spellings that activate both phonology and morphology. More generally: Writing systems appear to seek a balance between exposure of the language's phonology and exposure of its morphology, with an optimal balance point manifesting itself for a given language (Frost, 2012; Seidenberg, 2012).

These trade-offs of morphology and phonology in the writing system can further affect the procedural details for word identification. Models of reading developed on the basis of a single language and single orthography thus have limited generalizability unless compared across languages. In contrast, the parallel-distributed-processing (PDP) models originally developed for English (e.g., Plaut, McClelland, Seidenberg & Patterson, 1996) contain highly generalized procedures that may thus be applicable to the problem of learning to associate a graphic input with a language output in any language, as Yang, Zevin, Shu, McCandliss, and Li (2006) have shown for Chinese.

Universal 3: Familiarity Shifts Word Reading from Computation to Retrieval   Perfetti et al. (1992) suggest a third potential reading universal, namely that the divergence of sublexical (grapheme–phoneme; grapheme–syllable) phonology from lexical phonology (word pronunciation) tends to be restricted to high-frequency words. In keeping with this, irregular English spellings tend to occur more often among high-frequency English words. Similarly, in Chinese, the pronunciation of a compound character (which contains two or more components or radicals) is more likely to diverge from the pronunciation of its phonetic components when the character has a high frequency. Conversely, the semantic radical gives a valid cue to meaning more often in low- than high-frequency characters in Chinese.

These cross-language patterns of similarity can not only be cast as a generalization about the working of written language but also be shown to have deeper connections to underlying cognitive processing routines. For less familiar word forms, computational routines are generally called upon. That is, sublexical mappings to phonology (or morphology) are used to arrive at the pronunciation (or meaning) of the whole word. With increased familiarity, these computational routines become less necessary and retrieval from memory on the basis of the identified features of the whole word will occur. This assumption about the cognitive processing underlying word retrieval is part of the dual-route theory of English word pronunciation and an explanation of why regularity effects are restricted to low-frequency words (Coltheart, Rastle, Perry, Langdon & Ziegler, 2001). But the assumption also represents a more general observation about the nature of human memory-based information processing, which allows non-computational retrieval processes to operate more frequently as experience establishes addressable memory forms. This cognitive generalization aligns with observations of a range of frequency-based reading effects across languages – including the general effects of word frequency on word processing across languages, the minimal obstacles posed by irregularity for skilled readers of English, and the importance of character study for learning to read in Chinese.

1.2.2   Universals in Reading Comprehension

Comprehending what is read requires an array of cognitive resources that range from word identification, meaning retrieval, sentence parsing, referential

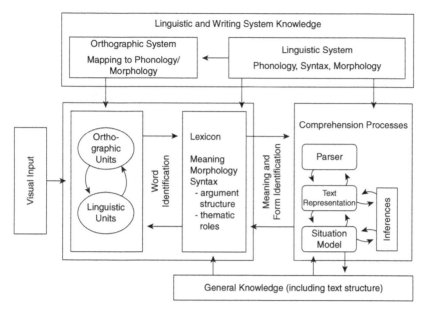

Figure 1.3 Reading Systems Framework linking the word identification system with the comprehension system using linguistic and orthographic knowledge and more general knowledge sources. (Adapted from Perfetti & Stafura, 2014)

binding, and text memory to relevant knowledge and the guidance provided by general cognitive structures. These reading comprehension processes are universal to the extent that they are part of the human cognitive capacity. They can be expected to vary across languages in relation to specific linguistic structures (e.g., word order, which effects parsing and referential binding) and writing conventions (e.g., word spacing, use of grammatically related graphemes such as apostrophes, commas, capital letters). However, the main influence of variation in writing systems is on word identification and its immediate outcome, the retrieval of meaning.

The Reading Systems Framework (Perfetti, 1999; Perfetti & Stafura, 2014), as depicted in Figure 1.3, provides a generalized model that captures the universal aspects of reading comprehension by linking lower lexical level with higher cognitive level knowledge sources and the processes they support.

Universal 4: Reading Comprehension is Driven by Word Knowledge (Lexical Quality) Both knowledge of word meanings (vocabulary) and the ability to retrieve this knowledge from written words are critical for reading comprehension. In other words, the reading comprehension of both children and adults is supported by knowledge of words and thus the reader's orthographic, phonological, and semantic representations, which can vary in their precision and interconnectedness (so-called lexical quality). Skilled readers are better able to take advantage of word training by remembering a new association between an orthographic form and a meaning than less skilled readers, for example (Anderson & Freebody, 1981).

According to the so-called lexical quality hypothesis (Perfetti & Hart, 2001), not only the quality of the reader's lexical representations but also the sheer number of available words can directly affect reading comprehension. In fact, there is strong evidence for an association between vocabulary size and reading comprehension (cf. Torgeson, Wagner, Rashotte, Burgess & Hecht, 1997; Verhoeven, 2000; Verhoeven & Perfetti, 2011b). Estimates further show large individual differences in the vocabulary knowledge of not only children but also other learners (Verhoeven, van Leeuwe & Vermeer, 2011). These differences can have major consequences for the reading comprehension process. According to Carver (1993), for example, deep comprehension of a text requires knowledge of virtually all of the words in the text. According to Wilson and Anderson (1986), moreover, large vocabularies provide increased opportunities for ideational scaffolding, inferential elaboration, orderly searches of memory, efficient editing and summary, and inferential reconstruction. In groups of people with high versus low knowledge of a particular domain, a strongly facilitating effect of vocabulary size on reading comprehension has also been found (Adams, Bell & Perfetti, 1995).

It should be noted that the association between vocabulary and reading comprehension may be reciprocal: The more one reads, the more one can deduce word meanings from surrounding text and, conversely, the more one comprehends, the more one's vocabulary may grow. In any case, reading comprehension can be successful only when word forms are readily identified and word meanings are easily accessed, which places considerable demands on the underlying linguistic capacities of the child.

Universal 5: Reading Comprehension = f (Word Decoding, Language Comprehension)   In the "simple view of reading," as proposed by Hoover and Gough (1990), reading comprehension is completely accounted for by word decoding and listening comprehension, with the functional relation simply the product of the two. Essentially, this perspective reflects the assumption that reading comprehension is the same as listening comprehension, once decoding (or word identification; Tunmer & Hoover, 1993) is at its asymptotic value. Thus, reading comprehension processes – the parsing of sentences into their constituent components, the drawing of inferences to establish sufficiently explicit relations within and between sentences, the facilitation thereby of the integration of information, and the identification of the propositional structure (micro structure) and global gist (macro structure) of a text – are all accounted for by strictly the reader's spoken language skill. This two-factor approach has indeed been found to account for most of the variance in reading comprehension as determined using standard assessments of decoding skill and vocabulary knowledge but also various assessments of spoken language skill (Verhoeven & van Leeuwe, 2008). The two-factor approach also illuminates the relative roles of decoding and listening comprehension in the development of reading comprehension. Decoding has been shown to be the main limiting factor for beginning readers while listening comprehension has been shown to be the main limiting factor for more advanced readers (cf. Carver, 1993; Bast & Reitsma, 1998).

For the two-factor approach to understanding reading comprehension to work as well as it does, two basic assumptions are necessary. (i) Vocabulary is assumed to be a component of spoken language rather than a separate third component. (ii) Listening and reading are assessed using equivalent texts, which are typically derived in actual practice from written rather than spoken discourse. These assumptions allow this simple view to indeed account for nearly all of the variance observed for reading comprehension (cf. Protopapas, Simos, Sideridis & Mouzaki, 2012). However, both of the aforementioned assumptions can be questioned. To allow the simple view to be useful for generalization across languages and writing systems but also sufficiently specific, we suggest the following: *For a given text in any language and any writing system: A reader can comprehend that text in its written form to the same extent as in its spoken form, if (and only if) the reader can identify all the words of the text and retrieve their meanings in their written form to the same extent as in their spoken form.* This formulation seems generally useful but, like the original simple view, its definition of reading comprehension in terms of two broad factors that exhaust both its meaning and its measurement borders on tautology. Described this way, the modified simple view is about the comprehensibility of a text rather than the reader's ability to comprehend. Comprehensibility, and particularly whether a text can be understood in its written as well as spoken form, obviously depends on the words and other aspects of language (syntax, morphology, paragraph structure, style, etc.). It is nevertheless also possible that a given text may, in fact, be more comprehensible in its spoken form than its written form (e.g., a speech or dialogue), or vice versa (e.g., a mathematical paper).

Whatever universals can be attributed to reading on the basis of the logic of spoken and written language, additional factors come into play for children to learn to read, which we refer to as operating principles.

1.3   Operating Principles in Learning to Read across Languages and Writing Systems

If reading development implies learning how a writing system encodes language, then operating principles can be posited that enable children to perceive, analyze, and use written language in ways that lead to the mastery of a particular orthography. Such operating principles for learning to read can be considered parallel to those proposed by Slobin (1985) for learning to speak.

Operating principles for learning to read are posited to enable the processing of linguistic input and the organization or reorganization of stored representations in order for the learner to acquire implicit knowledge of how a given writing system relates to spoken language or a given linguistic system. Figure 1.4 illustrates the general perceptual-cognitive framework that enables the development of the implicit knowledge needed to read. The central claim is that the same operating principles hold across languages and writing systems.

1.3.1   *Operating Principles for Becoming Linguistically Aware*

OP1: Attend to Salient Stretches of Speech as Indicated by Stress, Intonation, Rhythm   The acquisition of reading is supported by a learned sensitivity to the units of spoken language. To the extent that visual word identification in a language requires the connection of a familiar phonological form to a familiar or to-be-learned orthographic form, the quality of the child's phonological knowledge and processing will be essential. This is most

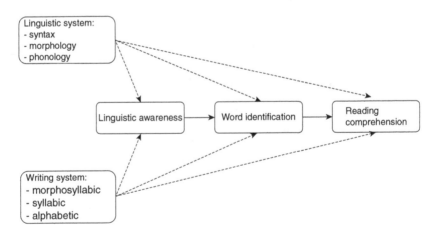

Figure 1.4 Model of how characteristics of the linguistic system and the writing system impact the development of linguistic awareness, word identification, and reading comprehension.

clearly the case when the phonological grain size is at the level of the phoneme, as for alphabetic reading.

Acquiring the alphabetic principle requires representations of phonemes. However, the speech signal is continuous and rapid with sharp modulations in both frequency and amplitude. The same speech sound can manifest itself differently, moreover, depending on the phonetic environment, speaker, and rate of speech. To solve the variability problem, the speech signal can be normalized, which then allows acoustic variations to be mapped onto canonical phonemes and thus onto spoken word representations within the mental lexicon (see McQueen & Cutler, 1997). With exposure to speech, infants can begin to parse the incoming acoustic signal into consistent, replicable chunks that come to represent phonemes (cf. Kuhl et al., 1997). By then attending to salient stretches of speech, which are typically indicated by stress, intonation, and rhythm, children can next build high-quality speech-based lexical representations. Moreover, stable and precise representations at the level of the phoneme are exactly what are needed for the efficient retrieval of word identities. The quality of word representation is thus dependent on the degree of specification, and only partially specified word representations may set the stage for impoverished reading development.

OP2: Attend to Any Salient Syllabic, Onset-Rime, or Phoneme Boundaries in Words   Learning to read in an alphabetic orthography builds upon a child's phonological awareness (Goswami, 2000; Snowling, 2000) or, in other words, their ability to attend to the sounds of language independent of meaning. Broadly, this awareness entails the ability to isolate words in sentences. Narrowly, phonological awareness entails the ability to identify sublexical units, syllables, rhymes, the beginnings of words, the ends of words, and phonemes. Phonological awareness is usually assessed using tasks that measure segmentation, blending, or the manipulation of speech sounds. It has been found to progress from the syllable and onset-rime levels to the phoneme level (cf. Liberman & Shankweiler, 1985; Shankweiler & Liberman, 1989; Treiman & Zukowski, 1996). In recent research, Moll et al. (2014) compared the roles of phonological processing (phonological awareness and memory) and rapid automatized naming (RAN) in reading development. They did this for a large sample of European elementary school children acquiring alphabetic orthographies that varied in the degree of grapheme–phoneme consistency (English, French, German, Hungarian, Finnish). Across orthographies, they found RAN to be the best predictor of reading speed but phonological processing to account for higher amounts of unique variance in reading accuracy and spelling. Interestingly, the predictive patterns tended to be stronger in the relatively opaque orthography of English than in all other orthographies. In other research, Shu, Peng, and

McBride-Chang (2008) examined the nature of phonological awareness in 4- to 6-year-old Chinese children. They found syllable and rime awareness but also tone awareness to gradually and steadily increase while awareness of phoneme onset remained at chance levels until the start of instruction on phonological coding (Pinyin) in first grade. In first grade, the variance in Chinese character recognition was best explained by tasks measuring syllable awareness, tone awareness, and speeded naming speed.

McBride-Chang, Bialystok, Chong, and Li (2004) investigated the role of phonological awareness for syllable phoneme onset levels in relation to the reading of Chinese and English by individuals from the Xian (China), Hong Kong, and Toronto cultures. Native Chinese speakers reached the same level of second-language English syllable awareness as native English speakers, indicating that the Chinese language may promote syllable-level awareness in children. The Hong Kong children read more words in both English and Chinese but performed poorer than the Xian children on both syllable and phoneme onset deletion tasks, suggesting that Pinyin training (given in only Xian) may promote phonological awareness even at the level of the syllable. In both Xian and Hong Kong, measures of syllable awareness consistently predicted Chinese character recognition better than phoneme onset awareness did. In contrast, English word reading was predicted differently by syllable and phoneme onset awareness across cultures. These results show both the languages and the writing systems to affect the development of children's phonological awareness.

Given that phonological awareness requires children to reflect upon the phonological segments of spoken words and manipulate these, an additional operating principle can be suggested: Attend to the sounds of language, as independent of meaning. This allows the distinct representation of multiple levels of speech units that can then provide the basis for the mapping functions of written language.

OP3: Attend to Written Language Signals for Their Connection to Language   Interaction with symbols in the environment and literate others helps children learn that print carries meaning, that written texts may have various forms and functions, and that ideas can be expressed with spontaneous (non)conventional writing (see Yaden, Rowe & MacGillivray, 2000). In the case of alphabetic writing, children learn that words consist of letters, which are linked to speech sounds. There is also general agreement that the development of literacy and mastery of an alphabetic writing system involves discovery of the principles of phonological recoding (Ehri, 2005, 2014; Leininger, 2014).

In the process of understanding alphabetic writing prior to instruction, children may begin with a limited collection of written words that have personal meaning for them. On the basis of an anlysis of the constituent sounds and letters encountered in these words, the alphabetic principle may then be discovered. And phonological recoding can be viewed as an inductive learning mechanism which helps children associate letters with sounds when they attempt to read a word (see Share, 1995, 2004).

If learning to read entails learning how one's writing system encodes one's language (Perfetti, 2003), then children must learn at least the following: (1) the inventory of graphic forms for a given writing system, (2) the orthographic units (graphemes) that connect to spoken language units (phonemes and morphemes), and (3) how specific orthographic units map onto specific phonological and morphological units of the spoken language. At a very young age, children may thus discover written language as a new modality of communication. By paying attention to salient script signs in the environment, they will gain knowledge at all three of the aforementioned levels. As a result of further analysis of the constituent sounds (phonemes, syllables) and graphemes of familiar words, they may then discover the more general mapping principle. Such self-learning is likely to be applicable across writing systems and orthographies.

However, for alphabetic orthographies, research suggests that such self-discovery is of limited use for most children. A more systematic approach that directly instructs children on the alphabetic principle and specific grapheme–phoneme correspondences is therefore required. For shallow alphabetic orthographies, such instruction is straightforward and noncontroversial. For deeper orthographies like English and the less reliable correspondences that occur in these, less straightforward manners of instruction have been explored. Nevertheless, even in English – or in English in particular – explicit teaching of specific grapheme correspondences still carries the day (National Reading Panel, 2000).

For beginning reading, the three operating principles discussed here reflect the importance of not only attending to spoken and written language but also having opportunities to link the spoken and written forms. Only then can the basic links between spoken and written language become apparent and an inventory of familiar written words be established or, in other words, the beginnings of the orthographic lexicon which is needed to learn to read. Additional operating principles are needed for the continued development of word identification ability.

1.3.2   Operating Principles for the Development of Word Identification

OP4: Increase the Orthographic Inventory The development of word identification requires the additional learning of graphic forms that might extend beyond beginning reading experiences, depending on the writing system. An alphabetic writing system has the advantage of calling upon a relatively small inventory of graphs (letters) across its various scripts; for example, twenty-four in Greek and Korean; thirty-three in Russian; forty-six in Slovak (Latin alphabet). This inventory can be mastered in the first year of instruction or even prior. However, the alphasyllabaries of South and Southeast Asia are more demanding due to generally more graphs and greater variation among consonant graphs containing implicit vowels. Chinese requires the largest inventory, with over 6,000 graphs commonly in use among the simplified set and many more in dictionaries containing traditional characters. Chinese therefore places the greatest demands on learning and requires more continuous learning than other languages. Note that there is no clear analogy between the semantic radicals found in Chinese characters and words spelled using an alphabet in other languages. In Chinese, for example, it is possible to have some idea of the meaning of a character without accessing its sound, which is typically not the case for alphabetic orthographies. Chinese words rely more heavily on lexical compounding, moreover, making them often more semantically transparent than words in other languages.

Even in alphabetic systems in which the number of letters is less than the number of phonemes, children must master more than just the letters to become literate. English, in particular, requires mastery of letter combinations that have become functional graphemes: *ea, ie, oa, th, sh*, and others. During initial phonics instruction, a small set of grapheme–phoneme correspondences is first presented and practiced within meaningful word contexts. Subsequent sets of graphemes are incrementally added to the baseline set of graphemes, and every time that a set of new graphemes is added, the full set of graphemes is again practiced within meaningful word contexts. In such a manner, children are given an opportunity to consolidate the grapheme–phoneme correspondence rules that they have acquired (Ellis & Ralph, 2000). There is clear evidence that systematic phonics instruction is highly effective for teaching children word decoding and spelling in alphabetic writing systems (De Graaff, Bosman, Hasselman & Verhoeven, 2009). Spelling practice helps children internalize the relevant rules in an efficient manner (Treiman, 1998). In a similar vein, Perfetti et al. (2013) have shown that the repeated writing of Chinese characters can improve the quality of the underlying visual or orthographic representations.

OP5: Increase the Inventory of Familiar Words through Reading In all languages, written words can become familiar perceptual objects that are then recognized more quickly. Learning to read fluently builds on this increasing familiarity.

Turning the unfamiliar into the familiar is relatively simple in shallow alphabetic writing. The first encounter with a new written word leads to decoding of the written form into its phonological form and initial familiarity; greater exposure may be needed for familiarity with deeper orthographies to grow. A mechanism that serves alphabetic reading of both deeper and shallower orthographies is the self-teaching device identified by Jorm and Share (1983) and Share (1995). An encounter with a word leads to phonological recoding, which is then, in turn, fed back to the word's orthography, initiating the word-specific identification process. Using this mechanism, only a few exposures to the same word can be sufficient for storage of the word's orthographic representation (see Share, 2004).

A high-quality orthographic representation can then emerge from this (Perfetti, 1992; 2007), with precision (this letter, not that; in this position, not that) and redundancy (phonology linked to both word parts and whole words, making the representation recoverable when one link is missing). The result is word identification driven, in part, by a familiarity-based memory retrieval process. Retrieval of word representations on the basis of familiarity can be assumed to be universal. And if such familiarity-based retrieval is functional in alphabetic reading – where it is not strictly necessary for the reading of a reliable (i.e., shallow) alphabetic orthography such as Finnish – then its importance in a language such as Chinese may be even greater.

When a systematic comparison of the development of word decoding in different alphabetic languages was undertaken by Seymour, Aro, and Erskine (2003), the speed and accuracy of the reading of familiar words by normal readers was found to be highly affected by both syllabic complexity and orthographic depth. Syllabic complexity involved the distinction between open consonant-vowel (CV) syllables with few initial or final consonant clusters and closed consonant-vowel-consonant (CVC) syllables with complex consonant clusters in both the onset and the coda positions. Orthographic depth involved the degree to which relevant orthographic patterns did not reflect and parallel phonemic representations. Decoding performance was relatively high in French, Portuguese, and Danish, while the performance of English-speaking first graders fell *far* below the levels of the other groups. English was classified as having the deepest orthography with many multi-letter graphemes, context-dependent rules, and irregularities. French, Portuguese, and Danish were also classified at the deep end of the scale. Orthographic depth effects parallel to those for the reading of familiar words were also found for the reading of simple nonwords: Faster and more accurate decoding was apparent for the simple syllable languages of French, Portuguese, and Danish; for the more complex syllable languages of Swedish and Dutch, this occurred to a lesser extent. The most striking outcome was the evidence of profound delays in the development of simple decoding skills in English (Seymour et al., 2003, p. 160). The high level of inconsistency of English orthography makes it hard to interpret the growth of word decoding over the years in terms of stages (cf. Aro & Wimmer, 2003; Ziegler & Goswami, 2005) and appears to call for an incremental learning process instead (Reichle & Perfetti, 2003).

OP6: Read to Gain Word Identification Fluency   Beyond establishing words as familiar, reading can also produce gains in word reading fluency. Highly fluent word reading is an effortless perceptual response that can include the automatization of word decoding, familiarity-based memory retrieval, and the attainment of fluent skilled reading. Moreover, these developments allow cognitive resources to be redirected to comprehension (Perfetti, 1992; Stanovich, 2000; Verhoeven & van Leeuwe, 2009).

Across different orthographies, the data show that parallel developmental gains in both word decoding speed and accuracy occur very rapidly after the start of explicit reading instruction, while steady improvements in the speed and accuracy of word decoding occurred in the years thereafter. The initially rapid building of the speed and accuracy of word decoding together with their steady and closely related development thereafter is fully commensurate with the restricted interactive model of lexical presentation (Perfetti, 1992). In this model, word decoding is assumed to increase the number of orthographically addressable words and modify already existing word representations. The sharp increase in the speed and accuracy of word decoding during the early stages of reading instruction suggests, moreover, that specific word representations develop fast but further improvement entailing increased numbers of redundant phonemic representations occurs more slowly. Thus, the development of word decoding can be defined as the acquisition of increased specificity and redundancy for lexical representations.

The cross-linguistic data also provide empirical evidence for the proposition put forth by Logan (1997), namely that reading automaticity should be conceptualized as a continuum and not a dichotomy. The learning curves that initially increase exponentially and later level off are similarly in keeping with the logistic learning functions featured in neural networks posited for the reading process under conditions of supervised learning (cf. Seidenberg & McClelland, 1989). It can thus be assumed that growth in word decoding entails children establishing strong connections between letters and sounds for a growing variety of words but also frequent retrieval of word forms, which fosters increased reading fluency and automaticity of word decoding. With this development and practice, children thus proceed from partially specified to fully specified representations of written words with the strength of the association between print and sound (or sound and print, for that matter) becoming increasingly automated. And it can be assumed that with sufficient reading practice, words are recognized by sight and the direct route to word decoding without the need for letter–sound conversion is opened up (Coltheart et al., 2001).

1.3.3   Operating Principles for the Development of Reading Comprehension

Automatic word identification allows mental resources to be devoted to the meaning of a text and thereby reading to be used as a tool for the acquisition of new information and knowledge. Figure 1.5 shows how word-to-text integration builds on incremental word identification during reading comprehension (cf. Perfetti & Stafura, 2014; Verhoeven & Perfetti, 2008).

OP7: Attend to Morphological Affixes   Current models of reading have focused on how letter strings are converted to phonological strings (pronunciations), essentially ignoring any internal structure that words have as morpheme units. However, reading more complex words across languages and writing systems may involve processes of morphological decomposition as well as identification of grapheme–phoneme connections and whole-word look-up. Morphological decomposition can be seen as a learned sensitivity to the systematic relationships among the surface forms of words and their underlying meanings (cf. Plaut & Gonnerman, 2000; Seidenberg & Gonnerman, 2000). Decomposition can be construed as a graded rather than all-or-none phenomenon with effects that vary as a function of the degree of morphophonological and semantic transparency of words in a language. Thus morphology, from such a connectionist perspective, emerges as a graded, inter-level activation pattern that reflects correlations among orthography, phonology, and semantics.

Theories of the morphological processes involved in reading can be classified according to their explanations of the identification and production of polymorphemic words – explanations ranging from full listing to total decomposition (cf. Verhoeven & Perfetti, 2003, 2011a). These two accounts have also been combined to create more interactive models that propose both a direct lexical route involving access to full form representations and a parsing route (cf. Schreuder & Baayen, 1995). In such hybrid theories, a race model with fully parallel routes is often proposed. A direct route applies when a full-form representation is accessed and mapped onto its associated lemma (meaning) node, which then activates the relevant semantic representations. The parallel parsing route includes segmentation and licensing processes. Segmentation implies that representations of affixes and stems are activated along with full-form representations. With the help of morphological knowledge, the constituent morphemes in polymorphemic words are identified. Final word identification is achieved when a unique entry in the mental lexicon is activated on the basis of the phonological, morphological, and semantic information associated with the lexical item.

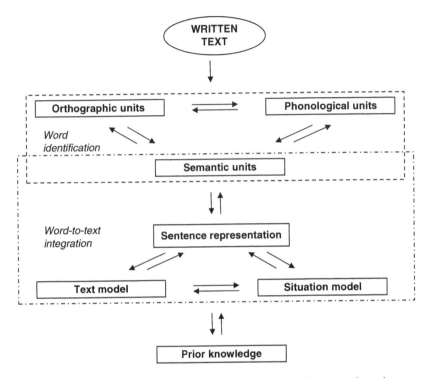

Figure 1.5 How word-to-text integration builds on incremental word
identification during reading comprehension.

The frequency of morphemes and their family sizes greatly impact the
speed and accuracy of word identification. Commonly used words are easier
to access and responded to faster than less commonly used words (Schilling,
Rayner & Chumbley, 1998). Family size or the number of words sharing
a given morpheme impedes word identification when it is small and facilitates
word identification when it is large. Schreuder and Baayen (1997) have
shown that the larger the morphological family, the faster the responses of
subjects on a visual lexical decision task in Dutch. Similar morphological
productivity effects have been found for a wide variety of languages, including Finnish (Hyönä & Pollatsek, 1998) and Hebrew (Feldman, Pnini & Frost,
1995). These findings can be interpreted as showing spreading activation
along morphological lines when morphological family members are co-
activated during the reading of a word. The more global the activation in
the mental lexicon, the easier it is to identify the target word as indeed an
existing word.

OP8: Parse the Text into Word Group Constituents and Sentence Boundaries Understanding sentences requires the identification of words. As a word is identified, the reader connects it to a continuously updated representation of the text. Studies of eye movements (cf. Reichle, Fisher, Rayner & Pollatsek, 1998) have revealed some important aspects of sentence comprehension during reading. First, even skilled readers fixate on most of the words they read. This suggests that word identification may lie at the heart of reading comprehension. Second, interpretation immediately followed recognition ("immediacy assumption"). And third, fixations tend to be longer at the ends of sentences. The latter finding indicates that integrative comprehension processes must take place at mostly sentence endings. Sentence comprehension can then be best understood as an operation which uses both sentence structure and word meanings to formulate hypotheses about the meaning of a sentence. The immediacy assumption, derived from studies of eye movements during reading, expresses this idea at a more general level.

Different theories about how words are attached to syntactic structures (Frazier & Clifton, 1996; MacDonald, Perlmutter & Seidenberg, 1994) agree on the conclusion that each word is immediately attached to a syntactic phrase. Neurocognitive studies provide further evidence for a neural (ERP) component sensitive specifically to processes that determine constituent structures (cf. Hagoort, 2005). In addition to the attachment of a word to a syntactic phrase, the word's referential meaning is attached to a semantic representation of the text. In such a manner, word-by-word processing leads to word-to-text integration. This so-called referential integration is necessary to maintain comprehension of the situation described by a text.

OP9: Pay Attention to Text Titles, Headings, and Paragraph Structures Titles and headings can be seen as signaling devices in expository texts. Both cognitive and educational psychology research has also demonstrated substantial effects of titles and headings on text processing. Titles have been shown to help activate prior knowledge on the part of the reader. When readers are given a disambiguating title for a text containing ambiguous referents, for example, they are found to be better able to recall text content and report better comprehension than without such a title (Wiley & Rayner, 2000). Furthermore, headings and paragraph structures have been shown to improve memory for text organization and promote text comprehension via the activation of prior knowledge on the part of readers (Lorch & Lorch, 1996).

For text comprehension, readers must combine the meaning of each sentence with the message accumulated up to a given point on the basis of prior text. This memory-based approach views comprehension as the product of the ongoing evaluation of the information from a text. Major models of text comprehension, including the construction-integration model (Kintsch, 1988), the landscape model (van den Broek, Risden, Fletcher & Thurlow, 1996), and the resonance model (Gerrig & McKoon, 1998), have all shown that text comprehension cannot be accomplished on the basis of only the information present in the text; readers must call upon prior knowledge to construct new knowledge that is relevant to their individual experiences and situations.

OP10: Supplement the Literal Meaning of the Text with Relevant Knowledge and Inferences   The propositional structure of the content of a passage of text delineates two types of structures: micro-propositional structure referring to the coherence of propositions with close proximity in the text and macro-propositional structure referring to the more global level of coherence and meaning. In keeping with this line of thought, readers are assumed to construct situation models involving two levels of representation as they attempt to comprehend text: first, a model of the propositions of the text (the text model); second, a model of what the text is about (the situation model). Basic meaning is extracted from sentences, progressively built with the reading of successive sentences, and supplemented with inferences, when needed, to make the text coherent. Because texts are never fully explicit, there are abundant occasions on which readers must make inferences about what a text is about and thereby draw upon their prior knowledge. It is this level of text comprehension that requires a situation model and calls for additional information to be added to/incorporated into purely linguistic-based accounts of text comprehension.

A situation model can help readers to identify and define problems, specify options for solving identified problems, generate problem-solving strategies, and observe the results of attempted solutions. The basic premise is that text comprehension requires a mental simulation of a referential situation and that these mental simulations are constrained by the linguistic and pictorial information contained in a text, the processing capacity of the human brain, and the nature of human interaction (Zwaan & Radvansky, 1998). The components of a situation model can include information from the text, inferences based on the text, relevant prior knowledge, and inferences connecting the text and prior knowledge (see Kintsch, 1998).

1.4 Learning to Read across Languages and Writing Systems

Reading engages cognitive language processes that are initiated by visual input from graphic strings. Cognitive and neurocognitive research has provided a variety of theoretical models for these processes and their acquisition. Nevertheless, the bulk of such research has been conducted on the English language, which raises doubts about the generalizability of the proposed models of reading and learning to read (see Share, 2008). A cross-linguistic perspective with dual lenses to view the language-specific properties of reading and the universal properties common to reading in all languages and orthographies can thus provide a fuller view of reading and learning to read. The present volume aims to facilitate this process with systematic analyses of a variety of languages, writing systems, and orthographies in relation to reading and its acquisition.

To achieve this aim, we brought together experts with a variety of multidisciplinary backgrounds (including neurocognitive science, cognitive psychology, developmental cognitive science, psycholinguistics, and education) to consider reading and its development in a variety of written languages. Our claim is that reading reflects a learned sensitivity to the systematic relationships between the surface forms of words and their meanings. This can be seen as a universal aspect of reading. Given that writing systems vary in how they represent the languages that they encode and languages substantially vary in their phonological, morphological, and semantic properties, however, we expect a wide variety of specific effects to reveal themselves across writing systems and orthographies. To address the role of universals and particulars in learning to read, we chose a broad grouping of languages and writing systems: Asian (Chinese, Japanese, Korean, Kannada), West-Semitic (Arabic, Hebrew), Latinate (Italian, French, Spanish), Germanic (German, Dutch, English), Slavic (Czech, Slovak, Russian), Greek, Finnish, and Turkish. These languages also represent the major writing systems, namely the syllabic, morpho-syllabic, alphasyllabic, abjad, and alphabetic writing systems.

Table 1.1 shows the distribution of languages and writing systems considered in this volume. The languages are grouped for convenient reference rather than according to linguistic typologies. For example, Chinese and Japanese are linguistically unrelated but nevertheless listed in the East Asian group.

When reading this volume, please keep in mind the extent of written language and the massive variety of languages read around the world. Our inclusion of seventeen languages is but a small sample of the world's languages and certainly underrepresents the languages read in South Asia

Table 1.1 *Distribution of languages and writing systems in this volume*

Language grouping	Language	Writing system
East Asian		
Sino-Tibetan	Chinese (Mandarin)	Morphosyllabic
Japonic	Japanese (Kanji)	Morphosyllabic
	Japanese (Kana)	Syllabic
Koreanic	Korean	Alphabetic (syllabic alphabet)
South Asian		
Dravidian	Kannada	Alphasyllabic
West Semitic		
	Arabic	Alphabetic: consonantal (abjad)
	Hebrew	Alphabetic: consonantal (abjad)
European/intercontinental		
Greek	Greek	Alphabetic
Latin	Italian	Alphabetic
	French	Alphabetic
	Spanish	Alphabetic
Germanic	German	Alphabetic
	Dutch	Alphabetic
	English	Alphabetic
Slavic	Czech & Slovak	Alphabetic
	Russian	Alphabetic
Uralic	Finnish	Alphabetic
Turkic	Turkish	Alphabetic

and sub-Saharan Africa. The languages we have sampled are nevertheless spoken by more than 3.7 billion people, which is more than half the earth's population.

In the present volume, the individual language chapters follow a common format to facilitate comparison across languages and writing systems. Basic information is provided on the language and writing system. Available research is then reviewed on the development of linguistic awareness of phonemes and morphemes, learning to identify and spell words, and the development of text comprehension. The implications of the findings for the process of learning to read are then presented to conclude each chapter.

This volume closes with a final chapter which discusses the universals and particulars in learning to read, as evidenced from the seventeen languages under consideration, and their implications for education.

References

Adams, B. C., Bell, L. C. & Perfetti, C. A. (1995). A trading relationship between reading skill and domain knowledge in children's text comprehension. *Discourse Processes*, *20*, 307–323.

Anderson, R. C. & Freebody, P. (1981). Vocabulary knowledge. In J. Guthrie (Ed.), *Comprehension and teaching: Research reviews* (pp. 77–117). Newark, DE: International Reading Association.

Aro, M. & Wimmer, H. (2003). Learning to read: English in comparison to six more regular orthographies. *Applied Psycholinguistics*, *24*, 621–635.

Bast, J. & Reitsma, P. (1998). Analyzing the development of individual differences in terms of Matthew effects in reading: Results from a Dutch longitudinal study. *Developmental Psychology*, *34*, 1373–1399.

Carver, R. P. (1993). Merging the simple view of reading with rauding theory. *Journal of Reading Behavior*, *25*, 439–455.

Coltheart, M., Rastle, K., Perry, C., Langdon, R. & Ziegler, J. (2001). DRC: A dual route cascaded model of visual word recognition and reading aloud. *Psychological Review*, *108*, 204–256.

Daniels, P. T. & Bright, W. (1996). *The world's writing systems*. New York: Oxford University Press.

De Graaff, S., Bosman, A., Hasselman, F. & Verhoeven, L. (2009). Benefits of systematic phonics instruction. *Scientific Studies of Reading*, *13*(4), 318–333.

Ehri, L. C. (2005). Learning to read words: Theory, findings and issues. *Scientific Studies of Reading*, *9*, 167–189.

    (2014). Orthographic mapping in the acquisition of sight word reading, spelling memory and vocabulary learning. *Scientific Studies of Reading*, *18*, 5–21.

Ellis, A. W. & Lambon Ralph, M. A. (2000). Age of acquisition effects in adult lexical processing reflect loss of plasticity in maturing systems: Insights from connectionist networks. *Journal of Experimental Psychology: Learning, Memory and Cognition*, 26, 1103–1123.

Ellis, N. C. & Hooper, A. M. (2001). Why learning to read is easier in Welsh than in English: Orthographic transparency effects evinced with frequency-matched tests. *Applied Psycholinguistics*, *22*(4), 571–599.

Feldman, L. B., Pnini, T. & Frost, R. (1995). Decomposing words into their constituent morphemes: Evidence from English and Hebrew. *Journal of Experimental Psychology*, *21*, 947–960.

Frazier, L. & Clifton, C. (1996). *Construal*. Cambridge, MA: MIT Press.

Frith, U., Wimmer, H. & Landerl, K. (1998). Differences in phonological recoding in German- and English-speaking children. *Scientific Studies of Reading*, *2*, 31–54.

Frost, R. (2012). Towards a universal model of reading. *Behavioral and Brain Sciences*, *35*(5), 263–279.

Frost, R., Katz, L. & Bentin, S. (1987). Strategies for visual word recognition and orthographic depth: A multilingual comparison. *Journal of Experimental Psychology: Human Perception and Performance*, *13*, 104–115.

Gelb, I. J. (1952). *A study of writing*. University of Chicago Press.

Gerrig, R. & McKoon, G. (1998). The readiness is all: The functionality of memory-based text processing. *Discourse Processes*, *26*, 67–86.

Goswami, U. (2000). Phonological and lexical processes. In M. L. Kamil, P. B. Rosenthal, P. D. Pearson & R. Barr (Eds.), *Handbook of reading research*, Vol. III (pp. 251–268). Mahwah, NJ: Lawrence Erlbaum.

Goswami, U., Gombert, J. E. & de Barrera, L. F. (1998). Children's orthographic representations and linguistic transparency: Nonsense word reading in English, French and Spanish. *Applied Psycholinguistics, 19*, 19–52.

Goswami, U., Porpodas, C. & Wheelwright, S. (1997). Children's orthographic representations in English and Greek. *Journal of Memory and Language, 45*, 648–664.

Hagoort, P. (2005). On Broca, brain, and binding: A new framework. *Trends in Cognitive Sciences, 9*, 416–423.

Hoover, W. A. & Gough, P. B. (1990). The simple view of reading. *Reading and Writing: An Interdisciplinary Journal, 2*, 127–160.

Hyönä, J. & Pollatsek, A. (1998). Reading Finnish compound words: Eye fixations are affected by component morphemes. *Journal of Experimental Psychology: Human Perception and Performance, 24*, 1612–1627.

Jorm, A. F. & Share, D. L. (1983). Phonological recoding and reading acquisition. *Applied Psycholinguistics, 4*, 103–147.

Kintsch, W. (1988). The use of knowledge in discourse processing: A construction-integration model. *Psychological Review, 95*, 163–182.

Kintsch, W. (1998). *Comprehension: A paradigm for cognition*. Cambridge University Press.

Kuhl, P. K., Andruski, J. E., Chistovich, I. A., Chistovich, L. A., Kozhevnikova, E. V., Ryskina, V. L., Stolyarova, E. I., Sundberg, U. & Lacerda, F. (1997). Cross-language analysis of phonetic units in language addressed to infants. *Science, 277*, 684–686.

Leininger, M. (2014). Phonological coding during reading. *Psychological Bulletin, 140*, 1534–1555.

Liberman, I. Y. & Shankweiler, D. (1985). Phonology and the problems of learning to read and write. Topical Issue (I. Y. Liberman, Guest Editor), *Remedial and Special Education, 6*(6), 8–17.

Logan, G. D. (1997). Automaticity and reading: Perspectives from the instance theory of automatization. *Reading and Writing Quarterly, 13*, 123–146.

Lorch, R. F. & Lorch, E. P. (1996). Effects of headings on text recall and summarization. *Contemporary Educational Psychology, 21*(3), 261–278.

MacDonald, M. C., Perlmutter, N. J. & Seidenberg, M. S. (1994). The lexical nature of syntactic ambiguity resolution. *Psychological Review, 101*, 676–703.

McBride-Chang, C., Bialystok, E., Chong, K. K. Y. & Li, Y. (2004). Levels of phonological awareness in three cultures. *Journal of Experimental Child Psychology, 89*(2), 93–111.

McBride-Chang, C., Tardif, T., Cho, J.-R., Shu, Hua, Fletcher, P., Stokes, S. F., Wong, A. M.-Y. & Leung, K. W. (2008). What's in a word? Morphological awareness and vocabulary knowledge in three languages. *Applied Psycholinguistics, 29*(3), 413–436.

McQueen, J. M. & Cutler, A. (1997). Cognitive processes in spoken-word recognition. In W. J. Hardcastle & J. D. M. H. Laver (Eds.), *The handbook of phonetic sciences* (pp. 566–585). Oxford: Blackwell.

Moll, K., Ramus, F., Bartling, J., Bruder, J., Kunze, S., Neuhoff, N., Streiftau, S., Lyytinen, H., Leppänen, P. H. T, Lohvansuu, K., et al. (2014). Cognitive mechanisms underlying reading and spelling development in five European orthographies: Is English an outlier orthography? *Learning and Instruction, 29,* 65–77.

National Reading Panel (2000). *Teaching children to read: An evidence-based assessment of the scientific research literature on reading and its implications for reading instruction.* Washington, DC: The National Institute of Child Health and Human Development.

Olson, D. R. (1977). Oral and written language and the cognitive processes of children. *Journal of Communication,* 27, 10–26.

Patel, T. K., Snowling, M. J. & de Jong, P. (2004). A cross-linguistic comparison of children learning to read in English and Dutch. *Journal of Educational Psychology, 96,* 785–797.

Perfetti, C. A. (1992). The representation problem in reading acquisition. In P. B. Gough, L. C. Ehri & R. Treiman (Eds.), *Reading acquisition* (pp. 145–174). Hillsdale, NJ: Lawrence Erlbaum.

(1997). The psycholinguistics of spelling and reading. In C. A. Perfetti, L. Rieben & M. Fayol (Eds.), *Learning to spell: Research, theory, and practice across languages* (pp. 21–38). Mahwah, NJ: Lawrence Erlbaum.

(1999). Comprehending written language: A blueprint of the reader. In C. M. Brown & P. Hagoort (Eds.), *The neurocognition of language processing* (pp. 167–208). Oxford University Press.

(2003). The universal grammar of reading. *Scientific Studies of Reading,* 7(1), 3–24.

(2007). Reading ability: Lexical quality to comprehension. *Scientific Studies of Reading,* 11, 357–383.

Perfetti, C. A. & Harris, L. N. (2013). Universal reading processes are modulated by language and writing system. *Language Learning and Development,* 9(4), 296–316.

Perfetti, C. A. & Hart, L. (2001). The lexical quality hypothesis. In L. Verhoeven, C. Elbro & P. Reitsma (Eds.), *Precursors of functional literacy* (pp. 189–214). Amsterdam and Philadelphia: John Benjamins.

Perfetti, C. & Stafura, J. (2014). Word knowledge in a theory of reading comprehension. *Scientific Studies of Reading,* 18(1), 22–37.

Perfetti, C. A., Cao, F. & Booth, J. (2013). Specialization and universals in the development of reading skill: How Chinese research informs a universal science of reading. *Scientific Studies of Reading,* 17(1), 5–21.

Perfetti, C. A., Liu, Y. & Tan, L. H. (2005). The Lexical Constituency Model: Some implications of research on Chinese for general theories of reading. *Psychological Review, 12*(11), 43–59.

Perfetti, C. A., Zhang, S. & Berent, I. (1992). Reading in English and Chinese: Evidence for a "universal" phonological principle. In R. Frost & L. Katz (Eds.), *Orthography, phonology, morphology, and meaning* (pp. 227–248). Amsterdam: North-Holland.

Plaut, D. C. & Gonnerman, L. M. (2000). Are nonsemantic morphological effects incompatible with a distributed connectionist approach to lexical processing? *Language and Cognitive Processing,* 15, 445–485.

Plaut, D. C., McClelland, J. L., Seidenberg, M. S. & Patterson, K. (1996). Understanding normal and impaired word reading: Computational principles in quasi-regular domains. *Psychological Review, 103*, 56–115.

Protopapas, A., Simos, P. G., Sideridis, G. D., Mouzaki, A. (2012). The components of the simple view of reading: A confirmatory factor analysis. *Reading Psychology, 33*(3), 217–240.

Reichle, E. D. & Perfetti, C. A. (2003). Morphology in word identification. *Scientific Studies of Reading, 7*, 219–238.

Reichle, E. D., Pollatsek, A., Fisher, D. L. & Rayner, K. (1998). Toward a model of eye-movement control in reading. *Psychological Review, 105*, 125–157.

Sampson, G. (1985). *Writing systems: A linguistic introduction.* Stanford University Press.

Schilling, H. E. H., Rayner, K. & Chumbley, J. I. (1998). Comparing naming, lexical decision, and eye fixation times: Word frequency effects and individual differences. *Memory & Cognition, 26*, 1270–1281.

Schreuder, R. & Baayen, R. H. (1995). Modeling morphological processing. In L. Feldman (Ed.), *Morphological aspects of language processing* (pp. 131–157). Hillsdale, NJ: Lawrence Erlbaum.

(1997). How complex simplex word scan be. *Journal of Memory and Language, 37*, 118–139.

Seidenberg, M. S. (2012). Writing systems: Not optimal but good enough. *Behavioral and Brain Sciences, 35*, 305–307.

Seidenberg, M. S. & Gonnerman, L. M. (2000). Explaining derivational morphology as the convergence of codes. *Trends in Cognitive Sciences, 4*, 353–361.

Seidenberg, M. S. & McClelland, J. L. (1989). A distributed, developmental model of word recognition and naming. *Psychological Review, 96*, 523–568.

Seymour, P. H., Aro, M. & Erskine, J. M. (2003). Foundation literacy in European orthographies. *British Journal of Psychology, 94*, 143–174.

Shankweiler, D. & Liberman, I. (1989). *Phonology and reading disability.* Ann Arbor: University of Michigan Press.

Share, D. L. (1995). Phonological recoding and self-teaching: Sine qua non of reading acquisition. *Cognition, 55*, 151–218.

(2004). Orthographic learning at a glance: On the time course and developmental onset of reading. *Journal of Experimental Child Psychology, 87*, 267–298.

(2008). On the Anglocentricities of current reading research and practice: The perils of overreliance on an "outlier" orthography. *Psychological Bulletin, 134*, 584–615.

Slobin, D. I. (1985). *The cross-linguistic study of language acquisition, Vol. II.* Hillsdale, NJ: Lawrence Erlbaum.

Snowling, M. J. (2000). Language and literacy skills: Who is at risk and why? In D. V. M. Bishop and L. B. Leonard (Eds.), *Speech and language impairment in children: Causes, characteristics, interventions and outcome* (pp. 245–260). Hove, UK: Psychology Press.

Stanovich, K. E. (2000). *Progress in understanding reading: Scientific foundations and new frontiers.* New York: Guilford Press.

Torgeson, J. K., Wagner, R. K., Rashotte, C. A., Burgess, S. & Hecht, S. (1997). Contributions of phonological awareness and rapid automatic naming ability to the growth of word-reading skills in second-to fifth-grade children. *Scientific Study of Reading, 1,* 161–195.

Treiman, R. (1998). Why spelling?: The benefits of incorporating spelling into beginning reading instruction. In J. Metsala & L. Ehri (Eds.), *Word recognition in beginning literacy* (pp. 289–313). Mahwah, NJ: Lawrence Erlbaum.

Treiman, R. & Zukowski, A. (1996). Children's sensitivity to syllables, onsets, rimes, and phonemes. *Journal of Experimental Child Psychology, 61,* 193–215.

Tunmer, W. & Hoover, W. (1993). Components of variance models of language-related factors in reading disability: A conceptual overview. In R. J. Joshi & C. K. Leong (Eds.), *Reading disabilities: Diagnosis and component processes* (pp. 135–173). Dordrecht: Kluwer.

United Nations (2014). *Human development report.* Geneva: UN Office.

van den Broek, P. W., Risden, K., Fletcher, C. R. & Thurlow, R. (1996). A "landscape" view of reading: Fluctuating patterns of activation and the construction of a stable memory representation. In B. K. Britton & A. C. Graesser (Eds.), *Models of understanding text* (pp. 165–187). Hillsdale, NJ: Lawrence Erlbaum.

Verhoeven, L. (2000). Components in early second language reading and spelling. *Scientific Studies of Reading, 4,* 313–330.

Verhoeven, L. & Perfetti, C. A. (2003). The role of morphology in learning to read. *Scientific Studies of Reading, 7,* 209–217.

(2008). Advances in text comprehension: Model, process and development. *Applied Cognitive Psychology, 22,* 293–301.

(2011a). Morphological processing in reading acquisition: A cross-linguistic perspective. *Applied Psycholinguistics, 32,* 457–466.

(2011b). Vocabulary growth and reading skill. *Scientific Studies of Reading 15,* 1–7.

Verhoeven, L. & van Leeuwe, J. (2008). Prediction of the development of reading comprehension: A longitudinal study. *Applied Cognitive Psychology, 22,* 407–423.

(2009). Modeling the growth of word decoding skills: Evidence from Dutch. *Scientific Studies of Reading, 13,* 205–223.

Verhoeven, L., van Leeuwe, J. & Vermeer, A. (2011). Vocabulary growth and reading development across the elementary school years. *Scientific Studies of Reading, 15* (1), 8–25.

Wiley, J. & Rayner, K. (2000). Effects of titles on the processing of text and lexically ambiguous words: Evidence from eye movements. *Memory and Cognition,* 28(6), 1011–1021.

Wilson, P. T. & Anderson, R. C. (1986). What they don't know will hurt them: The role of prior knowledge in comprehension. In J. Orasanu (Ed.), *Reading comprehension: From research to practice* (pp. 31–48). Hillsdale, NJ: LEA.

Yaden, D., Rowe, D. & MacGillivray, L. (2000). Emergent literacy: A matter (polyphony) of perspectives. In M. L. Kamil, P. B. Mosenthal, P. D. Pearson & R. Barr (Eds.), *Handbook of reading research, Vol. III* (pp. 425–454). Mahwah, NJ: Lawrence Erlbaum.

Yang, J., Zevin, J. D., Shu, H., McCandliss, B. D. & Li, P. (2006) *A triangle model of Chinese reading: Proceedings of the Twenty-Eighth Annual Conference of the Cognitive Science Society* (pp. 912–918). Mahwah, NJ: Lawrence Erlbaum.

Ziegler, J. C. & Goswami, U. (2005). Reading acquisition, developmental dyslexia and skilled reading across languages: A psycholinguistic grain size theory. *Psychological Bulletin, 131*, 3–29.

Zwaan, R. A. & Radvansky, G. A. (1998). Situation models in language comprehension and memory. *Psychological Bulletin, 123*, 162–185.

2   Learning to Read Chinese

Xi Chen and Adrian Pasquarella

2.1   Introduction

2.1.1   Chinese and Its Orthography

Chinese, while often referred to as a single language, represents a group of related language varieties. In Mainland China alone, Chinese is the native language of over 1.3 billion people. Chinese is also spoken in Hong Kong and Macao, both of which now belong to the People's Republic of China, as well as in Taiwan and Singapore. According to Yuan (1989), there are seven dialect families in China. The Mandarin family is the largest with over 70 percent of the speakers. Standard Chinese,[1] which is based on Beijing Mandarin, is the official language of Mainland China and Taiwan. Cantonese, the best-known dialect of the Yue family, is spoken in Hong Kong and Southern China.

A striking feature of Chinese dialects is that some of them are mutually unintelligible. Because of this, they are considered by some to be different languages (Mair, 1991). However, Chinese dialects are united by the same written language and essentially the same grammar (Duanmu, 2007). All Chinese dialects have tones. In a tone language, the pitch contour over a syllable distinguishes morpheme meanings. For example, 买 /mai3/ 'buy' and 卖 /mai4/ 'sell' are two different morphemes in Mandarin. In Mainland China, all children, regardless of their language background, are schooled in Mandarin only through immersion. In Hong Kong, Cantonese is the medium of instruction in most schools,[2] with Mandarin taught as a school subject (Pan, 2000). In Taiwan, Mandarin is the medium of instruction, while Min and Hakka are offered as school subjects.

---

[1] Standard Chinese is called *Putonghua* (common language) in the People's Republic of China, *Guoyu* (national language) in Taiwan, and *Huayu* (Chinese language) in Singapore. We will refer to Standard Chinese as "Mandarin" in this chapter.

[2] Hong Kong also has schools that use English as the medium of instruction, where Cantonese and Mandarin are both taught as school subjects.

The Chinese writing system is logographic in nature. Many prefer to use the term "morpho-syllabic," which emphasizes the fact that each Chinese character corresponds to one morpheme and one syllable in the spoken language. This unique writing system enables speakers of different Chinese dialects to share a common written language, thereby bringing a sense of unity to the vast and heterogeneous Chinese community (Dronjic, 2011; Hanley, Tzeng & Huang, 1999). Strokes, the building blocks of characters, do not map onto phonological or meaning units. For example, 口 /kou3/ 'mouth' is written in three strokes, a vertical stroke on the left, a horizontal and vertical stroke that forms the top and right part of the character, and a horizontal stroke on the bottom, in that exact order. While there are more than 40,000 characters in total, about 3,500 common characters are needed for functional literacy (Taylor & Taylor, 1995).

2.1.2   *Synchronic and Diachronic Characterization*

The Chinese script is one of the oldest in the world. In fact, among the few scripts in use before 1000 BC, Chinese is the only one still used (Taylor & Taylor, 1995). The earliest Chinese characters were pictograms; however, over time Chinese evolved into a logographic script (DeFrancis, 1984). Today, there is considerable diversity both in the Chinese script itself and in reading instruction across the different Chinese-speaking societies. The Chinese government simplified 2,238 commonly used characters in 1964.[3] Simplified characters are now used in Mainland China and Singapore, whereas traditional characters have been kept in Hong Kong and Taiwan. Although most Chinese children receive reading instruction in only simplified or traditional characters, it seems relatively easy for an educated person to read the other form. However, simplification is highly controversial, because characters not only represent a writing system but also embody a 5,000-year-old culture and tradition. *Pinyin* is used as an auxiliary alphabet in Mainland China to denote character pronunciation. Pinyin consists of the twenty-six letters of the Roman alphabet plus ü and is completely transparent in letter–sound correspondences. *Zhuyinfuhao* (phonetic symbols), a phonetic system made up of ancient characters and character components, is used in Taiwan. No transliteration systems are used in Hong Kong.

2.1.3   *Literacy and Schooling*

In both Mainland China and Taiwan, reading instruction officially begins in Grade 1. Children receive intensive training in Pinyin/Zhuyinfuhao in the first ten weeks, followed by systematic instruction in Chinese characters.

---

[3] Only simplified characters are given as examples in this chapter.

In Hong Kong, children start to learn characters in kindergarten when they are 3–4 years old. Across the three regions, a child is expected to master about 2,500 characters by the end of Grade 6 (Shu, Chen, Anderson, Wu & Xuan, 2003; Taylor & Taylor, 1995). With respect to the method of instruction, it seems that teachers in Mainland China sometimes draw children's attention to the internal structure of compound characters (e.g., 明 'bright' consists of 日 'sun' and 月 'moon'), although this is not done in a systematic fashion (Wu, Li & Anderson, 1999). Teachers in Hong Kong, on other hand, seem to prefer the "look-and-say" approach. Regardless, it is a challenging task to master thousands of characters. For Chinese children, a typical homework assignment is to copy each new character many times, and a typical class activity is to perform dictation tasks.

2.2 Description of Chinese and Its Written Forms

As mentioned above, there is considerable diversity within the Chinese language and script. Literacy practices also vary across different countries and regions. Since most reading studies involving Chinese children have examined speakers of Mandarin or Cantonese, we focus on these two dialects in this chapter. In what follows, we describe the important phonological, morphological, and orthographic features of the Chinese writing system that shape the linguistic and cognitive processes required for Chinese reading. Using English as a reference, we highlight the unique features of the Chinese writing system whenever applicable.

2.2.1 *Linguistic System*

2.2.1.1 Phonology How many sounds does Chinese have? Arguably Mandarin has twenty-one initial consonants, three glides, and six vowels[4] (Duanmu, 2007). Linguists usually describe the maximum Mandarin syllable as CGVX, where C is a consonant, G a glide, V a vowel, and X an offglide of a diphthong or a consonant (Cheng, 1973; Duanmu, 2007; Lin, 1989). Since a consonant glide combination is considered a single sound, Mandarin does not have consonant clusters. Thus, the maximal size of a Mandarin syllable can be categorized as CVC. The vowel slot can be filled with a single vowel or a diphthong. Mandarin has only two final consonants, /n/ and /ng/. Cantonese has eight vowels and nineteen consonants, six of which can appear at the syllable-final position (Chan & Li, 2000). Both Mandarin and Cantonese have four major syllable types, V, CV, VC, and CVC. By comparison, syllable structure can be much more complex in English. For example, the structure of

---

[4] The number of vowels may be five or six, depending on whether the retroflex vowel is counted.

Table 2.1 *Syllable structure in Mandarin (denoted in Pinyin)*

Initial phonemes (21)	b, p, m, f, d, t, n, l, g, k, h, j, q, x, z, c, s, zh, ch, sh, r
Vowels (glides) (6)	i (yi), u (wu), ü (yü), a, o, e
Final consonants (2)	n, ng
Diphthongs (4)	ai, ei, ao, ou
All final combinations (35)	i, u, ü, a, o, e, ai, ao, ei, ia, iao, ie, ou, iou, ua, uai, üe, ui, uo, an, en, ian, in, uan, üan, uen, ün, ang, eng, iang, ing, iong, ong, uang, ueng
Syllable types	V: 鹅 /e2/, 物 /wu4/, 爱 /ai4/, 欧 /ou1/
	CV: 大 /da4/, 瓜 /gua1/, 飞 /fei1/, 怪 /guai4/
	VC: 安 /an1/, 恩 /en1/, 昂 /ang2/, 英 /ying1/
	CVC: 坦 /tan3/, 同 /tong2/, 文 /wen2/, 黄 /huang2/

the word *strengths* is CCCVCCCC. Table 2.1 presents Mandarin sounds and syllables.

Mandarin and Cantonese are both tone languages. There are four tones in Mandarin, high level, rising, fall-rise, and falling, indicated by tone marks, ˉ ˊ ˇ ˋ in Pinyin. For typographical convenience, numbers 1, 2, 3, and 4 are often used instead. Cantonese has six tones: high level, high rising, mid-level, mid-low falling, mid-low rising, and mid-low level. In addition, there are three stopped tones. The stopped tones have the same contours as the high-level, mid-level, and mid-low level tones, but they are carried by syllables ending with /p/, /t/, and /k/ and have shorter syllable durations. Contemporary linguists maintain that Cantonese has six tones, as the three stopped tones are allotones (Bauer & Benedict, 1997; Matthews & Yip, 2011). Tone is traditionally considered a suprasegmental feature that belongs to units larger than segments. However, phonetic studies have shown that the expected contour does not start until the rhyme starts (e.g., Xu, 1999). Duanmu (2007) argues that the tone-bearing unit is the moraic segment.

Chinese has a relatively simple phonological structure. Mandarin has only about 400 basic syllables. Because some syllables carry fewer than four tones, the total number of tone syllables is about 1,300. Cantonese has 627 basic syllables and about 1,760 tone syllables. In comparison, English has more than 6,000 syllables (Duanmu, 2007). Homophone density is high in Chinese. Since in most cases, a character represents a morpheme, each tone syllable on average corresponds to five different characters/morphemes based on an analysis of 6,000 characters in Mandarin (Duanmu, 2007). However, the homophone load is not distributed evenly. A small number of syllables each corresponds to a large number of characters. For example, the tone syllable /yi4/ can correspond to characters 意, 易, 宜, 益, 亦, 译, 议, and many more. In English, the average homophone density is just 1.4, less than a third of that in Mandarin.

2.2.1.2 Morphology   A Chinese morpheme typically maps onto one syllable in the spoken language and one character in print, e.g., 猫 /mao1/ 'cat'. In comparison, an English morpheme can be smaller than one syllable, e.g., -*s* (plural), one syllable, e.g., *dog*, or larger than one syllable, e.g., *table*. A small number of Chinese morphemes are larger than one syllable, e.g., 葡萄 /pu2tao2/ 'grape'. These morphemes represent loan words, in which characters are merely used to indicate sound and have nothing to do with meaning. Some characters can represent different morphemes. For example, 面 /mian4/ means 'flour' in 面包 /mian4bao1/ (bread) and 'surface' in 面孔 /mian4kong3/ (face). These two morphemes are called *homographs*. A similar example in English is *bank*, which can mean a 'financial institution' or a 'riverbank'.

Chinese morphemes can be *free* or *bound*. Free morphemes are potentially independent words, e.g., 鱼 /yu2/ 'fish'. Bound morphemes can only appear with other morphemes, e.g., 民 /min2/ 'people' in 人民 /ren2min2/ 'people'. Traditionally, Chinese morphemes have also been divided into *content* and *function*. Content morphemes describe things, actions, and qualities, whereas function morphemes serve grammatical functions. Based on the criteria of free-bound and content-function, Packard (2000) classifies four types of Chinese morphemes. A free, function morpheme is a function word, e.g., 是 /shi4/ 'to be'. A free, content morpheme is a root word, e.g., 鱼 /yu2/ 'fish'. A bound content morpheme is a bound root, e.g., 民 /min2/ 'people'. A bound grammatical morpheme is an affix. The *grammatical affix* is similar to the inflectional affix in English. For example, 们 /men2/ (plural for human noun) can combine with 我 /wo3/ 'I' to form 我们 'we'. The *word forming affix* resembles the derivational affix in English. For example, 无 /wu2/ (negation) can combine with 良 /liang2/ 'moral' to form 无良 'immoral'. Unlike English, Chinese does not possess grammatical agreement, morphological paradigms, and morphophonemic alternation. For example, while the base in a derived word may undergo phonological and/or orthographic changes in English, e.g., *deep–depth*, similar changes do not occur in Chinese.

There are four types of complex words[5] in Chinese (Packard, 2000). A *compound word* is formed by two root words, e.g., 冰山 /bing1shan1/ 'ice mountain: iceberg'. A *bound root word* consists of a root word and a bound root or two bound roots, e.g., 电脑 /dian4nao3/ 'electric brain: computer'. Most reading studies do not distinguish between these two types and refer to both as compound words. An *inflected word* consists of a root word and a grammatical affix, e.g., 去了 /qu4le/ 'go' plus the affix 了: 'went'. A *derived word* consists of a bound root or a root word and a word forming affix, e.g., 房子 /fang2zi/

---

[5] 复合词 in Chinese, which literally translates to 'compound word' in English, traditionally refers to any word that has more than one syllable.

Table 2.2 *Morphological structure of Chinese nouns and verbs*

	Compound noun	Compound verb
Noun-Noun	熊猫 /xiong2mao1/ (bear cat: panda)	左右 /zuo3you4/ (left right: influence)
Verb-Noun	摇椅 /yao2yi3/ (rock chair: rocking chair)	出版 /chu1ban3/ (emit edition: publish)
Noun-Verb	职守 /zhi1shou3/ (job defend: duty)	瓜分 /gua1fen1/ (melon divide: partition)
Verb-Verb	动作 /dong4zuo4/ (move do: action)	帮助 /bang1zhu4/ (help help: help)
	Derived Noun	Derived Verb
Noun-Affix	房子 /fang2zi/ (house plus affix 子: house)	石化 /shi2hua4/ (stone plus affix化: petrify)
Affix-Noun	阿哥 /a1ge1/ (affix 阿 plus brother: dear brother)	可脚 /ke3jiao3/ (affix 可 plus foot: to fit one's feet)
Verb-Affix	弹性 /tan2xing4/ (bounce plus the affix 性: elasticity)	退化 /tui4hua4/ (retreat plus affix化: degenerate)
Affix-Verb	阿飞 /a1fei1/ (affix阿 plus fly: juvenile delinquent)	复发 /fu4fa1/ (affix 复 plus occur: relapse)
	Grammatical Noun	Grammatical Verb
Noun/Verb-Affix	我们 /wo3men/ (I plus affix 们: we)	走了 /zou3le/ (walk plus affix 了: walked)

'house' plus the affix 子: 'house'. In a count of about 6,000 common Chinese words, about one-third comprises one morpheme (Suen, 1986) and about two-thirds are two-morpheme words. A small percentage of Chinese words consist of three and more morphemes, e.g., 动物园 /dong4wu4yuan2/ 'animal park: zoo'. A distinguishing feature of Chinese morphology is that there are a lot more compound words than inflected or derived words (Duanmu, 1998; Sun, Huang, Sun, Li & Xing, 1997). With respect to form class, most Chinese words (about 88%) are nouns and verbs (Huang, 1998). According to the headedness principle, the majority of bisyllabic nouns have a noun morpheme on the right, and the majority of the bisyllabic verbs have a verb morpheme on the left. Table 2.2 shows Chinese nouns and verbs of different structures.

2.2.2   Writing System

2.2.2.1   Script and Punctuation   The Chinese script is composed of visually complex characters and each character has to be written following a fixed stroke order. The majority of characters have seven to twelve strokes, though some characters have more than twenty strokes. Each character, regardless of the number of strokes, occupies a square area of the same size. Chinese texts are written with equal space between characters. For example, "We are good friends" is written as 我们是好朋友, not as 我们 是 好 朋友. There is no extra space between words 我们 /wo3men2/ 'we', 是 /shi4/ 'to be', 好 /hao3/ 'good', and 朋友 /peng2you3/ 'friend'. The way Chinese texts are written reflects the fact that the character is the most salient unit in Chinese. Interestingly, even educated native speakers of Chinese do not always agree on word boundaries in simple sentences (Hoosain, 1992) and inserting inter-word spacing does not necessarily facilitate reading (e.g., Bai, Yan, Liversedge, Zang & Rayner, 2008).

Traditionally Chinese texts are arranged from the top to the bottom of a page, with the columns moving from right to left. Texts written in classical Chinese do not contain punctuation. Contemporary Chinese texts are printed from left to right, in the same way as English texts. While children in Mainland China are exposed only to horizontal writing in school, children in Hong Kong and Taiwan are exposed to both horizontal and vertical writing. Punctuation marks are used in modern Chinese. Many punctuation marks, including question (?), exclamation (!), colon (:), semi-colon (;), comma (,), single and double quotation marks ('')and (""), are the same as in English. The Chinese period (。) has the same function as its western counterpart. The Chinese system also has some distinctive punctuation marks, such as the enumeration comma (、) used to separate items in a list and the book title mark 《》 used to indicate the title of a book.

2.2.2.2 Orthography Broadly speaking, there are two categories of characters, simple characters and compound characters. Most simple characters are either *pictographs*, originally created to resemble the objects they represent, e.g., 口 /kou3/ 'mouth', or *indicators*, which are graphical representations of abstract ideas, e.g., 一 /yi1/ 'one', 二 /er4/ 'two', 三 /san1/ (three). A simple character may contain subcomponents, e.g., 吕 /lv3/ 'a family name', but subcomponents do not indicate the pronunciation or meaning of the character. Compound characters are made up of radicals. An *ideographic compound character* comprises two semantic radicals, both contributing to the meaning of the character. For example, 林 /lin2/ 'forest' is formed by combining two 木 /mu4/ 'tree'. A *semantic-phonetic compound character*, e.g., 妈 /ma1/ 'mother', comprises a semantic radical, 女 (female) and a phonetic radical, 马 /ma3/. The former gives information about the meaning of the character, whereas the latter gives information about the character's pronunciation.

About 80% of the Chinese characters are semantic-phonetic compound characters. However, as displayed in Table 2.3, there is wide variability in their *semantic transparency* and *phonetic regularity*. Shu et al. (2003) found that among the semantic-phonetic compound characters taught in primary school in Mainland China, 58% have semantic radicals that are informative

Table 2.3 *Different types of semantic-phonetic compound characters*

Phonetic regularity	Character and phonetic radical
Regular	清 /qing1/-青 /qing1/, 伴 /ban4/-半/ban4/
Tone different	妈 /ma1/-马 /ma3/, 饼 /bing3/-并/bing4/
Onset different	红 /hong2/-工 /gong1/, 跑 /pao3/-包/bao1/
Rime different	打 /da3/-丁/ding1/, 杯 /bei1/-不/bu4/
Irregular	研 /yan2/-开 /kai1/, 训/xun4/-川/chuan1/

Semantic transparency	Character and semantic radical
Transparent	嘴 (mouth) -口 (mouth), 爸 (father)-父 (father)
Closely related	姐 (sister) -女 (female), 橱 (cabinet), -木 (wood)
Somewhat related	浮 (float) -氵 (the water radical), 请 (invite), -讠 (the "word" radical)
Opaque	软 (soft), -车(vehicle), 坏 (bad), -土(earth)

and 30% have semantic radicals that are somewhat informative. With respect to phonology, only 23% of the compound characters taught in primary school have the same tone syllable as their phonetic radicals (Shu et al., 2003). The percentage increases to 39% if tone is not considered. In another estimate, DeFrancis (1984) examined 500 characters across a range of frequencies. For the 100 most frequent characters, 18 contain useful phonetics. For the 100 least frequent characters in his sampling, 57 contained useful phonetics. Generally, both semantic transparency and phonetic regularity increase as frequency of usage decreases (DeFrancis, 1984; Perfetti, Zhang & Berent, 1992; Shu et al., 2003).

Most semantic-phonetic compound characters have a left-right structure, with semantic radicals on the left and phonetic radicals on the right (Shu et al., 2003). The phonetic radical (e.g., 工) can also appear on the left, 功 /gong1/, on the top, e.g., 贡 /gong4/, on the bottom, 空 /kong1/ of a semantic-phonetic compound character. In addition, the phonetic radical (e.g., 元 /yuan2/) can be half surrounded, e.g., 远 /yuan3/, or completely surrounded, e.g., 园 /yuan2/ by the semantic radical. Most semantic and phonetic radicals are independent characters, but a small number of them are bound forms.

2.2.3   Conclusion

Chinese has many unique features both in terms of the spoken language and writing system. With respect to phonology, Chinese is a tonal language with a simple syllable structure and high homophone density. Morphemes are particularly salient in Chinese, as they correspond to syllables in the spoken language and characters in print. The majority of words in Chinese are compound words formed by combining two content morphemes. The number of simple words is small, so are the numbers of derived and inflected words, each formed by combining a content morpheme with a grammatical morpheme. The Chinese script distinguishes itself with thousands of visually complex characters. The majority of Chinese characters are semantic-phonetic compound characters, where the semantic radical provides information about meaning and phonetic radical provides information about pronunciation, although these cues are not always reliable. Chinese texts are written with equal space between characters with no additional interword spacing. As a result, word boundaries are relatively arbitrary in Chinese.

2.3   Acquisition of Reading and Spelling in Chinese

Reading in any writing system entails processing the visual-orthographic form of a linguistic unit and activating its pronunciation and meaning (Perfetti, 2003). Phonological awareness, morphological awareness, and orthographic processing have been found to contribute to reading and spelling across different writing systems (e.g., McBride-Chang et al., 2005; Perfetti, Cao & Booth, 2013). On the other hand, writing systems differ in mapping principles between the script and spoken language, as well as in specific phonological, morphological, and orthographic features (Perfetti, 2003). These differences in turn lead to differences in reading processes. In this section, we discuss how the specific features of the Chinese writing system affect the development of phonological awareness, morphological awareness, and orthographic processing and how each aspect of metalinguistic awareness contributes to Chinese reading and spelling.

2.3.1   Becoming Linguistically Aware

2.3.1.1   Phonological Development and Phonological Awareness   Like English, Chinese has three nested aspects of phonological awareness, *syllable awareness*, *onset and rime awareness*, and *phoneme awareness. Tone awareness* is an additional aspect of phonological awareness unique for Chinese and other tone languages. Syllable awareness is the understanding that spoken words are made up of syllables. The syllable is a salient phonological unit in Chinese, as one syllable typically represents one morpheme. Onset and rime awareness refers to the recognition that a syllable can be divided into an onset and a rime. Rimes (e.g., /an/, /ang/) are treated as single units and are not further divided into phonemes in school instruction. As a result, phonemic awareness, the ability to segment syllables into phonemes, can be difficult to acquire for Chinese children (Chen, Fen, Nguyen, Hong & Wang, 2010). A child with tone awareness is able to distinguish between morphemes that share the same

syllable but have different tones, such as 清 /qing1/ 'clear' and 请 /qing3/ 'please'. Phonological awareness is often measured with detection, oddity, and judgment tasks focusing on onsets, rimes, and tones in Chinese (e.g., Chen et al., 2004; Ho & Bryant, 1997a). Deletion tasks at onset, rime, and phoneme levels are also used (e.g., McBride-Chang & Ho, 2005; Chen et al., 2010). Segmentation and blending tasks are rare because these skills are not required to read or spell Chinese.

With respect to the development of phonological awareness, Chinese children become aware of large sound segments before smaller ones (Ho & Bryant, 1997a; Shu, Peng & McBride-Chang, 2008). Shu et al. (2008) reported that Mandarin-speaking children as young as 3 years performed above chance on a syllable detection task. Only children who were 4 years old and above performed above chance on rime and tone detection measures. These findings were confirmed by Ho and Bryant (1997a) among Cantonese-speaking Hong Kong children. In both studies, only first-grade children achieved above-chance performance on onset detection measures. Since Chinese syllables do not allow consonant clusters, onset awareness measures are also measures of initial phonemes. These studies suggest Chinese children develop syllable awareness first, followed by rime and tone awareness, and onset/phoneme awareness last. This sequence is similar to the sequence observed among English-speaking children (Treiman & Zukowski, 1991).

Given that Chinese is represented by a logographic script and its syllables are decomposed into onsets and rimes but not phonemes, Chinese children appear to develop phonological awareness more slowly than children from many other language backgrounds. Ho and Bryant (1997a) reported that Hong Kong children performed lower on tasks measuring rime awareness and phoneme onset awareness than English-speaking children of similar ages. Notably, experience with a phonetic coding system enhances Chinese children's phonological awareness. Children in Mainland China and Taiwan, who received instruction in Pinyin and in Zuyinfuhao, respectively, outperformed their peers in Hong Kong on phonological awareness measures (Huang & Hanley, 1995; McBride-Chang, Bialystok, Chong & Li, 2004). In a similar vein, Chinese children who had experience of learning English, an alphabetic language, also developed more advanced phonemic awareness than their peers with less or no such experience (Bialystok, McBride-Chang & Luk, 2005; Chen et al., 2010).

2.3.1.2 Morphological Development and Morphological Awareness The majority of words used in modern Chinese are compound words formed through lexical compounding. Chinese also has inflected and derived words, formed by combining a content morpheme with a grammatical affix and with a word forming affix, respectively. In this sense, just like in English, morphological awareness in Chinese consists of compound awareness, inflectional awareness, and derivational awareness. However, it is not always easy to differentiate among different types of words in Chinese. For example, 学者 /xue2zhe3/ 'scholar' is a derived word, but 学员 / xue2yuan2/ 'student' is a compound word.[6] Alternatively, one can define two aspects of morphological awareness: the ability to recognize morpheme meaning and the ability to understand and manipulate morphological structure in a morphologically complex word (Liu & McBride-Chang, 2010; Liu, McBride-Chang, Wong, Shu & Wong, 2013).

Owing to the high homophone density in Chinese, research studies examining morpheme meaning typically focus on homophone awareness and employ measures that request children to distinguish morphemes with the same pronunciation but different meanings. For example, in a morpheme judgment task, children are orally presented with a word containing a target morpheme, e.g., 口袋 /kou3 dai4/ 'mouth pocket: pocket' with 袋 as the target morpheme, followed by options each containing a morpheme that has the same pronunciation as the target morpheme, e.g., 带鱼 /dai4 yu2/ 'belt fish: cutlassfish' and 袋鼠 /dai4 shu3/ 'pocket mouse: kangaroo', and are requested to choose the option containing the same morpheme (e.g., Hao, Chen, Dronjic, Shu & Anderson, 2013; McBride-Chang, Shu, Zhou, Wat & Wagner, 2003). Sometimes a morpheme production task is used, in which a target morpheme is identified, e.g., 草 /cao3/ 'grass' in 草地 /cao3di4/ 'grass land: lawn', and children are asked to produce a word that contains the same morpheme, e.g., 小草 /xiao3cao3/ 'small grass: grass', and a word that contains a homograph of the morpheme, e.g., 草率 /cao3shuai4/ 'cursory' (Shu, McBride-Chang, Wu & Liu, 2006).

The other aspect of morphological awareness centers on the ability to manipulate morphological structure and is typically measured with a morphological construction task (Chen, Hao, Geva, Zhu & Shu, 2009; McBride-Chang et al., 2003, McBride-Chang et al., 2005). In this task, the experimenter orally provides the definition of a familiar object and asks children to create a morphologically complex word in order to name an imaginary object that bears some resemblance to it. For example, 斑马是身上有斑纹的一种马，那么身上有斑纹的牛我们叫什么? 'Striped horse (Zebra) is a kind of horse with stripes on the body. What should we call a cow with stripes on the body?' The answer is 斑牛 'striped cow'. A modified version created by Liu and McBride-Chang (2010) directly asks children to produce a novel word in response to a question. For example, 我们把味道酸酸的雾气叫什么? 'What do we call mist that smells sour?' The answer is 酸雾 'sour mist'. This modified task does not require analogical

---

[6] The explanation is that, compared to bound roots, word forming affixes are more general and abstract in meaning, and also more productive in word formation (Packard, 2000).

reasoning as in the original form. Finally, several previous studies have asked children to identify the head of a compound noun (Chen et al., 2009; Wang, Cheng & Chen, 2006). For example, 给穿着衣服的鱼起个名字, 鱼衣和衣鱼, 你看哪个更好? 'Which is a better name for a fish that wears a dress? A fish dress or a dress fish?' The answer is 衣鱼 'dress fish'.

Only a small number of studies have examined the development of morphological awareness among Chinese children. Ku and Anderson (2003), in a comprehensive study that tapped both morpheme meaning and word formation, found that children's performance steadily increased from Grade 2 to Grade 6. Furthermore, children generally scored higher on compound words than derived words, which is consistent with the fact that there are more compound words than derived words in Chinese. In a short-term longitudinal study, Hao et al. (2013) found that the identification of a morpheme in homophone awareness measures was facilitated when words containing it were closely related in meaning (e.g., 电视 /dian4 shi4/ 'electric vision: television' and 电话 /dian4 hua4/ 'electric talk: telephone') and when the morpheme was free. As children grew older, they became better at identifying a morpheme appearing in distantly related words (e.g., 假山 /jia3shan1/ 'artificial mountain: rockery' – 假发 /jia3fa4/ 'artificial hair: wig'). Finally, Liu and McBride-Chang (2010) reported that it was easier for children to produce noun compound words of subordinate and coordinative structures than those of subject-predicate and verb-object structures, probably because the last two types contained verb morphemes.

2.3.1.3 Development of Orthographic Processing Skills   Orthographic processing in Chinese is a complex construct that consists of several different, albeit related, aspects. An aspect often assessed in young children requires them to distinguish between drawings and orthographic units. Another aspect focuses on the regularity of radical positions (e.g., Wang, Perfetti & Liu, 2005). Children are asked to choose between a pair of pseudo-characters the one that looks more like a real character, e.g., 奵, 对. The choice with radicals in legal positions is the correct answer (奵). Yet another aspect of orthographic processing involves knowledge of radicals and subcomponents. For example, 汇 is not a real character whereas 江 is, because the "water" radical is misspelled in the former with an additional dot.

Since orthographic processing is a print-based skill, Chinese children seem to acquire this knowledge through repeated exposure to characters. Generally speaking, even young kindergarten children can differentiate between drawings and orthographic units (Luo, Chen, Deacon & Li, 2011). However, kindergarten children do not have a good understanding about either radical positions or radical forms (e.g., Ho, Yau & Au, 2003; Li, Shu, McBride-Chang, Liu & Peng, 2012; Luo et al., 2011). Knowledge of these aspects of orthographic processing starts to grow steadily once they enter Grade 1, likely due to increased formal literacy instruction (Li et al., 2012; Luo et al., 2011), and reaches relatively high levels by grade three (Ho, Ng & Ng, 2003; Ho, Yau & Au, 2003; Li et al., 2012).

A body of research conducted mostly in the 1990s and early 2000s examined children's ability to use the information in semantic and phonetic radicals in reading compound characters. These skills are sometimes called "radical awareness" and "phonetic awareness," respectively (e.g., Shu & Anderson, 1997; Shu, Anderson & Wu, 2000), though it may be more appropriate to categorize both as orthographic processing skills. Ho and colleagues (Ho, Ng & Ng, 2003; Ho, Yau & Au, 2003) have labeled this aspect of orthographic processing the "functional regularity of radicals." Research has shown that school-age children are capable of using semantic radicals to figure out meanings of unfamiliar compound characters (e.g., Chan & Nunes, 1998; Ho, Wong & Chan, 1999; Shu & Anderson, 1997, 1998). Similarly, they can use phonetic radicals to derive or memorize pronunciations of new compound characters (e.g., Anderson, Li, Ku, Shu & Wu, 2003; Ho & Bryant, 1997b; Ho et al., 1999; Shu et al., 2000).

2.3.2   Development of Word Identification

2.3.2.1   Word Decoding Development   Studies have examined the impact of different aspects of metalinguistic awareness on Chinese character and word reading. There is strong evidence that phonological awareness is related to Chinese reading (e.g., Chow, McBride-Chang & Burgess, 2005; Ho & Bryant, 1997c; Hu & Catts, 1998; McBride-Chang & Ho, 2005; McBride-Chang et al., 2008). Across studies, the effects of phonological awareness remained significant after controlling for other reading-related variables such as age, nonverbal reasoning, and speeded naming. Among different aspects of phonological awareness, syllable awareness appears to be a particularly strong predictor of Chinese reading (McBride-Chang et al., 2004; McBride-Chang & Ho, 2005; McBride-Chang & Kail, 2002). In addition, a couple of studies reported significant contributions of phonological awareness to oral vocabulary (i.e., Cheung et al., 2010; McBride-Chang, Cheung, Chow, Chow & Choi, 2006). The absence of grapheme–phoneme correspondences in Chinese renders the link between phonological awareness and reading less apparent. Nonetheless, according to the universal phonological principle, reading involves activating phonology at the smallest unit allowed by the writing system (Perfetti et al., 1992). This unit is the syllable in Chinese.

Morphological awareness has also been found to contribute to Chinese reading (e.g., Chen et al., 2009; Li et al., 2012; McBride-Chang et al., 2003; McBride-Chang et al., 2005; Shu et al., 2006; Tong & McBride-Chang, 2010;

Tong, McBride-Chang, Shu & Wong, 2009; Yeung et al., 2011). Since the majority of Chinese words are compound words, they are the focus of most studies. A couple of intervention studies demonstrated that morphological awareness training enhanced character reading among kindergarteners (Chow, McBride-Chang, Cheung & Chow, 2008; Zhou, McBride-Chang, Fong, Wong & Cheung, 2012), pointing to a causal link between the two constructs. Furthermore, there is strong evidence that morphological awareness is a significant contributor to vocabulary (e.g., Chen et al., 2009; Li, Anderson, Nagy & Zhang, 2002; McBride-Chang et al., 2006, 2008; McBride-Chang, Shu, Ng, Meng & Penney, 2007). Notably, morphological awareness was a stronger predictor of vocabulary than phonological awareness in most studies that included both aspects of metalinguistic awareness.

There are several reasons why morphological awareness, in particular compound awareness, plays an important role in Chinese literacy development (e.g., Hoosain, 1992; Nagy & Anderson, 1998; Shu, Anderson & Zhang, 1995). First, Chinese characters represent morphemes. This clear grapheme–morpheme association, coupled with less systematic representation of phonological information, encourages children to focus on meaning as opposed to pronunciation (McBride-Chang, 2004). Second, Chinese contains a large number of homophones. As a result, children must distinguish morphemes with identical pronunciation but different meanings. Furthermore, Chinese morphemes are highly productive and compound words tend to be transparent in meaning (Shu et al., 2006; Yin, 1984; Yuan & Huang, 1998). Given these features, Chinese children with more advanced morphological awareness read words and acquire new vocabulary more effectively.

Owing to the visual complexity of Chinese characters, visual processing, defined as the ability to process and remember geometric figures such as shapes, lines, etc., is believed to be important for Chinese reading. The empirical evidence, however, is not conclusive. Several studies showed that visual processing was related to Chinese character reading in young readers (Ho & Bryant, 1997c; McBride-Chang et al., 2005; Siok & Fletcher, 2001), whereas other studies failed to detect a significant relationship between visual processing and Chinese reading (Hu & Catts, 1998; Huang & Hanley, 1997; Li et al., 2012; McBride-Chang & Kail, 2002). The inconsistent results may be attributed to age difference, as most of the studies that observed a significant relationship involved children in kindergarten or Grade 1. Additionally, it seems that the relationship becomes more difficult to detect with added controls, suggesting that visual processing is not a strong predictor of Chinese reading.

Orthographic processing, which involves primarily knowledge of radical positions and forms, appears to be a reliable predictor of Chinese reading among school-age children (Li et al., 2012; Tong & McBride-Chang, 2010).

Li et al. (2012), for example, observed that a comprehensive orthographic measure was significantly related to character reading among children in Grades 1 to 3 after controlling for other reading-related variables. Furthermore, there is consistent evidence that Chinese children can use information in semantic and phonetic radicals to identify character meanings and pronunciations (e.g., Ho, Ng & Ng, 2003; Shu & Anderson, 1997; Shu et al., 2000). However, it is not clear whether this aspect of orthographic processing is related to character reading after controlling for other reading skills such as phonological awareness and morphological awareness.

What might a developmental word reading model look like in Chinese? Several researchers (e.g., Chen, Anderson, Li & Shu, 2013; Ho & Bryant, 1997c; Siok & Fletcher, 2001) proposed a theory that resembles Ehri's (1991) model of English reading in which beginning readers rely on visual features to recognize words, whereas more advanced readers use phonological information. Recently, several large-scale studies examined word reading comprehensively among hundreds of children from different age groups (Li et al., 2012; Tong & McBride-Chang, 2010). These studies showed that phonological awareness, morphological awareness, and orthographic processing were significant predictors of reading in kindergarten and primary school children, though the relative importance and the underlying structure of the variables varied in different age groups.

2.3.2.2 Word Spelling Development Until now only a small number of studies have examined spelling development in Chinese. The findings of these studies point to similarities in the component skills that support reading and spelling development in Chinese. For example, both orthographic processing and morphological awareness have been found to predict spelling among Chinese children in kindergarten and primary school (e.g., Tong et al., 2009; Yeung, Ho, Wong, et al., 2013; Yeung et al., 2011). In addition, rapid naming appears to be a strong predictor of Chinese spelling (Tong et al., 2009; Yeung et al., 2011). By contrast, there is mixed evidence with regard to the role of phonological awareness in Chinese spelling. While a significant relationship was reported by a couple of studies (e.g., Shen & Bear, 2000; Yeung, Ho, Wong, et al., 2013), the same relationship was not observed in other studies (e.g., Tong et al., 2009; Yeung et al., 2011). Generally speaking, these findings are consistent with the nature of the writing system – Chinese characters are visually complex orthographic forms, and they correspond to morphemes, rather than phonemes, in the spoken language.

Based on Shen and Bear (2000), Chinese children's spelling errors are typically classified into three categories: orthographic errors, phonological errors, and semantic (morpho-lexical) errors. Orthographic errors are common in Chinese spelling. They include substituting the target character with a character that has a similar visual form (e.g., 知 for 和), substituting a radical or reversing radicals within the character and adding, subtracting, or modifying strokes (e.g., 天 for 夫). The prevalence of orthographic errors highlights the importance of orthographic processing in Chinese spelling development. To spell a character correctly, children must rely on their orthographic skills to retrieve its written form from the mental lexicon. Chinese children also commit phonological and semantic errors in spelling. Phonological errors include homophone (e.g., 在 /zai4/ for 再 /zai4/) and similar sound character (e.g., 新 /xin1/ for 星 /xing1/) substitutions. Semantic errors refer to substitutions of synonyms (e.g., 脸 'face' for 面 'face') or semantically related characters (e.g., 时 'time' for 钟 'clock'). Interestingly, in Chinese, both phonological and semantic errors are affected by morphological awareness. Phonological errors suggest that children fail to distinguish among homophonic morphemes, whereas semantic errors reveal that children retrieve a character by identifying the meaning of the morpheme. Taken together, the saliency of phonological and semantic errors underscores the central role of morphological awareness in Chinese spelling.

2.3.2.3 Reading and Spelling Difficulties   The incidence of reading disability among Chinese children is roughly the same as among their western counterparts (e.g., Stevenson, Stigler, Lucker, Hsu & Kitamura, 1982). In a series of studies, Ho and her colleagues (Ho, 2010; Ho, Chan, Lee, Tsang & Luan, 2004; Ho, Chan, Tsang & Lee, 2002) identified rapid naming and orthographic deficits as the two most prevalent types of cognitive deficits in Chinese developmental dyslexia. They argued that children with deficits in these areas have difficulties in developing a strong and stable orthographic representation of Chinese characters. By contrast, most English dyslexic readers have a phonological deficit (e.g., Morris et al., 1998), which highlights the central role of phonological awareness in reading an alphabetic language.

Research has identified several other deficits in Chinese dyslexic children. McBride-Chang, Shu, and colleagues (Lei et al., 2011; McBride-Chang et al., 2011; Shu et al., 2006) suggest that morphological awareness may be a core cognitive construct in understanding developmental dyslexia in Chinese. On the other hand, results were inconsistent with regard to the prevalence of phonological deficits. While some studies showed that Chinese dyslexic children performed poorly on phonological awareness and memory measures (Cheung et al., 2009; Ho & Lai, 1999; Ho, Law & Ng, 2000; Huang & Zhang, 1997; Li & Ho, 2011; Wang, Georgiou, Das & Li, 2012), Ho et al. (2002, 2004) found that phonological deficits were less frequent than deficits in rapid naming and orthographic processing. Interestingly, a couple of studies showed that Chinese dyslexic children were impaired in tone awareness and perception (Li & Ho, 2011; Cheung et al., 2009; Li & Ho, 2011), again suggesting that Chinese readers and readers of alphabetic languages may face different challenges.

2.3.3   Reading Comprehension

Recent research has identified skills important for Chinese reading comprehension. First, there is strong evidence that morphological awareness and vocabulary knowledge are concurrent and longitudinal predictors of reading comprehension. The relationships remain significant after controlling for other reading related skills (Tong et al., 2009; Shu et al., 2006; Zhang et al., 2012; Zhang et al., 2014). Word reading has also been found to predict reading comprehension in Chinese (e.g., Chik et al., 2012; Yeung, Ho, Chan, Chung & Wong, 2013; Zhang et al., 2012). Other identified predictors include phonological awareness, rapid naming, and orthographic processing, and verbal working memory (Chik et al., 2012; Leong, Tse, Loh & Han, 2008; Shu et al., 2006; Tong, et al., 2009; Zhang et al., 2012; Zhang et al., 2014; Yeung, Ho, Chan, et al., 2013). The contributions of these variables, however, are often weaker than those of word-level reading and semantic skills.

A couple of studies have investigated the role of syntactic awareness in reading comprehension. Syntactic awareness refers to the ability to reflect on and manipulate the grammatical structure of a language (Cain, 2007; Chik et al., 2012; Yeung, Ho, Chan, et al., 2013). For example, Chik et al. (2012) indicated that first-grade syntactic skills, measured with an oral sentence completion task, made an independent contribution to sentence comprehension in Grade 2. Taken together, models of Chinese reading comprehension are similar to models of English in that word-level reading and semantic skills, as well as oral language and text-level skills, are important components of comprehension (Cain, 2007; Carlisle, 2000; Gough & Tunmer, 1986; Hoover & Gough, 1990).

2.3.4   Conclusion

Metalinguistic awareness is important for literacy development in Chinese children. Phonological awareness in Chinese includes tone awareness in addition to syllable, onset-rime, and phonemic awareness. Similar to English, awareness of large phonological units (e.g., syllable, rime) develops before small units (phoneme) in Chinese. However, syllable awareness rather than phonemic awareness plays a central role in Chinese word reading, due to the morpho-syllabic nature of the Chinese writing system. Research on morphological awareness in Chinese has focused on compound awareness. Specifically, researchers have examined the abilities to recognize morpheme meaning (i.e., distinguish meanings of homophones) and manipulate morphological structure and found both to be related to

Chinese word reading. Morphological awareness develops with age and is influenced by morpheme status (free vs. bound), word structure, and word meaning. Orthographic processing in Chinese is characterized by awareness of radical position and form. Orthographic processing develops through repeated exposure to print and is closely related to Chinese word reading.

While all three aspects of metalinguistic awareness mentioned above are associated with word reading, morphological awareness and orthographic processing are also related to Chinese spelling and are core constructs underlying developmental dyslexia in Chinese readers. By contrast, the roles of phonological awareness in these areas are less clear. These findings again highlight the morpho-syllabic nature of the Chinese writing system. Finally, both morphological awareness and syntactic awareness make important contributions to text comprehension in Chinese.

2.4   Discussion

2.4.1   Challenges in Learning to Read Chinese

Chinese children face several unique challenges in learning to read. The Chinese writing system lacks grapheme–phoneme correspondences. It represents phonological information in the form of phonetic radicals, but the majority of phonetic radicals do not provide complete information about character pronunciation. As a result, children have to memorize thousands of visually complex characters. Learning to read in Chinese is a gradual and laborious process. Chinese children add 200–700 characters per year to their sight vocabularies to acquire about 3,000 characters by the end of grade 6 (Shu et al., 2003). Learning to spell Chinese is also an arduous undertaking, exacerbated by the emphasis on producing the strokes of a character in a fixed sequence. Literacy development in Chinese is further complicated by the high homophone density in the spoken language. Children often fail to distinguish meanings of homophonic morphemes in reading, and they produce homophone substitutions in spelling. Consistent with the "morpho-syllabic" nature of the Chinese writing system, the contribution of phonological awareness to Chinese reading and spelling is somewhat limited, whereas morphological awareness and orthographic processing play more important roles in these processes.

2.4.2   Implications for Instruction

Based on the research findings, instructional activities that focus on various aspects of metalinguistic awareness may facilitate literacy development among Chinese children. Because Chinese is represented by a logographic writing system, Chinese teachers rarely carry out phonological awareness activities in the classroom. Phonological awareness games and activities such as deletion, blending, segmentation, especially at the levels of syllable and onset-rime, may be beneficial for Chinese children in the early primary grades. Learning an alphabetic transliteration system, such as Pinyin and Zhuyinfuhao, enhances phonological awareness. However, no such system is used in Hong Kong.

With respect to morphological awareness, activities can be designed to help children identify morpheme meaning and manipulate word structure. Activities that enable children to differentiate among homophones may be particularly useful given the high homophone density in Chinese and the frequent occurrence of homophone errors in young children. Chinese teachers understand the importance of meaning for reading acquisition. They have traditionally incorporated elements of morphological awareness in their instruction. For example, they often ask children to define and compare word and morpheme meanings and to form multiple words with the same morpheme. However, morphological instruction should be implemented in a more explicit and systematic manner throughout primary and secondary grades than it has been in the past.

As for orthographic processing, activities that highlight the internal structure of compound characters, including both the position and function of semantic and phonetic radicals, may be particularly beneficial. Semantic radicals are taught explicitly in Chinese classrooms due to the emphasis on meaning in reading instruction and the fact that they are used as search indexes in Chinese dictionaries. Phonetic radicals, on the other hand, are often ignored because the majority of them do not provide complete information for character pronunciation. However, research has demonstrated that more skilled readers are better able to use the information in phonetic radicals to predict and memorize character pronunciations than poor readers (e.g., Anderson et al., 2003; Shu et al., 2000). Thus, phonetic radicals, especially the ones with a high level of regularity, should be taught systematically. Chinese children are required to master spelling through repeated practice, which is also critical for developing orthographic skills.

2.5   Final Conclusion

Although the number of studies on Chinese reading is growing rapidly, many areas remain to be explored. Research on morphological awareness has primarily focused on noun-noun compound words. Compound words of other structures have not been studied. There are essentially no studies on awareness of derived or inflected words, under the misconception that they do not exist in Chinese. The number of studies investigating the relationship between orthographic processing and Chinese reading is still relatively small. Moreover, relatively little is known about the development of the various aspects of metalinguistic awareness. With respect to the outcome variable, the largest number of reading studies focus on predictors of word reading. More research is needed to reveal the factors that contribute to reading comprehension.

Chinese reading research has not taken into consideration the diversity within the Chinese language and script. It is not clear how research findings are influenced by differences in Chinese dialects and scripts. No studies have specifically looked at how Chinese children who speak another dialect learn to read the writing system based on Mandarin, and how well these children function in Mandarin immersion education. The primary goal of the research to date has been to advance reading theory, and the findings have limited impact on practice. With respect to research design, most studies are cross-sectional, though the number of longitudinal studies is increasing. Intervention studies remain rare. Addressing these issues is a challenging task faced collectively by a new generation of Chinese reading researchers.

In sum, research has consistently demonstrated that phonological awareness, morphological awareness, and orthographic processing are important factors in Chinese children's reading development. The same metalinguistic skills, together with vocabulary and syntactic awareness, are important for text comprehension. By contrast, the impact of visual processing on Chinese reading appears to be weak. These patterns echo research findings from alphabetic languages and point to universal processes in reading. On the other hand, reading in Chinese is shaped by the unique characteristics of the Chinese language and writing system. Syllable awareness seems to be the most prominent predictor of reading among different levels of phonological awareness. Compound awareness is the aspect of morphological awareness that is most strongly related to reading in Chinese. Finally, orthographic processing in Chinese focuses on knowledge of radicals and is very different from orthographic processing in alphabetic languages.

References

Anderson, R. C., Li, W., Ku, Y., Shu, H. & Wu, N. (2003). Use of partial information in learning to read Chinese characters. *Journal of Educational Psychology, 95,* 52–57.

Bai, X., Yan, G., Liversedge, S., Zang, C. & Rayner, K. (2008). Reading spaced and unspaced Chinese text: Evidence from eye movements. *Journal of Experimental Psychology: Human Perception and Performance, 34,* 1277–1287.

Bauer, R. S. & Benedict, P. K. (1997). *Modern Cantonese phonology*. Berlin: Mouton de Gruyter.

Bialystok, E., McBride-Chang, C. & Luk, G. (2005). Bilingualism, language proficiency, and learning to read in two writing systems. *Journal of Educational Psychology, 97,* 580–590.

Cain, K. (2007). Syntactic awareness and reading ability: Is there any evidence for a special relationship? *Applied Psycholinguistics, 28,* 679–694.

Carlisle, J. F. (2000). Awareness of the structure and meaning of morphologically complex words: Impact on reading. *Reading and Writing*, *12*, 169–190.

Chan, A. Y. W. & Li, D. C. S. (2000). English and Cantonese phonology in contrast: Explaining Cantonese ESL learners' English pronunciation problems. *Language, Culture and Curriculum*, *13*, 67–85.

Chan, L. & Nunes, T. (1998). Children's understanding of the formal and functional characteristics of written Chinese. *Applied Psycholinguistics*, *19*, 115–131.

Chen, X., Anderson, R. C., Li, W., Hao, M., Wu, X. & Shu, H. (2004). Phonological awareness of monolingual and bilingual Chinese children. *Journal of Educational Psychology*, *96*, 142–151.

Chen, X., Anderson, R. C., Li, H. & Shu, H. (2013). Visual, phonological and ortho-graphic strategies in learning to read Chinese. In X. Chen, L. Wang & Y. Luo (Eds.), *Reading development and difficulties in monolingual and bilingual Chinese children* (pp. 23–48). Dordrecht: Springer.

Chen, X., Fen, X., Nguyen, T.-K., Hong, G. & Wang, Y. (2010). Effects of cross-language transfer on first language phonological awareness and literacy skills in Chinese children receiving English instruction. *Journal of Educational Psychology*, *102*, 712–728.

Chen, X., Hao, M., Geva, E., Zhu, J. & Shu, H. (2009). The role of compound awareness in Chinese children's vocabulary acquisition and character reading. *Reading and Writing*, *22*, 615–631.

Cheng, C.-C. (1973). *A synchronic phonology of Mandarin Chinese*. Monographs on Linguistic Analysis no. 4. The Hague: Mouton.

Cheung, H., Chung, K. K. H., Wong, S. W. L., McBride-Chang, C., Penney, T. B. & Ho, C. S.-H. (2009). Perception of tone and aspiration contrasts in Chinese children with dyslexia. *Journal of Child Psychology and Psychiatry*, *50*, 726–733.

(2010). Speech perception, metalinguistic awareness, reading, and vocabulary in Chinese–English bilingual children. *Journal of Educational Psychology*, *102*, 367–380.

Chik, P. P.-M., Ho, C. S.-H., Yeung, P.-S., Chan, D. W.-O., Chung, K. K.-H., Luan, H., Lo, L.-Y. & Lau, W. S.-Y. (2012). Syntactic skills in sentence reading comprehension among Chinese elementary school children. *Reading and Writing*, *25*, 679–699.

Chow, B. W.-Y., McBride-Chang, C. & Burgess, S. (2005). Phonological processing skills and early reading abilities in Hong Kong Chinese kindergarteners learn-ing to read English as a second language. *Journal of Educational Psychology*, *97*, 81–87.

Chow, B. W.-Y., McBride-Chang, C., Cheung, H. & Chow, C. S.-L. (2008). Dialogic reading and morphology training in Chinese children: Effects on language and literacy. *Developmental Psychology*, *44*, 233–244.

DeFrancis, J. (1984). *The Chinese language: Fact and fantasy*. Honolulu: University of Hawaii Press.

Dronjic, V. (2011). Mandarin Chinese compounds, their representation, and processing in the visual modality. *Writing Systems Research*, *3*, 5–21.

Duanmu, S. (1998). Wordhood in Chinese. In J. Packard (Ed.), *New approaches to Chinese word formation: Morphology, phonology and the lexicon in modern and ancient Chinese* (pp. 135–196). Berlin: Mouton de Gruyter.

(2007). *The phonology of standard Chinese*, 2nd edn. Oxford University Press.

Ehri, L. (1991). Development of the ability to read words. In R. Barr, M. Kamil, P. Mosenthal & P. Pearson (Eds.), *Handbook of reading research*, Vol. II (pp. 383–417). New York: Longman.

Gough, P. B. & Tunmer, W. E. (1986). Decoding, reading, and reading ability. *RASE: Remedial & Special Education, 7*, 6–10.

Hanley, J. R., Tzeng, O. & Huang, H. S. (1999). Learning to read Chinese. In M. Harris and G. Hatano (Eds.), *Learning to read and write: A Cross-linguistic perspective* (pp. 173–95). Cambridge University Press.

Hao, M. L., Chen, X., Dronjic, V., Shu, H. & Anderson, R. C. (2013). The development of young Chinese children's morphological awareness: The role of semantic relatedness and morpheme type. *Applied Psycholinguistics, 34*, 45–67.

Ho, C. S.-H. (2010). Understanding reading disability in Chinese: From basic research to intervention. In M. H. Bond (Ed.), *Handbook of Chinese Psychology*, 2nd edn. (pp. 109–121). New York: Oxford Press.

Ho, C. S.-H. & Bryant, P. (1997a). Development of phonological awareness of Chinese children in Hong Kong. *Journal of Psycholinguistic Research, 26*, 109–126.

(1997b). Learning to read Chinese beyond the logographic phase. *Reading Research Quarterly, 32*, 276–289.

(1997c). Phonological skills are important in learning to read Chinese. *Developmental Psychology, 6*, 946–951.

Ho, C. S.-H., Chan, D. W.-O., Lee, S.-H., Tsang, S.-H. & Luan, V. H. (2004). Cognitive profiling and preliminary subtyping in Chinese developmental dyslexia. *Cognition, 91*, 43–75.

Ho, C. S.-H., Chan, D. W.-O., Tsang, S.-H. & Lee, S.-H. (2002). The cognitive profile and multiple-deficit hypothesis in Chinese developmental dyslexia. *Developmental Psychology, 38*, 543–553.

Ho, C. S.-H. & Lai, D. N.-C. (1999). Naming-speed deficits and phonological memory deficits in Chinese developmental dyslexia. *Learning and Individual Differences, 11*, 173–186.

Ho, C. S.-H., Law, T. P.-S. & Ng, P. M. (2000). The phonological deficit hypothesis in Chinese developmental dyslexia. *Reading and Writing: An Interdisciplinary Journal, 13*, 57–79.

Ho, C. S.-H., Ng, T.-T. & Ng, W.-K. (2003). A "radical" approach to reading development in Chinese: The role of semantic radicals and phonetic radicals. *Journal of Literacy Research, 35*, 849–878.

Ho, C. S.-H., Wong, W.-L. & Chan, W.-S. (1999). The use of orthographic analogies in learning to read Chinese. *Journal of Child Psychology and Psychiatry, 40*, 393–403.

Ho, C. S.-H., Yau, P.W.-Y. & Au, A. (2003). Development of orthographic knowledge and its relationship with reading and spelling among Chinese kindergarten and primary school children. In C. McBride-Chang & H.-C. Chen (Eds.), *Reading Development in Chinese Children* (pp. 51–71). Westport, CT: Greenwood Publishing Group Inc.

Hoosain, R. (1992). Psychological reality of the word in Chinese. In H. C. Chen & O. Tzeng (Eds.), *Language processing in Chinese* (pp. 111–130). New York: North-Holland Elsevier Science Publisher.

Hoover, W. A. & Gough, P. B. (1990). The simple view of reading. *Reading and Writing, 2*, 127–160.

Hu, C. -F. & Catts, H. W. (1998). The role of phonological processing in early reading ability: What we can learn from Chinese. *Scientific Studies of Reading, 2*, 55–79.

Huang, H. S. & Hanley, J. R. (1995). Phonological awareness and visual skills in learning to read Chinese and English. *Cognition, 54*, 73–98.

——— (1997). A longitudinal study of phonological awareness, visual skills, and Chinese reading acquisition among first-graders in Taiwan. *International Journal of Behavioral Development, 20*, 249–268.

Huang, H. S. & Zhang, H. R. (1997). An analysis of phonemic awareness, word awareness and tone awareness among dyslexic children. *Bulletin of Special Education and Rehabilitation, 5*, 125–138.

Huang, S. (1998). Chinese as a headless language in compounding morphology. In J. Packard (Ed.), *New approaches to Chinese word formation: Morphology, phonology and the lexicon in modern and ancient Chinese* (pp. 261–283). Berlin and New York: Mouton de Gruyter.

Ku, Y. & Anderson, R. C. (2003). Development of morphological awareness in Chinese and English. *Reading and Writing, 16*, 399–422.

Lei, L., Pan, J., Liu, H., McBride-Chang, C., Li, H., Zhang, Y., Chen, L., Tardif, T., Liang, W., Zhang, Z. & Shu, H. (2011). Developmental trajectories of reading development and impairment from ages 3 to 8 years in Chinese children. *The Journal of Child Psychology and Psychiatry, 52*, 212–220.

Leong, C. K., Tse, S. K., Loh, K. Y. & Hau, K. T. (2008). Text comprehension in Chinese children: Relative contribution of verbal working memory, pseudoword reading, rapid automated naming, and onset-rime phonological segmentation. *Journal of Educational Psychology, 100*, 135–149.

Li, W., Anderson, R. C., Nagy, W. & Zhang, H. (2002). Facets of metalinguistic awareness that contribute to Chinese literacy. In W. Li, J. S. Gaffney & J. L. Packard (Eds.), *Chinese children's reading acquisition: Theoretical and pedagogical issues* (pp. 87–106). Norwell, MA: Kluwer Academic Press.

Li, W.-S. & Ho, C. S.-H. (2011). Lexical tone awareness among Chinese children with developmental dyslexia. *Journal of Child Language, 38*, 793–808.

Li, H., Shu, H., McBride-Chang, C., Liu, H. & Peng, H. (2012). Chinese children's character recognition: Viso-orthographic, phonological processing and morphological skills. *Journal of Research in Reading, 35*, 287–307.

Lin, Y.-H. (1989). *Autosegmental treatment of segmental processes in Chinese phonology*. Doctoral dissertation, University of Texas, Austin.

Liu, P. D. & McBride-Chang, C. (2010). What is morphological awareness: Tapping lexical compounding awareness in Chinese third graders. *Journal of Educational Psychology, 102*, 62–73.

Liu, P. D., McBride-Chang, C., Wong, T. T.-Y., Shu, H. & Wong, A. M.-Y. (2013). Morphological awareness in Chinese: Unique associations of homophone awareness and lexical compounding to word reading and vocabulary knowledge in Chinese children. *Applied Psycholinguistics, 34*, 755–775.

Luo, Y. C., Chen, X., Deacon, S. H. & Li, H. (2011). Development of Chinese orthographic processing: A cross-cultural perspective. *Writing Systems Research, 3*, 69–86.

Mair, V. H. (1991). What is a Chinese "dialect/topolect"? Reflections on some key Sino-English linguistic terms. *Sino-Platonic Papers, 29*, 1–31.

Matthews, S. & Yip, V. (2011). *Cantonese: A comprehensive grammar*, 2nd edn. London: Routledge.

McBride-Chang, C. (2004). *Children's literacy development*. London: Edward Arnold.

McBride-Chang, C., Bialystok, E., Chong, K. & Li, Y. P. (2004). Levels of phonological awareness in three cultures. *Journal of Experimental Child Psychology, 89*, 93–111.

McBride-Chang, C., Cheung, H., Chow, B. W.-Y., Chow, C. S.-L. & Choi, L. (2006). Metalinguistic skills and vocabulary knowledge in Chinese (L1) and English (L2). *Reading and Writing, 19*, 695–716.

McBride-Chang, C., Cho, J., Liu, H., Wagner, R. K., Shu, H., Zhou, A. & Muse, A. (2005). Changing models across culture: Associations of phonological awareness and morphological structure with vocabulary and word recognition in second graders from Beijing, Hong Kong, Korea, and the United States. *Journal of Experimental Child Psychology, 92*, 140–160.

McBride-Chang, C. & Ho, C. S.-H. (2005). Predictors of beginning reading in Chinese and English: A 2-year longitudinal study of Chinese kindergartners. *Scientific Studies of Reading, 9*, 117–144.

McBride-Chang, C. & Kail, R. (2002). Cross-cultural similarities in the predictors of reading acquisition. *Child Development, 73*, 1392–1407.

McBride-Chang, C., Lam, F., Lam, C., Chan, B., Fong, C. Y.-C., Wong, T. T.-Y. & Wong, S. W.-L. (2011). Early predictors of dyslexia in Chinese children: Familial history of dyslexia, language delay, and cognitive profiles. *Journal of Child Psychology and Psychiatry, 52*, 204–211.

McBride-Chang, C., Shu, H., Ng, J. Y. W., Meng, X. & Penney, T. (2007). Morphological structure awareness, vocabulary, and reading. In R. K. Wagner, A. E. Muse & K. R. Tannenbaum (Eds.), *Vocabulary acquisition: Implications for reading comprehension* (pp. 104–122). New York: Guilford Press.

McBride-Chang, C., Shu, H., Zhou, A., Wat, C. P. & Wagner, R. K. (2003). Morphological awareness uniquely predicts young children's Chinese character reading. *Journal of Experimental Psychology, 95*, 743–751.

McBride-Chang, C., Tong, X., Shu, H., Wong, A. M.-Y., Leung, K. & Tardif, T. (2008). Syllable, phoneme, and tone: Psycholinguistic units in early Chinese and English word recognition. *Scientific Studies of Reading, 12*, 171–194.

Morris, R. D., Stuebing, K. K., Fletcher, J. M., Shaywitz, S. E., Lyon, G. R., Shankweiler, D. P., Katz, L., Francis, D. J. & Shaywitz, B. A. (1998). Subtypes of reading disability: Variability around a phonological core. *Journal of Educational Psychology, 90*, 347–373.

Nagy, W. E. & Anderson, R. C. (1998). Metalinguistic awareness and the acquisition of literacy in different languages. In D. Wagner, R. Venezky & B. Street (Eds.), *Literacy: An international handbook* (pp. 155–160). Boulder, CO: Westview Press.

Packard, J. (2000). *The morphology of Chinese: A linguistic and cognitive approach*. Cambridge University Press.

Pan, Y. (2000). Code-switching and social change in Guangzhou and Hong Kong. *International Journal of the Sociology of Language, 146*, 21–41.

Perfetti, C. A. (2003). The universal grammar of reading. *Scientific Studies of Reading, 7*, 3–24.

Perfetti, C. A., Cao, F. & Booth, J. (2013). Specialization and universals in the development of reading skill: How Chinese research informs a universal science of reading. *Scientific Studies of Reading, 17*, 5–21.

Perfetti, C. A., Zhang, S. & Berent, I. (1992). Reading in English and Chinese: Evidence for a "universal" phonological principle. In R. Frost & L. Katz (Eds.), *Orthography, phonology, morphology, and meaning* (pp. 227–248). Amsterdam: North-Holland.

Shen, H. H. & Bear, D. R. (2000). Development of orthographic skills in Chinese children. *Reading and Writing, 13*, 197–236.

Shu, H. & Anderson, R. C. (1997). Role of radical awareness in the character and word acquisition of Chinese children. *Reading Research Quarterly, 32*, 78–89.

(1998). Learning to read Chinese: The development of metalinguistic awareness. In J. Wang, A. W. Inhoff & H.-C. Chen (Eds.), *Reading Chinese script: A cognitive analysis* (pp. 1–18). Mahwah, NJ: Lawrence Erlbaum.

Shu, H., Anderson, R. C. & Wu, N. (2000). Phonetic awareness: Knowledge of orthography-phonology relationships in the character acquisition of Chinese children. *Journal of Educational Psychology, 92*, 56–62.

Shu, H., Anderson, R. C. & Zhang, H. (1995). Incidental learning of word meanings while reading: A Chinese and American cross-cultural study. *Reading Research Quarterly, 39*, 76–94.

Shu, H., Chen, X., Anderson, R. C., Wu, N. & Xuan, Y. (2003). Properties of school Chinese: Implications for learning to read. *Child Development, 74*, 27–47.

Shu, H., McBride-Chang, C., Wu, S. & Liu, H. (2006). Understanding Chinese developmental dyslexia: Morphological awareness as a core cognitive construct. *Journal of Educational Psychology, 98*, 122–133.

Shu, H., Peng, H. & McBride-Chang, C. (2008). Phonological awareness in young Chinese children. *Developmental Science, 11*, 171–181.

Siok, W. T. & Fletcher, P. (2001). The role of phonological awareness and visual-orthographic skills in Chinese reading acquisition. *Developmental Psychology, 37*, 886–899.

Stevenson, H. W., Stigler, J. W., Lucker, G. W., Hsu, C. & Kitamura, S. (1982). Reading disabilities: The case of Chinese, Japanese, and English. *Child Development, 53*, 1164–1181.

Suen, C.-Y. (1986). *Computational studies of the most frequent Chinese words and sounds*. Singapore: World Scientific.

Sun, H. L., Huang, J. P., Sun, D. J., Li, D. J. & Xing, H. B. (1997). Introduction to language corpus system of modern Chinese study. In M. Y. Hu (Ed.), *Paper collection for the 5th World Chinese Teaching Symposium* (pp. 459–466). Beijing: Peking University Publisher.

Taylor, I. & Taylor, M. M. (1995). *Writing and literacy in Chinese, Korean and Japanese*. Amsterdam: John Benjamins.

Tong, X. & McBride-Chang, C. (2010). Chinese-English biscriptal reading: Cognitive component skills across orthographies. *Reading and Writing, 23*, 293–310.

Tong, X., McBride-Chang, C., Shu, H. & Wong, A. M.-Y. (2009). Morphological awareness, orthographic knowledge and spelling errors: Keys to understanding early Chinese literacy acquisition. *Scientific Studies of Reading, 13*, 426–452.

Treiman, R. & Zukowski, A. (1991). Levels of phonological awareness. In S. A. Brady & D. P. Shankweiler (Eds.), *Phonological processing in literacy: A tribute to Isabelle Y. Liberman* (pp. 67–83). Hillsdale, NJ: Lawrence Erlbaum.

Wang, M., Cheng, C. & Chen, S. (2006). Contribution of morphological awareness to Chinese–English biliteracy acquisition. *Journal of Educational Psychology*, *98*, 542–553.

Wang, X., Georgiou, G. K., Das, J. P. & Li, Q. (2012). Cognitive processing skills and developmental dyslexia in Chinese. *Journal of Learning Disabilities*, *45*, 526–537.

Wang, M., Perfetti, C. A. & Liu, Y. (2005). Chinese-English biliteracy acquisition: Cross-language and writing system transfer. *Cognition*, *97*, 67–88.

Wu, X., Li, W. & Anderson, R. C. (1999). Reading instruction in China. *Journal of Curriculum Studies*, *31*, 571–586.

Xu, Y. (1999). Effects of tone and focus on the formation and alignment of f_0 contours. *Journal of Phonetics*, *27*, 55–105.

Yeung, P.-S., Ho, C. S.-H., Chan, D. W.-O., Chung, K. K.-H. & Wong, Y.-K. (2013). A model of reading comprehension in Chinese elementary school children. *Learning and Individual Differences*, *25*, 55–66.

Yeung, P.-S., Ho, C. S.-H., Chik, P. P.-M., Lo, L.-Y., Luan, H., Chan, D. W.-O. & Chung, K. K.-H. (2011). Reading and spelling Chinese among beginning readers: What skills make a difference? *Scientific Studies of Reading*, *15*, 285–313.

Yeung, P.-S., Ho, C. S.-H., Wong, Y.-K., Chan, D. W.-O., Chung, K. K.-H. & Lo, L.-Y. (2013). Longitudinal predictors of Chinese word reading and spelling among elementary grade students. *Applied Psycholinguistics*, *34*, 1245–1277.

Yin, B. (1984). A quantitative research of Chinese morphemes. *Zhongguo Yuwen*, *5*, 338–347.

Yuan, Y. (1989). *Hanyu Fangyan Gaiyao* [Outline of Chinese dialets], 2nd edn. Beijing: Wenzi Gaige Chubanshe.

Yuan, C. & Huang, C. (1998). The study of Chinese morphemes and word formation based on the morpheme data bank. *Applied Linguistics*, *3*, 83–88.

Zhang, J., McBride-Chang, C., Tong, X., Anita, M.-Y., Shu, H. & Fong, C. Y.-C. (2012). Reading with meaning: The contributions of meaning-related variables at the word and subword levels to early Chinese reading comprehension. *Reading and Writing*, *25*, 2183–2203.

Zhang, J., McBride-Chang, C., Wong, A. M.-Y., Tardif, T., Shu, H. & Zhang, Y. (2014). Longitudinal correlates of reading comprehension difficulties in Chinese children. *Reading and Writing*, *27*, 481–501. DOI: 10.1007/s11145-013-9453-4.

Zhou, Y.-L., McBride-Chang, C., Fong, C. Y.-C., Wong, T. T.-Y. & Cheung, S. K. (2012). A comparison of phonological awareness, lexical compounding, and homophone training for Chinese word reading in Hong Kong kindergartners. *Early Education and Development*, *23*, 475–492.

3   Learning to Read Japanese

Keiko Koda

3.1   Introduction

3.1.1   *Japanese and Its Orthography*

The Japanese language is written using two typologically distinct writing systems: phonographic Kana and morpheme-based Kanji. Because the two systems map onto relatively large units of language, they have considerably greater numbers of symbols than English and other alphabetic systems. During the six years of primary school education, Japanese children learn 105 Kana symbols in two forms (Hiragana and Katakana) and 1,006 Kanji characters in 2,005 pronunciations (Kess & Miyamoto, 1999). In addition, they must also learn which linguistic element is graphically encoded in each system. It may seem impractical to use multiple writing systems concurrently in running text, but such a convention does not occur accidentally. It exemplifies the culmination of collective creativity and wisdom deployed by the Japanese in establishing their written language. Despite the ostensive intricacies, the written Japanese language has its logic that children can learn and use to facilitate literacy learning. This chapter describes the evolution of Kana and Kanji through diverse adaptation strategies, multiple complexities that arose from the adaptations, and the impacts of such complexities on reading acquisition in Japanese.

3.1.2   *Synchronic and Diachronic Characterization*

Chinese characters were brought to Japan between the fourth and fifth centuries by Korean scholars to introduce Chinese culture and technologies to small groups of Japanese elites and royal family members, most of whom were not familiar with the Chinese language. Technology and other related concepts were therefore taught through Chinese characters, and the Chinese pronunciations corresponding to those concepts were used as their phonetic labels. Morpheme-based Chinese characters were well studied for transmitting semantic information across languages. Gradually, people began to extend the use of Chinese characters to write their own language. To do so, however, borrowed characters must be substantially modified through two basic, meaning-based and sound-based, adaptation strategies (Coulmas, 1989).

In the meaning-based adaptation, a Chinese character was selected to write a Japanese word that conveys the same meaning as the Chinese word for which the character was used. As noted above, the Chinese pronunciation of the word was also adopted along with the character. The spoken sound of the Japanese word was then added to the character as its lexical identity. The attachment of additional sounds could be easily accomplished in morpheme-based characters because the sounds of morphemes are holistically associated with their graphemes. This allowed a borrowed character to represent simultaneously its generally monosyllabic Chinese pronunciation and the spoken sound of the Japanese word that semantically corresponds to the Chinese word for which the character is used. Such flexibility led to a massive influx of Chinese words into the Japanese lexicon. Two major consequences arose: (1) the majority of Kanji have two or more readings; and (2) Sino-Japanese words constitute more than half the contemporary Japanese lexicon (Matsushita, 2012).

The sound-based adaptation came into use as a complementary device to the meaning-based strategy to meet the need for using characters phonetically, irrespective of the morphological information they encode, to convey grammatical and other non-semantic information that is unique to the Japanese language. Initially, there were considerable variations in the sounds to be transcribed and the characters used to transcribe those sounds. The variations decreased dramatically over time as the transcribing method was conventionalized based on the "one character for one sound" principle (Taylor & Taylor, 1995).

Katakana evolved directly from the stylized characters as phonetic indicators. Initially, they appeared only as auxiliary marks in conjunction with Kanji. Hiragana, on the other hand, were derived from Katakana specifically for transcribing the grammatical elements, and as such, their use was independent of and complementary to Kanji. The emergence of Hiragana is said to be instrumental in the establishment of the current convention of using multiple writing systems concurrently, as shown in the example below, in standard written texts in Japanese.

私は毎朝コーヒーを飲む。

私	は	毎朝	コー ヒー	を	飲む
watashi	wa	maiasa	kōhī	wo	nomu

I drink coffee every morning

| I | topic
marker | every
morning | coffee | object
marker | drink-nonpast |

3.1.3 Literacy and Schooling

Ensuring the acquisition of basic literacy is a major goal of compulsory education. In Japan, the highly centralized educational system regulates both instructional approaches and contents in all subjects, including reading and language arts. The guidelines issued by the Ministry of Education, for example, stipulate which writing systems (and how many symbols in each system) are to be taught in each grade.

Formal literacy instruction commences in primary school. In Grade 1, Hiragana are taught throughout the year. Many children learn most Hiragana symbols before entering primary school (Sakamoto & Makita, 1973). Katakana are taught over three years in Grades 2 through 4. Most children master the basic Katakana symbols by the end of Grade 3 (National Language Research Institute, 1964).

Kanji are taught over the nine years of compulsory education. Kanji instruction begins in the second term of first grade. In each grade, Kanji words are introduced in sentences or texts without Kana (phonetic) annotations. In the initial grades, each character is taught with the meaning and the spoken sound of the word it denotes and stroke order. The general expectation is that children can read all the characters that are taught explicitly in each grade and write most of them by the end of the grade (Taylor & Taylor, 1995). Children are also expected to learn characters by copying them repeatedly in specified orders of strokes (Naka & Naoi, 1995).

In first grade, only eighty characters are taught, mostly in Kun readings (Japanese pronunciations), because they holistically represent spoken words that are familiar to children. Once learned, those characters offer instant and direct access to the meaning and the sound of the words they encode. The first-grade characters are mostly single-unit, structurally simple, characters. Beyond the initial grades, the proportions of compound characters increase dramatically. A compound character consists of two functionally distinct graphic components, each conveying a Chinese pronunciation of the character (phonetic component) or partial information on the meaning of the word it represents (semantic component). As shown in Figure 3.1, over 60 percent of the words taught in Grade 4 to Grade 6 are multi-syllabic Sino-Japanese words (Wada, 2000), such as 冷蔵庫 /rei-zō-ko/ 'refrigerator' (冷 /rei/ 'to chill' + 蔵 /zō/ 'to store', 庫 /ko/ 'space').

3.2   Description of Japanese and Its Written Forms

Several unique features of the Japanese language do not allow any simple typological categorization. Although the language shares many morphosyntactic properties with members of the Altaic language family, historically, its

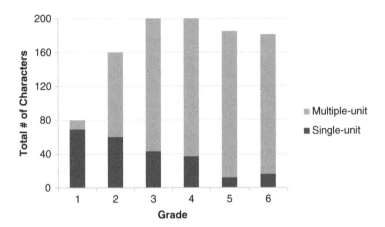

Figure 3.1 Single vs. multiple-unit characters. Based on "Redefining phonological awareness in Japanese literacy acquisition" (Master's thesis), by Y. Wada, 2000, Carnegie Mellon University, PA.

formation was heavily influenced by intense contact and heavy borrowings from Melo-Polynesian languages and Chinese (Clancy, 1985). Reflecting the multilingual contacts, the Japanese lexicon comprises four types of words, including native Japanese, Sino-Japanese (those borrowed from Chinese), foreign loan (those borrowed from various languages other than Chinese), and hybrids (those consisting of loan word stems with Japanese affixes) (Taylor & Taylor, 1995). Japanese has numerous dialects, many of which are mutually unintelligible. The majority of native Japanese speakers living in Japan are fluent in Tokyo dialect, which constitutes the modern standard.

3.2.1 Linguistic System

3.2.1.1 Phonology Japanese has a simple sound system, consisting of five vowels (/a/, /e/, /i/, /o/, /u/) and sixteen consonants (/p/, /t/, /k/, /b/, /d/, /g/, /s/, /h/, /z/, /j/, /r/, /m/, /n/, /w/, nasal N, and geminate consonant Q). Japanese consonants appear only in the initial position of a syllable with two exceptions. The nasal consonant N occurs only in the final position of a syllable, and the geminate consonant Q is placed only in the medial position of a word. The small inventory of phonemes produces an extremely small number (roughly 110) of structurally simple syllables, or more precisely, morae. As a sub-syllabic rhythmic unit, a mora may consist of a single vowel or any of the consonants (except for N and Q) in combination with any of the five vowels. Because mora is a short beat (the time to pronounce a short syllable), the duration of uttering one mora, be it /i/ or /ki/, is constant. A long vowel and a sequence of two vowels are counted as two morae. Vowel length alters the meaning, as in /chi/ 'blood' and /chī/ 'status'. Most Japanese sounds are relatively stable because they do not change in different phonetic contexts with a few exceptions for smooth articulation. The simple sound system of Japanese could not discriminate tonal differences in Sino-Japanese words that were adopted through early contact with Chinese. As a result, there are a large number of homophones in the present-day lexicon and an even larger number of homophonous characters.

3.2.1.2 Inflectional Morphology Syntactically, Japanese is classified as a subject-object-verb (SOV) language, exhibiting many of the grammatical features associated with this classification. There is relative freedom of word order because postpositional case markers indicate the syntactic roles of the noun phrases in a sentence. The case markers include particles, such as が /-ga/ (nominative or subject), を /-wo/ (accusative or direct object), and に /-ni/ (dative or indirect object). Although the case markers allow the use of other, non-canonical, word orders, they can be omitted when the syntactic function of a noun phrase can be predicted from the word order or contextual information. Also, sentential elements, such as pronominals, can be omitted when they are predictable from the discourse context.

When the subject or direct object of a sentence is topicalized, the topic marker /-wa/ replaces the designated case particle, as shown in (1) and (2) below. When topicalization occurs to other nominal arguments, such as dative and locative, the topic marker is added to the case particle as seen in (3). In the appropriate conversational context, any of the nouns could be postposed to sentence-final position following the verb, or reoriented with respect to one another in preverbal position. In face-to-face conversations, it is common for Japanese sentences to deviate from the canonical word order.

(1) watashi **wa**   tsukue *o*   tatai*ta*
     I   topic   desk   nominative   hit-past
              marker   marker
              (replacing the nominative marker /-ga/)

(2) tsukue **wa**   watashi *ga*   tataki*ta*
     desk   topic   I   nominative hit-past
             marker   marker
             (replacing the accusative marker /-o/)

(3) Hanako ni   **wa**   tsukue o   age*ta*
     Hanako dative   topic   desk   accusative give-past
            marker   marker   marker

Japanese morphology is typologically mixed in that nouns are analytic and predicate words (verbs and adjectives) are synthetic. Japanese nouns are largely uninflected because Japanese does not morphologically mark for gender, number, and person on nouns. Such information may be conveyed lexically through the addition of separate words. Like nouns, Japanese verbs have no agreement in number, gender, or person, but unlike nouns, suffixation is prominent in verb formation because verbal roots are bound morphemes. A fully formed verb includes at minimum a root and a termination suffix (Kondo, 2008). For example, the verb 見る /mi-ru/ 'to see' consists of the root /mi-/ and the non-past termination suffix /-ru/. Japanese verbs also have an assortment of inflectional suffixes, which may be added to verb roots to convey information such as tense, aspect, voice, mood, negation, potential, causation, formality, and conditionality. Adjectives are also inflected for tense, negation, conditionality, and formality.

3.2.1.3 Word Formation Processes   Japanese derivational affixes include prefixes and suffixes. Grammatical categories can be changed through the use of derivational suffixes. For example, nouns can be derived from adjectives by replacing the adjective termination suffix /-i/ with the nominalizer suffix /-sa/, as in 美しい /utsukushi-i/ 'beautiful' to 美しさ /utsukushi-sa/ 'beauty'. Similarly, adverbs can be generated from adjectives by replacing the adjective termination suffix /-i/ with the adverb-making suffix /-ku/, as in 美しい /utsukushi-i/ to 美しく /utsukushi-ku/ 'beautifully'.

Derivational affixes may be added to modify or limit a word's meaning without changing its grammatical category. For example, a negative meaning can be expressed by attaching negative prefixes, such as 非 /hi-/, 不 /fu-/, 無 /mu-/, and 未 /mi-/ (roughly corresponding to English prefixes *im-, in-, dis-, un-, non-, de-, ir-*). There are also agent suffixes that may be used to designate persons based on their occupation or attribute, including 者 /-sha/, 家 /-ka/, 人 /-ji/, and 士 /-shi/ (roughly equivalent to English suffixes *-er, -or, -ist*).

Compounding plays a major role in Japanese word formation. In particular, Sino-Japanese words are highly productive in that a new word can be easily coined by combining them with other lexical morphemes or combining forms, such as 教習所 /kyōshū-jo/ 'driving school' (/kyōshū/ 'training' and /-jo/ 'place'). There are three types of compound formation (nominal, verbal, and adjectival). A nominal compound consists of a nominal head and another nominal element, both of which can be a noun or a noun equivalent (i.e., nominalized verb or adjective). According to Iwasaki (2002), of the nine possible combination patterns, the most productive pattern is the N+N combination, wherein the two constituents are both nouns, such as 山頂 /san-chō/ 'mountain peak' (/san/ 'mountain' and /cho/ 'peak'). The Nv+N combination is the second most productive pattern, in which a nominalized verb is followed by either its direct object or intransitive subject, as in 読書 /doku-sho/ (/doku/ 'to read' and /sho/ 'document'). A compound verb consists of a verbal head and a noun or a noun equivalent, as in 気付く /ki-zuk-u/ 'notice' (/ki/ 'spirit' + /tsuk-u/ 'to turn on').

3.2.2 Writing System

3.2.2.1 Script and Punctuation Standard Japanese texts are written using morpheme-based Kanji and two forms of Kana syllabary (Hiragana and Katakana). The three scripts are used to encode distinct classes of words. In principle, Kanji are used for writing nouns and verbal/adjectival/adverbial roots, Hiragana for conveying grammatical information, and Katakana for transcribing foreign loan words and onomatopoeias.

Japanese sentences can be written horizontally or vertically, and punctuation marks adapt to this change in direction. In running text, there is no space between words regardless of their formational types (e.g., compounds, derived/inflected words, and pronouns). Similarly, no space is given between the morphological constituents within a word, or between a noun phrase and the case-marking particle attached to the noun phrase. In a new paragraph, a single space is left before the first symbol. Most punctuation marks in modern Japanese, such as period and comma, serve similar functions to their English equivalents.

3.2.2.2 Orthography

Kana Hiragana and Katakana each comprises seventy-one standard symbols, consisting of forty-six basic symbols that represent voiceless consonants and twenty-five additional symbols that are created by adding one of the two diacritic marks to twenty-five of the basic symbols to represent their voiced counterparts (e.g., か /ka/ and が /ga/). An additional set of compound symbols is created by combining eleven of the standard symbols with semi-vowel /y/ to encode contracted sounds, such as きゃ /kya/, きゅ /kyu/, and きょ /kyo/. The small size つ /tsu/ is used for transcribing double consonants, as in かっこ /ka<u>kk</u>o/ 'parenthesis' (as opposed to かこ /ka<u>k</u>o/ 'past'). The number of symbols in each form of Kana totals up to 105, including 46 basic symbols, 25 additional symbols, 33 compound symbols, and 1 symbol for double consonants. This allows Kana to assign a unique symbol to each of the 110 morae in spoken Japanese. Nearly perfect one-to-one grapheme–phonology correspondences make Kana one of the most phonologically transparent writing systems.

Hiragana and Katakana are taught with a Kana matrix, in which the basic symbols are organized in five horizontal vowel rows and ten vertical consonant

Figure 3.2 Hiragana Matrix.

columns. As shown in Figure 3.2, the symbols for the morae sharing the same consonant (e.g., か /ka/ and き /ki/) appear vertically in the same column, and those for the morae sharing the same vowel (e.g., か /ka/ and さ /sa/) line up horizontally in the same row. In Kana instruction, children are required to memorize the symbols in the strict order (from top to bottom and from left to right) in which they appear in the matrix. The order is culturally important because it is used to organize entries in socially meaningful lists, such as dictionaries and directories.

Kanji: Grapheme–Phonology Relationships   There are as many as 50,000 characters listed in typical Kanji dictionaries, but roughly 2,000 characters are designated as "characters for common use" and taught during the nine years of compulsory education. In Kanji, graphemes encode morphemes, and the sounds of the morpheme for which a character is used are assigned holistically to the character. In principle, each character has two sounds, one based on its Chinese pronunciation (On reading) and the other representing the spoken sound of the equivalent word in Japanese (Kun reading). Because in Kun readings, graphemes map onto Japanese spoken words regardless of the number of morae, Kun sounds vary in length. As an illustration, the Kun reading of the character 尾 'tail' is a single vowel /o/, while that of the character 頂 'peak' is /i-ta-da-ki/, consisting of four morae.

Owing to the sizable proportion of Sino-Japanese words in the Japanese lexicon, there are more On readings than Kun readings. Of the 1,945 Common Use Kanji, 1,168 have both On and Kun readings, 737 have only On readings

Table 3.1 *Morphological and phonological composition in compound Kanji and words*

Grapheme	Semantic component	Phonetic component	Character type	Character/Word meaning	Character/Word sound
空	穴 'roof'	工 /kō/	composite	'sky'	Kun: /sora/ On: /kū/
港	氵 'water'	巷 /kō/	composite	'port'	Kun: /minato/ On: /kō/
空港	–	–	compound	'air port'	/kū kō/

and 40 have only Kun readings (Taylor & Taylor, 1995). Because On readings do not directly correspond to any meaningful unit in spoken Japanese, they rarely appear alone. Multiple character words are generally (but not always) read in On sounds.

Kanji: Grapheme–Morpheme Relationships   Suffixation plays a central role in Japanese verb formation. Since verbal roots and suffixes are written in different writing systems (Kanji and Hiragana, respectively), the morphological composition of verbs is visually accessible. In nouns, however, the grapheme–morpheme relationships are differentially transparent between single-unit and compound characters, as well as between mono-morphemic and mutli-morphemic words. As shown in Table 3.1, in a compound character morphological information is coded in two graphic units, including the semantic component of the character and the character itself, whereas in multi-morphemic words, the information is represented in three graphic units, including the semantic component of each constituent character, the constituent characters, and the word. As such, the morphological composition in multiple character words is not as transparent, because strings of characters in those words represent different types of words, including mono-morphemic words (e.g., 学校 /gakko/ 'school'), derived words (e.g., 無 /mu/ 'non-' +神経 /shinkei/ 'nerve' ➔ 'insensitive') and compounds (e.g., 健康 /kenkō/ 'health' + 保険 /hoken/ 'insurance' ➔ 'health insurance').

3.2.3   Conclusion

The grapheme–language relationships markedly vary between phonographic Kana and morpheme-based Kanji. In Kana, each symbol corresponds to a sub-syllabic rhythmic unit, mora. A total of 105 Kana symbols represent 110 morae in spoken Japanese with nearly perfect grapheme–phonology correspondences. In contrast, the grapheme–phonology relationships in Kanji are varied and complex because each character represents two fundamentally different sounds (Kun/Japanese and On/Chinese). While, in Kun sounds, graphemes map directly onto spoken words, in On readings, each character represents a Chinese pronunciation of the morpheme it encodes. The grapheme–morpheme relationships differ in verbs and nouns. In verbs, the morphological composition is visually accessible, but in nouns, the morphological structure is less transparent because linearly concatenated characters do not reveal their semantic relationships.

3.3   Acquisition of Reading and Spelling in Japanese

Learning to read entails learning to map between graphic symbols and spoken language elements, and as such, it relies on children's metalinguistic insight into the abstract structure of language. Owing to the distinct grapheme–language relationships in Kana and Kanji, reading acquisition in the two systems necessitates unique facets of metalinguistic awareness. The following sections describe how children develop sensitivity to the phonological and morphological structures of spoken words in Japanese.

3.3.1   *Becoming Linguistically Aware*

3.3.1.1 Phonological Development and Phonological Awareness   The acquisition of the language-specific phonemic inventory occurs in stages. According to Ota (2006), vowels are among the first sounds to be productive in Japanese. By 2 years of age, most children produce the vowels with high levels of accuracy. Of the sixteen consonants, the nasals and the alveolo-palatal affricates are acquired relatively early. Late-acquired sounds include the three allophones of /h/, the flap, and alveolar sibilants. Some children have difficulty in articulating these late-acquired phonemes until about age 3.

Japanese has durational contrasts in morae, as in /to/ 'door' and /tō/ 'ten'. Because durational contrasts are graphically distinguished in Kana, as in と /to/ and と う /tō/, the ability to discriminate vowel length in speech is relevant to Kana reading development. Although children show sensitivity to the distinction between long and short vowels as early as 1 year of age, it takes several years for their early sensitivity to be adult-like in production (Ota, 2006).

Speech segmentation is another area of phonology that is relevant to reading acquisition. Adult Tokyo dialect speakers tend to segment words at points that correspond to mora boundaries even when they break the integrity of the syllable, as in /ho-n/ 'book' (Kubozono, 2006). Sensitivity to mora boundaries in speech begins to appear at around age 4 (Amano, 1970; Ito & Kagawa, 2001; Ito & Tatsumi, 1997). Around this time, children start playing with spoken sounds in word games, such as *sakasa kotoba* (reversing morae in words) and *shiritori* (finding a word whose first mora is the same as the last mora of a given word).

Although mora biases in speech perception and production are formed well before schooling, it appears that explicit sub-syllabic representations emerge through formal literacy (Hiragana, in specific) instruction in primary school. The nature of phonological awareness in Japanese children has been investigated in relation to Kana learning in the formal educational context. Inagaki, Hatano, and Otake (2000), for example, compared strategies for speech segmentation between kindergarten and first-grade children (aged 5–7). They found a notable change in segmentation strategies between the two age groups. While the kindergarteners used a mixture of mora-based and syllable-based strategies, the first-grade children relied almost exclusively on mora-based strategies. The observed difference was taken as indicating that phonological awareness is refined in first grade through formal Kana instruction. From a cross-linguistic perspective, Mann (1986) compared phonological manipulation skills between age-matched children (aged 5–7) in the USA and Japan. She found an interesting contrast between the two language groups. While Japanese children were more adept at mora-level analysis, their American counterparts excelled at phonemic manipulation. The comparative strengths of the groups' phonological manipulation skills at the distinct levels were interpreted as suggesting that cumulative experience with a particular writing system plays a decisive role in shaping phonological awareness.

If, indeed, the formation of phonological awareness were entirely script dependent, Japanese children, in theory, would never develop phoneme-level sensitivity because neither Kana nor Kanji requires phoneme-level analysis. This does not seem to be the case, however. Mann (1986) reported that Japanese fourth-grade children were skilled at phonemic segmentation and manipulation. In an attempt to explain the unexpected presence of phonemic skills in older Japanese children, Mann points out that phonemic analysis is indeed required for Kana learning. For example, the symbols for the vowels (/a/, /i/, /u/, /e/, /o/) and the nasal /N/) represent mora units that also correspond to phonemes. She also contends that voiced and voiceless contrast pairs, such as /ka/ and /ga/, might also promote phonemic sensitivity because the same basic symbol is used for the voiced and voiceless morae in each contrast pair, such as か /ka/ and が /ga/.

It has been hypothesized that the method of Kana instruction also contributes to the formation of phonemic awareness in Japanese children. As described earlier, Hiragana and Katakana instruction heavily relies on the Kana matrix that organizes the standard Kana symbols in vowel rows and consonant columns (see Figure 3.2). Such organization is likely to promote children's explicit awareness of shared consonants and vowels in subgroups of Kana symbols. In a training study, Goetry, Urbain, Morais, and Kolinsky (2005) tested the hypothesized facilitation stemming from the use of the Kana matrix in the refinement of phonological awareness in beginning readers (aged 5–7). Their results demonstrated that explicit reference to the symbol organization in the matrix led to improved phonemic manipulation performance. Interestingly, however, they also noted that even after the training, most children continued to use mora-based strategies, whenever possible, in tasks requiring phoneme-level analysis, such as phoneme counting and deletion.

3.3.1.2 Morphological Development and Morphological Awareness   Japanese verbs have well-developed inflectional suffixes. Child language acquisition studies have focused on the acquisition of verbal inflections as an index of morphological development in Japanese children. According to Clancy (1985), the system of verbal inflectional suffixes develops between 18 to 30 months. Even before 2 years of age, a few inflectional suffixes, including the imperative and the past tense, appear in utterances. During the subsequent period (24 to 30 months), high-frequency inflections, such as the present progressive/resultative, the non-past tense, and the completed past, become productive. At around this time, children dramatically expand their repertoire of verbal inflections. Some children begin to express their sense of social distance by means of polite inflectional suffixes. In the month around the child's third birthday, verbal inflections for passive, causative, and obligation are learned along with additional polite suffixes. It appears that most verbal suffixes and suffixation rules are acquired well before formal literacy instruction commences.

A critical question is what structural generalizations arise from the acquisition of verbal suffixes and other types of morphemes during speech development. Clarification of such generalizations is essential as they evolve into "conscious awareness" (Carlisle, 1995) of the morphological structure of words later through literacy experience. To date, little information is available on morphological awareness in Japanese children. The only study on record (Hayashi & Murphy, 2013) directly addressing morphological awareness involves two groups of English–Japanese bilingual children in the UK, who received little, if any, formal education in Japan, and as such, provides limited information on the development of morphological awareness in Japanese in relation to literacy learning. In the absence of empirical data, this section describes likely generalizations that might occur as a result of spoken language development based on the characteristics of Japanese morphology described above.

Verbal suffixation is the most likely type of Japanese morphemes that induce structural generalizations as a by-product of spoken language development. The relatively simple concatenation rules and regularity in their implementation should enable children to understand the abstract structure of Japanese verbs. The productive use of inflectional suffixes reported in child language studies implies that such awareness does emerge in early years of language development.

Caution is necessary, however, because the grapheme–morpheme relationships are not uniformly transparent in all verb types. In consonant-root verbs, wherein verbal roots end with a consonant, as in 飲む /nom-u/ 'drink', the morphological composition is not reflected in their graphic forms. In writing consonant-root verbs, the final consonant of a root (/m/ in /nom-/ in the example above) is detached from the root to be attached to the verb terminal suffix immediately following the root (/-u/ in the example). The maneuver is necessary because mora-based Hiragana cannot transcribe single consonants. As a result, their graphic forms conform to mora (/no-mu/), rather than morphological (/nom-u/), boundaries.

Class-changing derivational suffixes are another type of morphemes whose acquisition may induce structural generalizations. Since they are abundant and productive (Iwasaki, 2002), their occurrences in the language input seem sufficient for allowing children to uncover their structural regularities. Other types of derivational morphemes, such as class-changing prefixes, are limited in number and low in productivity, and generally convey varied and idiosyncratic information. It is highly unlikely that the acquisition of these morphemes generates generalizations that can guide children in grapheme-to-morpheme mapping learning.

Compounding awareness entails an understanding of the linear structure of compound words that contain a sequence of two or more lexical morphemes or combining forms. It includes generalizations about the semantic relationship between the constituent morphemes in conjunction with their order in the sequence. Given the prominence of nominal compounding in Japanese, the likely generalization to occur is that the last element of a compound word is the head of the word. It has been found that such a generalization is a central facet of morphological awareness in Chinese-speaking children. Structural understanding of this sort enables young children to recognize that "dress fish" and "fish dress" refer to very different objects (Chen, Hao, Geva, Zhu & Shu, 2009; McBride-Chang, Cheung, Chow, Chow & Choi, 2006). Although compound awareness is known to emerge as early as 2.5 years of age (Clark, 1993), it is commonly assumed that the initial structural insight becomes explicit only through literacy instruction and experience (Ku & Anderson, 2003).

3.3.2   *Development of Word Identification*

3.3.2.1 Word Decoding Development   Word-reading skills are acquired at different rates and in different manners in Kana and Kanji. In phonologically transparent Kana, word-reading skills develop with considerable ease. Many children learn most Hiragana symbols before they enter primary school.

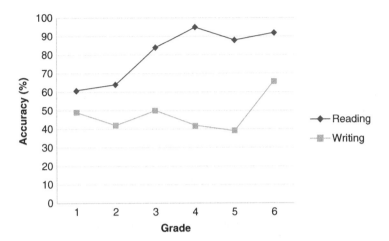

Figure 3.3 Kanji reading and writing development. Based on
The development of language abilities in elementary school children:
A six-year follow-up study of the same children. The National Language
Research Institute Research Report 26, by National Language Research
Institute, 1964, Tokyo: Meijitosho Publishing Co.

Roughly 60 percent of 4-year-olds know some Hiragana symbols (Shimamura
& Mikami, 1994); and by age 5, more than 60 percent of children recognize
sixty or more (out of seventy-one) standard Hiragana symbols (Taylor &
Taylor, 1995). All Hiragana symbols are mastered by the end of Grade 1, and
most Kataka symbols are learned by the end of Grade 3 (National Language
Research Institute, 1964). It has also been demonstrated that the ability to
manipulate morae in spoken Japanese is a strong predictor of Kana word
reading (Amano, 1989; Dairoku, 1995; Kobayashi, Haynes, Macaruso, Hook
& Kato, 2005; Koyama, Hansen & Stein, 2008).

In contrast, Kanji reading ability develops gradually. A large-scale survey
involving seventeen schools (National Language Research Institute, 1964)
documented some of the characteristics of Kanji reading development in
primary school children. Their main findings are summarized below:

- Kanji reading accuracy improves as children move through grade levels
  (61.4 percent [of the 50 characters tested] in Grade 1 to 91.5 percent [of
  the 881 characters tested] in Grade 6).
- Children make faster progress in Kanji decoding between Grade 3 and Grade
  4 when the two Kana forms have been completely mastered.
- Kanji writing development lags behind Kanji reading development.
  The difference between reading and writing abilities widens gradually
  through upper grades, as shown in Figure 3.3.

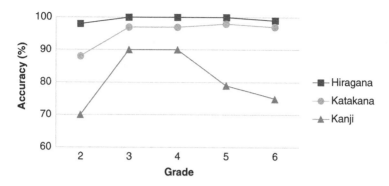

Figure 3.4 Word reading accuracy across grade level. Based on "Relationship between reading/writing skills and cognitive abilities among Japanese primary-school children: Normal readers versus poor readers (dyslexics)," by A. Uno, T. Wydell, N. Haruhara, M. Kaneko, and N. Shinya, 2009, *Reading and Writing*, *22*, 755–789.

- In Grade 5 and Grade 6, many children are able to read commonly used Kanji that are not taught in school.
- Learned Kanji are easily forgotten unless they are encountered frequently in out-of-school reading materials, such as newspapers, magazines, and comic books.

Considering the number of characters children learn in primary school, the reported Kanji reading accuracy rates, based on the number of correctly pronounced Kanji words presented in isolation, are impressive particularly in the upper grades. High accuracy rates have been reported in more recent studies, including 92.9 percent in Grade 4 children (Koyama et al., 2008) and 98 percent in Grade 6 children (Uno, Wydell, Haruhara, Kaneko & Shinya, 2009; see Figure 3.4). The reported rates alone, however, do not tell the whole story. Unlike Hiragana, Kanji learning entails substantial challenges. In particular, many children struggle to cope with the complex grapheme–phonology relationships stemming from the multiple reading assignments (Kun/Japanese and On/Chinese) (Coulmas, 1989; Taylor & Taylor, 1995; Yamada, 1992). Since Kun readings and On readings correspond to spoken sounds in two unrelated languages, Kanji decoding requires qualitatively different grapheme-to-phonology mappings in the two sounds.

Kanji decoding in Kun reading is procedurally simple as it entails holistic mappings between characters and spoken words, allowing decoding skills to be acquired with relative ease. In Grade 1, in fact, the majority of Kanji (86 percent) are taught in Kun readings (Wada, 2000). A subset of the data from the above survey revealed that most preschool children (aged 5–6) had some knowledge of Kanji, and, on average, could read fifty-six characters accurately

(Muraishi & Amano, 1972). The connection between Kun reading ability and oral vocabulary knowledge was explored in an experimental study involving adult native speakers (Yamazaki, Ellis, Morrison & Lambon Ralph, 1997). Their findings showed that Kun word naming speed was predicted strongly by two age factors – the age at which the tested words were acquired in speech and the age at which their written forms were learned in school.

In contrast, On reading skills take longer to acquire (Kayamoto, Yamada & Takashima, 1998; Yamada, 1992) mainly because there are more On readings than Kun readings. In general, in a compound character, an On reading of the phonetic component is used as the On reading of the character, as in 同 /dō/ in the compound character 銅 / dō/ 'copper'. On readings thus serve as phonetic indicators in phonologically opaque Kanji and, as such, should greatly facilitate Kanji decoding. However, several factors make their utility less salient. For example, the grapheme–phonology correspondences are far less regular to be useful for children to grasp generalizable grapheme–phonology relationships, as shown in the grapheme 青 pronounced /jō/ in 情, /shō/ in 精, and /sē/ in 清. Their small family sizes (the mean family size = 3.23; Shu et al., 2003) also contribute to the phonological opacity in compound characters.

In addition, there are roughly fifteen times more On readings (approximately 1,800) than syllables in spoken Japanese (about 110). Inevitably, Kanji decoding in On readings involves many-to-one grapheme-to-phonology mappings. To illustrate, the four characters, 家, 可, 科, 火 all share /ka/ as their On reading. Since the sound /ka/ alone, as an On reading, does not correspond to any meaningful unit in spoken Japanese, these characters are used as a phonological (and morphological) constituent in disyllabic words, such as 家 in 家庭 /ka-tei/ 'home', 可 in 可能 /ka-nō/ 'possible', 科 in 科目 /ka-moku/ 'subject', and 火 in 火事 /ka-ji/ 'fire'. The On sound /ka/ is linked to the Japanese lexicon only as a phonological segment of a number of disyllabic words, which are semantically unrelated, as shown above. It hence follows that the grapheme–phonology connection in a constituent character of a disyllabic word is not likely to be represented saliently in lexical memory, making phonological segmentation far more challenging in disyllabic words. In fact, phonological confusion is the most commonly observed error type in Kanji naming and spelling (National Language Research Institute, 1964; Yamada, 1992). Typical errors in Kanji reading identification include Kun-sound substitution (indicating a Kun sound to name a character when its On-sound is requested), homophone substitution (using a homophonous character in dictation), and phonological reversal (using a sound of a wrong constituent character in a disyllabic word).

Further, the graphic complexity of characters adds further demands to Kanji learning and processing. As shown in the examples, many single-unit characters look alike as they share similar patterns of strokes (日、白、百、目、自).

When these characters are used as components of compound characters, as in 時、間、眺，暇, a close visual inspection becomes a critical step for extracting phonological and morphological information from those characters. The importance of visual skills has been investigated in a study involving Grade 2 and Grade 4 children (Koyama et al., 2008). By comparing the relative contributions of audio-phonological skills and visual-orthographic skills to word reading development in Kana and Kanji, the researchers demonstrated that visual long-term memory was a strong predictor of Kanji reading ability, while phonological awareness played a more prominent role in predicting Kana reading performance. Importantly, orthographic skills and phonological short-term memory were both found to be significant factors in Kana and Kanji reading development.

Uno et al. (2009) compared the contributions of a wider variety of sub-skills to word reading and writing development in Grade 2 to Grade 6 children. They found that, in all grade levels except for Grade 6, vocabulary knowledge was the strongest predictor of Kanji word reading. In the Grade 6 data, however, phonological memory and analysis skills were more powerful predictors of Kanji reading performance. A similar pattern was found in the analysis of Kanji writing development. While kanji writing ability was closely associated with Katakana writing and Kanji reading abilities in all (but Grade 6) groups, writing performance of the Grade 6 children was predicted by arithmetic skills and vocabulary knowledge. The observed differences in Grade 6 children were taken as indicating that qualitative changes in Kanji word learning might have occurred in the upper grades as a result of cognitive maturation.

3.3.2.2 Word Spelling Development   In word spelling development, spelling skills are acquired at different rates in Hiragana and Katakana. This is perhaps due to the much lower proportion of Katakana relative to Hiragana words in standard Japanese texts (roughly 4 percent and 47 percent, respectively; Taylor & Taylor, 1995). According to the survey conducted by the National Language Research Institute (1964), spelling skills are mastered by the end of Grade 2 in Hiragana, but the acquisition of Katakana spelling skills requires an additional year to complete. In both Hiragana and Katakana, spelling development is slower for words containing compound symbols, such as those representing contracted sounds きゃく /kyaku/ and double consonants みっか /mikka/. A relatively small number of children have difficulty until around Grade 5 in learning some spelling conventions associated with the use of Hiragana as case-marking particles. For example, the topic marker /wa/ is written with は /ha/, instead of わ /wa/. In the study involving Grade 2 to Grade 6 children, mentioned above, Uno et al. (2009) presented a similar pattern of spelling development. Their results showed that while no difference existed in Hiragana spelling performance across all grade levels, in Katakana, Grade 2 children performed notably more poorly than the other grade groups.

3.3.2.3 Reading and Spelling Difficulties   In a widely cited publication, Makita (1968) claimed that reading disabilities (RD) are extremely rare in Japan based on his estimate of less than 0.1 percent of the instance rate of RD. Since the mid 1980s, Makita's claim has been challenged and subjected to empirical examinations. In the studies on record, the notion of RD is generally defined as reading performance at or below -1.5 to $-.2$ SDs. Cumulative evidence, though still limited, suggests that reading problems are not a rarity in Japan. Stevenson et al. (1982), for example, found that 5.4 percent of fifth-grade children performed two grade levels below on a researcher-constructed test designed to measure the ability to understand textural information presented in clauses, phrases, and sentences. Using a similar definition of RD, Hirose and Hatta (1988) reported a much higher rate of RD instance (11 percent) among   fifth-grade   children.   Their   results   demonstrated   that reading impairments were attributable to an inferiority of sentence memory and reasoning abilities and that reading problems were not associated with word discrimination skills. Focusing on word-level reading and writing disabilities (WD), Uno et al. (2009) found that proportions of children with disabilities varied across writing systems, as well as between reading and writing (Hiragana, 0.2% RD and 1.6% WD; Katakana, 1.4% RD and 3.8% WD; and Kanji, 6.9% RD and 6% WD) and that the R/WD children performed markedly poorly on abstract word comprehension, arithmetic, and short-term visual memory tasks relative to their normally developing counterparts.

3.3.3   Reading Comprehension

3.3.3.1 Predictors of Reading Comprehension   As a process of text meaning construction, passage comprehension entails a number of sub-skills that are required for integrating linguistic information extracted from printed words. To date, only a handful of studies have explored text-level reading development in Japanese children. In one such study, Kobayashi et al. (2005) compared the relative contributions of four sub-skills to oral reading fluency and short text comprehension in kindergarten and first-grade children. Their analysis revealed that performance on Rapid Automated Naming (RAN; Hiragana and number) predicted both oral reading fluency and accuracy in the kindergarten children, but RAN predicted only oral reading fluency in the first-grade children. Oral reading accuracy in the first-grade children was predicted by phonological analysis skills, instead. All measured sub-skills, except for visual processing, significantly contributed to short text comprehension in the first-grade children. Viewed together, their results seem to suggest that naming speed and phonological skills are significant predictors of reading ability in the initial phase of literacy acquisition. These findings thus corroborate what has been known about early reading development in English-speaking children (Adams, 1990; Badian, 1994; Torgesen, Wagner & Rashotte, 1994; Wolf & Bowers, 1999).

Findings from a study involving fifth-grade children (Kuhara-Kojima, Hatano, Saito & Haebara, 1996) provide additional support for the significance of naming efficiency as a factor separating skilled and less skilled comprehenders. In the study, vocalization latencies (defined as the elapsed time from the presentation of a word to initial vocalization) were compared between two reading ability groups across five word type conditions, including real words in Hiragana, real words in special Hiragana symbols, pseudowords in Hiragana, real words in Kanji and pseudowords in Kanji. The children in the higher ability group were significantly faster and more accurate than their less skilled counterparts when all types of words were presented together in a random sequence. However, the two groups did not differ in two Hiragana word conditions (real and pseudoword) when each type of word was presented separately. Two findings are particularly germane: (1) Hiragana reading efficiency did not differentiate skilled and less skilled readers in Grade 5; and (2) efficiency differences between the two ability groups were parallel between the real word and pseudoword Hiragana word conditions. The findings point out the facility with which Hiragana decoding is acquired, as well as its inadequacy as a predictor of successful text comprehension in the upper grades.

3.3.3.2 Word-Level Effects in Comprehending Text   In a series of studies, Takahashi investigated the relative contributions of basic cognitive skills and decoding efficiency across three grade groups (kindergarten, Grade 1, and Grade 3; Takahashi, 1993), as well as longitudinally between kindergarten and Grade 1 (Takahashi, 1996). In both studies, Hiragana naming efficiency was the only factor that was consistently significant in predicting standardized reading test scores. In a subsequent study, Takahashi (2001) examined developmental changes in the pattern of sub-skills contributions to reading ability over a span of five years. The longitudinal analysis revealed that Hiragana naming efficiency increased until Grade 3 and then leveled off. Correspondingly, its contribution to reading ability was significant in Grade 1, but not thereafter. Vocabulary knowledge was significant across all grade levels. In Grade 5, two highly correlated variables, vocabulary knowledge and Kanji knowledge, were both significant predictors of reading performance and Grade 5 vocabulary knowledge was predicted by Grade 3 reading comprehension scores. Thus, the picture emerging from the longer-span longitudinal study (Takahashi, 2001) is remarkably similar to those emanating from studies investigating comprehension sub-skills development in English-speaking children. In particular, the reported pattern of changes in the predictive strength of decoding and vocabulary knowledge is consistent with the predictions made within the *simple view of reading* (Gough & Tunmer, 1986; Hoover & Gough, 1990).

3.3.4   Conclusion

Word reading development in Kana and Kanji necessitates distinct sub-skills. In phonographic Kana, sensitivity to mora boundaries plays a role in word reading development. In contrast, Kanji reading acquisition depends heavily on vocabulary knowledge and visual skills, such as visual memory and analysis. Collectively, currently available data suggest that word reading development in Japanese necessitates a combination of general cognitive abilities and script-specific sub-skills.

As for reading comprehension, the extant research base, though still heavily limited, has shown that text reading development relies on a broad range of sub-skills, including basic cognitive abilities, phonological skills, vocabulary knowledge, and decoding efficiency. The findings to date seem to imply that the trajectories of text-level reading development in Japanese and the sub-skills that contribute to the trajectories are similar to those found in a number of comprehension studies conducted with English-speaking children.

3.4   Discussion

3.4.1   Challenges in Learning to Read Japanese

Japanese employs phonographic Kana and morpheme-based Kanji to encode its spoken language. Their combined use in running text was conventionalized over time in the process of fitting borrowed Chinese characters to the Japanese language. Although morpheme-based characters efficiently transmitted semantic information across languages, they were not well suited for expressing non-semantic information, such as inflectional suffixes and case-marking particles. The emergence of Kana thus was an inevitable consequence of the need for using morpheme-based characters phonetically to encode the grammatical elements of Japanese, and the concurrent use of Kana and Kanji was a practical solution to the problems that arose from the incompatibilities between the Chinese writing system and the Japanese language.

The combined use of the two writing systems makes Japanese one of the most complicated written languages to learn. An obvious challenge children face in literacy acquisition is the sheer volume of work necessitated for learning literally thousands of symbols through repetitive exercise. Rote learning, by any measure, is an arduous undertaking particularly when it involves colossal amounts of cumulative information. Japanese literacy thus demands sustained devotion to laborious practice over the nine years of compulsory education.

Another challenge lies in the distinct representational properties of Kanji taught in different grade levels. While, in the initial grades, Kanji are taught as a morphographic system in conjunction with spoken words, in the upper grades, Kanji are treated as syllabic, as well as morphological, constituents of multi-syllabic/multi-morphemic words. Hence, the core requisite for Kanji learning shifts from holistic grapheme–word association building to sublexical information analysis. Such a shift makes Kanji learning radically discontinuous, adding further complications to the already complex undertaking. Ideally, instruction prepares children to meet the fundamentally different challenges they face in the upper grades. In actuality, however, Kanji instruction largely remains memory intensive in the upper grades, emphasizing repeated writing as the primary means of learning (Hatano, 1986; Stevenson et al., 1982).

3.4.2 *Implications for Instruction*

Orthographic consistency has direct bearing on reading skills development in diverse writing systems. Decoding development occurs with considerable ease in orthographically consistent systems, in which words can be read, once their symbols are mastered, by applying simple grapheme-to-phonology mapping rules. In less consistent systems, the opacity of the grapheme–phonology relationships demands diverse learning procedures, including, in addition to rule application, word segmentation and analogical inference. It has been suggested that word reading acquisition in orthographically less consistent systems, such as English, is affected by how reading is taught, to a greater extent, than in consistent systems (Nunes & Bryant, 2006; Ziegler & Goswami, 2006). Optimally, reading instruction in all languages should help children focus on the specific unit of language and the unit of grapheme that corresponds most consistently in their writing system.

In phonologically opaque Kanji, reading instruction should take into account the distinct nature of the grapheme–phonology relationships in morphographic and morphosyllabic characters taught in different grade levels. In the initial stages, Kanji instruction typically highlights one-to-one grapheme–word associations in mainly single-unit characters. Since many of these basic characters are used as components of a large number of compound characters, a firm grasp of these characters is vital for laying a solid grapho-morphological foundation for Kanji learning in the subsequent developmental stages. It is therefore essential that children's grapho-morphological readiness be assessed and ascertained before the instructional foci shift to structurally complex compound characters.

In the upper grades, Kanji learning is more segmental and analytical as it involves sublexical information. As a morphosyllabic system, compound characters encode phonological and morphological information simultaneously, yet independently, and as such, serve as the building blocks of multi-syllabic words. This simply means that any increase in the number of morphosyllabic characters in Kanji instruction leads to an exponential increase in the number of multisyllabic words for children to learn. Clearly, rote memorization alone is far from sufficient for coping with the growing demands stemming from the dramatic increase in incoming information to be absorbed and then analyzed in conjunction with the large amounts of stored information. The clear implication is that children need to develop an explicit understanding of the structural principle of compound characters and to acquire the skills to use the insight efficiently in learning and processing structurally complex characters and words.

3.5   Final Conclusion

In an attempt to clarify the nature of the challenges Japanese children face in learning to read, this chapter has described how the written Japanese language evolved from Chinese characters, what kinds of complexities resulted from the evolution, and how such complexities affect reading acquisition in Japanese. An emerging body of evidence, though still heavily limited, suggests that the acquisition of word-reading skills in Kana and Kanji depends on different sub-skills in different degrees. While phonological awareness plays a significant role in Kana reading development, vocabulary knowledge and visual skills are uniquely associated with Kanji reading ability. Phonological short-term memory and orthographic knowledge are seemingly common contributors to word reading development in the two writing systems. Beyond word-level reading, however, the developmental trajectories of comprehension sub-skills in Japanese children appear to be similar to those found in studies conducted with English-speaking children. All in all, Japanese reading acquisition necessitates two diverse sets of script-specific sub-skills, knowledge of spoken language, and general cognitive abilities that are required for mapping spoken Japanese onto its written form.

References

Adams, M. J. (1990). *Beginning to read*. Cambridge, MA: The MIT Press.

Amano, K. (1970). Formation of the act of analyzing phonemic structure of words and its relation to learning syllabic characters (Kanamoji). *Japanese Journal of Educational Psychology, 18*, 76–89.

(1989). Phonological analysis and acquisition of reading and writing in children. *Psychologia, 32*, 16–32.

Badian, N. A. (1994). Preschool prediction: Orthographic and phonological skills, and reading. *Annals of Dyslexia, 44*, 87–100.

Carlisle, J. F. (1995). Morphological awareness and early reading achievement. In L. B. Feldman (Ed.), *Morphological aspects of language processing* (pp. 189–210). Hillsdale, NJ: Lawrence Erlbaum.

Chen, X., Hao, M., Geva, E., Zhu, J. & Shu, H. (2009). The role of compound awareness in Chinese children's vocabulary acquisition and character reading. *Reading and Writing, 22*, 615–631.

Clancy, P. M. (1985). The acquisition of Japanese. In D. I. Slobin (Ed.), *The cross-linguistic study of language acquisition, Vol I: The data* (pp. 373–524). Hillsdale, NJ: Lawrence Erlbaum.

Clark, E. V. (1993). *The lexicon in acquisition.* Cambridge University Press.

Coulmas, F. (1989). *The writing systems of the world.* Cambridge, MA: Blackwell.

Dairoku, H. (1995). Is awareness of morae a requisite for acquisition of kana reading? *The Japanese Journal of Psychology, 66*, 253–260.

Goetry, V., Urbain, S., Morais, J. & Kolinsky, R. (2005). Paths to phonemic awareness in Japanese: Evidence from a training study. *Applied Psycholinguistics, 26*, 285–309.

Gough, P. & Tunmer, W. (1986). Decoding, reading, and reading disability. *RASE: Remedial & Special Education, 7*, 6–10.

Hatano, G. (1986). How do Japanese children learn to read?: Orthographic and eco-cultural variables. In B. R. Foorman & A. W. Siegel (Eds.), *Acquisition of reading skills: Cultural constraints and cognitive universals* (pp. 81–114). Hillsdale, NJ: Lawrence Erlbaum.

Hayashi, Y. & Murphy, V. A. (2013). On the nature of morphological awareness in Japanese-English bilingual children: A cross-linguistic perspective. *Bilingualism: Language and Cognition, 16*, 49–67.

Hirose, T. & Hatta, T. (1988). Reading disabilities in modern Japanese children. *Journal of Research in Reading, 11*, 152–160.

Hoover, W. A. & Gough, P. B. (1990). The simple view of reading. *Reading and Writing, 2*, 127–160.

Inagaki, K., Hatano, G. & Otake, T. (2000). The effect of Kana literacy acquisition on the speech segmentation unit used by Japanese young children. *Journal of Experimental Child Psychology, 75*, 70–91.

Ito, T. & Kagawa, A. (2001). Moji kakutoku mae no yooji ni okeru onritsu tan'i no hattatsu [Development of sensitivity to a rhythmic unit in pre-literate children]. *Onsei Gengo Igaku, 38*, 196–203.

Ito, T. & Tatsumi, I. F. (1997). Tokushuhaku ni taisuru metagengo chishiki no hattatsu [Development of mora awareness]. *Onsei Gengo Igaku, 38*, 196–203.

Iwasaki, S. (2002). *Japanese.* Philadelphia, PA: John Benjamins.

Kayamoto, Y., Yamada, J. & Takashima, H. (1998). The consistency of multiple-pronunciation effects in reading: The case of Japanese logographs. *Journal of Psycholinguistic Research, 27*, 619–637.

Kess, J. F. & Miyamoto, T. (1999). *The Japanese mental lexicon: Psycholinguistic studies of Kana and Kanji processing.* Amsterdam: John Benjamins.

Kobayashi, M. S., Haynes, C. W., Macaruso, P., Hook, P. E. & Kato, J. (2005). Effects of mora deletion, nonword repetition, rapid naming, and visual search performance on beginning reading in Japanese. *Annals of dyslexia, 55*, 105–128.

Kondo, A. (2008). *Nihongo-gaku nyuumon* [Introduction to Japanese language studies]. Tokyo: Kenkyusha.

Koyama, M. K., Hansen, P. C. & Stein, J. F. (2008). Logographic Kanji versus phonographic Kana in literacy acquisition: How important are visual and phonological skills? *Annual N.Y. Academic Science, 1145*, 41–55.

Ku, Y.-M. & Anderson, R. C. (2003). Development of morphological awareness in Chinese and English. *Reading and Writing, 16*, 399–422.

Kubozono, H. (2006). The phonetic and phonological organization of speech in Japanese. In M. Nakayama, R. Mazuka & Y. Shirai (Eds.), *The handbook of East Asian psycholinguistics* (pp. 191–200). New York: Cambridge University Press.

Kuhara-Kojima, K., Hatano, G., Saito, H. & Haebara, T. (1996). Vocalization latencies of skilled and less skilled comprehenders for words written in hiragana and kanji. *Reading Research Quarterly, 31*, 158–171.

Makita, K. (1968). Rarity of reading disability in Japanese children. *American Journal of Orthopsychiatry, 38*, 599–614.

Mann, V. A. (1986). Phonological awareness: The role of reading experience. *Cognition, 24*, 65–92.

Matsushita, T. (2012). In what order should learners learn Japanese vocabulary? A corpus-based approach (Doctoral dissertation). Victoria University of Wellington, New Zealand.

McBride-Chang, C., Cheung, H., Chow, B. W.-Y., Chow, C. S.-L. & Choi, L. (2006). Metalinguistic skills and vocabulary knowledge in Chinese (L1) and English (L2). *Reading and Writing, 19*, 695–716.

Muraishi, S. & Amano, K. (1972). *Reading and writing ability in pre-school children.* The National Language Research Institute Report 45. Tokyo: Tokyo-Shoseki.

Naka, M. & Naoi, H. (1995). The effect of repeated writing on memory. *Journal of Memory and Cognition, 23*, 201–212.

National Language Research Institute. (1964). *The development of language abilities in elementary school children: A six-year follow-up study of the same children.* The National Language Research Institute Research Report 26. Tokyo: Meijitosho Publishing Co.

Nunes, T. & Bryant, P. (2006). *Improving literacy by teaching morphemes.* London: Routledge.

Ota, M. (2006). Phonological acquisition. In M. Nakayama, R. Mazuka & Y. Shirai (Eds.), *The handbook of East Asian psycholinguistics, Vol. II: Japanese* (pp. 41–47). New York: Cambridge University Press.

Sakamoto, T. & Makita, K. (1973). Japan. In J. Downing (Ed.), *Comparative reading* (pp. 440–465). New York: Macmillan.

Shimamura, N. & Mikami, H. (1994). Acquisition of Hiragana letters by pre-school children: A comparison with the 1967 survey by the National Language research Institute. *Kyoiku Shinrigaku Kenkyuu, 42*, 70–76.

Shu, H., Chen, X., Anderson, R. C., Wu, N. & Xuan, Y. (2003). Properties of school Chinese: Implications for learning to read. *Child Development, 74*, 27–47.

Stevenson, H. W., Stigler, J. W., Lucker, G. W., Lee, S.-Y., Hsu, C.-C. & Kitamura, S. (1982). Reading disabilities: The case of Chinese, Japanese, and English. *Child Development, 53*, 1164–1181.

Takahashi, N. (1993). Becoming skillful at reading in beginners. *Japanese Journal of Educational Psychology, 41*, 264–274.

———— (1996). Development of reading ability in preschool and first grade years: A longitudinal analysis. *Japanese Journal of Educational Psychology, 44*, 166–175.

———— (2001). Developmental changes in reading ability: A longitudinal analysis of Japanese children from first to fifth grade. *Japanese Journal of Educational Psychology, 49*, 1–10.

Taylor, I. & Taylor, M. M. (1995). *Writing and literacy in Chinese, Korean and Japanese*. Philadelphia, PA: John Benjamins.

Torgesen, J. K., Wagner, R. K. & Rashotte, C. A. (1994). Longitudinal studies of phonological processing and reading. *Journal of Learning Disabilities, 27*, 276–286.

Uno, A., Wydell, T., Haruhara, N., Kaneko, M. & Shinya, N. (2009). Relationship between reading/writing skills and cognitive abilities among Japanese primary-school children: Normal readers versus poor readers (dyslexics). *Reading and Writing, 22*, 755–789.

Wada, Y. (2000). Redefining phonological awareness in Japanese literacy acquisition (Master's thesis). Carnegie Mellon University, PA.

Wolf, M. & Bowers, P. G. (1999). The double-deficits, developmental dyslexia and a specific deficit hypothesis. *Brain and Language, 42*, 219–247.

Yamada, J. (1992). Asymmetries of reading and writing Kanji by Japanese children. *Journal of Psycholinguistic Research, 21*, 563–580.

Yamazaki, M., Ellis, A. W., Morrison, C. M. & Lambon Ralph, M. A. (1997). Two age of acquisition effects in the reading of Japanese Kanji. *British Journal of Psychology, 88*, 407–421.

Ziegler, J. C. & Goswami, U. (2006). Becoming literate in different languages: Similar problems, different solutions. *Developmental Sciences, 9*, 425–436.

4   Learning to Read Korean

Min Wang, Jeung-Ryeul Cho, and Chuchu Li

4.1   Introduction

4.1.1   Korean and Its Orthography

Different writing systems in the world select different units of spoken language for mapping. An alphabetic system selects phonemes; a syllabary system selects syllables; and a logographic system, traditionally considered, selects morphemes or words to represent spoken language. Korean Hangul can be considered a transparent alphabetic system, in which graphemes map directly onto phonemes, as in English, Russian, and Italian. However, unlike these alphabetic systems, Korean Hangul orthographic structure is nonlinear: The composition of letters is shaped into a square-like syllable block. The letters are arranged from left to right and from top to bottom. Its overall shape makes Korean appear more similar to Chinese than to its fellow alphabetic orthographies. Because the Hangul syllable blocks are separated, there is a clear syllable boundary within a Korean Hangul word. As a result, Korean Hangul is sometimes called an alphabetic syllabary or syllabic alphabet.

4.1.2   Synchronic and Diachronic Characterization

The Korean language is different from Chinese and English in terms of its linguistic family. Chinese and English belong to the Sino-Tibetan and Indo-European families, respectively. Although a small number of historical linguists think that Korean might be related to the Altaic language family (e.g., Taylor & Taylor, 1995), the majority of scholars consider Korean to be a language isolate (e.g., Kim, 1992; Song, 2005). The Korean language includes three types of vocabulary words: native Korean, Sino-Korean, and European loan words. Sino-Korean words were borrowed from China and have been used in the Korean language for over a thousand years. More than a half of Korean vocabulary words are Sino-Korean words, representing content information such as abstract concepts and technical terms. Sino-Korean words can be written in both Hangul and Chinese characters, whereas native Korean words and grammatical morphemes are written in Hangul only.

Unlike other writing systems in the world, Korean Hangul is *invented*; there is no historical evolution involved. Prior to the invention of the Korean alphabet (Hangul) and until the fifteenth century, Korean used two written forms. One was in the form of Chinese characters for the upper class and the other was an incomplete traditional notational system borrowed from limited Chinese meanings and sounds (see Pae, 2011). Because of the complexity that resulted and the inconsistency between the native Korean language and the sounds of Chinese characters, King Sejong (1417–1450) invented (with assistance from several scholars) an alphabet system and mandated it for universal adoption by the public. The King designed the system with a clear idea in his mind: that it should be much easier to read and write using the invented alphabets rather than the logographic Chinese characters.

The Korean alphabets were designed with the careful consideration of phonetic features and philosophical ideology of the graphs. The visual shape of the consonant symbols closely represents the place and manner of articulation. For instance, the letter ㄱ for the /g/ or /k/ shows the roots of the tongue closing the throat; the letter ㄴ /n/ shows the tongue touching the upper gum; the letter ㅁ /m/ shows the closed mouth; the letter ㅅ for the /s/ shows the tongue tip meeting the gum just above the front teeth; and the letter ㅇ for the sound /ŋ/ shows the open throat (Taylor & Taylor, 1995). Related consonant letters are created by adding one or two strokes to the five basic simple consonant letters. For example, the stop consonant letter /t/ or /d/ represented by ㄷ is created by adding one stroke above the letter ㄴ /n/. As to the vowels, the King first created three core vowel graphemes,., ㅡ, ㅣ, to represent heaven, earth, and human. Then by adding one stroke to each of the core vowels, four additional vowels were constructed, ㅗ, ㅏ, ㅜ, ㅓ. Finally, by adding one extra stroke to these four vowels, another four vowels, ㅛ, ㅑ, ㅠ, ㅕ, were constructed.

4.1.3   *Literacy and Schooling*

South and North Korea use Korean language and Hangul script. Because Korea has been divided into two different countries since 1945, each country has different vocabularies and language policies. For example, South Korea uses both Hangul and Hanja (characters borrowed from the Chinese writing system), whereas North Korea has a policy to use Hangul only. In addition, the spelling of some words is different in the two countries. For example, in South Korea 'tree leaves' is written 나뭇잎, whereas in North Korea it is written 나무잎. South Korea adds ㅅ /t/ between the two nouns (e.g., 나무 'tree' and 잎 'leaf') to reflect a sound change when making a compound word (e.g., 나뭇잎), whereas North Korea does not. In other words, South Korea tends to adopt phonemic changes in the writing of compound words, whereas North Korea tends to keep morphemes transparent (e.g., Bae & Yi, 2012). The standard language of South Korea refers to the modern language of Seoul, although regional dialects are available in South Korea. This chapter is based on literature that deals with the standard language of South Korea.

In contrast to children in parts of the world that use alphabetic orthographies, who start to learn alphabetic letters first, Korean children are first taught with Hangul syllables, particularly CV syllables around the age of 4 at home (see Cho, 2009). Around the age of 5, Korean children are taught letter names and letter sounds as well as combination rules of consonants with vowels. Later, around the age of 5 to 6, Korean children are taught to add a consonant letter at a coda position to a CV syllable to form a CVC syllable. Finally, at the age of 6, when children enter primary school, they master reading CVC syllables. Cho (2009) showed that 4- and 5-year-old Korean children are able to identify 78% and 96% of CV syllables, but only 54% and 76% of consonant letter names, and 29% and 68% of consonant sounds, respectively. This result suggests that Korean children develop knowledge about CV first, then letter names, and finally letter sounds. In Cho's study (2009), CV syllable knowledge explained unique variance of word reading longitudinally, after controlling for reading and letter knowledge measured earlier. However, letter name and letter sound knowledge did not predict word reading when controlling for reading and CV syllable knowledge measured at the earlier time point.

One of the reasons that Korean children learn alphabet letter names later than CV syllables might be related to the features of Korean letter names. While English letter names are mostly mono-syllabic, the names of Korean basic consonants consist of two syllables in a CV VC or CV CVC form (Cho, 2009; Kim, 2012). For instance, the letter ㄱ has the name 기역 /gi.yeg/ and represents the sound /g/ or /k/, and the letter ㅁ has the name 미음 /mi.um/ representing the sound /m/. Therefore, each consonant name starts with its own sound and ends with the sound value of the letter made at the syllable-final position. Each Korean consonant has a name and represents one sound, whereas each vowel has the same name as the sound it represents. Kim (2012) examined the relation between letter names and letter sound knowledge among Korean kindergarteners. She found that the relation between the letter names and letter sound knowledge was somewhat inconsistent and was overall smaller than what has been found for English-speaking children. Kim (2012) speculated that abstracting letter sounds from letter names is more difficult for two-syllable letter names in the case of Korean than for single-syllable letter names in the case of English.

Korean children start kindergarten at the age of 4 or 5. Kindergartens are independent from primary schools in South Korea. They consist of two grade levels, roughly corresponding to children aged either 4 or 5. In general, kindergartens are for children from middle-income families, whereas the so-called

Vokale / Konson.	ㅏ / a	ㅑ / ya	ㅓ / ŏ	ㅕ / yeo	ㅗ / o	ㅛ / yo	ㅜ / u	ㅠ / yu	ㅡ / eu	ㅣ / i
ㄱ / g(k)	가	갸	거	겨	고	교	구	규	그	기
ㄴ / n	나	냐	너	녀	노	뇨	누	뉴	느	니
ㄷ / d	다	댜	더	뎌	도	됴	두	듀	드	디
ㄹ / r(l)	라	랴	러	려	로	료	루	류	르	리
ㅁ / m	마	먀	머	며	모	묘	무	뮤	므	미
ㅂ / b	바	뱌	버	벼	보	뵤	부	뷰	브	비
ㅅ / s	사	샤	서	셔	소	쇼	수	슈	스	시
ㅇ / ※	아	야	어	여	오	요	우	유	으	이
ㅈ / j	자	쟈	저	져	조	죠	주	쥬	즈	지
ㅊ / ch	차	챠	처	쳐	초	쵸	추	츄	츠	치
ㅋ / k	카	캬	커	켜	코	쿄	쿠	큐	크	키
ㅌ / t	타	탸	터	텨	토	툐	투	튜	트	티
ㅍ / p	파	퍄	퍼	펴	포	표	푸	퓨	프	피
ㅎ / h	하	햐	허	혀	호	효	후	휴	흐	히

Figure 4.1 Korean syllable chart.

"children's house," established by the Ministry of Welfare, offers childcare facilities for working mothers and lower-income families. About 57.8% and 68.7% of 4- and 5-year-old Korean children, respectively, attend kindergarten and the children's house (Na & Moon, 2004). Based on the national curriculum for literacy, kindergartens are not supposed to explicitly teach Hangul alphabet and decoding skills. Kindergartens are supposed to enhance children's interest and motivation to read and write (Ministry of Education and Human Resource Development, 1998). Since the 1990s, kindergarten teachers have used a whole-word reading method in literacy instruction. Meanwhile, about 85% of children have had additional learning opportunities at home, such as studying commercially available workbooks as home education or enrolling in commercial institutions (e.g., Korean Association of Child Studies & Hangul Education Research Center, 2002). These after-school reading programs often employ phonics instruction (Lee & Lee, 2007). Although a CV syllable chart is not widely used these days, it was considered as an effective method for less educated people before the twentieth century (Taylor & Taylor, 1995). In a typical CV chart (see Figure 4.1), 14 basic consonant letters are arranged in a column, and 10 basic vowel letters are arranged in a row to form 140 CV syllable blocks. Within the CV chart, children are often taught to read the entire syllable blocks in order.

Korean children enter first grade at the age of 6. When they enter a primary school, most children learn to master regular words that could be read by the grapheme-to-phoneme correspondence rules (e.g., Cho & McBride-Chang, 2005b). In primary schools, children are taught various morphophonological rules that alter the phonology of some words, such as through resyllabification, simplifications of multiple coda, and consonantal assimilation. Hanja is learned in secondary schools and students are expected to master about 1,800 characters. Nowadays, however, most primary schools teach Hanja for elective classes.

4.2   Description of Korean and Its Written Forms

This section provides a description of Korean linguistic and writing systems. The description of the linguistic system focuses on Korean phonology and morphology. The description of phonology includes basic consonants, vowels, and phonological alterations within a syllable and across syllables in a multi-syllable word. Korean language has a rich morphology; the description of morphology includes three types of morphological structure: inflection, derivation, and compounding. The writing system of Korean Hangul has some interesting characteristics, especially the *left to right* and *top to bottom* arrangement of letters to form a square-like syllable block. The description of the writing system focuses on the constraints of letter arrangement within a syllable block and phonological changes for some consonant letters across syllable blocks.

4.2.1   Linguistic System

4.2.1.1 Phonology   The Korean language has fourteen basic consonants (e.g., /k, n, t, l/) and ten basic vowels (e.g., /a, ja, o, jo/). Some Korean phonemes are the same as English phonemes (e.g., /m/ and /n/). However, Korean does not have the two English *th* sounds, as in *this* and *think*; there is also no /f/ or /v/ sound. Just like Chinese and Japanese speakers, Koreans have difficulty distinguishing /l/ and /r/ sounds in English. The syllable is an important unit in Korean, but its syllable structure is simpler compared to English. Korean syllables can be in the form of CV (e.g., 가 /ga/), CVC (e.g., 먹 /muk/), and CVCC (e.g., 닭 /dak/) structures. There are no initial consonant clusters in Korean syllables; final consonant clusters are limited. Most words contain one to three syllables. This simpler syllable structure may pose less of a phonemic-level phonological decoding challenge for learning to read Korean in comparison to learning to read English. There is no word- or syllable-level stress information in Korean (Jun, 1995). Each syllable is equally stressed in multi-syllabic words. However, there is a phrasal intonation pattern available, the so-called *accentual phrase*. The default pitch pattern in Seoul Korean is *low-high-low-high* (LHLH) (Jun, 1998, 2000).

There are four major phonological alternations in Korean words depending on the contexts. The first is called *simplification*, meaning that a consonant in a final consonant cluster in Korean CVCC words is not pronounced. For example, in 닭 /dak/ chicken, /l/ sound prior to /k/ sound is not pronounced. In 값 /gap/ price, the /t/ sound after the /p/ is not pronounced. The second is called *assimilation*. Only seven final consonants or codas are allowed, /k/, /t/, /p/, /n/, /m/, /ŋ/, and /l/. The final consonants, /k/, /t/, /p/, are to be changed to /ŋ/, /n/, /m/ when followed by an initial nasal consonant in the second syllable, for example, 먹는다 'eat' /muk.neun.da/ will be changed to 멍는다 /muŋ.neun.da/. The third is called *resyllabification*. The sound of the final consonant of a first syllable moves to the first consonant of a second syllable if the second syllable starts with a vowel, for example, 군인 'soldier' /gun.in/ will be changed to 구닌 /gu.nin/. The final one is called *palatalization*. The sounds of coda /t/ and /d/ will be changed to the sounds of /ch/ and /j/, respectively, if they follow a vowel /i/. For example, 같이 /gat.i/ 'together' will be changed to 가치 /ga.chi/ 'value'.

4.2.1.2 Morphology The Korean language has a rich morphology. Some morphemes in the Korean language are monosyllabic; however, many of them are composed of two or more syllables. Korean shares the three major types of morphological structures with English: inflection, derivation, and compounding.

Inflectional Morphology In Korean, suffixation in verbs and adjectives is the most productive and complex formation of inflectional words. The four common inflection forms are as follows: (a) plural inflection: 나무 /na.mu/ 'tree' ➔ 나무들/na.mu.deul/ 'trees'; (b) tense inflection: 노래한다 /no.rae.han.da/ 'sing' ➔ 노래했다 /no.rae.hat.da/ 'sang'; (c) honorific inflection that is used to show respect or honors to seniors: 온다 /on.da/ 'come' ➔ 오셨다 /o.sut.da/; (d) conjunctive inflection: 자다 /ja.da/ 'sleep' ➔ 자고 /ja.go/ 'sleep and'. In particular, conjugation of Korean verbs and adjectives is complex. For example, adding a pre-final ending (e.g., 었 /ət/, 겠 /get/) and a final ending (e.g., 다 /da/, 고 /go/) to the verb stem 먹 /mək/ produces many different verb forms (e.g., 먹었다 /mək.ət.da/ 'ate', 먹겠다 /mək.get.da/ 'will eat', 먹었고 /mək.ət.go/ 'ate and', 먹겠고 /mək.get.go/ 'will eat and').

Derivational Morphology Korean has very productive, derivational complex word formation, just like English. Most derivations are generated through affixation. Suffixes are more important than prefixes in deriving new words in Korean: they are more productive and carry more syntactic functions (Sohn, 1999). For example, many adjectives and verbs can be derived from nouns by adding the suffixes 하다 /ha.da/ or 롭다 /lop.da/, such as in 조용하다 /dʒo.jo ŋ. ha.da/ 'be quiet', 사랑하다 /sa.raŋ.ha.da/ 'love', 향기롭다 /hjaŋ.gi.lop.da/ 'be fragrant'. Many nouns can be derived from verbs or adjectives by adding the suffixes 음 /im/ or 이 /i/, such as in 믿음 /mit.im/ 'belief', 웃음 /ut.im/ 'laugh', 먹이 /mug.i/ 'food', and 길이 /gil.i/ 'length'. In addition, the suffix 이 and 게 can be added to adjective stems such as 많 'many' and 밝 'bright', respectively, to form adverbs 많이 'much' and 밝게 'brightly'. It is important to note that the morphemic information in Korean is preserved without much complicated alteration to its phonology, in contrast to English. The medial vowels in Korean Hangul never undergo phonological changes after adding the derivational suffixes, although the final consonants undergo assimilation or resyllabification processes.

Compounding Morphology   The Korean language has as many compounds and homophones as the Chinese language. In fact, more than half of Korean vocabulary consists of Sino-Korean words that originated in the Chinese language and have been used in Korea since ancient times. Sino-Korean words can be written in both Hangul and Chinese characters such as 학교 and 學校 /hak.gjo/ 'school'. Most of the multi-syllable Sino-Korean words (美國 /mi.guk/ 'USA', 中國 /juŋ.guk/ 'China', 英國 /jəŋ. guk/ 'UK') as well as many native Korean words (손목 /son.mok/ 'wrist', 발목 /bal.mok/ 'ankle') are compounds. Homophones are prevalent in Korean as well. For example, 사 /sa/ has sixty-five meanings including 四 'four', 死 'death', 思 'think', 史 'history' in a morpheme dictionary (Baek, 2012).

4.2.2   Writing System

4.2.2.1 Script and Punctuation   Hangul syllable boundaries are marked by character separation. A phrase called *eojeol* in Korean is a unit of separation by a big space in a Korean sentence. Eojeol consists of a lexical unit (e.g., a word) and a functional unit (e.g., a subject marker). An example of a Korean sentence is 당신은 학교에 가십니까? /da ŋ.sin.in hag.gjo.e ga.sip.ni.k'a?/ meaning 'Do you go to school?' The sentence has three eojeol consisting of a pronoun ('you', 당신 /da ŋ.sin/) + a subject marker (은 /in/), a noun ('school', 학교 /hag.gjo/) + a postposition (에 /e/), and a verb phrase. Sentences in Korean are marked by a period, a question mark, or a exclamation mark at the end. Paragraphs are usually marked by inserting two spaces before the first word of the paragraph to the right.

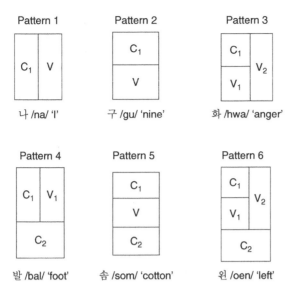

Figure 4.2 Six Hangul syllable block patterns. Modified from "Subsyllabic units in reading: A difference between Korean and English," by H.-K. Yoon, D. J. Bolger, O.-S. Kwon, and C. A. Perfetti, 2002. In L. Verhoeven, C. Elbro, and P. Reitsma (Eds.), *Precursors of functional literacy* (pp. 139–163), Amsterdam: John Benjamins.

4.2.2.2 Orthography   The nature of the Korean writing system, Hangul, is alphabetic; it maps letters onto phonemes just like English, French, and Italian do. The letters in a Hangul syllable block are arranged from left to right and from top to bottom. Each Hangul syllable is built from two to four symbols that in various combinations represent each of the twenty-four phonemes. There are six possible patterns of syllable block structure in Hangul (see Figure 4.2). The spatial arrangement of consonants and vowels is varied across different patterns. The overall shape of the Hangul syllable makes Korean appear more similar to Chinese than to its fellow alphabetic orthographies. Each Hangul letter contains between one and eight strokes, compared to English letters that contain between one and four strokes. The simplest syllable block contains two strokes (e.g., 이 /i/), and the most complex block has thirteen strokes (e.g., 빨 /bbal/). Taylor and Taylor (1995) pointed out that the uneven visual complexity of Hangul syllable blocks should help recognition because the more varied the visual shapes of graphs, the more easily they are distinguished from one another.

There are some letter position constraints for Hangul syllables (Simpson & Kang, 2004). A horizontal vowel is always placed under an initial consonant (e.g., 소 /so/, 'cow'). A vertical vowel is always placed to the immediate right of the initial consonant (e.g., 나 /na/, 'I'). A written syllable always starts with a consonant (or a null consonant that does not have a pronunciation). There are also constraints on final consonant clusters and simple vowel combinations; certain combinations of two consonants will lead to illegal final clusters. Likewise, certain combinations of two simple vowels will lead to illegal Hangul syllables.

Because the Hangul syllable blocks are separated, there is a clear syllable boundary for a Hangul word (e.g., 안녕하십니까, /an njəŋ ha sim ni ka/, 'hello'). As a result, Korean Hangul is sometimes called an alphabetic syllabary or syllabic alphabet. It is noteworthy that the syllabary aspect of Hangul is different from Japanese Kana, which is a true syllabary system. The Japanese Kana syllables cannot be further segmented into consonants and vowels; therefore, memorization of the existent Kana syllables is necessary for beginning learners. Hangul learners, on the other hand, do not need to memorize the syllable blocks; instead, they need to learn the alphabetic symbols and the simple and reliable rules to package them. Hence, Hangul is a shallow orthography.

It is noteworthy that a consonant (the first or the second) in the final consonant cluster in a Korean CVCC word is not pronounced when it stands alone. In other words, the final consonant cluster is represented in the orthography; however, it is not pronounced completely in spoken language. The initial consonant and medial vowel are fairly transparent in reading single syllables; there is a direct one-to-one mapping between the letters and phonemes. However, phonological alternations occur in reading multi-syllable words. For example, four (/k, t, p, n/) of the seven final consonants (/k, t, p, n, m, g, l/) go through an assimilation process. The stops /k/, /t/, and /p/ at the end of a first syllable are changed to /g/, /n/, or /m/, respectively, when followed by an initial nasal consonant in a second syllable. The consonant assimilation process, however, is systematic and consistent across all the syllables.

4.2.3   Conclusions

Korean is a language with unique linguistic and orthographic characteristics. In terms of phonology, the syllable is a salient phonological unit largely because of the prominent visual space across syllables. Simplification, assimilation, resyllabification, and palatalization are four major phonological alternations in Korean. In addition, Korean is a language without tone or word-level stress. Instead, it has pitch patterns at the phrase level. With regard to morphology, the major types of morphological structure are inflection, derivation, and compounding. Although various types of inflection and derivation forms exist, suffixation is primarily used for the formation of both inflectional and derivational words. With respect to the writing system, Korean Hangul is an alphabetic syllabary writing system with a shallow orthography. Each Hangul syllable block is composed of alphabetic symbols that can be consistently mapped onto phonemes. These linguistic and orthographic features have cognitive consequences on the development of reading and spelling abilities among Korean children.

4.3 Acquisition of Reading and Spelling in Korean

Learning to read is essentially learning to map sounds to letters and to seek meaning from written words and texts. Learning to spell is essentially learning to assign letters to sounds in written words. Both reading and spelling abilities entail the mapping process between written and spoken language, which is largely influenced by the linguistic and orthographic features of the language. In this section, we discuss the development of reading and spelling abilities among Korean children and how the features of Korean language and orthography influence their development. First, we discuss the development of linguistic awareness, including phonological and morphological awareness, which have been shown to significantly relate to Korean children's later reading success. Second, we discuss children's development of reading and spelling skills at the word level. Finally, we discuss reading development at a higher level, including comprehending a written text and various linguistic and word-level variables that contribute to reading comprehension.

4.3.1 Becoming Linguistically Aware

4.3.1.1 Phonological Development and Phonological Awareness Phonology is important in reading Korean Hangul, just like other alphabetic orthographies. Research has shown that reading Hangul words involves prelexical phonological information processing and that prelexical phonology is activated rapidly and automatically even in semantic processing of Korean words (e.g., Kim, 1999; Yoon, Bolger, Kwon & Perfetti, 2002). Cho and Chen (1999) found that Korean readers demonstrated strong homophone interference effects for pseudo-homophones in a category judgment task. That is, phonologically similar stimuli (e.g., *sute* for the category 'an article of clothing') caused greater confusion for Hangul readers when making semantic judgments than stimuli with control items (e.g., *blane* for the same category). Although the participants also made more errors on visually similar trials than on controls, the effect size for homophone interference was much larger than that for visual similarity. In another study suggesting the importance of phonology in reading Hangul, Kim and Davis (2004) found that Korean poor readers performed badly on Korean phonological awareness measures when compared with good readers. Cho and McBride-Chang (2005a) studied Korean children who learn to read Hangul in kindergarten and Grade 2 and found that both syllabic- and phonemic-level skills uniquely predicted Hangul word recognition. This finding suggests that the Korean Hangul system requires children to be sensitive to both the syllabic and the phonemic level of linguistic units.

One important characteristic of phonological development and awareness in Korean is that the salient and prominent subsyllabic structure is CV-V, in contrast to C-VC structure for English. Yoon et al. (2002) found that Korean kindergarteners could read nonwords two times better when clue words and tested nonwords shared the CV syllable body than when they shared the VC unit. For example, the 먀 /mjag/ (clue word) – 먄 /mjan/ (test word) pairs that share a CV unit was read better than the 먀/mjag/ (clue word) – 냑 /njag/ (test word) pairs that share a VC unit. Similarly, Korean kindergartners performed two times better in the tasks of coda deletion from a CVC syllable than in onset deletion (Cho, McBride-Chang & Park, 2008); for example, coda deletion in 감 /gam/ (answer: 가/ga/) was better performed than onset deletion in 감/gam/ (answer: 암/am/).

The saliency of the CV unit in spoken and written Korean words can be attributed to the distributional properties of the Korean language; for instance, many syllables in Korean are of the CV type (Kim, 2007). Another explanation is that this saliency is a result of Korean children's early acquisition of CV syllable knowledge. CV syllable knowledge is taught to Korean children at an early stage, at least earlier than letter knowledge. The syllable chart is used even in preschool to facilitate Korean children's emerging literacy.

4.3.1.2 Morphological Development and Morphological Awareness   McBride-Chang et al. (2005) compared reading skills of second-grade children in mainland China, Hong Kong, South Korea, and the United States. The researchers used a cluster of oral vocabulary, phonological, speeded naming, and morphological awareness tasks to predict word recognition in the different orthographies. Their results showed that for native Korean-speaking children, both phonological and morphological awareness predicted word recognition. However, for native English-speaking children only phonological awareness significantly contributed to word reading. For Chinese children, on the other hand, morphological awareness was the only significant predictor. These interesting findings provide strong evidence suggesting that the relative importance of phonology and morphology in learning to read is dependent upon the specific orthography. It seems that reading Korean Hangul orthography in early grades entails both phonological and morphological skills. The morphological task used in their study was a compound production task in which the child was asked to construct a compound word following a two- or three-sentence scenario.

Wang, Ko, and Choi (2009) tested Korean–English bilingual children in Grades 2 to 4 on a set of comparable Korean and English tasks tapping into oral vocabulary, phonemic awareness, morphological awareness of derivations, and word reading skills. Results showed that morphological awareness explained a significant amount of variance in word reading within both Korean Hangul and English, suggesting that morphological awareness is important not only in an opaque orthography such as English but also in a transparent orthography such as Korean Hangul.

4.3.2   *Development of Word Identification*

4.3.2.1   Word Decoding Development   At age 4, Korean children start to learn CV syllables. At age 5, they are able to combine CV and coda, and by age 6, they are able to read CVC regular words very well. Children start to learn phonological alterations in written words, including simplification, assimilation, resyllabification, and palatalization, in early grades in primary schools. When comparing decoding skills between phonological regular versus phonological irregular words, phonological irregular words refer to those words involved with phonological alterations. Cho et al. (2008) found that kindergarteners were poorer in decoding irregular words than regular words. Furthermore, the researchers showed that reading regular words was strongly related to phonological awareness at syllable, onset, and coda levels, whereas reading irregular words was strongly related to morphological awareness and coda awareness. During elementary school years, children gradually master the reading of irregular words. Cho and Lee (2010) found that sixth graders were 93% correct on average in the reading of irregular Hangul words and that their reading outcome was associated with morphological awareness and vocabulary but not with phonological awareness. These findings suggest that there are different cognitive demands in reading regular versus irregular words. Reading irregular words is likely to utilize the lexical route, whereas reading regular words is likely to utilize the phonological route, consistent with the dual-route reading model.

4.3.2.2   Word Spelling Development   Spelling in Korean is relatively difficult as compared to reading in Korean. In the transparent Hangul orthography, the consistency of phoneme-to-grapheme correspondences is lower than the consistency of grapheme-to-phoneme correspondences, similar to the patterns of other regular orthographies such as German. For example, Korean has the constraints that only seven out of nineteen consonant phonemes can occur in the final position of a syllable. In particular, the sound of /t/ in the coda position can be written in many consonant letters such as ㅅ, ㅆ, ㅈ, ㅉ, ㅊ, ㄷ, ㄸ, ㅌ. Thus, Hangul spelling requires phonological awareness to access and establish multiple associations between the letters and sounds just as in other alphabetic orthographies (e.g., Landerl & Wimmer, 2008).

Korean spelling is morphophonemic. Korean spelling must maintain a certain syllable shape and keep morphemes' underlying representations together (Kim-Renaud, 1997). An example of derivational morphology is 깊이 'depth', where the suffix 이 is added to a stem 깊 'deep', and its pronunciation is 기피 /gi.pi/ 'avoidance' due to the resyllabification phenomenon of the Korean language. Thus, a strong association between morphological awareness and Hangul word spelling is expected as in those studies related to English (Bryant & Nunes, 2004; Green et al., 2003; Kemp, 2006; Nagy, Berninger, Abbott, Vaughan & Vermeulen, 2003; Nunes & Hatano, 2004). As expected, Korean phonological and morphological awareness are strongly associated with Hangul spelling among kindergarteners (Kim, 2010) and longitudinally from Grades 4 to 6 (Cho, Chiu & McBride-Chang, 2011).

Kim (2010) found that kindergartners, when spelling phonologically transparent Hangul words that are involved with consistent grapheme-to-phoneme correspondence rules, made 58% of the errors in the coda position but 19% in onset position. This suggests that the coda may be particularly difficult for spelling Hangul words, probably as a result of the constraint that only seven consonant phonemes can occur in the final position in a syllable. In her study, children made twice as many legal errors as illegal errors for phonologically opaque words. Legal errors are phonemically correct but conventionally incorrect. In another study (Cho, 2004), Korean first graders made more errors in writing words with complex vowels than simple vowels, more errors in spelling low-frequency words than high-frequency words, and more errors in phonologically transparent words than opaque words.

4.3.2.3 Reading and Spelling Difficulties   Just like children who speak other languages, Korean children may suffer from reading and spelling difficulties. Phonological and naming deficits are prominent in Korean poor readers and spellers (Cho & Ji, 2011). Compared with average Korean readers of the same age, more than 70% of poor readers and spellers at Grade 3 showed a phonological deficit, either in isolation or with other deficits. The phonological deficit was reflected in poor readers' and spellers' significantly worse performance on tasks that tapped into phonological awareness, such as syllable and phoneme onset deletion tasks. Results from picture and digit naming speed tasks showed that 50% of the poor readers and spellers had a naming deficit, although the deficit was always in association with other deficits, such as phonological deficit or visual deficit. Park and Uno (2012) consistently found that Korean children with poor reading and spelling skills showed significantly worse performance on tasks that measured phonemic awareness and naming speed. The phonemic awareness of Grade 3 children was measured in an onset oddity task and their naming speed was measured in a rapid automatized naming task, which required them to name sets of drawings and digits within a minute. These findings are consistent with previous literature suggesting that phonological awareness and naming speed are two important predictors of reading and spelling skills in Korean (Cho et al., 2008; Cho & McBride-Chang, 2005b; Kim, 2007).

Reading and spelling difficulties in Korean may be explained by the properties of the Hangul orthographic system. Similar to other alphabetic orthographies such as English, alphabets represent phonemes in Hangul. This explains why phonemic awareness is a unique predictor of reading and spelling difficulties in Hangul (Park & Uno, 2012). However, unlike other alphabetic orthographies in which letters are organized in a horizontal linear string, Hangul is organized via square-like syllable blocks (Kang & Simpson, 1996). Thus, Hangul reading may require some specific visual skills such as location processing. This may help explain why poor readers and spellers in Korean may also have visual deficits. Cho and Ji (2011) showed that poor readers and spellers were more likely to have worse performance than normal readers on Gardner's (1996) Test of Visual-Perceptual Skills (non-motor) Revised, which served as an index of the visual perceptual deficit. For example, poor readers and spellers had difficulties finding out a figure on a page that differed in orientation from the other four.

4.3.3   Reading Comprehension

4.3.3.1   Predictors of Reading Comprehension   Word decoding skill is a significant predictor of reading comprehension among young Korean children at age 5 (Kim, 2011). However, it no longer predicts reading comprehension among children at higher grades of elementary school (Lee & Cho, 2003). Kim, Yoo, and Kim (2010) found that word recognition, phonological working memory, and listening comprehension contributed to reading comprehension of passages among 7-year-old children in Korea. Cho, Kim, and Kim (2013) tested Korean kindergarteners aged 4–5 for one year to examine the relations of word recognition, semantic knowledge, listening comprehension, and reading comprehension of sentences. Results showed that word recognition at Time 1 uniquely explained listening and reading comprehension at Time 2. Data at Time 2 showed that word reading, morphological awareness, and listening comprehension explained the unique variance of reading comprehension after controlling for nonverbal intelligence, vocabulary, and mother's education. These findings suggest that word reading and language comprehension skills jointly contribute to reading comprehension in Korean among young children.

4.3.3.2 Word-Level Effects in Comprehending Text Kim (2011) studied several latent factors that may predict Korean children's reading abilities. Results showed that word reading and semantic knowledge were the only two direct and significant predictors of reading comprehension (β = .47 and .53, respectively). Phonological awareness was the only direct and significant predictor of word reading (β = .92), but alphabet knowledge and semantic knowledge contributed to word reading indirectly via relating to phonological awareness (β = .62 and .82, respectively). Word reading was significantly related to oral reading fluency (ORF) (β = .81), but ORF did not contribute to reading comprehension directly. In Kim's study, seventy-nine 5-year-old native Korean-speaking children were recruited at the end of the school year. Their alphabet knowledge, phonological awareness, semantic knowledge, word reading, ORF, and reading comprehension were measured. Alphabet knowledge was measured by letter-name and letter-sound identification tasks. Phonological awareness was measured at syllable level and phoneme level. Syllable deletion and coda deletion tasks were used as the measurement. In terms of semantic knowledge, an expressive vocabulary task and two morphological awareness tasks were used. The morphological awareness tasks included a *come-from* task, in which children were asked to decide whether a word was derived from another word (e.g., 책상 /ʧek.saŋ/ 'desk', comes from 책 /ʧek/ 'book'), and a compound construction task, in which children were asked to construct compound words based on some scenarios (e.g., a refrigerator that keeps flowers in it should be called a flower refrigerator). Children's performance on reading phonologically transparent and opaque words were used as indicators of their word reading performance; their accuracy and speed when reading three passages were taken as indicators of ORF. In terms of children's reading comprehension ability, the indicators were their accuracy in answering questions about three short passages. Open-ended questions, multiple-choice questions, and oral cloze tasks were used for the three passages, respectively.

The absence of a unique contribution of ORF to reading comprehension may be due to the fact that children read words without comprehending them. They may be able to decode text at single-word level, but fail to understand the meaning of sentences or paragraphs because they treat the text as a simple combination of unrelated words. To understand passages not only requires readers to recognize a single word but also requires them to integrate the meaning of each word into text. On the other hand, morphological awareness entails readers' ability to recognize individual morphemes and to combine them into a new integral unit to represent the meaning of the whole complex word. Particularly, morphology plays an important role in Korean word learning considering that Korean spelling is morphophonemic. Together, vocabulary and morphological awareness jointly contribute to reading comprehension.

The significant contribution of semantic knowledge to reading comprehension was also found in older Korean children (Wang et al., 2009). For native Korean-speaking children from Grades 2 to 4, both their vocabulary and derivational morphological awareness were positively and significantly related to their reading comprehension performance.

4.3.4 Conclusion

Literacy development among Korean children and native English-speaking children seems to share common processes. Phonological information is important and is activated automatically in reading Hangul. Phonological awareness is an important predictor of Hangul word recognition. These findings support the universal phonological principle in reading acquisition. However, there are several unique features about reading acquisition among Korean children. A CV unit is a salient subsyllabic unit in the development of word decoding and spelling skills in comparison to English in which the VC unit has been shown to be a reliable and preferred unit (Treiman, Mullennix, Bijeljac-Babic & Richmond-Welty, 1995). The spelling of coda appears to be a challenging task for Korean preschool children. Morphological awareness serves as a significant predictor of word recognition, word spelling, and reading comprehension. The saliency of CV structure and morphological units may be a joint function of linguistic properties and how children are taught to read.

4.4 Discussion

4.4.1 Challenges in Learning to Read Korean

Although Korean Hangul orthography is a fairly transparent alphabetic orthography, there is still a certain degree of complexity involved that would pose learning challenges. First, the nonlinear composition of Korean alphabets may add to the challenges in learning Korean orthography. As mentioned in Section 4.2.2.2, Korean alphabets are arranged in a syllable block and there are six possible patterns to form the syllable block. For many of the Indo-European alphabetic orthographies, letters are arranged linearly from left to right. It becomes essential for Korean Hangul learners to memorize the six syllable-block patterns when reading and spelling words. Similar to Chinese characters, Korean orthography may require relatively greater visual-spatial skill in processing orthographic information. In reading and spelling Chinese characters, learners need to identify and locate various strokes at the correct positions in a square-like block. Likewise, in reading and spelling Korean Hangul, learners need to identify and locate various letters at the correct positions in a square-like block.

Second, various phonological alterations increase the orthographic complexity at word level. For instance, according to the rule of simplification, in 닭 /dak/ 'chicken', the /l/ sound prior to the /k/ sound is not pronounced, but in the spelling the letter needs to be represented. Korean orthography does not allow a vowel to start a syllable; a null consonant is always required at the beginning of the word.

Third, coda consonants are particularly difficult for children to spell given the variations in mapping a coda consonant to a letter. Taking these orthographic features and constraints together, there is a certain degree of opacity in phoneme-to-grapheme correspondences in Korean Hangul. Children need to understand and gradually store the irregular mappings in memory through instruction and practice.

In addition to the opaque phoneme-to-grapheme correspondences, the mapping between the morpheme, grapheme, and phoneme may pose challenges to Korean learners. Korean has a rich morphology. In Korean there are far more types of inflections than in English. In particular, inflections on verbs and adjectives are complex, involving various functions. Morphological awareness is an important predictor of Korean children's reading success. It is beneficial for children to memorize the rich spelling of various morphemes. Furthermore, the orthographic representations of morphemic units need to be preserved after the formation of derivational or inflectional new words even at the cost of phonological shifts. For example, after the suffix 이 is added to a stem 깊 'deep' to form the new word 깊이 'depth', its pronunciation becomes 기피 /gi. pi/ 'avoidance' due to the resyllabification rule. However, the spelling is still kept as 깊이.

In summary, Korean orthographic features and Korean's indirect mapping between orthography and phonology, morphology and phonology may pose challenges to young Korean learners. Learning to read and spell Korean entails visual-orthographic and morphological processing skills. These challenges have implications for reading instruction in Korean.

4.4.2   *Implications for Instruction*

Given that Korean Hangul has a nonlinear visual-orthographic structure, classroom instruction should draw children's attention to the spatial configuration of a syllable block. The specific location of each grapheme should be marked explicitly within the syllable block so that children can view and remember them easily. Phonological alterations in multi-syllable words should also be explicitly marked to draw students' close attention.

Since CV and coda are considered salient subsyllabic units in Korean orthography as opposed to onset and rime in English, initial instruction for Hangul acquisition should focus on CV syllables and coda. It would be desirable to teach young children with CV syllables in a syllable chart at first and then practice with coda six months later. A syllable chart has each Korean consonant in a column and each vowel in a row in order to make CV syllables. The syllable chart was used to teach Hangul to the lower class and to women from the fifteenth century, when Hangul was created, until the mid-twentieth century. The syllable chart is not popular nowadays, because of the strong influence of the western educational approach. In contrast, public kindergartens adopt a whole word approach, a key policy of the Korean government for literacy education. However, the private learning centers in Korea adopt a phonics approach to teaching reading. Given the inconsistent approaches in literacy instruction across the country and the salient CV structure in Korean Hangul orthography, more attention needs to be given to the syllable unit in teaching. We suggest that the use of the syllable chart may be especially beneficial for young children with reading problems and in less privileged environments. Future research may need training and intervention studies with a syllable chart to establish the potential causal effect of the syllable chart on reading success.

Morphological awareness is important in Hangul reading and writing for young children (Cho et al., 2008), primary school students (Cho et al., 2011; Wang et al., 2009), and college students (Bae & Yi, 2012) in Korea. Classroom instruction needs to help children establish a good understanding of individual constituent morphemes in morphologically complex words. Children need to learn how to decompose and recompose complex words, taking phonological shifts into consideration while preserving the morphemic units. Korean has a productive derivational and inflectional morphology. Given the complexity of Korean inflectional and derivational morphology, classroom instruction needs to make extra efforts in helping children understand a variety of inflectional and derivational morphemes and the process of affixation to form the morphologically complex words. Korean vocabulary includes as many compounds containing homophones as in Chinese. Children should be given ample opportunities to practice detecting the meaning differences in homophones in different compounds. Specific training and intervention programs are needed to enhance morphological awareness for less skilled readers.

To conclude, given the saliency of syllables and the CV unit within a syllable, the CV syllable chart may be an effective tool to enhance young children's phonological awareness, which in turn improves children's reading skill. Owing to the richness of Korea's morphological system and the importance of morphological awareness for word decoding and spelling development, explicit classroom instruction in the processes of morphological decomposition and recomposition may be needed to facilitate word learning.

4.5   Final Conclusion

In this chapter we examined the acquisition of reading in Korean orthography. The Korean language is considered a language isolate and the Korean orthography Hangul is considered a transparent alphabetic writing system. A syllable is a salient phonological and orthographic unit in Korean. The composition of letters is shaped into a square-like syllable block, ranging from left to right and from top to bottom. Phonological awareness at both syllable and phoneme level is an important predictor of Hangul word recognition in Korean children. Phonological and naming deficits are prominent poor readers and spellers of Korean. A CV unit is a salient subsyllabic unit in the development of word decoding and spelling skills. The spelling of coda appears to be a challenging task among Korean preschool children because a coda phoneme can often be spelled in multiple ways. Morphological awareness plays an important role in word recognition, word spelling, and reading comprehension among school-aged children. The indirect mapping between orthography and phonology, especially for the coda phonemes, and between morphology and phonology as a result of phonological assimilation, provides challenges for young Korean readers. Learning to read and spell Korean entails both visual-orthographic and morphological processing skills. These challenges have implications for reading instruction in Korean.

Acknowledgement

This work was partially supported by the National Research Foundation of Korea Grant funded by the Korean Government (NRF-2013S1A3A2054928) to Jeung-Ryeul Cho.

References

Bae, S. & Yi, K.(2012). Processing of Korean compounds with Saisios. *Korean Journal of Cognitive Science, 23*, 349–366.

Baek, M.-S. (2012). *Korean morpheme dictionary.* Seoul: Parkyijung.

Bryant, P. & Nunes, T. (2004). Morphology and spelling. In T. Nunes & P. Bryant (Eds.), *Handbook of children's literacy* (pp. 91–118). London: Kluwer.

Cho, B. E. (2004). Issues concerning Korean learners of English: English education in Korea and some common difficulties of Korean students. *The East Asian Learner, 1*(2), 31–36.

Cho, J.-R. (2009). Syllable and letter knowledge in early Korean Hangul reading. *Journal of Educational Psychology, 101*, 938–947.

Cho, J.-R. & Chen, H. C. (1999). Orthographic and phonological activation in the semantic processing of Korean Hanja and Hangul. *Language and Cognitive Processes, 14*, 481–502.

Cho, J.-R., Chiu, M. M. & McBride-Chang, C. (2011). Morphological awareness, phonological awareness, and literacy development in Korean and English: A 2-year longitudinal study. *Scientific Studies of Reading*, *15*, 383–408. DOI:10.1080/10888438.2010.487143.

Cho, J.-R. & Ji, Y.-K. (2011). Cognitive profiles of Korean poor readers. *Dyslexia*, *17*, 312–326.

Cho, J.-R., Kim, B.-H. & Kim, Y.-S. (2013). Semantic knowledge in listening and reading comprehension among Korean children living in urban and rural communities: A 1-year longitudinal study. Paper presented at 20th Annual Meeting Society for the Scientific Study of Reading, Hong Kong.

Cho, J. R. & Lee, J. Y. (2010). Transfer of morphological and phonological awareness to reading in English and logographic Hanja among Korean children. *Journal of Cognitive Science*, *11*, 57–78.

Cho, J. R. & McBride-Chang, C. (2005a). Correlates of Korean Hangul acquisition among kindergartners and second graders. *Scientific Studies of Reading*, *9*, 3–16.

(2005b). Levels of phonological awareness in Korean and English: A 1-year longitudinal study. *Journal of Educational Psychology*, *97*, 564–571.

Cho, J.-R., McBride-Chang, C. & Park, S.-G. (2008). Phonological awareness and morphological awareness: Differential associations to regular and irregular word recognition in early Korean Hangul readers. *Reading and Writing*, *21*, 255–274.

Gardner, M. F. (1996). *Test of visual-perceptual skills (non-motor)*. Burlingame, CA: Psychological and Educational Publications.

Green, L., McCutchen, D., Schwiebert, C., Quinlan, T., Eva-Wood, A. & Juelis, J. (2003). Morphological development in children's writing. *Journal of Educational Psychology*, *95*, 752–761.

Jun, S.-A. (1995). A phonetic study of stress in Korean. Paper presented at the 130th Acoustical Society of America meeting, St. Louis, MO.

(1998). The accentual phrase in the Korean prosodic hierarchy. *Phonology*, *15*, 189–226.

(2000). K-ToBI (Korean ToBI) labelling conventions: Version 3. *Speech Sciences*, *7*, 143–170.

Kang, H. & Simpson, G. B. (1996). Development of semantic and phonological priming in a shallow orthography. *Developmental Psychology*, *32*, 860–866.

Kemp, N. (2006). Children's spelling of base, inflected, and derived words: Links with morphological awareness. *Reading and Writing*, *19*, 737–765.

Kim, A.-H., Yoo, H.-S. & Kim, U. (2010). Prediction of word recognition, reading fluency, and reading comprehension: A longitudinal study of 5-year-old and 6-year-old children. *Korean Journal of Elementary Education*, *23*, 427–453.

Kim, H.-J. (2012). Syllable structure, frequency, analogy, and phonetics: Factors in North Kyungsang Korean accentuation of novel words. Doctoral dissertation, State University of New York at Stony Brook.

Kim, J. (1999). Investigating phonological processing in visual word recognition: The use of Korean Hangul (alphabetic) and Hanja (logographic) scripts. *Dissertation Abstracts International: Section B: The Sciences and Engineering*, *59*(11-B), 6093.

Kim, J. & Davis, C. (2004). Characteristics of poor readers of Korean Hangul: Auditory, visual and phonological processing. *Reading and Writing*, *17*, 153–185.

Kim, N. (1992). Korean. *International Encyclopedia of Linguistics*, *2*, 366–370.

Kim, Y.-S. (2007). Phonological awareness and literacy skills in Korean: An examination of the unique role of body-coda units. *Applied Psycholinguistics*, *28*, 69–94.

———— (2010). Componential skills in early spelling development in Korean. *Scientific Studies of Reading*, *14*, 137–158.

———— (2011). Proximal and distal predictors of reading comprehension: Evidence from young Korean readers. *Scientific Studies of Reading*, *15*, 167–190.

Kim-Renaud, Y.-K. (Ed.) (1997). *The Korean alphabet: Its history and structure*. Honolulu, HI: University of Hawaii.

Korean Association of Child Studies & Hansol Education Research Center (2002). *Child development report 2001*. Seoul: Hansol Education.

Landerl, K. & Wimmer, H. (2008). Development of word reading fluency and spelling in a consistent orthography: An 8-year follow-up. *Journal of Educational Psychology*, *100*, 150–161.

Lee, I.-S. & Cho, J.-R. (2003). Causal relations between Hangul reading and cognitive-linguistic variables in primary school children. *Korean Journal of Developmental Psychology*, *16*, 211–225.

Lee, K. & Lee, S. (2007). A study on the beginning literacy instruction through the analysis of commercial Korean language textbooks. *New Korean Education*, *75*, 215–248.

McBride-Chang, C., Cho, J.-R., Liu, H., Wagner, R. K., Shu, H., Zhou, A., Cheuk, C. S.-M. & Muse, A. (2005). Changing models across cultures: Associations of phonological and morphological awareness to reading in Beijing, Hong Kong, Korea, and America. *Journal of Experimental Child Psychology*, *92*, 140–160.

Ministry of Education and Human Resource Development (1998). *Korean kindergarten curriculum*. Seoul: Special Education Publishing.

Na, J. & Moon, M. (2004). *Early childhood education and care policies in the republic of Korea* (OECD Thematic Review of Early Childhood Education and Care Policy: Background Report). Seoul: Korean Educational Development Institute. www.oecd.org/dataoecd/25/57/27856763.pdf.

Nagy, W., Berninger, V., Abbott, R., Vaughan, K. & Vermeulen, K. (2003). Relationship of morphology and other language skills to literacy skills in at-risk second-grade readers and at-risk fourth-grade writers. *Journal of Educational Psychology*, *95*, 730–742.

Nunes, T. & Hatano, G. (2004). Morphology, reading and spelling: Looking across languages. In T. Nunes & P. Bryant (Eds.), *Handbook of children's literacy* (pp. 651–672). Dordrecht: Kluwer Academic Publishers.

Pae, H. K. (2011). Is Korean a syllabic alphabet or an alphabetic syllabary? *Writing Systems Research*, *3*, 103–115. DOI:10.1093/wsr/wsr002.

Park, H. R. & Uno, A. (2012). Investigation of cognitive abilities related to reading and spelling in Korean: Readers with high, average, and low skill levels. *Dyslexia*, *18*, 199–215.

Simpson, G. B. & Kang, H. (2004). Syllable processing in alphabetic Korean. *Reading and Writing*, *17*, 137–151.

Sohn, H.-M. (1999). *The Korean language*. Cambridge University Press.

Song, J. J. (2005). *The Korean language: Structure, use and context*. New York: Routledge.

Taylor, I. & Taylor, M. M. (1995). *Writing and literacy in Chinese, Korean, and Japanese, Vol. III*. Amsterdam: John Benjamins.

Treiman, R., Mullennix, J., Bijeljac-Babic, R. & Richmond-Welty, E. D. (1995). The special role of rimes in the description use and acquisition of English orthography. *Journal of Experimental Psychology: General, 124*, 107–136.

Wang, M., Ko, I.-Y. & Choi, J. (2009). The importance of morphological awareness in Korean–English biliteracy acquisition. *Contemporary Educational Psychology, 34*, 132–142.

Yoon, H.-K., Bolger, D. J., Kwon, O.-S. & Perfetti, C. A. (2002). Subsyllabic units in reading: A difference between Korean and English. In L. Verhoeven, C. Elbro & P. Reitsma (Eds.), *Precursors of functional literacy* (pp. 139–163). Amsterdam: John Benjamins.

5   Learning to Read Kannada and Other Languages of South Asia

Sonali Nag

5.1   Introduction

South Asia is rich in linguistic diversity, and a robust body of research is available to describe the distinct features of the multiple languages of the region (e.g., Dravidian languages, Krishnamurti, 2003; Indo-Aryan languages, Masica, 1991). Many South Asian languages share a common early history and have experienced similar waves of language contact over the centuries, leading to a phenomenon of convergence in lexicon, grammar, and writing system. The overarching presence of such commonalities led to the region being called *a linguistic area* (*Sprachbund*; Emeneau, 1956). Acquisition research is available in several languages of South Asia, but the body of evidence is small in each language. In this chapter, research from Kannada, a southern Dravidian language, will provide the backdrop for reviewing literacy development in Indic writing systems, and where available, cross-linguistic evidence will be used to explore commonalities and particularities. It is also critical to note that socioeconomic inequalities run deep in the South Asian region. Socio-political and socio-linguistic issues are therefore inextricably woven into any discussion on literacy development and schooling in the region (cf. Sen, 2010). While this chapter introduces some of the issues involved, the focus will be on the psycholinguistic and cognitive-behavioral aspects of literacy learning.

5.1.1   South Asian Languages and Their Writing System

The orthographies of a large number of languages of South Asia are descendants of the ancient Indic writing system called Brahmi. There are other writing systems in the region including the Arabic-derived scripts of Urdu and Pashto, and the Latin-based script of Khasi, but these are not covered here.

Akshara is a basic symbol unit of the Indic writing system. While many akshara are constructed from phonemic markers (alphabet-like), some are representations of syllables with no discernible phonemic markers (syllabary-like). A typological description for the writing system is the *alphasyllabary*

(Bright, 1996; Salomon, 2000), although it would be erroneous to infer from the term that the akshara system is merely a hybrid with part-solutions borrowed from an alphabet and a syllabary (a point also made by Bright, 1996, and Salomon, 2000). Other names for this writing system include syllabo-alphabetic (Patel & Soper, 1987), syllabic alphabet (Coulmas, 1996), *abugida* (Daniels, 1996), and sub-syllabic (Vaid & Padakannaya, 2004). Figure 5.1 (column 1) gives a selection of akshara in four South Asian languages.

The akshara is minimally a vowel (/V/), lengthened by combining prevocalic consonants (/CV/, /CCV/, /CCCV/). A subset carries an inherent vowel (/Ca/) which has been said to offer articulatory ease to spoken consonants (Pandey, 2007a; Patel, 1996, 2004, 2007). Depending on the language, the inherent vowel is a mid-central [ə], open-central [a] or open-mid back rounded [ɔ] vowel. The automatically assumed inherent vowel in a consonant may be nullified by adding a vowel-suppression marker or by constructing conjoint consonants where a consonant gives up the inherent vowel by ligaturing to another consonant (see akshara marked as 1, 6, and 7 in Figure 5.1). The former vowel-suppression marker is common in some but not all languages (compare Tamil with other language in Figure 5.1). Taken together, the phenomena of inherent vowel and *consonantal conjoints* are considered defining features of the writing system (Salomon, 2000). Finally, a less transparent instance of vowel suppression occurs where a /Ca/ akshara represents a vowel-less consonant ⟨C^O⟩, with the phonological context needed for this inference (e.g., from Hindi: coda /r/ written with inherent vowel (/ra/) but read as /karna/ 'to do').

A principle of *surface organization* moderates transcription of the spoken language such that markers for sound units fall into a series of block-like arrangements. Each vowel and consonant has a primary and a secondary form (e.g., in Hindi: /i/ = इ, ि; /k/ = क, क्), and positional rules govern their use. For vowels, the primary form is typically used in word-initial position and for morphemic vowels, with the secondary form reserved for the post-consonantal position. Among consonants, the primary form is for syllable-initial consonants and the secondary form for consonants in a cluster. The visuospatial arrangement of some akshara may be non-linear, with phoneme markers placed in one of the four quarters of the symbol space (e.g., vowel markers in Hindi: ि, ी, ॖ, ॢ, /i/, /ī/, /e/, /u/).

A principle of *complete phonemic transcription* governs written representation of spoken words (Figure 5.1, last column). For this, the rule is to represent the coda (syllable-final consonant(s)) as the *next* akshara. This resyllabification phenomenon is carried intact from ancestral forms of the writing system into most contemporary varieties (Patel, 2007; Salomon, 2000; but see Miller, 2013). Resyllabification for purposes of writing maintains the surface arrangement of symbol blocks. The coda has one of three possible representations: (a) a /Ca/ akshara with the inherent vowel assumed

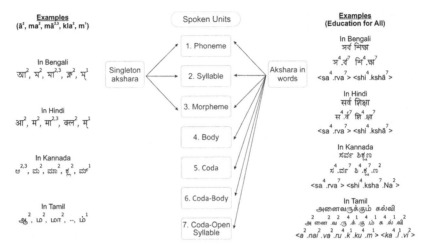

Note: For each orthographic example the level of mapping to language is shown in superscript.

Figure 5.1 Schematic representation of the akshara writing system: orthographic examples and levels of mapping to language.

as suppressed, (b) an akshara with vowel suppression marker, (c) an akshara that also carries information from the next syllable as either a coda-body or coda-syllable mapping (illustrated in Figure 5.1). A /CVC.CV/ word may thus be written as ⟨CV.C^O.CV⟩, ⟨CV.C.CV⟩, or ⟨CV.CCV⟩, and among these, it is the context-sensitive interpretation of the /Ca/ as ⟨C^O⟩ that introduces opacity in an otherwise transparent system. The choice of the appropriate coda representation depends on rules of syllabification of the specific South Asian language, and the etymological, morphological, and morphophonological characteristics of individual words. The forward-pinning of codas to the next phonological syllable may form akshara representing a coda-syllable mapping or a coda-body mapping. The mapping of the writing system to spoken language is therefore at multiple levels (Figure 5.1). Consequently, the construct of orthographic depth (Frost, Katz & Bentin, 1987) is to be analyzed at two levels in the akshara writing system. Within akshara, transparency is bound by positional rules for use of primary and secondary forms. Within a word, accommodation of resyllabification has transparent options (⟨CCV⟩, ⟨C⟩) and the opaque option of a /Ca/ akshara with suppression of the inherent vowel.

In summary, it is useful to think of the akshara for what it represents when single and when embedded within a word. As a singleton akshara, the unit is an *orthographic syllable* with the exception of the phonemic consonant. In a word context, the akshara additionally may represent resyllabification of the spoken string. We see below that insights about the links between the linguistic and orthographic layers are critical for literacy development in this writing system.

5.1.2   Synchronic and Diachronic Characterization

The ancestral roots of akshara are in the Brahmi writing system. Theoretical accounts have given weight to influences of both the Classical Sanskrit heritage (e.g., Pandey, 2007b; Patel, 2007), and the Prakrit (vernacular) varieties including Pali (Masica, 1991; Rimzhim, Katz & Fowler, 2013), Sinhala Prakrit and Early Tamil (Deraniyagala & Abeyratne, 2000; Mahadevan, 2003). In the Prakrits-influenced accounts, the architecture of the akshara writing system first represented a language with only open syllables, with new solutions emerging to accommodate the historical drift toward closed final syllables. Over the centuries, Brahmi diversified to become distinctive orthographies for multiple languages (cf. Lew, 2013; Masica, 1991; Miller, 2013; Singh, 2007). In the more recent past, spelling reforms and negotiations to reduce diglossia have had a strong influence on written language (e.g., Telugu: Krishnamurti, 1979; Tamil: Geetha, 2012; Bengali: Dasgupta & Sengupta, 2003; Hindi: Pandey, 2007c, 2013). In addition, ongoing influences of language contact are evident at all linguistic levels: reduced integration of loan words, wholesale borrowings into native lexicon, and subtle yet distinctive changes in syntax (e.g., English on Odiya: Patnaik & Pandit, 1986; Hindi on Maithili: Kumar, 2001).

5.1.3   Literacy and Schooling

The quality of teaching environments varies significantly across South Asia (Dyer, 2008; Govinda & Bandopadhyay, 2011). Schools in resource-poor communities have interrupted educational programs because of either irregular teaching or children who are "long absent." School effects on literacy attainments is not yet an area of systematic research, though descriptive studies confirm that many schools in the region do not have an adequate supply of reading materials. Such poorly functioning schools slow down the pace of literacy learning by about one year (Nag, 2007). An inherent requirement in the region is multilingual education (e.g., UNESCO, 2003), but the provision of mother tongue-based multilingual education appears unmet and it is common for children to learn to read in a second or third language. Other challenges include addressing home literacy environments, finding culturally accepted orthographies for languages that do not have a literary tradition, producing books with appropriate cultural material, showing sensitivity to the issues of diglossia, and addressing teacher supply (e.g., Nag, Chiat, Torgerson & Snowling, 2013).

5.2   Description of Kannada and Its Written Forms

Kannada is a major language of India with a concentration of speakers in the southern state of Karnataka and a rapidly growing diaspora. This section gives a brief description of the phonology, morphology, and orthography of Kannada. For a more comprehensive description, see Sridhar (1990), and for a comparative analysis with neighboring Dravidian languages, see Krishnamurti (2003).

5.2.1   Linguistic System

5.2.1.1 Phonology   Modern Standard Kannada is spoken by the educated people of the Bangalore-Mysore region, with several phonological changes seen in the coastal (Mangalore) and northern (Dharwad) varieties, and in the dialects within each variety. In Standard Colloquial Kannada, most words are bi-syllabic or longer. The canonical syllable at the minimum is the syllabic vowel which can be either short or long in length. Other syllables may have up to three consonants before and after the vowel (Sridhar, 1990). Of the variety available, the consonant-vowel syllable is the most common.

Kannada has five pairs of voiceless–voiced consonant pairs (e.g., /k/–/g/, /p/–/b/) with aspirated equivalents (/kh/, /gh/, /ph/, /bh/). Apart from the set of plosives and affricates, the other consonants are nasals (/m/, /n/, /ṇ/), approximants (/v/, /j/), lateral approximants (/l/, /ḷ/), and the fricatives (/s/, /ṣ/, /š/). The glottal /h/ and the consonants /f/ and /z/ are reserved for loan words. Among vowels, there are five long and short pairs (/i/–/ī/, /e/–/ē/, /a/–/ā/, /o/–/ō/, and /u/–/ū/) and two diphthongs (/ai/, /au/). The phonotactics of the language allow all vowels but no consonants in the word-final position. Loan words that end with a consonant are generally followed by /u/ to end the syllable, except for the glide /y/, when /i/ is added. All vowels and consonants are allowed in the word-initial position except /ṇ/ and /ḷ/. The word-initial /y/ glide is followed by a back vowel (/u/, /o/) and the off glide /v/ by a front vowel (/a/, /æ/, /i/, /e/). Syllabic vowel sequences are not permitted in the language. Both geminates and mixed clusters are present. Historically, clusters were permitted only in the medial position, but with successive inclusion of loan words, consonant clusters are now found in all word positions. A nativizing trend of such clusters would be to insert vowels in initial clusters (/prema/ to /perema/) and to enunciate the final cluster with a vowel (/mask/ to /masku/).

Many of these phonological characteristics are seen in an adult written language corpus of 100,000 words (Ranganatha, 1982): Forty-six of the fifty highest-frequency syllables and half of the remaining lower-frequency syllables in the corpus are simple, open syllables (e.g., /pa/, /te/, /ni/). Syllables containing three phonemes are /CCV/ and /CVC/ combinations (e.g., /svā/, /sid/, /dal/), and

Table 5.1 *Two simple Kannada sentences with notation of their inflectional content*

ರಾಜಿ ಹುಡುಗನಿಗೆ ಆರು ಚಮಚಗಳನ್ನು ಕೊಟ್ಟಳು.
raaji huDugan[ige] aaru chamacha[gaLannu] koTT[aLu].
Raaji gave six spoons to the boy.
- Nom case on raaji
- Genitive *[ige]*
- Plural + accusative *[gaLannu]*
- Past tense stem + agr 3rd person feminine singular *[aLu]*

ಅಂಗಳದಲ್ಲಿ ಚಿಕ್ಕಪ್ಪ ಹಳೆಯ ರೇಡಿಯೊ ಕೇಳುತ್ತಿದ್ದರು.
angaLa[dalli] chikkappa haLe[ya] radio keeL[uttiddaru].
Uncle was listening to the old radio in the courtyard.
- Locative *[dalli]*
- Genetive *[ya]*
- Present participle or tense marker *[utt-]*; past + agr 3rd person honorific *[idd-aru]*

approximately 10 percent of syllables carry four phonemes (e.g., /sval/, /vyak/, /gran/). Five-phoneme syllables are rare and appear to be mostly for loan words (/byank/, 'bank').

5.2.1.2 Inflectional Morphology   Kannada is an agglutinating language, rich in inflectional details (illustrated in Table 5.1). Inflections on verbs include person, number, gender, tense, passive, and causative markers. Inflections on nouns include markers for case and number. Case markers are bound suffixes attached to the noun phrase. Semantic and syntactic factors influence the realization of specific inflections (Amritavalli, 2008; Sridhar, 1990). The Ranganatha corpus (1982) of 100,000 written words has 179 inflectional suffixes and examples of the most common, with token frequency between 3,000 and 4,000, are the case markers *-annu* (accusative), *-da* (genitive), and *-alli* (locative).

5.2.1.3 Word Formation Processes   In Kannada, stringing of suffixes to root words is common, making some words six to seven syllables long (*kadambari.gal.annu*, noun + plural + accusative, 'magazines'). Compound words are also common (*chikka + appa = chikkappa*, 'uncle', literally: 'little' + 'father'). Morphophonological rules called *sandhi* govern all such multi-morphemic constructions both within words (the root + suffix) and between words (compounding). As with most Indic languages, the sandhi rules in Kannada often involve phonemic changes at the boundary. For example, the accusative *-annu*, may occur with /v/ (*pustaka.vannu* 'book') but also /y/ (*guri.yannu* 'target'). Similarly, the genitive marker (*-a*) may combine with *-n*, *-d*, or *-in*.

Two prominent sandhi rules in Kannada are the loss of the word-final vowel and the insertion of a glide in boundaries where there are no vowels.

5.2.2   Writing System

5.2.2.1   Script and Punctuation   The old Kannada script of the tenth century is the predecessor of two closely related scripts: the Kannada script and the Telugu script. Both are written from left to right.

5.2.2.2   Orthography   Kannada has an *extensive orthography* comprising a large register of symbols (Nag, 2007). The akshara set includes syllabic vowels (/V/, 12 units), phonemic consonants (/C/, 34 units), consonants with inherent vowels (/Ca/, 34 X 1 = 34 units), consonants with other vowels (/CV/, 34 X 11 = 374 units), and consonant clusters (/CCV/). Theoretically, thousands of /CCV/s may be constructed (34 X 34 X 12 = 13,872), but many among these are neither valid phonotactically nor likely to be called upon to represent the resyllabification principal. Also available is the very productive but rarely needed akshara for longer consonant clusters (e.g., /CCCV/). Finally, coda representation in Kannada is primarily through resyllabification into /CCV/ akshara (thus /CVC.CV/ becomes ‹CV.CCV›).

An analysis of a child-directed print corpus of 8,549 words from 101 story cards (Chili Pili Cheela, 2007) returned 703 akshara (Patel, Bapi & Nag, 2013). This number is not inclusive of the *anuswara* (o), an exception in the symbol set because it represents more than one sound (nasals and /m/). Patterns of akshara use in the child corpus mirrors the adult corpus (Ranganatha, 1982): Among the high-frequency akshara, most are /CV/, closely followed by /Ca/ with a few /CCV/s. Among the low-frequency akshara, /CV/ and /CCV/ are common, with a few phonemic consonants, and the /CCCV/ is extremely rare (only /kshmi/ in the child corpus). A point to note is that several consonant clusters in both print corpora are from word-medial positions and are the result of the resyllabification principle. In other words, viewed within a lexical context, these /CCV/ akshara are not phonological syllables but map to coda-body or coda-syllable pairs.

Taking the large size of the symbol set together with the patterns of occurrence of orthographic units in the child corpus, two points become clear: (a) young readers do not encounter all the symbols possible in the system, but among those encountered, the *variety* is high; (b) akshara-phonology mapping may be at the level of syllables but also body, coda, and phonemes (see Figure 5.1). This orthographic experience is more or less similar in the other akshara-based languages of South Asia.

A final point is the visuospatial arrangements in the Kannada akshara. The block-like surface organization is enhanced in Kannada because more phoneme markers within the akshara are stacked off-the-line than in the Devanagari-based (e.g., Hindi, Marathi) and other orthographies (e.g., Malayalam, Sinhala, Tamil). In Kannada, vowel diacritics are placed above, below, and after the base consonant (e.g., ಅ, ಿ, ು, ೆ, ೖ, ಅ, /ā/, /ī/, /ū/, /ē/, /æ/, /au/), and the secondary forms of consonants are like a subscript (e.g., ಪ್ರ and ್ for second consonants in /prā/ and /svā/: ಪ್ರ, ಸ್ವ). An orthography-specific non-linearity in Kannada akshara is the ligaturing of the vowel in a /CCV/ akshara to the first rather than the immediately preceding consonant (thus in the examples above, the vowel diacritic /ā/ (ಾ) is attached to /p/ and /s/, ಪ್ರಾ, ಸ್ವಾ).

5.2.3   Conclusion

Kannada is an agglutinating language with conditional morphophonological rules governing the formation of multi-morphemic words. A near-perfect correspondence exists between phonology and orthography. The rich morphology and morphophonology, together with an extensive symbol set, complete phonemic transcription, and a surface organization of stacking phoneme markers make Kannada an exemplar system for examining literacy learning in the akshara-based languages of South Asia.

5.3   Acquisition of Reading and Spelling in South Asian Languages

Children bring to the task of acquiring literacy a variety of cognitive and linguistic skills. It is interesting that writing system theorists have tended to invoke native-like proficiency to explain the learning of the akshara system. Thus learning, particularly those features that seemingly have no transparent linguistic rule, is seen to occur because of "the intuitive understanding of the native speaker" (Salomon, 2000, p. 93), "lexical knowledge ... is presumed" (Pandey, 2013, p. 6), and because the reader is "simply expected to know" (Dasgupta & Sengupta, 2003, p. 15). However, these explanations are unsatisfactory, both from a theory-building point of view about the architecture and processing of a writing system, and for the practical concern of how children may best be supported to learn to read and write. The following sections try to untangle what these native-like proficiencies might be, while also showing that even among native learners of a writing system there are individual differences.

5.3.1   Becoming Linguistically Aware

5.3.1.1 Phonological Development and Phonological Awareness   This section focuses on phonological development, examining intuitive syllabification and sub-syllabic processing skills. In intuitive syllabification, decisions about the position of syllable boundaries in a word can reflect phonological knowledge about the principles of sonority and legality. The akshara-based organization may also help to align syllabification with the orthographic syllables rather than phonological syllables, with the nature of coda representation, in particular, exerting influence. Among Hindi adult readers this was indeed found to be the case; if ‹CV.C^O.CV› then segmentation was /CVC.CV/, but if ‹CV.CCV› then /CV.CCV/ (Ohala, 1999). Similar mapping of syllable segmentation to orthographic organization is also reported in Malayalam (Mohanan, 1989), while in Telugu the evidence comes from the selective treatment of the nasal coda called anuswara, which, unlike the ‹CV.CCV› representations of all other codas, is an orthographically distinct marker without the forward pinning to form a /CCV/ akshara (Murty, Otake & Cutler, 2007; Sailaja, 2007). Turning to intuitive syllabification in children, the trends are far from clear. In Bengali, intuitive syllabification of CVCCV nonwords by 6- to 10-year-olds showed a preference for a single consonant onset (/CVC.CV/) overriding both sonority and legality principles (Sircar & Nag, 2013b). Inferences about the influence of akshara-based representations could not be reliably made in this study because in Bengali both ‹CV.C^O.CV› and ‹CV.CCV› representations are available for the coda, and it was not clear which one might have been invoked by the child for the aurally presented nonword stimuli. This ambiguity is not there in Kannada where ‹CV.CCV› representation is the norm. A survey with 5- to 8-year-olds found two distinct strategies on CVCCV nonwords. For 54 percent of the sample, segmentations were essentially akshara-by-akshara (/CV.CCV/), suggesting a large influence of orthography on spoken language processing. But for the rest, a /CVC. CV/ syllabification was restricted to certain items and structured around Kannada phonotactics, suggesting that these children ignored the orthographic layer. More research is clearly needed to understand the influence of literacy in the akshara systems on syllabic processing. It is plausible that greater akshara knowledge increases akshara-based syllabification. But if better akshara knowledge is itself shaped by a greater understanding of the phonology of the language, then it may also be that the mediation of orthographic organization reduces with greater akshara knowledge.

Turning to sub-syllabic processing, the Kannada language is replete with word pairs minimally distinct at the phonemic level (*āne – āme*, ‘elephant’ – ‘tortoise’; *bēga – bīga*, ‘fast’ – ‘lock’; *kūgi – kūgu*, verb forms for ‘crying out’). Despite this demand in the spoken language for implicit phonemic awareness, children show a slow pace of attainment on tasks requiring explicit phonemic processing. Surveys by Nag and colleagues (Nag, 2007; Nag & Snowling, 2012, 2013) showed phonemic processing to be associated with increasing Kannada orthographic experience, with more fluent readers better on a phoneme deletion task. The relationship appeared to be one of reciprocal influence between characteristics of the writing system and the fine-tuning of the phonological domain. Importantly, 22 percent of a middle school cohort of 8- to 12-year-olds continued to be near zero in phonemic processing tasks. These findings confirm earlier indications in the literature of a spurt in explicit phonemic processing approximately three years after literacy instruction, with performance of some children remaining exceptionally low (Kannada: Prakash, Rekha, Nigam & Karanth, 1993; Gujarati: Patel & Soper, 1987). It is important to note that children in all the above studies were in instructional contexts that treated the writing system more or less like a syllabary. Findings are strikingly different in literacy environments that actively demonstrate the use of phonemic markers, and thus arguably reduce the syllabary-like notion of the writing system. In one such instruction setting, children in Grades 2 to 3 scored well above chance on phoneme deletion tasks (Bengali: Sircar & Nag, 2013a). Clearly, there is a need to examine the quality of insights that literacy instruction provides about the akshara and how these interact with children's phonological development.

5.3.1.2 Morphological Development and Morphological Awareness The two simple sentences in Table 5.1 show some of the ways that inflectional morphemes convey event semantics (who-did-what-to-whom) and other grammatical information in Kannada. In the first sentence, even if we do not know whether Raaji is a girl or a boy, the gender marker on the verb (last word) gives this information, while the last word (verb) in the second sentence carries the tense marker for when uncle played the radio. Systematic acquisition studies on Kannada's morphosyntax in school-age children are not available (but for studies with preliterate children, see Devaki, 1991; Lidz, Gleitman & Gleitman, 2003). The relationship between development of morphological, morphosyntactic, morphophonological (sandhi) knowledge and literacy may be a reciprocal one. Seeing in print the morphophonological alteration in word boundaries, for example, may help to consolidate learning about sandhi changes in the index word and similar other words in the child's lexicon. In addition, knowing many such instances may help with recognizing these words more quickly in print. There may even be links between reading and spelling of multi-morphemic words, and an awareness of their morphosyntactic functions. A preliminary indication that this may be so is the better performance found on a Kannada grammaticality judgment task among in-school children when compared to a never-enrolled group (Karanth, Kudva & Vijayan, 1995). There is also evidence that 4- to 7-year-old children with more exposure to Kannada oral narratives and book reading at home are more accurate with morphosyntactic details on a repetition task of just-heard sentences of differing syntactic complexity (Nag, Mirković & Snowling, 2012).

5.3.2   Development of Word Identification

Two issues about akshara learning have implications for word identification. First is the obvious: words become easy to identify when individual akshara are accurately recognized. The factors influencing the learning of the full complement of akshara are several, some of which have only recently begun to receive research attention. In the perceptual domain, visuospatial factors, particularly non-linear arrangements, influence processing (Vaid & Gupta, 2002; Wali, Sproat, Padakannaya & Bhuvaneshwari, 2009). In the experiential domain, frequency of occurrence in child-directed texts varies (e.g., Patel et al., 2013), and along with sequence and scope of instruction, influences pace of learning (Nag, 2007, 2011, 2013). Some of the key cognitive-linguistic factors that matter at the onset of literacy learning are vocabulary, visual memory, phonological processing skills, phonological memory, and rapid automatized naming (RAN) (Kannada: Nag & Snowling, 2012; Sinhala: Wijayathilake & Parrila, 2013). The last perhaps taps the efficiency of cross-modal learning between the visual and verbal domains. During the primary school years, a reciprocal relationship between fine-grained phonological processing and greater analytical skills for phonemic markers appears to define the akshara learning system (see Nag, 2007, 2011; Nag & Snowling, 2012, 2013). By middle school, a marker for a poor reader is a child who struggles to recognize less frequent akshara or akshara with two or more phoneme markers (Nag, 2011; Nag & Snowling, 2011a).

The cognitive-linguistic process of accurate mapping of akshara to oral language also aids word identification. Recall that in this writing system, a guiding principle for transcription is to represent all sound segments and that the principle of surface organization into symbol blocks moderates this process. Akshara in the context of words therefore may map on to phonological syllables, the body or coda, and successive syllables either as coda-body or coda-full-syllable concatenations (see Figure 5.1). In Kannada, as is the case with other languages of South Asia that allow closed syllables, the resyllabification phenomenon of forward pinning of the coda to the next orthographic syllable (‹CV.CCV›) implies that the /CCV/ akshara is exceptionally productive. It is therefore understood that even advanced readers will encounter unfamiliar /CCV/ akshara in the course of reading literary texts or because unusual /CCV/ akshara have been put together to transcribe foreign words (e.g., 'phosphate', 'acquire'). It would also appear therefore that both insights into the principles of the writing system and recognizing cues from the lexical context would aid word identification.

5.3.2.1   Word Decoding Development   A growing body of research shows moderate to strong associations between development of Kannada word decoding skills, akshara knowledge, and phonological skills, and these trends appear in other languages of South Asia as well. Grades 1 to 4 are a period of actively expanding skills for decoding words (Nag, 2007; Prema, 1998). The challenge is particular to more complex akshara in words, as also reported in Bengali (Sircar & Nag, 2013a), Sinhala (Wijayathilake & Parrila, 2013), and Gujarati (Patel, 2004). Over these years, akshara knowledge expands and sub-syllabic processing improves both in Kannada (Nag, 2007; Prakash et al., 1993) and in other languages (e.g., Patel, 2004; Sircar & Nag, 2013a; Tiwari, Nair & Krishnan, 2011). Evidence from naming (Nag, 2007; Vaid & Gupta, 2002) and parsing (Patel, 2004) suggests that an analytic approach to word identification underpins this development. Awareness of phonemic markers and multiple levels of mapping to phonology support children moving from being global to more analytic and strategic in their processing of words.

Further insights into word identification processes come from an analysis of component skills of reading fluency, where speed and accuracy are both expected. Nag & Snowling (2012), examining performance of middle schoolers, found that *both* syllable- and phoneme-level performance explained individual differences in Kannada reading accuracy, whereas for reading rate, only phoneme-level scores were significant. It would appear that the orthographic properties of syllabic symbols and phonemic markers maintain sensitivity of both syllable- and phoneme-level processing. When the child cracks the akshara code and gains alphasyllabic competence, the biggest gains are on words with complex akshara. RAN was also a unique predictor of both components, perhaps because RAN is related to well-automatized processes for access and retrieval from the extensive symbol set.

Another important factor in word identification is oral language beyond phonology. Strong associations between phrase repetition and word identification in phrases by 4- to 7-year-olds point to the possible links between spoken and written language (Ramachandra & Karanth, 2007). However, among older readers (15- to 45-year-olds), unusual akshara-phonology mapping and not semantic features of concreteness-abstractness influenced naming latencies (Karanth, Mathew & Kurien, 2004), suggesting the very important role of orthographic processing in Kannada word identification. In other South Asian languages, individual differences have been found in primary schoolers' accuracy on word-level parsing tasks (e.g., Gujarati: Patel, 2004; Sinhala: Wijayathilake & Parrila, 2013). Here again it is difficult to draw any firm conclusions about the role of morphological processing in word identification because no morphological analysis is reported. Nonetheless, using one's lexical repertoire is a valuable strategy, particularly since akshara learning takes time to reach a high level of efficiency. Moreover, wider lexical knowledge, including implicit knowledge of phonotactics, etymological conventions, and morphophonological rules is a valuable resource when akshara-phonology (and phonology-akshara) mappings are ambiguous. One preliminary line of evidence for this proposal comes from a Bengali nonword reading task. Sircar and Nag (2013a) exploited the nature of coda representation in Bengali – the medial akshara in ‹CVCaCV› may map either to /CVCaCV/ or /CVC^{O}CV/ – to examine decoding strategies. Phonological analogies in the lexicon appeared to aid decoding at points of ambiguity. Thus, the nonword ‹piraṣa› was decoded by typically developing readers in Grades 3 to 4 as a /CVCaCV/ in keeping with words like *Dhāranā* ('assumption') and *prerana* ('inspiration'), while ‹DaTakā› was decoded as /CVC^{O}CV/ in keeping with common words like *maTka* ('pot') and *paTka* ('firecrackers'). Importantly, while typically developing readers made a distinction between the two nonwords, less skilled and younger readers were unquestioning of orthography, reading both nonwords as /CVCaCV/. Quality lexical representations, it appears, makes for a more discerning identification of written words.

5.3.2.2 Word Spelling Development   A bidirectional mapping between phonology-akshara and akshara-phonology is involved in spelling. Accurate phonology-akshara mapping put down in the right sequence of orthographic syllables best describes the process of spelling in South Asian languages. Among primary and middle school children, individual differences in spelling accuracy are at the level of both mapping and selection of appropriate orthographic syllables (Hindi: Vaid & Gupta, 2002; Gujarati: Patel, 2004; Telugu: Vasanta, 2004). A study by Nag, Treiman, and Snowling (2010) of the Kannada spellings of middle schoolers captures many of the key issues in learning the component skills of this process. Spelling shorter words with only akshara that have the inherent vowel /Ca/ is easier than spelling longer words and words with multiple phonemic markers. Consonant segments within akshara are usually easier to spell, though phonologically close neighbors (e.g., the fricatives /s/, / ṣ /, / ś /) are prone to error, and, as in reading, consonants in the /CCV/ akshara need particular attention. Common errors with vowels are (a) omitting to write their phonemic markers (appearing then to revert to the inherent vowel), and (b) a phonological mix-up within the short–long vowel pair (e.g., /i/ for /ī/).

   Moving next to factors in akshara-phonology mapping that influence spelling, Nag (2013) found that when words were matched for age of acquisition and frequency in child-directed print, children in Grade 3 did better on those akshara that represented a phonological syllable (/d^{h}ya/ in /d^{h}ya.na/) than those that represented successive syllables (/bda/ in /sʰab.da/). There were large individual differences in children's awareness of the principles of akshara-phonology mapping, making it clear that the cognitive-linguistic underpinnings of akshara-based spelling is more than mere recall of individual symbols.

Two socio-linguistic processes also influence spelling in Kannada, and other languages of South Asia (e.g., Patnaik & Pandit, 1986; Sugathapala De Silva, 1986). First is diglossia (e.g., the dropping of the glottal fricative /h/ in certain dialects of Kannada so /halva/ spelled as ‹alva›; Nag et al., 2010). Second is the process of nativizing loan words, and confusion about phonological and morphophonological alterations. Examples of spelling versions of English words in Kannada are television (*televijan, televishan*), ticket + plural marker (*ticket.tannu, ticketu.galannu*), and tender + plural marker (*tendaru.galannu, tendar.galannu*) (Ranganatha, 1982).

5.3.2.3 Reading and Spelling Difficulties   A current view of reading difficulties is that poor reading can be caused by an accumulation of cognitive risk factors with some cognitive factors also acting as protective influences that moderate the impact of a risk factor (Snowling, 2008). Findings from the few available studies on children with atypical literacy development confirm such a multi-factorial explanation for the reading and spelling difficulties in the languages of South Asia. Cognitive profiles of poor readers show that single deficit profiles are rare and lower attainments are recorded in symbol learning and sub-syllabic processing (Hindi: Gupta, 2004; Kannada: Nag & Snowling, 2011a; Ramaa, Miles & Lalithamma, 1993), as well as knowledge of vocabulary and awareness of the morpho-syntax of the language (Nag & Snowling, 2011a). Reduced speed during RAN is also reported for children in the lower end of the distribution (Nag & Snowling, 2012; for Sinhala, see Wijayathilake & Parrila, 2013). The available data suggest two hypotheses about dyslexia in the akshara-based languages: one related to a deficit in phonological processing and the other to a mapping problem which could in principle stem from the phonological deficit (Snowling & Nag, 2011). Figure 5.2 gives a summary of the type of deficits that might characterize each. Within this profile of deficits, it is possible that high-quality semantic and morpho-syntactic knowledge may act as a protective factor. Systematic case studies as well as group comparison studies are needed to test these hypotheses.

5.3.3   Reading Comprehension

Reading comprehension surveys in the languages of South Asia report three reading profiles (e.g., Gujarati: Patel, 2004; Bengali: Nag & Sircar, 2008; Kannada: Nag, 2008). One group of children reads fluently and is typically

Dyslexia as a Language Deficit (Phonology)	Dyslexia as a Mapping Problem (Learning)
• Difficulties with syllable-level processing	• Slow pace of akshara learning
• Difficulties with phoneme-level processing	• Poor spelling particularly when phonology-akshara mapping is ambiguous
• Difficulties with morpho-phonological boundaries in multi-morphemic words	• Deficits in rapid automatized naming (RAN)

Figure 5.2 Types of deficits related to two hypotheses about dyslexia in South Asian languages.

accurate on factual questions about the text, a second group reads *akshara-by-akshara* but shows average reading comprehension scores, and a third group fails in both decoding and reading comprehension. It would appear that the quality of orthographic representation of words in these subgroups is different. Also children vary in the extent to which they draw upon lexical representations to disambiguate written words and therefore scaffold comprehension. Extending such a proposal to a study of middle school reading, Nag and Snowling (2011b) predicted that Kannada reading comprehension would be associated with lexical awareness, assessed by vocabulary definitions and a test of accuracy when recalling the content of richly inflected sentences. By contrast, those with lower levels of reading comprehension would show diminished vocabulary knowledge and mapping of morphosyntactic information to meaning. Analysis of data from ninety-five fourth- to sixth-grade children in twelve schools confirmed these predictions: significant positive correlations were found between reading comprehension and vocabulary (.340) and inflection knowledge (.354). Strong correlations were also found between reading comprehension and accuracy (.644) and phonological processing (.594). Overall, children who were better at reading comprehension were also better in reading accuracy, phonological processing, vocabulary, and inflectional morphology.

5.3.3.1 Predictors of Reading Comprehension   Turning to concurrent predictors in the same group of Kannada-speaking children, reading accuracy and phonological processing measures together accounted for 44 percent of variance in reading comprehension, after controlling for age. In a third step of the analysis, children's vocabulary scores or scores on the inflection knowledge task were entered separately. Each measure predicted unique variance in reading comprehension: vocabulary predicted 4.8 percent and inflection knowledge 2.2 percent. This model gives the cognitive-linguistic underpinnings of reading comprehension in Kannada and is perhaps as relevant for the other akshara-based languages of South Asia. First, since reading comprehension is essentially dependent on accurate word identification, and some aspects of akshara knowledge are still being mastered in the middle school years (Nag, 2007, 2013), it is not surprising that a substantial proportion of the variance in reading comprehension was explained by skills for decoding and phonological processing. Second, vocabulary and grammar knowledge support the generation of meaning from the text, and therefore, again as predicted, these aspects of broader oral language explained variance in reading comprehension.

Inference making is another factor contributing to individual differences in reading comprehension. Small-scale surveys show primary school children can make connections between idea units to draw simple inferences, but there is also a lot of variation in attainments on this skill (Bengali: Nag & Sircar, 2008; Kannada: Nag, 2008). It is important to note that the instruction methods available to the children in these surveys did not actively encourage inference making, a contextual factor that is quite widespread in South Asia (Gujarati: Dyer, 2008; Patel, 2004; Tamil: Geetha, 2012; Hindi: Jayaram, 2008a, 2008b). Research that disentangles instruction effects from spontaneous individual differences in inference making is needed to throw light on reading comprehension processes in such contexts. Also of interest is how phenomena such as causality, transitivity, and other aspects of events are encoded in South Asian languages, and what this might mean for reading comprehension (e.g., ambiguities in causality in Kannada: Lidz et al., 2003; and ambiguities in word order in Hindi: Mishra, Pandey & Srinivasan, 2010).

5.3.3.2 Word-Level Effects in Comprehending Text Words take root in the phonological, morphosyntactic, morphophonological, and orthographic domains, and the more detailed their representation in each domain, the higher their "lexical quality" (Perfetti, 2007). Several strands of evidence in the preceding sections from Kannada and other languages of South Asia point to the influence that these multiple dimensions of lexical quality play in akshara-based reading. In addition, there is the domain of morpho-orthography, details of which are not yet available from child studies, although preliminary evidence from skilled adult readers suggests word-level effects (Hindi: Rao, Soni & Chatterjee-Singh, 2012).

5.3.4   Conclusion

There are reciprocal links between linguistic awareness and literacy development. Insights into akshara formation and improved automaticity in accessing and retrieving mapping details when reading and spelling are intricately and reciprocally associated with phonological and morphological awareness. Further, literacy instruction has a far-reaching effect, from the development of explicit phonemic awareness to inference making during text reading.

5.4   Discussion

5.4.1   Challenges in Learning to Read South Asian Languages

The akshara orthographies are almost as productive as the Chinese sets, with one crucial difference: a combinatorial principal dramatically reduces the number of akshara to be individually learned. Thus, if the consonant is fixed as the base for constructing the symbol block, then the object of learning is reduced to a consonant–vowel matrix. But even then, the challenge of size remains because, as shown in the preceding sections, any number of akshara with consonant clusters must be constructed and most of these are not explicitly taught. Learning hurdles also come from the visual complexity of the symbols, phonological confusability, and mis-sequences in visuospatial arrangements. A final challenge is knowing which phonological units in a word an akshara encodes, and vice versa. Linguistic knowledge about syllabification, etymology, and morphology provides insights for gaining mastery over these orthographic complexities.

5.4.2   Implications for Instruction

This section discusses issues related to recitation, copywriting, and reading prescribed books, because these activities dominate many early literacy classrooms in South Asia, especially in public-funded schools (Dyer, 2008; Geetha, 2012; Jayaram, 2008a, 2008b; Nag, 2007; Patel, 2004, 2007; Vagh, 2010).

Recitation and copywriting. An efficiently laid-out synthetic phonics scheme provides the material for sound drills in all akshara-based languages of South Asia: Among consonants, the unvoiced and voiced sounds, and unaspirated–aspirated pairs are laid out in strings (e.g., /ka, kha, ga, gha/, /pa, pha, ba, bha/). The confusing nasals (variations of /n/) are given prominence individually at the end of each phonics string. The fricatives (variations on /s/) come in a sequence, with the trills (/r/), liquids (variations on /l/), and aspirants (like /j/ and /v/) interspersed for maximum perceptual distinctiveness. Short and long vowel pairs (/a – ā/, /i – ī /) make another set. Among the close and close-mid vowels, perceptual distinctiveness is enhanced by inter-leaving front vowels with back vowels (thus /i-u-e-o/). A final akshara set, reserved for Grades 2 to 3 usually, has a small collection of high-frequency consonant clusters. The potential of such phonics materials for developing phonological awareness seems obvious, though it does not contribute to explicit phonological processing at the sub-syllabic level.

Akshara charts are prominently displayed in classrooms and are an easy-to-refer-to visual toolkit for the beginning reader. Copywriting of these akshara is common. The parallel practice of copywriting and recitation arguably draw attention to fine-grained visuospatial details and their linkages to sound. But since no explicit attention is brought to the phonemic markers in these decon-textualized lists of symbols, the accompanying sound drills can promote a syllabary-like notion of the writing system. Incidental learning then becomes important for children to extract the underlying rules of akshara formation.

The available research does not provide a clear account of the learning mechanisms targeted by these indigenous methods of literacy instruction though there are several pointers to make them more efficient: First, the traditional phonics charts described above do not have to be an invariant sequence for teaching about the akshara. A better starting point is instead with high-frequency akshara, particularly those akshara that help construct words common in early vocabulary. Second, explicit instruction of parts of an akshara help children abstract combinatorial rules, including copywriting of the same phonemic marker (e.g., the vowel markers) with the whole comple-ment of consonants. Third, the separation of symbol sets into /V/, /Ca/, /CV/, and /CCV/ is artificial and does not reflect the phonological patterns of the spoken language. Children learn about all of these potentially easily recog-nizable akshara from encounters within known words, and hence there is no need to sanitize early grade readers of all complex akshara (like /mma/ in /amma/ 'mother'). Finally, akshara charts do not address the mapping issue. What appears to strengthen insights is good-quality lexical representation of words, and a large vocabulary. Hence, a robust oral language program must accompany akshara practice, even when the language is the home language of the child.

Reading books. If akshara learning is frequency-sensitive, then the more words in which they come embedded, the greater the chance of quickly gaining mastery. Thus, while reading practice with books is growing in most South Asian classrooms, the value of the practice needs to be qualified – repeated reading of the same book (e.g., one prescribed textbook) severely limits opportunities for implicit akshara learning. Similarly, artificially graded books with restricted vocabularies cannot offer the variety needed for akshara learning. Moving to higher order engagement with texts, the evidence suggests that reduced vocabulary and limited grammatical knowledge slow down attainments. An important implication from akshara literacy research is to introduce children of all ages to variety and complexity in narratives, at the spoken and written level.

5.5   Final Conclusion

The state of literacy research in the languages of South Asia is mainly descriptive, giving information of associations between variables. The evidence available gives more information on what-goes-with-what during literacy learning in this writing system. A very small set of studies contain sequential and process data that can give an account of "what comes from what" or "what leads to what." From the evidence available, it appears that literacy development moves from a global view of the akshara to an analytic understanding. This transition is possibly driven by an awareness about component phonemic markers and their mapping to multiple levels of phonology. Morphological awareness and akshara knowledge related to resyllabification are further factors that support word-level processing. Turning to atypical development, hypotheses under consideration for literacy difficulties are a phonological processing deficit, and a deficit in the mapping principle. Difficulties with vocabulary and grammar learning are additionally common among poor readers, with the intersecting domains of morphophonology and morpho-orthography yet to be explored. Taken together, the picture is clear that gaining mastery in Indic writing systems requires insights into the intricate mapping between the spoken language and its written form, and knowledge about the complexities of its vocabulary and grammar.

References

Amritavalli, R. (2008). The origins of functional and lexical categories: Tense-aspect and adjectives in Dravidian. *Nanzan Linguistics*, *4*, 1–20.

Bright, W. (1996). Kannada and Telugu writing. In P. T. Daniels & W. Bright (Eds.), *The world's writing systems* (pp. 413–419). New York: Oxford University Press.

Chili Pili Cheela (2007). *Kannada reading cards*. Bangalore: The Promise Foundation, National Institute of Advanced Studies and Sarva Shiksha Abhiyan (Karnataka).

Coulmas, F. (1996). *The Blackwell encyclopedia of writing systems*. Oxford: Blackwell.

Daniels, P. T. (1996). Grammatology. In P. T. Daniels & W. Bright (Eds.), *The world's writing systems* (pp. 3–5). New York: Oxford University Press.

Dasgupta, P. & Sengupta, G. (2003). The Bangla-Asamiya script and its representation in Unicode. In P. Bhaskararao (Ed.), *Indic scripts: Past and future*. ILCAA, Tokyo University of Foreign Studies.

Deraniyagala, S. U. & Abeyratne, A. (2000). Radiocarbon chronology of AnurÅdhpura, Sri Lanka: A revised age of estimate. In M. Taddei & G. De Marco (Eds.), *South Asian archaeology 1977* (pp. 759–791). Rome: Instituto Italiano per l'Africa e l'Oriente.

Devaki, L. (1991). *Development of morphological rules in children*. Mysore: Central Institute of Indian Languages.

Dyer, C. (2008). Early years literacy in Indian urban schools: Structural, social and pedagogical issues. *Language and Education, 22*, 237–253.

Emeneau, M. (1956). India as a linguistic area. *Language, 32*, 3–16.

Frost, R., Katz, L. & Bentin, S. (1987). Strategies for visual word recognition and orthographic depth: A multilingual comparison. *Journal of Experimental Psychology: Human Perception and Performance, 13*, 104–115.

Geetha, V. (2012). Literacy and reading: A Tamil experiment. *Contemporary Education Dialogue, 9*, 63–84.

Govinda, R. & Bandopadhyay, M. (2011). *Overcoming exclusion through quality schooling: Pathways to access*. Research Monograph No. 65. Brighton: Create.

Gupta, A. (2004). Reading difficulties of Hindi speaking children with developmental dyslexia. *Reading and Writing, 17*, 79–99.

Jayaram, K. (2008a). Early literacy project: Explorations and reflections. Part 1: Theoretical perspectives. *Contemporary Education Dialogue, 5*, 133–174.

(2008b). Early literacy project: Explorations and reflections. Part 2: Interventions in Hindi classrooms. *Contemporary Education Dialogue, 5*, 175–211.

Karanth, P., Kudva, A. & Vijayan, A. (1995). Literacy and linguistic awareness. In B. de Gelder & J. Morais (Eds.), *Speech and reading: A comparative approach* (pp. 303–316), Hove, UK: Lawrence Erlbaum.

Karanth, P., Mathew A. & Kurien, P. (2004). Orthography and reading speed: Data from native readers of Kannada. *Reading and Writing, 17*, 101–120.

Krishnamurti, Bh. (1979). Classical or modern: A controversy of styles in education in Telugu. In E. Annamalai (Ed.), *Language movements in India*. CIIL Conferences and Seminars Series, 5 (pp. 1–29). Mysore: Central Institute of Indian Languages.

(2003). *The Dravidian languages*. Cambridge University Press.

Kumar, R. (2001). Shift from Maithili to Hindi: A sociolinguistic study. *Studies in the Linguistic Sciences, 31*(2), 127–141.

Lew, S. (2013). A linguistic analysis of the Lao writing system and its suitability for minority language orthographies. *Writing Systems Research, 6*, 25–40. DOI:10.1080/17586801.2013.846843.

Lidz, J., Gleitman, H. & Gleitman, L. (2003). Understanding how input matters: Verb learning and the footprint of universal grammar. *Cognition, 87*, 151–178.

Mahadevan, I. (2003). *Early Tamil epigraphy: From the earliest to the sixth century A.D.* Chennai: Cre-A and Cambridge, MA: Department of Sanskrit and Indian Studies, Harvard University.

Masica, C. P. (1991). *The Indo-Aryan languages*. Cambridge: Cambridge University Press.

Miller, C. (2013). Devanagari's descendants in North and South India, Indonesia and the Philippines. *Writing Systems Research, 6*, 10–24. DOI:10.1080/17586801.2013.857288.

Mishra, R. K., Pandey, A. & Srinivasan, N. (2010). Revisiting the scrambling complexity hypothesis in sentence processing: A self-paced reading study on anomaly detection and scrambling in Hindi. *Reading and Writing, 24*(6), 709–727.

Mohanan, T. (1989). Syllable structure in Malayalam. *Linguistic Inquiry, 20*, 589–625.

Murty, L., Otake, T. & Cutler, A. (2007). Perceptual tests of rhythmic similarity: I. Mora rhythm. *Language and Speech, 50*, 77–99.

Nag, S. (2007). Early reading in Kannada: The pace of acquisition of orthographic knowledge and phonemic awareness. *Journal of Research in Reading, 30*, 7–22.

(2008). Promoting controlled inferences when reading: Reflections from a Language Programme in India. Paper presented in ESRC Seminar, University of Sussex.

(2011). The akshara languages: What do they tell us about children's literacy learning? In R. Mishra & N. Srinivasan (Eds.), *Language-cognition: State of the art* (pp. 291–310). Munich: Lincom Publishers.

(2013). Akshara-phonology mappings: The common yet uncommon case of the consonant cluster. *Writing Systems Research, 6*, 105–119. DOI:10.1080/17586801.2013.855621.

Nag, S., Chiat, S., Torgerson C. & Snowling, M. J. (2013). *Literacy, foundation learning and assessment in developing countries: Report of a rigorous review.* London: Department of International Development.

Nag, S., Mirkovic, J. & Snowling, M. J. (2012). Sentence repetitions of bilingual children: A multi-factorial study examining individual differences in the first language. Paper presented at International Conference on bilingualism and comparative linguistics, Chinese University of Hong Kong.

Nag, S. & Sircar, S. (2008). *Learning to read in Bengali: Report of a survey in five Kolkata primary schools.* Bangalore: The Promise Foundation.

Nag, S. & Snowling, M. J. (2011a). Cognitive profiles of poor readers of Kannada. *Reading and Writing, 24*, 657–676. DOI:10.1007/s11145-010–9258-7.

(2011b). Reading comprehension, decoding and oral language. *The EFLU Journal, English and Foreign Languages University, 2*(2), 75–93.

(2012). Reading in an alphasyllabary: Implications for a language-universal theory of learning to read. *Scientific Studies of Reading, 16*, 404–423.

(2013). Children's reading development: Learning about sounds, symbols and cross-modal mappings. In B. Kar (Ed.), *Cognition and brain development: Converging evidence from various methodologies* (pp. 253–270). New York: American Psychological Association.

Nag, S., Treiman, R. & Snowling, M. J. (2010). Learning to spell in an alphasyllabary: The case of Kannada. *Writing Systems Research, 2*, 41–52. DOI:10.1093/wsr/wsq001.

Ohala, M. (1999). The syllable in Hindi. In H. van der Hulst & N. A. Ritter (Eds.), *The syllable: Views and facts* (pp. 93–112). The Hague: Mouton de Gruyter.

Pandey, P. K. (2007a). Akshara as the minimum articulatory unit. In P. G. Patel, P. Pandey & D. Rajgor (Eds.), *The Indic scripts: Palaeographic and linguistic perspectives* (pp. 167–232). New Delhi: DK Printworld.

(2007b). Phonological and generative aspects of Brāhmī and its derivatives. In P. G. Patel, P. Pandey & D. Rajgor (Eds.), *The Indic scripts: Palaeographic and linguistic perspectives* (pp. 233–248). New Delhi: DK Printworld.

(2007c). Phonology–orthography interface in Devanagari for Hindi. *Written Language & Literacy, 10*, 139–156.

(2013). Akshara-to-sound rules for Hindi. *Writing Systems Research*, *6*, 54–72. DOI:10.1080/17586801.2013.855622.

Patel, J., Bapi, R. S. & Nag, S. (2013). Akshara counts in child-directed print: A pilot study with 101 texts. Manuscript.

Patel, P. G. (1996). Linguistic and cognitive aspects of the orality-literacy complex in ancient India. *Language and Communication*, *16*, 315–329.

(2004). *Reading acquisition in India: Models of learning and dyslexia*. New Delhi: Sage Publishers.

(2007). Akshara as a linguistic unit in Brāhmī scripts. In P. G. Patel, P. Pandey & D. Rajgor (Eds.), *The Indic scripts: Paleographic and linguistic perspectives* (pp. 167–215). New Delhi: DK Printworld.

Patel, P. G. & Soper, H. V. (1987). Acquisition of reading and spelling in a syllabo-alphabetic writing system. *Language and Speech*, *30*, 69–81.

Patnaik, B. N. & Pandit, I. (1986). Englishization of Oriya. In Bh. Krishnamurti (Ed.), *South Asian languages: Structure, convergence and diglossia* (pp. 232–243). Delhi: Motilal Banarasidass.

Perfetti, C. (2007). Reading ability: Lexical quality to comprehension. *Scientific Studies of Reading*, *11*, 357–383.

Prakash, P., Rekha, D., Nigam, R. & Karanth, P. (1993). Phonological awareness, orthography and literacy. In R. J. Scholes (Ed.), *Literacy and language analysis* (pp. 55–70). Hillsdale, NJ: Lawrence Erlbaum.

Prema, K. S. (1998). Reading acquisition profile in Kannada. Doctoral dissertation, University of Mysore, India.

Ramaa, S., Miles, T. R. & Lalithamma, M. S. (1993). Dyslexia: Symbol processing difficulty in Kannada language. *Reading and Writing*, *5*, 29–41.

Ramachandra, V. & Karanth, P. (2007). The role of literacy in the conceptualization of words: Data from Kannada-speaking children and non-literate adults. *Reading and Writing*, *20*, 173–199.

Ranganatha, M. R. (1982). *Morphophonemic analysis of the Kannada language: Relative frequency of phonemes and morphemes in Kannada*. CIIL Occasional Monograph Series, 17. Mysore: Central Institute of Indian Languages.

Rao, C., Soni, S. & Chatterjee Singh, N. (2012). The case of the neglected alphasyllabary: Orthographic processing in Devanagari. *Brain and Behavioural Sciences*, *35*, 302–303. DOI:10.1017/S0140525X12000313.

Rimzhim, R., Katz, L. & Fowler, C. (2013). The Brahmi-derived writing system is alphabetic. *Writing Systems Research*, *6*, 41–53. DOI:10.1080/17586801. 2013.855618.

Sailaja, P. (2007). Writing systems and phonological awareness. In J. Bayer, T. Bhattacharya & M. T. H. Batra (Eds.), *Linguistic theory and south Asian languages: Essays in honour of K. A. Jayaseelan* (pp. 249–265). Amsterdam: John Benjamins.

Salomon, R. (2000). Typological observations on the Indic script group and its relationship to other alphasyllabaries. *Studies in the Linguistic Sciences*, *30*(1), 87–104.

Sen, A. (2010). Primary schooling in West Bengal. *Prospects: Quarterly Review of Comparative Education*, *40*, 311–320.

Singh, A. K. (2007). Progress of modification of Brāhmī alphabet as revealed by the inscriptions of sixth-eighth centuries. In P. G. Patel, P. Pandey & D. Rajgor (Eds.),

The Indic scripts: Paleographic and linguistic perspectives (pp. 85–107). New Delhi: DK Printworld.

Sircar, S. & Nag, S. (2013a). Akshara-syllable mappings in Bengali: A language-specific skill for reading. In H. Winskell & P. Padakanayya (Eds.), *South and South-East Asian psycholinguistics* (pp. 202–211). Cambridge University Press.

——— (2013b). Children's intuitive syllabification of intervocalic consonant clusters in Bengali: The role of sonority, phonotactics and akshara. *The EFL Journal, 4*(2), 35–52.

Sridhar, S. N. (1990). *Kannada*. London: Routledge.

Snowling, M. J. (2008). Specific disorders and broader phenotypes: The case of dyslexia. *Quarterly Journal of Experimental Psychology, 61*, 142–156.

Snowling, M. J. & Nag, S. (2011). Impairments of reading and language: From theory to practice. Paper presented at the Symposium on Language, Literacy and Cognitive Development, The Promise Foundation & University of York, Bangalore, India.

Sugathapala De Silva, M. W. (1986). Typology of diglossia and its implications for literacy. In Bh. Krishnamurti (Ed.), *South Asian languages: Structure, convergence and diglossia* (pp. 304–311). Delhi: Motilal Banarasidass.

Tiwari, S., Nair, R. & Krishnan, G. (2011). A preliminary investigation of akshara knowledge in the Malayalam alphasyllabary: Extension of Nag's (2007) study. *Writing Systems Research, 3*, 145–151.

UNESCO (2003). *Education in a multilingual world: UNESCO Education Position Paper*. Paris: UNESCO.

Vagh, S. B. (2010). Learning at home and at school: A longitudinal study of Hindi language and emergent literacy skills of young children from low-income families in India. Unpublished doctoral dissertation, Harvard University, MA.

Vaid, J. & Gupta, A. (2002). Exploring word recognition in a semi-alphabetic script: The case of Devanagari. *Brain and Language, 81*, 679–690.

Vaid, J. & Padakannaya, P. (2004). Reading and writing in semi-syllabic scripts: An introduction. *Reading and Writing, 17*, 1–6.

Vasanta, D. (2004). Processing phonological information in a semi-syllabic script: Developmental data from Telugu. *Reading and Writing, 17*, 59–78.

Wali, A., Sproat, R., Padakannaya, P. & Bhuvaneshwari, B. (2009). Model for phonemic awareness in readers of Indian script. *Written Language & Literacy, 12*, 161–169.

Wijayathilake, D. & Parrila, R. (2013). Predictors of word reading in good and struggling readers in Sinhalese. *Writing Systems Research, 6*, 120–131. DOI:10.1080/17586801.2013.846844.

6 Learning to Read Arabic

Elinor Saiegh-Haddad

6.1 Introduction

6.1.1 Arabic and Its Orthography

Arabic is the official language of twenty-two Member States of UNESCO and is used by more than 422 million speakers in the Arab world (Bokova, 2012). Arabic is also the religious and liturgical language of more than 1.5 billion Muslims (Bokova, 2012). The sociolinguistic context of Arabic is a typical *diglossia* (Ferguson, 1959). In diglossic Arabic, a local dialect of a spoken variety of the language is spontaneously acquired by all native speakers as their mother tongue. This variety is known as *Spoken Arabic* or *Colloquial Arabic*. In contrast with Spoken Arabic, the literary variety of Arabic, called *(Modern) Standard Arabic*, has no native speakers. It is the only variety considered proper for the writing of Arabic and is, thus, the only language of literacy (Maamouri, 1998; Saiegh-Haddad, 2012; Saiegh-Haddad & Henkin-Roitfarb, 2014).

Diglossia is defined as:

A relatively stable language situation in which, in addition to the primary dialects of the language ... there is a very divergent, highly codified (often grammatically more complex) superposed variety ... which is largely learned by formal education and is used for most written and formal spoken purposes, but is not used by any sector of the community for ordinary conversation. (Ferguson, 1959, p. 345)

Though Ferguson proposes a dichotomy between a spoken and a written variety, the linguistic situation in Arabic diglossia has been described in terms of levels, or a continuum, with speakers shifting between as many as four (Meiseles, 1980) or five (Badawi, 1973) varieties, ranging between colloquial/ vernacular and literary/standard forms, resulting in levels that are neither fully standard nor fully colloquial. As such, there are "gradual transitions" (Blanc, 1960) between the various varieties, and "theoretically an infinite number of levels" (Basiouny, 2009, p. 15).

6.1.2   Synchronic and Diachronic Characterization

Arabic diglossia was established at the latest with the standardization of Arabic in the eighth and ninth centuries AD when the early grammarians produced a set of linguistic norms for the written form of the language that they called *(ʔal-luɣa) l-fuṣḥa:* 'the most eloquent/correct (language)'. Over the course of years, the use of fixed prescriptive rules for written Arabic led to remarkable differences between the constantly changing spoken varieties and the written form, making the two linguistically distant. At present, the linguistic distance between spoken and written Arabic traverses all areas of structure and usage, including not only lexicon and phonology but also syntax and morphology, as documented in a range of studies in the past several decades (e.g., Bateson, 2003; Eid, 1990; Geva-Kleinberger, 2000; Henkin, 2010; Ibrahim, 1983; Kay, 1994; Levin, 1995; Meiseles, 1980; Versteegh, 1997, 2014; Wright, 1898).

In all literate societies, spoken and written languages are used in different socio-cultural contexts. Therefore, the two forms of linguistic expression tend to be somewhat different. Yet what is unique to Arabic diglossia, although possibly to some other sociolinguistically analogous situations (Myhill, 2014), is that the spoken and written varieties are so different in lexicon, phonology, morphology, and syntax that the two have been shown to be cognitively represented as two distinct languages (Ibrahim & Aharon-Peretz, 2005; Khamis-Dakwar & Froud, 2007). For example, the two varieties differ in their phonemic inventories, syllable structure, and stress patterns. They vary in inflectional categories, with a less varied system of inflections in Spoken than in Standard Arabic. They vary in their use of nominal constructions and passivization, with nominal constructions and passive verbs being far more common in Spoken than in Standard Arabic (Laks, 2013; Laks & Berman, 2014; Rosenhouse, 1990, 2008). Finally, the lexicons of Spoken and Standard Arabic coincide only partially, with as many as 80 percent of the spoken words in the lexicon of young 5-year-old children having different surface phonological forms in the two varieties (Saiegh-Haddad & Spolsky, 2014).

6.1.3   Literacy and Schooling

In diglossic Arabic, children start out speaking a local variety of Spoken Arabic, the one used at home and in the neighborhood. Once they enter school, at age 6, they are formally exposed to Standard Arabic as the language of reading and writing, while Spoken Arabic remains the language of informal speech. Academic school-related speech is conducted in a semi-standard variety, Educated Spoken Arabic (Badawi, 1973), except in Arabic language classes where Standard Arabic is more dominant, at least in aspiration (Amara, 1995). Outside the school milieu, there is a similarly stable coexistence of the two major varieties, each serving distinct spheres of social communication. Spoken Arabic is used by all native speakers: young and old, educated and uneducated, for informal and intimate speech in the home, at work, in the community, and so forth. On the other hand, Standard Arabic, alternating with Educated Spoken Arabic, is expected to be used for formal oral interactions. Thus, while Spoken Arabic is undoubtedly the primary language of spoken usage, native speakers of Arabic, including young children, are actively and constantly engaged with Standard Arabic as well. Yet, the limited functions of Standard Arabic compounded with the remarkable linguistic gulf between this variety and Spoken Arabic makes achievement of proficiency (oral and written) extraordinarily difficult. It is hardly surprising then that research-oriented experimental exposure to Standard Arabic was shown to contribute to proficiency in this language and to reading comprehension (Abu-Rabia, 2000; Feitelson, Goldstein, Iraqi & Share, 1993). Yet not all exposure programs are equally effective; naturalistic-exposure programs may not be sufficiently rich or varied to enable implicit and incidental learning of the linguistic system encoded in print. Rather, controlled and structured exposure together with explicit mediation of the linguistic system of Standard Arabic may prove more successful (SaieClearingh-Haddad, 2011b, 2012; Saieegh-Haddad & Spolsky, 2014; Zozovsky, 2010).

6.2 Description of Arabic and Its Written Forms

Arabic is a member of the Semitic language family that encompasses a number of languages with shared phonology, morphology, basic lexicon, and a common putative origin called "Proto-Semitic" (Holes, 2004, p. 10). In this section, we will briefly outline the phonological and morphological structure of Semitic Arabic. Then, we will describe the Arabic writing system.

6.2.1 Linguistic System

6.2.1.1 Phonology   Standard Arabic comprises twenty-eight consonantal phonemes, including two glides /w/ and /y/ and six vowel phonemes: three short vowels: low /a/, high front /i/, and high back /u/, and three corresponding long vowels: /a:/, /i:/, and /u:/. All syllables in Standard Arabic begin with a single consonant (C) serving as the syllable onset and necessarily followed by a vowel (V), as the syllable nucleus/peak. The syllabic structure of Arabic is relatively simple with CV and CVC types the most predominant. Initial pre-vocalic consonantal clusters are not permitted in Arabic and postvocalic bi-consonantal clusters are rare and phonotactically constrained. It is noteworthy that the phonological structure of Standard Arabic may be at variance with that of Spoken Arabic. For instance, in some dialects of *Palestinian Arabic* spoken in Israel, interdental consonants are not used. Similarly, prevocalic consonantal clusters are frequent, whereas postvocalic clusters are not preferred. Arabic syllabic boundaries are flexible and vary with agglutination. Arabic stress is non-phonemic (Holes, 2004, p. 62) and it is predictable from the number of syllables and syllable weight.

A pervasive phonological process influencing the surface phonetic structure of Arabic words is *emphasis spread* or *velarization spread* (Holes, 2004). In this process, velarized and velar phonemes trigger a phonological assimilation process which results in allophonic lowering and backing of neighboring vowels and in the velarization of surrounding consonants. This process is not marked in the spelling of words, with interesting psycholinguistic implications (Saiegh-Haddad, 2013).

6.2.1.2 Inflectional Morphology   Arabic words have traditionally been classified into three lexical categories: noun, verb, and particle. In Arabic, both nouns and verbs (perfective and imperfective) inflect for gender (masculine, feminine) and number (singular, dual, plural), and verbs also inflect for person (first, second, and third). Yet the morphemes marking these categories vary in the two classes. Such inflectional procedures are usually described as linear (utilizing prefixes and suffixes). However, they often involve predictable stem-internal vocalic changes as well.

A predominant inflectional system common to both nouns and verbs in Standard Arabic involves stem-final vowels called *ʔiʕra:b-endings*, which denote the syntactic categories of case for nouns and adjectives, and mood for verbs (Saiegh-Haddad & Henkin-Roitfarb, 2014). These inflectional categories have disappeared from all dialects of Spoken Arabic.

6.2.1.3 Word Formation Processes   A compelling feature of Semitic Arabic is its non-linear or non-concatenative morphological structure (Larcher, 2006; McCarthy, 1981) with interesting psycholinguistic implications (Ravid, 2012; Saiegh-Haddad, 2013). Words in Arabic are minimally bi-morphemic comprising two unpronounceable bound morphemes: a consonantal root, e.g., {KTB} that provides the core semantic information, and a word pattern (e.g., Ca:CeC or maCCu:C), a fixed phonological/prosodic template with fixed slots for the root consonants, and which specifies the surface phonological structure and the morpho-syntactic properties of the resultant lexical item. For instance, all the words pertaining to writing, closely or remotely, will embody the consonantal root {KTB}, such as *ka:teb* 'writer', *maktaba* 'library', *maktab* 'desk, office', *kataba* 'he wrote', *kita:b* 'book', *maktu:b* 'letter, written', etc. By the same token, the word-pattern links a number of words together as having a shared prosodic structure (stress, vowels, and sometimes also some consonants) and a similar categorical meaning, such nouns denoting a profession, e.g., *najja:r* 'carpenter', *hadda:d* 'black smith', *ṭabba:x* 'cook', *rassa:m* 'painter', *dahha:n* 'painter (wall painting)', *fanna:n* 'artist', *sawwaq* 'driver'.

All twenty-eight Arabic consonants may function as root radicals, and a small subset of these can also participate in the formation of some word patterns. Consonantal roots are mapped in a transparent way in the spelling of words, even in the case of velarization spread. However, when one of the root consonants is a glide, the insertion of the consonants within the word-pattern results in phonological and orthographic shifting (for examples, see Saiegh-Haddad & Henkin-Roitfarb, 2014).

It is possible to categorize word patterns in Arabic into two classes: verbal patterns and nominal patterns. Verbal patterns combine with roots to derive verbs, whereas nominal patterns combine with roots to derive nouns (and adjectives). There are fifteen distinct verbal patterns in Arabic, ten of which are still productive in Modern Standard Arabic. In contrast, nominal patterns form a very large set. For example, Boudelaa and Marslen-Wilson (2010) report the occurrence of 2,324 different patterns in current use in Modern Standard Arabic.

The morphological structure of Arabic also comprises a rich system of clitics (prepositions, conjunctions, direct object pronouns, etc.). Clitics may attach to the word only as prefixes or suffixes and can co-occur within the same word, resulting in single-word phrases/clauses. Table 6.1 shows the combination of roots with word patterns and the addition of inflections and clitics to form words in Arabic.

6.2.2 Writing System

6.2.2.1 Script and Punctuation   Arabic is written from right to left in a cursive script, in which all but six letters, "kicking letters" و ذ ز ر (ا), may ligate forward to a following letter. All letters can ligate backward to a preceding letter unless that happens to be a kicking letter. In order for a letter to ligate to a preceding or a following letter, the letter has to take a ligature. This results in four allographic variants (shapes) per letter. These shapes may be quite distinct (e.g., ‏خ ‏غ ‏ـغ ‏ـخ‎ all representing the sound /ɣ/ or ‏ھ ‏ﻬ ‏ﻫ ‏ﻩ‎ all representing the sound /h/) or rather similar and varying only in the ligature (e.g., ‏ح ‏ﺧ ‏ـح ‏ـخ‎ representing the sound /x/, or ‏ﻛ ‏ﻚ ‏ﻙ ‏ﻜ‎ representing the sound /k/).

The Arabic script is believed to have originated in the earlier Nabatean descending from the Aramaic alphabet (Bateson, 2003). As Arabic had more consonants than Aramaic, the script was modified to represent the extra Arabic consonants. This was accomplished by developing a system of consonant pointing (dotting) which consisted in the use of distinguishing dots. This explains the fact that the modern Arabic alphabet consists of sets of letters

Table 6.1 *Morphological structure of Arabic words*

| Prefixes | | Stem | | Suffixes | | |
Clitics	Inflections	Root	Word pattern	Inflections	Clitics	Resultant word
wa 'and' *sa* 'will'	*ya* 'imperfective verb inflection'	{KTB}	CaCaCa (internal vocalic change CCuC)	*u* 'mood inflection' *u:na* 'they: plural verb inflection'	*ha:* 'it'	وَسَيَكْتُبُونَها *wa-sa-ya-ktub- (u)-u:na-ha:* 'and they will write it (feminine)'
bi 'in'		{KTB}	Ca:CeC	*a* 'feminine gender inflection' *a:t* 'feminine plural inflection' *i* 'case inflection' *na:* 'possessive inflection'		بكاتباتِنا *bi-ka:tib-(a)- a:t-i-na:* 'in/of our (female) writers'

that share a basic shape and vary in the number of dots (1–3) and their position (above or below).

The adapted Nabatean alphabet did not represent vowels either. Therefore, in addition to the compulsory letter dots, a system of optional diacritics was developed to represent two sets of linguistic structure: (a) the short vowels of Arabic as well as other features of phonemic structure, including consonant doubling (lengthening); and (b) the morpho-syntactic *ʔiʕra:b-endings* denoting case and mood on nouns and verbs, respectively (for a detailed description, see Saiegh-Haddad & Henkin-Roitfarb, 2014).

6.2.2.2 Orthography The Arabic writing system consists of a system of letters, mapping mainly the consonants of the language, and an optional system of diacritics, mapping mainly the phonemic short vowels and the morpho-syntactic *ʔiʕra:b-endings*. This results in two orthographies: a fully voweled (vowelized) and an unvoweled orthography. The bulk of Arabic script is unvoweled, while vowelization is commonly used only in reading primers, religious texts, and children's literature. It is also sporadically used in ordinary texts when an ambiguity of pronunciation might arise.

All twenty-eight letters of the alphabet represent consonants, except for the first letter, aleph, which, however, may act as a "bearer" of an additional sign, *hamza*, representing the twenty-eighth consonant, a glottal stop. Three of the letters, ي و ا act as *matres lectionis* 'mothers of reading' and are used to represent the three Standard Arabic long vowels: /i:/, /u:/, and /a:/, respectively. The Arabic alphabet is thus considered as an *abjad* (Daniels, 1992): a type of writing system where each symbol always or usually stands for a consonant, leaving the reader to supply the appropriate vowels. According to other accounts, the Arabic unvoweled writing system is a mora-based system in which the letters represent CV moras within syllables (Ratcliffe, 2001).

Arabic orthography is primarily a representation of Standard Arabic; it maps Standard Arabic phonology, morphology, syntax, and lexicon. This means that linguistic features of Spoken Arabic, including sounds, words, and syntactic constructions, may not have a conventional form of representation in Arabic spelling.

Arabic orthography maps Standard Arabic consonants and long vowels in a rather regular way, with an almost one-to-one relationship between graphemes and phonemes. When Arabic is voweled, this results in a transparent orthography with all phonological information required for word decoding completely and regularly represented. When Arabic is unvoweled, the orthography becomes less transparent. Yet the opacity of unvoweled Arabic is not the result of equivocal graphemes but is the result of the absence of the optional diacritics. The unvoweled orthography, though phonologically underspecified, is a fully specified and consistent consonantry with a regular mapping between the consonantal material of words and their orthographic representation. The morphological structure of this consonantry is likewise transparent, with a regular and uninterrupted representation (except by the mothers of reading) of the consonantal root morpheme (excluding weak verbs) and of the consonantal material (as well as the long vowels) of word patterns. Table 6.2 illustrates the consonantal structure of the letter-based unvoweled Arabic orthography.

Despite a rather high degree of feedforward consistency not only in the voweled orthography but also in the consonantal unvoweled orthography, as Table 6.2 shows, Arabic features a few instances of feedback inconsistency. The most notorious source of such opacity is the hamza (originally a diacritic but now a full-fledged letter) which represents the glottal stop; hamza has a variety of different phonologically conditioned orthographic forms depending on preceding and following vowels and their alleged relative "strength." This makes the spelling of hamza relatively difficult and lexically acquired.

Another source of feedback inconsistency is velarization spread and the assimilation of non-velarized with velarized sounds. Because primary velarization is phonemic in Arabic, the phonetic realization of these secondarily velarized consonants might coincide with the phonemic representation of other letters in the Arabic alphabet. Consequently, some letters become

Table 6.2 *Consonantal structure of unvoweled Arabic words by morphological structure*

| | Prefixes | | Stem | | Suffixes | | Resultant word |
	Clitics	Inflections	Root	Word pattern	Inflections	Clitics	
Written form	W S	Y	KTB	KaTaBa (KTuB)	-	H	وسيكتبونه WSYKTBWNH
Spoken form	wa sa	ya	{KTB}	ktubu	u u:na	hu	wa-sa-ya-ktub-(u)-u:-na-hu
Gloss	'and' 'will'	'imperfective verb inflection'			'mood inflection' 'they: plural verb inflection'	'it'	'and they will write it (masculine)'
Written word	B		KTB	MKTWB	H	H	بمكتوبه BMKTWBH
Spoken word	bi		{KTB}	maktu:b	i h i		bi-maktu:b-i-hi
Gloss	'in'				'case inflection' 'his' 'case inflection'		'In his letter'

homographic, leading to difficulty in the orthographic encoding of sounds, or spelling.

6.2.3   Conclusion

The Arabic script may be considered consistent in both its voweled and its unvoweled orthographies. In the voweled orthography, consistency is furnished by the full representation and regular mapping of all phonological information required for word pronunciation; in the unvoweled orthography, consistency is the outcome of the regular mapping of the consonantal material (and long vowels) of the word's morphological structure (root, word pattern, and clitics). Thus, equipped with a root and word-pattern lexicon, Arabic speakers can reliably use the consonantal orthographic form of the word to recover the phonological form and to identify a word. As for non-proficient speakers of the language or foreign language learners, however, the absence of the short vowel diacritics might render the unvoweled orthography psycholinguistically opaque.

Despite a high degree of transparency in the relationship between the orthographic structure of the word and the word's sound structure in Standard Arabic, this relationship may still be argued to be non-transparent when the relationship between the orthographic structure of the word and its phonological form in the mental lexicon of native speakers is considered. In other words, the mapping from the spelling of the word to the sound of the word in Standard Arabic is regular. Yet because of the linguistic (primarily phonological and lexical) distance between Spoken and Standard Arabic, this relationship may be deemed psycholinguistically opaque because the sound of the Standard Arabic word may be different from its sound in Spoken Arabic. The same argument is valid for processing in other linguistic domains (Khamis-Dakwar, Froud & Gordon, 2012; Khamis-Dakwar & Machul, 2014).

6.3   Acquisition of Reading and Spelling in Arabic

Empirical research into the acquisition of reading and spelling in Arabic has addressed five broad questions. These questions are: (a) What is the effect of the linguistic distance between Spoken Arabic and Standard Arabic on the acquisition of linguistic awareness and word reading in Arabic diglossia? (b) What is the effect of diacritical vowelization on word reading in Arabic? (c) What is the effect of orthographic features of Arabic (letter similarity and letter connectedness) on word reading in Arabic? (d) What is the role of non-linear morphology in lexical representation and processing in Arabic? and (e) What are the cognitive and linguistic predictors of normal reading development and reading disability in Arabic?

6.3.1   Becoming Linguistically Aware

6.3.1.1   Phonological Development and Phonological Awareness   Arabic's

phonological and morpho-phonological structure lead to two predictions regarding the development of phonological awareness, neither of which has been systematically tested. First, syllable awareness should develop rather early in children, probably earlier than reported in other languages like English (Liberman, Shankweiler, Fischer & Carter, 1974). This is because of the multi-syllabic nature of Arabic words, which applies to almost 85 percent of the spoken lexicon of 5-year-olds (Saiegh-Haddad & Spolsky, 2014). Second, phonological awareness of consonants may precede awareness of vowels. This is because of two reasons: (a) differences in the function of consonants versus vowels in the morphological structure of words (consonantal semantic root versus vocalic categorical word pattern), and (b) the difference in the salience of consonants versus vowels in the orthographic representation of words (consonantal letters versus vocalic diacritics). These differences in the linguistic and orthographic features of consonants versus vowels might explain the observed tendency among Arabic native speakers to delete vowels when reading English as a foreign language (Ryan & Meara, 1991).

Regarding evidence-based insights, research addressing phonological awareness has demonstrated the role of two Arabic-specific linguistic factors. The first is linguistic and pertains to the phonological distance between the phonological structure of words in Spoken Arabic and Standard Arabic and the effect that this distance has on the quality of phonological representations of words. The second is metalinguistic and pertains to the internal sub-syllabic structure of Arabic syllables and its effect on the relative accessibility of syllable-initial versus syllable-final consonants.

In diglossic Arabic, the differences between the phonological system of the child's spoken language and the standard language extend to the phonemic inventory; some standard phonemes are not available in the spoken language of children, and there are differences in the internal composition of the syllable in the two language varieties. In a series of studies, Saiegh-Haddad tested the effect of this feature on phonological awareness in native speakers of *Palestinian Arabic* residing in the north of Israel (Saiegh-Haddad, 2003, 2004, 2007a). This research compared the same child's awareness of phonological units that varied in their linguistic affiliation (Spoken Arabic versus Standard Arabic). It was shown that the linguistic affiliation of phonemes had a significant impact on the child's ability to access phonemes. Specifically, Standard Arabic phonemes were more difficult to operate on than Spoken Arabic phonemes, even when pronunciation was intact. This factor was found to have cross-dialectal external validity (Saiegh-Haddad, 2007a). Furthermore, it was shown to predict performance across the elementary grades and to impact performance on phonological production phoneme isolation tasks as well as phonological recognition picture choice tasks (Saiegh-Haddad, Levin, Hende & Ziv, 2011). The linguistic affiliation of larger linguistic units (syllables and lexical items) showed a similar pattern with kindergarten children finding Standard Arabic phonemes embedded within Standard Arabic syllables (Saiegh-Haddad, 2003) and Standard Arabic words (Saiegh-Haddad, 2004) particularly more difficult to access. These effects were found to be attributed to low-quality phonological representations. Specifically, we have shown that these effects stem from problems in the phonological encoding of Standard Arabic words in the speakers' lexicons (Saiegh-Haddad et al., 2011; Saiegh-Haddad & Haj, 2016). Similar patterns have been observed in L2 reading (Russak & Saiegh-Haddad, 2011).

A second factor impacting phonological awareness in Arabic is the internal structure of the Arabic syllable. Contrary to the *rime cohesion hypothesis* (e.g., Treiman, 1983, 1985, 1988), Arabic-speaking children found initial phonemes more difficult to isolate than final phonemes (Saiegh-Haddad, 2003, 2004, 2007a). This was the case among preliterate kindergarteners as well as school-age children and was hence argued to be rooted not only in the unvoweled nature of the Arabic orthography that maps CV units but also in the CV-based phonology of Arabic. Nonetheless, it seems that facility in accessing final versus initial phonemes interacts with the nature of the task (epilinguistic implicit versus metalinguistic explicit) with explicit phoneme isolation tasks showing more sensitivity to internal syllabic structure (Saiegh-Haddad, 2007b; Saiegh-Haddad, Kogan & Walters, 2010; Share & Blum, 2005).

6.3.1.2 Morphological development and morphological awareness   Arabic's root and word-pattern morphological structure implies the representation of this structure in the mental representation of words (Beland & Mimouni, 2001; Boudelaa & Marslen-Wilson, 2000, 2004, 2011, 2015; Idrissi, Prunet & Beland, 2008; Mimouni, Kehaya & Jarema, 1998; Perea, Abu Mallouh & Carreiras, 2010; Prunet, Beland & Idrissi, 2000). It also predicts Arabic-speaking children to be able to extract abstract morphological regularities and develop morphological awareness early in their linguistic development. Taha & Saiegh-Haddad (2016a) investigated root and word-pattern morphological awareness in Arabic native-speaking children in Grades 2, 4, and 6 using word-relatedness tasks. The study showed that while root awareness appears to develop before word-pattern awareness, both aspects of morphological awareness develop rather early in children.

6.3.2   Development of Word Identification

6.3.2.1   Word Decoding Development   Arabic's voweled orthography is shallow and is expected to result in a rather easy and speedy development of decoding accuracy and speed (Seymour, Aro & Erskine, 2003). However, this does not seem to be the case (Saiegh-Haddad & Schiff, 2016). Abu-Ahmad, Ibrahim, and Share (2014) tested word and pseudoword decoding accuracy of voweled words in Grade 2 and showed that accuracy rates were rather low (67 and 63 percent, respectively). Similar results were reported in Jayusi (2013) with readers at just 80 percent on both tasks even in Grade 8. Saiegh-Haddad (2005) showed that pseudoword decoding speed was also remarkably low and lower than expected in a shallow orthography. Several factors have been proposed to explain such unexpected findings, including Arabic diglossia and particularly the linguistic distance between Standard Arabic and Spoken Arabic discussed above (Saiegh-Haddad, 2011a, 2012; Saiegh-Haddad & Schiff, 2016). Another was Arabic's orthographic properties (Eviatar & Ibrahim, 2014), including the use of diacritics to represent short vowels, letter similarity, and letter connectedness. These orthographic factors are discussed below.

Diacritical vowelization was the first orthographic feature of Arabic to attract psycholinguistic research attention. This research compared indices of word reading accuracy and speed for voweled and unvoweled words and texts in beginning and skilled readers, using mainly reading aloud tasks. It showed that reading rates (for words in isolation and in context) as well as silent reading comprehension were higher when words were vowelized, both in beginning (Abu-Rabia, 1997a, 1997b, 1997c, 1998, 1999) and in adult readers (Abu-Rabia, 2001, 2007). This was interpreted as replicating the cost in word naming efficiency (accuracy and speed) usually observed in an orthography that does not provide a full or regular account of the word's phonological structure. It is important to note in this regard that Arabic has two systems of diacritics mapping two distinct vocalic systems: one is primarily phonemic and is necessary for word identification. The second is morpho-syntactic and is rarely required for word identification or text comprehension (see Saiegh-Haddad & Henkin-Roitfarb, 2014). The latter type may become necessary only sporadically when reading literary works that manipulate word order to serve a stylistic literary purpose. While some research on vowelization has accounted for the difference between the two systems of vowelization in their error scoring rubric, it has never treated the two systems independently. This might have confounded the results reported and is a question for future research to pursue.

Vowelization diacritics, especially the phonemic diacritics, may be conducive to word identification in early reading development. However, they might inhibit reading fluency among more skilled readers not in need of the full representation of vowels to identify words accurately, especially given the rich morphological structure of spoken and written Arabic words. Moreover, diacritics, although useful in decreasing phonological ambiguity, might require excessive visuo-spatial processing and might hence disrupt achievement of fluency in phonological recoding. No study has yet tested the independent effects of type of diacritical vowelization (phonemic, morpho-syntactic) or the interaction of this factor with developmental factors principally grade level and reading skill. In a recent study, Saiegh-Haddad and Schiff (2016) tested these questions and showed that phonemic vowelization did not influence reading accuracy but disrupted reading fluency in readers in Grades 2 to 10.

Another orthographic feature is letter dotting (the use of diacritical dots to discriminate among letters that share a basic shape) and the subsequent visual similarity of letters. In a number of studies, Ibrahim, Eviatar, and colleagues tested the effect of this factor on letter and word identification (Abdelhadi, Ibrahim & Eviatar, 2011; Eviatar & Ibrahim, 2004, 2007, 2014; Ibrahim & Eviatar, 2009; Ibrahim, Eviatar & Aharon-Peretz, 2002). For example, Eviatar, Ibrahim, and Ganayim (2004) presented pairs of letters in Hebrew and in Arabic and asked participants to decide if the two letters were physically identical or not. The Arab students were bilinguals and could read both Arabic and Hebrew, whereas the Hebrew speakers could not read Arabic. They found that, in both groups, response to pairs of Arabic letters was slower than to pairs of Hebrew letters. Visual letter similarity was also found to explain some of the problems observed by kindergarteners in learning the Arabic alphabet (Levin, Saiegh-Haddad, Hende & Ziv, 2008) and also among adult foreign language learners of Arabic (Russak & Fragman, 2014).

A third orthographic facet is letter connectivity. It has been assumed that, because Arabic script is cursive, letter connectivity might add an additional layer of complexity to word decoding in Arabic. However, evidence appears to refute this hypothesis. For example, Abdelhadi et al. (2011) examined vowel (diacritic) identification in third and sixth graders and showed the highest speed of detection to be with connected rather than unconnected letters. Similarly, Taha, Ibrahim, and Khateb (2013) tested the behavioral and neural consequences of letter connectivity and found that fully connected words were read more accurately and rapidly than partially connected or unconnected words. Recently, Dai, Ibrahim, and Share (2013) attempted to disentangle the impact of letter connectivity and letter dotting. This study showed that letter dotting slowed reading accuracy considerably. However, letter connectedness, while being a transient source of difficulty, promoted orthographic learning. Given the aforementioned orthographic peculiarities of Arabic, it is hardly surprising for some research studies to have demonstrated the implication of orthographic processing in normal Arabic reading and in Arabic dyslexia (Abu-Ahmad et al., 2014; Abu-Rabia, Share & Mansour, 2003; Elbeheri, Everatt, Mahfoudhi, Al-Diyar & Taibah, 2011; Jayusi, 2013).

Moving to linguistic factors, research has shown that both phonological and morphological factors impact word identification in Arabic. Yet, no conclusive argument may be made about the relative contribution of these two linguistic factors to reading in Arabic. This is because no systematic experimental comparison has yet been conducted. Evidence for phonological processing in Arabic reading comes from various studies varying in objective and design. One is a body of research testing the effect of the phonological distance between Spoken and Standard Arabic on word decoding. This research showed that young children found it more difficult to decode pseudowords that embodied Standard Arabic phonemes and syllable structures and that their errors reflected the use of Spoken Arabic phonological representations instead (Saiegh-Haddad, 2003). Further evidence comes from research investigating correlates of normal reading development and reading disability in Arabic, demonstrating a positive correlation between phonological awareness and word reading (Abu-Ahmad et al., 2014; Abu-Rabia et al., 2003; Al-Mannai & Everatt, 2005; Elbeheri & Everatt, 2007; Taouk & Coltheart, 2004). For instance, Taibah and Haynes (2011) administered a number of reading accuracy and fluency tasks to kindergarten through Grade 3 Arabic-speaking children in Jeddah, Saudi Arabia, and found that phonological awareness was a strong predictor of reading accuracy and fluency; even stronger than rapid naming or memory, in all grades. This finding contrasts, however, with the results reported in Saiegh-Haddad (2005) who found an indirect role of phonological awareness in reading fluency at the end of the first grade. In this study, memory and rapid naming were found to be direct predictors of reading fluency. This latter finding was argued to be the result of the phonological distance between Spoken and Standard Arabic, which might result in less reliance on phonological skills and more on lexical processes (Mahfoudhi, Everatt & Elbeheri, 2011). This explanation is particularly viable when diglossia is compounded with reading instructional methods that are not phonetic in nature, like the whole-language-based approach that had been used in Arab schools in Israel until recently (Ministry of Education, 2008; Saiegh-Haddad & Everatt, 2017).

Now we turn to the role of the non-linear morphological structure of Arabic in lexical representation and processing. Here, research has demonstrated implicit and explicit root and word-pattern morphological decomposition in spoken and written word recognition (Boudelaa, 2014; Boudelaa & Marslen-Wilson, 2000, 2004, 2011, 2015). Further, it has been shown that there may be a difference in the timeline of activation of the two morphological units with the root being activated earlier in the word recognition process than the word pattern (Boudelaa & Marslen-Wilson, 2005). Given the centrality of morphology, in both the structure of Arabic words and their orthographic representation, research has demonstrated morphological decomposition in word reading, unvoweled and even voweled, in monolinguals (Abu-Ahmad et al., 2014; Abu-Rabia et al., 2003; Saiegh-Haddad & Taha, 2014; Taha, 2009) and bilinguals (Farran, Bingham, Mathews & Mona, 2012; Saiegh-Haddad & Geva, 2008).

Convergent evidence in support of the role of phonological and morphological processing in Arabic word decoding comes from an intervention study that examined the relative contribution of phonological versus morphological training to Arabic word reading in Grade 2, 4, and 6 Arabic native-speaking children (Saiegh-Haddad & Taha, 2014). This study showed that both phonological and morphological intervention programs were effective in producing gains in voweled and unvoweled word reading and pseudoword decoding. At the same time, the type of intervention program interacted with age and orthography; older children benefited more from morphological than phonological intervention, and morphological intervention contributed more to reading unvoweled than voweled Arabic.

6.3.2.2 Word Spelling Development   There are far fewer studies on spelling development in Arabic than on reading. Furthermore, most studies use a similar design that analyzes spelling errors as mainly phonological or visual-orthographic (Abu-Rabia & Sammour, 2013; Abu-Rabia & Taha, 2004, 2006; Azzam, 1984, 1993). For instance, Abu-Rabia and Taha (2004) examined spelling errors among fifth-grade dyslexic, age-matched, and reading-matched control groups. They categorize the errors they observed as phonetic, semiphonetic, dysphonetic, visual letter confusion, irregular spelling, and word omission and found that phonetic errors were the most predominant in all groups. Using the same rubric, Abu-Rabia and Taha (2006), examined the spelling errors made by native Arabic-speaking pupils in Grades 1 through 9 and reported that the most prominent type of error across grade levels was phonetic, representing 50 percent of all errors. Recently, Abu-Rabia and Sammour (2013) analyzed the spelling errors in native Arabic-speaking eighth-grade dyslexic and spelling-matched controls. Using a similar rubric, they reported that phonetic errors were the most prevalent. These results led the authors to conclude that "phonology poses the greatest challenge to students developing spelling skills in Arabic" (Abu-Rabia & Sammour, 2013, p. 60). While the rubric used in the above studies accounts for phonological, visual, and orthographic errors, it is agnostic of the role of other factors, such as morphology. Morphology is critical in Arabic word spelling for two reasons: The first is the predominance of morphological structure in the linguistic and orthographic structure of Arabic words. The second is velarization spread, a widespread phonological assimilation process operating across morpheme boundaries in Arabic and not marked in the spelling of words (Saiegh-Haddad, 2013; Saiegh-Haddad & Henkin-Roitfarb, 2014). Another factor that has been ignored in research on Arabic spelling is diglossia, and the role of the phonological distance between the sound of the word in Spoken and Standard Arabic on spelling in general and on the reported plethora of phonological errors that have been observed. This factor has been shown to affect phonological

Table 6.3 *Regular and Irregular* ت *‹t› in root, word-pattern, and affix morphemes*

Morpheme	Root	Word pattern	Affix (prefix)	Affix (suffix)
Regular ‹t›	KTB	ʔistaCCaCa	taCCaC	CaCeCat
Example	مكتوب	استعمل	تلعب	لعبت
Phonological form	*maktu:b*	*ʔista ʕmala*	*tal ʕab*	*la ʕibat*
Gloss	'letter', 'written'	'he used'	'she plays'	'she played'
Irregular ‹t›	QTL	ʔistaCCaCa	taCCuC	CaCaCat
Example	مقتول	استقبل	ترقص	رقصت
Phonological form	*maqtu:l*	*ʔistaqbala*	*tarquṣ*	*raqaṣat*
Gloss	'is killed'	'he welcomed'	'she dances'	'she danced'

processes in reading (Saiegh-Haddad, 2003, 2004, 2007a). It has also been shown to disrupt phonological encoding by Arabic L1 spellers in English L2 (Allaith & Joshi, 2011) and by Hebrew L1 spellers in Arabic L2 (Russak & Fragman, 2014).

In a recent study, the role of morphology in early spelling in Arabic was tested (Saiegh-Haddad, 2013). The study examined the spelling of the letter ‹t› in Arabic among children in Grades 1 through 5. The spelling development of the letter ‹t› is interesting because this letter may become orthographically irregular (or homographic) due to velarization spread and might as a result encode not only the default voiceless dental-alveolar stop /t/ but also its allophonic variant [t]. Furthermore, this letter participates in the encoding of three productive morphemes: derivational root, derivational word pattern, and inflectional affix. The effect of velarization spread on the sound of the letter ‹t› in different morphological affiliations (root, word pattern, and affix) is illustrated in Table 6.3.

An analysis of the spelling of regular versus irregular ‹t› as a function of morphological affiliation showed that even young first-grade children use morphological processing to spell irregular letters in Arabic. The results also showed that there are differences in the degree of morphological processing in spelling as a function of the specific morphological unit targeted with first graders spelling irregular root and affix letters more accurately than irregular word-pattern letters.

6.3.2.3 Reading and Spelling Difficulties Arabic, despite its peculiar linguistic and orthographic properties, appears to share features with other languages, including English, in the sort of underlying phonological variables that predict variation in basic literacy skills (Al-Mannai & Everatt, 2005; Elbeheri & Everatt, 2007; Jayusi, 2013; Saiegh-Haddad & Taha, 2014; Smythe et al., 2008; Taha & Saiegh-Haddad, 2016a, 2016b). Reading and spelling difficulties appear to also incriminate derivational (root and word-pattern) morphological awareness deficits too (Abu-Rabia, 2007; Abu-Rabia et al., 2003; Jayusi, 2013; Saiegh-Haddad & Taha, 2014; Taha & Saiegh-Haddad, 2014). Yet research into morphological awareness in Arabic has focused exclusively on derivational morphological awareness to the exclusion of inflectional awareness. Furthermore, the field is lacking in research that systematically compares the development of these two facets of morphology, or the relative role of deficits in each to developmental reading or spelling difficulties.

The study of the relationship between spelling and reading deficits in Arabic suggests a weak dissociation between the two (Azzam, 1993; Mohamed, Elbert & Landerl, 2011), hence implying reliance on similar processing mechanisms to the establishment of both skills. For instance, a recent epidemiological survey of reading and spelling deficits in young Arabic-speaking children in Egypt showed that the rate of combined deficits in reading and spelling was high (12.6 percent). Yet isolated deficits in reading or spelling were very low (0.9 percent and 1.1 percent, respectively) and lower than those reported in other shallow orthographies (Mohamed, Landerl & Elbert, 2014).

6.3.3   Reading Comprehension

6.3.3.1   Predictors of Reading Comprehension   There is little psycholinguistic research on reading comprehension in Arabic. Nonetheless, the research available provides a mixed picture with comprehension in Arabic being predicted primarily by sub-lexical, but also by supra-lexical processes. For instance, Abu-Ahmad et al. (2014) tested the contribution of sub-lexical versus supra-lexical processes to word decoding and reading comprehension among second-grade children. This study showed that sub-lexical processes, including phonological awareness (the strongest predictor) as well as morphological awareness, explained close to one-half of the variance in reading comprehension (yet only around one-third of the variance in word recognition). Supra-lexical factors, including syntactic and semantic processing, explained just over one-quarter of the variance in reading comprehension (and a modest albeit significant 11 percent of the variance in word recognition). Mahfoudhi, Elbeheri, Al-Rashidi, and Everatt (2010) detected unique variance in comprehension fluency among mainstream children explained by morphological awareness, beyond that explained by measures of phonological skills and general nonverbal ability. Finally, Elbeheri et al. (2011) demonstrated that orthographic processing predicted unique variance in reading comprehension fluency (speeded sentence completion) among older mainstream children (Grades 4, 5) in Kuwait but not among younger ones (Grades 2, 3).

6.3.3.2   Word-Level Effects in Comprehending Text   While no research has directly tested word-level effects in comprehending text in Arabic, two studies have addressed the quality of lexical representation in Arabic and the role of Arabic diglossia, particularly the lexical-phonological distance between Standard and Spoken Arabic, on lexical representation and processing. In Arabic, the lexical-phonological distance between Spoken and Standard Arabic is a prominent phenomenon with as many as 40 percent of the words in the lexicon of 5-year-olds having two different, yet related, phonological forms in the two language varieties.[1] These words are called paired lexical items (Ferguson, 1959) or cognates. Saiegh-Haddad et al. (2011) tested kindergarten children's phonological representations for paired lexical items that varied in the phonological distance between their form in Spoken and Standard Arabic: Words that encode a Standard Arabic phoneme in word-initial position but which are otherwise identical in Spoken and Standard Arabic versus words that have a completely identical phonological form in the two varieties. Children were presented with triplets of pictures representing line drawings of familiar objects and were asked to point to the word from a pair that began with the same phoneme as the third word in the triplet. The results showed that words encoding a Standard Arabic phoneme were harder for children, and that children were particularly distracted by words that began with a Spoken phoneme that was phonetically close to the target Standard phoneme. These findings were argued to reflect difficulty in the phonological encoding of Standard Arabic words in the mental lexicon of children.

With the same objective in mind, Saiegh-Haddad and Haj (2016) used a lexical decision task to test the lexical representation of paired lexical items (as against identical and unique words) among kindergarten, first-grade, second-grade, and fifth-grade children. All words were familiar to children in their Spoken Arabic form. The researchers systematically manipulated the phonological structure of the words and presented them together with a picture for lexical decision. The results showed that lexical representation for identical words was the most accurate and stable. These were followed by paired lexical items, and finally by unique words. This finding implied that the lexicon of Standard Arabic, the language of print and reading, comprises many words that have low-quality phonological representations, including high-frequency words that may be conceptually, yet not lexico-phonologically familiar to children. This is a lexical representation reflex of the diglossic linguistic distance between Spoken and Standard Arabic, and one that is expected to have an adverse effect on lexical processes in reading comprehension (Perfetti, 2007).

---

[1]   The remaining words in the lexicon were found to be divided between identical words (20%) and unique words (40%) (Saiegh-Haddad & Spolsky, 2014).

6.3.4   Conclusion

Despite the Semitic nature of Arabic script and the diglossic context of Arabic, reading development and disability in Arabic appear to implicate similar phonological variables. Yet the possibly transient and indirect nature of the role of phonological variables, especially when reading fluency is tested (Saiegh-Haddad, 2005) or when unvoweled words are targeted (Taha & Saiegh-Haddad, 2016a, 2016b), as well as the early and concurrent reliance on morphological mechanisms too (Saiegh-Haddad, 2013) position Arabic in contradistinction to other languages. Furthermore, the orthographic peculiarities that inhere in the Arabic writing system and confront beginning readers and spellers make embarking on the Arabic literacy journey particularly challenging (Smythe et al., 2008). Last but not least, the diglossic linguistic context, with the gulf it entails between the spoken language of children and the language of reading and writing, naturally means that reading in Arabic, even at the very initial stages, involves learning not only an orthographic system but also the linguistic system that it maps. This is undoubtedly a formidable task.

6.4   Discussion

6.4.1   Challenges in Learning to Read Arabic

Three features of orthographic complexity converge in making reading acquisition in Arabic theoretically interesting yet practically challenging. The first is the diglossic nature of Arabic with the result that the orthographic system of Arabic maps a linguistic system that is remarkably different from the language naturally spoken by native readers. This linguistic distance traverses all domains of language, including the phonological domain, and implies that even the very initial attempts of simple word decoding or spelling will engage the reader in activating linguistic units that they have not yet acquired, including phonemic, morpho-syntactic, and lexical units (Aram et al., 2013; Korat, Aram, Hassunha-Arafat, Saiegh-Haddad & Hag-Yehiya-Iraki, 2014).

The second challenge pertains to the complex orthographic structure of Arabic including the complex system of letters which constitutes sets that are identical in their basic shape but vary in the number and position of dots, letter connectivity, and diacritical vowelization to mark the word's phonemes (primarily short vowel) as well as its morpho-syntactic properties (Standard Arabic case and mood). This results in the fact that, even when voweled, printed Arabic words are not only visually and orthographically dense but also psycholinguistically non-transparent and map linguistic information that is absent from and hence not used in natural lexical processing in Spoken Arabic (Saiegh-Haddad & Henkin-Roitfarb, 2014).

6.4.2   Implications for Instruction

What is mostly warranted in reading instruction in Arabic is transition from misconceptions and practices that are ideologically based and empirically unfounded to evidence-based practice. The psycholinguistic evidence points to three areas that deserve particular attention in Arabic literacy instruction. The first is the linguistic distance between Spoken and Standard Arabic. This linguistic distance and the remarkable orality-literacy gap that it confronts young readers with has been shown to be daunting and not easily or quickly bridged. Therefore, reading instruction in Arabic, even at the initial stages, should aim at explicitly mediating to children the linguistic system of Standard Arabic by making them aware of the structure of Standard Arabic and the differences and similarities between Standard and Spoken Arabic. Children should be assisted in constructing proper linguistic representations for the language of literacy at all linguistic levels, principally at the phonological level in early reading stages, in order to enhance the learning of the systematic mapping between language and orthography. It is to be remembered in this regard that while the Standard and Spoken Arabic vary considerably from each other, they also share many linguistic features. These shared linguistic features of phonology, morphology, syntax, and lexicon are a linguistic asset that the child brings to the task of reading acquisition and should, therefore, be used as the stepping stones to leverage Standard Arabic language and reading acquisition (Saiegh-Haddad & Spolsky, 2014).

Reading instruction in Arabic should also become attuned to the ortho-graphic structure of Arabic and to the functionality in reading of the different orthographic peculiarities of Arabic. Letter complexity, allography, and letter connectedness may be a stumbling block for beginning readers (Dai et al., 2013; Ibrahim et al., 2002). Therefore, these features have to all be referred to children as early as possible and as part of their preschool literacy activities. Similarly, the sounds that letters represent, especially when these sounds are not part of the phonemic inventory of the Spoken Arabic dialect of children, have to be mediated to children, and their ability to discriminate, articulate, represent, and become phonologically aware of these sounds should be seen as another preschool literacy objective (Saiegh-Haddad, Hadieh & Ravid, 2012).

Reading instruction should exploit the rich morphological structure of Arabic as early as possible, as research has shown this linguistic information to be used in the organization of the mental lexicon of Arabic native speakers and in their access to it (Boudelaa, 2014). It has also been shown to be naturally used in early word decoding and spelling (Saiegh-Haddad, 2013). Helping children develop morphological awareness, especially at the level of the root and the word-pattern, and helping them to use the morphological structure of words for word learning should be seen as another preschool literacy preparation objective as well as a processing strategy that must be targeted in beginning Arabic reading instruction.

6.5   Final Conclusion

The review suggests that reading acquisition in Arabic, despite the orthography's spelling-sound consistency, confronts the beginning reader with numerous challenges. These pertain primarily to diglossia, which probably has an enduring effect on reading development, as well as to the complex orthographic system whose impact may be more powerful in the initial stages of reading acquisition. So far, research on the former has been restricted to initial reading processes, such as phonological processing and word decoding. Future research should address the effect of diglossia on vocabulary acquisition, syntactic processing and comprehension.

As in other languages, phonological awareness appears to be a strong correlate with reading development and disability in Arabic. This underscores the crucial role of the alphabetic/phonological foundation of reading in Arabic. Yet the importance of phonological awareness as against other processing mechanisms (such as morphological or orthographic ones) might interact with the nature of the task (accuracy versus fluency, naming versus lexical decision, and word versus text reading), type of orthography (voweled versus unvoweled), type of vowelization (phonemic versus morpho-syntactic), and reading skill. The interactions between these factors have not been systematically tested and therefore the role of phonological processing as against other processing mechanisms in reading Arabic has not been fully understood.

References

Abdelhadi, S., Ibrahim, R. & Eviatar. Z. (2011). Perceptual load in the reading of Arabic: Effects of orthographic visual complexity on detection. *Writing Systems Research, 3*, 117–127.

Abu-Ahmad, H., Ibrahim, R. & Share, D. L. (2014). Cognitive predictors of early reading ability in Arabic: A longitudinal study from kindergarten to grade 2. In E. Saiegh-Haddad & M. Joshi (Eds.), *Handbook of Arabic literacy: Insights and perspectives* (pp. 171–194). Dordrecht: Springer.

Abu-Rabia, S. (1997a). The need for cross-cultural considerations in reading theory: The effects of Arabic sentence context in skilled and poor readers. *Journal of Research in Reading, 20*, 137–147.

(1997b). Reading in Arabic orthography: The effect of vowels and context on reading accuracy of poor and skilled native Arabic readers in reading paragraphs, sentences, and isolated words. *Journal of Psycholinguistic Research, 26*, 465–482.

(1997c). Reading in Arabic orthography: The effect of vowels and context on reading accuracy of poor and skilled native Arabic readers. *Reading and Writing, 9*, 65–78.

(1998). Reading Arabic texts: Effects of text type, reader type and vowelization. *Reading and Writing, 10*, 105–119.

(1999). The effect of Arabic vowels on the reading comprehension of second- and sixth-grade native Arab children. *Journal of Psycholinguistic Research, 28*, 93–101.

(2000). Effects of exposure to literary Arabic on reading comprehension in a diglossic situation. *Reading and Writing, 13*, 147–157.

(2001). The role of vowels in reading Semitic scripts: Data from Arabic and Hebrew. *Reading and Writing, 14*, 39–59.

(2007). The role of morphology and short vowelization in reading Arabic among normal and dyslexic readers in grades 3, 6, 9, and 12. *Journal of Psycholinguistic Research, 36*, 89–106.

Abu-Rabia, S. & Sammour, R. (2013). Spelling errors' analysis of regular and dyslexic bilingual Arabic-English students. *Open Journal of Modern Linguistics, 3*, 58–68.

Abu-Rabia, S., Share, D. & Mansour, M. A. (2003). Word recognition and basic cognitive processes among reading-disabled and normal readers in Arabic. *Reading and Writing, 16*, 423–442.

Abu-Rabia, S. & Taha, H. (2004). Reading and spelling error analysis of native Arabic dyslexic readers. *Reading and Writing, 17*, 651–689.

(2006). Phonological errors predominate in Arabic spelling across grades 1–9. *Journal of Psycholinguistic Research, 35*, 167–188.

Allaith, Z. A. & Joshi, M. R. (2011). Spelling performance of English consonants among students whose first language is Arabic. *Reading and Writing, 24*, 1089–1110.

Al-Mannai, H. & Everatt, J. (2005). Phonological processing skills as predictors of literacy amongst Arabic speaking Bahraini children. *Dyslexia, 11*, 269–291.

Amara, M. H. (1995). Arabic diglossia in the classroom: Assumptions and reality. In S. Izre'el & R. Drory (Eds.), *Language and Culture in the Near East.* Israel Oriental Studies, Vol. 15 (pp.131–142). Leiden: E. J. Brill.

Aram, D., Korat, O., Saiegh-Haddad, E., Hassunha Arafat, S., Khoury, R. & Hija, J. (2013). Early literacy among Arabic speaking kindergartners: The role of socio-economic status, home literacy environment and maternal mediation of writing. *Cognitive Development, 28*, 193–208.

Azzam, R. (1984). Orthography and reading of the Arabic language. In J. Aaron & R. M. Joshi (Eds.), *Reading and writing disorders in different orthographic systems* (pp. 1–29). Dordrecht: Kluwer Academic.

(1993). The nature of Arabic reading and spelling errors of young children. *Reading and Writing, 5*, 355–385.

Badawi, E. (1973). *Mustawayat al-arabiyya l-mu'assira fi misr* [Levels of Modern Arabic in Egypt]. Cairo: Daral-ma'arif.

Basiouny, R. (2009). *Arabic sociolinguistics.* Edinburgh University Press.

Bateson, M. C. (2003). *Arabic language handbook.* Washington, DC: Georgetown University Press.

Beland, R. & Mimouni, Z. (2001). Deep dyslexia in the two languages of an Arabic–French bilingual patient. *Cognition, 82*, 77–126.

Blanc, H. (1960). Style variations in spoken Arabic: A sample of inter-dialectal conversation. In C. Ferguson (Ed.), *Contributions to Arabic linguistics* (pp. 81–158). Cambridge, MA: Harvard University Press.

Bokova, I. (2012, December 18). Online message delivered on the occasion of the first World Arabic Language Day. Retrieved from www.unesco.org/new/en/unesco/ev ents/prizes-and-celebrations/celebrations/international-days/world-arabic-lan guage-day/.

Boudelaa, S. (2014). Is the Arabic mental lexicon morpheme-based or stem-based? Implications for spoken and written word recognition. In E. Saiegh-Haddad & M. Joshi (Eds.), *Handbook of Arabic literacy: Insights and perspectives* (pp. 31–54). Dordrecht: Springer.

Boudelaa, S. & Marslen-Wilson, W. D. (2000). Non-concatenative morphemes in language processing: Evidence from Modern Standard Arabic. In J. McQueen & A. Cutler (Eds.), *Proceedings of the Workshop on Spoken Word Access Processes* (pp. 23–26). Nijmegen: MPI for Psycholinguistics.

(2004). Allomorphic variation in Arabic: Implications for lexical processing and representation. *Brain and Language, 90,* 106–116.

(2005). Discontinuous morphology in time: Incremental masked priming in Arabic. *Language and Cognitive Processes, 20,* 207–260.

(2010). Aralex: A lexical database for Modern Standard Arabic. *Behavior Research Methods, 42,* 481–487.

(2011). Productivity and priming: Morphemic decomposition in Arabic. *Language and Cognitive Processes, 26,* 624–652.

(2015). Structure, form, and meaning in the mental lexicon: Evidence from Arabic. *Language, Cognition and Neuroscience, 30*(8), 955–992. DOI:10.1080/23273798.2015.1048258.

Dai, J., Ibrahim, R. & Share, D. L. (2013). The influence of orthographic structure on printed word learning in Arabic. *Writing Systems Research, 5,* 189–213.

Daniels, P. T. (1992). The syllabic origin of writing and the segmental origin of the alphabet. In P. Downing, S. D. Lima & M. Noonan (Eds.), *The linguistics of literacy* (pp. 83–110). Amsterdam: John Benjamins.

Eid, M. (1990). Arabic linguistics: The current scene. In M. Eid (Ed.), *Perspectives on Arabic linguistics* (pp. 3–38). Amsterdam: John Benjamins.

Elbeheri, G. & Everatt, J. (2007). Literacy ability and phonological processing skills amongst dyslexic and non-dyslexic speakers of Arabic. *Reading and Writing, 20,* 273–294.

Elbeheri, G., Everatt, J., Mahfoudhi, A., Al-Diyar, M. A. & Taibah, N. (2011). Orthographic processing and reading comprehension among Arabic speaking mainstream and LD children. *Dyslexia, 17,* 123–142.

Eviatar, Z. & Ibrahim, R. (2004). Morphological and orthographic effects on hemispheric processing of nonwords: A cross-linguistic comparison. *Reading and Writing, 17,* 691–705.

(2007). Morphological structure and hemispheric functioning: The contribution of the right hemisphere to reading in different languages. *Neuropsychology, 21,* 470–484.

(2014). Why is it hard to read Arabic? In E. Saiegh-Haddad & M. Joshi (Eds.), *Handbook of Arabic literacy: Insights and perspectives* (pp. 77–96). Dordrecht: Springer.

Eviatar, Z., Ibrahim, R. & Ganayim, D. (2004). Orthography and the hemispheres: Visual and linguistic aspects of letter processing. *Neuropsychology, 18,* 174–184.

Farran, L. K., Bingham, G. E. & Mathews, M. W. (2012). The relationship between language and reading in bilingual English-Arabic children. *Reading and Writing, 25*, 2153–2181.

Feitelson, D., Goldstein, Z., Iraqi, J. & Share, D. L. (1993). Effects of listening to story reading on aspects of literacy acquisition in a diglossic situation. *Reading Research Quarterly, 28*, 71–79.

Ferguson, C. A. (1959). Diglossia. *Word, 14*, 47–56.

Geva-Kleinberger, A. (2000). Aspects of the dialects of Arabic today. In A. Youssi, F. Benjelloun, M. Dahbi & Z. Iraqui-Sinaceur (Eds.), *Proceeding of the Association International de Dialectologie Arabe 4 in Honour of Professor David Cohen* (pp. 473–479). Rabat: Amapatril.

Henkin, R. (2010). *Negev Arabic: Dialectal, sociolinguistic, and stylistic variation. Semitica viva series.* Wiesbaden: Otto Harrassowitz.

Holes, C. (2004). *Modern Arabic: Structures, functions, and varieties.* Washington, DC: Georgetown University Press.

Ibrahim, M. (1983). Linguistic distance and literacy in Arabic. *Journal of Pragmatics, 7*, 507–515.

Ibrahim, R. (2013). Reading in Arabic: New evidence for the role of vowel signs. *Creative Education, 4*, 248–253.

Ibrahim, R. & Aharon-Peretz, J. (2005). Is literary Arabic a second language for native Arab speakers? Evidence from a semantic priming study. *The Journal of Psycholinguistic Research, 34*, 51–70.

Ibrahim, R. & Eviatar, Z. (2009). Language status and hemispheric involvement in reading: Evidence from trilingual Arabic speakers tested in Arabic, Hebrew, and English. *Neuropsychology, 23*, 240–254.

Ibrahim, R., Eviatar, Z. & Aharon Peretz, J. (2002). The characteristics of the Arabic orthography slow its cognitive processing. *Neuropsychology, 16*, 322–326.

Iddrissi, A., Prunet, J.-F. & Beland, R. (2008). On the mental representation of Arabic roots. *Linguistic Inquiry, 39*, 221–259.

Jayusi, A. (2013). Developing early triliteracy: The effect of metalinguistic awareness on reading within and across three languages. Ph.D. thesis, Bar-Ilan University, Israel.

Kay, A. S. (1994). Formal vs. informal Arabic: Diglossia, triglossia, tetraglossia etc., polyglossia – multiglossia viewed as a continuum. *Zeitschrift für Arabische Linguistik, 27*, 47–66.

Khamis-Dakwar, R. & Froud, K. (2007). Lexical processing in two language varieties: An event related brain potential study of Arabic native speakers. In M. Mughazy (Ed.), *Perspectives on Arabic linguistics XX* (pp. 153–166). Amsterdam: John Benjamins.

Khamis-Dakwar, R., Froud, K. & Gordon, P. (2012). Acquiring diglossia: Mutual influences of formal and colloquial Arabic on children's grammaticality judgments. *Journal of Child Language, 39*, 1–29.

Khamis-Dakwar, R. & Machul, B. (2014). Diglossic knowledge development in typically developing native Arabic-speaking children and the development of ADAT (Arabic Diglossic Knowledge and Awareness Test). In E. Saiegh-Haddad & M. Joshi (Eds.), *Handbook of Arabic literacy: Insights and perspectives* (pp. 279–300). Dordrecht: Springer.

Korat, O., Aram, D., Hassunha-Arafat, S., Saiegh-Haddad, E. & Hag-Yehiya Iraki, H. (2014). Mother–child literacy activities and early literacy in the Israeli Arab Family. In E. Saiegh-Haddad & M. Joshi (Eds.), *Handbook of Arabic literacy: Insights and perspectives* (pp. 323–350). Dordrecht: Springer.

Laks, L. (2013). Passive formation in Palestinian and Standard Arabic: Lexical vs. syntactic operations. *Word Structure, 6*, 156–180. DOI:10.3366/word.2013.0043.

Laks, L. & Berman, R. A. (2014). A new look at diglossia: Modality-driven distinctions between spoken and written narratives in Jordanian Arabic. In E. Saiegh-Haddad & M. Joshi (Eds.), *Handbook of Arabic literacy: Insights and perspectives* (pp. 241–354). Dordrecht: Springer.

Larcher, P. (2006). Derivation. In L. Edzard & R. de Jong (Eds.), *Encyclopedia of Arabic language and linguistics* (pp. 573–579). Leiden: Brill.

Levin, A. (1995). *The grammar of the Arabic dialect of Jerusalem.* Jerusalem: Magnes. [In Hebrew]

Levin, I., Saiegh-Haddad, E., Hende, N. & Ziv, M. (2008). Early literacy in Arabic: An intervention with Israeli Palestinian kindergarteners. *Applied Psycholinguistics, 29*, 413–436.

Liberman, I. Y., Shankweiler, D., Fischer, F. W. & Carter, B. (1974). Explicit segmentation of syllable and phoneme segmentation in the young child. *Journal of Experimental Child Psychology, 18*, 201–212.

Maamouri, M. (1998). Language education and human development: Arabic diglossia and its impact on the quality of education in the Arab region. Paper presented at the Mediterranean Development Forum of the World Bank, Marrakech, Morocco.

Mahfoudhi, A., Elbeheri, G., Al-Rashidi, M. & Everatt, J. (2010). The role of morphological awareness in reading comprehension among typical and learning disabled native Arabic speakers. *Journal of Learning Disabilities, 43*, 500–514.

Mahfoudhi, A., Everatt, J. & Elbeheri, G. (2011). Introduction to the special issue on literacy in Arabic. *Reading and Writing, 24*, 1011–1018.

McCarthy, J. (1981). A prosodic theory of non-concatenative morphology. *Linguistic Inquiry, 12*, 373–418.

Meiseles, G. (1980). Educated spoken Arabic and the Arabic language continuum. *Archivum Linguisticum, 11*, 118–143.

Mimouni, Z., Kehaya, E. & Jarema, G. (1998). The mental representation of singular and plural nouns in Algerian Arabic as revealed through auditory priming in agramatic aphasia patients. *Brain & Language, 61*, 63–87.

Ministry of Education (2008). *The new curriculum of Arabic language education for elementary school (grades 1–6).* Israel: Ministry of Education. Retrieved from http://meyda.education.gov.il/files/Tochniyot_Limudim/Arabic/ChinuchLeshoni.pdf. [In Hebrew]

Mohamed, W., Elbert, T. & Landerl, K. (2011). The development of reading and spelling abilities in the first three years of learning Arabic. *Reading and Writing, 24*, 1043–1060.

Mohamed, W., Landerl, K. & Elbert, T. (2014). An epidemiological survey of specific reading and spelling disabilities in Arabic speaking children in Egypt. In E. Saiegh-Haddad & M. Joshi (Eds.), *Handbook of Arabic literacy: Insights and perspectives* (pp. 99–118). Dordrecht: Springer.

Myhill, J. (2014). The effect of diglossia on literacy in Arabic and other languages. In E. Saiegh-Haddad & M. Joshi (Eds.), *Handbook of Arabic literacy: Insights and perspectives* (pp. 197–223). Dordrecht: Springer.

Perea, M., Abu Mallouh, R. & Carreiras, M. (2010). The search of an input coding scheme: Transposed-letter priming in Arabic. *Psychonomic Bulletin and Review, 17*, 375–380.

Perfetti, C. (2007). Reading ability: Lexical quality to comprehension. *Scientific Studies of Reading, 11*, 1–27.

Prunet, J.-F., Beland, R. & Idrissi, A. (2000). The mental representation of Semitic words. *Linguistic Inquiry, 4*, 609–648.

Ratcliffe, R. R. (2001). What do "phonemic" writing systems represent? *Written Language and Literacy, 4*, 1–14.

Ravid, D. (2012). *Spelling Hebrew: The psycholinguistics of Hebrew spelling.* New York: Springer.

Rosenhouse, Y. (1990). Tendencies to nominalization in modern literary Arabic as compared with Classical Arabic. *Zeitschrift für Arabische Linguistik (Z.A.L.), 22*, 23–43.

Rosenhouse, Y. (2008). Verbal Nouns. In L. Edzard & R. de Jong (Eds.), *Encyclopedia of Arabic language and linguistics* (pp. 659–665). Leiden: Brill.

Russak, S. & Fragman, A. (2014). The development of grapho-phonemic representations among native Hebrew speakers learning Arabic as a foreign language. In E. Saiegh-Haddad & M. Joshi (Eds.), *Handbook of Arabic literacy: Insights and perspectives* (pp. 381–394). Dordrecht: Springer.

Russak, S. & Saiegh-Haddad, E. (2011). Phonological awareness in Hebrew (L1) and English (L2) in normal and disabled readers. *Reading and Writing, 24*, 427–440.

Ryan, A. & Meara, P. (1991). The case of the invisible vowels: Arabic speakers reading English words. *Reading in a Foreign Language, 5*, 531–540.

Saiegh-Haddad, E. (2003). Linguistic distance and initial reading acquisition: The case of Arabic diglossia. *Applied Psycholinguistics, 24*, 431–451.

(2004). The impact of phonemic and lexical distance on the phonological analysis of words and pseudowords in a diglossic context. *Applied Psycholinguistics, 25*, 495–512.

(2005). Correlates of reading fluency in Arabic: Diglossic and orthographic factors. *Reading and Writing, 18*, 559–582.

(2007a). Linguistic constraints on children's ability to isolate phonemes in Arabic. *Applied Psycholinguistics, 28*, 605–625.

(2007b). Epilinguistic and metalinguistic phonological awareness may be subject to different constraints: Evidence from Hebrew. *First Language, 27*, 385–405.

(2011a). Phonological processing in diglossic Arabic: The role of linguistic distance. In E. Broselow & H. Ouli (Eds.), *Perspectives on Arabic Linguistics XXII* (pp. 269–280). Amsterdam: John Benjamins.

(2011b).The effect of exposure to Standard Arabic and linguistic distance from Spoken Arabic on lexical processing in Standard Arabic. In D. Aram & O. Korat (Eds.), *Literacy and Language: Interaction, bilingualism, and difficulties* (pp. 321–336). Jerusalem: Magnes Press. [In Hebrew]

(2012). Literacy reflexes of Arabic diglossia. In M. Leikin, M. Schwartz & Y. Tobin (Eds.), *Current issues in bilingualism: Cognitive and sociolinguistic perspectives* (pp. 43–55). Dordrecht: Springer.

(2013). A tale of one letter: Morphological processing in early Arabic spelling. *Writing Systems Research, 5,* 169–188.

Saiegh-Haddad, E. & Everatt, J. (2017). Literacy Education in Arabic. In N. Kucirkova, C. Snow, V. Grover, and C. McBride-Chang (Eds.), *The Routledge International Handbook of Early Literacy Education* (pp. 185–199). USA: Taylor & Francis Routledge.

Saiegh-Haddad, E. & Geva, E. (2008). Morphological awareness, phonological awareness, and reading in English-Arabic bilingual children. *Reading and Writing, 21,* 481–504.

Saiegh-Haddad, E., Hadieh, A. & Ravid, D. (2012). Acquiring noun plurals in Arabic: Morphology, familiarity, and pattern frequency. *Language Learning, 62,* 1079–1109.

Saiegh-Haddad, E. & Haj, L. (2016). Phonological representations in the diglossic mental lexicon. Ms. in preparation.

Saiegh-Haddad, E. & Henkin-Roitfarb, R. (2014). *The structure of Arabic language and orthography.* In E. Saiegh-Haddad & M. Joshi (Eds.), *Handbook of Arabic literacy: Insights and perspectives* (pp. 3–28). Dordrecht: Springer.

Saiegh-Haddad, E., Kogan, N. & Walters, J. (2010). Universal and language-specific constraints on phonemic awareness: Evidence from Russian–Hebrew bilingual children. *Reading and Writing, 23,* 359–384.

Saiegh-Haddad, E., Levin, I., Hende, N. & Ziv, M. (2011). The linguistic affiliation constraint and phoneme recognition in diglossic Arabic. *Journal of Child Language, 38,* 297–315.

Saiegh-Haddad, E. & Schiff, R. (2016). The impact of diglossia on voweled and unvoweled word reading in Arabic: A developmental study from childhood to dolescence. *Scientific Studies of Reading, 20,* 311–324.

Saiegh-Haddad, E. & Spolsky, B. (2014). *Enhancing mother tongue literacy in diglossic Arabic: Problems and prospects.* In E. Saiegh-Haddad & M. Joshi (Eds.), *Handbook of Arabic literacy: Insights and perspectives* (pp. 225–240). Dordrecht: Springer.

Seymour, P. H. K., Aro, M. & Erskine, J. M. (2003). Foundation literacy skills in European orthographies. *British Journal of Psychology, 94,* 143–174.

Share, D. & Blum, P. (2005). Syllable splitting in literate and preliterate Hebrew speakers: Onsets and rimes or bodies and codas? *Journal of Experimental Child Psychology, 92,* 182–202.

Smythe, I., Everatt, J., Al-Menaye, N., He, X., Capillini, S., Gyarmathy, E. & Siegel, L. (2008). Predictors of word-level literacy amongst grade 3 children in five diverse languages. *Dyslexia, 14,* 170–187.

Taha, H. (2009). The contribution of phonological versus morphological intervention to reading and spelling in Arabic: A developmental perspective. Ph.D. thesis, Bar-Ilan University, Israel.

Taha, H., Ibrahim, R. & Khateb, A. (2013). How does Arabic orthographic connectivity modulate brain activity during visual word recognition: An ERP study. *Brain Topography, 26,* 292–302.

Taha, H. & Saiegh-Haddad, E. (2014). Linguistic intervention and spelling development in Arabic. Manuscript submitted for publication.

Taha, H. & Saiegh-Haddad, E. (2016a). The role of phonological versus morphological skills in the development of Arabic spelling: An intervention study. *Journal of Psycholinguistic Research, 45,* 507–535.

(2016b). Morphology and spelling in Arabic: Development and interface. *Journal of Psycholinguistic research.* Available online.

Taibah, N. J. & Haynes, C. W. (2011). Contributions of phonological processing skills to reading skills in Arabic speaking children. *Reading and Writing, 24,* 1019–1042.

Taouk, M. & Coltheart, M. (2004). The cognitive processes involved in learning to read in Arabic. *Reading and Writing, 17,* 27–57.

Treiman, R. (1983). The structure of spoken syllables: Evidence from novel word games. *Cognition, 15,* 49–74.

(1985). Onsets and rimes as units of spoken syllables: Evidence from children. *Journal of Experimental Child Psychology, 39,* 161–181.

(1988). The internal structure of the syllable. In G. Carlson & M. Tanenhaus (Eds.), *Linguistic structure in language processing* (pp. 27–52). Norwell, MA: Kluwer Academic.

Versteegh, K. (1997). *The Arabic language.* Edinburgh University Press.

(2014). *The Arabic language.* 2nd edn. Edinburgh University Press.

Wright, W. (1898). *A grammar of the Arabic language.* Cambridge University Press.

Zozovsky, R. (2010). The impact of socioeconomic versus linguistic factors on achievement gaps between Hebrew-speaking and Arabic-speaking students in Israel in reading literacy and in mathematics and science achievement. *Studies in Educational Evaluation, 36,* 153–161.

7   Learning to Read Hebrew

David L. Share

7.1   Introduction

7.1.1   *Hebrew and Its Orthography*

There has been growing concern among social scientists that conclusions from studies conducted on highly educated populations from wealthy European cultures (especially English-speaking) may have limited generalizability regarding human behavior in general (Henrich, Heine & Norenzayan, 2010). These reservations also extend to the field of language (Beveridge & Bak, 2012; Evans & Levinson, 2009) and literacy (Frost, 2012; Share, 2008). Research on reading, in particular, has been overwhelmingly dominated by work on English, which, unfortunately, appears to be an outlier among European alphabets (Share, 2008, 2012). Around the globe, however, most individuals are not native English speakers and neither do they acquire literacy in a European alphabet. The study of reading acquisition in Hebrew, therefore, presents an intriguing case study of learning to read and write in a non-European non-alphabetic orthography.

Since a detailed review of this literature was published in 1999 together with my late colleague, Iris Levin (Share & Levin, 1999), this chapter will pick up where the previous review left off by first summarizing prior findings and conclusions (which I will shorthand as S&L99) before moving on to a sketch of current and possible future research trends. Beyond the scope of the present chapter is important work on second language Hebrew learning (Frost, Siegelman, Narkiss & Afek, 2013), and on special populations such as bilinguals (Geva, 2008; Leikin, Schwartz & Tobin, 2011), the deaf (Miller, 2009), dyslexics (Share, 2003), and socio-economically disadvantaged groups (Aram, 2005; Korat, 2005; Schiff & Lotem, 2011).

7.1.2   *Synchronic and Diachronic Characterization*

Hebrew, the language of the Jewish bible, the Christian Old Testament, has a long and unbroken history. Used continuously from antiquity until today, its reformed version became the official language of the modern state of

Israel. Contrary to popular belief, Hebrew was never a dead language. Even after the Biblical period (circa 1300 BCE to 200 BCE), Hebrew continued to evolve, and although colloquial usage ceased for some 1,500 years, it remained in continual use not only in liturgy and reading of sacred texts but also in correspondence, and in scientific and creative writing (Berman, 1997; Hetzron, 1987).

Although Hebrew is not one of the world's major languages (with only some 10 million speakers), Semitic languages are the native tongue of some hundreds of millions, and the consonantal writing systems (abjads) first developed nearly 4,000 years ago by Semitic speakers are the progenitor of writing systems now used daily by billions (Daniels & Bright, 1996; Diringer, 1948; Naveh, 1982). The many offspring of the original Semitic abjad include today's Semitic (e.g., Hebrew, Arabic) and non-Semitic abjads, (e.g., Urdu, Malay), and all European alphabets originating with the Greeks' borrowing of the Semitic (Phoenician) abjad. This first alphabet later gave birth to the Roman alphabet which was disseminated first throughout Europe, and then across the globe by traders, empire-builders, and missionaries. Eastward, the Semitic abjad evolved into the abugidas (alphasyllabaries) of India, South-East Asia, and many parts of central Asia (Daniels & Bright, 1996; Gnanadesikan, 2009).

7.1.3   Literacy and Schooling

In Israel, formal reading instruction begins in Grade 1, around age 6, when children are introduced to the pointed (fully vocalized) Hebrew script. However, as in North America, there is a great deal of informal literacy teaching in the preschool years emphasizing phonological awareness, letter knowledge, writing and invented spelling, storybook reading, print conventions, language development, and varieties of discourse structure. On entry to school, children are normally taught via systematic phonic-emphasis methods, but the unit of instruction is typically *not* the individual letter but an integral CV syllable block (termed a /tʃeruf/ 'combination') consisting of a consonant letter with a small (diacritic-like) vowel sign underneath. Owing to its regularity, children are expected to master pointed script by the end of the first year or even earlier. Around Grade 3, the vowel points are dropped and children are expected to be able to read unpointed (i.e., partly vocalized) text. (In their writing, children are not expected to write the vowel points at any stage.)

Among the language-majority Hebrew-speaking (Jewish) population of Israel, literacy levels are very high and, according to international comparisons such as the Progress in International Reading Literacy Study (PIRLS), among the highest in the world.

7.2 Description of Hebrew and Its Written Forms

7.2.1 Linguistic System

7.2.1.1 Phonology Modern Hebrew (Ivrit) has a simple vowel system consisting of five vowels; high front /i/ and back /u/, midfront /ɛ/, back /o/ and low /a/ – all pronounced close to the cardinal vowels (Glinert, 1994). There are three dipthongs, /aj/, /oj/, /uj/, each with a glide. There is no longer any phonemic contrast between short and long vowels or single versus geminate vowels (or consonants). In addition to consonants familiar to English speakers (/p, b, t, d, k, g, f, v, s, z, ʃ, m, n, l/), and the semivowel (/j/), Hebrew has an unvoiced uvular liquid /ʁ/, a voiceless velar fricative /x/, the affricate /ts/, and, of late, the loan /w/. Biblical Hebrew's Semitic pharyngeals have been neutralized to /x/ and the glottal stop to zero. Emphatics, too, have disappeared in Modern Hebrew. Nonnative affricates now exist in loan words (/tʃ/ for 'chips', /dʒ/ for 'jeep'). The glottal stop and /h/ are now pronounced as zero in most environments. Of the six original stop-spirant alternations, only three (/p/, /b/, /k/) now have fricative counterparts, distinguished in pointed Hebrew script by a dot (spirantization *dagesh)* inserted into the letter (see Table 7.1). The numerous historical neutralizations create considerable challenges for spelling, with six of Hebrew's nineteen consonantal phonemes represented by at least two letters (see Table 7.1). Few words are monosyllabic, most consisting of two and three syllables and, owing to extensive clitics and inflections, possessives and pronominals, can range up to five or more syllables.

Spoken Hebrew has a very extensive range of consonant clusters (e.g., /gz/, /pts/, /tsx/, etc.; Glinert, 1994; Schwarzwald, 2002), but because written forms consist exclusively of CV sequences (consonant letter plus vowel sign), it is often misrepresented as a language with a simple CV/CVC phonology – a classic case of confusion between the written signary and the spoken language.

In summary, a once extensive inventory of phonemes (vowels and consonants) has now been whittled down to a deceptively small set. Unfortunately for the speller, the orthography adamantly preserves all these once-distinct phonemes. Nonetheless, the orthography makes up for this spelling complexity somewhat by simplifying the task of learning to read.

7.2.1.2 Inflectional Morphology Modern Hebrew has a rich inflectional morphology that permits considerable versatility in word order. Nouns and adjectives are marked linearly for number, near-arbitrary gender, and definiteness; verbs are marked for number, gender, and person and take infinitive, imperative, or indicative moods including past tense, future, and present or participial forms. There is no grammatical marking of verb aspect.

Table 7.1 *Old (Paleo-)Hebrew letters, Modern Hebrew letters, their names, and phonemic values*

Biblical sign	Modern sign (word-final form)	Letter name	Reading phonemic value	Spelling alternatives
✗	א	Alef	ʔ/Ø	א ה ע
ﬤ	ב	Bet	/b/ ב, /v/ ב	(/v/) ו ב
∧	ג	Gimel	/g/	
⊿	ד	Dalet	/d/	
ﬡ	ה	He	h/ʔ/Ø	
ﬠ	ו	Vav	/v/	
∼	ז	Zayin	/z/	
ﬡ	ח	Xet	/x/	ח כ
⊖	ט	Tet	/t/	ת ט
𝑚	׳	Yod	/j/	
ꓘ	כ (ך)	Kaf	/k/ כ, /x/ כ	ק פ
ﬥ	ל	Lamed	/l/	
ﬖ	מ (ם)	Mem	/m/	
ﬤ	נ (ן)	Nun	/n/	
ﬡ	ס	Samex	/s/	שׂ ס
○	ע	Ayin	/ʔ/Ø	
⟩	פ (ף)	Pe	/p/ /f/ פ פ	
ﬡ	צ (ץ)	Tsadi	/ts/	
ﬡ	ק	Kof	/k/	
ﬡ	ר	Resh	/ʁ/	
ﬡ	שׁ	Shin/Sin	/ʃ/ /s/	
ﬠ	ת	Tav	/t/	

Note. The final column labeled "Spelling alternatives" lists the letters sharing the same phonemic value.

7.2.1.3 *Word Formation Processes*

Hebrew is a synthetic (S)VO language with a highly productive morphology (Berman, 1985; Ravid, 1990). Whereas English has many different lexemes for semantically related words such as *play* and *game*, Hebrew uses derivational devices that operate on a limited number of common tri-consonantal roots (leSaXeK 'to play', miSXaK 'game'). Possibly because the lexical base of Old (Biblical) Hebrew mainly consisted of just three consonants (allowing only around 8,000 (20^3) possible roots), the morphology assumed the burden of word-making. Many mono-morphemic words (particularly Aramaic) entered the lexicon at a later time, but the root-and-pattern word formation apparatus remains dominant. This system, in many ways, is the key to understanding the Hebrew writing system and the nature of learning to read and write in Hebrew.

The heart of Hebrew word formation is the uniquely Semitic root-and-pattern system (McCarthy, 1981). Most Hebrew content words are poly-morphemic combinations of a tri-consonantal skeleton interwoven with a vowel pattern (via infixing, with or without affixed consonants). These morpho-phonemic vowel patterns convert an unpronounceable and discontinuous consonantal root (e.g., בגד, B,G,D) into a pronounceable word BeGeD (בֶּגֶד 'article of clothing').[1] The consonantal root is the semantic core of most content words; hence, it is a fundamental unit of processing in both the spoken and the written language. To illustrate, verbs derived from the tri-consonantal root קלט KLT include KaLaT ('he grasped'), niKLaT ('was grasped/absorbed'), hiKLiT ('he recorded'), and many more. Most noun forms operate on the same root-plus-pattern principle, e.g., KLiTah ('absorption'), miKLaT ('shelter'), KoLTan ('receptor'), and many adjectives too, e.g., KaLiT ('absorbant/accessible'). Notice, again, that where English has distinct lexemes, Hebrew has the common KLT root morpheme. While some noun patterns represent semantic categories (e.g., the form CaCaC is characteristic of professions; KaTaV 'journalist', NaGaR 'carpenter'), many are highly unpredictable.

In contrast to the English-speaking child's early lexicon, the core lexicon encountered by beginning readers in Hebrew is multi-morphemic (Ravid, 2001). Even many common everyday nouns are morphologically complex and hence oblige the Hebrew reader to attend to word-internal structure. Some additional Hebrew word formation devices include the increasingly common linear derivations (Berman, 2003), e.g., SaFRan 'librarian', SaFRan-ut 'librarianship', (hyphenated) prefixes bɛn- ('inter-'), as in בין-תחומי (bɛn-TXuMi, 'inter-disciplinary'), blends – מדרחוב (miDRaXoV), merging מדרכה (miDRaXa 'sidewalk'), and רחוב (ReXoV 'street') to generate 'pedestrian mall'. Straight non-native borrowings are very popular nowadays (e.g., איי-פון /ajfon/ 'i-phone').

In new word formation, verbs can be formed only by combining a root with one of the seven verb patterns (*binyanim*). These patterns express transitivity, reciprocity, reflexivity, causitivity, and inchoativeness. For example, GaDaL 'he grew' (simple intransitive), GiDeL 'he grew' (transitive), hiGDiL 'he enlarged' (causative), and so on. Borrowed verbs must be adapted to an existing Hebrew pattern but nouns can be borrowed intact (e.g., /intɛʁnɛt/ 'internet'; Hoberman & Aronoff, 2003).

In contrast to content words, most Hebrew grammatical morphemes are monosyllabic and mono-morphemic, including prepositions (e.g., /im/ 'with'), conjunctions (e.g., /ki/ 'because'), pronouns (e.g., /at / 'you'), quantifiers (e.g., /kol/ 'all'), and articles (e.g., /zɛ/ 'this').

---

[1] I adopt the common convention of representing the root letters with capital letters and the vowels (and any non-root affixed consonants) with lowercase letters. This is somewhat misleading because Hebrew vowel diacritics (in pointed script) mostly appear directly *beneath* (not beside) consonants.

As a highly synthetic language, many grammatical morphemes in Hebrew are affixed to a stem, creating long poly-morphemic strings where a single letter string can express an entire English sentence (cf. Turkish or Greek) thereby placing considerable demands on morphemic analysis, and perhaps also slowing reading rate (Shimron & Sivan, 1994).

Summarizing, Hebrew is heavily inflected, permitting flexible word order, with word formation primarily via non-linear (root-and-pattern) morphology, although linear structures and direct borrowings are becoming increasingly common. The poly-morphemic nature of even simple words calls for considerable morphemic unpacking but, as we see below, the architecture of the writing system excels in making the morphology transparent.

7.2.2   Writing System

Hebrew is an abjad or consonantal writing system (Daniels, 1990). This observation has far-reaching implications for literacy learning, instruction, and assessment. Hebrew represents all consonants as full-fledged letters linearly arrayed from right to left. Vowels, however, either are omitted or have only subordinate status. And although Hebrew writing has had many opportunities to become a "true" alphabet, it has never abandoned its consonantal architecture. Thus, vowels neither are, nor ever were, on an equal footing with consonants. Yiddish (an Indo-European, Germanic language), in contrast, is also written with Hebrew letters, but with full-sized vowel and consonant letters arrayed linearly side by side as in all European alphabets.

7.2.2.1 Script and Punctuation   Since biblical times Hebrew was a purely consonantal script, practically identical with the Phoenician abjad (see the leftmost column of Table 7.1). By the end of the sixth century BCE, however, the biblical script was gradually replaced by an Aramaic script which evolved into the so-called Jewish *square* script – the standard script used today (Goerwitz, 1996). As in ancient times, Hebrew has twenty-two consonantal letters, five of which take a word-final form. Three letters have an added apostrophe marking borrowed palatals and affricates (ג' /ʒ/, צ' /ʧ/, and ז' /ʤ/).

Unlike Arabic, Hebrew letters are never ligatured. Three letters represent predictable stop/fricative alternations *b/v, k/x, p/f* which, in pointed Hebrew, are marked by inserting a dot or point (*dagesh*) into the letter (e.g., ב בּ).[2]

With the post-biblical demise of spoken Hebrew, the introduction of vowel signs became a necessity. Two separate systems of vocalization evolved. The first, called *mothers of reading*, employs four consonantal letters (AHVY, אהוי) to serve

---

[2] These stop/fricative alternatives are not entirely predictable (e.g., מכר 'he sold', מכר 'acquaintance'); hence the absence of this point in unpointed script adds consonantal ambiguity.

כל בני האדם נולדו בני חורין ושווים בערכם
ובזכויותיהם. כולם חוננו בתבונה ובמצפון, לפיכך
חובה עליהם לנהוג איש ברעהו ברוח של אחווה.

כָּל בְּנֵי הָאָדָם נוֹלְדוּ בְּנֵי חוֹרִין וְשָׁוִים בְּעֶרְכָּם
וּבְזְכֻיוֹתֵיהֶם. כֻּלָּם חוֹנְנוּ בַּתְּבוּנָה וּבְמַצְפּוּן, לְפִיכָךְ
חוֹבָה עֲלֵיהֶם לִנְהוֹג אִישׁ בְּרֵעֵהוּ בְּרוּחַ שֶׁל אַחֲוָה.

Figure 7.1 The same text in standard unpointed and pointed Hebrew.

the dual function of signifying vowels as well as consonants (e.g., כתיבה, /KTiVa/ 'writing'; כתוב /KaTuV/ 'written'). This system is the standard *unpointed* version of Hebrew appearing in periodicals and books but is inconsistent and incomplete (Ravid & Schiff, 2006; Shimron, 1993) creating extensive phonological under-specification as well as pervasive homography (Bar-On, forthcoming).

A second system of vocalization, developed in the eighth century CE (Chomsky, 1941), employs diacritic-like dots or points. So-called *pointed* Hebrew is largely restricted to poetry, sacred texts, and materials for beginning readers. This vocalization system provides a complete and virtually unambiguous representation of the vowels by means of relatively inconspicuous dots and dashes appearing mostly under, but sometimes also above and between, the letters. For example: דְּ /di/, דּוֹ /do/, דֻּ /du/, דָּ /da/, דֶּ /dε/. Note that each of these consonant–vowel combinations forms a graphically integral CV syllable block. These same units are the basic phonic building blocks of pointed Hebrew and are also, as mentioned above, the unit of initial instruction in most Israeli schools. However, duplication abounds in this system, with numerous signs preserving historically neutralized phonemic distinctions such as vowel length. Children learn to read in pointed Hebrew, which has almost perfect letter-to-phoneme correspondence, negligible homophony, and no homography. This phonological consistency allows beginning readers to rely entirely on serial bottom-up letter–sound translation to identify novel printed words with little need for supplementary contextual or higher-order lexical or morpho-phonological information (see Shatil & Share, 2003).

Punctuation in standard Hebrew text adheres to the same conventions as in English (as seen in Figure 7.1).

7.2.2.2 Orthography The strict adherence to the consonantal principle derives from the consonantal nature of the roots that provide the core meaning of a Hebrew content word. The orthography highlights the root consonants by transforming the phonologically discontinuous spoken root into an orthographically *continuous* unit which is easily unitized as an integral (linear) lexical-orthographic representation. Consider the following derivations from the common root KTV denoting the concept of writing.

The listener hears /katav/ ('he wrote'), /jixtov/ ('he will write'), /ktuba/ ('marriage contract'), and so on. These words often have little in common (/jixtov/ and /ktuba/ share only a single phoneme) but appear in print as follows, כתובה כתב יכתוב; the three (bolded) root letters appearing as a continuous or near-continuous string; only the relatively unobtrusive VAV ו and YOD י are interpolated between the root letters. Thus, as in the case of English morphemic transparency (e.g., *soft/soften, two/twice*), Hebrew provides a fine example of morpheme constancy (Rogers, 1995), consistently marking phonologically distinct allomorphs.

Owing to its synthetic nature, Hebrew words are highly dense morphemically. Not only are tense, person, number, etc., usually indicated by inflecting roots, but many function words (*to, from, the*, etc.) and possessives (*my, his*) are frequently affixed to both nouns and pronouns. For example, the first (right-most) six-syllable word on the second line of Figure 7.1 (ובזכויותיהם) translates into four English words 'and by their rights'. As a consequence, Hebrew texts are significantly shorter than the same text in English. This demands considerable morphemic unpacking by the reader and creates an additional source of homography.

Owing to its distinctive morphology, full representation of vowels in Hebrew, at least for the skilled reader, may well be unnecessary to distinguish basic morphemic contrasts. Compare words derived from the root SPR (root letters again bolded); SiPeR (סיפר) 'he told', SiPuR (סיפור) 'story', SuPaR (סופר) 'narrated', and so on. In English, words sharing the same consonants, but with different vowels, are typically unrelated morphemes (e.g., *SPRee, SPooR, SuPeR, aSPiRe*, etc.). By adding full-fledged vowel letters, Greek, an Indo-European language like English, became the first fully vocalized segmental script, that is, an alphabet. Not only is vowel information less critical for the Hebrew speaker, but this information is far more easily inferred in printed Hebrew owing to the small inventory of vowels and the limited number of morpho-phonological patterns. Yiddish uses Hebrew script alphabetically, with full and equal representation of vowels. Ancient Egyptian, a Semitic language, experimented briefly with alphabetization at one point, before abandoning the idea (Gnanadesikan, 2009).

Unlike letter-to-phoneme correspondence, however, phoneme-to-letter relations are not one-to-one with six pairs of (once phonemically distinct) graphemes each representing the same phoneme (see Table 7.1, column headed "Spelling"). The vast majority of Hebrew words, therefore, contain consonants and vowels which could be spelled with alternate letters.

7.2.3   Conclusion

The bi-scriptal (pointed/unpointed) Hebrew abjad seems ideally suited to preserving and highlighting root morphemes (essential for the skilled reader) as well as providing phonological transparency (via the addition of pointing) for the beginning reader. From a writing systems perspective, the common appellation *alphabet* is simply incorrect because this typically implies representation of *all* phonemes – both consonants and vowels – thereby helping legitimize the mistaken notion of unpointed Hebrew as a "defective" script on the misguided assumption that full and equal (European-style) representation of vowels and consonants is necessarily superior to a script (i.e., Semitic abjad) that "fails" to represent vowels systematically. This is far from a mere debate over nomenclature, and has far-reaching implications for reading and writing assessment, literacy instruction, and even definitions of dyslexia.

7.3   Acquisition of Reading and Spelling in Hebrew

7.3.1   Becoming Linguistically Aware

7.3.1.1 Phonological Development and Phonological Awareness   The small number of longitudinal/predictive and training studies of phonological awareness in Hebrew reviewed by S&L99 largely converged with the English language findings: Access to sub-lexical phonological units *including* phonemes is a significant predictor of later reading and, when trained, has a significant and durable impact on later reading ability. Over the last decade, this conclusion has been adopted by the Israeli Ministry of Education and incorporated into the Israeli curriculum both in preschool and in grade school. More recent work has explored phonological awareness (PA) in the upper-elementary grades, and also the question of precisely which phonological units are the crucial ones in Hebrew. Related to this is the growing interest in the question of awareness of vowels versus consonants. Several cross-linguistic studies by Tolchinsky, Levin, and colleagues provide a valuable backdrop for understanding the development of PA in the Hebrew abjad as opposed to alphabetic and non-segmental writing systems.

Evidence is accumulating that phonemes are not the only sub-lexical unit important for Hebrew, and, furthermore, among phonemes, awareness of consonants (particularly syllable-final consonants) may be more important than awareness of vowels. Several studies across a range of ages from preschoolers to adults have shown that CV (body) units (*not* rimes, as in English) are more accessible than isolated phonemes among native Hebrew speakers (Ben-Dror, Bentin & Frost, 1995; Bentin, Deutsh & Liberman, 1990; Share & Blum, 2005). In addition, access to single (consonant) phonemes has been found to shift from an early pre-literacy advantage for initial phonemes to a literacy-engendered preference for final phonemes (codas) (Saiegh-Haddad, 2007; Share & Blum, 2005). Bar-Kochva (2013) recently reported that final consonant isolation tended to be more strongly correlated with first-grade word identification than initial phoneme isolation. CV deletion also correlated well with first-grade reading, reaffirming that both consonantal phonemes *and* sub-syllabic (CV) bodies are important for Hebrew reading.

Several studies have now shown that young children more easily identify and isolate consonants than vowels (Lapidot, Tubul & Wohl, 1995–1996; Tolchinsky & Teberosky, 1998). In a study of phonological awareness in 5-year-old native speakers of Spanish, Hebrew, and Cantonese, Tolchinsky, Levin, Aram, and McBride-Chang (2012) found no significant differences between the three languages in initial phoneme (consonantal) isolation, but a significant advantage emerged in final phoneme isolation in Hebrew. Both final (but not initial) phoneme isolation and CV isolation correlated well with Hebrew word writing and reading. It seems that syllable-*initial* consonant awareness may be less critical than awareness of syllable-final consonants which are not bound to a vowel in a CV conglomerate. A CV response was frequently supplied in the initial phoneme isolation task, but rarely a VC (rime) in the final phoneme isolation task. In learning to read Hebrew, it appears that individual consonants (particularly final consonants) *and* CV units are the critical elements of phonology.

Recently, a number of cross-linguistic studies have questioned whether the PA-reading connection is equally strong in deep and shallow alphabets. S&L99 cited several studies reporting weaker correlations between Hebrew reading and phonological awareness at the end of Grade 1 compared to English, but they also noted that Bentin and Leshem (1993) reported a strong correlation between Hebrew reading and PA in the *middle* of Grade 1 when most children are still learning basic letter–sound correspondences. Share (2008) went on to suggest that, at this point in development, decoding skill may be more comparable to those of English speakers later in the year. This led to the *functional opacity hypothesis* (Share, 2008), according to which the PA-reading association is strongest when the spelling–sound code is opaque owing either to intrinsic spelling–sound irregularities in the orthography or to incomplete mastery of a regular code. This implies that the intrinsic relationship between phonological awareness and reading may be equally strong in both languages, the only difference being one of timing and duration. Several recent Hebrew studies of PA in older upper-elementary children have reported data bearing on this issue (Bar-Kochva, 2013; Bar-Kochva & Breznitz, 2014; Cohen-Mimran, 2009; Katzir, Schiff & Kim, 2012). Unfortunately the findings conflict, probably owing, at least in part, to the use of different measures and different sample ages. One possible interpretation is that PA correlates with reading accuracy but not fluency or comprehension. This tentative interpretation, if correct, would seem to refute Share's functional opacity hypothesis because both Katzir et al. (2012) and Bar-Kochva & Breznitz (2014) found substantial correlations in Grade 4 between reading accuracy in *pointed* (highly regular) and not just unpointed text. However, the declining knowledge of vowel diacritics after Grade 1 (see section 7.3.1.2) essentially reinstates a level of functional opacity (for vowels and occasionally consonants too) that places new demands on phoneme awareness among these older readers.

Summing up, research undertaken over the past fifteen years has confirmed the importance of phonological awareness in learning to read Hebrew. It appears that both individual phonemes (particularly final consonants) *and* CV bodies are the critical phonological elements in learning Hebrew. The hypothesis that the PA-reading link is strong only in the presence of decoding ambiguity may be sustained if a U-shaped developmental curve is assumed: During initial learning of consonant and vowel correspondences, decoding ambiguity is high, declining by the end of Grade 1 when the code is mastered, then re-emerging again later in Grade 2 (and beyond) when knowledge of the vowel diacritics diminishes thereby reinstating functional opacity for vowels. The role of CV bodies is now well established. The integral CV syllable block has the advantage of obviating the well-known problems of co-articulating consonants and vowels within a syllable, that is, blending (Feitelson, 1988), thereby reducing working memory demands (see also Abu-Ahmad, 2015). It appears that whereas initial consonants are intimately linked to the following vowel in an indivisible CV unit, access to final singleton phonemes is important because these phonemes still need to be integrated into closed (CVC) syllables. Future research will need to track the development of vowel and consonant awareness across the early years and examine its role in both silent and oral reading of pointed and unpointed text.

7.3.1.2 Morphological Development and Morphological Awareness   Given the central role of morphology in spoken Hebrew (Berman, 1985; Ravid, 2001) and especially the unique Semitic root-and-pattern morphology, it is not surprising that the association between morphological awareness and early reading and spelling has received a good deal of attention in the reading research literature.

The earlier pre-S&L99 work focused on the general question of whether morphological awareness/knowledge is related to reading. The answer then, as now, is a resounding yes. Post-S&L99 studies have almost unanimously reported significant and unique contributions of morphological awareness to reading and spelling in pointed/unpointed, silent/oral, and older/younger samples (e.g., Bar-Kochva, 2013; Bar-Kochva & Breznitz, 2014; Cohen-Mimran,

2009; Gur, 2005; Ravid & Mashraki, 2007; Schiff, Schwartz-Nahshon & Nagar, 2011). Indeed, some studies have found evidence that morphological awareness in Hebrew has a stronger association with reading than phonological awareness. Today, measures of morphology are now included as standard practice in all investigations of Hebrew literacy development. The task ahead will be to fill in the finer details – *which* aspects of morphology are related to *which* aspects of reading and spelling and *when*. To date, different measures of morphology (and often reading too) have typically been used interchangeably.

7.3.2   Development of Word Identification

7.3.2.1   Word Decoding Development   The rapid early mastery of Hebrew's phonologically transparent pointed script, discussed in S&L99, has again been confirmed in numerous studies conducted in recent years, notably Shany, Bar-On, and Katzir's (2012) definitive study of a large nationally representative sample.

S&L99 reviewed a number of studies indicating that vowel diacritics facilitated oral reading speed and accuracy among young readers, mainly by reducing vowel errors. More recent work has taken a more genuinely developmental approach posing the question of how pointing influences reading at *different* developmental points.

Gur's (2005) longitudinal study found that the advantage of oral text reading accuracy for pointed (as opposed to unpointed) script in Grade 1 was substantial (pointed 94%, unpointed 85%), narrowing in Grade 2 (95%, 92%), before disappearing by the end of Grade 3 (96%, 95%). This trend has since been replicated for accuracy and extended to reading rate (Bar-Kochva & Breznitz, 2014; Schiff, Katzir & Shoshan, 2013). These data reaffirm that pointed word reading is mastered by the end of Grade 1 and maintained thereafter at consistently high levels. The less familiar unpointed script seems to take some getting used to initially but is eventually mastered by late Grade 3. What is typically labeled an "advantage" of pointing (for speed and accuracy) might perhaps better be characterized as developmental "catch-up" with the initial "disadvantage" for (unfamiliar) unpointed text overcome by Grade 3. Simply asking whether diacritics help or hinder may be missing the fuller developmental picture.

The direct investigation of the diacritical system per se has recently emerged as a topic worthy of study in its own right, rather than merely as a tool for addressing the classic debate on the role of phonology in word reading.[3] Gur

---

[3] In what appears to be a case of "reverse-Anglocentrism," it is important to recognize that the difference between pointed and unpointed Hebrew is primarily vowel phonology, and accordingly plays a very different linguistic role to the "phonology" tapped in the classic regular/ exception word contrast in English. The unspoken assumption underlying numerous Hebrew

(2005) examined the issue of vowel diacritics in a longitudinal sample followed from Grade 1 to Grade 3 at a single school. Children read aloud vowel diacritics under seven conditions; first in isolation, then in a variety of morphological, lexical, and sentential contexts (in additive fashion).

Overall knowledge of diacritics presented in print actually *diminished* over the three grades (Share & Gur, in preparation). The same trend was reported by Shany, Bar-On, and Katzir (2012) in their large nationally representative (cross-sectional) sample. This is a startling finding when one considers the fact that steadily *improving* knowledge of the spelling–sound code as witnessed in increasing letter–sound knowledge and pseudoword reading accuracy (among normally developing populations at least) is an axiomatic, indeed *unquestioned*, finding in the English-language literature. These data underscore the pedagogical role of Hebrew diacritics in providing full phonological specification for the learner. Gradually, the diacritics become less crucial as reading skill advances and the reader relies to a greater extent on higher-order word-level lexical and morphological information.

Another unexpected finding emerged in both these investigations. Contrary to popular belief, the easiest diacritic was not the ubiquitous *kamats* (ָ) /a/ which accounts for some 25% of all vowel signs, but the *hiriq*. Gur hypothesized that the advantage of the *hiriq* is due to its spelling–sound consistency; it alone among the vowel diacritics has a single phonemic value (/i/).[4] In addition to consistency, Gur found frequency correlated strongly with reading accuracy but not visual-spatial complexity (number and position of dots) (see also Bar-Kochva, 2013).

Gur also found that diacritical mastery correlated ($r = .86$) with pseudoword reading in both Grade 1 and Grade 2, showing unambiguously that pseudoword reading in the Hebrew abjad depends largely on vowel diacritics rather than consonants. Consistent with the increasing role of lexico-morpho-orthographic processing in developing readers, the correlation between word decoding and vowel diacritic mastery diminished (to .61) by Grade 3. The decreasing reliance on phonology and growing lexical-morphological influences is also seen in the fact that two measures of morphological awareness were uncorrelated in Grade 1 with any of the CV reading tasks but did show significant moderate correlations by Grade 3.

studies that the role of "phonology" in word identification, as gauged by within-item pointed/unpointed comparisons, is functionally equivalent to the classic regular/exception word contrast in English may be ill-founded.

[4] The *kamats* has two inconsistent values. One is the so-called *kamats katan* which appears in a single but very high-frequency item: /kol/ 'all'. The second is the *hataf kamats* /o/ which appears in a few dozen fairly common nouns. It appears that even a very high-frequency diacritic, if not entirely consistent, creates ambiguity for the beginning reader.

The S&L99 review included several studies attesting to a growing influence of lexico-morphological knowledge across age. For example, reading accuracy increases across age for pseudowords that conform to a familiar morpho-phonological pattern as opposed to "unpatterned" pseudowords. In addition, the tendency to misread incorrectly pointed items in accordance with the correct vocalization pattern also increases. But before surveying more recent work, it is important to recap Ravid's (1996) groundbreaking study examining the oral reading of highly literate forms that are unfamiliar to young children. First graders read these forms more accurately than fourth-grade readers, suggesting that novice readers rely mostly on bottom-up serial spelling–sound (assembled) decoding, whereas the older, more skilled readers rely more on lexico-orthographic (addressed) phonology, disregarding the vowel diacritics and generating the more common spoken forms. This general developmental progression has been confirmed in the newer studies.

Gur (2005) compared the reading of morphologically *unpatterned* pseudo-words that were phonologically and orthographically legal at the syllable (CV) level, but did not conform to a Hebrew morpho-phonological pattern with a matched list consisting of *patterned* pseudowords that conformed to a familiar morpho-phonological pattern. A list of real words with the identical morpho-phonological patterns to the patterned pseudoword list was also presented.

In Grade 1, children's pronunciation accuracy was unaffected by either morphological patterning (i.e., well-formedness) or even word-specific lexical support (real words), but by Grade 2 there was a clear differentiation manifest mainly as declining accuracy for unpatterned pseudowords together with lexical benefits for real words (i.e., word superiority effect). This pattern of findings was reproduced in the reaction time data. Once again (and confirming the earlier study by Ravid [1996]), pure ("unassisted") grapheme–phoneme decoding actually declines after Grade 1, hand in hand with growing sensitivity to higher-order (word-level) morphological and lexical constraints.

Turning to unpointed orthography, the two major challenges for the developing reader are the pronunciation of unpointed words and the rampant homography. Only a single study in Hebrew was published at the time of the earlier S&L99 review. Bentin, Deutsch, and Liberman (1990) identified young disabled readers who experienced selective difficulties with unpointed but not pointed text. Members of this group were characterized by difficulties in the domain of syntax.

More recently, Bar-On and Ravid (2011) investigated the role of morphology in the reading of (non-homographic) unpointed words across a wide range of ages. Participants read aloud unpointed pseudowords constructed from a pseudoroot and a genuine pattern (e.g., כלסן KaLSan). Responses were scored as either a true Hebrew morpho-phonological pattern (KaLSan), as unpatterned responses that constituted a permissible grapho-phonemic decoding (at the syllable level) but did not conform to any Hebrew morpho-phonological pattern (e.g., KaLeSan), or basic grapho-phonemic errors (KaLMaN).

In early Grade 2, unpatterned responses predominated (50%), followed by grapho-phonemic errors (20%) with 30% correct pattern responses. Thereafter, the trend shifted to mostly correct pattern identification, with around one-third unpatterned responses, and grapho-phonemic errors extremely rare. The authors labeled this a transition from phonological to morphological reading, and described the change from early Grade 2 to late Grade 2 as a "watershed" period in reading acquisition (cf. Share & Shalev, 2004). The authors concluded that morphology is the key to determining lexical identity in unpointed script, eliminating multiple alternative pronunciations.

Bar-On and Ravid's second study addressed the issue of homography. They presented the homographic pseudoword מִשְׁגָּף, which can be assigned four different pronunciations depending on context. The most common forms – present tense verb and a noun – were correctly identified by the end of Grade 2, but the more complex and lower-frequency alternatives were only mastered around Grade 7.

In a follow-up study, Bar-On (forthcoming) showed that extensive homography poses little problem for the reader of unpointed text (indeed, skilled readers were found to be largely oblivious to these ambiguities) because almost all alternatives were found to possess distinct morpho-syntactic features such as nouns versus verbs (consider *wind/wind* in English). Bar-On identified several sources of homography including the interwoven (non-linear) root-plus-pattern structure of most content words, and linear affixation. Bar-On concludes with the insightful observation that the context-dependent nature of printed words in standard unpointed Hebrew text raises questions about the role of models and assessment practices founded on isolated word recognition.

Consistent with the context-dependent nature of unpointed reading, several correlational studies have demonstrated that semantic and syntactic measures contribute selectively to unpointed but not pointed reading (Shatil & Share, 2003), whereas morphological knowledge is important for both scripts (Cohen-Mimran, 2009).

7.3.2.2 Word Spelling Development The pioneering work of Levin, Tolchinsky, and colleagues on preschool writing/spelling aimed at tracing the developmental stages characterizing children's early attempts at producing written language prior to school entry. More recent research has extended this work by delving into the social/environmental factors (e.g., maternal mediation) that help or hinder growth in early writing (e.g., Aram & Levin, 2004; Korat, 2005; Schiff & Lotem, 2011) as well as cross-linguistic comparisons between Hebrew and other orthographies (e.g., Levin, Aram, Tolchinsky

& McBride, 2013; Tolchinsky et al., 2012). A new strand of research led by Ravid and Schiff has focused on the role of morphology among school-aged children, thereby providing a more complete picture of writing development both before and after school entry.

A series of studies summarized by Levin (1997) documented the early emergence of both the universal properties of writing systems and Hebrew-specific features. This work culminated in a developmental scale of Hebrew writing (Levin, Korat & Amsterdamer, 1996; Shatil, Share & Levin, 2000) which has proven popular with researchers and educators alike.

In all these investigations, children's representation of consonants has been found to be more advanced than that of vowels. Newer developmental (e.g., Ravid & Kubi, 2003) and cross-linguistic work (e.g., Tolchinsky et al., 2012) has confirmed the advantage of consonants over vowels.

A new generation of research into spelling in school has also addressed the biggest challenge in Hebrew spelling – producing orthographically correct (conventional) spellings, given the many options for transcribing so many phonemes (see Table 7.1).

In an analysis of naturally occurring spelling errors in compositions produced by children from Grades 1 to 6, Ravid (2001) compared content words with grammatical words, and, *within* content words, root letters versus non-root letters. As anticipated, Ravid (2001) found that errors in content words far outnumbered errors in grammatical words, with content word errors high in Grade 1 (29%) and Grade 2 (20%) and declining steeply thereafter. Grammatical errors were rare after Grade 1 (19%). Letter-level analyses of errors within content words replicated this pattern.

In a follow-up study in Grades 2, 3, and 4, Ravid dictated a set of words each containing root and function letters. Again, root letter errors for homophonous letters were far more numerous than function letter errors. This finding has since been replicated and extended by Ravid and Bar-On (2005) and Gillis and Ravid (2006).

7.3.2.3 Reading and Spelling Difficulties   The defining feature of reading difficulty in Hebrew is not reading accuracy (as in English) but reading speed. Hebrew dyslexics are typically found to read at half the rate of age-matched normal readers (see, e.g., Breznitz, 1997). Phonological awareness deficits are also characteristic of poor readers in Hebrew, but morphological deficits seem to be equally important. Syntax and semantics are not crucial given Hebrew's phonologically transparent script but are essential for dealing with ambiguity in unpointed text.

The influential English-language subtyping taxonomy spawned by the dual route model (phonological versus surface dyslexics) may have limited applicability to Hebrew. Recently Shany and colleagues (e.g., Shany & Share, 2011;

Shany & Breznitz, 2011) have proposed a promising subtyping scheme based on rate versus accuracy, adducing evidence for true double dissociations between rate-disabled and accuracy-disabled readers.

Spelling difficulties in Hebrew are rarely manifest in phonologically implausible spellings (see, e.g., Lamm & Epstein, 1994) but are in orthographically incorrect spellings involving the many homophonic letters (Ravid, 2012).

7.3.3   Reading Comprehension

7.3.3.1   Predictors of Reading Comprehension   Only a few studies have addressed this topic in Hebrew. In a large-scale longitudinal study, Shatil and Share (2003) examined the contribution of a host of kindergarten predictors to first-grade decoding and reading comprehension (of pointed text). Predictors included both "domain-specific" variables (visual-orthographic processing, phonological awareness, phonological memory, and early literacy) and "domain-general" (general intelligence, metacognitive functioning, and oral language). Whereas domain-general measures (which included oral vocabulary and syntax) explained very little of the variance in first-grade decoding (a speed and accuracy composite), both domain-specific and domain-general blocks each contributed significant and substantial portions of variance to the prediction of first-grade reading comprehension.

In the research thus far, morphological awareness has repeatedly been found to explain significant and substantial variance in reading comprehension throughout the elementary years. In a longitudinal study, Bar-Kochva (2013) found that morphological awareness and phonological working memory were the best kindergarten predictors of first-grade (pointed) reading comprehension, followed by vocabulary and phonological awareness. Rapid automatized naming (RAN) correlated well with fluency measures but somewhat less well with comprehension. Visual-spatial measures using non-symbolic material were uncorrelated with any reading measure.

In a second longitudinal study, Bar-Kochva and Breznitz (2014) compared the predictors of pointed and unpointed comprehension in Grades 3 and 4. Pointed comprehension in Grade 3 was most strongly predicted by phonological awareness (.4), and also, but more weakly, by Raven, Peabody vocabulary, morphology, RAN, and digit-span (all around .3), but again uncorrelated with visual processing speed. Interestingly, neither pseudoword reading accuracy nor speed was correlated with comprehension (reinforcing early comments about the questionable relevance of vowel diacritics beyond Grade 1). The picture was largely unaltered for unpointed comprehension except that Raven and Peabody were more strongly correlated than with pointed, suggesting that unpointed text depends more on higher-order reasoning.

In Grade 4, the results for pointed comprehension were roughly similar, although this time Raven did not correlate more strongly with unpointed comprehension, and phonological awareness was a little weaker. Pseudoword reading accuracy in this grade correlated significantly (but very weakly) with unpointed comprehension. On the whole, therefore, the predictors of pointed and unpointed comprehension were fairly similar, consistent with the idea that the common consonantal infrastructure of both versions of the orthography is the core of reading in both orthographies.

7.3.3.2 Word-Level Effects in Comprehending Text   A small number of studies have focused on word-level effects in comprehending test. Ravid and Mashraki (2007) found that an aggregated score on morphology (combining five separate morphology measures) correlated .64 with fourth-grade reading comprehension. It also correlated well with prosodic reading fluency but made a unique contribution to comprehension even after partialling out prosodic fluency. Word-level comprehension questions correlated very highly with higher-order comprehension (.81), indicating that lexical/morphological processing is central to higher-order reading comprehension, consistent with Perfetti's "lexical quality" hypothesis (Perfetti, 2007; Perfetti & Hart, 2002).

Schiff et al. (2011) also found moderate to strong correlations between morphological awareness and reading comprehension in Grades 3 and 7. Furthermore, the contribution of morphology remained significant after controlling both word decoding and phonological awareness.

7.3.4   Conclusion

Learning to read Hebrew, like all segmental orthographies, depends on phonological awareness, but one in which the critical phonological units only partly overlap with European alphabets; the supra-phonemic sub-syllabic CV unit, and, at the phoneme level, consonants more than vowels. Morphology has also been shown to be crucial in Hebrew for word-level, sentence-level, and text-level reading. The initial pointed and highly phonologically transparent script, like other transparent scripts, is acquired rapidly. Interestingly, the challenges of learning the diacritic-like vowel system appear to stem not from its visual-spatial complexity but from phonological inconsistency. The "all-phonological" and sequential nature of beginning reading gradually shifts in Grade 2 to a more rapid, more parallel lexico-morphological-orthographic mode of word identification that lays the foundations for faster, more fluent reading. It also provides the platform for a successful transition to unpointed text (with its rampant homography) which depends heavily on syntactic and semantic-pragmatic contextual support that would not be possible without a certain level of word reading fluency (Perfetti, 1985).

7.4   Discussion

7.4.1   Challenges in Learning to Read Hebrew

A wide-angled overview of Hebrew reading acquisition reveals important commonalities with alphabetic reading acquisition – this follows from the fact that both writing systems are primarily segmental. Close up, at a finer grain, there are fundamental differences; this too follows from the fact that one is alphabetic, the other an abjad. Both perspectives, the wide-angled lens and the close-up, provide valuable insights.

The wide-angled view reveals important universals (at least for segmental writing systems) including the indispensability of phonological awareness and a developmental shift from small-unit sequential phonological recoding to a higher-order or larger-unit morpheme-level or morpho-orthographic mode of processing which is faster and more efficient. One way to characterize this general shift without making commitments to specifics such as unit size or timing issues is the *unfamiliar-to-familiar/novice-to-expert* dualism (Share, 2008). This is a shift, common to all skill learning, from slow, effortful, piece-by-piece unskilled performance to rapid one-step large-unit skilled performance. This dualism also converges with the dualistic nature of an efficient orthography which must serve the needs of the novice for *decipherability* (via phonological transparency) as well as the expert for *unitizability* and *automatizability* (via morphemic transparency). Hebrew performs this balancing act with aplomb, employing diacritics to supply the beginner with a consistent, phonologically well-specified script, while helping the expert-to-be unitize the basic meaning-bearing units (roots) of the orthography by transforming abstract, discontinuous spoken roots into concrete, continuous, and therefore unitizable orthographic units. However, a dualistic approach focused exclusively at the level of individual words falls short of providing a complete picture of Hebrew reading acquisition: There appear to be three rather than two major aspects of learning to read Hebrew. These can be broadly characterized as a cumulative progression from lower-order phonological (*sub-lexical*) sequential spelling-to-sound translation through higher-order string-level (*intra-lexical*) lexico-morphological processing up to a *supra-lexical* contextual level essential for unpointed script with its pervasive homography. Each aspect or mode of processing adds to, not replaces, the previous one.

7.4.2   Implications for Instruction

In order to draw out the instructional implications of this three-phase model of reading development, a closer examination of the three modes is required. First, the sub-lexical phonological recoding level of the beginner is *not* the separate segments (vowels and consonants) of an alphabet, but primarily CV syllables and syllable-final consonants. Vowels appear to play only a subordinate role, if any. This initial entry-level spelling–sound translation is a relatively "pure," almost exclusively low-level decoding, akin to the bottom-up processes characteristic of regular alphabetic orthographies. But unlike alphabets, blending is completely bypassed in the case of open syllables, although, for closed syllables, final consonants may have to be appended to CV units. Direct observational studies of beginner's decoding will be needed to confirm this picture and determine how it varies across instructional practices. Note that even the common term "grapheme-phoneme" is theoretically loaded; there are no digraphs in Hebrew and hence no need for a term other than "letter," and the basic graphic units may not only be phonemes but multi-phonemic CV units, as already noted.

The second phase of this progression also brings to light fundamental differences between the Hebrew abjad and European alphabets, with major implications for teaching. In the course of Grade 2, the "watershed" year of reading development, the Hebrew reader shifts gear to a faster, more efficient word-level or morpheme-level lexico-morphological-orthographic reading strategy based on larger, higher-order units that primarily reflect consonantal roots and morphophonological patterns. The highly productive word formation structures in Hebrew, both non-linear and linear, underpin reading at this point even though children are still reading mostly pointed script. The term "lexical" comes to mind here but, if conceptualized in the classic dual-route sense, it is problematic for Hebrew because most words, even the early lexicon of beginning readers, are not mono-morphemic but multi-morphemic, representing the intersection of two abstract entities, a root and pattern (each discontinuous and unpronounceable). Although the result is a specific pronounceable unit, the dozens of content word inflections and affixes raise doubts about the utility of the notion of an orthographic lexicon (as conceptualized in the English-language literature) as a list or directory of discrete, self-contained ("encapsulated" or "autonomous") word-specific entries. Rather than the minimally inflected, and hence largely constant string of letters in an English word, most Hebrew words (if that term can be applied) are far less "stable" but more chameleon-like entities or families of overlapping resemblances (recall yiXToV, KTuBa).

The most startling and "unalphabetic" feature of this second phase of reading development, and one with profound implications not only for instruction but also assessment, is a decline in knowledge and use of vowel signs (as witnessed in deteriorating pseudoword reading accuracy), a finding that stands in complete opposition to a universal almost axiomatic feature of normal alphabetic reading development. At this point, the role of morphology in Hebrew emerges again and again as crucial, even outweighing phonological awareness in some studies.

The transition to unpointed Hebrew (around Grades 3 and 4) with its pervasive homography again highlights glaring alphabet/abjad differences with far-reaching implications not only for instruction and assessment but even the definition of reading disability. In Hebrew, the significance of supra-lexical contextual information sets it well apart from English and even more so from regular European alphabets. Given the ubiquity of homographs in unpointed text, reliance on contextual information appears to be both central and indispensable (even among highly skilled readers; see, e.g., Benuck & Peverly, 2004). By contrast, the developmental literature in English describes the marginal and *declining* role of context that accompanies growing word recognition skill (Stanovich, 1986, 2000), with increasing word reading modularity made possible by self-contained written forms (spellings). On a note of concord, it is interesting to observe that the diminishing role of vowel diacritics in Hebrew and extra-lexical context in English (particularly in the case of irregular words; Ricketts, Nation & Bishop, 2007; Tunmer & Chapman, 2012) both appear to serve a similar assistive function for developing readers.

7.5   Final Conclusion

The study of Hebrew reading acquisition offers valuable insights into one of the fundamental dilemmas of all writing systems; the trade-off between the needs of the novice versus the expert (Share, 2008). This is the antinomy between the *decipherability* needed by learners encountering massive numbers of unfamiliar words, as opposed to the expert-to-be's need for *automatizability* and *unitizability*, that is, between phonological transparency and morphemic transparency. The ingenious bi-scriptal solution achieved by means of optional diacritics provides both a phonologically well-specified script to assist the novice (so-called *pointed* Hebrew) and later, by shedding its vowel diacritics (and pedagogical intent), a phonologically under-specified script (*unpointed* Hebrew) emphasizing morphology.

The study of Hebrew literacy acquisition also widens the researcher's angle of vision on many issues on the global research agenda including the phonological awareness–reading connection in a non-alphabetic orthography, the transition from a phonologically well-specified orthography to an under-specified one, pervasive homography, morphemic analysis of poly-morphemic strings, the processing of diacritics, and the classic problems of learning to spell a writing system that, like English, preserves many now-neutralized consonant and vowel distinctions in spelling.

Above all, the study of Hebrew reading offers all reading researchers some refreshing insights into literacy learning outside the familiar box of European alphabets, one that provides a wider angle of vision on all orthographies.

176   *David L. Share*

References

Abu-Ahmad, H. (2015). Learning to read Arabic syllabically versus alphabetically: psycholinguistics, grammatological and pedagogical aspects. Ph.D. dissertation, University of Haifa.

Aram, D. (2005). Continuity in children's literacy achievements: A longitudinal perspective from kindergarten to school. *First Language, 3*, 259–289.

Aram, D. & Levin, I. (2004). The role of maternal mediation of writing to kindergartners in promoting literacy achievements in second grade: A longitudinal perspective. *Reading and Writing, 17*, 387–409.

Bar-Kochva, I. (2013). What are the underlying skills of silent reading acquisition? A developmental study from kindergarten to the 2nd grade. *Reading and Writing, 26*, 1417–1436.

Bar-Kochva, I. & Breznitz, Z. (2014). Reading scripts that differ in orthographic transparency: A within-participant-and-language investigation of underlying skills. *Journal of Experimental Child Psychology, 121*, 12–27.

Bar-On, A. (forthcoming). *kriya betzel hahomografia: haba'aya hi gam hapitaron* [Reading in the shadow of homography: The problem is the solution]. *Safa Ve'Oriyanut.* [In Hebrew]

Bar-On, A. & Ravid, D. (2011). Morphological analysis in learning to read psseudo-words in Hebrew. *Applied Psycholinguistics, 32*, 553–581.

Ben-Dror, I., Bentin, S. & Frost, R. (1995). Semantic, phonologic, and morphologic skills in reading disabled and normal children: Evidence from perception and production of spoken Hebrew. *Reading Research Quarterly, 30*, 876–893.

Bentin, S., Deutsch, A. & Liberman, I. Y. (1990). Syntactic competence and reading ability in children. *Journal of Experimental Child Psychology, 48*, 147–172.

Bentin, S. & Leshem, H. (1993). On the interaction of phonologic awareness and reading acquisition: It's a two-way street. *Psychological Science, 2*, 271–274.

Benuck, M. B. & Peverly, S. T. (2004). The effect of orthographic depth on reliance upon semantic context for oral reading in English and Hebrew. *Journal of Research in Reading, 27*, 281–299.

Berman, R. (1985). Acquisition of Hebrew. In D. I. Slobin (Ed.), *The cross-linguistic study of language acquisition*, Vol. I (pp. 255–371). Hillsdale, NJ: Lawrence Erlbaum.

(1997). Modern Hebrew. In R. Hetzron (Ed.), *The semitic languages* (pp. 312–333). Abingdon: Routledge.

(2003). Children's lexical innovations: Developmental perspectives on Hebrew verb-structure. In J. Shimron (Ed.), *Language processing and acquisition in languages of Semitic root-based morphology* (pp. 243–291). Amsterdam: John Benjamins.

Beveridge, M. E. L. & Bak, T. H. (2012). Beyond one-way streets: The interaction of phonology, morphology, and culture with orthography. *Behavioral and Brain Sciences, 35*, 18–19.

Breznitz, Z. (1997). Effects of accelerated reading rate on memory for text among dyslexic readers. *Journal of Educational Psychology, 89*, 289–297.

Chomsky, W. (1941). The history of our vowel-system in Hebrew. *The Jewish Quarterly Review, 32*, 27–49.

Cohen-Mimran, R. (2009). The contribution of language skills to reading fluency: A comparison of two orthographies for Hebrew. *Journal of Child Language, 36*, 657–672.

Daniels, P. T. (1990). Fundamentals of grammatology. *Journal of the American Oriental Society, 110*, 727–731.

Daniels, P. T. & Bright, W. (Eds.) (1996). *The world's writing systems*. New York: Oxford University Press.

Diringer, D. (1948). *The Alphabet: A Key to the History of Mankind*. London: Thames & Hudson.

Evans, N. & Levinson, S. C. (2009). The myth of language universals: Language diversity and its importance for cognitive science. *Behavioral and Brain Science 32*, 429–492.

Feitelson, D. (1988). *Facts and fads in beginning reading*. New York: Ablex.

Frost, R. (2012). Towards a universal model of reading. *Behavioral and Brain Sciences, 35*, 263–279.

Frost, R., Siegelman, N., Narkiss, A. & Afek, L. (2013). What predicts successful literacy acquisition in a second language? *Psychological Science, 24*, 1243–1252.

Geva, E. (2008). Facets of metalinguistic awareness related to reading development in Hebrew: Evidence from monolingual and bilingual children. In K. Koda & A. Zehler (Eds.), *Learning to read across languages* (pp. 154–187). New York: Routledge.

Gillis, S. & Ravid, D. (2006). Typological effects on spelling development: A crosslinguistic study of Hebrew and Dutch. *Journal of Child Language, 33*, 621–659.

Glinert, L. H. (1994). Israeli Hebrew. In R. E. Asher & J. M. Y. Simpson (Eds.), *The encyclopedia of language and linguistics* (pp. 1538–1541). Oxford: Pergamon Press.

Gnanadesikan, A. E. (2009). *The writing revolution: Cuneiform to the internet*. Chichester: Wiley-Blackwell.

Goerwitz, R. L. (1996). The Jewish scripts. In P. T. Daniels & W. Bright (Eds.), *The world's writing systems* (pp. 489–494). New York: Oxford University Press.

Gur, T. (2005). Reading Hebrew vowel diacritics: A longitudinal investigation from Grade 1 to Grade 3. Unpublished doctoral dissertation, University of Haifa.

Henrich, J., Heine, S. J. & Norenzayan, A. (2010). The weirdest people in the world? *Behavioural and Brain Sciences, 33*, 61–135.

Hetzron, R. (1987). Hebrew. In B. Comrie (Ed.), *The world's major languages* (pp. 578–593). London: Croom Helm.

Hoberman, R. D. & Aronoff, M. (2003). The verb morphology of Maltese: From Semitic to Romance. In J. Shimron (Ed.), *Language processing and acquisition in languages of Sematic, root-based, morphology* (pp. 61–78). Amsterdam: John Benjamins.

Katzir, T., Schiff, R. & Kim, Y.-S. (2012). The effects of orthographic consistency on reading development: A within and between cross-linguistic study of fluency and accuracy among fourth grade English- and Hebrew-speaking children. *Learning and Individual Differences, 22*, 673–679.

Korat, O. (2005). Contextual and non-contextual knowledge in emergent literacy development: A comparison between children from low SES and middle SES communities. *Early Childhood Research Quarterly, 20*, 220–238.

Lamm, O. & Epstein, R. (1994). Dichotic listening performance under high and low lexical work load in subtypes of developmental dyslexia. *Neuropsychologia, 32*, 757–785.

Lapidot, M., Tubul, G. & Wohl, A. (1995–1996). Mivchan eranut fonologit kekli nibui lerechishat hakri'a [A test of phonological awareness as a predictor of reading acquisition]. *Chelkat Lashon, 19–20*, 169–188. [In Hebrew]

Leikin, M., Schwartz, M. & Tobin, Y. (2011). *Current issues in bilingualism: Cognitive and socio-linguistic perspectives.* Dordrecht: Springer.

Levin I. (1997). Hitpatxut haktiva hamukdemet be'Ivrit [The early development of writing in Hebrew]. In J. Shimron (Ed.), *Mexkarim bepsixologia shel halashon beyisrael: rexishat lashon, kriya vektiva* [Studies in the psychology of language in Israel: Language acquisition, reading and writing]. Jerusalem: Magnus. [In Hebrew]

Levin, I., Aram, D., Tolchinsky, L. & McBride, C. (2013). Maternal mediation of writing and children's early spelling and reading: The Semitic abjad versus the European alphabet. *Writing Systems Research, 5*, 134–155.

Levin, I., Korat, O. & Amsterdamer, P. (1996). Emergent writing among kindergartners: Cross-linguistic commonalities and Hebrew-specific issues. In G. Rijlaarsdam, H. van der Bergh & M. Couzijn (Eds.), *Current trends in writing research: Theories, models and methodology* (pp. 398–419). Amsterdam University Press.

McCarthy, J. J. (1981). A prosodic theory of nonconcatenative morphology. *Linguistic Inquiry, 12*, 373–418.

Miller, P. (2009). Learning in a world of silence: Insight from 30 years of work and research with deaf and hard of hearing children. In D. Aram & O. Korat (Eds.), *Literacy and language: Interactions, bilingualism, and difficulties* (pp. 471–491). Jerusalem: Maganes Press.

Naveh, J. (1982). *Early history of the alphabet: An introduction to West Semitic epigraphy and palaeography.* Jerusalem: Magnes Press.

Perfetti, C. A. (1985). *Reading ability.* New York: Oxford University Press.

(2007). Reading ability: Lexical quality to comprehension. *Scientific Studies of Reading, 11*, 357–383.

Perfetti, C. A. & Hart, L. (2002). The lexical quality hypothesis. In L. Verhoeven, C. Elbro & P. Reitsma (Eds.), *Precursors of functional literacy* (pp. 189–213). Amsterdam: John Benjamins.

Ravid, D. (1990). Internal structure constraints on new-word formation devices in Modern Hebrew. *Folia Linguistica, 24*, 289–346.

(1996). Accessing the mental lexicon: Evidence from incompatibility between representation of spoken and written morphology. *Linguistics, 34*, 1219–1246.

(2001). Learning to spell in Hebrew: Phonological and morphological factors. *Reading and Writing, 14*, 459–485.

(2012). *Spelling morphology.* New York: Springer.

Ravid, D. & Bar-On, A. (2005). Manipulating written Hebrew roots across development: The interface of semantic, phonological, and orthographic factors. *Reading and Writing, 18*, 231–256.

Ravid, D. & Kubi, E. (2003). What is a spelling error? The discrepancy between perception and reality. *Faits de Langues, 22*, 87–98.

Ravid, D. & Mashraki, Y. E. (2007). Prosodic reading, reading comprehension and morphological skills in Hebrew-speaking fourth graders. *Journal of Research in Reading, 30*, 140–150.

Ravid, D. & Schiff, R. (2006). Roots and patterns in Hebrew language development: Evidence from written morphological analogies. *Reading and Writing*, *19*, 789–818.

Ricketts, J., Nation, K. & Bishop, D. V. M. (2007). Vocabulary is important for some, but not all reading skills. *Scientific Studies of Reading*, *11*, 235–257.

Rogers, H. (1995). Optimal orthographies. In I. Taylor & D. R. Olson (Eds.), *Scripts and Literacy* (pp. 31–43). Dordrecht: Kluwer Academic Publishers.

Saiegh-Haddad, E. (2007). Epilinguistic and metalinguistic phonological awareness may be subject to different constraints: Evidence from Hebrew. *First Language*, *27*, 385–405.

Schiff, R., Katzir, T. & Shoshan, N. (2013). Reading accuracy and speed of vowelized and unvowelized scripts among dyslexic readers of Hebrew: The road not taken. *Annals of Dyslexia*, *63*, 171–185.

Schiff, R. & Lotem, M. (2011). Effects of phonological and morphological awareness on children's word reading development from two socioeconomic backgrounds. *First Language*, *31*, 139–163.

Schiff, R., Schwartz-Nahshon, S. & Nagar, R. (2011). Effect of phonological and morphological awareness on reading comprehension in Hebrew-speaking adolescents with reading disabilities. *Annals of Dyslexia*, *61*, 44–63.

Schwarzwald, O. R. (2002). *Modern Hebrew morphology*. Tel Aviv: Open University. [In Hebrew]

Shany, M., Bar-On, A. & Katzir, T. (2012). Reading different orthographic structures in the shallow-pointed Hebrew script: A cross-grade study in elementary school. *Reading and Writing*, *25*, 1217–1238.

Shany, M. & Breznitz, Z. (2011). Rate- and accuracy-disabled subtype profiles among adults with dyslexia in the Hebrew orthography. *Developmental Neuropsychology*, *37*, 889–913.

Shany, M. & Share, D. L. (2011). Subtypes of reading disability in a shallow orthography: A double dissociation between accuracy-disabled and rate-disabled reading in Hebrew. *Annals of Dyslexia*, *61*, 64–84.

Share, D. L. (2003). Dyslexia in Hebrew. In N. Goulandris (Ed.), *Dyslexia in different languages: Cross-linguistic comparisons* (pp. 208–234). London: Whurr.

(2008). On the Anglocentricities of current reading research and practice: The perils of over-reliance on an "outlier" orthography. *Psychological Bulletin*, *134*, 584–616.

(2012). Frost and fogs, or sunny skies? Orthography, reading, and misplaced optimalism. *Behavioral and Brain Sciences*, *35*, 45–46.

Share, D. L. & Blum, P. (2005). Syllable splitting among literate and pre-literate Hebrew-speakers. *Journal of Experimental Child Psychology*, *92*, 182–202.

Share, D. L. & Gur, T. (in preparation). When less is more: Declining code knowledge signals progress in reading in a Semitic abjad.

Share, D. L. & Levin, I. (1999). Learning to read and write in Hebrew. In M. Harris & G. Hatano (Eds.), *Learning to read and write* (pp. 89–111). Cambridge University Press.

Share, D. L. & Shalev, C. (2004). Self-teaching in normal and disabled readers. *Reading and Writing*, *17*, 1–31.

Shatil, E. & Share, D. L. (2003). Cognitive antecedents of early reading ability: A test of the modularity hypothesis. *Journal of Experimental Child Psychology*, *86*, 1–31.

Shatil, E., Share, D. L. & Levin, I. (2000). On the contribution of kindergarten writing to Grade 1 literacy: A longitudinal study in Hebrew. *Applied Psycholinguistics*, *28*, 1–25.

Shimron, J. (1993). The role of vowels in reading: A review of studies of English and Hebrew. *Psychological Bulletin*, *114*, 52–67.

Shimron, J. & Sivan, T. (1994). Reading proficiency and orthography: Evidence from Hebrew and English. *Language Learning*, *44*, 5–27.

Stanovich, K. E. (1986). Matthew effects in reading: Some consequences of individual differences in the acquisition of literacy. *Reading Research Quarterly*, *21*, 360–406.

(2000). *Progress in understanding reading: Scientific foundations and new frontiers.* New York: Guilford.

Tolchinsky, L., Levin, I., Aram, D. & McBride-Chang, C. (2012). Building literacy in alphabetic, abjad and morphosyllabic systems. *Reading and Writing*, *25*, 1573–1598.

Tolchinsky, L. & Teberosky, A. (1998). The development of word segmentation and writing in two scripts. *Cognitive Development*, *13*, 1–14.

Tunmer, W. E. & Chapman, J. W. (2012). Does the set for variability mediate the influence of vocabulary knowledged on the development of word recognition skills. *Scientific Studies of Reading*, *16*, 122–140.

8 Learning to Read Greek

Athanassios Protopapas

8.1 Introduction

8.1.1 Greek and Its Orthography

Greek (in Greek: *ελληνικά* /elinika/) is spoken by an estimated total of 13 million people worldwide, including in Greece, where it is the national language, and by expatriates in many other countries.[1] It is written with the Greek script, a "true alphabet" from its beginnings many centuries ago (*c.* 740 BCE; Threatte, 1996), which was derived from the Phoenician script (Swiggers, 1996; Voutyras, 2001) and adopted for the ancient Greek dialects in archaic times (Karali, 2001).

8.1.2 Synchronic and Diachronic Characterization

Standard Modern Greek is a descendant of Koine, the language of the Hellenistic era, lying on the Greek branch of the Indoeuropean family of languages (Tonnet, 1995). Attempts to "purify" the language toward ancient attic resulted in *katharevousa* forms, leading to problems of diglossia in recent centuries. Today the spoken language has settled near the southern regional dialects of the Ottoman and modern era, enriched with a wealth of loan words and minor grammatical innovations. Modern "demotic" Greek (with elements of katharevousa) was officially adopted by the Greek state in 1976 (Holton, Mackridge & Philippaki-Warburton, 1997). See Christidis (2001, 2007) for a history of the ancient language up to the Hellenistic years, Tonnet (1995) for a discussion of the trajectory from the Koine toward the modern language, Petrounias (2002) for recent developments, and Mackridge (2009) for the associated sociolinguistic saga.

Very briefly, through the millennia since the classical era Greek has become more analytic, with fewer grammatical types and classes and somewhat more restrictive word order. The phonetic repertoire has expanded in consonants and diminished in vowels. Orthography has not followed the phonetic evolution,

---

[1] See www.ethnologue.com/language/ell (Lewis, Simons & Fennig, 2016).

resulting in a system rife with spelling ambiguities, as phonetic shifts and neutralizations have taken place in the context of relatively stable spelling. As a result, there are several ways to spell certain phonemes, permitting lexical disambiguation through complex spelling patterns.

A number of reforms and attempted reforms of the spoken and written language have punctuated the evolution of Greek from ancient through modern times (Petrounias, 2002; Tonnet, 1995). The adoption of demotic in 1976 was followed by a spelling reform in 1981 in which Hellenistic breathing and pitch accent marks no longer relevant in contemporary pronunciation were officially abolished, replacing *polytonic* (multi-accent) spelling with the *monotonic* (single-accent) system, in which only a single stress diacritic remained. Additional reforms are still proposed, on a variety of grounds, or said to be imminent (e.g., Tzakosta, 2012; Tzakosta, Christianou & Kalisperaki, 2011).

8.1.3   Literacy and Schooling

The Greek educational system is highly centralized via a compulsory national curriculum that applies to every accredited school, public or private. The national curriculum lists detailed educational goals and methods along a specific progression of instructional units through preschool, elementary, and secondary education. By law, all children begin Grade 1 in the year of their sixth birthday. Pre-kindergarten attendance (at 4 years of age) is optional but starting with kindergarten, at 5 years of age, attendance is mandatory through Grade 9 (third grade of junior high school), for a total of ten years of compulsory education (K-9). Primary school attendance has been compulsory since the early days of the modern Greek state, but actual attendance in the 1830s was very low and limited to two to three years (Hadjistefanidis, 1990). It has reached 97% in recent decades, with large disparities between major cities and rural areas (Ministry of National Education and Religious Affairs, 1995). Compulsory attendance of kindergarten for all children was introduced in the 2007–2008 school year (Manolitsis & Tafa, 2011); prior to that kindergarten attendance was about 50% (Ministry of National Education and Religious Affairs, 1995).

As described by Aidinis (2012), the kindergarten language arts curriculum includes early literacy activities capitalizing on home experience to develop skills, knowledge, and concepts. Children are encouraged to read and write and are presented with a variety of texts, contexts, and opportunities, without systematic teaching of phonics. Manolitsis and Tafa (2011) relate the current emergent literacy activities to the 2003 reform of the National Kindergarten Curriculum, which put emphasis on alphabet letters and phonological awareness without teaching children to read and write.

In Grade 1, children are taught to read using systematic phonics intruction through an *analytic-synthetic* method (Aidinis, 2012) with syllabic and supra-syllabic elements. This includes teaching of letter shapes and sounds, articulation and blending drills, and emphasis on decoding at the single-word level. Children begin to write texts by the second semester of Grade 1. Most children can read simple words by February of Grade 1. Long and complex words and pseudowords are mastered by the majority of children by Grade 3 or earlier.

The overall instruction approach is evidently effective: Compared with Cypriot children,[2] who were taught using a whole-language approach, Greek children in Grade 1 were significantly better in pseudoword decoding and other phonological and cognitive tasks (but not in real word reading accuracy) (Papadopoulos, 2001).

8.2   Description of Greek and Its Written Forms

Greek is a language with average-size vowel and consonant inventories, complex syllable structure, and lexical stress. It is strongly suffixing and fusional with respect to inflectional morphemes, SVO/VSO with respect to the dominant order of subject, verb, and object, and uses prepositions (preceding the noun phrase) (Dryer, 2011).

8.2.1   Linguistic System

8.2.1.1 Phonology   The Greek phonemic inventory includes five vowels (see Table 8.1). There is no consensus as far as consonants are concerned: Their number ranges from 15 to 31 depending on the theoretical and empirical criteria applied by different researchers (cf. Holton et al. 1997; Holton, Mackridge, Philippaki-Warburton & Spyropoulos, 2012; Klairis & Babiniotis, 2004; Mennen & Okalidou, 2006; Okalidou, 2008; see Arvaniti, 2007; and Petrounias, 2002, for extensive discussions). It seems that twenty-six consonants (see Table 8.1) are phonetically distinctive and require individual treatment in artificial speech synthesis (Bakamidis & Carayannis, 1987) and in tracking phonological development (e.g., Mennen & Okalidou, 2006). This set

---

[2] Studies in both Greece and Cyprus are included in this chapter. Standard Greek is the language spoken throughout Greece at home, with minor dialectic variation, and the sole language of administration and education. In contrast, in Cyprus the home language is Cypriot Greek, a dialect with no standardized or written form, but the language of administration and education is very similar to standard Greek, in a situation of diglossia (Hadjioannou, Tsiplakou & Kappler, 2011). There are differences between standard and Cypriot Greek in most linguistic domains, and the two dialects are not entirely mutually intelligible (see discussion and references in Arvaniti, 2006, 2010). Although many phonological awareness tasks may be largely equivalent when used in Greece and Cyprus, it might be kept in mind that Cypriot children are taught and tested in a nonnative linguistic system.

Table 8.1 *Greek phonemic inventory with 26 consonants and 5 vowels*

b	d	ɟ	g	p	t	c	k	v	ð	z	j	ʝ	f	θ	s	ç	x	m	n	ɲ	l	ʎ	r	ts	dz
a	e	i	o	u																					

includes six palatal consonants (Petrounias, 2002) and two affricates (Tzakosta & Vis, 2009) and is most likely the relevant inventory for the child becoming phonologically aware.[3]

Greek has relatively few monosyllables, most of which are closed-class (grammatical) words or otherwise atypical (e.g., recent loans from English, acronyms and abbreviations). Mean word length is 5.4 letters, 5.0 phonemes, 2.4 syllables, by token count (Protopapas, Tzakosta, Chalamandaris & Tsiakoulis, 2012). With a few exceptions, content words are multisyllabic and bear lexical stress. A relative majority (28%) of all words is stressed on the penultimate syllable (Protopapas, 2006). Syllables are predominantly open (estimated at 86%; with CV accounting for 56% and V for 17%; Protopapas, Tzakosta, et al., 2012) with only a few codas permitted, mainly /n/ and /s/. A variety of complex onset clusters are allowed (Holton et al., 1997), ranging on a continuum of acceptability (Tzakosta & Karra, 2011), with two or three consonants being relatively common (estimated at 15% of syllable tokens). A corpus-based analysis suggests that approximately 900 syllables account for 99% of all syllable tokens, whereas the total number of different syllables appearing at least once in the corpus is less than 2,000.

8.2.1.2 Inflectional Morphology   Greek is characterized by an extensive system of inflectional morphology. Nouns and adjectives are inflected for gender, number, and case. There are three genders (masculine, feminine, and neuter, for adjectives; each noun belongs to a single gender), two numbers (singular and plural), and four cases (nominative, genitive, accusative, and vocative). Some of the corresponding inflectional suffixes are phonologically identical (homonymous). Masculine nouns and adjectives have up to seven distinct forms (suffixes), whereas feminine and neuter ones have only four.

Verb forms include a stem and an inflectional ending, both of which may be simple or complex (Ralli, 2003). An *augment* prefix is added to certain past tense forms. Verb inflections involve stem changes, suffixes, and a variety of particles indicating moods and modalities. There is a basic set of forty-eight word forms for each verb, twenty-four for each of two voices (active and non-active), including two aspects (perfective and imperfective), two tenses (past and non-past), two numbers, and three persons. In addition, there are up to four imperative forms for each voice. These word forms are combined with particles and auxiliaries to form the complete structure of verb types (see Holton et al., 1997, 2012; and Klairis & Babiniotis, 2004, for comprehensive descriptions). Homonymy among verb forms is very limited.

---

[3] In addition, the velar nasal /ŋ/, though nondistinctive, is associated with specific orthographic patterns and appears in transparency analyses.

Distinct inflectional classes (verb conjugations and nominal declensions) are recognized both in verbs and in nouns/adjectives. Ralli (2003, 2005) postulates eight general noun declensions, not distinguished by gender, whereas Holton et al. (1997, 2012) list more than twenty noun classes, classified by gender, and twelve adjective classes, plus variants and exceptions. Two major verb conjugations are generally recognized. Stem variation is present in both verbs and nouns/adjectives, with different *allomorph* stems used in different contexts (e.g., perfective vs. imperfective aspect, for verbs, and singular vs. plural, for nouns; Ralli, 2003).

8.2.1.3 Word Formation Processes   Word formation in Greek includes systematic derivational processes, especially for nouns (based on verb stems) and adjectives (based on verb and noun stems). A variety of derivational suffixes has been described in the literature (Ralli, 2003), ranging from one to three syllables long. There is a much richer variety (an order of magnitude) of derivational suffixes producing nouns and adjectives, compared to verbs (cf. the tables of suffixes in Papanastasiou, 2008, pp. 303–317, or Ralli, 2005, pp. 147–153). Prefixation, both with bound and free morphemes, is also extensive in Greek and produces a variety of verbs, nouns, and adjectives (Papanastasiou, 2008; Ralli, 2003). Derivational affixes often carry their specific stress pattern, systematically affecting derived words (Revithiadou, 1999).

Compounding is a highly productive process in Greek whereby new adjectives, nouns, and verbs can be created from existing stems and words (Ralli, 2005; including bound stems appearing only in compounds; Ralli, 2003). The semantics of compounds may be transparent or noncompositional. Stress rules apply in compound formation; moreover, a linking vowel is inserted between the two constituents under certain morphophonological conditions. See Ralli (2003, 2005) for more information.

8.2.2   Writing System

8.2.2.1 Script and Punctuation   Modern Greek uses twenty-four letters, which come in uppercase and lowercase variants, plus a lowercase-only variant for word-final sigma (see Table 8.2). Seven letters correspond to vowels in isolation, namely ‹α, ε, η, ι, ο, υ, ω›. In lowercase, stress is marked on the vowel of the stressed syllable with an acute accent. A diaeresis diacritic is used to indicate that an iota or upsilon does not constitute a digraph with the preceding letter but stands on its own (e.g., ‹εϊ›, ‹αϋ›; also on uppercase: ‹Ϊ›, ‹Ϋ›; combined with stress: ‹ΐ›, ‹ΰ›).

Greek punctuation is similar to that of other European languages with the exception of the semicolon (;) which is used as a question mark, while *ano*

Table 8.2 Modern Greek: 24 letters, in uppercase and lowercase variants

Α	Β	Γ	Δ	Ε	Ζ	Η	Θ	Ι	Κ	Λ	Μ	Ν	Ξ	Ο	Π	Ρ	Σ	Τ	Υ	Φ	Χ	Ψ	Ω
α	β	γ	δ	ε	ζ	η	θ	ι	κ	λ	μ	ν	ξ	ο	π	ρ	σ ς	τ	υ	φ	χ	ψ	ω

teleia (the upper dot of the colon) plays the role of the semicolon. Period, comma, exclamation point, parentheses, and apostrophe have a similar shape and function to their English equivalents. Quotation marks appear as double angle brackets (« »). The hyphen is used to break words at the end of a line. It also appears in certain multi-word compounds though not as extensively as in English. For more details, examples, and additional rare symbols and uses, see Papanastasiou (2008, chapter 13).

8.2.2.2 Orthography   Letters and letter combinations correspond to phonemes in a largely systematic manner. Petrounias (2002) described a set of mappings allowing graphophonemic and phonographemic transcription. A "rule" system derived from these mappings achieves word-level regularity of reading around 95% (Protopapas & Vlahou, 2009), indicating that phonemes can be determined from letter sequences in the great majority of cases. There is no comparable estimate of spelling regularity.

Greek orthographic transparency is convenient to analyze because the string of phonemes making up each word corresponds to a string of letters or contiguous letter groups in the same order without gaps or jumps. Every orthographic string can be segmented into phoneme-size chunks, termed *graphemes*, when the corresponding phoneme string is known. The consistency of Greek orthography has been calculated at about 95% for reading (i.e., 95% of individual grapheme tokens map to their most frequent phoneme) and about 80% for spelling. There are 84 graphemes in a total of 118 graphophonemic mappings. See Protopapas and Vlahou (2009) for tables of mappings and frequencies.

Of the eighty-four graphemes, thirty-six consist of a single letter and cumulatively account for 91.1% of phoneme tokens, thirty-seven are composed of two letters (digraphs) and account for 8.9%, and eleven are three letters long and account for only 0.01%. Thus the great majority of mappings involve single letters to single phonemes or vice versa, even though not all of them are either consistent or predictable.

Here are a few frequent word examples: *λέξη* →/leksi/ 'word'; *κάτι* →/kati/ 'something'; *και* →/ce/ 'and'; *είναι* →/ine/ 'is'; *γιατί* →/jati/ 'why'; *πολύ* →/poli/ 'much'; *αυτά* →/afta/ 'these'; *παιδιά* →/peðja/ 'children'; *μου* →/mu/ 'my'; *μπορείς* →/boris/ 'you can'. These spelling patterns are not uncommon and exemplify many features of the Greek orthographic system, including mostly single-letter graphemes and a variety of complexities and inconsistencies. For example, /b/ is spelled with the digraph ⟨μπ⟩, ⟨κ⟩ corresponds to both /k/ and /c/ in different contexts, ⟨ξ⟩ spells the phoneme pair /ks/, both ⟨γι⟩ and ⟨ι⟩ (and other graphemes) can map to /j/, /e/ can be spelled with ⟨ε⟩ or ⟨αι⟩, /i/ can be spelled with ⟨η⟩, ⟨ι⟩, ⟨υ⟩, ⟨ει⟩ (and other digraphs), and ⟨υ⟩ can map to the vowel /i/ or the consonant /f/, or to /u/ as part of the ⟨ου⟩ digraph. Still, almost all mappings from letters to phonemes are predictable, even though the reverse mappings (from phonemes to letters) are less so.

In addition to these complexities, there is a genuinely ambiguous orthographic pattern, which occurs in every case of a consonant letter followed by a letter or letter sequence that can spell /i/ followed by a vowel. This *CiV* (consonant-i-vowel) pattern occurs in an estimated 7% of word tokens (18% of types; Protopapas & Vlahou, 2009). In every such case there are two possible readings: one that includes the /i/ phoneme and one without /i/. For example, the letter string ‹δια› can spell the single syllable /ðja/ (as in *σανίδια* /sa.ni.ðja/ 'planks') and the two-syllable string /ði.a/ (as in *σακίδια* /sa.ci.ði.a/ 'backpacks'). In real words the ambiguity is resolved lexically because readers know which of the two readings corresponds to a word. In rare cases both readings are words, constituting homographs. None of the two alternatives is irregular, as both are used productively in pseudoword reading (Protopapas & Nomikou, 2009).

The diacritic placed on the vowel of the stressed syllable is obligatory on every word with two or more syllables. It is not allowed on monosyllables except in a few prescribed cases. This makes it perfectly regular for the speller but is sometimes at odds with phonological stress (Petrounias, 2002). The stress diacritic resolves ambiguities between minimal stress pairs, such as *μέτρο* 'meter' – *μετρό* 'metro'. However, the necessity of the diacritic for lexical disambiguation has been estimated at less than 1% and possibly well below that taking context into account (Protopapas, 2006).

Morphology has extensive orthographic consequences insofar as derivational and grammatical suffixes are associated with specific spellings, which also serve to disambiguate homonyms. For example, in a certain class of adjectives, singular feminine nominative and accusative both end in /i/, like plural masculine nominative and vocative, but the singular suffixes are spelled with ‹η› whereas the plural ones are spelled with ‹οι›. Similarly, some verb suffixes are distinguished orthographically. For example, a final /e/ is found in several forms but is spelled with ‹ε› in some cases and ‹αι› in others. Thus homonymy and partial homography are not completely overlapping. Knowledge of the inflectional type is often required for the correct spelling of adjective, noun, and verb suffixes.

8.2.3   Conclusion

The complexities of Greek spelling are a consequence of the phonetic evolution of the spoken language through the centuries. As the vowel inventory has diminished, distinctions have been neutralized. Therefore, letters and letter combinations used to denote different vowels or diphthongs in ancient Greek are now used as alternative spellings for the same vowel. In contrast, the consonant repertoire has expanded. As a result, there are not enough letters to spell all the modern consonants, necessitating digraphs and context-sensitive combinations. The neutralization of phonologically double consonants has left behind additional relics of "historic orthography" in the form of letter doubling lacking synchronic motivation.

The combination of these factors has resulted in a situation in which individual phonemes map onto more than one spelling pattern each. The reverse is less common insofar as most individual graphemes map onto a single phoneme. In other words, the sets of multiple alternative spelling patterns of different phonemes are largely mutually exclusive. Setting aside the issue of frank ambiguities (CiV), this situation makes reading highly predictable. As far as spelling is concerned, difficulties arise from having to choose from a set of alternatives, but the consequences of erroneous choices are phonologically neutral, that is, the word may be orthographically incorrect but remains phonologically as intended. Thus, the orthographic system makes it difficult to produce the correct spelling but easy to produce the intended phoneme string. The ease of learning to read accurately and the very low rate of phonological spelling errors, as documented below, are both consistent with these properties of the orthography.

8.3   Acquisition of Reading and Spelling in Greek

Learning to read and spell in Greek has been studied since the 1980s (see Porpodas, 1999, 2002) and continues at an increasing rate, driven primarily by the pragmatic needs of educators and observations on children manifesting severe and persistent difficulties.

8.3.1   Becoming Linguistically Aware

8.3.1.1 Phonological Development and Phonological Awareness   Greek children acquire most phonemes by the age of 4 years and 6 months. The full inventory is acquired by six years, including all two-element consonant clusters and most three-element clusters in word-initial position (Mennen & Okalidou, 2006; Papathanasiou, Dimitrakopoulou, Ntaountaki & Vasiliou, 2012).

Children become phonologically aware in preschool and by Grade 1 they are generally thought to exhibit adequate phonological processing. Precocious readers enter school with a phonological awareness advantage, which may dissipate by the end of Grade 2 (Papadopoulos, Kendeou, Ktisti & Fella, 2012; Tafa & Manolitsis, 2008; cf. Tafa & Manolitsis, 2012). Syllabic awareness appears earlier than phonemic awareness, but they subsequently develop in parallel (Papadopoulos, Kendeou & Spanoudis, 2012) and both predict reading independently (Aidinis & Nunes, 2001; Papadopoulos, Spanoudis & Kendeou, 2009). Studies have examined the sequence of phonological awareness skills over a wide combined age range (3 years and 10 months to Grade 3). Syllable segmentation and blending are among the easiest tasks, in which performance approaches ceiling by mid-kindergarten. Rhyme identification, syllable matching, and initial and final phoneme matching exceed floor performance in kindergarten and continue to improve in Grade 1. Phoneme segmentation, elision, and blending exhibit rapid development, from floor kindergarten performance to near ceiling by the end of Grade 1. Syllable and phoneme transposition do not approach ceiling before Grade 3 (Aidinis, 2007, 2012; Giannetopoulou, 2003; Papadopoulos, Kendeou & Spanoudis, 2012; Papadopoulos, Spanoudis & Kendeou, 2009).

The relative difficulty of these tasks may depend on specific properties of the materials. The aforementioned studies used short items, composed of mostly open syllables with simple onsets. When task demands are increased, using long pseudowords with consonant clusters, reliable performance differences in phoneme deletion can be detected in Grades 3 to 4 (Protopapas, Skaloumbakas & Bali, 2008) and, in children with reading difficulties, through secondary education (Anastasiou & Protopapas, 2015; Protopapas & Skaloumbakas, 2007).

The dimensionality of phonological awareness has received some research attention. One set of studies has resulted in a structure of three correlated factors distinguishing performance in *base level*, *epi-phonological*, and *meta-phonological* tasks (Aidinis, 2007, 2012). Other researchers have argued in favor of an overall unidimensional trajectory, augmented by nested factors accounting for residuals in phonemic and supraphonemic sensitivity skills (Papadopoulos, Kendeou & Spanoudis, 2012; Papadopoulos, Spanoudis & Kendeou, 2009).

8.3.1.2 Morphological Development and Morphological Awareness   Research in morphological development and awareness remains limited. It is generally thought that by the age of entering elementary education most children have mastered the inflectional paradigms of the language to a large extent, at least as far as the suffixes with orthographic consequences are concerned (i.e., case, gender, and number, for adjectives and nouns, and person and number, for verbs). Normally developing kindergarten children approach ceiling performance in the production of verb past tense and noun gender, number, and case (Mastropavlou, 2006), although persistent difficulties with verb aspectual formation and noun gender are observed in certain word classes with unusual properties (Stavrakaki & Clahsen, 2009; Varlokosta & Nerantzini, 2013, 2015). Thus, morphological acquisition is largely but not entirely completed by Grade 1.

The study of metamorphological skill is still in its infancy. Nunes, Aidinis, and Bryant (2006) published a battery of morphological awareness tasks and presented only their predictive power for spelling (see also Aidinis & Paraschou, 2004; Bryant, Nunes & Aidinis, 1999; Harris & Giannouli, 1999; but cf. Pittas & Nunes, 2014). Aidinis and Dalakli (2006) tested children with morphosyntactic tasks such as grammaticality judgment, word order reconstruction, and number/tense transposition. They found that performance increased from Grade 1 to Grade 2 but was still well below ceiling. This is interpreted as ongoing morphosyntactic development, considering that Grade 6 children approached ceiling on these tasks (Aidinis & Paraschou, 2004).

Several researchers have noted the potential importance of morphological awareness for the development of reading and spelling skills (but its unique contribution remains equivocal; cf. Pittas & Nunes, 2014; Rothou & Padeliadu, 2014). Morphological knowledge is sometimes surmised on the basis of postulating spelling strategies by qualitative analysis of children's spellings (e.g., Chliounaki & Bryant, 2002, 2007; Diakogiorgi, Baris & Valmas, 2005; Diamanti, Goulandris, Stuart & Campbell, 2014). In a related vein, Tsesmeli and Koutselaki (2013) found that semantic understanding of compounds is related to their correct spelling.

8.3.2   Development of Word Identification

Most Greek children enter school with some literacy background. By the end of kindergarten, children know on average about half of the letters of the alphabet (Aidinis, 2006; Dalakli & Aidinis, 2010; Manolitsis & Tafa, 2011). About a third know no letters and about a quarter know all of the letters (Aidinis, 2006). Children are more familiar with uppercase than lowercase letters and with letter sounds than letter names, consistent with the emphasis on letter sounds and lack of teaching letter names.

According to Dalakli and Aidinis (2010; as cited in Aidinis, 2012), 55% of children at the end of kindergarten (May) and 30% at the beginning of Grade 1 (September–October) cannot read any single words at all, whereas 28% and 25%, respectively, cannot write at all. About 16% of children at the end of kindergarten and 30% at the beginning of Grade 1 can read sentences fluently, whereas 17% and 35%, respectively, can write alphabetically correct texts.

8.3.2.1 Word Decoding Development   According to Porpodas (2001, 2002), Greek children do not go through an initial logographic stage but approach reading directly by an alphabetic process. Letter knowledge and phonological awareness at or prior to school entry predict later word and pseudoword reading (Georgiou, Manolitsis, Nurmi & Parrila, 2010; Georgiou, Torppa, Manolitsis, Lyytinen & Parrila, 2012; Harris & Giannouli, 1999; Mouzaki, Protopapas & Tsantoula, 2008; Papadimitriou & Vlachos, 2014), whereas home literacy environment does not (Manolitsis, Georgiou & Parrila, 2011). Phonemic awareness is concurrently correlated with word and pseudoword reading in the early grades (Porpodas, 1992, 1999), but its effects may diminish by Grade 3 (Porpodas, 2002; cf. Rothou & Padeliadu, 2014). Accurate phonological decoding (alphabetic reading) is observed before the end of Grade 1 (Porpodas, 1999, 2001), including children with difficulties (Porpodas, 2002). Although accuracy is not a major issue with reading difficulties (Nikolopoulos, Goulandris & Snowling, 2003), individual differences in accuracy persist through elementary grades, at least to Grade 7 (Protopapas, Simos, Sideridis & Mouzaki, 2012; Protopapas & Skaloumbakas, 2007; Protopapas et al., 2008).

Word accuracy and fluency develop rapidly throughout the elementary grades (see, e.g., tables for Grades 2 to 5 in Protopapas, Mouzaki, Sideridis, Kotsolakou & Simos, 2013; Protopapas, Sideridis, Mouzaki & Simos, 2007). Fluency follows an almost linear trajectory through Grades 2 to 6, with little divergence between the most and least fluent children (Protopapas, Parrila & Simos, 2016). Precocious readers enter school with a naming advantage and retain a fluency advantage through Grade 6 (Papadopoulos, Kendeou, et al., 2012; Tafa & Manolitsis, 2012). There is little evidence for a primarily sublexical (graphophonemic) mode of word recognition past the early stages; findings from a stress assignment study are consistent with effective sight-word reading by the end of Grade 2 (Protopapas & Gerakaki, 2009).

Reading fluency is concurrently and longitudinally predicted by rapid serial naming (digits, colors, and objects)[4] throughout the elementary grades. Strong concurrent correlations have been documented in Grades 1 to 6 (Antoniou & Patsiodimou, 2009; Georgiou, Papadopoulos & Kaizer, 2014; Georgiou, Parrila, Cui & Papadopoulos, 2013; Nikolopoulos, Goulandris, Hulme & Snowling, 2006; Protopapas, Altani & Georgiou, 2013), increasing somewhat in higher grades. Moderate to strong longitudinal correlations have been reported from kindergarten through Grade 10 (Georgiou, Manolitsis, et al., 2010; Georgiou, Papadopoulos, Fella & Parrila, 2012; Georgiou, Papadopoulos & Kaizer, 2014; Georgiou, Parrila & Papadopoulos, 2008; Georgiou, Torppa, et al., 2012; Nikolopoulos et al., 2006). Articulation time (i.e., the total duration of articulated items) is more strongly related to reading fluency than pause time (i.e., the silent intervals between items), in contrast to English and Chinese (Georgiou, Aro, Liao & Parrila, 2015; Georgiou, Parrila & Liao, 2008), and increasingly over time (Georgiou, Papadopoulos & Kaizer, 2014). It remains unclear whether the longitudinal contribution from rapid automatized naming

---

[4] The lack of teaching letter names and the exclusive focus on letter sounds prevents early assessment using rapid naming of letters because children cannot respond fluently with the letter names, as required for the task.

(RAN) to reading goes beyond the autoregressive effect (cf. Georgiou, Papadopoulos, Fella & Parrila, 2012; Nikolopoulos et al., 2006).

Despite long-standing expectations that words and pseudowords might index separate domains or aspects of readng skills, studies show that word and pseudoword reading performance lies along the same dimensions of accuracy and speed (Protopapas, Simos, et al., 2012; Protopapas & Skaloumbakas, 2007; Protopapas et al., 2008; but see Douklias, Masterson & Hanley, 2009, for a different opinion).

Processing of the stress diacritic has been studied from Grade 2 through adulthood. Despite explicit teaching in Grade 1, the diacritic is not fully adhered to, especially in the early grades (Protopapas & Gerakaki, 2009). This is rarely noticed in word reading, presumably because children recognize the words from the letter sequence and pronounce them based on their knowledge of the correct stress pattern. In contrast, in pseudoword reading, stress assignment errors (i.e., inconsistent with the diacritic) are prominent through Grade 7 (Protopapas, 2006; Protopapas & Gerakaki, 2009; Protopapas, Gerakaki & Alexandri, 2006). Highly proficient adult readers make very few stress assignment errors and are delayed when the diacritic is misplaced; however, they are not affected by its omission (Protopapas, Gerakaki & Alexandri, 2007).

8.3.2.2   Word Spelling Development   Five stages of spelling development are identified in Greek, including pre-alphabetic, partially alphabetic, fully alphabetic, transitional/morphographic, and fully developed or morpho-phonemic spelling (Aidinis, 2010a, 2012; Aidinis & Dalakli, 2006; Mouzaki, 2010a, 2010b). In each stage, a mixture of spelling strategies is employed, including invention, memory, analogy, and morphology (Aidinis, 2010a, 2012). Development of the morphological strategy is not yet fully acquired by Grade 6 (Aidinis, 2010b, 2010c). The developmental trajectory of spelling through Grades 2 to 6 exhibits evidence for divergence in performance between the highest- and lowest-performing children consistent with *Matthew effects* (Protopapas et al., 2014).

Children employ phonological recoding to spell as early as Grade 1, producing correct alphabetic spellings of words and pseudowords (Loizidou-Ieridou, Masterson & Hanley, 2010; Porpodas, 1999, 2001; Sarris & Porpodas, 2012). Mnemonic strategies for orthographic spelling are employed at the end of Grade 1 (Sarris & Porpodas, 2012). Spelling performance is longitudinally predicted by phonological awareness from kindergarten throughout elementary education (Diamanti, Ioannou, Mouzaki & Protopapas, 2012; Georgiou, Manolitsis, et al., 2010; Georgiou, Torppa, et al., 2012; Harris & Giannouli, 1999; Mouzaki et al., 2008; Nikolopoulos et al., 2006), even after controlling for earlier spelling skill. Spelling is also concurrently correlated with phonological and morphological awareness, controlling for age and verbal ability (Aidinis, 2010b; Aidinis & Dalakli, 2006; Aidinis & Nunes, 2001; Nunes et al., 2006; cf. Papadopoulos & Georgiou, 2010, for orthographic choice).

Phonological spelling errors, that is, errors resulting in words that would be pronounced differently from the intended word, are relatively rare in the general population and in children with difficulties (Aidinis & Paraschou, 2004; Andreou & Baseki, 2012; Loizidou-Ieridou et al., 2010; Nikolopoulos et al., 2003; Niolaki & Masterson, 2012; Protopapas, Fakou, Drakopoulou, Skaloumbakas & Mouzaki, 2013).

Nonphonological errors make up the bulk of error counts for children with typical and impaired spelling performance alike. These include grammatical errors, that is, misspelled inflections of adjective, noun, and verb suffixes, and orthographic errors, namely, misspellings of word stems. The relative proportion of grammatical and orthographic errors remains controversial (cf. Aidinis, 2010b, 2010c; Aidinis & Paraschou, 2004; Protopapas, Fakou, et al., 2013; Tzakosta et al., 2011). However, within-word comparisons are particularly challenging to interpret because the relative difficulty of different word parts cannot be independently controlled. Moreover, if there are several vowel phonemes in a stem that can be misspelled but only one in the inflectional suffix, then it is not surprising that a higher absolute number of errors will be observed on the stem than on the inflection. Notably, verb inflections, which are more numerous and less consistent, are spelled less accurately than noun inflections (Diamanti et al., 2014; Tzakosta & Dimtsa, 2012). Errors on derivational morphemes are observed with elevated relative frequency (Diamanti et al., 2014; Protopapas, Fakou, et al., 2013).

Morphological spelling, that is, spelling of grammatical suffixes, proceeds from indiscriminate early use of preferred spelling patterns to gradual enrichment of the orthographic repertoire with alternative spelling patterns. Alternative spellings are initially mixed but are eventually used in the grammatically appropriate situations (Bryant et al., 1999; Chliounaki & Bryant, 2002; Nunes et al., 2006). Learning of grammatical spelling patterns is associated with specific word experience rather than abstract grammatical knowledge (Chliounaki & Bryant, 2007). An explicit morphological strategy can be detected by Grade 3 in the spellings of grammatical suffixes and lexical stems, which remains incomplete and continues to develop throughout the elementary grades (Aidinis, 2010b, 2010c).

Spelling of the stress diacritic is an area of protracted development, as children make many errors, almost exclusively omissions. A nonnegligible proportion of children fail to use the diacritic entirely in their writing, including normally developing readers in the early elementary grades as well as children with reading difficulties through secondary education (Anastasiou & Protopapas, 2015; Protopapas, Fakou, et al., 2013).

8.3.2.3 Reading and Spelling Difficulties   Although dyslexia is officially recognized in Greek law as one form of specific learning disability, there is no official definition and no widespread standardized assessment practice; it is typically diagnosed on the basis of a discrepancy between intellectual ability and nonstandardized measures of reading and spelling achievement (Anastasiou & Polychronopoulou, 2009).

Greek children with dyslexia exhibit deficits in phonological awareness, RAN, word and pseudoword reading accuracy and speed, spelling, stress assignment, and verbal working memory, through primary and secondary education (Anastasiou & Protopapas, 2015; Constantinidou & Evripidou, 2012; Constantinidou & Stainthorp, 2009; Hatzidaki, Gianneli, Petrakis, Makaronas & Aslanides, 2011; Protopapas & Skaloumbakas, 2007, 2008; Protopapas et al., 2008). They also exhibit more and longer fixations in their eye movements (Hatzidaki et al., 2011) but no systematic deficits in auditory processing (Georgiou, Papadopoulos, Zarouna & Parrila, 2012; Georgiou, Protopapas, Papadopoulos, Skaloumbakas & Parrila, 2010; Papadopoulos, Georgiou & Parrila, 2012).

Timed measures of reading constitute the "crucial index" of difficulty in reading acquisition from the earliest stages of learning to read (Porpodas, 1999) throughout the middle elementary grades (Constantinidou & Stainthorp, 2009; Protopapas et al., 2008) and onto secondary education (Anastasiou & Protopapas, 2015; Protopapas & Skaloumbakas, 2007). Reading fluency, a measure combining accuracy and speed into a *words per minute* metric, is the single most reliable measure distinguishing children with reading difficulties from the general population (Protopapas & Skaloumbakas, 2008). This conflation of accuracy with speed muddles the dimensional structure because, when measured separately, accuracy and speed constitute distinct dimensions (cf. Protopapas, Simos, et al., 2012) on both of which children with reading difficulties can be significantly impaired (Mouzaki & Sideridis, 2007; Protopapas & Skaloumbakas, 2007; Protopapas et al., 2008), in a pattern also consistent with the double-deficit hypothesis (Papadopoulos, Georgiou & Kendeou, 2009; cf. Niolaki, Terzopoulos & Masterson, 2014, for a subtyping interpretation).

Spelling is typically the domain of greatest and most persistent impairment, with orthographic and grammatical errors being most common. Children with reading and spelling problems employ phonological recoding to spell by Grade 1, achieving only 25% accurate word spelling but 88% correct (i.e., phonologically acceptable) pseudoword spelling (Porpodas, 1999). The proportion of phonological spelling errors made by children with dyslexia in later grades is less than would be expected on the basis of their overall elevated error rate (Protopapas, Fakou, et al., 2013). Nevertheless, children with dyslexia make more phonological spelling errors than typically developing readers (Diamanti,

2006; Protopapas, Fakou, et al., 2013). With the exception of the stress diacritic, the spelling profile of reading-impaired children is indistinguishable from that of younger typically developing spellers matched in reading and phonological awareness, consistent with an interpretation of spelling problems in dyslexia as reflecting delay rather than deviance (Diamanti, 2006; Diamanti et al., 2014; Protopapas, Fakou, et al., 2013).

8.3.3   Reading Comprehension

The development of reading comprehension has been studied in children spanning a wide age range. Aidinis (2003, cited in Aidinis, 2012) found that passage comprehension was relatively poor in Grades 1 to 2 despite successful identification of individual words. Inadequate inference from multiple pieces of information was found even in Grade 6 (Hatziathanasiou & Aidinis, 2006, cited in Aidinis, 2012). No evidence for Matthew effects has been detected in reading comprehension, as lower-performing children seem more likely to catch up rather than fall behind through the elementary grades 2–6 (Protopapas, Sideridis, Mouzaki & Simos, 2011); and precocious readers fail to retain their comprehension advantage through Grade 6 (Tafa & Manolitsis, 2012).

8.3.3.1   Predictors of Reading Comprehension   Word reading accuracy, fluency, and spelling are concurrently correlated with comprehension in the general population (Padeliadou & Antoniou, 2014; Protopapas, Sideridis, et al., 2007). However, by Grade 3 fluency no longer has a unique concurrent contribution and neither accuracy nor fluency are unique longitudinal predictors (Protopapas, Mouzaki, et al., 2013; the situation may differ for children with reading difficulties, cf. Constantinidou & Stainthorp, 2009). Comprehension typically loads on a different factor from word reading accuracy and fluency, more closely related to cognitive ability tasks (Protopapas & Skaloumbakas, 2007, 2008; Protopapas et al., 2008).

The relationship between comprehension and word-level reading skills has also been examined in poor readers. Children in Grades 2 to 4 identified on the basis of their poor word reading skills achieved on average lower reading comprehension scores than unimpaired readers (Constantinidou & Stainthorp, 2009; Mouzaki & Sideridis, 2007). In other studies, no significant difference in reading comprehension was found between children with and without dyslexia matched in age and nonverbal ability in Grades 3 to 4 (Protopapas & Skaloumbakas, 2008; Protopapas et al., 2008) and in Grades 7 to 12 (Anastasiou & Protopapas, 2015). In contrast, Grade 7 children with dyslexia scored significantly lower on reading comprehension but the corresponding effect size was smaller than reading and spelling tests and similar to that of WISC (Wechsler Intelligence Scale for Children) subscales (Protopapas & Skaloumbakas, 2007, 2008).

These findings concern comprehension tests composed of brief passages followed by multiple-choice questions. Other forms of testing might have led to different results (cf. Maridaki-Kassotaki, 1998) as different reading comprehension tests make diverse demands on cognitive and language skills (Kendeou, Papadopoulos & Spanoudis, 2012; Papadopoulos, Kendeou & Shiakalli, 2014). For example, Papadopoulos, Georgiou, and Kendeou (2009) found impaired reading comprehension among Grade 1 children with a phonological deficit using sentence completion tests. Conversely, poor performance in three different reading comprehension tests in Grade 2 was associated with distinct profiles in cognitive, language, and reading performance in Grades K-2 (Papadopoulos, Kendeou & Shiakalli, 2014).

Reading comprehension is strongly correlated with listening comprehension, both concurrently and longitudinally, beyond autoregressive effects (Protopapas, Mouzaki, et al., 2013). The relationship may become stronger with age (Diakidoy, Stylianou, Karefillidou & Papageorgiou, 2005).

8.3.3.2 Word-Level Effects in Comprehending Text   Throughout the elementary grades, vocabulary is the strongest concurrent and longitudinal predictor of reading comprehension, even controlling for autoregressive effects (Protopapas, Mouzaki, et al., 2013; Papadimitriou & Vlachos, 2014; Protopapas, Sideridis, et al., 2007; Rothou & Padeliadu, 2014; but cf. Georgiou, Manolitsis, et al., 2010). Vocabulary shares most of the reading comprehension variance accounted for by *print-dependent* skills even though it is usually assessed orally (Protopapas, Mouzaki, et al., 2013). The relative separability of two constructs presumably related to future reading comprehension is evident already in kindergarten, but vocabulary aligns with precursors of print-dependent skills rather than listening comprehension (Kendeou, Papadopoulos & Kotzapoulou, 2013). Much more work will be required to elucidate the relationship of vocabulary with reading comprehension.

8.3.4   Conclusion

Early acquisition of reading and spelling Greek has been studied from a perspective of phonological awareness and application of the alphabetic principle. Because most children can read accurately very early on, researchers subsequently focused on the development and assessment of reading fluency. Spelling has received a lot of attention because it constitutes a domain of substantial difficulties for typically developing children and an area of protracted and persistent frustration and failure for children with reading problems. The systematic mappings from morphology to orthography have led a number of researchers to consider the role of morphological knowledge and awareness in learning to read and spell.

Comprehension has received comparatively less attention and therefore not much is yet known about how children learning to read and write Greek approach and process texts and how linguistic levels beyond morphology, such as syntax and pragmatics, may affect their understanding and creation of meaningful passages and communicative situations.

8.4   Discussion

8.4.1   Challenges in Learning to Read Greek

Greek has a relatively low orthographic complexity, with contiguous graphemes, most of them composed of single letters, mapping onto phonemes in a largely (but not entirely) predictable manner, despite a variety of inconsistencies and context dependencies. As a result, learning to read accurately is rapid as is the development of phoneme-level phonological awareness. Accuracy problems are barely detectable in the general population and not very substantial even in impaired readers. Failures or delays in learning to read primarily concern the development of fluency or, in the case of concomitant problems in oral language or general learning ability, may also concern passage comprehension.

Spelling is not as predictable as reading, but the alternative spellings of different phonemes do not overlap. As a result, phonologically accurate spelling does not present substantial challenges to Greek children. However, to attain the final stage in spelling development and produce consistently correct spellings is not so easy. Inflectional suffixes are frequent and apply to large classes of words, so most children learn to spell them correctly, eventually, presumably as they become familiar with the inflection system and its orthographic consequences. Derivational affixes are not as broadly applicable or as frequent as inflectional ones, but their spelling is every bit as arbitrary and lexically unmotivated as that of inflections. These present the greatest and most persistent challenges for the developing spellers.

At the other end, word stems are specific to particular word families but are lexically supported to the extent that one is familiar with a set of words and their associated meanings. In the absence of difficulties with visual orthographic memory, children learn to spell the majority of word stems correctly, although not before the late elementary grades. Words containing multiple challenges with conflicting solutions (e.g., μυρμήγκι /mirmiɟi/ 'ant', or ξυπνητήρι /ksipnitiri/ 'alarm clock', in both of which three different spellings of /i/ are found) are, naturally, most demanding and take a long time to secure an orthographic representation.

The orthographically salient inflectional morphology may also support processing of texts insofar as words display information about their syntactic roles on their suffixes and may therefore be grammatically deciphered without recourse to other phrase elements. This word-heavy approach, once mastered, may be beneficial for the assembly of sentence meaning if its implications for syntactic processing turn out to be facilitatory (order-light and perhaps memory-light; a hypothesis for psycholinguists to consider).

8.4.2   Implications for Instruction

At the word level the current system of instruction seems fully adequate. Letter sounds and phonological awareness activities in kindergarten, followed by an analytic-synthetic approach in Grade 1, seem to work well in supporting the great majority of children to progress rapidly in word decoding and identification, on to word fluency and passages. In this respect educators would be wise to leave well enough alone and steer clear of recurring calls to turn to whole-language approaches.

However, the point of reading is to understand the text. So it remains crucial to ensure that children engage with texts and acquire knowledge and pleasure from them. This includes both motivational and informational elements and may require additional instructional efforts to help children understand how to process texts, how to approach them in a systematic way, navigating text structure and monitoring their comprehension along the way. The elementary curriculum includes many passages and guidelines to engage them in the classroom, but the extent to which this is achieved in actual practice remains unknown and requires more research.

Spelling presents great challenges to learners and may benefit from additional steps toward systematic teaching. A solid foundation of phonological (alphabetic) spelling may be required before the complexity of the system can be fully processed. Explicit emphasis on morphology may help children understand that different parts of words depend on different kinds of information. Thus, explicit teaching of inflections, by relation to grammar; derivations, by relation to word formation processes; and stems, by relation to meanings, etymology, and word families, may provide additional support toward the development of strong orthographic skills.

Finally, a largely neglected aspect of written language development concerns writing. Researchers have focused on the development of word reading accuracy and fluency and how that eventually supports passage comprehension. But there is comparatively little theoretical or empirical work on children's communicative efforts in the form of text production. Children with impaired reading exhibit notable difficulties in putting in writing thoughts they can express orally. Perhaps future assessments of spelling fluency may help us understand the low-level foundation that is necessary for expressive written language, in conjunction with the high-level expressive oral language skills. This is a challenge for both researchers and educators.

8.5   Final Conclusion

The Greek orthography employs an alphabetic system with high feedforward (reading) consistency but substantial ambiguities in the feedback (spelling) direction. Learning to read Greek therefore presents a relatively minor challenge to the majority of schoolchildren, resulting in highly accurate word reading as early as Grade 1. In contrast, learning to spell posits significant demands that are never fully met for a substantial proportion of the general population. Difficulties in learning to read, expressed primarily in low reading fluency, are concurrently and longitudinally associated with poor phonological awareness and rapid naming performance. Imperfect or inadequate processing of the stress diacritic in reading and spelling may be related to its low utility for lexical access and disambiguation. Spelling difficulties are manifested in patterns of spelling errors that are common across levels of performance and can be accounted for by the properties of the orthographic system. Specifically, as several vowels have alternative spellings, either lexically or morphologically determined, spelling of vowels depends on word knowledge and morphological awareness and remains the most obvious domain of difficulty throughout elementary and secondary education. Further research is needed to elucidate the processes of reading comprehension and the limits imposed by word reading and lexical development.

Acknowledgments

I am grateful to several colleagues for helpful discussions, suggestions, and advice in their domain of expertise, and comments on the manuscript, including Athanasios Aidinis, Amalia Arvaniti, Vassiliki Diamanti, George Georgiou, Timothy Papadopoulos, Ilias Papathanasiou, Marina Tzakosta, and Spyridoula Varlokosta.

Preparation of this chapter was supported by the European Union (European Social Fund – ESF) and Greek national funds through the Operational Program "Education and Lifelong Learning" of the National Strategic Reference Framework (NSRF) – Research Funding Program THALIS-UOA-COGMEK: Cognitive Mechanisms in the Perception, Representation, and Organization of Knowledge.

References

Aidinis, A. (2006). Η ανάπτυξη της φωνολογικής ενημερότητας και η σχέση της με την απόκτηση του γραμματισμού [The development of phonological awareness and its relation to literacy acquisition]. *Hellenic Journal of Psychology (Psychological Society of Northern Greece)*, *4*, 17–42.

(2007). Δομή και ανάπτυξη της φωνολογικής ενημερότητας στην ελληνική γλώσσα [Structure and development of phonological awareness in the Greek language]. In M. Vlassopoulou, A. Giannetopoulou, M. Diamanti, L. Kirpotin, P. Levantis, K. Leftheris & Y. Sakellariou. (Eds.), *Γλωσσικές δυσκολίες και γραπτός λόγος στο πλαίσιο της σχολικής μάθησης* [Language difficulties and written language in the context of school learning] (pp. 223–244). Athens: Grigori.

(2010a). Στρατηγικές ορθογραφημένης γραφής και η ανάπτυξή τους στο δημοτικό σχολείο [Spelling strategies and their development in elementary school]. In A. Mouzaki & A. Protopapas (Eds.), *Ορθογραφία: Μάθηση και διαταραχές* [Spelling: Learning and disorders] (pp. 137–150). Athens: Gutenberg.

(2010b). Η ανάπτυξη των στρατηγικών ορθογραφημένης γραφής στα ελληνικά [The development of spelling strategies in Greek]. In A. Mouzaki & A. Protopapas (Eds.), *Ορθογραφία: Μάθηση και διαταραχές* [Spelling: Learning and disorders] (pp. 151–164). Athens: Gutenberg.

(2010c). Ο ρόλος της μορφολογικής γνώσης στη γραφή του θέματος των λέξεων [The role of morphological knowledge in the spelling of word stems]. In A. Mouzaki & A. Protopapas (Eds.), *Ορθογραφία: Μάθηση και διαταραχές* [Spelling: Learning and disorders] (pp. 165–177). Athens: Gutenberg.

(2012). *Γραμματισμός στην πρώτη σχολική ηλικία: Μια ψυχογλωσσολογική προσέγγιση* [Literacy in the early primary school age: A psycholinguistic approach]. Athens: Gutenberg.

Aidinis, A. & Dalakli, C. (2006). Από τη γραφή στην ορθογραφημένη γραφή: Η επίδραση της φωνολογικής και μορφοσυντακτικής επίγνωσης [From writing to spelling: the effects of phonological and morphosyntactic awareness]. In P. Papoulia-Tzelepi, A. Fterniati & K. Thivaios (Eds.), *Έρευνα και πρακτική του γραμματισμού στην ελληνική κοινωνία* [Literacy research and practice in the Greek society] (pp. 41–64). Athens: Ellinika Grammata.

Aidinis, A. & Nunes, T. (2001). The role of different levels of phonological awareness in the development of reading and spelling in Greek. *Reading and Writing*, *14*, 145–177.

Aidinis, A. & Paraschou, D. (2004). Ανάπτυξη της ορθογραφημένης γραφής στο δημοτικό σχολείο: Λάθη και στρατηγικές των παιδιών [Spelling development in elementary education: Children's errors and strategies]. In N. Makris & D. Desli (Eds.), *Η γνωστική ψυχολογία σήμερα: Γέφυρες για τη μελέτη της νόησης* [Cognitive psychology today: Bridges for the study of cognition] (pp. 245–252). Athens: Typothito/Dardanos.

Anastasiou, D. & Polychronopoulou, S. (2009). Identification and overidentification of specific learning disabilities (dyslexia) in Greece. *Learning Disability Quarterly*, *32*, 55–69.

Anastasiou, D. & Protopapas, A., (2015). Difficulties in lexical stress versus difficulties in segmental phonology among adolescents with dyslexia. *Scientific Studies of Reading*, *19*, 31–50.

Andreou, G. & Baseki, J. (2012). Phonological and spelling mistakes among dyslexic and non-dyslexic children learning two different languages: Greek vs. English. *Psychology, 3*, 595–600.

Antoniou, F. & Patsiodimou, A. (2009). Η σχέση μεταξύ της αυτόματης κατονομασίας και της αναγνωστικής αποκωδικοποίησης στην Α΄ τάξη του δημοτικού σχολείου [The relationship between automatized naming and reading decoding in elementary Grade 1]. In E. Tafa & G. Manolitsis (Eds.), *Αναδυόμενος γραμματισμός: Έρευνα και εφαρμογές* [Emergent literacy: Research and applications] (pp. 93–106). Athens: Pedio.

Arvaniti, A. (2006). Erasure as a means of maintaining diglossia in Cyprus. *San Diego Linguistic Papers, 2*, 25–38.

(2007). Greek phonetics: The state of the art. *Journal of Greek Linguistics, 8*, 97–208.

(2010). Linguistic practices in Cyprus and the emergence of Cypriot standard Greek. *Mediterranean Language Review, 17*, 15–45.

Bakamidis, S. & Carayannis, G. (1987). "Phonemia": A phoneme transcription system for speech synthesis in Modern Greek. *Speech Communication, 6*, 159–169.

Bryant, P., Nunes, T. & Aidinis, A. (1999). Different morphemes, same spelling problems: Cross-linguistic developmental studies. In M. Harris & G. Hatano (Eds.), *Learning to read and write: A cross-linguistic perspective* (pp. 112–133). Cambridge University Press.

Chliounaki, K. & Bryant, P. (2002). Construction and learning to spell. *Cognitive Development, 17*, 1489–1499.

(2007). How children learn about morphological spelling rules. *Child Development, 78*, 1360–1373.

Christidis, A.-F. (Ed.) (2001). *Ιστορία της ελληνικής γλώσσας: Από τις αρχές έως την ύστερη αρχαιότητα* [History of the Greek language: From the beginnings to late antiquity]. Institute of Modern Greek Studies, Aristotle University of Thessaloniki.

(Ed.) (2007). *A history of ancient Greek: From the beginnings to late antiquity.* Cambridge University Press.

Constantinidou, F. & Evripidou, C. (2012). Stimulus modality and working memory performance in Greek children with reading disabilities: Additional evidence for the pictorial superiority hypothesis. *Child Neuropsychology, 18*, 256–280.

Constantinidou, M. & Stainthorp, R. (2009). Phonological awareness and reading speed deficits in reading disabled Greek-speaking children. *Educational Psychology, 29*, 171–186.

Dalakli, C. & Aidinis, A. (2010). Από τον αναδυόμενο γραμματισμό στην πρώτη ανάγνωση και γραφή [From emergent literacy to early reading and writing]. In P. Papoulia-Tzelepi & A. Fterniati (Eds.), *Proceedings of the fifth International Conference on Literacy of the Hellenic Association for Language and Literacy* (pp. 109–131). University of Patras, and Hellenic Association for Language and Literacy.

Diakidoy, I. A. N., Stylianou, P., Karefillidou, C. & Papageorgiou, P. (2005). The relationship between listening and reading comprehension of different types of text at increasing grade levels. *Reading Psychology, 26*, 55–80.

Diakogiorgi, K., Baris, T. & Valmas, T. (2005). Ικανότητα χρήσης μορφολογικών στρατηγικών στην ορθογραφημένη γραφή από μαθητές της Α' τάξης του δημοτικού [First graders' ability to use morphological strategies in spelling]. *Psychology: The Journal of the Hellenic Psychological Society, 12*, 568–586.

Diamanti, V. (2006). Dyslexia and dysgraphia in Greek in relation to normal development: Cross-linguistic and longitudinal studies. Doctoral dissertation, Department of Human Communication Science, University College London.

Diamanti, V., Goulandris, N., Stuart, M. & Campbell, R. (2014). Spelling of derivational and inflectional suffixes by Greek-speaking children with and without dyslexia. *Reading and Writing, 27*, 337–358.

Diamanti, V., Ioannou, D., Mouzaki, A. & Protopapas, A. (2012, July). Predictors of spelling ability in Greek: Morphological vs. phonological awareness. Oral presentation at the nineteenth Annual Meeting of the Society for the Scientific Study of Reading, Montreal, Canada.

Douklias, S. D., Masterson, J. & Hanley, J. R. (2009). Surface and phonological developmental dyslexia in Greek. *Cognitive Neuropsychology, 26*, 705–723.

Dryer, M. S. (2011). Language page for Greek (Modern). In M. S. Dryer & M. Haspelmath (Eds.), *The world atlas of language structures online*. Munich: Max Planck Institute for Evolutionary Anthropology. Retrieved March 31, 2013, from http://wals.info/languoid/lect/wals_code_grk.

Georgiou, G. K., Aro, M., Liao, C.-H. & Parrila, R. (2015). The contribution of RAN pause time and articulation time to reading across languages: Evidence from a more representative sample of children. *Scientific Studies of Reading, 19*, 135–144 .

Georgiou, G. K., Manolitsis, G., Nurmi, J. E. & Parrila, R. (2010). Does task-focused versus task-avoidance behavior matter for literacy development in an orthographically consistent language? *Contemporary Educational Psychology, 35*, 1–10.

Georgiou, G. K., Papadopoulos, T. C., Fella, A. & Parrila, R. (2012). Rapid naming speed components and reading development in a consistent orthography. *Journal of Experimental Child Psychology, 112*, 1–17.

Georgiou, G. K., Papadopoulos, T. C. & Kaizer, E. L. (2014). Different RAN components relate to reading at different points in time. *Reading and Writing, 27*, 1379–1394. DOI: 10.1007/s11145-014-9496-1.

Georgiou, G. K., Papadopoulos, T. C., Zarouna, E. & Parrila, R. (2012). Are auditory and visual processing deficits related to developmental dyslexia? *Dyslexia, 18*, 110–129.

Georgiou, G. K., Parrila, R., Cui, Y. & Papadopoulos, T. C. (2013). Why is rapid automatized naming related to reading? *Journal of Experimental Child Psychology, 115*, 218–225.

Georgiou, G. K., Parrila, R. & Liao, C. H. (2008). Rapid naming speed and reading across languages that vary in orthographic consistency. *Reading and Writing, 21*, 885–903.

Georgiou, G. K., Parrila, R. & Papadopoulos, T. C. (2008). Predictors of word decoding and reading fluency across languages varying in orthographic consistency. *Journal of Educational Psychology, 100*, 566–580.

Georgiou, G. K., Protopapas, A., Papadopoulos, T. C., Skaloumbakas, C. & Parrila, R. (2010). Auditory temporal processing and dyslexia in an orthographically consistent language. *Cortex, 46*, 1330–1344.

Georgiou, G. K., Torppa, M., Manolitsis, G., Lyytinen, H. & Parrila, R. (2012). Longitudinal predictors of reading and spelling across languages varying in orthographic consistency. *Reading and Writing, 25,* 321–346.

Giannetopoulou, A. (2003). Από τον προφορικό στο γραπτό λόγο: Έρευνα για την ανάπτυξη της φωνολογικής επίγνωσης στην ελληνική γλώσσα [From oral to written language: Research on the development of phonological awareness in the Greek language]. In M. Glykas & G. Kalomoiris (Eds.), *Διαταραχές επικοινωνίας και λόγου* [Disorders of communication and language] (pp. 143–169). Athens: Ellinika Grammata.

Hadjioannou, X., Tsiplakou, S. & Kappler, M. (2011). Language policy and language planning in Cyprus. *Current Issues in Language Planning, 12,* 503–569.

Hadjistefanidis, T. D. (1990). *Ιστορία της νεοελληνικής εκπαίδευσης (1821–1986)* [History of modern Greek education (1821–1986)], 2nd edn. Athens: Papadimas.

Harris, M. & Giannouli, V. (1999). Learning to read and spell in Greek: The importance of letter knowledge and morphological awareness. In M. Harris and G. Hatano (Eds.), *Learning to read and write: A cross-linguistic perspective* (pp. 51–70). Cambridge University Press.

Hatzidaki, A., Gianneli, M., Petrakis, E., Makaronas, N. & Aslanides, I. M. (2011). Reading and visual processing in Greek dyslexic children: An eye-movement study. *Dyslexia, 17,* 85–104.

Holton, D., Mackridge, P. & Philippaki-Warburton, I. (1997). *Greek: A comprehensive grammar of the modern language.* London: Routledge.

Holton, D., Mackridge, P., Philippaki-Warburton, I. & Spyropoulos, V. (2012). *Greek: A comprehensive grammar,* 2nd edn. London: Routledge.

Karali, M. (2001). Συστήματα γραφής [Writing systems]. In A. F. Christidis (Ed.), *Ιστορία της ελληνικής γλώσσας: Από τις αρχές έως την ύστερη αρχαιότητα* [History of the Greek language: From the beginnings to late antiquity] (pp. 157–164). Institute of Modern Greek Studies, Aristotle University of Thessaloniki.

Kendeou, P., Papadopoulos, T. C. & Kotzapoulou, M. (2013). Evidence for the early emergence of the simple view of reading in a transparent orthography. *Reading and Writing, 26,* 189–204.

Kendeou, P., Papadopoulos, T. C. & Spanoudis, G. (2012). Processing demands of reading comprehension tests in young readers. *Learning and Instruction, 22,* 354–367.

Klairis, C. & Babiniotis, G. (2004). *Γραμματική της νέας ελληνικής: Δομολειτουργική-επικοινωνιακή* [Grammar of modern Greek: Structural/functional-communicative]. Athens: Ellinika Grammata.

Lewis, M. P., Simons, G. F. & Fennig, C. D. (Eds.) (2016). *Ethnologue: Languages of the World, Nineteenth edition.* Dallas, TX: SIL International. Online version: www.ethnologue.com.

Loizidou-Ieridou, N., Masterson, J. & Hanley, J. R. (2010). Spelling development in 6–11-year-old Greek-speaking Cypriot children. *Journal of Research in Reading, 33,* 247–262.

Mackridge, P. (2009). *Language and national identity in Greece, 1766–1976.* Oxford University Press.

Manolitsis, G., Georgiou, G. K. & Parrila, R. (2011). Revisiting the home literacy model of reading development in an orthographically consistent language. *Learning and Instruction, 21,* 496–505.

Manolitsis, G. & Tafa, E. (2011). Letter-name letter-sound and phonological awareness: Evidence from Greek-speaking kindergarten children. *Reading and Writing, 24,* 27–53.

Maridaki-Kassotaki, A. (1998). Ικανότητα βραχύχρονης συγκράτησης φωνολογικών πληροφοριών και επίδοση στην ανάγνωση: Μια προσπάθεια διερεύνησης της μεταξύ τους σχέσης [Evaluation of the relationship between phonological working memory and reading ability in Greak-speaking children]. *Psychology: The Journal of the Hellenic Psychological Society, 5,* 44–52.

Mastropavlou, M. (2006). The role of phonological salience and feature interpretability in the grammar of typically developing and language impaired children. Doctoral dissertation, Department of Theoretical and Applied Linguistics, Aristotle University of Thessaloniki.

Mennen, I. & Okalidou, A. (2006). Acquisition of Greek phonology: An overview. *QMUC Speech Science Research Centre Working Paper, WP-11.* Edinburgh: Queen Margaret University College.

Ministry of National Education and Religious Affairs (1995). *Επισκόπηση του ελληνικού εκπαιδευτικού συστήματος: Έκθεση για τον ΟΟΣΑ* [Review of the Greek Educational System: A report to the Organizations for Economic Co-Operation and Development]. J. Panaretos (Ed.). Retrieved from www.stat-at hens.aueb.gr/~jpan/oosa-background-report.html.

Mouzaki, A. (2010a). Αξιολόγηση της ορθογραφικής δεξιότητας [Assessment of spelling skill]. In A. Mouzaki & A. Protopapas (Eds.), *Ορθογραφία: Μάθηση και διαταραχές* [Spelling: Learning and disorders] (pp. 307–325). Athens: Gutenberg.

(2010b). Η ανάπτυξη της ορθογραφικής δεξιότητας [The development of spelling skill]. In A. Mouzaki & A. Protopapas (Eds.), *Ορθογραφία: Μάθηση και διαταραχές* [Spelling: Learning and disorders] (pp. 29–52). Athens: Gutenberg.

Mouzaki, A., Protopapas, A. & Tsantoula, D. (2008). Προσχολικοί δείκτες πρόγνωσης αναγνωστικών δεξιοτήτων στην Α΄ Δημοτικού [Preschool indices predicting the development of reading skills in 1st grade]. *Επιστήμες της Αγωγής [Education Sciences], 1,* 71–88.

Mouzaki, A. & Sideridis, G. D. (2007). Poor readers' profiles among Greek students of elementary school. *Hellenic Journal of Psychology, 4,* 205–232.

Nikolopoulos, D., Goulandris, N., Hulme, C. & Snowling, M. J. (2006). The cognitive bases of learning to read and spell in Greek: Evidence from a longitudinal study. *Journal of Experimental Child Psychology, 94,* 1–17.

Nikolopoulos, D., Goulandris, N. & Snowling, M. J. (2003). Developmental dyslexia in Greek. In N. Goulandris (Ed.), *Dyslexia in different languages: Cross-linguistic comparisons* (pp. 53–67). London: Whurr.

Niolaki, G. Z. & Masterson, J. (2012). Transfer effects in spelling from transparent Greek to opaque English in seven-to-ten-year-old children. *Bilingualism: Language and Cognition, 15,* 757–770.

Niolaki, G. Z., Terzopoulos, A. R. & Masterson, J. (2014). Varieties of developmental dyslexia in Greek children. *Writing Systems Research, 6,* 230–256.

Nunes, T., Aidinis, A. & Bryant, P. (2006). The acquisition of written morphology in Greek. In R. M. Joshi & P. G. Aaron (Eds.), *Handbook of orthography and literacy* (pp. 201–218). Mahwah, NJ: Lawrence Erlbaum.

Okalidou, A. (2008). Ομιλία: Ανάπτυξη και διαταραχές τεμαχιακής δομής [Speech: Development and disorders of segmental structure]. In D. Nikolopoulos (Ed.), *Γλωσσική ανάπτυξη και διαταραχές* [Language development and disorders] (pp. 175–229). Athens: Topos.

Padeliadou, S. & Antoniou, F. (2014). The relationship between reading comprehension, decoding, and fluency in Greek: A cross-sectional study. *Reading and Writing, 30*, 1–31.

Papadimitriou, A. M. & Vlachos, F. M. (2014). Which specific skills developing during preschool years predict the reading performance in the first and second grade of primary school? *Early Child Development and Care, 184*, 1706–1722.

Papadopoulos, T. C. (2001). Phonological and cognitive correlates of word-reading acquisition under two different instructional approaches. *European Journal of Psychology of Education, 16*, 549–568.

Papadopoulos, T. C. & Georgiou, G. K (2010). Ορθογραφική επεξεργασία και γνωσιακή ανάπτυξη [Orthographic processing and cognitive development]. In A. Mouzaki & A. Protopapas (Eds.), *Ορθογραφία: Μάθηση και διαταραχές [Spelling: Learning and disorders]* (pp. 53–66). Athens: Gutenberg.

Papadopoulos, T. C., Georgiou, G. K. & Kendeou, P. (2009). Investigating the double-deficit hypothesis in Greek: Findings from a longitudinal study. *Journal of Learning Disabilities, 42*, 528–547.

Papadopoulos, T. C., Georgiou, G. K. & Parrila, R. K. (2012). Low-level deficits in beat perception: Neither necessary nor sufficient for explaining developmental dyslexia in a consistent orthography. *Research in Developmental Disabilities, 33*, 1841–1856.

Papadopoulos, T. C., Kendeou, P., Ktisti, C. & Fella, A. (2012, July). Precocious readers: A cognitive or a linguistic advantage? Paper presented at the annual meeting of the Society for the Scientific Study of Reading, Montreal, Canada.

Papadopoulos, T. C., Kendeou, P. & Shiakalli, M. (2014). Reading comprehension tests and poor comprehenders: Do different processing demands mean different profiles? *Topics in Cognitive Psychology, 114*, 725–753.

Papadopoulos, T. C., Kendeou, P. & Spanoudis, G. (2012). Investigating the factor structure and measurement invariance of phonological abilities in a sufficiently transparent language. *Journal of Educational Psychology, 104*, 321–336.

Papadopoulos, T. C., Spanoudis, G. & Kendeou, P. (2009). The dimensionality of phonological abilities in Greek. *Reading Research Quarterly, 44*, 127–143.

Papanastasiou, G. (2008). *Νεοελληνική ορθογραφία: Ιστορία, θεωρία, εφαρμογή* [Modern Greek spelling: History, theory, application]. Institute of Modern Greek Studies, Aristotle University of Thessaloniki.

Papathanasiou, I., Dimitrakopoulou, I., Ntaountaki, M. & Vasiliou, K. (2012, November). Phonetic and phonological development in Greek children aged 4;0–6;0. Presented at the 2012 ASHA Convention, Atlanta, GA.

Petrounias, E. V. (2002). *Νεοελληνική γραμματική και συγκριτική (αντιπαραθετική) ανάλυση, τ. Α΄: Φωνητική και εισαγωγή στη φωνολογία* [Modern Greek grammar and comparative (contrastive) analysis, vol. I: Phonetics and introduction to phonology]. Thessaloniki: Ziti.

Pittas, E. & Nunes, T. (2014). The relation between morphological awareness and reading and spelling in Greek: a longitudinal study. *Reading and Writing, 27*, 1507–1527. DOI:10.1007/s11145-014-9503-6.

Porpodas, C. D. (1992). Η εκμάθηση της ανάγνωσης και ορθογραφίας σε σχέση με την ηλικία και τη φωνημική ενημερότητα [Learning to read and spell in relation to age and phonemic awareness]. *Psychology: The Journal of the Hellenic Psychological Society, 1*, 30–43.

(1999). Patterns of phonological and memory processing in beginning readers and spellers of Greek. *Journal of Learning Disabilities, 32*, 406–416.

(2001). Cognitive processes in first grade reading and spelling of Greek. *Psychology: The Journal of the Hellenic Psychological Society, 8*, 384–400.

(2002). Η ανάγνωση [Reading]. Patra: Author.

Protopapas, A. (2006). On the use and usefulness of stress diacritics in reading Greek. *Reading and Writing, 19*, 171–198.

Protopapas, A., Altani, A. & Georgiou, G. K. (2013). Development of serial processing in reading and rapid naming. *Journal of Experimental Child Psychology, 116*, 914–929.

Protopapas, A., Fakou, A., Drakopoulou, S., Skaloumbakas, C. & Mouzaki, A. (2013). What do spelling errors tell us? Classification and analysis of errors made by Greek schoolchildren with and without dyslexia. *Reading and Writing, 26* 615–646.

Protopapas, A. & Gerakaki, S. (2009). Development of processing stress diacritics in reading Greek. *Scientific Studies of Reading, 13*, 453–483.

Protopapas, A., Gerakaki, S. & Alexandri, S. (2006). Lexical and default stress assignment in reading Greek. *Journal of Research in Reading, 29*, 418–432.

(2007). Sources of information for stress assignment in reading Greek. *Applied Psycholinguistics, 28*, 695–720.

Protopapas, A., Mouzaki, A., Sideridis, G. D., Kotsolakou, A. & Simos, P. G. (2013). The role of vocabulary in the context of the simple view of reading. *Reading and Writing Quarterly, 29*, 168–202.

Protopapas, A. & Nomikou, E. (2009). Rules vs. lexical statistics in Greek nonword reading. In N. A. Taatgen & H. van Rijn (Eds.), *Proceedings of the 31st Annual Conference of the Cognitive Science Society* (pp. 1030–1035). Austin, TX: Cognitive Science Society.

Protopapas, A., Parrila, R. & Simos, P. G. (2016). In search of Matthew effects in reading. *Journal of Learning Disabilities, 49*, 499–514.

Protopapas, A., Sideridis, G. D., Mouzaki, A. & Simos, P. G. (2007). Development of lexical mediation in the relation between reading comprehension and word reading skills in Greek. *Scientific Studies of Reading, 11*, 165–197.

(2011). Matthew effects in reading comprehension Myth or reality? *Journal of Learning Disabilities, 44*, 402–420.

Protopapas, A., Simos, P. G., Sideridis, G. D. & Mouzaki, A. (2012). The components of the simple view of reading: A confirmatory factor analysis. *Reading Psychology, 33*, 217–240.

Protopapas, A. & Skaloumbakas, C. (2007). Traditional and computer-based screening and diagnosis of reading disabilities in Greek. *Journal of Learning Disabilities, 40*, 15–36.

(2008). Η αξιολόγηση της αναγνωστικής ευχέρειας για τον εντοπισμό αναγνωστικών δυσκολιών [Assessment of reading fluency for the identification of reading difficulties]. *Psychology: The Journal of the Hellenic Psychological Society, 15*, 267–289.

Protopapas, A., Skaloumbakas, C. & Bali, P. (2008). Validation of unsupervised computer-based screening for reading disability in Greek elementary grades 3 and 4. *Learning Disabilities: A Contemporary Journal, 6*, 45–69.

Protopapas, A., Tzakosta, M., Chalamandaris, A. & Tsiakoulis, P. (2012). IPLR: An online resource for Greek word-level and sublexical information. *Language Resources and Evaluation, 46*, 449–459.

Protopapas, A. & Vlahou, E. L. (2009). A comparative quantitative analysis of Greek orthographic transparency. *Behavior Research Methods, 41*, 991–1008.

Ralli, A. (2003). Morphology in Greek linguistics: The state of the art. *Journal of Greek Linguistics, 4*, 77–129.

(2005). *Μορφολογία* [Morphology]. Athens: Patakis.

Revithiadou, A. (1999). *Headmost accent wins: Head dominance and ideal prosodic form in lexical accent systems.* LOT Dissertation Series 15 (HIL/Leiden University). The Hague: Holland Academic Graphics.

Rothou, K. M. & Padeliadu, S. (2014). Inflectional morphological awareness and word reading and reading comprehension in Greek. *Applied Psycholinguistics.* Advance online publication. DOI: 10.1017/S0142716414000022.

Sarris, M. & Porpodas, K. (2012). Μάθηση της ορθογραφημένης γραφής της ελληνικής γλώσσας: Στρατηγικές που χρησιμοποιούν οι μαθητές της Α΄ τάξης στη γραφή [Learning to spell in Greek: Strategies used in spelling by first graders]. *Psychology: The Journal of the Hellenic Psychological Society, 19*, 373–397.

Stavrakaki, S. & Clahsen, H. (2009). The perfective past tense in Greek child language. *Journal of Child Language, 36*, 113–142.

Swiggers, P. (1996). Transmission of the Phoenician script to the west. In P. T. Daniels & W. Bright (Eds.), *The world's writing systems* (pp. 261–270). New York: Oxford University Press.

Tafa, E. & Manolitsis, G. (2008). A longitudinal literacy profile of Greek precocious readers. *Reading Research Quarterly, 43*, 165–185.

(2012). The literacy profile of Greek precocious readers: A follow-up study. *Journal of Research in Reading, 35*, 337–352.

Threatte, L. (1996). The Greek alphabet. In P. T. Daniels & W. Bright (Eds.), *The world's writing systems* (pp. 271–280). Oxford University Press.

Tonnet, H. (1995). *Ιστορία της νέας ελληνικής γλώσσας* [*Histoire du grec moderne*] (M. Karamanou & P. Lialiatsis, Trans.). Athens: Papadima. (Originally published 1993.)

Tsesmeli, S. N. & Koutselaki, D. (2013). Spelling performance and semantic understanding of compound words by Greek students with learning disabilities. *Journal of Learning Disabilities, 46*, 241–251.

Tzakosta, M. (2012). Ιστορικές μεταρρυθμίσεις του ορθογραφικού συστήματος της ελληνικής: μια αναθεώρηση που επίκειται [Historical revisions of the orthographic system of Greek: A revision is eminent]. In S. Bouzakis (Ed.), *Proceedings of the sixth Scientific Conference of the History in Education – Topic: Greek language and education.* (pp. 510–521). University of Patras. Retrieved from www.eriande. elemedu.upatras.gr/?section=1119&language=el_GR.

Tzakosta, M., Christianou, C. & Kalisperaki, F. (2011). The role of phonological perception in learning the orthographic system of Greek: Is there anything that needs to change? In *Proceedings of the 31st Annual Meeting of Greek Linguistics* (pp. 541–553). Aristotle University of Thessaloniki.

Tzakosta, M. & Dimtsa, A. (2012). Obstacles in learning the Greek orthography: the case of students with learning disabilities. In *Proceedings of the 32nd Annual Meeting of Greek Linguistics* (pp. 454–463). Aristotle University of Thessaloniki.

Tzakosta, M. & Karra, A. (2011). A typological and comparative account of CL and CC clusters in Greek dialects. In M. Janse, B. Joseph, P. Pavlou, A. Ralli & S. Armosti (Eds.), *Studies in Modern Greek dialects and linguistic theory I* (pp. 95–105). Nicosia: Kykkos Cultural Research Centre.

Tzakosta, M. & Vis, J. (2009). Phonological representations of consonant sequences: the case of affricates vs. 'true' clusters. In G. K. Giannakis, M. Baltazani, G. I. Xydopoulos & T. Tsaggalidis (Eds.), *E-proceedings of the eighth International Conference of Greek Linguistics (8ICGL)* (pp. 558–573). University of Ioannina.

Varlokosta, S. & Nerantzini, M. (2013). Grammatical gender in specific language impairment: Evidence from determiner-noun contexts in Greek. *Psychology: The Journal of the Hellenic Psychological Society, 20*, 338–357.

——— (2015). The acquisition of past tense by Greek-speaking children with specific language impairment: The role of phonological saliency, regularity, and frequency. In S. Stavrakaki (Ed.), *Advances in Research on Specific Language Impairment* (pp. 253–286). Amsterdam: John Benjamins.

Voutyras, E. (2001). Η εισαγωγή του αλφαβήτου [The introduction of the alphabet]. In A. F. Christidis (Ed.), *Ιστορία της ελληνικής γλώσσας: Από τις αρχές έως την ύστερη αρχαιότητα [History of the Greek language: From the beginnings to late antiquity]* (pp. 210–217). Institute of Modern Greek Studies, Aristotle University of Thessaloniki.

9 Learning to Read Italian

Cristina Burani, Anna M. Thornton, and Pierluigi Zoccolotti

9.1 Introduction

9.1.1 Italian Language and Its Orthography

Italian (It. *italiano*) is the statutory national language of Italy and of the Republic of San Marino, and one of the four languages of Switzerland. It has about 60 million native speakers. The Italian orthography is a transparent alphabetic writing system with mostly consistent letter-to-phoneme correspondences largely independent of context (but see Section 9.2.2.2).

9.1.2 Synchronic and Diachronic Characterization

Italian belongs to the Romance branch of the Indo-European family; it derives from Latin. Latin had an alphabetic orthography, with a high rate of univocal phoneme-to-grapheme and grapheme-to-phoneme correspondence in rendering consonants (the only non-univocal correspondences were: ‹i› for both /i/ and /j/, ‹u› for both /u/ and /w/, and /k/ written as ‹k›, ‹c› and ‹q› in different, largely complementary, contexts). Italian has always been written by means of the Latin alphabet. At the beginning of the written tradition (tenth century CE), the main problem was the rendering of Italian phonemes that were absent in Latin (/ts, dz, tʃ, dʒ, v, z, ʃ, ʎ/) and of geminate consonants (for greater detail, see Chapter 10, this volume, on French). A great variability in the solutions adopted is found in the first centuries of written tradition; this variability is abated with the beginning of printing (Biffi & Maraschio, 2008).

9.1.3 Literacy and Schooling

From the age of 3 to 6, Italian children are engaged in *scuola dell'infanzia* or kindergarten, which is not mandatory. Since 2000, schooling has been mandatory for ten years, between 6 and 16 years of age; prior to this, eight years had been mandatory since 1923, but this was enforced only from 1962; before that, five years of primary school were usually completed. Formal instruction in reading and writing begins in primary school when children are 6 years old. Reading and spelling are mainly taught through phonics by training sound–letter and letter–sound correspondences.

In 2001 only 25% of the adult population had a high-school diploma, and only 7.1% had a university degree, while about 10% had not completed even the lowest cycle of schooling and 2% of the population was illiterate (ISTAT, 2011). Results of the OECD PISA (Programme for International Student Assessment) 2009 Survey show that Italian 15-year-olds perform slightly but significantly below the mean of OECD countries in reading tasks, with big differences within the country (Invalsi, 2009). In 2011, Italy was the OECD country with the lowest percentage of public expenditure on education (OECD, 2011).

9.2   Description of Italian and Its Written Forms

9.2.1   Linguistic System

Good descriptions of the Italian language are provided by Lepschy and Lepschy (1991) and Vincent (1988). Below we give an overview of the main characteristics of the Italian linguistic system that are relevant for reading acquisition.

9.2.1.1 Phonology   We describe the phonology of standard Italian, a variety not spoken natively by anybody as such, based on educated spoken Florentine. A good overview is provided by Bertinetto and Loporcaro (2005). The consonant phonemes of standard Italian are shown in Table 9.1.[1]

Consonant length opposition is distinctive in Italian: There are minimal pairs such as /ˈpala/ 'shovel' vs. /ˈpalla/ 'ball'.

A number of observations on the consonantal inventory is in order. The status of the glides [j] and [w] is debated. According to some authors they are allophones of the vowels /i/ and /u/ when they occupy a non-nuclear position in a syllable. Minimal pairs between a glide and the corresponding vowel always involve a morphological boundary, as in [ˈspjan.ti] 'uproot.IND. PRS.2SG' (where morpheme boundaries are the following: s+pjant+i) vs. [ˈspi. an.ti] 'spy.PRS.PTCP.PL' (where morpheme boundaries are the following: spi+a+nt+i), [laˈkwa.le] 'REL.F.SG' (la=kwal+e) vs. [la.kuˈa.le] 'lacustrine' (laku+al+e) (Lepschy, 1978). However, there are minimal pairs opposing the

---

[1] Phonetic and phonological transcriptions are in IPA (International Phonetic Alphabet) (www.internationalphoneticassociation.org/sites/default/files/ipa-Kiel-2015.pdf). Orthographic transcriptions are between ⟨⟩. Information on the morphosyntactic specification of words is given in the Leipzig Glossing Rules format, which is becoming an international standard for annotation in morphology (www.eva.mpg.de/lingua/resources/glossing-rules.php).

Table 9.1 *Consonant phonemes of standard Italian*

	Bilabial	Labiodental	Dental	Alveolar	Palato-alveolar	Palatal	Velar	Labial-velar
Stops	p b		t d				k g	
Affricates				ts dz	tʃ dʒ			
Nasals	m			n		ɲ		
Fricatives		f v		s (z)	ʃ (ʒ)			
Laterals				l		ʎ		
Trills				r				
Approximants						j		w

Note. Following the IPA style, when two consonants appear in the same cell, the one on the left is voiceless, the one on the right is voiced.

two glides with each other, such as [ˈfjɔko] 'feeble' vs. [ˈfwɔko] 'fire', or with other consonants such as [ˈpjana] 'flat.F.SG' / [ˈplana] 'glide.IND.PRS.3SG' / [ˈprana] 'id.', [ˈtwɔno] 'thunder' / [ˈtrɔno] 'throne' (cf. D'Achille, 2006, p. 88). Marotta (1991) observes that [w] has a restricted distribution: It is either followed by /ɔ/ or preceded by a velar stop. She concludes that /wɔ/ constitutes a complex nucleus and that /kʷ/ and /gʷ/ are complex labiovelar obstruents, rather than sequences of two phonemes.

The phonemic opposition between /s/ and /z/ obtains intervocalically only in conservative Tuscan varieties, as in the minimal pair [ˈfuso] 'spindle' vs. [ˈfuzo] 'fuse.PST.PTCP.M.SG'; in Northern varieties of Italian, only [z] occurs intervocalically, while in the Roman variety only [s] does, but the possibility of intervocalic voicing is spreading due to the prestige of Northern varieties, so that intervocalic [s] and [z] appear in stylistically and socially conditioned free variation in non-Northern varieties. In pre-consonantal position, there is voice assimilation between the alveolar fricative and the following C. In word-initial prevocalic position, only [s] occurs. [ʒ] occurs only in loanwords, mostly of French origin, such as [gaˈraʒ] 'garage'.

Only in a few cases do minimal pairs oppose the two alveolar affricates, such as /ˈrattsa/ 'breed, race' vs. /ˈraddza/ 'ray' (kind of fish); however, /ts/ and /dz/ are not freely interchangeable in most words and are unanimously recognized as different phonemes. /ts, dz, ɲ, ʎ, ʃ/ are always long in intervocalic position; /z/ and /ʒ/ are always short.

Phonological processes relevant when discussing orthography are the following: Nasals assimilate in place with obstruents following them, both word-internally and across word boundaries; therefore, there is total neutralization of the opposition between nasal consonants in pre-consonantal position;

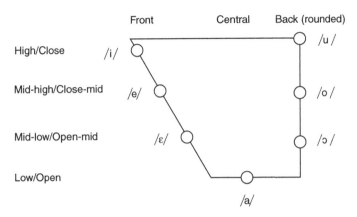

Figure 9.1 Vowel phonemes of standard Italian (in stressed syllables).

this is reflected in spelling only with bilabial nasals and word-internally (e.g., *impossibile* < *in+possibile* 'impossible'). When followed by sonorants, nasals undergo total regressive assimilation across morphological boundaries, and this is reflected by the orthography word-internally (e.g., *illeggibile* < *in+leggibile* 'illegible', *irreale* < *in+reale* 'unreal').

Vowel length is not contrastive in Italian; stressed vowels are lengthened in open syllables in penultimate and (to a lesser extent) antepenultimate position. The vowel phonemes of standard Italian are shown in Figure 9.1.

The opposition between mid-high and mid-low vowels obtains only in stressed syllables (it is neutralized in unstressed ones), in standard Italian and in certain regional varieties that have minimal pairs such as /'botte/ 'barrel' vs. /'bɔtte/ 'blows, hits', /'peska/ 'fish.IND.PRS.3SG' vs. /'pɛska/ 'peach'.

With respect to syllables and word length, several sources (Bortolini, 1976; Mancini & Voghera, 1994a, 1994b; Schmid, 1999) provide information on the inventory of syllable types in written and spoken Italian. Data are not immediately comparable, as some studies mark certain phonemes (/s/, glides) separately and others do not. The number of syllable types recognized in these studies ranges from nineteen (Mancini & Voghera, 1994a) to twenty-six (Schmid, 1999). There are eight uncontroversial open types (syllables ending in a V: CV, V, CCV, CGV, GV, CCCV, CCGV, CGGV). CV is the most frequent syllable type, covering 56% and 58% of syllable tokens in written and spoken corpora, respectively. Overall, 77% of syllable tokens in the spoken corpus is constituted by open syllables.

As for the number of different forms of syllables (e.g., /a/, /ta/, /del/, etc.), the phonItalia database (http://phonitalia.org/), based on a corpus of about 2 million tokens, lists 3,626 different phonological syllable forms (Goslin,

Galluzzi & Romani, 2014). The Italian syllable frequency database (Stella & Job, 2001), based on a corpus of about 11.8 million tokens, does not distinguish between homographic, but phonologically different, syllables (e.g., ‹sfug› represents both /sfug/ and /sfudʒ/, and is counted only once) and lists 2,720 different forms of syllables. The difference between the two counts indicates that as many as 33% of orthographic syllables in Italian may be ambiguous, representing more than one phonological syllable.

Word-form length in syllables ranges between one and twelve in the LIP corpus of spoken Italian (De Mauro, Mancini, Vedovelli & Voghera, 1993) but the only forms above eight syllables are numbers (e.g., spoken version of "1994" and the like). About 90% of the word forms in this corpus are one to three syllables long (Mancini & Voghera, 1994b).

The mode length of Italian lexemes (GRADIT; De Mauro, 1999) is four syllables, and three in the Italian Basic dictionary (BDVDB; Thornton, Iacobini & Burani, 1997). The mean length in syllables of word tokens in Stella and Job's corpus is 2.27. This is due to the fact that many monosyllabic words are among the most frequent forms, as shown also by Mancini and Voghera (1994a, 1994b).

With regard to word stress, it is important to note that native content words in Italian end in a vowel. Recently, this constraint has been relaxed, due to massive borrowings from English.

Stress falls on one of the last three syllables. It is not phonologically predictable, as (semi)minimal pairs such as /ˈkapito/ 'happen.IND.PRS.1SG', /kaˈpito/ 'understand.PST.PTCP.M.SG', /kapiˈtɔ/ 'happen.PST.PFV.3SG' show. Heavy penultimates almost invariably attract stress (there is a handful of exceptions, such as /ˈmandorla/ 'almond', /ˈtaranto/ (placename)). If enclitics are added to the right of a morphological word, stress can end up further away from the phonological word's rightmost end, as in *carica=lo* /ˈkarikalo/ 'upload.IMP.2SG=3SG.M.ACC', i.e., 'upload it/him'. Words are typically stressed on the penultimate (83.6% of the citation forms of the lexemes in the Italian Basic Dictionary, vs. 12.2% on the antepenultimate and 4.2% on the last syllable: Thornton et al., 1997).

9.2.1.2 Inflectional Morphology Inflecting word classes are nouns, adjectives, articles, pronouns, and verbs.

Italian nouns have inherent gender (masculine or feminine) and inflect for number; a typical noun has two forms, singular and plural. Nouns distribute in several inflectional classes, as shown in Table 9.2. Typically, the number opposition is signaled by a single word-final unstressed vowel, as in *cas-a/ cas-e* 'house-SG/house-PL'. A few nouns have isolated types of stem allomorphy: *uom-o/uomin-i* 'man/men', *di-o/de-i* 'god/gods', *bu-e/buoi-i* 'ox/oxen'. A few nouns in class 1 have a stem-final alternation between /k/ in the SG and /tʃ/ in the PL (e.g., /aˈmiko/ vs. /aˈmitʃi/ 'friend'); very few alternate

Table 9.2 *Italian noun inflection*

Class	Endings (SG/PL)	Examples	Gender
1	-o/-i	*libro/libri* 'book'	M except *mano/mani* 'hand' F
2	-a/-e	*casa/case* 'house'	F
3	-e/-i	*fiore/fiori* 'flower' *siepe/siepi* 'hedge' *cantante/cantanti* 'singer'	M 44.4%, F 43.4%, M/F 12%
4	-a/-i	*poeta/poeti* 'poet'	M except *ala/ali* 'wing' F, *arma/armi* 'weapon' F
5	-o/-a	*uovo/uova* 'egg'	SG. M, PL. F
6	invariabile	*re, gru, brindisi, crisi, caffè, città, foto ...* 'king, crane, toast, crisis, coffee, city, snapshot ... '	M 48.6%, F 51.4%

between stem-final /g/ and /dʒ/ (e.g., /kiˈrurgo/ vs. /kiˈrurdʒi/ 'surgeon'. Class 6 contains uninflectable nouns.

Adjectives inflect for gender and number similarly to nouns, with which they agree. There are three adjectival inflectional classes: so-called 4-endings (e.g., *rosso/rossa/rossi/rosse* 'red.M.SG/F.SG/M.PL/F.PL'), so-called 2-endings (which neutralizes gender oppositions, e.g., *verde/verdi* 'green.SG/PL'), and indeclinables (e.g., *blu* 'blue').

The definite article inflects for gender and number, like adjectives, and in addition has several shapes conditioned by the following word's initial phoneme or cluster, as in *il cane / l'asino / lo struzzo* 'the dog / the donkey / the ostrich'. The indefinite article inflects for gender and has only singular forms, conditioned by the following phoneme or cluster.

Pronouns inflect for person, number, and case, and for gender as well in the third person; their paradigms display several cases of syncretism and suppletion (e.g., *io* 'ISG.NOM' vs. *me* 'ISG.OBL'); in addition, pronouns divide in two series, stressed and unstressed (clitic).

Verbs inflect for person, number, tense-aspect, and mood in finite forms, and for gender and number in the past participle. A verb paradigm contains at least forty-eight synthetic and forty-four periphrastic forms. Italian verbs are traditionally described as belonging to three conjugations, recognizable by the theme vowel (/a/, /e/ or /i/) that precedes the infinitival ending -*re*. However, some modern scholars (Dressler & Thornton, 1991; Vincent, 1988) maintain that the main distinction is between two classes, the overwhelmingly regular /a/

conjugation and the "other" conjugation that hosts all sorts of stem alternations (Maiden, 1992). A verb can have up to six phonologically different stems (Pirrelli & Battista, 2000); their distribution is constrained by an "overall distribution schema" and is independent of their phonological makeup. Most inflectional endings are stable across conjugations (e.g., -o 'IND.PRS.1SG'), others distinguish the two main classes (e.g., -a vs. -e 'IND.PRS.3SG').

Verb inflection interacts with word stress in several ways: IND.PRS.3PL forms of verbs with stress on the antepenultimate syllable in the singular are stressed on the ante-antepenultimate: e.g., /'kariko/ 'charge.IND.PRS.1SG', /'karikano/ 'charge.IND.PRS.3PL'; simple perfective past (It. *passato remoto*) 3SG forms are always stressed on the last syllable (/a'mɔ/ 'love.PST.PFV.3SG', /te'me/ 'fear. PST.PFV.3SG', /sen'ti/ 'hear.PST.PFV.3SG'); FUT.1SG and FUT.3SG are stressed on the last syllable. As already observed, Italian word stress is not fully phonologically predictable, but morphology often carries information on where stress falls.

9.2.1.3 Word Formation Processes Italian has a rich system of lexeme formation processes (Grossmann & Rainer, 2004). Suffixation is the most used technique, although it is difficult to estimate the incidence of compounds, as those written as separate words orthographically are not listed in dictionaries (Iacobini & Thornton, 1992). The relative incidence of suffixed words appears the same in written and spoken corpora (Iacobini & Adinolfi, 2008).

Thornton et al. (1997) provide data on the morphological complexity of lexemes belonging to the Italian Basic Dictionary (De Mauro, 1989), containing about 7,000 high-frequency or high-availability lexemes. Only 36.6% of these are non-complex; 27.2% are suffixed, 19.1% are the result of conversion/ zero-derivation, 11.9% are prefixed, and 5.2% are compounds.

Most denominal and de-adjectival suffixes are vowel-initial (e.g., -*ista*, -*aio* for agent nouns, -*ino*, -*etto* for diminutives). Deverbal suffixes are usually consonant-initial (e.g., -*zione*, -*tura* for action nouns, -*tore* for agent nouns, -*bile* for adjectives expressing potentiality). In denominal derivatives the base usually appears devoid of the final vowel displayed by inflected forms (e.g., *dente* 'tooth' → *dentista* 'dentist', **denteista*), while in deverbal derivatives and compounds the base verb appears in a form that is usually homophonous and homographic with one or more free forms (e.g., *osservare* 'observe' → *osservatore* 'observer', cf. *osserva* 'observe.IND.PRS.3SG/IMP.2SG').

Morphotactic transparency of suffixed deverbal derivatives can be very high for derivatives based on the most basic verb stem (verb's root + theme vowel), as in *osservatore*. However, certain suffixes of high type and token frequency attach to a different verb stem, sometimes homophonous (and homographic) with the stem found in the PST.PTCP and the PFV.PST, sometimes specific to derivatives: e.g., *escludere* 'exclude' → *esclusione* 'exclusion' (cf. *escluso*

'exclude.PST.PTCP', *esclusi* 'exclude.PFV.PST.1SG'); *corrompere* 'corrupt' →
corruzione 'corruption' (cf. *corruppi* 'corrupt.PFV.PST.1SG', *corrotto* 'corrupt.
PST.PTCP'). Therefore, the degree of transparency must be assessed separately
for each specific lexeme and suffix. Prefixes usually agglutinate to their base,
but prefixes ending in a nasal consonant assimilate the nasal as described in
Section 9.2.1.1. In these cases, it is the prefix identity, rather than the base's
one, that is altered (e.g., *in+reale* → *irreale* 'unreal').

9.2.2   Writing System

9.2.2.1   Script and Punctuation   The Latin alphabet is used. Traditionally,
twenty-one letters are considered part of the Italian alphabet: ⟨a, b, c, d, e, f, g,
h, i, l, m, n, o, p, q, r, s, t, u, v, z⟩; the five "foreign" letters ⟨j, k, w, x, y⟩ are used
in the spelling of loanwords. There are spaces between words. Capital initial
letters are used after full stops (periods) and for proper names and names of
certain institutions. Punctuation is in line with most systems using the Latin
alphabet: the signs ⟨. , ; : ? ! ⟩ are used; besides, accent marks on some vowels
(⟨à, è, é, ì, ò, ó, ù⟩) and the apostrophe ⟨'⟩ are used in cases which will be
detailed below.

9.2.2.2   Orthography   "The Italian spelling system exhibits a fairly regular
pattern of phoneme–grapheme correspondences" (Vincent, 1988, p. 285).
Overall, Italian can be considered an (almost) "pure phonemic system,"
where the phonological structure of base words rarely changes with derivational morphology. Italian spoken words have morphological structures that are
largely phonologically transparent and are reflected in the orthography, where
the morpho-phonemic structure is transparently realized. In this respect Italian
orthography is in sharp contrast with morpho-phonemic spelling systems, such
as English, in which morphology is represented by the orthography in spite of
extensive phonological variations often resulting in changes of pronunciation
(e.g., *heal – health*; see Frost, 2012).

Cases of non-univocal correspondences are the following:

1. ⟨h⟩ appears word-initially in certain forms of the IND.PRS of the verb *avere*
   'have' (*ho, hai, ha, hanno*), where it does not correspond to any phoneme.
2. /k/ and /g/ are represented by digraphs ⟨ch⟩ and ⟨gh⟩ when followed by
   front vowels. The sequence /kw/ is sometimes represented by ⟨cu⟩, other
   times by ⟨qu⟩: e.g., *cuoco* /ˈkwɔko/ 'cook' vs. *quota* /ˈkwɔta/ 'share'. /kkw/
   is represented by ⟨cqu⟩, except in the single word *soqquadro* 'mess,
   disorder' and its derivatives.
3. /tʃ/, /dʒ/ are represented by ⟨c⟩,⟨g⟩ when followed by front vowels, by ⟨ci⟩,
   ⟨gi⟩ elsewhere. However, there is some variation in rendering /tʃɛ/ and /tʃe/,
   /dʒɛ/ and / dʒe/, which are written ⟨cie⟩, ⟨gie⟩ in some words and ⟨ce⟩, ⟨ge⟩

in other ones: e.g., *cieco* /ˈtʃɛko/ 'blind' vs. *ceco* /ˈtʃɛko/ 'Czech', *specie* /ˈspɛtʃe/ 'species' vs. *radice* /raˈditʃe/ 'root', *igiene* /iˈdʒɛne/ 'hygiene' vs. *gelo* /ˈdʒɛlo/ 'frost'.

4. /ʃ/ is represented by ⟨sc⟩ when followed by front vowels, by ⟨sci⟩ elsewhere. The nouns *scienza* /ˈʃɛntsa/ 'science', *coscienza* /koʃˈʃɛntsa/ 'conscience', *usciere* /uʃˈʃɛre/ 'janitor', and their derivatives (e.g., *scientifico* /ʃenˈtifiko/ 'scientific') contain the sequence ⟨scie⟩, while in all other words /ʃɛ/ and /ʃe/ are represented by ⟨sce⟩ (e.g., *adolescenza* /adoleʃ ˈʃɛntsa/ 'adolescence'). Notice that ⟨sc⟩ represents /sk/ when followed by ⟨a,o,u⟩.

5. /ɲ/ is represented by ⟨gn⟩; ⟨gn⟩ represents /gn/ in extremely rare technical terms, belonging to the non-native stratum of the lexicon, such as *gneiss* 'id.'.

6. /ʎ/ is represented by ⟨gl⟩ when followed by /i/, by ⟨gli⟩ elsewhere. On the other hand, ⟨gl⟩ stands for /gl/ in certain words, e.g., *glicine* 'wisteria'. This causes uncertainty in how to read uncommon words, such as *geroglifico* 'hieroglyphic(al)'.

7. /s/ and /z/ (to the extent that /z/ occurs as a distinct phoneme) are both represented by ⟨s⟩.

8. ⟨z⟩ represents both /ts/ and /dz/; besides, while these affricates are always long in intervocalic position, rules of orthography in some cases prescribe a single ⟨z⟩: e.g., *mazzo* /ˈmattso/ 'bunch' vs. *Lazio* /ˈlattsjo/ (placename).

9. ⟨e⟩ represents both /e/ and /ɛ/, ⟨o⟩ represents both /o/ and /ɔ/, so, e.g., *pesca* spells both 'peach' and 'fish.IND.PRS.3SG'.

10. ⟨i⟩ represents both /i/ and /j/, ⟨u⟩ represents both /u/ and /w/ (although ⟨y⟩ is used for /j/ and ⟨w⟩ for /w/ in loanwords, such as *yogurt, whisky*).

Geminate consonants are represented by doubling a letter, with the exception of some occurrences of /tts/. Word stress is represented only when it falls on the last syllable. In this case, the opposition between grave and acute accent is exploited to express vowel height: *caffè* /kafˈfɛ/ 'coffee', *perché* /perˈke/ 'why, because'. Monosyllables are usually written without stress, but when there are two homophonous monosyllables an orthographic accent is prescribed on one of the two for diacritic purposes: e.g., *da* 'from' vs. *dà* 'give.IND.PRS.3SG'. Many people do not observe this rule. There are homographic non-homophonous pairs of words, distinguished by having their accent on the penultimate vs. antepenultimate syllable (e.g., *ancora* /ˈankora/ 'anchor' vs. *ancora* /anˈkora/ 'still, yet').

An apostrophe is used in spelling prevocalic shapes of the definite article. The prevocalic shape of the indefinite article is /un/ for both M.SG and F.SG: orthography prescribes an apostrophe after the feminine form, but not after the masculine: *un amico* 'a (male) friend' vs. *un'amica* 'a (female) friend'.

Spelling mistakes are common and spread in both directions (i.e., apostrophe is used in the M.SG or dropped in the F.SG).

9.2.3   Conclusion

Italian has relatively regular correspondences between letters and phonemes. Most cases in which more than one letter or sequence of letters can correspond to the same phoneme or sequence of phonemes are such that they will cause difficulty in writing rather than in reading: e.g., writing <ha> instead of <a> or vice versa is a common spelling mistake, but the two spellings are both read as /a/. The main areas in which spelling does not point to a univocal phonological representation are the mid-vowels <e> and <o>, each one of which corresponds to two phonemes in standard Italian; the use of certain digraphs (<gl>, <gn>); the lack of representation of stress, except when it falls on the last syllable.

9.3   Acquisition of Reading and Spelling in Italian

The characteristics of the Italian language (and orthography) play a critical role in some areas of acquisition, such as morphological processing, word decoding, and spelling, and much less in other areas, such as reading comprehension, which are largely language-independent.

9.3.1   Becoming Linguistically Aware

9.3.1.1   Phonological Development and Phonological Awareness   Phonological segmentation ability was examined in a study comparing Italian and English (Cossu, Shankweiler, Liberman, Katz & Tola, 1988). Performance of Italian and American children followed a similar pattern: Phoneme segmentation ability was low in nursery and kindergarten and peaked only after formal instruction. Syllable segmentation ability was generally higher and less sensitive to school beginning. Notably, success rate was higher for Italian than American children in all age and task comparisons.

Subsequent studies examined the relationship between phonological processes and reading using segmentation and blending tasks (Cossu, Gugliotta, Villani, Cristante & Emiliani, 1990; Tressoldi, 1989; Tressoldi, Vio & Maschietto, 1989) as well as phonological short-term memory tasks (D'Amico, 2000). These studies reported a significant correlation between performance in phonological and meta-phonological tasks and reading ability.

Two main questions are of interest in evaluating this relationship. One concerns its specificity. While phonological awareness is related to reading, one may wonder whether this is the only (or main) predictor or other cognitive abilities play a specific (and independent) role. A second issue concerns whether the association between phonological awareness and reading indicates a unidirectional, causal relationship or the two variables show a more complex (e.g., interactive) bi-directional relationship. This question goes back to the observations on illiterate Portuguese adults by Morais, Gary, Alegria, and Betelson (1979) who proposed that awareness of words as being made of a sequence of phones occurs due to formal training to read, not as a spontaneous consequence of cognitive development (but see, for the proposal of a reciprocal relation, Perfetti, Beck, Bell & Hughes, 1987).

As to the first question, some studies tried to predict the acquisition of literacy skills, examining a variety of target cognitive abilities. Orsolini et al. (2003) reported that several variables independently contributed in predicting reading ability: conceptualization of written language, lexical skills, non-word repetition, visual symbol search, letter knowledge, and phoneme segmentation.

In another extensive study by Scalisi, Desimoni, and Pelagaggi (2009), performance in different cognitive tests before school entrance predicted reading accuracy, speed, and comprehension in Grades 1 and 3. In Grade 1, low performance in all areas of reading was predicted by low performance in working memory tests, while low performance in reading speed was associated with defective performance in a visual search task. Furthermore, performance in Rapid Automatized Naming (RAN) tasks was a good predictor of reading in Grade 3. In the same vein, a cross-sectional study of RAN in Grades 1 to 6 indicated that speed in naming colors (digits or objects) predicted reading speed and accuracy (but not comprehension) at all ages (Di Filippo et al., 2005).

Overall, a variety of cognitive skills, other than meta-phonological skills, exert a significant influence on predicting reading performance. This occurs both when the early stages of reading acquisition are examined and when a larger spectrum of ages is considered.

The second question concerns the nature of the association between meta-phonological skills and reading acquisition. Empirical results generally confirmed this relationship in Italian children (Cossu et al., 1988, 1990; D'Amico, 2000; Tressoldi, 1989; Tressoldi et al., 1989). However, other evidence militates against a causal interpretation of this association. In a longitudinal study, Cossu et al. (1990) reported the presence of individual double dissociations with excellent reading skills in children with low performance in segmentation or elision tasks and excellent segmentation skills in children with no progress in reading throughout Grade 1. Surprising dissociations also emerge in pathological samples. Thus, retarded children may show good reading skills in the presence of poor meta-phonological abilities (Cossu & Marshall, 1990; Cossu, Rossini & Marshall, 1993). Finally, some young children showed outstanding transcoding skills for reading and writing words and non-words (hyper-lexia) but were unable to perform meta-phonological tasks (Cossu & Marshall, 1986).

Evidence on the role of schooling instruction on meta-phonological ability also comes from studies comparing children who start school later than expected with children matched for age but differing for school experience, as well as with children matched for schooling but differing for age (e.g., Cunningham & Carroll, 2011). One recent study compared large groups of Italian children with the same age (in the 5–7 years range) but with a six-month difference in school experience (Scalisi, Desimoni & Di Vito Curmini, 2013). When age and schooling effects were separated, the schooling effect was significant only for syllable segmentation and blending, indicating the effect of reading training over and above that of age. By contrast, performance on RAN tasks showed a linear age increase and was not affected by schooling.

Finally, complementary evidence on the role of phonological and meta-phonological skills on reading derives from studies on developmental dyslexics. Deficits in phonological awareness tasks were reported in a large study comparing children with dyslexia with peer proficient readers; notably, other non-phonological abilities (including visual-spatial and motion perception, selective and sustained attention and executive functions) significantly contributed in explaining variance in word and non-word reading (Menghini et al., 2010).

On a different line of research, selective deficits in meta-phonological (spoonerism and phonemic fluency) and verbal short-term memory tasks were found for children with dyslexia with a previous history of language delay, while they were negligible in those without such a history (Brizzolara et al., 2006). A similar pattern was obtained in two further studies examining a greater variety of linguistic tasks, including expressive and receptive vocabulary (Chilosi et al., 2009; Scuccimarra et al., 2008).

Overall, data indicate a statistical association between meta-phonological skills and reading acquisition. However, large individual differences are present. Furthermore, evidence indicates an important role of formal instruction in mediating this relationship. It appears that a simple directional relationship is unlikely to express such association and an interactive bi-directional relationship is a more likely candidate.

9.3.1.2 Morphological Development and Morphological Awareness   An interesting question concerns whether word morphology is used by developing readers for word comprehension and vocabulary learning (for a review, see Bimonte & Burani, 2005). Some studies pointed to the role of semantic and phonological transparency of derived words with respect to their bases in favoring the use of morphemes in word decoding and comprehension.

Furthermore, the frequency and productivity of derivational suffixes has proven relevant for morpho-lexical reading and comprehension.

Lo Duca (1990) documented the importance of semantic transparency in the neologisms produced by 4- to 8-year-old children. The study focused on the development of word formation rules for agent nouns, i.e., nouns designating "a person who does something," that can be derived by means of suffixes (e.g., *lattaio* 'somebody who sells milk', from *latte* 'milk') or compounds (e.g., *tagliaboschi* 'lumberjack' from *tagliare* 'to cut' and *boschi* 'woods'). All children, including the youngest ones, knew the basic word formation procedures. Furthermore, the derived words coined by the children were prevalently phonologically and semantically transparent relative to their base. In another study, 4- to 8-year-old children mainly used productive derivational suffixes such as *-ista* and *-tore* in naming persons' activities (Martina, 2001).

When presented with unfamiliar suffixed derived words, 6- to 8-year-old children were able to define them if the words included a familiar root and a frequently occurring suffix (e.g., *parolaio*, 'windbag' made up of *parola* 'word' and *-aio*; Lo Duca, 1987). Other studies demonstrated that second to fourth graders (including young persons with Williams syndrome) have access to word formation morphology and employ knowledge of roots and suffixes to understand the meaning of unfamiliar words (Bimonte, 2002; Burani, Bimonte, Barca & Vicari, 2006).

Overall, children can extract the meaning of derived unfamiliar words, analyzing and combining the meaning of the word's morphemic constituents (root and affix). Developing readers are also sensitive to the quantitative properties of suffixes (frequency and productivity): The more productive and frequent a suffix, the easier for children to understand a derived word.

Studies in English and French showed that morphological awareness is a predictor of reading and comprehension abilities, which adds to the contribution of phonological awareness from the end of Grade 1 (Carlisle & Nomabody, 1993) or Grade 2 (Casalis & Louis-Alexandre, 2000). Morphological awareness as a predictor of reading ability has not yet been investigated in Italian. However, several studies show that morphemes develop early as reading units in Italian (see Section 9.3.2.1).

9.3.2   Development of Word Identification

9.3.2.1   Word Decoding Development   Because of the transparency of the Italian orthographic system (see Section 9.2.2.2), the acquisition of reading can, in principle, be accomplished relying on small grain-size units that consistently map onto single phonemic units (Ziegler & Goswami, 2005). This is confirmed by the finding that Italian children become rapidly accurate in reading words as well as non-words. By the end of Grade 1, they read correctly *c.* 95% of content words and function words, as well as *c.* 90% of simple non-words (Seymour, Aro & Erskine, 2003). These values place Italian among the easiest languages in terms of word decoding (Seymour et al., 2003). Other studies (on Italian children only) generally confirmed these high figures in Grade 1 (e.g., Cossu, Shankweiler, Liberman & Gugliotta, 1995; Zoccolotti, De Luca, Di Filippo, Judica & Martelli, 2009).

It is therefore particularly interesting to examine children at the very early phases of reading acquisition. Orsolini, Fanari, Tosi, De Nigris, and Carrieri (2006) examined the oral production of children attempting to read a list of simple words after three months of formal instruction. They observed marked individual differences. Some children ("Phonetic cues" subgroup) relied in a non-sequential way on phonetic cues. Thus, after correctly identifying the word *gatto* /gat:o/ 'cat', a child maintains the phonetic content associated with the letter ⟨g⟩ and promptly responds *gatto* when later confronted with the word *aglio* /ˈao o/ 'garlic'. These children obtained a very low rate of word recognition although some identification of graphemes was present; interestingly, they often produced non-target words. Other children ("Alphabetic 1 beginners") engaged in systematic orthography–phonology conversion; however, this occurred predominantly at the level of single graphemes, and children were often unsuccessful in blending the phonemes. Thus, while they were relatively correct in reading single graphemes, word recognition rate was low, resulting often in non-words. Other children ("Alphabetic 2 intermediate") also showed systematic orthography–phonology conversion, but prevalently at the level of syllabic units, and blending proved more effective. Thus, word accuracy was higher and production of non-words lower. Finally, a fourth subgroup ("Alphabetic 3 advanced") tended to pronounce strings as whole-word forms with no previous aloud conversion of small orthographic units. They obtained a high rate of word recognition in spite of the very short period of literacy training.

An in-depth analysis of misreadings was carried out by Cossu, Shankweiler, et al. (1995) who examined first and second graders using phonetically and orthographically controlled materials. Italian beginning readers generally made few decoding errors (particularly when compared to American children examined with similar materials). Within the subset of spatially reversible graphs, visual similarity contributed to the reading difficulties of beginners; however, it was only when visual similarity was associated with phonological similarity (as in ⟨b⟩ and ⟨d⟩) that misreadings tended to occur. Therefore, the pattern of errors "reflects not the spatial characteristics of the misread letters but their functions within the linguistic system and its [*sic*] orthographic manifestation" (Cossu, Shankweiler, et al., 1995, p. 250).

As accuracy asymptotes quickly, reading time measures are largely used to examine reading, particularly at later stages of development.

The acquisition of reading skill was studied in children in Grades 1 to 8 using lists of words and non-words (Zoccolotti et al., 2009). Accuracy saturated rapidly, particularly in the case of words. By contrast, reading times showed a progressive decrease closely following the law of practice (i.e., an improvement progressively smaller over time; Newell & Rosenbloom, 1981). Using a z-score normalization (Faust, Balota, Spieler & Ferraro, 1999) allowed examining the size of the various psycholinguistic effects independent of the large global performance change occurring with age. Length modulated performance at early stages of learning and progressively less later on; in the case of non-words, the effect of length was large but did not change as a function of grade. The lexicality effect, present at all ages for high-frequency words and, by Grade 3, for low-frequency words too, increased with reading practice, indicating a progressive differentiation in the ability to read words and non-words. Finally, the effect of word frequency was highest in Grade 3 and then decreased.

The large change in the effect of length with age/reading experience was confirmed in a study examining vocal reaction times (RTs) of children in Grades 1 to 3 (Zoccolotti, De Luca, Gasperini, Judica & Spinelli, 2005): RTs became faster and less sensitive to word length as a function of age. Notably, third graders with dyslexia behaved very similarly to skilled first graders, i.e., they showed a marked effect of word length.

In a study by Marcolini, Donato, Stella, and Burani (2006), the interaction among word length and morphological effects in reading aloud low-frequency words was investigated in primary school children. Derived words were read faster than simple words only when they were long, namely when lexical access to the word's whole form was difficult. No difference was found in the use of morphological analysis in relation to children's grade, confirming the early structuring in morphemes of the child's lexicon.

Morpheme-based reading was also investigated by Burani, Marcolini, and Stella (2002) in third to fifth graders. For all age groups pseudowords made up of roots and derivational suffixes resulting in nonexistent combinations (e.g., *donnista*, 'womanist', composed of *donn-*, 'woman', and *-ista*, '-ist') were recognized more frequently as possible words and were named more quickly and accurately than matched pseudowords with no morphological constituents.

A subsequent study confirmed that children (in Grades 2/3 or 6) read pseudowords composed of root and suffix faster and more accurately than simple pseudowords (Burani, Marcolini, De Luca & Zoccolotti, 2008). Skilled children in Grades 2/3 benefited from morphological structure also in reading aloud words; i.e., they were faster in reading words composed of a root and a derivational suffix (e.g., *cassiere*, 'cashier') than corresponding simple words (e.g., *cammello*, 'camel'). A similar pattern was observed in sixth graders with dyslexia (Burani et al., 2008). In contrast, there was no advantage of complex vs. simple words in skilled sixth graders who could effectively use whole-word recognition.

Further work showed that this morphological effect is modulated by word frequency as well as type of morphological constituents: young skilled readers named low- but not high-frequency morphologically complex words faster than simple words (Marcolini, Traficante, Zoccolotti & Burani, 2011); RTs depended exclusively on roots, with no effect of suffixes, which affected only accuracy (Traficante, Marcolini, Luci, Zoccolotti & Burani, 2011).

Overall, morpheme-based reading is important for obtaining reading fluency (rather than accuracy) particularly for low-frequency words and in children who do not yet fully master whole-word processing (for a review, see Burani, 2010). The availability of preassembled morphemic units favors efficient naming relative to the laborious and slower non-lexical process of segmenting, converting, and reassembling smaller units necessary for reading new words with no morphological structure.

An interesting question concerns the development of the non-lexical procedure of reading. Evidence on this issue derives from the study of words containing context-sensitive rules. As stated in Section 9.2.2.2, the pronunciation of sequences involving the letters ⟨c⟩ and ⟨g⟩ are determined by rules that depend on the letters that follow them. Italian adult readers are slower in reading words containing contextual rules than words wihout them, an effect present for low- but not high-frequency words (Burani, Barca & Ellis, 2006), indicating that rule complexity effects arise from sublexical procedures that are more involved in reading low-frequency words. The same effects were reported in children in Grades 3 and 5, including the presence of a frequency effect (Barca, Ellis & Burani, 2007). The absence of any interaction with grade indicates that Italian third graders have already developed an efficient system of lexical reading for more familiar words.

The early presence of lexical reading in Italian children was confirmed in other studies. A high-frequency word neighbor had an inhibitory effect on non-word processing in third and fifth graders, i.e., the activation of a lexical representation conflicted with the assembly of the non-word phonemic sequence (Marcolini, Burani & Colombo, 2009).

The interaction between the lexical and the sublexical serial procedure (Coltheart, Rastle, Perry, Langdon & Ziegler, 2001) can be approached examining the position of the diverging letter (PDL) effect: Non-words derived from words are read faster when the single diverging letter is toward the end of the string than when it is at the beginning (Mulatti, Peressotti & Job, 2007). The PDL effect found in adults was also observed in fourth graders; by contrast, second graders showed a reversed pattern with slower responses for late than early diverging non-words (Peressotti, Mulatti & Job, 2010). Apparently, lexical information was activated slowly but still dominated phonology computation afterwards. Evidence on the PDL effect indicates a development in the balance between the sublexical and lexical procedures as the latter becomes more efficient with increasing reading experience.

Information on the interaction between lexical and sublexical knowledge comes from studies on stress assignment in developing readers. As described above (Section 9.2.1.1), word stress is practically the only source of unpredictability in reading Italian. Consequently, the reader must know the word in order to correctly assign stress. However, two main sources of statistical information on stress distribution in the language can be exploited in assigning stress to newly encountered words. The first one is stress dominance: stress on the penultimate syllable is the dominant stress pattern, whereas stress on the antepenultimate is the non-dominant one (Thornton et al., 1997). The second is stress neighborhood, i.e., the proportion and number of words sharing orthographic ending and stress pattern: Stress assignment is facilitated when a word has a final sequence shared by a majority of stress friends (Burani & Arduino, 2004; Colombo, 1992).

Both stress dominance and stress neighborhood affected young readers in assigning stress to non-words. However, there was also a developmental trend in the acquisition of statistical information, going from more general to more specific knowledge of stress: second graders were more likely than fourth graders to overgeneralize dominant stress (i.e., assign penultimate stress; Sulpizio, Boureaux, Burani, Deguchi & Colombo, 2012; Sulpizio & Colombo, 2013).

In reading aloud, both second and fourth graders showed word-specific knowledge: high-frequency words were assigned stress correctly irrespective of stress dominance (Burani, Paizi & Sulpizio, 2013; Paizi, Zoccolotti & Burani, 2011; Sulpizio & Colombo, 2013). However, when reading unfamiliar words, fourth and sixth graders relied more on stress neighborhood than on stress dominance (Burani et al., 2013; Paizi et al., 2011). Only young readers with dyslexia assigned the dominant stress pattern more frequently to low-frequency words (Paizi et al., 2011).

The role of breadth of lexical knowledge in assigning stress was recently reported in a study examining children learning Italian as L2: Only children with a smaller Italian vocabulary size (but not those with a larger vocabulary) assigned dominant stress to low-frequency three-syllable words more frequently than native Italian readers (Bellocchi, Bonifacci & Burani, 2013).

Overall, in learning the statistical regularities of the language (of the stress system in particular) readers develop a graded sensitivity to the probabilistic constraints of the lexicon.

9.3.2.2 Word Spelling Development   Cossu, Gugliotta, and Marshall (1995) compared the acquisition of reading and spelling using the same stimulus materials in first and second graders. Lexicality and length effects were present already in Grade 1. Furthermore, spelling proved more difficult than reading at both ages, in keeping with the idea that spelling is more challenging because, unlike reading, it requires fully specified orthographic lexical representations (e.g., Tainturier & Rapp, 2001). Partially discrepant results were obtained by Tressoldi (1996) who examined children in Grades 1 to 8 but did not obtain differences between spelling words and non-words. Tressoldi (1996) also used a task involving sentences containing contrasting homophonic but non-homographic sequences (e.g., *l'ago* 'the needle' vs. *lago* 'lake'), thereby requiring lexical look-up. For this task, acquisition proved particularly slow.

In evaluating the role of the lexicon, it is important to consider that some ambiguity in phoneme-to-grapheme conversion is present; i.e., a given phono-logical string may have more than one orthographic solution, though only one is correct. An example (see Section 9.2.2.2) concerns words with the phono-logical sequence /kw/, that can be transcribed as ‹cu› or ‹qu›, before ‹o› (e.g., *cuore* 'heart' vs. *liquore* 'liqueur'). The sublexical procedure does not allow choosing among spelling solutions; thus, a child with poor lexical knowledge may write **cuota* instead of *quota* 'share' or **squola* instead of *scuola* 'school'. Another example is the sequence /tte/, which may be spelled as ‹ce› or ‹cie› (as in *radice* 'root' and *specie* 'species').

A large study examining children in Grades 1 to 8 investigated the acquisi-tion of the sublexical and lexical spelling procedures comparing different word categories[2] (Notarnicola, Angelelli, Judica & Zoccolotti, 2012):

- *Regular* words with a 1:1 phoneme–grapheme correspondence, varying in phonetic-phonological complexity (including continuant versus non-continuant consonants, presence of CV syllables versus consonant clusters, and doubled consonants and bisyllables versus polysyllables);
- *Context-sensitive* words requiring the application of context-sensitive sound-to-spelling rules (e.g., /k/ is spelled ‹c› in *casa* /'kasa/ 'home', but ‹ch› in *chiesa* /'kjɛza/ 'church');
- *Ambiguous* words with two or more possible spellings (e.g., words contain-ing /kw/, /tʃɛ/, etc.);
- *Regular* pseudowords (non-lexical units with one-phoneme-to-one-letter correspondence; items were controlled for the same sources of phonological complexity as the regular words).

Based on the dual-route model (e.g., Tainturier & Rapp, 2001), the effects of regularity (regular words and pseudowords vs. ambiguous words) and

---

[2] These stimuli are part of the DDO (Diagnosis of Orthographic Deficits in Childhood; Angelelli et al., 2008).

orthographic complexity (regular words with one-phoneme-to-one letter correspondence vs. context-sensitive words) would involve the sublexical procedure while the effect of lexicality (words vs. pseudowords) would mark the lexical one.

Early reliance on the sublexical procedure was indicated by the analysis of the regularity and orthographic complexity effects. As to the former, children were more accurate on regular stimuli (words or pseudowords) than on ambiguous words at all grades. As to the latter, regular words were spelled more accurately than context-sensitive words at all grades. However, early lexical processing was also detected. Regular words were spelled more accurately than regular pseudowords already in Grade 1, confirming data from Cossu, Gugliotta, and Marshall (1995). Notably, regular pseudowords were spelled more accurately than ambiguous words, indicating that the regularity effect was stronger than the lexicality one.

Lexical and sublexical processes showed different developmental trends. Accuracy on pseudoword spelling showed a rapid increase followed by a plateau around Grades 3/4 indicating a rapid development of the sublexical procedure. Accuracy on ambiguous words increased throughout the period tested, indicating a more gradual acquisition of the lexical procedure.

Notarnicola et al. (2012) also examined the error types at different ages, distinguishing between phonologically plausible and non-plausible errors. The former indicate errors that result in a string that could be read as homophonous to the target: They include errors in the absence of an orthographic rule (e.g., *cuota instead of quota 'share'), and errors violating an orthographic rule (e.g., *digha instead of diga 'dam'). So-called non-phonologically plausible errors included errors that result in a string not homophonous with the target, because of substitution or permutation of graphemes (e.g., fino 'until' instead of vino 'wine'), doubling of a single consonant or de-doubling of a double consonant.

Phonologically plausible errors were prevalent at all grades and decreased slowly throughout the period considered. By contrast, the other types of errors decreased substantially within the first three grades. These data indicate an earlier and more rapid development for the sublexical procedure and a slower acquisition of the lexical one. However, facilitating effects of morphological structure on accuracy in spelling pseudowords have been recently reported for both third- and fifth-grade children (Angelelli, Marinelli & Burani, 2014).

9.3.2.3 Reading and Spelling Difficulties   Some children show a selective difficulty in acquiring reading (about 3% of cases, two-thirds of which may remain undiagnosed; Barbiero et al., 2012). The difficulty is expressed most clearly in terms of reading slowness, while accuracy may be relatively preserved (Zoccolotti et al., 1999). Analysis of eye movements indicates very small rightward saccades (De Luca, Di Pace, Judica, Spinelli & Zoccolotti, 1999), particularly in the case of long stimuli (De Luca, Borrelli, Judica, Spinelli & Zoccolotti, 2002). Consistently, RTs of children with dyslexia grow monotonically as a function of word length (e.g., Spinelli et al., 2005), an effect present in typically developing children only in the very early phases of reading acquisition (Zoccolotti et al., 2005). The effect of length is partially compensated for in the case of morphologically complex words; thus, the morpheme is a unit of intermediate grain size that proves useful in the processing of words in children who did not fully develop mastering of whole-word processing (Burani et al., 2008; Marcolini et al., 2011).

Studies examining the effect of frequency (e.g., Barca, Burani, Di Filippo & Zoccolotti, 2006) or lexicality (e.g., Zoccolotti, De Luca, Judica & Spinelli, 2008) generally revealed spared lexical activation. While the effects of frequency and lexicality are quantitatively larger in children with dyslexia, this group difference vanishes when the general slowness in processing orthographic stimuli is controlled (Zoccolotti et al., 2008; Paizi, De Luca, Zoccolotti & Burani, 2013). These findings contrast with the hypothesis that Italian children with dyslexia show a selective impairment in either lexical or nonlexical processing. Alternatively, the reading difficulty has been ascribed to a deficit at a prelexical level of analysis which is expressed as a general slowness in processing visually presented orthographic strings independent of lexical quality (Zoccolotti et al., 2008; Paizi et al., 2013).

As for writing, analysis of spelling performance indicates different profiles of difficulties at different ages (Angelelli, Notarnicola, Judica, Zoccolotti & Luzzatti, 2010). In Grade 3, children show a spelling deficit encompassing all stimulus categories; by contrast, by Grade 5, only errors in writing ambiguous words (and phonologically plausible errors) remain in the foreground (Angelelli, Judica, Spinelli, Zoccolotti & Luzzatti, 2004; Angelelli et al., 2010). It has been reported that reading and spelling deficits are closely associated (Angelelli et al., 2004). One hypothesis is that this parallelism is due to a single defective lexicon, rather than to separate orthographic input and output lexicons (Angelelli, Marinelli & Zoccolotti, 2010).

9.3.3   Reading Comprehension

9.3.3.1 Predictors of Reading Comprehension   In Italian, reading comprehension has been studied more in relationship to the presence of developmental disturbances than to the issue of development per se. In this vein, it has been noted that children with developmental dyslexia show a selective deficit in word decoding but a smaller and variable disturbance in the comprehension of texts (Zoccolotti et al., 1999). This dissociation is clearer if children are given comprehension tests without time limits so that word decoding is less crucial and other parameters (see below) come to the foreground.

However, it is possible to identify children with selective difficulties in reading comprehension. Studies compared poor and good comprehenders matched for general cognitive abilities to detect which cognitive components are crucial for reading comprehension. For example, Cataldo and Cornoldi (1998) reported that poor comprehenders were particularly defective in responding to questions at the end of the text and ascribed this failure to lack of a strategy in searching for appropriate information. When instructed to search in the text for the appropriate information, readers appreciably improved their comprehension performance.

There is a large consensus that working memory is important for reading comprehension (e.g., Swanson & Berninger, 1995). A critical working memory operation may regard the updating of relevant information, particularly in discounting items that are no longer relevant (Palladino, Cornoldi, De Beni & Pazzaglia, 2001). Accordingly, poor comprehenders were more likely to intrude items maintained longer in memory (Carretti, Cornoldi, De Beni & Romanò, 2005; De Beni & Palladino, 2000).

One battery of tests for testing Italian children during school years was developed by De Beni, Cornoldi, Caretti, and Meneghetti (2003). Two factors account for the performance in the various tests (Meneghetti, Carretti & De Beni, 2006): One involves aspects requiring continuous work on the text and allows for basic understanding of the text, while another concerns self-regulated aspects of cognition. This includes abilities such as constructing a mental model of the text, monitoring the level of comprehension, and checking for congruent and incongruent information in the text. Skills related to the first factor evolved more rapidly than the "complex" abilities related to the second (Carretti, Meneghetti & De Beni, 2005). Notably, scholastic achievement correlated more with the complex, than the basic, abilities (Meneghetti et al., 2006).

9.3.3.2 Word-Level Effects in Comprehending Text   Examining the predictive and concurrent relationships between different literacy skills in Italian and their changes across grades was the aim of a recent longitudinal study (Desimoni, Scalisi & Orsolini, 2012). Children were assessed for reading accuracy, speed, text comprehension, and spelling first in Grade 1 and subsequently in Grade 3. Reading speed (but not accuracy) was a significant predictor of later literacy. Spelling was the most stable measure and predicted text comprehension and reading speed. An asymmetry was also observed between reading and spelling errors, with reading errors predicting later spelling errors and a non-significant result in the opposite direction.

As for reading comprehension, the contribution of decoding was stronger in Grade 1 than 3; by contrast, spelling predicted comprehension in both grades. Finally, reading speed was a significant predictor only in Grade 3. Desimoni et al. (2012) propose that, in Grade 1, the effective acquisition of phoneme–grapheme conversion rules strengthens grapheme–phoneme processes (and vice versa), improving accurate reading. This in turn leaves more attentional resources available for comprehension. In Grade 3, lexically driven word recognition helps children to quicken their reading rate, enhancing reading comprehension.

9.3.4   Conclusion

Evidence confirms the relatively fast acquisition of accuracy in reading Italian, similar to other transparent orthographies. By contrast, optimal reading speed is obtained slowly through the whole scholastic curriculum. Critically, acquisition of reading speed depends upon the characteristics of the stimuli. In particular, morphemes play an important role as phonologically transparent units to foster speed of word decoding. This indicates that reading acquisition is based on lexical units of a larger grain-size than the single letters. Importantly, reading speed is a good predictor of reading comprehension indicating that an appropriate level of fluency is necessary to effectively master text comprehension.

Contrary to the idea that sublexical processing may be sufficient in transparent orthographies, much evidence indicates the importance of lexical knowledge in reading and spelling acquisition. This is especially clear for stress assignment: Children pass from using more general information (i.e., stress dominance) to more specific knowledge (i.e., stress neighborhood). In spelling, the presence of phoneme-to-grapheme ambiguities allows a distinction between the development of the sublexical and lexical procedures, with the former being much faster than the latter.

Several issues are still open. The Italian language has a large prevalence of open syllables (see Section 9.2.1.1), and a relatively low number of syllable types. Consequently, the number of syllable forms is low (about 3,500, see Section 9.2.1.1) compared to English, which has well above 10,000 syllable forms (see Perfetti & Harris, 2013). Surprisingly, to our knowledge, there have not yet been investigations of the possible role of syllables as reading units.

A related issue worthy of further investigation is how far and under which circumstances the word as a whole may act as a reading unit. Italian words are quite long as compared to the mean word length of languages such as English. Therefore, the developing readers might be often forced to adopt shorter reading units to bypass the limitations of their developing visual-perceptual system.

9.4   Discussion

9.4.1   Challenges in Learning to Read Italian

There are two main characteristics of Italian orthography that influence reading acquisition. First, because of the high degree of regularity, accuracy asymptotes early and already by the end of Grade 1 children make relatively few reading errors. Second, owing to the relatively long words, length has a powerful effect on reading speed during the early grades (and holds as a critical factor for a minority of children with selective reading deficits).

The acquisition of an appropriate reading speed is important to allow children to master texts of increasing complexity as they progress in their scholastic curriculum. We have seen how reading speed is a significant predictor of text comprehension. Specific rehabilitation intervention has been proposed to foster reading speed in children with dyslexia (e.g., Judica, De Luca, Spinelli & Zoccolotti, 2002).

9.4.2   Implications for Instruction

There has been a growing interest in recent years in studying the acquisition of reading and spelling in Italian. Parallel interest was also expressed by the Italian health and educational institutions. Two consensus conferences were devoted to learning disabilities (Consensus Conference, 2006/2007; Istituto Superiore di Sanità, 2010/2011). Their objective was to establish agreement between practitioners on the diagnostic procedures as well as on the rehabilitative treatments. Legislative initiatives from the Department of Education also focused on this question. The Italian Parliament recently approved Law no. 170 (2010) that established a series of policies in favor of children with dyslexia. A subsequent decree (Decreto N. 5669, 2011) contained "guidelines for the right to study of students with specific learning disabilities."

Even though specific rehabilitation may on occasion be necessary to cope with severe disturbances, much can be obtained directly in school by tailoring the characteristics of instruction to the specific needs of children.

Two issues seem to come to the foreground. First, the acquisition of an appropriate reading speed is an important educational goal to allow a child's progression to texts of higher complexity. Even in typically developing children, the acquisition of optimal reading speed is a slow process requiring appropriate levels of exposure to print and reading practice. One key problem in dyslexic children is that they do not enjoy reading. Accordingly, they read much less than their peers and do not engage themselves in reading texts apart from those required in school. This creates a vicious circle aggravating their difficulties. School teachers and operators should be sensitive to this issue and make efforts to find interesting materials stimulating the children's interest. Some educational programs have been developed with this aim (e.g., Judica, Baldoni, Chirri, Cucciaioni & Del Vento, 2006).

Second, lexical processing, and processing based on morphemes in particular, is important in mediating reading and spelling acquisition (Traficante, 2012). The reviewed studies indicate that morphological abilities develop early in Italian as contrasted to English-speaking children who might develop knowledge of word morphology much later (Freyd & Baron, 1982). As presented in Section 9.3.2.1, morphemes are available early as reading units in Italian, again in contrast to English-speaking readers for whom the morphographic level of representation may be an advanced phase of literacy acquisition available on top of orthographic knowledge (Seymour, 1997). Consequently, focusing on morphological constituents may help in training young Italian readers.

We have illustrated markers of deficiencies in lexical processing. In reading, they may be probed by difficulties in stress assignment (Paizi et al., 2011), and in writing, by difficulties in spelling words which have more than one spelling possibility. It seems important that school teachers be made sensitive to these deficiencies in order to facilitate early detection and intervention.

9.5   Final Conclusion

We have described the up-to-date evidence on Italian children's acquisition of reading and spelling skills. A brief description of the Italian language is provided, including its phonology, inflectional morphology, and word formation processes. The basic rules of schooling and how they developed in recent years are also illustrated.

The orthography of Italian exhibits a fairly regular pattern of phoneme–grapheme correspondences, but a few cases of non-univocal correspondences are present and prove important in the evaluation of reading and spelling acquisition. Reading accuracy asymptotes quickly, and by the end of Grade 1 typically developing children read correctly over 90% of content and function words. However, reading speed develops more slowly, and this parameter proves more sensitive than accuracy in detecting the developmental trajectory of effects such as lexicality, word length, and frequency. Findings indicate an early mastering of grapheme to phoneme correspondences but also early evidence of lexical competence, and sensitivity to morphological structure and lexical stress. Evidence on spelling acquisition indicates a relatively rapid development of the sublexical procedure and a more gradual acquisition of the lexical procedure (as indicated by the spelling of the few Italian words which have more than one possible spelling).

Overall, contrary to the idea that sublexical processing may be sufficient in transparent orthographies, much evidence indicates the importance of lexical knowledge in reading and spelling acquisition. This is particularly important in the acquisition of reading fluency which, in turn, represents a prerequisite of appropriate levels of reading comprehension (though other factors are also involved in this process). The implications of this body of evidence for fostering literacy instruction were briefly discussed.

References

Angelelli, P., Judica, A., Spinelli, D., Zoccolotti, P. & Luzzatti, C. (2004). Characteristics of writing disorders in Italian dyslexic children. *Cognitive and Behavioral Neurology, 17*, 18–31.

Angelelli, P., Marinelli, C. & Burani, C. (2014). The effect of morphology on spelling and reading accuracy: A study on Italian children. *Frontiers in Psychology*, 8, 875.

Angelelli, P., Marinelli, C. V. & Zoccolotti, P. (2010). Single or dual orthographic representations for reading and spelling? A study on Italian dyslexic and dysgraphic children. *Cognitive Neuropsychology, 27*, 305–333.

Angelelli, P., Notarnicola, A., Costabile, D., Marinelli, C. V., Judica, A., Zoccolotti, P. & Luzzatti, C. (2008). *DDO–Diagnosi dei disturbi ortografici in etá evolutiva* [Diagnosis of orthographic deficits in childhood]. Trento: Erickson.

Angelelli, P., Notarnicola, A., Judica, A., Zoccolotti, P. & Luzzatti, C. (2010). Spelling impairment in Italian dyslexic children: Does the phenomenology change with age? *Cortex, 46*, 1299–1311.

Barbiero, C., Lonciari, I., Montico, M., Monasta, L., Penge, R., Vio, C., Tressoldi, P. E., Ferluga, V., Bigoni, A., Tullio, A., Carrozzi, M. & Ronfani, L. (2012). The submerged dyslexia iceberg: How many school children are not diagnosed? Results from an Italian study. *PloS one, 7*, e48082.

Barca, L., Burani, C., Di Filippo, G. & Zoccolotti, P. (2006). Italian developmental dyslexic and proficient readers: Where are the differences? *Brain and Language, 98*, 347–351.

Barca, L., Ellis, A. W. & Burani, C. (2007). Context-sensitive rules and word naming in Italian children. *Reading and Writing, 20*, 495–509.

Bellocchi, S., Bonifacci, P. & Burani, C. (2013). Lexicality, frequency and stress assignment effects in bilingual children reading Italian as a second language. Ms. submitted for publication.

Bertinetto, P. M. & Loporcaro, M. (2005). The sound pattern of Standard Italian, as compared with the varietes spoken in Florence, Milan and Rome. *Journal of the International Phonetic Association, 35*, 131–151.

Biffi, M. & Maraschio, N. (2008). Storia interna dell'italiano: Sistema fonico e grafico. In G. Ernst, M.-D. Gleßgen, C. Schmitt & W. Schweickard (Eds.), *Romanische Sprachgeschichte* (pp. 2810–2830). Berlin: De Gruyter.

Bimonte, D. (2002). "La conigliera è un collare per conigli ... ": Morfologia derivazionale e acquisizione del vocabolario in bambini di scuola elementare. Unpublished thesis, University of Roma-La Sapienza.

Bimonte, D. & Burani, C. (2005). Studi sullo sviluppo della conoscenza della morfologia derivazionale. *Età Evolutiva, 80,* 101–115.

Bortolini, U. (1976). Tipologia sillabica dell'italiano: Studio statistico. In R. Simone, U. Vignuzzi & G. Ruggiero (Eds.), *Studi di fonetica e fonologia* (pp. 5–22). Rome: Bulzoni.

Brizzolara, D., Pecini, C., Chilosi, A., Cipriani, P., Gasperini, F., Mazzotti, S., Di Filippo, G. & Zoccolotti, P. (2006). Do phonological and rapid automatized naming deficits differentially affect dyslexic children with and without a history of language delay? A study on Italian dyslexic children. *Cognitive and Behavioural Neurology, 19,* 141–149.

Burani, C. (2010). Word morphology enhances reading fluency in children with developmental dyslexia. *Lingue e Linguaggio, 9,* 177–198.

Burani, C. & Arduino, L. S. (2004). Stress regularity or consistency? Reading aloud Italian polysyllables with different stress patterns. *Brain and Language, 90,* 318–325.

Burani, C., Barca, L. & Ellis, A. W. (2006). Orthographic complexity and word naming in Italian: Some words are more transparent than others. *Psychonomic Bulletin & Review, 13,* 346–352.

Burani, C., Bimonte, D., Barca, L. & Vicari, S. (2006). Word morphology and lexical comprehension in Williams Syndrome. *Brain and Language, 99,* 112–113.

Burani, C., Marcolini, S., De Luca, M. & Zoccolotti, P. (2008). Morpheme-based reading aloud: Evidence from dyslexic and skilled Italian readers. *Cognition, 108,* 243–262.

Burani, C., Marcolini, S. & Stella, G. (2002). How early does morpholexical reading develop in readers of a shallow orthography? *Brain and Language, 81,* 568–586.

Burani, C., Paizi, D. & Sulpizio, S. (2013). Stress assignment in Italian: Friendship outweighs dominance. *Memory & Cognition, 42,* 662–675.

Carlisle, J. F. & Nomabody, D. M. (1993). Phonological and morphological awareness in first grades. *Applied Psycholinguistics, 14,* 177–195.

Carretti, B., Cornoldi, C., De Beni, R. & Romanò, M. (2005). Updating in working memory: A comparison of good and poor comprehenders. *Journal of Experimental Child Psychology, 91,* 45–66.

Carretti, B., Meneghetti, C. & De Beni, R. (2005). Evoluzione delle abilità di comprensione in studenti dalla 3a elementare alla 1a media [The evolution of reading comprehension abilities in students from third to sixth grade]. *Età Evolutiva, 80,* 5–16.

Casalis, S. & Louis-Alexandre, M.-F. (2000). Morphological analysis, phonological analysis and learning to read French: A longitudinal study. *Reading and Writing, 12,* 303–335.

Cataldo, M. G. & Cornoldi, C. (1998). Self-monitoring in poor and good reading comprehenders and their use of strategy. *British Journal of Developmental Psychology, 16,* 155–165.

Chilosi, A. M., Brizzolara, D., Lami, L., Pizzoli, C., Gasperini, F., Pecini, C. & Zoccolotti, P. (2009). Reading and spelling disabilities in children with and without a history of early language delay: A neuropsychological and linguistic study. *Child Neuropsychology, 15,* 582–604.

Colombo, L. (1992). Lexical stress effect and its interaction with frequency in word pronunciation. *Journal of Experimental Psychology: Human Perception and Performance, 18,* 987–1003.

Coltheart, M., Rastle, K., Perry, C., Langdon, R. & Ziegler, J. (2001). DRC: A dual route cascaded model of visual word recognition and reading aloud. *Psychological Review, 108,* 204–256.

Consensus Conference (2006, September/2007, January). *Disturbi evolutivi specifici di Apprendimento: Raccomandazioni per la pratica clinica definite con il metodo della Consensus Conference* [Specific Developmental disturbances: Recommandations for clinical practice defined with the method of Consensus Conference]. 22–23 September 2006, Montecatini Terme (sentenza della giuria: 26 January 2007, Milan. Retrieved from http://hubmiur.pubblica.istruzione.it/alfresco/d/d/work space/SpacesStore/a9cf25e3-2cd0-471a-9b44-f2d12d17e5a3/raccomandazio nidsa2007.pdf.

Cossu, G., Gugliotta, M. & Marshall, J. C. (1995). Acquisition of reading and written spelling in a trasparent orthography: Two non parallel processes? *Reading and Writing, 7,* 9–22.

Cossu, G., Gugliotta, M., Villani, D., Cristante, F. & Emiliani, M. (1990). Consapevolezza fonemica e acquisizione della lettura [Phonemic awareness and reading acquisition]. *Saggi, 16,* 47–60.

Cossu, G. & Marshall, J. C. (1986). Theoretical implications of the hyperlexia syndrome: Two new Italian cases. *Cortex, 22,* 579–589.

(1990). Are cognitive skills a prerequisite for learning to read and write? *Cognitive Neuropsychology, 7,* 21–40.

Cossu, G., Rossini, F. & Marshall, J. C. (1993). When reading is acquired but phonemic awareness is not: A study of literacy in Down's Syndrome. *Cognition, 4,* 129–138.

Cossu, G., Shankweiler, D., Liberman, I. Y. & Gugliotta, M. (1995). Visual and phonological determinants of misreading in a transparent orthography. *Reading and Writing, 17,* 247–256.

Cossu, G., Shankweiler, D. P., Liberman, I. Y., Katz, L. & Tola, G. (1988). Awareness of phonological segments and reading ability in Italian children. *Applied Psycholinguistics, 9,* 1–16.

Cunningham, A. J. & Carroll, J. M. (2011). Reading-related skills in earlier- and later-schooled children. *Scientific Studies of Reading, 15,* 244–266.

D'Achille, P. (2006). *L'italiano contemporaneo.* Bologna: Il Mulino.

D'Amico, A. (2000). Il ruolo della memoria fonologica e della consapevolezza fonemica nell'apprendimento della lettura: Ricerca longitudinale [The role of phonological memory in the learning of reading: A longitudinal study]. *Psicologia Clinica Dello Sviluppo, 4,* 125–144.

De Beni, R., Cornoldi, C., Carretti, B. & Meneghetti, C. (2003). *Nuova guida alla comprensione del testo* [A new guide to reading comprehension], Vol. I. Trento: Edizioni Erickson.

De Beni, R. & Palladino, P. (2000). Intrusion errors in working memory tasks: Are they related to reading comprehension ability? *Learning and Individual Differences, 12,* 131–143.

De Luca, M., Borrelli, M., Judica, A., Spinelli, D. & Zoccolotti, P. (2002). Reading words and pseudo-words: An eye movement study of developmental dyslexia. *Brain and Language, 80*, 617–626.

De Luca, M., Di Pace, E., Judica, A., Spinelli, D. & Zoccolotti, P. (1999). Eye movement patterns in linguistic and non-linguistic tasks in developmental surface dyslexia. *Neuropsychologia, 37*, 1407–1420.

De Mauro, T. (1989). *Guida all'uso delle parole*. Rome: Editori Riuniti.

(1999). *Grande dizionario italiano dell'uso*. Turin: UTET.

De Mauro, T., Mancini F., Vedovelli, M. & Voghera, M. (1993). *Lessico di frequenza dell'italiano parlato*. Milan: ETASLIBRI.

Decreto N. 5669 (2011, July 12). *Linee guida per il diritto allo studio degli alunni e degli studenti con dsa* [Guidelines for the "right to study" of students with specific learning disabilities]. Rome: Il Ministro dell'Istruzione dell' Università e della Ricerca.

Desimoni, M., Scalisi, T. G. & Orsolini, M. (2012). Predictive and concurrent relations between literacy skills in Grades 1 and 3: A longitudinal study of Italian children. *Learning and Instruction, 22*, 340–353.

Di Filippo, G., Brizzolara, D., Chilosi, A., De Luca, M., Judica, A., Pecini, C., Spinelli, D. & Zoccolotti, P. (2005). Rapid naming, but not cancellation speed or articulation rate, predicts reading in an orthographically regular language (Italian). *Child Neuropsychology, 11*, 349–361.

Dressler, W. U. & Thornton, A. M. (1991). Doppie basi e binarismo nella morfologia italiana. *Rivista di Linguistica, 3*, 3–22.

Faust, M. E., Balota, D. A., Spieler, D. H. & Ferraro, F. R. (1999). Individual differences in information processing rate and amount: Implications for group differences in response latency. *Psychological Bulletin, 125*, 777–799.

Freyd, P. & Baron, J. (1982). Individual differences in the acquisition of derivational morphology. *Journal of Verbal Learning and Verbal Behaviour, 21*, 282–295.

Frost, R. (2012). Towards a universal model of reading. *Behavioral and Brain Sciences, 35*, 263–329.

Goslin, J., Galluzzi, C. & Romani, C. (2014). PhonItalia: A phonological lexicon for Italian. *Behavior Research Methods, 46*, 872–886.

Grossmann, M. & Rainer, F. (Eds.) (2004). *La formazione delle parole in italiano*. Tübingen: Niemeyer.

Iacobini, C. & Adinolfi, A. (2008). La derivazione suffissale nel parlato dell'italiano messa a confronto con quella dello scritto. In M. Pettorino, A. Giannini, M. Vallone & R. Savy (Eds.), *Proceedings of the Conference "La comunicazione parlata" (Spoken Communication)* (pp. 494–512). Naples: Liguori.

Iacobini, C. & Thornton, A. M. (1992). Tendenze nella formazione delle parole nell'italiano del ventesimo secolo. In B. Moretti, D. Petrini & S. Bianconi (Eds.), *Linee di tendenza dell'italiano contemporaneo* (pp. 25–55). Rome: Bulzoni.

Invalsi (2009). *Le competenze in lettura, matematica, e scienze degli studenti quindicenni Italiani. Rapporto Nazionale PISA 2009*, Frascati: Author. Retrieved from www.invalsi.it/invalsi/ri/Pisa2009/documenti/RAPPORTO_PISA_2009.pdf.

ISTAT (2011). *Italia in cifre 2011*. Rome: Author. Retrieved from www.istat.it/it/files/2011/06/italiaincifre2011.pdf.

Istituto Superiore di Sanità (2010, December/2011, June). *Consensus conference. Disturbi specifici dell'apprendimento* [Specific learning disturbances], Published in June, 2011, Rome. Retrieved from www.snlg-iss.it/cms/files/Cc_Disturbi_App rendimento_sito.pdf.

Judica, A., Baldoni, L., Chirri, L., Cucciaioni, C. & Del Vento, G. (2006). *Parole in corso: Materiale per il recupero delle difficoltà di lettura* [Running words: Materials for the recovery from reading difficulties]. Trento: Erickson.

Judica, A., De Luca, M., Spinelli, D. & Zoccolotti, P. (2002). Training of developmental surface dyslexia improves reading performance and shortens eye fixation duration in reading. *Neuropsychological Rehabilitation, 12,* 177–197.

Law no. 170 (2010). Nuove norme in materia di disturbi specifici di apprendimento in ambito scolastico [New rules for learning disabilities at school]. In *Gazzetta Ufficiale N. 24.* October 18, 2010.

Lepschy, A. L. & Lepschy, G. C. (1991). *The Italian language today.* London: Routledge.

Lepschy, G. C. (1978). Note sulla fonematica italiana. In G. C. Lepschy, *Saggi di linguistica italiana* (pp. 63–75). Bologna: Il Mulino.

Lo Duca, M. G. (1987). I bambini e le parole: Su alcuni procedimenti di scoperta del significato. *Quaderni di Semantica, 8,* 69–93.

(1990). *Creatività e regole, studio sull'acquisizione della morfologia derivativa dell'italiano.* Bologna: Il Mulino.

Maiden, M. (1992). Irregularity as a determinant of morphological change. *Journal of Linguistics, 28,* 285–312.

Mancini, F. & Voghera, M. (1994a). Lunghezza, tipi di sillabe e accento in italiano. In T. De Mauro (Ed.), *Come parlano gli italiani* (pp. 217–245). Scandicci: La Nuova Italia Editrice.

Mancini, F. & Voghera, M. (1994b). Lunghezza, tipi di sillabe e accento in italiano. *Archivio Glottologico Italiano, 79,* 51–77.

Marcolini, S., Burani, C. & Colombo, L. (2009). Lexical effects on children's pseudo-word reading in a transparent orthography. *Reading and Writing, 22,* 531–544.

Marcolini, S., Donato, T., Stella, G. & Burani, C. (2006). Lunghezza e morfologia della parola: Come interagiscono nella lettura dei bambini? *Giornale Italiano di Psicologia, 33,* 649–659.

Marcolini, S., Traficante, D., Zoccolotti, C. & Burani, C. (2011). Word frequency modulates morpheme-based reading in poor and skilled Italian readers. *Applied Psycholinguistics, 32,* 513–532.

Marotta, G. (1991). The Italian diphthongs and the autosegmental framework. In P. M. Bertinetto & M. Loporcaro (Eds.), *Certamen phonologicum* (pp. 389–420). Turin: Rosenberg & Sellier.

Martina, A. (2001). Studio sperimentale sull'acquisizione della morfologia derivazionale da parte di bambini italiani: Un approccio neurolinguistico. Unpublished thesis, University of Pisa.

Meneghetti, C., Carretti, B. & De Beni, R. (2006). Components of reading comprehension and scholastic achievement. *Learning and Individual Differences, 16,* 291–301.

Menghini, D., Finzi, A., Benassi, M., Bolzani, R., Facoetti, A., Giovagnoli, S., Ruffino, M. & Vicari, S. (2010). Different underlying neurocognitive deficits in developmental dyslexia: A comparative study. *Neuropsychologia, 48,* 863–872.

Morais, J., Gary, L., Alegria, J. & Bertelson, P. (1979). Does awareness of speech as a sequence of phones arise spontaneously? *Cognition, 7*, 323–331.

Mulatti, C., Peressotti, F. & Job, R. (2007). Zeading and reazing: Which is faster? The position of the diverging letter in a pseudoword determines reading time. *The Quarterly Journal of Experimental Psychology, 60*, 1005–1014.

Newell, A. & Rosenbloom, P. S. (1981). Mechanisms of skill acquisition and the law of practice. In J. R. Anderson (Ed.), *Cognitive skills and their acquisition* (pp. 1–55). Hillsdale, NJ: Lawrence Erlbaum.

Notarnicola, A., Angelelli, P., Judica, A. & Zoccolotti, P. (2012). Development of spelling skills in a shallow orthography: The case of Italian language. *Reading and Writing, 25*, 1171–1194.

OECD (2011). *Education at a glance 2011: OECD indicators.* Retrieved from www .oecd.org/education/school/educationataglance2011oecdindicators.htm#Data.

Orsolini, M., Fanari, R., Serra, G., Cioce, R., Rotondi, A., Dassisti, A. & Maronato, C. (2003). Primi progressi nell'apprendimento della lettura: Una riconsiderazione del ruolo della consapevolezza fonologica [Initial progress in reading learning: A reconsideration of the role of phonological awareness]. *Psicologia Clinica Dello Sviluppo, 7*, 403–436.

Orsolini, M., Fanari, R., Tosi, V., De Nigris, B. & Carrieri, R. (2006). From phonological recoding to lexical reading: A longitudinal study on reading development in Italian. *Language and Cognitive Processes, 21*, 576–607.

Paizi, D., De Luca, M., Zoccolotti, P. & Burani, C. (2013). A comprehensive evaluation of lexical reading in Italian developmental dyslexics. *Journal of Research in Reading, 36*, 303–329.

Paizi, D., Zoccolotti, P. & Burani, C. (2011). Lexical stress assignment in Italian developmental dyslexia. *Reading and Writing, 24*, 443–461.

Palladino, P., Cornoldi, C., De Beni, R. & Pazzaglia, F. (2001). Working memory and updating processes in reading comprehension. *Memory & Cognition, 29*, 344–354.

Peressotti, F., Mulatti, C. & Job, R. (2010). The development of lexical representations: Evidence from the position of the diverging letter effect. *Journal of Experimental Child Psychology, 106*, 177–183.

Perfetti, C. A., Beck, I., Bell, L. C. & Hughes, C. (1987). Phonemic knowledge and learning to read are reciprocal: A longitudinal study of first grade children. *Merrill-Palmer Quarterly, 33*, 283–319.

Perfetti, C. A. & Harris, L. N. (2013). Universal reading processes are modulated by language and writing system. *Language Learning and Development, 9*, 296–316.

Pirrelli, V. & Battista, M. (2000). The paradigmatic dimension of stem allomorphy in Italian verb inflection. *Rivista di linguistica, 12*, 307–380.

Scalisi, T. G., Desimoni, M. & Di Vito Curmini, L. (2013). Age and schooling effects on the development of phonological awareness (PA) and rapid automatized naming (RAN) in Italian children aged 5–7 years. *Rivista di Psicolinguistica Applicata/ Journal of Applied Psycholinguistics, 13*, 45–60.

Scalisi, T. G., Desimoni, M. & Pelagaggi, D. (2009). Validità delle prove PAC-SI nella previsione della lettura in prima e terza primaria [Validity of the PAC-SI tests in the prediction of reading in first and third grade]. *Psicologia Dell'Educazione, 3*, 255–280.

Schmid, S. (1999). *Fonetica e fonologia dell'italiano.* Turin: Paravia.

Scuccimarra, G., Cutolo, L., Fiorillo, P., Lembo, C., Pirone, T. & Cossu, G. (2008). Is there a distinct form of developmental dyslexia in children with specific language impairment? Findings from an orthographically regular language. *Cognitive and Behavioral Neurology*, *21*, 221–226.

Seymour, P. H. K. (1997). Foundations of orthographic development. In C. Perfetti, L. Rieben & M. Fayol (Eds.), *Learning to Spell* (pp. 319–337). Hillsdale, NJ: Lawrence Erlbaum.

Seymour, P. H. K., Aro, M. & Erskine, J. M. (2003). Foundation literacy acquisition in European orthographies. *British Journal of Psychology*, *94*, 143–174.

Spinelli, D., De Luca, M., Di Filippo, G., Mancini, M., Martelli, M. & Zoccolotti, P. (2005). Length effect in word naming latencies: Role of reading experience and reading deficit. *Developmental Neuropsychology*, *27*, 217–235.

Stella, V. & Job, R. (2001). Le sillabe PD/DPSS: Una base di dati sulla frequenza sillabica dell'italiano scritto. *Giornale Italiano di Psicologia*, *28*, 633–639.

Sulpizio, S., Boureux, M., Burani, C., Deguchi, C. & Colombo, L. (2012). Stress assignment in the development of reading aloud: Nonword priming effects on Italian children. In N. Miyake, D. Peebles & R. P. Cooper (Eds.), *Proceedings of the 34th Annual Conference of the Cognitive Science Society* (pp. 2369–2374). Austin, TX: Cognitive Science Society.

Sulpizio, S. & Colombo, L. (2013). Lexical stress, frequency, and stress neighborhood effects in the early stages of Italian reading development. *The Quarterly Journal of Experimental Psychology*, *66*, 2073–2084.

Swanson, H. L. & Berninger, V. (1995). The role of working memory in skilled and less skilled readers' comprehension. *Intelligence*, *21*, 83–108.

Tainturier, M. J. & Rapp, B. (2001). Spelling words. In B. Rapp (Ed.), *What deficits reveal about the human mind/brain: A handbook of cognitive neuropsychology* (pp. 263–289). Philadelphia, PA: Psychology Press.

Thornton, A. M., Iacobini, C. & Burani, C. (1997). *BDVDB. Una base di dati per il vocabolario di base della lingua italiana*, 2nd edn. Rome: Bulzoni.

Traficante, D. (2012). From graphemes to morphemes: An alternative way to improve skills in children with dyslexia. *Revista de investigación en Logopedia*, *2*, 163–185.

Traficante, D., Marcolini, S., Luci, A., Zoccolotti, P. & Burani, C. (2011). How do root and suffix influence reading of morphological pseudowords: A study of young Italian dyslexic children. *Language and Cognitive Processes*, *26*, 777–793.

Tressoldi, P. E. (1989). Lo sviluppo della lettura e della scrittura: Segmentazione e fusione fonemica [Reading and writing development: Phonemic analysis and synthesis]. *Età Evolutiva*, *33*, 53–58.

(1996). L'evoluzione della lettura e della scrittura dalla 2a elementare alla 3a media: Dati per un modello di sviluppo e per la diagnosi dei disturbi specifici [The evolution of reading and spelling from 2nd elementary class to 3rd middle class: Data for a developmental model and for the diagnosis of specific disturbances]. *Età evolutiva*, *56*, 43–55.

Tressoldi, P. E., Vio, C. & Maschietto, D. (1989). Valore predittivo della consapevolezza fonemica sul livello di lettura e scrittura nel primo anno di scuola elementare [Predictive value of phonemic awareness on reading and writing levels in the first class]. *Giornale Italiano di Psicologia*, *16*, 279–292.

Vincent, N. (1988). Italian. In M. Harris & N. Vincent (Eds.), *The Romance languages* (pp. 279–313). New York: Oxford University Press.

Ziegler, J. C. & Goswami, U. (2005). Reading acquisition, developmental dyslexia and skilled reading across languages: A psycholinguistic grain size theory. *Psychological Bullettin, 131,* 3–29.

Zoccolotti, P., De Luca, M., Di Filippo, G., Judica, A. & Martelli, M. (2009). Reading development in an orthographically regular language: Effects of length, frequency, lexicality and global processing ability. *Reading and Writing, 22,* 1053–1079.

Zoccolotti, P., De Luca, M., Di Pace, E., Judica, A., Orlandi, M. & Spinelli, D. (1999). Markers of developmental surface dyslexia in a language (Italian) with high grapheme–phoneme correspondence. *Applied Psycholinguistics, 20,* 191–216.

Zoccolotti, P., De Luca, M., Gasperini, F., Judica, A. & Spinelli, D. (2005). Word length effect in early reading and in developmental dyslexia. *Brain and Language, 93,* 369–373.

Zoccolotti, P., De Luca, M., Judica, A. & Spinelli, D. (2008). Isolating global and specific factors in developmental dyslexia: A study based on the rate and amount model (RAM). *Experimental Brain Research, 186,* 551–560.

10   Learning to Read French

S. Hélène Deacon, Alain Desrochers,
and Kyle Levesque

10.1   Introduction

10.1.1   French and Its Orthography

Recent estimates indicate that French is the main language of communication of more than 200 million people distributed over five continents and seventy countries (Lewis, Simons & Fennig, 2013; L'Observatoire de la Langue française, 2010). Although the spoken form of the language within the Francophone world is colored by regional accents and lexical specificities, its written form is governed by a common set of rules and practices monitored by institutions, such as the *Académie de la langue française* in France and the *Office de la langue française* in Québec, Canada.

10.1.2   Synchronic and Diachronic Characterization

The term *orthography* implies the application of a norm that dictates the "correct" way of spelling words. This concept became relevant to French in the seventeenth century only with the creation of the French Academy as a regulatory body. Let's begin with the process by which French became a written language and acquired a genuine orthographic system (Catach, 2001; Perret, 2008; Rey, Duval & Siouffi, 2007). This language is a daughter language of a vernacular form of Latin spoken by soldiers, settlers, and merchants of the Roman Empire. Vernacular (or vulgar) Latin is to be distinguished from the classical form of the language spoken and written by the Roman upper classes. Through the expansion of the Roman Empire, vernacular Latin eventually became the primary language of oral and written communication over continental Western Europe. After the fall of the Empire in the fifth century, varieties of vernacular Latin started to diverge and evolve into different typologies and ultimately distinct so-called Romance dialects (from *romanice loqui*, meaning 'speaking Latin'), each with unique phonology, morphology, and lexicon. Over the present geographical area of France, these dialects formed the Gallo-Romance family and divided into two branches, *langue d'oïl* north of the Loire River and *langue d'oc* in the south. French emerged from the former branch and ultimately became the dominant language in both Northern and Southern France.

The transcription of Gallo-Romance evolved gradually from a casual recording device to a genuine orthographic system (Rey et al., 2007, part 3). Initially, side notes were added to Latin texts; these notes were intended to be read aloud to illiterate people with a poor command of spoken Latin (e.g., *Reichenau Glosses, Oaths of Strasbourg, Cantilène de Sainte Eulalie*). Written Gallo-Romance originally mapped the sound of the spoken language onto Latin graphemes, with the addition of Latin scripting habits (e.g., the use of abbreviations). These correspondences were not consensual or integrated into a unified system; instead, they varied widely within and across manuscripts. The transcription of Romance phonemes that did not exist in Latin, particularly diphthongs and triphthongs, was challenging and led to a long period of scripting experimentation (Biedermann-Pasques & Baddeley, 2008). By the twelfth century an early form of French, dubbed *Old French*, had emerged and its written form involved one-to-one phoneme–grapheme correspondences. Although Latin remained the language of prestige, the social status of French was rising, as reflected in its use in religious texts and administrative and juridical acts, as well as literary and scholarly works.

During the Renaissance, French made significant gains both as a spoken and as a written language. King François I officially made it the sole language of state administration, and legal and juridical acts in 1539 and, thereby, demoted Latin in state affairs management. Several developments gradually led writers of French to adopt a set of common rules and practices: the publication of glossaries and dictionaries (*Estienne, Nicot*), scholarly works on grammar (e.g., by Dubois, Meigret, Palsgrave, Tory; see Rey et al., 2007) and reading instruction methods (e.g., Le Gaygnard; Morin, 2008). Printers proposed many improvements to increase the readability of written French, such as the use of auxiliary marks (e.g., accents, dieresis, and cedilla) and the addition of *j* and *v* to the alphabet. Paradoxically, two antagonistic trends began to influence the shape of French orthography. One consisted in dressing up French words as Latin words by inserting mute *etymological* letters (e.g., *g* in *doigt* 'finger' from Latin *digitum*). The other, promoted by printers and poets, was to implement strictly one-to-one grapheme–phoneme correspondences.

The opposing forces between an etymological and a phonetic orthography hindered the development of a coherent orthographic system and fed lengthy disputes even after the creation of the French Academy by King Louis XIII in

1635. Even though important orthographic changes were made between 1650 and 1835 (Chervel, 2008, chap. 2), the present form of French orthography had essentially been established in the fourth edition (1762) of the Academy's dictionary. Despite significant efforts at developing a coherent system, French orthography is still struggling with inconsistencies today. All orthographic reforms attempted in the twentieth century have failed (Blanche-Benveniste & Chervel, 1969), but a modest set of rectifications, proposed in 1989, is gaining acceptance (Catach, 2001; Goosse, 1991; Séguin & Desrochers, 2008).

10.1.3 Literacy and Schooling

Following the Prussian model (Van Horn Melton, 1988), schooling became compulsory and free in most European and North American French-speaking communities during the nineteenth or twentieth century. Schooling spans about ten years, from the age of five or six years. In emerging countries on the African continent, access to reading instruction remains a concern (Organisation internationale de la Francophonie, 2012).

10.2   Description of French and Its Written Forms

Jaffré and Fayol (1997; Jaffré, 2003) argue that all written languages have two levels of articulation. The phonographic level specifies how speech is encoded, if at all, into print, and the semiographic level specifies how meaning is encoded into print. This distinction leads us to characterize the linguistic system in order to understand how it is captured by its written form.

10.2.1 Linguistic System

10.2.1.1 Phonology The phonetic representation of French words in a standard dictionary (e.g., *Le Petit Robert*) involves a set of sixteen vowels, twenty consonants, and three semi-vowels (see Table 10.1). The sounds of French vowels vary along five dimensions: mouth aperture (four levels), lip positions (rounded or spread), locus (front, central, and back), sonority (oral or nasal), and length (short or long). French consonants are captured by four dimensions: sonority (oral or nasal), manner of articulation (e.g., stop, fricative, lateral), place of articulation, and voicing (voiced or unvoiced). A recent analysis of the distribution of phonemes in popular media indicates that consonants account respectively for 51% of token frequencies and 53% of type frequencies, vowels for 46% and 44%, and semi-vowels for 3.6% and 3.5%

Table 10.1 *Transcription of standard phonemes found in spoken French with associated graphemes*

Vowels		Consonants	
[a]	année 'year', chat 'cat'	[p]	père 'father', groupe 'group', appel 'call'
[ɑ]	âne 'donkey', bras 'arm'	[t]	terre 'earth', porte 'door', carotte 'carrot', thé 'tea'
[ə]	le 'the', cheval 'horse'	[k]	côté 'side, sac 'bag', accord 'agreement', queue 'tail', musique 'music', ski 'ski', chorale 'choir'
[e]	écrire 'to write', jouer 'to play'	[b]	bon 'good', jambe 'leg', abbaye 'abbey'
[ɛ]	après 'after', prêt 'ready', fer 'iron', maison 'house', neige 'snow'	[d]	dent 'tooth', monde 'world', addition 'addition'
[i]	il 'he', hygiène 'hygiene'	[g]	garçon 'boy', bague 'ring', agglomération 'agglomeration'
[o]	odeur 'odour', dôme 'dome', autre 'other', château 'castle'	[f]	feu 'fire', œuf 'egg', affiche 'poster', éléphant 'elephant'
[ɔ]	oreille 'ear', encore 'again'	[s]	soleil 'sun', ciel 'sky', leçon 'lesson', poisson 'fish', nation 'nation'
[u]	ouvert 'open', genou 'knee', août 'August'	[ʃ]	chat 'cat', bouche 'mouth', schéma 'diagram'
[y]	unité 'unit', perdu 'lost'	[v]	vent 'wind', rêve 'dream'
[ø]	euphorie 'euphoria', feu 'fire', jeûne 'fasting', nœud 'knot'	[z]	zèbre 'zebra', bronze 'bronze', chose 'thing'
[œ]	seul 'alone', cœur 'heart'	[ʒ]	jour 'day', girafe 'girafe', geôlier 'jailer', juge 'judge'
[ɛ̃]	insecte 'insect', important 'important', synthèse 'synthesis', symphonie 'symphony', main 'hand', faim 'hunger' plein 'full', examen 'exam'	[l]	lettre 'letter', cheval 'horse', balle 'ball'
[ɑ̃]	enfant 'child', ampoule 'light bulb', emploi 'job'	[ʀ]	rue 'street', mer 'sea', verre 'glass', rhume 'a cold'
[ɔ̃]	oncle 'uncle', ombre 'shadow'	[m]	mot 'word', plume 'feather', pomme 'apple'
[œ̃]	un 'one', humble 'humble'	[n]	nuit 'night', lune 'noir', personne 'person'
Semi-vowels		[ɲ]	agneau 'lamb', vigne 'grapevine'
[j]	yoga, fille 'girl'	[ŋ]	camping
[w]	oui 'yes', fouet 'whip'	[h]	hop!
[ɥ]	huile 'oil', lui 'him'	[x]	jota

(New & Spinelli, 2013). The three most frequent phonemes are [a], [e], and [ʀ], and the three least frequent phonemes are [ɲ], [ŋ], and [x].

The combination of French phonemes into syllables is commonly accounted for by Pulgram's (1970) segmentation rules. In the application of these rules the final printed schwa, which is typically mute, is discounted and the maximum onset principle is used to segment two medial consonants, albeit with some exception rules. French phonological syllables are constructed from forty-five different patterns of consonants, vowels, and semi-vowels, comprising 1 to 6 phonemes, with an average of 3.5 (Chetail & Mathey, 2010). The CV pattern accounts for 49% of phonological syllables and the CVC pattern for 21%, attesting to the dominance of CV syllables in the phonological formation of French words.

10.2.1.2 Inflectional Morphology   French grammatical morphology hinges primarily on the noun and the verb. The noun controls two forms of inflection: grammatical gender and number. Case inflection has ceased to be productive in modern French. All nouns are assigned to one of two gender classes, *masculine* and *feminine*; unlike other languages, French has not retained the Latin neuter class. Grammatical gender is thus a grammaticalized noun classification system distinctive from biological gender. For animate nouns there is a strong, but less than perfect, correlation between grammatical gender and biological gender. The assignment of inanimate nouns to gender classes, however, can be predicted with some accuracy from noun endings, which typically take the form of suffixes. Some word endings are more clearly differentiated in writing than they are in speech (e.g., final /ɛ/ can take several orthographic forms: *-aie, -ais, -et*, associated with different gender classes).

Number inflection is far more straightforward than gender inflection. Noun pluralization is typically marked by the adjunction of a final *-s* and exceptionally by *-x* (e.g., on nouns ending with *-eu, -oeu, -au*). In some cases the plural is not marked at all, such as mass nouns and nouns that end with letters *-s, -x*, and *-z*. Although plural marking bears resemblance in French and English, there is a major difference between the two: plural markers (*-s, -x*) have become mute in modern French.

Gender and number inflections spread to other words within a noun phrase (e.g., determiners and adjectives) and between phrases (e.g., participles; number for the verb) through *agreement* processes. These inflections also spread across sentences through *coreference*. Plural marking on these words again involves the adjunction of a final *-s* or *-x* in writing only. It is phonologically realized only indirectly, namely, in liaisons to avoid collisions between two spoken vowels (e.g., *petits enfants* [petiz̃ɑ̃fɑ̃] 'small children'). Gender agreement is realized through special paradigms for determiners, adjectives, and participles (e.g., by the adjunction of a final *-e* in writing; Gardes-Tamine, 2002, chap. 2).

The conjugation of French verbs involves three primary dimensions: person (first, second, third), mood (e.g., indicative, conditional, subjunctive), and tense (e.g., present, past, future). Verbs are constructed by combining a word base with a person-tense suffix (e.g., first person plural of 'sing': *chant + ons*). The person is specified by the chosen subject, whereas the mood and tense are determined by the intended meaning of the message. There are approximately 11,000 verbs in modern French, and they are traditionally sorted into three conjugation classes according to their infinitive suffix: *-er, -ir*, and *-oir* or *-re* (Dubois, Jouannon & Lagane, 1961). A few verbs are not captured by this scheme because their patterns of conjugation are irregular (e.g., *avoir* 'to have', *être* 'to be'). This three-class scheme has become obsolete over time, since nearly all new verbs created in the past century belong to the first conjugation class (*-er*), which include over 90% of present French verbs (Séguin, 1986). Compared to English, the mastery of French verb conjugation is arduous; the phonological and orthographic base of some verbs varies for different persons or tenses, and the number of person-tense suffixes to learn is relatively large. All aspects of French inflectional morphology must be taught explicitly and over a relatively long interval for its mastery to be achieved.

10.2.1.3 Word Formation Processes   The primitive lexical stock of modern French comes from Vulgar Latin and, to a much lesser extent, from the languages Roman settlers came in contact with, such as Gaulish and Frankish. Subsequently, the French lexicon expanded through a variety of linguistic processes, which Guilbert (1975) assigned to four distinct classes. Phonological processes yield onomatopoeias, abbreviations, acronyms, and assimilation of loanwords. Semantic processes lead to changes in meaning without ensuing changes in phonological form, such as polysemy, semantic mutation (e.g., *Picasso* as the artist and his paintings), and grammatical class conversion. Loanword processes in French are involved in lexical imports from many other languages (e.g., from English: *gadget, lobby, marketing*). Finally, morphological processes result in the combination of freestanding morphemes (i.e., compounding) or the combination of free and bound morphemes (derivation).

Given that derivation has contributed a large number of new words in French, we discuss it in more detail. French allows three forms of derivations: the adjunction of an affix before (prefix) or after (suffix) or on both sides of a word base (e.g., prefix + base + suffix ➜ *transformation* 'transformation'). Word bases are typically nouns, adjectives, or verbs; in rare cases, they can be acronyms, adverbs, compound words, or short idioms. The adjunction of a prefix typically leaves the word base unchanged (e.g., *unir* 'unite' ➜ *réunir* 'reunite'). Suffixation, however, typically entails a phonological or etymological substitution in the base word (e.g., *poil* 'hair' ➜*pelage* 'fur'), reducing its transparency. The adjunction of a prefix changes the meaning of the resulting word but not its grammatical class (e.g., *dire* 'tell' → *redire* 'retell'). Some prefixes come from Latin (e.g., *co-*, *dé-*) and many from Greek (e.g., *bi-*, *hémi-*; Grevisse & Goose, 2007). The adjunction of a suffix, however, is by far the most productive word creation procedure in French. Like the prefix, it changes the meaning of the resulting word and it can also change its grammatical class. Suffixes can be used to form new nouns, adjectives, verbs, and adverbs through the application of combination rules (Dubois, 1962; Thiele, 1987). Nominal suffixes have an additional property: many are almost exclusively associated to a particular grammatical gender class (e.g., *-ier* for masculine nouns; *-ière* for feminine nouns).

10.2.2 Writing System

10.2.2.1 Script and Punctuation   French inherited its alphabet from Latin and various additions or adjustments were made over time. It is currently written using twenty-six letters and two ligatures (i.e., ‹æ›, ‹œ›). Because these characters are insufficient to represent all French phonemes, they have been supplemented over time by three scripting procedures. The first consists in adding a diacritical mark on top of vowels (to modify their phonological value: acute, grave, or circumflex accent; to indicate a hiatus: the dieresis mark) or under the letter *c* (to shift /k/ to /s/: the cedilla). The second involves the use of multiletter graphemes to represent single phonemes (e.g., ‹ou› [u], ‹ch› [ʃ]). Finally, the third procedure makes the phonological realization of some letters dependent on their context in the word structure (e.g., hard and soft *c* or *g*). French letters are capitalized only at the beginning of sentences, proper names (e.g., person, country), and special nouns (e.g., forms of address, titles). Other auxiliary marks include the apostrophe (e.g., for the elision of letters) and the hyphen (e.g., for joining words). The use of Arab digits has almost entirely replaced that of Roman digits, except for particular functions (e.g., numbering centuries or sovereigns).

Written French makes use of fourteen different punctuation marks: the period (.), the question mark (?), the exclamation mark (!), the comma (,), the semi-colon (;), the colon (:), suspension marks (. . .), parentheses (), square brackets [], angle brackets (<>), quotation marks (« »), the hyphen (-), the oblique mark (/), and the asterisk (*). Each of these marks serves specific functions (for details, see Grevisse & Gosse, 2007, chap. 2; Tanguay, 2006), and some marks traditionally indicate pauses of different durations in oral reading (e.g., period > semi-colon > comma; Codaire, 2008).

10.2.2.2 Orthography   In the twelfth century, French spelling involved one-to-one grapheme–phoneme correspondences. Over time pronunciation changed without systematic orthographic adjustments. For instance, many bigrams (e.g., ⟨au⟩, ⟨eu⟩) and trigrams (e.g., ⟨eau⟩, ⟨ain⟩) once represented distinct strings of phonemes, but they were later reduced to single phonemes. Many French words have preserved mute etymological letters (e.g., *baptiser* 'to baptise', *corps* 'body') and word-final letters that have become mute over time (e.g., *porc* 'pork', *gant* 'glove'; Grevisse & Goose, 2007). The progressive dissociation between orthography and pronunciation resulted in (a) graphemic redundancy (e.g., several phonemes are now represented by multiple graphemes; /o/ ➜ ⟨o⟩, ⟨au⟩, ⟨eau⟩); (b) multiple mute letters (e.g., *seringue* 'serynge' ➜ /sʀɛ̃g/); and (c) patterns of orthographic syllables that are more diverse than those of phonological syllables. Chetail and Mathey (2010) have identified 148 types of orthographic syllables, comprising 1 to 10 letters, with an average of 4.32. The CV pattern accounts for 26.4% of orthographic syllables and the CVC pattern for 15.4%, again attesting the dominance of the former in written French.

Catach (1980) has identified some 130 distinct graphemes in modern French (see Table 10.1 for common examples). Quantitative analyses show that grapheme-to-phoneme (G–P) consistency is generally higher than phoneme-to-grapheme (P–G) consistency, but these estimates vary over different serial positions (Peereman & Content, 1999; Peereman, Lété & Sprenger-Charolles, 2007; Ziegler, Jacobs & Stone, 1996). For instance, Peereman et al. (2007) have shown that the percentage of G–P consistency is 96% in initial position, 80% in middle positions, and 92% in final position. In comparison, the percentage of P-G consistency is 91% in initial position, 76% in middle positions, and 45% in final position. These findings lead to the prediction that learning to read French words aloud should be easier than learning to spell them out, at least for final letters.

10.2.3   Conclusion

Many factors contribute to the present French orthography. Through its alphabetic script, it provides important information about word pronunciation, albeit with some complexity. Through its historical and etymological letters, it preserves links with its origin and prior states of its evolution (e.g., obsolete pronunciations). Through its morphology, it conveys essential information about gender, number, person, mood, and tense. Moreover, it manages to differentiate homophones (e.g., /vɛʀ/: *ver* 'worm', *verre* 'glass', *vers* 'toward', and *vert* 'green'). These features have increased the complexity of French graphemes and reduced the transparency of grapheme–phoneme and phoneme–grapheme correspondences, all making French orthography harder to master than that of more transparent alphabetic languages. Although the efficiency of French orthography can still be optimized, recent reformation attempts have been met with resistance.

10.3   Acquisition of Reading and Spelling in French

Both phonological and morphological development reflects features of the French language system, and word reading and spelling reflect the orthography. Young Francophone children acquire word reading skill at a reasonably fast rate. As an example, by the end of Grade 1, Francophone children read about 87% of words and 80% of nonwords accurately (Sprenger-Charolles, Siegel & Bonnet, 1998). Young Francophone readers outperform their Anglophone peers (e.g., Bruck, Genesee & Caravolas, 1997), although both groups are outperformed by young readers of more phonologically transparent orthographies (e.g., Spanish; Caravolas et al., 2012; Goswami, Gombert & de Barrera, 1998; Seymour, Aro & Erskine, 2003; Ziegler et al., 2010). As in several other orthographies (e.g., Bruck & Waters, 1988; Wimmer & Hummer, 1990), French spelling poses more challenges than reading to both the learner and the expert (Leybaert & Content, 1995; Sprenger-Charolles & Casalis, 1995; Sprenger-Charolles et al., 1998).

10.3.1   Becoming Linguistically Aware

10.3.1.1 Phonological Development and Phonological Awareness The developmental trajectory of phonological production is quite similar in French and English (for French, see Aicart-De Falco & Vion, 1987; Rondal, 1997; for English, see Sander, 1972). Vowels are mastered first (often before age 2), followed by stop consonants (often before age 3). The mastery of fricative and lateral consonants is typically late emerging, overlapping with the onset of both phonological awareness and beginning reading.

Francophone children's phonological awareness reflects the high transparency of their language syllabic structure (Wioland, 1985). For instance, they show particularly strong syllabic awareness (Bruck et al., 1997; Ecalle & Magnan, 2002, 2007). They outperform same-aged Anglophone peers on syllabic awareness tasks but underperform them on phonemic awareness tasks (see Figure 10.1). Francophone children continue to perform more strongly on syllable- than phoneme-level awareness tasks throughout the elementary school years (Cormier, Desrochers & Sénéchal, 2006; Demont & Gombert, 1996; Sprenger-Charolles, Colé, Béchennec & Kipffer-Piquard, 2005). This advantage is often attributed to the time-based nature of the French syllable, the clarity of syllable boundaries (Goslin & Floccia, 2007), and the abundance of open syllables in French (e.g., CV or CCV; Chetail & Mathey, 2010; Wioland, 1985).

As in other alphabetic orthographies, phonological awareness predicts reading outcomes in young Francophone children. Several recent studies demonstrate this relationship, beyond multiple control measures (Ecalle & Magnan,

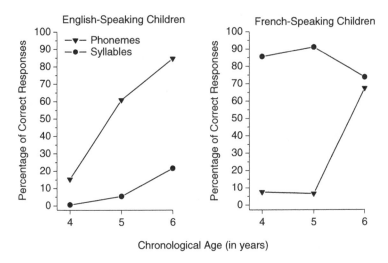

Figure 10.1 Percentage of correct responses as a function of segmental unit type (phoneme or iambic-stressed syllable) in the word matching task and native language (English or French). Constructed from "Differing sequences of metaphonological development in French and English," by L. G. Duncan, P. Colé, P. H. Seymour & A. Magnan, 2006, *Journal of Child Language, 33*, p. 389.

2007; Plaza & Cohen, 2003, 2004; Sanchez, Magnan & Ecalle, 2012; Ziegler et al., 2010). A few studies have contrasted the contribution of awareness of different sized phonological units to children's reading with equivocal results. As an example, different studies of Grade 1 children, with appropriate control variables, support the greater role of awareness of each segmental unit: phoneme (Demont & Gombert, 1996; Sanchez et al., 2012), onset-rime (Colin, Magnan, Ecalle & Leybaert, 2007; see also Bruck et al., 1997), and syllable (Plaza & Cohen, 2007). There is, however, consistent evidence that phonemic awareness emerges as a consequence of learning to read (Bruck et al., 1997; Duncan et al., 2006; Ecalle & Magnan, 2002). While the exact role of different segmental units still needs to be elucidated, there is clear evidence that phonological awareness is a strong correlate of Francophone children's reading outcomes.

10.3.1.2 Morphological Development and Morphological Awareness   Production of morphological forms emerges early in young Francophone children's speech. By 3 years of age, Francophone children produce appropriate morphosyntactic markers, such as articles and auxiliaries (François, François, Sabeau-Jouannet & Sourdot, 1977; Parrisse & Le Normand, 2000), and accurate gender inflections based on specific suffixes (Karmiloff-Smith, 1979; Seigneuric, Zagar, Meunier & Spinelli, 2007). Children's early competence with morpho-syntactic markers might emerge in part because of the co-occurrence of specific parts of speech; as an example, children always hear determiner–noun pairs, such as *le lit* 'the bed' (masc.), and so they reproduce it as a cluster. Some of these morphosyntactic markers seem to be acquired implicitly on this basis.

Young Francophone children clearly improve in their morphological aware-ness skills across the elementary school period, with better performance on tasks requiring comprehension than production (e.g., Casalis & Louis-Alexandre, 2000; Colé, Royer, Leuwers & Casalis, 2004). As an example, Grade 1 and 2 Francophone children appear to be aware of the morphological status of endings prior to understanding the relationship between words sharing a base morpheme (Roy & Labelle, 2007). It seems that children then become aware of the grammatical functions of morphemes (e.g., that adding *-ette* typically forms a noun). Intriguingly, Duncan, Casalis, and Colé (2009) showed that young Francophone children outperform their Anglophone counterparts with a similar level of schooling on oral derivational production tasks (like Berko, 1958), although these differences only approached significance when the children were matched for chronological age (see also Clark & Hecht, 1982; Seidler, 1988). Duncan et al. (2009) argued that this potential advantage on derivational forms might reflect linguistic features, specifically the greater productivity and heightened salience of derivations in French than English. While such studies need to extend beyond the early elementary school period and to other morphemic features, there is clear evidence of growth in Francophone children's morphological awareness through this time period.

Morphological awareness is also correlated with Francophone children's reading outcomes. This connection is to be expected given that French spel-lings encode both phonemes and morphemes (Huot, 2001). Kindergarten children's skill in morphological awareness relates to children's later word decoding and reading comprehension (Casalis & Louis-Alexandre, 2000; Colé et al., 2004). Perhaps the strongest evidence comes from a recent study; Sanchez et al. (2012) showed that these relationships survive the added control of phonological awareness, when evaluated at Grades 1 and 2. Given that the studies to date have focused on early word reading skill, future studies clearly need to examine both older children (see e.g., Roman, Kirby, Parrila, Wade-Woolley & Deacon, 2009, in English) and reading comprehension (e.g., Carlisle, 2003).

10.3.2   Development of Word Identification

10.3.2.1 Word Decoding Development   As a first step into word decoding, Francophone children learn single-letter grapheme–phoneme relationships fairly quickly. By the end of kindergarten (age 5), many graphemes are mastered by most children; in contrast, practically none of the multi-letter grapheme–phoneme relationships are known. Francophone children master most single- and multi-letter graphemes by the end of their first year of formal schooling, especially when they are taught explicitly (Desrochers & Thompson, 2008; see also Seymour et al., 2003).

Francophone children use grapheme–phoneme correspondence knowledge in their early reading. This is evident in regularity effects that emerge from the middle of Grade 1, only four months after the onset of formal reading instruction. Children of 6 years and 6 months (middle of Grade 1) read words with regular grapheme–phoneme correspondences more accurately than words with irregular correspondences (Sprenger-Charolles et al., 1998; see also Sprenger-Charolles & Casalis, 1995; Sprenger-Charolles et al., 2005; Sprenger-Charolles, Siegel, Béchennec & Serniclaes, 2003). Sprenger-Charolles and her collaborators (2005) reported evidence (see Figure 10.2) that words with regular single-letter and multi-letter graphemes[1] are initially the easiest to decode, followed by contextual graphemes and irregular graphemes. The impact of the grapheme-type effect decreases as a function of schooling and reading experience (see also Eme & Golder, 2005; Leybaert & Content, 1995), but it is still detectable in adulthood (Content, 1991; Ziegler, Perry & Coltheart, 2003).

Two findings demonstrate young children's growing sight word reading skills emerging by the end of Grade 1. First, children are more accurate in reading frequent than infrequent words at the end of Grade 1 (roughly aged 7 years; Sprenger-Charolles & Casalis, 1995; Sprenger-Charolles et al., 1998). Second, children read real words more accurately than nonwords from the end of Grade 1 (Desrochers, 2007; Eme & Golder, 2005; Sprenger-Charolles et al., 2003; Springer-Charolles et al., 1998). Both regularity and lexicality effects remain in reading latency throughout the elementary school years (Ducrot, Lété, Sprenger-Charolles, Pynte & Billard, 2003; Dufau et al., 2010; Leybaert & Content, 1995; Sprenger-Charolles et al., 2003).

Francophone children also draw on their oral language knowledge in their early reading attempts, as reflected in their ability to read new words by analogy to familiar words. For example, they are more accurate in reading nonwords with analogous forms than those without (e.g., *roile* that shares a rhyme unit with *voile* versus *loave* with no such analogous form). This effect emerges in reading by the middle of Grade 1 (Goswami et al., 1998; Sprenger-Charolles et al., 1998) and in spelling by the end of Grade 1 (Bosse, Valdois & Tainturier, 2003; Sprenger-Charolles et al., 1998). These effects emerge in French

---

[1] In this study, words with single-letter and multi-letter graphemes were equated for total number of letters. With this control in place, words with multi-letter graphemes included fewer phonemes than words with single-letter graphemes, which likely led to faster reading latencies in early school grades as shown in Figure 10.2.

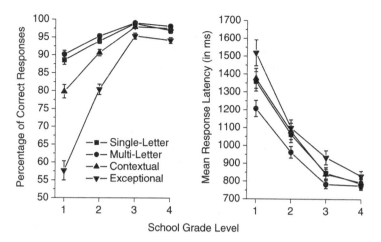

Figure 10.2 Percentage of correct responses (left panel) and response latency (in ms; right panel) in decoding words with different types of graphemes as a function of school grade level. Single-letter = words with regular single-letter graphemes; Multi-letter = words with regular multiple-letter graphemes; Contextual = words with regular contextual graphemes; Exceptional = words with irregular graphemes. Constructed from "French normative data on reading and related skills from EVALEC, a new computerized battery of tests (end Grade 1, Grade 2, Grade 3, and Grade 4)," by L. Sprenger-Charolles, P. Colé, D. Béchennec & A. Kipffer-Piquard, 2005, *Revue Européenne de Psychologie Appliquée, 55*(3), p. 166.

children's reading prior to other lexical factors, leading researchers to argue that reading by analogy reflects activation of related forms in the oral rather than written lexicon (Sprenger-Charolles et al., 1998).

Finally, by the end of Grade 1, Francophone children appear to access the morphemic components of real words as they read them. Prefixed words are read more accurately than pseudo-prefixed words (e.g., *refaire* versus *renifler*; Colé, Marec-Breton, Royer & Gombert, 2003). Similarly, Grade 2 and 3 children read pseudowords more accurately and faster when these are made up of real stem and real suffix (e.g., *chat-ure*) rather than a pseudo-stem and real suffix (e.g., *chot-ure*) or a pseudo-stem and a pseudo-suffix (e.g., *chot-ore*; Colé, Bouton, Leuwers, Casalis & Sprenger-Charolles, 2012; see also Marec-Breton, Gombert & Colé, 2005). Notably, morphemic effects during reading tasks are not entirely robust across all ages and morphemic types (e.g., Marec-Breton et al., 2005). Although research on children's word reading needs to be connected with the evidence of adults' automatic morphological analysis of complex words (e.g., Longtin, Segui & Hallé, 2003; see Quémart, Casalis & Colé, 2011), early sensitivity to morphemic structure is worthy of further investigation.

10.3.2.2 Word Spelling Development   In early spelling, as in early reading, children exploit the relationships between graphemes and phonemes, albeit in the other direction. Children make rapid progress in learning sound–letter correspondences. By the middle of Grade 1, children are more accurate in spelling regular than irregular words (Eme & Golder, 2005; Leybaert & Alegria, 1995; Leybaert & Content, 1995; Sénéchal, 2000; Sénéchal, Basque & Leclair, 2006; Sprenger-Charolles & Casalis, 1995; Sprenger-Charolles et al., 2003). By Grade 2, children are almost at ceiling in spelling consistent graphemes in pseudowords (Alegria & Mousty, 1996). These effects persist; children are more accurate in spelling phonemes and syllables with consistent sound-to-spelling correspondences through to Grade 5, with the greatest effects on long infrequent words (Lété, Peereman & Fayol, 2008).

Young Francophone children also demonstrate early sensitivity to graphotactic constraints, or regularities in the position and order of letters within words. Pacton, Perruchet, Fayol, and Cleeremans (2001) found that even at Grade 1, children were more likely to identify nonwords as word-like when these contained high- rather than low-frequency double consonants (e.g., *ll* versus *dd*). Clearly, young children have some knowledge about which letters can and cannot be doubled that is independent of, or in addition to, their knowledge of letter–sound mappings.

It takes children some time to master other aspects of the French orthography. For example, the spelling of certain phonemes, such as /s/, depends on the surrounding context; these are challenging even until Grade 5 (Alegria & Mousty, 1996). Similarly, Francophone children have long-standing difficulties in spelling final mute letters, which are common in French orthography (Bourdin, Leuwers & Bourbon, 2011; Fayol, Totereau & Barrouillet, 2006; Totereau, Thevenin & Fayol, 1997).

Sensitivity to morphological regularities in print can help children resolve the spelling of challenging orthographic features. The earliest evidence of children's use of morphemic regularities in spelling emerges at Grade 2, when they demonstrate sensitivity to the consistent spelling of bases across morphologically related words. Children are more accurate in choosing the correct spelling for final silent consonants when the letter can be deduced by reference to a related form (e.g., the *t* in *petit* by reference to *petite*) than when they cannot (e.g., *tabac*; Leybaert & Alegria, 1995; Leybaert & Content, 1995; Sénéchal, 2000; Sénéchal et al., 2006). It takes children much more time to work out which specific spelling to use at the end of inflected forms, another morphological regularity. As noted earlier, plurality of nouns and verbs is marked with *-s* and *-nt*, but these markers are mute. It is only at about 10 years of age that Francophone children use these markers appropriately (Fayol, Thenevin, Jarousse & Totereau, 1999; Totereau et al., 1997). Despite this lengthy process of learning, morphemic sensitivity is clearly at work in young children's spellings, and there is ongoing debate as to whether it emerges through statistical (e.g., Pacton, Fayol & Perruchet, 2005) or rule-based learning (e.g., Fayol et al., 1999).

10.3.2.3 Reading and Spelling Difficulties   In French, as in other alphabetic orthographies, there is good consensus that a phonological deficit explains the reading challenges experienced by individuals with dyslexia. As an example, Casalis (1995) found a particularly strong lexicality effect in both speed and accuracy for French dyslexics; that is, pseudowords were read less quickly and accurately than real words by all groups in their study (including reading age and chronological age controls), but this discrepancy was particularly large for the dyslexics. In contrast, the regularity effect (the difference between regular and irregular words) was just as large for all groups. This pattern has emerged in several studies, with the clearest deficits emerging in processing time, rather than accuracy (Casalis, 1995, 2003; Grainger, Bouttevin, Truc, Bastien & Ziegler, 2003; Sprenger-Charolles, Colé, Lacert & Serniclaes, 2000). Taken together, these results lend support to a phonological deficit explanation of the poor reading skills of French dyslexics. In contrast, there is some evidence of a relative strength in morphological skills of French children with dyslexia. Casalis, Colé, and Sopo (2004) confirmed deficient phonological skills of French dyslexic children in comparison to both reading and chronological age matches. However, dyslexics' performance on two morphological tasks (sentence completion and morphological blending) was on a par with reading-age matches. Casalis, Mathiot, Bécavin, and Colé (2003) even found that dyslexics outperformed reading-age matches on a modified sentence completion task in which children chose the correct word to complete the sentence. These findings leave us wondering as to whether morphological skills are a relative strength in French dyslexics. Nevertheless, we need to remain aware of the profound and lasting deficits in phonological skills in this population (Sprenger-Charolles et al., 2005).

10.3.3   Reading Comprehension

10.3.3.1 Predictors of Reading Comprehension   Reading comprehension in French, as in any orthography, is admittedly a complex activity, with an intricate interplay of lower-level processes necessary for single word reading and higher-order processes relating to comprehension monitoring, inference making, working memory, etc. (Ecalle & Magnan, 2010; Oakhill & Cain, 2007). The main bulk of research on French reading comprehension has been guided by the *simple view of reading* (e.g., Ecalle, Bouchafa, Potocki & Magnan, 2013; Fayol, David, Dubois & Rémond, 2000; Megherbi, Seigneuric & Ehrlich, 2006). This framework characterizes reading comprehension as the cross-product of word decoding and oral language comprehension (Gough & Tunmer, 1986; Hoover & Gough, 1990; Kirby & Savage, 2008).

The contribution of oral language comprehension appears to be particularly important for reading comprehension in the younger grades. Using the simple view approach, Megherbi and colleagues (2006) directly contrasted the contribution of nonword decoding with that of language comprehension. While both variables were independent and significant predictors of reading comprehension, language comprehension was the stronger predictor in both first- and second-grade French-speaking children's reading comprehension (approximately 30% of variance beyond decoding). Similarly, Ecalle, Magnan, and Bouchafa's (2008) study of Francophone children in Grades 2 and 3 found that oral sentence comprehension emerged as a much stronger predictor of written sentence comprehension than single word reading. Taken together, these findings articulate a predominant role of language comprehension on young Francophone children's reading comprehension.

The ability to decode letter strings is an indisputable requirement of understanding written text. With fourth- and fifth-grade children, Ecalle and colleagues (2008) found that real word decoding (i.e., single word reading) was the strongest predictor of written sentence comprehension, a contribution that was stronger than that of oral sentence comprehension and vocabulary. There is also evidence of its importance with younger children. Nonword decoding emerged as the strongest predictor of reading comprehension in a study of Francophone children in Grade 1 beyond age, working memory, and vocabulary (Seigneuric & Erhlich, 2005).

The importance of both word decoding and language comprehension in reading comprehension of Francophone children is further reinforced by the findings of studies contrasting *skilled* versus *less skilled* reading comprehenders (e.g., Ehrlich & Remond, 1997; Megherbi & Ehrlich, 2005; cf., Perfetti, 1985, 2007). Specifically, children characterized as less skilled comprehenders vary greatly in their decoding skills; for instance, as many as 50% of less skilled comprehenders have decoding skills on a par with skilled comprehenders (Ehrlich & Remond, 1997; Megherbi & Ehrlich, 2004, 2005; Megherbi et al., 2006), which supports the hypothesis that skilled word reading is not a sufficient requirement in written text comprehension (cf. Oakhill, Yuill & Parkin, 1986; Perfetti, 2007). Less skilled comprehenders with good decoding skills may exhibit comprehension difficulties that stem from deficits in higher-level processes shared between oral and reading comprehension (Megherbi & Ehrlich, 2004; Megherbi et al., 2006). However, the remaining children who are identified as less skilled comprehenders show difficulties in both word decoding *and* oral comprehension. Their lower reading comprehension skills might be due, at least in part, to specific deficits in word decoding occurring in combination with oral comprehension difficulties (Megherbi & Ehrlich, 2004).

It is worth mentioning a potential limitation of many of the abovementioned studies. Many investigations of French reading comprehension have measured the constructs of reading comprehension and oral comprehension with identical tasks presented in different modalities (i.e., visual presentation for reading comprehension and oral for language comprehension; e.g., Ecalle et al., 2008; Megherbi & Ehrlich, 2004, 2005; Megherbi et al., 2006). It is possible that presenting the same comprehension task in both visual *and* auditory forms in a single study is responsible for, at least in part, the high correlations between language comprehension and reading comprehension, as well as the shared patterns of deficits in language and reading comprehension in less skilled comprehenders. Future research on French reading comprehension might consider building on these tasks with more distinctive ways to assess reading and oral comprehension.

10.3.3.2 Word-Level Effects in Comprehending Text   There are remarkably few investigations into word-level effects on the reading comprehension skills of Francophone children. A set of studies, however, examined the effect of vocabulary, assessed by picture-word matching (e.g., French version of Peabody Picture Vocabulary Test [PPVT]: Dunn, Thériault-Whalen & Dunn, 1993) or indirectly by manipulating word frequency (e.g., with frequency norms: Lété, Sprenger-Charolles & Colé, 2004), on sentence comprehension. In third-grade children, Ecalle and colleagues (2013) found that receptive vocabulary knowledge (PPVT) ranked among the strongest predictors of reading comprehension after controlling for age. The contribution of vocabulary knowledge on French children's ability to understand written text has also been shown to increase during the early elementary grades. In a longitudinal study, Seigneuric and Ehrlich (2005) found that receptive vocabulary accounted for a unique 2% of the variance in reading comprehension (beyond age, nonword decoding, and working memory) in Grade 1, and this contribution increased in Grade 2 (18%) and became the strongest predictor in Grade 3 (21%). Studies manipulating word frequency with students spanning Grades 2 to 9 revealed word-frequency effects in the semantic comparison of sentences (Ecalle et al., 2013). Specifically, sentence pairs were more likely to be judged as semantically similar if they contained higher- rather than lower-frequency words. These findings offer compelling evidence for the prominent role of vocabulary in the reading comprehension of developing readers of French.

Word-level effects in text comprehension have also been observed in children's processing of anaphors. Anaphoric devices, such as pronouns, ensure cohesion and referential continuity of successive sentences. As such, anaphors are important in text comprehension because they help to construct a coherent representation of the text during reading. Researchers have found that less skilled comprehenders perform more poorly than skilled comprehenders on resolving anaphors, both in text (Ehrlich & Remond, 1997) and in spoken language (Megherbi & Ehrlich, 2005). These findings are consistent with the *lexical quality hypothesis* (Perfetti, 2007; Perfetti & Hart, 2002), which predicts that the word-to-text integration processes required for building coherent text representations are less effective in less skilled comprehenders.

Finally, we alluded earlier to the fact that empirical studies of reading comprehension in French-speaking individuals are scarce at this point in time, a situation likely due, in large part, to the paucity of standardized reading comprehension tests available in French. This is the case both for adults (Ehrlich, Brébion & Tardieu, 1994) and children (Megherbi & Ehrlich, 2005). Thus, future research might focus on developing reliable measures of French text comprehension standardized across the life span.

10.3.4   Conclusion

The body of research on reading and spelling development in French-speaking children is uneven across domains, with more detailed studies on the early stages of word reading or spelling and less on reading comprehension, a common situation across languages.

10.4   Discussion

10.4.1   Challenges in Learning to Read French

A striking feature of our review is the resemblance between the early literacy development of French-speaking children and that of native speakers of less orthographically transparent alphabetic languages (e.g., English). For instance, the production of phonemes is acquired in a similar sequence and at a similar rate. Children face similar obstacles in mastering grapheme–phoneme relationships and for the same reasons, such as the presence of single- or multiletter graphemes and contextual graphemes as well as irregular correspondences between graphemes and phonemes. Yet there is ample evidence that most beginning readers or spellers gradually learn to process efficiently different units of the written language: graphemes, derivational and inflectional morphemes, and sentences, for reading and for writing. Moreover, foundational skills often serve as significant predictors of subsequent reading outcomes.

10.4.2   Implications for Instruction

Developments in reading instruction methods have raised essentially the same controversies in French- as in English-speaking countries. The main one concerns the merits of two competing approaches to reading instruction (see Chall, 1967; Pressley, 2006): one based on the memorization of words as undividable units (e.g., the whole language method) and the other on the analysis of sublexical units (e.g., the phonics method). The former approach has been popular in France, Belgium, and French Canada in the late twentieth century, and it still has appeal today despite unfavorable empirical support and open criticisms (see Morais, 1994, chap. 5; Pierre, 2003; Sprenger-Charolles & Colé, 2013, chap. 6). Although reading instruction controversies continue to highlight the political charge of curriculum philosophy and question the criteria that should be used in educational decision making, steady progress is being made on three fronts. More detailed analyses of French words and sentence structures are yielding invaluable insights on the obstacles beginning readers/spellers need to overcome (e.g., Catach, 1980; Fayol & Jaffré, 2008; Pothier, 2011). In turn, these insights are progressively captured in theoretical models of written language processing (for reviews, Fayol, 2013; Sprenger-Charolles & Colé, 2013) and invested into more systematic and evidence-based approaches to reading and spelling instruction (e.g., Brissaud & Cogis, 2011; Gauthier, Bissonnette & Richard, 2013; Pothier & Pothier, 2008; Réseau canadien de recherche sur le langage et l'alphabétisation, 2009). As we are often reminded, however (e.g., Cook & Cook, 2013; Savage, 2009), instructional effectiveness should not be taken for granted; it should be empirically verified through rigorous intervention studies with reliable and valid assessment tools.

10.5   Final Conclusion

The orthography of modern French emerged through a long process of standardization and optimization. The complexity of this process results from several factors such as an alphabet that was and is still insufficient to represent the entire set of French phonemes in writing, the continuous evolution of word pronunciation, and competing approaches to orthographic decisions (e.g., one-to-one letter–sound relations vs. etymological traces). Despite the less than optimal level of orthographic transparency, there is clear evidence that French-speaking children succeed in mastering reading and spelling at an early age. Although their progress is faster than that of children learning English, it is significantly slower than that of children learning to read and write in more transparent orthographies. Notably, historical traces in French orthography (e.g., etymological and final mute letters) significantly raise the level of difficulty children need to overcome in learning to read and spell, with the latter being a particularly long-standing process. Over the course of our review, it has become clear that the greatest area in need of research lies in reading comprehension, a domain of investigation limited by both the empirical methods applied and the standardized measures available to date. However, the investigation of reading comprehension is admittedly a complex endeavor for all languages.

References

Aicart-De Falco, S. & Vion, M. (1987). La mise en place du système phonologique du français chez les enfants entre 3 et 6 ans: Une étude de la production. *Cahiers de Psychologie Cognitive, 7*, 247–266.

Alegria, J. & Mousty, P. (1996). The development of spelling procedures in French-speaking, normal and reading-disabled children: Effects of frequency and lexicality. *Journal of Experimental Child Psychology, 63*, 312–338.

Berko, J. (1958). The child's learning of English morphology. Doctoral dissertation, Radcliffe College, Cambridge, MA.

Biedermann-Pasques, L. & Baddeley, S. (2008). Histoire de l'orthographe à travers des manuscrits et des incunables (IXe – XVe siècle). In A. Desrochers, F. Martineau & Y. C. Morin (Eds.), *Orthographe française: Évolution et pratique* (pp. 29–49). Ottawa: Éditions David.

Blanche-Benveniste, C. & Chervel, A. (1969). *L'orthographe*. Paris: Librairie François Maspero.

Bosse, M.-L., Valdois, S. & Tainturier, M.-J. (2003). Analogy without priming in early spelling development. *Reading and Writing, 16*, 693–716.

Bourdin, B., Leuwers, C. & Bourbon, C. (2011). Impact des contraintes linguistiques et cognitives sur l'acquisition de l'accord en genre de l'adjectif en français écrit. *Psychologie Française, 56*, 133–143.

Brissaud, C. & Cogis, D. (2011). *Comment enseigner l'orthographe aujourd'hui?* Paris: Hatier.

Bruck, M., Genesee, F. & Caravolas, M. (1997). A cross-linguistic study of early literacy acquisition. In B. A. Blachman (Ed.), *Foundations of reading acquisition and dyslexia: Implications for early intervention* (pp. 145–162). Mahwah, NJ: Lawrence Erlbaum.

Bruck, M. & Waters, G. (1988). An analysis of spelling errors of children who differ in their reading and spelling skills. *Applied Psycholinguistics, 9*, 77–92.

Caravolas, M., Lervåg, A., Mousikou, P., Efrim, C., Litavský, M., Onochie-Quintanilla, E., Salas, N., Schöffelová, M., Defior, S., Mikulajová, M., Seidlová-Málková, G. & Hulme, C. (2012). Common patterns of prediction of literacy development in different alphabetic orthographies. *Psychological Science, 23*, 678–686.

Carlisle, J. F. (2003). Morphology matters in learning to read: A commentary. *Reading Psychology, 24*, 291–322.

Casalis, S (1995). *Lecture et dyslexies de l'enfant*. Paris: Presses Universitaires du Septentrion.

      (2003). The delay-type in developmental dyslexia: Reading processes. *Current Psychology Letters, 10*(1). Retrieved from http://cpl.revues.org/document95.html.

Casalis, S., Colé, P. & Sopo, D. (2004). Morphological awareness in developmental dyslexia. *Annals of Dyslexia*, *54*, 114–138.

Casalis, S. & Louis-Alexandre, M.-F. (2000). Morphological analysis, phonological analysis and learning to read in French: A longitudinal study. *Reading and Writing*, *12*, 303–335.

Casalis, S., Mathiot, E., Bécavin, A. S. & Colé, P. (2003). Conscience morphologique chez des lecteurs tout venant et en difficultés [Morphological awareness in average and below average readers]. *Silexicales*, *3*, 57–66.

Catach, N. (1980). *L'orthographe française: Traité théorique et pratique*. Paris: Nathan.

(2001). *Histoire de l'orthographe française*. Paris: Honoré Champion.

Chall, J. S. (1967). *Learning to read: The great debate*. New York: McGraw-Hill.

Chervel, A. (2008). *Histoire de l'enseignement du français du XVIIe au XXe siècle*. Paris: Retz.

Chetail, F. & Mathey, S. (2010). InfoSyll: A syllabary providing statistical information on phonological and orthographic syllables. *Journal of Psycholinguistic Research*, *39*, 485–504. DOI:10.1007/s10936-009-9146-y.

Clark, E. V. & Hecht, B. F. (1982). Learning to coin agent and instrument nouns. *Cognition*, *12*, 1–24.

Codaire, E. (2008). La ponctuation au siècle des Lumières. In A. Desrochers, F. Martineau & Y. C. Morin (Eds.), *Orthographe française: Évolution et pratique* (pp. 163–183). Ottawa: Éditions David.

Colé, P., Bouton, S., Leuwers, C., Casalis, S. & Sprenger-Charolles, L. (2012). Stem and derivational-suffix processing during reading by French second and third graders. *Applied Psycholinguistics*, *33*, 97–120.

Colé, P., Marec-Breton, N., Royer, C. & Gombert, J. E. (2003). Morphologie des mots et apprentissage de la lecture. *Rééducation Orthophonique*, *213*(1), 57–60.

Colé, P., Royer, C., Leuwers, C. & Casalis, S. (2004). Les connaissances morphologi-ques dérivationnelles et l'apprentissage de la lecture chez l'apprenti-lecteur français du CP au CE2. *L'Année Psychologique*, *104*, 701–750.

Colin, S., Magnan, A., Ecalle, J. & Leybaert, J. (2007). Relation between deaf children's phonological skills in kindergarten and word recognition performance in first grade. *Journal of Child Psychology and Psychiatry*, *48*, 139–146.

Content, A. (1991). The effect of spelling-to-sound regularity on naming in French. *Psychological Research*, *53*, 3–12.

Cook, B. G. & Cook, S. C. (2013). Unraveling evidence-based practices in special education. *Journal of Special Education*, *47*, 71–82. DOI:10.1177/0022466911420877.

Cormier, P., Desrochers, A. & Sénéchal, M. (2006). Validation et consistance interne d'une batterie de tests pour l'évaluation multidimensionnelle de la lecture en français. *Revue des Sciences de l'Éducation*, *32*, 205–225.

Demont, E. & Gombert, J. E. (1996). Phonological awareness as a predictor of recoding skills and syntactic awareness as a predictor of comprehension skills. *British Journal of Educational Psychology*, *66*, 315–322.

Desrochers, A. (2007). Le développement de la lecture orale chez les élèves du primaire. Keynote address at the annual conference of l'Association québécoise des enseig-nants du primaire (AQEP), Montreal, Canada.

Desrochers, A. & Thompson, G. (2008). De l'orthographe à la lecture orale. In A. Desrochers, F. Martineau & Y.-C. Morin (Eds.), *Orthographe française: Évolution et pratique.* Ottawa: Éditions David.

Dubois, J. (1962). *Étude sur la dérivation suffixale en français moderne et contemporain.* Paris: Librairie Larousse.

Dubois, J., Jouannon, G. & Lagane, R. (1961). *Grammaire française.* Paris: Librairie Larousse.

Ducrot, S., Lété, B., Sprenger-Charolles, L., Pynte, J. & Billard, C. (2003). The optimal viewing position effect in beginning and dyslexic readers. *Current Psychology Letters, 10*(1). Retrieved from http://cpl.revues.org/document99.html.

Dufau, E., Lété, B., Touzet, C., Glotin, H., Ziegler, J. C. & Grainger, J. (2010). A developmental perspective on visual word recognition: New evidence and a self-organising model. *European Journal of Cognitive Psychology, 22*, 669–694.

Duncan, L. G., Casalis, S. & Colé, P. (2009). Early metalinguistic awareness of derivational morphology: Observations from a comparison of English and French. *Applied Psycholinguistics, 30*, 405–440.

Duncan, L. G., Colé, P., Seymour, P. H. & Magnan, A. (2006). Differing sequences of metaphonological development in French and English. *Journal of Child Language, 33*, 369–399.

Dunn, L., Thériault-Whalen, C. & Dunn, L. (1993). *Echelle de vocabulaire en images Peabody: Adaptation française du Peabody vocabulary test-revised.* Toronto: Psycan.

Ecalle, J., Bouchafa, H., Potocki, A. & Magnan, A. (2013). Comprehension of written sentences as a core component of children's reading comprehension. *Journal of Research in Reading, 36*, 117–131. DOI:10.1111/j.1467–9817.2011.01491.x.

Ecalle, J. & Magnan, A. (2002). The development of epiphonological and metaphonological processing at the start of reading: A longitudinal study. *European Journal of Psychology of Education, 17*, 47–62.

(2007). Development of phonological skills and learning to read in French. *European Journal of Psychology of Education, 22*, 153–167.

(2010). *L'apprentissage de la lecture et ses difficultés.* Paris: Dunod.

Ecalle, J., Magnan, A. & Bouchafa, H. (2008). De la compréhension en lecture chez l'enfant de 7 à 15 ans: Étude d'un nouveau paradigme et analyse des déterminants. *Glossa, 105*, 36–48.

Eme, E. & Golder, C. (2005). Word-reading and word-spelling styles of French beginners: Do all children learn to read and spell in the same way? *Reading and Writing, 18*, 157–188.

Ehrlich, M.-F., Brébion, J. & Tardieu, H. (1994). Working-memory capacity and reading comprehension in young and older adults. *Psychological Research, 56*, 110–115.

Ehrlich, M.-F. & Remond, M. (1997). Skilled and less skilled comprehenders: French children's processing of anaphoric devices in written texts. *British Journal of Developmental Psychology, 15*, 291–309. DOI:10.1111/j.2044-835X.1997. tb00522.x.

Fayol, M. (2013). *L'acquisition de l'écrit.* Paris: Presses universitaires de France.

Fayol, M., David, J., Dubois, D. & Rémond, M. (2000). *Maîtriser la lecture: Poursuivre l'apprentissage de la lecture de 8 à 11 ans.* Paris: Éditions Odile Jacob.

Fayol, M. & Jaffré, J.-P. (2008). *Orthographier.* Paris: Presses universitaires de France.

Fayol, M., Thenevin, M.-G., Jarousse, J.-P. & Totereau, C. (1999). From learning to teaching to learning French written morphology. In T. Nunes (Ed.), *Learning to read: An integrated view from research and practice* (pp. 43–64). Dordrecht: Kluwer.

Fayol, M., Totereau, C. & Barrouillet, P. (2006). Disentangling the impact of semantic and formal factors in the acquisition of number inflections: Noun, adjective and verb agreement in written French. *Reading and Writing, 19*, 717–736.

François, F., François, D., Sabeau-Jouannet, E. & Sourdot, M. (1977). *Syntaxe de l'enfant avant 5 ans.* Paris: Larousse.

Gardes-Tamine, J. (2002). *La grammaire: 1. Phonologie, morphologie, lexicologie*, 3rd edn. Paris: Armand Colin.

Gauthier, C., Bissonnette, S. & Richard, M. (2013). *Enseignement explicite et réussite des élèves: La gestion des apprentissages.* Montréal: Pearson.

Goosse, A. (1991). *La « nouvelle » orthographe.: Exposé et commentaires.* Paris: Duculot.

Goslin, J. & Floccia, C. (2007). Comparing French syllabification in preliterate and adults. *Applied Psycholinguistics, 28,* 341–367. DOI:10.1017. S0142716407070178.

Goswami, U., Gombert, J. E. & de Barrera, L. F. (1998). Children's orthographic representations and linguistic transparency: Nonsense word reading in English, French and Spanish. *Applied Psycholinguistics, 19,* 19–52.

Gough, P. B. & Tunmer, W. E. (1986). Decoding, reading, and reading disability. *Remedial and Special Education, 7,* 6–10.

Grainger, J., Bouttevin, S., Truc, C., Bastien, M. & Ziegler, J. (2003). Word superiority, pseudoword superiority, and learning to read: A comparison of dyslexic and normal readers. *Brain and Language, 87,* 432–440.

Grevisse, M. & Goose, A. (2007). *Le bon usage: Grammaire française*, 14th edn. Paris: Duculot.

Guilbert, L. (1975). *La créativité lexicale.* Paris: Larousse.

Hoover, W. A. & Gough, P. B. (1990). The simple view of reading. *Reading and Writing, 2,* 127–160.

Huot, H. (2001). *La morphologie: Forme et sens des mots du français.* Paris: Armand Colin.

Jaffré, J.-P. (2003). La linguistique et la lecture-écriture: De la conscience phonologique à la variable «orthographe». *Revue des Sciences de l'Éducation, 29,* 37–49.

Jaffré, J.-P. & Fayol, M. (1997). *Orthographes: Des systèmes aux usages.* Paris: Flammarion.

Karmiloff-Smith, A. (1979). *A functional approach to child language: A study of determiners and reference.* Cambridge University Press.

Kirby, J. R. & Savage, R. S. (2008). Can the simple view deal with the complexities of reading? *Literacy, 42,* 75–82.

Lété, B., Peereman, R. & Fayol, M. (2008). Consistency and word-frequency effects on spelling among first- to fifth-grade French children: A regression-based study. *Journal of Memory and Language, 58,* 952–977.

Lété, B., Sprenger-Charolles, L. & Colé, P. (2004). MANULEX: A grade-level lexical database from French elementary school readers. *Behavior Research Methods, Instruments & Computers, 36,* 156–166.

Lewis, M. P., Simons, G. F. & Fennig, C. D. (Eds.) (2013). *Ethnologue: Languages of the world*, 17th edn. Dallas, TX: SIL International.

Leybaert, J. & Alegria, J. (1995). Spelling development in deaf and hearing children: Evidence for use of morpho-phonological regularities in French. *Reading and Writing, 7*, 89–109.

Leybaert, J. & Content, A. (1995). Reading and spelling acquisition in two different teaching methods: A test of the independence hypothesis. *Reading and Writing, 7*, 65–88.

Longtin, C.-M., Segui, J. & Hallé, P. (2003). Morphological priming without morphological relationship. *Language and Cognitive Processes, 18*, 313–334.

Marec-Breton, N., Gombert, J. É. & Colé, P. (2005). Traitements morphologiques lors de la reconnaissance des mots écrits chez des apprentis lecteurs. *L'Année Psychologique, 105*, 9–45.

Megherbi, H. & Ehrlich, M.-F. (2004). Compréhension de l'oral chez de jeunes enfants bons et mauvais compreneurs de textes écrits. *L'Année Psychologique, 104*, 433–489.

Megherbi, H. & Ehrlich, M.-F. (2005). Language impairment in less skilled comprehenders: The on-line processing of anaphoric pronouns in a listening situation. *Reading and Writing, 18*, 715–753. DOI:10.1007/s11145-005-8131-6.

Megherbi, H., Seigneuric, A. & Ehrlich, M.-F. (2006). Reading comprehension in French 1st and 2nd grade children: Contribution of decoding and language comprehension. *European Journal of Psychology of Education, 21*, 135–147.

Morais, J. (1994). *L'art de lire*. Paris: Odile Jacob.

Morin, Y. C. (2008). Le Gaygnard (1609): L'Ancienne orthographe, la nouvelle pédagogie et la réforme orthographique. In A. Desrochers, F. Martineau & Y. C. Morin (Eds.), *Orthographe française: Évolution et pratique* (pp. 51–90). Ottawa: Éditions David.

New, B. & Spinelli, E. (2013). Diphones-fr: A French database of diphone positional frequency. *Behavior Research Methods, 45*, 758–764. DOI:10.3758/s13428-012-0285-y.

Oakhill, J. & Cain, K. (2007). Introduction to comprehension development. In K. Cain & J. Oakhill (Eds.), *Children's comprehension problems in oral and written language: A cognitive perspective* (pp. 3–40). New York: Guilford Press.

Oakhill, J., Yuill, N. & Parkin, A. (1986). On the nature of the difference between skilled and less-skilled comprehenders. *Journal of Research in Reading, 9*, 80–91.

L'Observatoire de la Langue française (2010). *Le français dans le monde 2010*. Paris: Nathan.

Organisation internationale de la Francophonie (2012). *Rapport du Secrétaire général de la Francophonie: De Montreux à Kinshasa. 2010–2012*. Paris: Author.

Pacton, S., Fayol, M. & Perruchet, P. (2005). Children's implicit learning of graphotactic and morphological regularities. *Child Development, 76*, 324–339.

Pacton, S., Perruchet, P., Fayol, M. & Cleeremans, A. (2001). Implicit learning out of the lab: The case of orthographic regularities. *Journal of Experimental Psychology: General, 130*, 401–426.

Parisse, C. & Le Normand, M. T. (2000). How children build their morphosyntax: The case of French. *Journal of Child Language, 27*, 267–292.

Peereman, R. & Content, A. (1999). LEXOP: A lexical database providing orthography-phonology statistics for French monosyllabic words. *Behavior Research Methods, Instruments & Computers, 31*, 376–379.

Peereman, R., Lété, B. & Sprenger-Charolles, L. (2007). Manulex-Infra: Distributional characteristics of grapheme–phoneme mappings, and infralexical and lexical units in child-directed written material. *Behavior Research Methods*, *39*, 593–603. DOI:10.3758/BF03193029.

Perfetti, C. A. (1985). *Reading ability*. New York: Oxford University Press.

(2007). Reading ability: Lexical quality to comprehension. *Scientific Studies of Reading*, *11*, 357–383. DOI:10.1080/10888430701530730.

Perfetti, C. A. & Hart, L. (2002). The lexical quality hypothesis. In L. Verhoeven, C. Elbro & P. Reitsma (Eds.), *Precursors of functional literacy* (pp. 189–214). Amsterdam: John Benjamins.

Perret, M. (2008). *Introduction à l'histoire de la langue française*. Paris: Armand Colin.

Pierre, R. (2003). L'enseignement de la lecture au Québec de 1980 à 2000: Fondements historiques, épistémologiques et scientifiques. *Revue des Sciences de l'Éducation*, *29*, 3–35.

Plaza, M. & Cohen, H. (2003). The interaction between phonological processing, syntactic awareness, and naming speed in the reading and spelling performance of first-grade children. *Brain and Cognition*, *53*, 287–292.

Plaza, M. & Cohen, H. (2004). Predictive influence of phonological processing, morphological/syntactic skill, and naming speed on spelling performance. *Brain and Cognition*, *55*, 368–373.

Plaza, M. & Cohen, H. (2007). The contribution of phonological awareness and visual attention in early reading and spelling. *Dyslexia*, *13*, 67–76. DOI:10.1002/dys.330.

Pothier, B. (2011). *Contribution de la linguistique à l'enseignement du français*. Presses de l'Université du Québec.

Pothier, B. & Pothier, P. (2008). *Pour un apprentissage raisonné de l'orthographe syntaxique*. Paris: Retz.

Pressley, M. (2006). *Reading instruction that works: The case for balanced teaching*. New York: Guilford Press.

Pulgram, E. (1970). *Syllable, word, nexus, cursus*. The Hague: Mouton.

Quémart, P., Casalis, S. & Colé, P. (2011). The role of form and meaning in the processing of written morphology: A priming study in French developing readers. *Journal of Experimental Child Psychology*, *109*, 478–496.

Réseau canadien de recherche sur le langage et l'alphabétisation (2009). *Pour un enseignement efficace de la lecture et de l'écriture: Une trousse d'intervention appuyée par la recherche*. London: Author.

Rey, A., Duval, F. & Siouffi, G. (2007). *Mille ans de la langue française*. Paris: Perrin.

Roman, A. A., Kirby, J. R., Parrila, R. K., Wade-Woolley, L. & Deacon, S. H. (2009). Toward a comprehensive view of the skills involved in word reading in Grades 4, 6, and 8. *Journal of Experimental Child Psychology*, *102*, 96–113.

Rondal, J. A. (1997). *L'évaluation du langage*. Liege: Editions Mardaga.

Roy, C. & Labelle, M. (2007). Connaissance de la morphologie dérivationnelle chez les francophones et non-francophones de 6 à 8 ans. *Canadian Journal of Applied Linguistics / Revue Canadienne de Linguistique Appliquée*, *10*, 263–291.

Sanchez, M., Magnan, A. & Ecalle, J. (2012). Knowledge about word structure in beginning readers: What specific links are there with word reading and spelling?

European Journal of Psychological of Education, 27, 299–317. DOI:10.1007/s10212-011-0071-8.

Sander, E. K. (1972). When are speech sounds learned? *Journal of Speech and Hearing Disorders, 37,* 55–63.

Savage, R. S. (2009). *What would an evidence-based Canadian National Strategy for early literacy look like?* London: Canadian Language and Literacy Research Network.

Séguin, H. (1986). *Tous les verbes conjugués.* Montréal: Centre éducatif et culturel.

Séguin, H. & Desrochers, A. (2008). L'évolution de l'orthographe au fil des dictionnaires de l'académie française. In A. Desrochers, F. Martineau & Y. C. Morin (Eds.), *Orthographe française: Évolution et pratique* (pp. 91–137). Ottawa: Éditions David.

Seidler, S. (1988). Untersuchung zum Erwerb von Wortbildungsregeln Deverbativa Nomina (Agens und Instrument) im Franzosischen. Unpublished Master's thesis, Universitat Hamburg.

Seigneuric, A. & Ehrlich, M.-F. (2005). Contribution of working memory capacity to children's reading comprehension: A longitudinal investigation. *Reading and Writing, 18,* 617–656. DOI:10.1007/s11145-005-2038-0.

Seigneuric, A., Zagar, D., Meunier, F. & Spinelli, E. (2007). The relation between language and cognition in 3- to 9-year-olds: The acquisition of grammatical gender in French. *Journal of Experimental Child Psychology, 96,* 229–246.

Sénéchal, M. (2000). Morphological effects in children's spelling of French words. *Canadian Journal of Experimental Psychology / Revue Canadienne de Psychologie Expérimentale, 54,* 76–85.

Sénéchal, M., Basque, M. T. & Leclaire, T. (2006). Morphological knowledge as revealed in children's spelling accuracy and reports of spelling strategies. *Journal of Experimental Child Psychology, 95,* 231–254.

Seymour, P. H., Aro, M. & Erskine, J. M. (2003). Foundation literacy acquisition in European orthographies. *British Journal of Psychology, 94,* 143–174.

Sprenger-Charolles, L. & Casalis, S. (1995). Reading and spelling acquisition in French first graders: Longitudinal evidence. *Reading and Writing, 7,* 39–63.

Sprenger-Charolles, L. & Colé, P. (2013). *Lecture et dyslexie: Approche cognitive,* 2nd edn. Paris: Dunod.

Sprenger-Charolles, L., Colé, P., Béchennec, D. & Kipffer-Piquard, A. (2005). French normative data on reading and related skills from EVALEC, a new computerized battery of tests (end Grade 1, Grade 2, Grade 3, and Grade 4). *Revue Européenne de Psychologie Appliquée/European Review of Applied Psychology, 55,* 157–186.

Sprenger-Charolles, L., Colé, P., Lacert, P. & Serniclaes, W. (2000). On subtypes of developmental dyslexia: Evidence from processing time and accuracy scores. *Canadian Journal of Experimental Psychology / Revue Canadienne de Psychologie Expérimentale, 54,* 87–104.

Sprenger-Charolles, L., Siegel, L. S., Béchennec, D. & Serniclaes, W. (2003). Development of phonological and orthographic processing in reading aloud, in silent reading, and in spelling: A four-year longitudinal study. *Journal of Experimental Child Psychology, 84,* 194–217.

Sprenger-Charolles, L., Siegel, L. S. & Bonnet, P. (1998). Reading and spelling acquisition in French: The role of phonological mediation and orthographic factors. *Journal of Experimental Child Psychology, 68,* 134–165.

Tanguay, B. (2006). *L'art de ponctuer*. Montréal: Québec-Amérique.

Thiele, J. (1987). *La formation des mots en français moderne*. Montréal: Presses de l'Université de Montréal.

Totereau, C., Thevenin, M. G. & Fayol, M. (1997). Acquisition de la morphologie du nombre à l'écrit en français. In L. Rieben, M. Fayol & C.-A. Perfetti (Eds.), *Des orthographes et leur acquisition*. (pp. 147–167). Lausanne: Delachaux et Niestlé.

Van Horn Melton, J. (1988). *Absolutism and the eighteenth-century origins of compulsory schooling in Prussia and Austria*. New York: Cambridge University Press.

Wimmer, H. & Hummer, P. (1990). How German speaking first graders read and spell: Doubts on the importance of the logographic stage. *Applied Psycholinguistics, 11*, 349–368.

Wioland, F. (1985). *Les structures syllabiques du francais*. Geneva: Slatkine.

Ziegler, J. C., Bertrand, D., Tóth, D., Csépe, V., Reis, A., Faísca, L. & Blomert, L. (2010). Orthographic depth and its impact on universal predictors of reading: A cross-language investigation. *Psychological Science, 21*, 551–559.

Ziegler, J., Jacobs, A. M. & Stone, G. O. (1996). Statistical analyses of the bidirectional inconsistency of spelling and sound in French. *Behavior Research Methods, Instruments & Computers, 28*, 504–515.

Ziegler, J. C., Perry, C. & Coltheart, M. (2003). Speed of lexical and nonlexical processing in French: The case of the regularity effect. *Psychonomic Bulletin & Review, 10*, 947–953.

11   Learning to Read Spanish

Sylvia Defior and Francisca Serrano

11.1   Introduction

The origins of Spanish date from Roman times. After the Roman invasion of the Iberian Peninsula, Vulgar Latin became widely used. Over the centuries it evolved into Spanish; gradually it displaced all pre-Roman Hispanic languages except Basque, the only non-Indo-European language that survived the Latinization of Hispania. At the end of the eleventh century, a process of linguistic assimilation was underway, involving the central Romance dialects spoken in the Iberian Peninsula and culminating in the development of a common language, which incorporated different influences.

An important milestone in the development of the early forms of the Romance languages spoken in the Iberian Peninsula was the Moorish invasion of the eighth century. Another major event was the Renaissance period, when the kingdom of Castile and Aragon expanded greatly and the resulting contact with other European cultures greatly enriched the lexicon. The Spanish colonization that commenced in the sixteenth century spread the Spanish language through most of the Americas, where its lexicon was further enriched with borrowings from native languages.

By the eighteenth century, the state imposed a linguistic policy aimed at standardizing Spanish, slowing phonetic and morphosyntactic changes. The foundation of the Royal Spanish Academy (Real Academia Española, RAE henceforth) in 1713 contributed to this standardization. Spanish is today the common language throughout Spain, although it coexists with three other official languages (Catalan, Galician, and Basque), and also is the main language of most countries of Central and South America.

11.1.1   Spanish and Its Orthography

Spanish is the most widely spoken Romance language in the world today, with some 470 million speakers. It is the world's second language by number of native speakers and in terms of international communication (according to Instituto

Cervantes data in 2014); it has also an increasing importance in the United States and Brazil. Literacy rates are around 90%–100% in most of the twenty-one countries where Spanish is the national language; only in a few of them is the rate as low as 70%–79% (according to UNESCO Institute for Statistics (2013) data).

Spanish, like the other Romance languages, inherited its orthographic system from Latin, using the Roman alphabet. According to the RAE (2010), seven basic criteria underpin the Spanish orthographic system, although the primacy of the phonological criterion was a constant theme in the historical development of written Spanish.

11.1.2   Synchronic and Diachronic Characterization

The current Spanish orthography is the result of a gradual adaptation of the Latin spelling system and of several reforms guided by the ideal principle of one-to-one mapping of graphemes to phonemes (G–P). However, the vowel quantity distinction (long-short) and the declination system were lost in the process of Latin's evolution into the Spanish language. Consonants were reduced despite the addition of some new consonants. Verbal conjugations were reduced from four to three.

The first writings in a Spanish Romance language were the *Glosas Emilianenses* (eleventh century). During the reign of Alfonso X the Wise (1252–1284), the Romance language became firmly consolidated; a common syntax was developed and spelling was simplified. The arrival of printing helped to further fixate the Spanish language and regulate spelling. The first treatise on a Romance language was *Gramática castellana* by Antonio de Nebrija (1492); however, there was still great variability in the choice of spellings for phonemes.

Throughout the sixteenth and seventeenth centuries, important changes occurred to the phonological system. The phoneme–grapheme mappings remained unstable, given the absence of prescriptive rules and the importance attached to criteria such as pronunciation, etymology, and traditional usage. The situation changed with the founding of the RAE, which created a Spanish dictionary thereby fixing the spelling of words. The first *Orthographia española* appeared in 1741. In successive reforms, the RAE used all criteria, but primacy was given to the phonological criteria. Thus, ⟨ç⟩ to represent /θ/ was eliminated; Latinizing digraphs such as ⟨th, ch, ph, rh, ss, nn, ff⟩ were replaced by simple letters such as ⟨t, c/q, f, r, s, ñ, f⟩; ⟨ch⟩ was reserved for /ʧ/ and ⟨ll⟩ for /ʎ/; a new letter ⟨z⟩ was introduced to represent /θ/; double consonants and consonant clusters were reduced in number; ⟨v⟩ was fixed as a consonant and ⟨u⟩ as a vowel; ⟨h⟩ and ⟨v/b⟩ were maintained for etymological reasons; use of ⟨x⟩ was maintained for /ks/; and the acute accent (´) replaced the grave accent (`) (Echenique Elizondo & Martínez Alcalde, 2000).

Disputes surrounding the orthography persisted until 1844, when teaching according to RAE rules was made compulsory in all Spanish schools; all rules were gradually adopted in Latin America. As a result, Spanish orthography is nowadays standard, stable, and accepted by the entire Spanish-speaking community.

11.1.3 Literacy and Schooling

While oral language inevitably evolves, especially given the vast community of Spanish speakers, the written language is highly fixed throughout the Spanish-speaking world; however, despite some particularities in names and expressions, the range of variation is not very great and only rarely disrupts mutual comprehensibility. The RAE and Latin American language academies endeavor to preserve and maintain this common oral and written language.

In the mid-nineteenth century, through Moyano's Law in 1857, schooling became compulsory in Spain and functioned as a standardizing system. Compulsory schooling is currently from age 6 to 16 years. Children begin formal education in the calendar year in which they turn 6 years old. As the school year starts in September, the first year of primary education can hold children with age differences up to 11 months. The 0–6 schooling period, called *Educación Infantil*, is divided in two phases (age 0–3; age 3–6) and it is not compulsory. Nevertheless, 100% of 4- and 5-year-old children and a high percentage of 3-year-old children are enrolled in preschools. It is a common practice to familiarize 4-year-old children with the five vowels of the alphabet; 5-year-olds start to learn some of the consonants too, but reading is systematic and formally taught in the first year of compulsory education. A mixed teaching approach (phonics and whole language) is used. Children also complete metaphonological exercises, focused on syllabic structures and initial sounds of words. Children tend to learn the essentials rapidly and fully master the code principles by the end of their second year of primary school (Defior, Jiménez-Fernández & Serrano, 2009). Overall, parents support literacy development; there is an extended collection of children's books available for teachers and parents for that purpose.

11.2   Description of Spanish and Its Written Forms

From the point of view of the taxonomy of languages, Spanish is classified as an Indo-European language belonging to the Romance subfamily.

11.2.1 Linguistic System

Although the phonological system is quite simple, the morphosyntactic system is quite complex. Spanish is an inflected synthetic language (many morphemes

Table 11.1 *Inventory of Spanish vowels (adapted from Alarcos Llorach, 2007)*

	Front	Central	Back
Close or high vowel	/i/		/u/
Mid vowel	/e/		/o/
Open or low vowel		/a/	

per word) and fusional (tendency to overlay the morphemes). It has a distinctively syllabic character, and so, classified as a syllable-timed or, more appropriately, as a segment-timed language (Comrie, 2009).

The basic word order is SVO, but it admits a great deal of flexibility as SV is not mandatory except in sentences with an interrogative pronoun (*¿Quién es Rosa?*, but not *¿Quién Rosa es?*) and in clitics, in which the order must be OV (*Te vi*, but not *Vi a ti*). Spanish has, however, strong order constraints within the major syntactic elements constituting a sentence.

Compound sentences are governed by complex restrictions resulting from the distinction between indicative (reflecting real and factual) and subjunctive (reflecting hypothetical and counterfactual) moods. The use of the subjunctive is very characteristic of Spanish; e.g., see the contrast between *Seguro que Juan tiene* (indicative) *las entradas* ('Surely Juan has the tickets') and *Es probable que Juan tenga* (subjunctive) *las entradas* ('It is likely that Juan has the tickets'). Spanish is also characterized by the frequent use of the reflexive pronoun with a passive or impersonal meaning (*se venden patatas* 'potatoes are sold').

11.2.1.1 Phonology The Spanish phonological system consists of twenty-four phonemes. The vowel subsystem consists of five vowels (see Table 11.1). Overall vowel frequency is 47.13%; the most frequently used are /e/ and /a/ (13.46% each), followed by /o/ (9.55%), /i/ (7.51%), and /u/ (3.15%). There is no vowel reduction or weakening in unstressed syllables.

The consonant subsystem consists of nineteen phonemes (see Table 11.2); the most frequent is /s/ (9.24%), followed by /n/ (7.49%), /r/ (5.77%), /l/ (5.12%), /d/ (4.72%), and /t/ (4.31%), and the least frequent /ɲ/, /ʎ/, and /ʧ/. The only consonant that cannot appear in word-initial position is /r/.

Phonologies for geographical varieties of Spanish differ; e.g., loss of the distinction between /ʎ/ and /j/ (both pronounced /j/) or between /θ/ and /s/ (both /s/); loss of the /-s/ in the coda position of syllables. None of these differences causes comprehensibility problems between speakers.

A syllable can have a maximum of five phonemes, with a maximum of two consonants at the head that rarely appear in the coda position. The most

Table 11.2 *Inventory of Spanish consonants (adapted from Alarcos Llorach, 2007)*

Series | Order			Bilabial	Dental	Palatal	Velar
Stop (voiceless)			/p/	/t/	/ʧ/	/k/
Stop (voiced)			/b/	/d/	/j/	/g/
Fricative (voiceless)			/f/	/θ/	/s/	/x/
Nasal			/m/	/n/	/ɲ/	
Liquid	Lateral			/l/	/ʎ/	
	Vibrant	Simple (tap)		/ɾ/		
		Multiple (trill)		/r/		

frequent syllable structures are open (CV, CCV, V, CVV, and CCVV represent 65%–70% of syllable structures; CV, 52.64%). The most frequent closed structure is CVC (19%) and the less frequent is CCVCC (0.01%) (Guerra, 1983).

Suprasegmental elements of stress and intonation are fundamental in Spanish (Alarcos Llorach, 2007), generally referred to as prosodic features. Stress marks signal the strong and weak syllables in a word. Partly free, the accent falls on one of the last three syllables of the word, counting from the end. Paroxytone words, stressed on the penultimate syllable, are the most frequent in number and reflect the default or unmarked pattern. Next frequent are oxytone words, stressed on the last syllable, and the least frequent are proparoxytone words (mainly loan words), stressed on the third-from-last (antepenultimate) syllable. The stress is occasionally used to distinguish between similar words, e.g., /médico/ (nominal form), /medico/ and /medicó/ (present and past verbal forms, respectively).

Intonation is expressed via the melodic curve or sequence of tones that depicts the vocalization of a sentence. Spanish has five types of final inflection, depending on the tone direction and on curve amplitude, which reflect the distinctive features of assertion, interrogation, exclamation, and appeal (Alarcos Llorach, 2007).

11.2.1.2 Inflectional Morphology Word classes are determiners, nouns, adjectives, pronouns, and verbs, which are variable (i.e., capable of being inflected), and adverbs, prepositions, conjunctions, and interjections, which are invariable.

Compared to English, Spanish has a much more complex inflectional system, and it is considered a highly inflected language due to its wide use of inflection to indicate changes in grammar that have implications for syntactic relations (agreement) in a sentence. Inflection affects the meaning of words but not phonology, and it proceeds always by suffixation; it may be placed on nouns, verbs, adjectives, articles, and pronouns and can be in number, gender, person, and case (only for personal pronouns). Inflections of tense, aspect, and mood (indicative, subjunctive, and imperative) are unique to verbs, which must agree in number and person with the subject. Inflection can also be suprasegmentally performed via the positioning of the stress, e.g., *(yo) animo* versus *(él) animó*.

Number and gender matching is mandatory for all noun phrase modifiers (e.g., *el niñ-o/a alt-o/a*; *lo/a-s niñ-o/a-s alt-o/a-s*). Furthermore, number, person, and sometimes gender agreement between subject and verb is marked, so Spanish verb forms always include morphemes in fixed order that indicate person, number, mood, aspect, and tense (e.g., in *cantábamos*, *canta-* [lexical stem], *-ba-* [information on past tense, imperfect aspect, and indicative mood], *-mos* [information on first person and plural number]). No agreement is necessary between verb and object. Unlike non-pro-drop languages, which require an explicit lexical subject, Spanish permits the subject pronoun to be dropped (e.g., *Vendré mañana* does not need to indicate that the subject is *yo*).

11.2.1.3 Word Formation Processes Although 94% of the daily Spanish language has Vulgar Latin origin, the lexicon is the result of historical accretions (Comrie, 2009). A few pre-Roman words (*pizarra, manteca*) or Celtic (*cerveza, camisa*) are still in use as well as some Germanic words (*guerra, rico*). Nearly 4,000 words come from Arabic, almost all nouns, with a high proportion beginning with *a-* or *al-* due to the agglutination of the Arabic definite article (*aceite, alcalde*). Since the Renaissance, Spanish has borrowed extensively from other Romance languages, Greek and Latin, Amerindian languages, and most recently from English.

Lexical morphology relies on two fundamental word formation processes. One is derivation, whereby one affix or more is attached to a lexical base to form a new word, usually a noun, verb or adjective. The affixation process can be done by suffixation, attaching suffixes to the right of the root morpheme (*pescadería* from *pescad* and *-ería*), by prefixation, attaching prefixes to the left (*desprender* from *des* and *-prender*) or both (*desprendimiento* from *des-prend -i-miento*). The other process is composition, which combines two or more lexical bases (*boquiabierto* from *boca* and *abierto*). Yet another possibility is parasynthesis, which is the simultaneous application of derivation and composition (*centrocampista* from *centro, campo* and *-ista*).

Suffixed words represent 9.59% of the total number of Spanish words, whereas prefixed words reach only 2.06% (Gómez & Pérez, 2009); clearly, suffixation is the main word formation process as it is used both for inflection and for derivation, whereas prefixation is only derivational. Suffixes can be used to form new nouns, adjectives, verbs, and adverbs.

As for inflection, the derivation process implies changes in meaning but typically preserves word phonology; prefixes also leave the word class unchanged (*hacer* ➜ *deshacer*), contrary to suffixes that could change it (*cansar* ➜ *cansado*). Many Spanish words are morphologically complex and divisible into smaller components that encode both syntactic and semantic information: e.g., in *panaderos*, *pan-* (lexical base), *ad-ero* (occupation), *-s* (plurality); the same happens with the verb form *cantábamos*, as showed before.

11.2.2   Writing System

Spanish uses a highly consistent alphabetic system which is written from left to right, close to the shallow edge of the transparency continuum. The code consists of a set of general rules (mainly referring to P-G mappings), plus a set of particular rules applying to specific words, especially those for which a phoneme can be written in more than one way and result from a lengthy historical evolution, reflecting etymological, grammatical, and semantic inputs. Regularities in a group of these words take the form of rules, although most of them have exceptions.

11.2.2.1 Script and Punctuation   The constituent elements of Spanish script include:

- An alphabet of twenty-seven letters, existing in uppercase and lowercase: ⟨A, B, C, D, E, F, G, H, I, J, K, L, M, N, Ñ, O, P, Q, R, S, T, U, V, W, X, Y, Z⟩.
- Five digraphs: ⟨CH, LL, RR, GU, QU⟩. The last three are considered positional variants of the phonemes /r/, /g/, and /k/.
- Two diacritical marks written over vowels: the acute accent (´), indicating prosodic stress, and the dieresis (¨), placed over *u* to indicate that it is not part of the digraph ⟨gu⟩ when followed by ⟨e⟩, ⟨i⟩, and should be pronounced as a vowel (e.g., *cigüeña* vs. *guerra*).
- A set of punctuation marks which demarcate (full stop, comma, semicolon, colon), indicate the type of intonation (two punctuation marks for *question* and exclamation, i.e., *¿Hace frio?, ¡Hace frio!*), or indicate omission of part of a statement (ellipsis).
- An open set of typographical marks (hyphens, dashes, slashes, brackets, apostrophes, asterisks, etc.) with various functions.
- The white space to indicate boundaries between words.
- Abbreviations, acronyms, and symbols, used for scientific and technical concepts (e.g., Arabic and Roman numerical symbols).

Strict punctuation rules govern the use of the stress mark, according to word nature as oxytone (on all words ending in a vowel or in consonants ⟨n⟩ or ⟨s⟩; *rubí; cajón*), paroxytone (on words ending in a consonant other than ⟨n⟩ or ⟨s⟩; *mástil*), or proparoxytone (on all words; *látigo*).

11.2.2.2 Orthography   Since 1844, the orthography has been only slightly
modified by the RAE; last modification dates on December 2010. Today, the
Spanish code establishes that three vowel phonemes (/a/, /e/, /o/) are always
represented by a single grapheme (‹a›, ‹e›, ‹o›), /i/ can be represented by ‹i› or
‹y›, and /u/ can be represented by ‹u›, ‹ü›, or ‹w› (*kiui, kigüi* or *kiwi*). The vowel
phonemes can be written with an initial or final ‹h› in monosyllabic words, with
initial or intercalated ‹h› in polysyllabic words (*hijo, zanahoria*) and with
dieresis in the case of *u* (‹güi› as in *pingüino*).

There are two important facts about the written forms of consonants:

- Eleven are always displayed with the same grapheme/digraph: /ʧ, d, f, l, ʎ, m,
  n, ɲ, p, ɾ, t/, ‹ch, d, f, l, ll, m, n, ñ, p, r, t›, respectively.
- Eight can be represented by more than one grapheme/digraph: /b/ (‹b›, ‹v›,
  ‹w›); /k/ (‹k›, ‹qu›,‹c›); /g/ (‹g›, ‹gu›); /x/ (‹g›, ‹j›); /j/ (‹y›, ‹ll›[1]); /r/ (‹r›,
  ‹rr›); /θ/ (‹z›, ‹c›); /s/ (‹s›, ‹x›).

Moreover, graphemes representing different phonemes are ‹g› (/x/, /g/), ‹c› (/k/,
/θ/, /s/[2]), ‹y› (/i/, /j/, /ʎ/), and ‹r› (/r/, /ɾ/). Two special graphemes are ‹h› (silent)
and ‹x› (usually represents two phonemes /ks/). The graphemes ‹w› and ‹k› are
fairly rare (only in loan words or literary words).

In reading, the mapping G–P is predictable, as simple and complex (mainly
contextual and positional) rules determine the pronunciation of a ‹g›.
A competent reader can thus unambiguously correctly pronounce a written
word or pseudoword. This is not the case with writing, as P–G correspondences
are inconsistent.

In contrast to deep systems, when phonology and morphology are in conflict
regarding orthography, Spanish tends to preserve P–G correspondences and to
sacrifice morphology (Defior & Alegría, 2005); e.g., for verbs ending in *-ger*
and *-gir* (*escoger/corregir*), the letter ‹g› is replaced by ‹j› when it is followed
by /o/ or /a/ in conjugated forms such as *escojo* or *corrija* in order to respect
phonology. Likewise, the letter ‹c› of the word *vaca* changes to ‹qu› in derived
words like *vaquería* or *vaquero*.

11.2.3 Conclusion

The Spanish oral language is simultaneously characterized by phonological
simplicity (the trend to phonological reduction still continues today) and
morphosyntactic complexity.

Regarding orthography, throughout the historic evolution and subsequent
modifications by the RAE, the ideal of biunique correspondence has been
pursued to the point that contemporary Spanish orthography shows a high
degree of consistency between phonemes and graphemes and is considered

[1] In areas of yeismo.   [2] In areas of seseo.

as a transparent alphabetic script. A number of disparities significantly affect transparency, particularly in writing, which is governed by etymological and usage criteria as well as phonological rules; the result is a hybrid and strongly conventional system. Therefore, the claim that it is mostly phonographic is as widespread as it is erroneous. The inconsistencies in P-G mappings produce an imbalance between its highly transparent reading system, with high predictability about how to pronounce words (easy to read), and its less consistent writing system (difficult to spell). In writing the mapping P-G is much less consistent and, besides P-G correspondences, morphosyntactic, semantic, and etymological knowledge comes to play an important role.

11.3   Acquisition of Reading and Spelling in Spanish

11.3.1   Becoming Linguistically Aware

Research in written language acquisition has dealt with how children acquire the linguistic and metalinguistic abilities that are the foundation for literacy acquisition.

11.3.1.1 Phonological Development and Phonological Awareness   Spanish phonological development takes place early, and nearly all phonemes have emerged by the end of age 4 (Acevedo, 1993). As in other languages, though quicker, stop consonants are acquired first, followed by nasals, then fricatives and affricates, and finally liquids (for a detailed description, see Hernandez Pina, 1984).

Phonological awareness (PA) progresses from large to small units (Goikoetxea, 2005): the early ability to discriminate sounds in words to the sensitivity to rhyme and alliteration appears first, followed by the awareness of syllables and part of syllables, and finally, the deepest level is phoneme awareness (Denton, Hasbrouck, Weaver & Riccio, 2000).

Regarding awareness to intrasyllabic units (onset and rime), some studies have pointed out Spanish-speaking children's difficulty in distinguishing between them inside the syllable (e.g., Baños, 2000; Serrano & Defior, 2007). The relevance of the syllable in Spanish, considered a syllable-timed language, may account for these findings. Finally, another level of PA has been found relevant in Spanish studies, namely awareness of lexical rhyme or the ability to detect similar endings in words. Awareness of lexical rhyme develops after syllable awareness and before phoneme awareness (see Figure 11.1).

PA levels before and after literacy instruction was studied by Serrano and Defior (2007) with a longitudinal design (three testing points: T1–end of pre-school; T2–beginning of first grade; T3–end of first grade). Children showed better performance on syllabic and phoneme awareness than on lexical rhyme

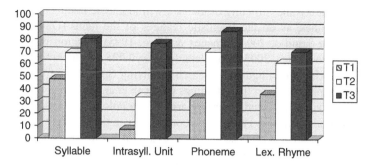

Figure 11.1 Mean percentage of correct answers in syllable, intrasyllabic unit, phoneme, and lexical rhyme level task, respectively, at each testing point, T1–end of preschool; T2–beginning of first grade; T3–end of first grade (Serrano & Defior, 2007).

detection and intrasyllabic awareness before literacy explicit instruction (T1–end of preschool). After the beginning of formal literacy instruction, a dramatic increase in children's performance was found, nearly the same for all the PA levels (note T3 results in Figure 11.1). This study shows the central role of formal literacy instruction in PA skills development. Carrillo (1994) showed similar findings studying sensitivity to rhyme and alliteration skills.

Although some basic level of PA can be observed before literacy acquisition, deeper levels of phonemic awareness are achieved only once literacy instruction has been started (Caravolas et al., 2012; Defior, Serrano & Herrera, 2006; Serrano, González Trujillo, Defior & Carpio, 2005; Suarez-Coalla, García-de-Castro & Cuetos, 2013). Some training studies have also shown a causal influence of phonemic awareness in literacy development in Spanish language (e.g., Defior & Tudela, 1994; Herrera, Defior & Lorenzo, 2007). Moreover, studies in dyslexia have shown that nearly transparent grapheme–phoneme correspondences would facilitate achievement in phonemic awareness tasks in children with dyslexia, making their performance in accuracy comparable to their peers (Serrano & Defior, 2005). However, when performance time is taken into account or the phonological demands of the task are increased, PA deficits appear, making time an important factor to detect dyslexia in Spanish (Serrano & Defior, 2008).

The strong influence of PA in literacy development when children are beginning readers decreases with schooling (*hot house effect*; Defior, 2008). Instead, other phonological abilities like rapid automatized naming (RAN) become more influential in more advanced school levels (Defior, Serrano, Onochie & Simpson, 2011). In the same regard, the influence of PA in literacy is placed in the background of linguistic awareness once participants are expert readers (Serrano, Defior & Martos, 2003).

The nature and difficulty of the task will modulate findings in PA development studies, as do the linguistic features of the items (Defior, Serrano & González Trujillo, 2004; Jiménez & Haro, 1995), position of the linguistic units (Goicoextea, 2005), word length and syllable structure (Jiménez & Haro, 1995). Also crosslinguistic research involving Spanish and other European orthographies support these findings (Duncan et al., 2013).

Finally, a "new" and emerging area of phonological development (suprasegmental phonology) namely *prosody* is now in the spotlight (see Gutiérrez-Palma, Defior & Calet, 2016, for a review in Spanish). Some studies have pointed out the relevance of prosody in reading acquisition (Calet, 2013; Calet, Defior & Gutiérrez-Palma, 2013; Calet, Gutiérrez-Palma, Simpson, González-Trujillo & Defior, 2015; González Trujillo, 2005), whereas others have associated low prosodic skills with low literacy in children with reading difficulties (Jiménez-Fernández, Gutiérrez-Palma & Defior, 2015).

11.3.1.2 Morphological Development and Morphological Awareness   Morphological development in Spanish is characterized by different patterns depending on age, the development being very dramatic from 3 to 4 years old, and then becoming more gradual until 6 years old (Pérez Pereira & Singer, 1984). Inflectional morphology is mastered before derivational morphology; children are able to deal with plurals even at 3 years old, while they struggle with some verb conjugations until 6 years old, especially with irregular verbs; i.e., children will use *yo pono* instead of *yo pongo* when trying to use the verb *poner*.

Morphological awareness development is first implicit and passive, relying on oral language abilities (for a detailed explanation, see Gathercole, Sebastián & Soto, 1999); as children progress in primary school, they become able to analyze and manipulate isolated words' morphemic structures. Clahsen, Aveledo, and Roca (2002) studied the evolution of morphology, analyzing verb inflections in Spanish-speaking children (age range: 1;7 to 4;7). Dissociation between regular and irregular verbs development was found; regular suffixes are over-extended to irregulars in children's inflection errors, but not vice versa. Also, overregularization errors at all ages was only a small minority of the children's irregular verbs errors, and the period of overregularization was preceded by a stage without errors. The development for person, tense, and number follows a scattered, piecemeal pattern (Gathercole, Sebastián & Soto, 2000).

Domínguez, Cuetos, and Segui (1999) studied inflectional morphology focusing on the processing of grammatical gender and number. Overall, while gender information is retrieved in a direct way during isolated word recognition, access to inflectional number information could be mediated by the lexical entry corresponding to the inflected singular form.

In contrast to deep orthographies, Spanish tends to give priority to phonology over morphology on word spelling (Defior & Alegría, 2005). Normally, the orthographical form of the root morpheme is sacrificed in order to respect the phoneme-to-grapheme correspondence rules (PGCR). Morphology is especially important in resolving ambiguities that arise when a spoken language form maps onto two different spellings. For example, the spoken form /as/ is ambiguous between the noun spelled "as" (meaning 'ace') and the verb spelled "has" ("you have" – the 'h' is unpronounced) (Defior & Alegría, 2005). Thus, Defior, Alegria, Titos, and Martos (2008) investigated how first- to third-grade Spanish-speaking children use inflectional morphology information to spell verbs and plural nouns. Participants from the Andalusia region, where consonantal -s sound at the end of a syllable is omitted in spoken language (mentioned in Section 11.2.1.1), performed a dictation task including plural nouns and verbs in second person all ending in ‹s› (morphological -s condition) and a control condition (nouns and verbs with lexical -s). Children used morphological knowledge to write the plural mark in nouns and the person mark in verbs even if it is omitted in spoken language, showing awareness of the morphological use of -s. This finding supports the idea of Spanish as a pro-drop language, contrary to French or English (non-pro-drop).

Similarly, Singson, Mahoney, and Mann (2000) evidenced that awareness of derivational suffixes made a unique contribution to decoding over and above vocabulary and phonemic awareness. More generally, morphological skills are relevant for the development of comprehension and thus broadly important for the development of literacy (Kieffer, Biancarosa & Mancilla-Martinez, 2013; Kieffer & Lesaux, 2007; Ramirez, Chen, Geva & Kiefer, 2010).

11.3.2   Development of Word Identification

In this section, processes involved in word decoding and spelling in Spanish written language are reviewed.

11.3.2.1 Word Decoding Development   Word decoding development in Spanish is characterized by a quick improvement on accuracy versus a gradual improvement on speed. Defior et al. (2011) found, using a longitudinal design with five testing points (from 5 years old to preschool to the beginning of second grade) and both accuracy and speed measures (see Figure 11.2a, b), that children quickly reached ceiling in accuracy (Figure 11.2a), whereas the improvement in speed took more time (Figure 11.2b).

As a result, speed would be a more suitable measure than accuracy for characterizing word decoding development in Spanish (also in dyslexia studies; Serrano & Defior, 2008).

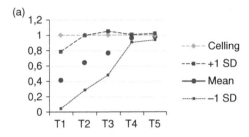

Figure 11.2a Accuracy measure: mean proportion of correct responses by testing point.

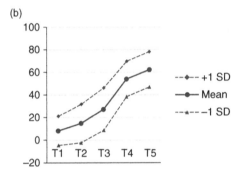

Figure 11.2b Speed measure: mean of time in correct words by testing point.

Transparency and regularity of the Spanish language affect this development. Thus, transparency has a positive effect on the rate of reading development, that is, Spanish children are quicker and more accurate in word decoding than children learning deeper languages, as shown in crosslinguistic research (e.g., Caravolas et al., 2012; Defior, Martos & Cary, 2002; Serrano et al., 2011; Seymour, Aro & Erskine, 2003); moreover, growth of reading skills follows a different trajectory (Caravolas et al., 2013). The number of vowels has been signaled as a crucial feature regarding the speed of reading acquisition (Serrano et al., 2011).

Other relevant factors are syllable structure, frequency, and lexical value. In general, the syllable will act as a useful sublexical unit during word identification (Carreiras, Álvarez & de Vega, 1993; Carreiras & Perea, 2004), in agreement with the syllable-timed language character of Spanish. Furthermore, frequent words are decoded more easily than less frequent ones (frequency effect), and word decoding is easier than pseudoword decoding (lexicality effect) (Defior, Justicia & Martos, 1996).

Finally, as in English, the development of word reading has been explained by both *dual-route* models (e.g., Defior et al., 1996; de Vega, Carreiras, Gutierrez Calvo & Alonso-Quecuty, 1990; Valle-Arroyo, 1989, 1996) and *parallel distributed processing* (PDP) models (Simpson & Defior, 2017).

11.3.2.2 Word Spelling Development   Spelling development poses a greater difficulty over reading acquisition in Spanish. Jiménez-Fernández, Defior, Cantos, and Serrano (2006) compared the acquisition of reading and spelling skills in a sample of Spanish-speaking first to fourth graders, finding that while a ceiling effect was reached in reading accuracy as early as the second year of primary education, spelling performance did not attain a high level even at the end of the fourth grade.

Mechanisms involved in learning to spell in Spanish were examined in Defior and Serrano (2005). They described a continuum course of development in learning to spell from 4- to 6-year-old children and how an almost transparent code such as Spanish allows learners to reach a high level of command in phonological spelling already in the same year they start to learn.

Crosslinguistic studies (Caravolas et al., 2013) confirm that Spanish children acquire spelling skills more quickly compared to children from other European orthographies (English, Czech); however, the same predictors (PA, letter knowledge, and RAN) for spelling skills are found in the compared languages. Similarly, Carrillo, Alegria, and Marin (2013) showed that children reach a high percentage of success in spelling acquisition sooner than French-speaking participants. The Spanish code characteristics may account for the early development of phonological segmentation skills and thus allow an earlier mastery of sound–letter correspondences that will be reflected in good spelling performance (Serrano et al., 2011).

However, Spanish orthography has some complexities. Defior et al. (2009) explored the influence of these complexities in learning to spell. Children's performance was better in simple graphonemes (P-G mappings 1:1) than in complex graphonemes, and both children's academic level and the type of complexity affected spelling performance. Children acquire spelling skills early in terms of PGCR, but lexical knowledge develops more slowly, affecting the spelling of inconsistent graphonemes and words with diacritical marks. Thus, to master spelling, phonological, orthographic, grammatical, semantic, and prosodic knowledge are required (Calet et al., 2015; Defior et al., 2008). Plus, the need of prosodic knowledge for the stress mark is considered an idiosyncratic characteristic of the Spanish language.

The consonant cluster (appearing only in syllable onset position) is also a noteworthy complexity affecting Spanish spelling development.

Children's difficulties in writing consonant clusters in early writing acquisition (Defior, Martos & Aguilar, 2003; Jiménez González & Jiménez Rodríguez, 1999) are explained by the major phonological demands of the cluster and the difficulty of segmenting it into separate phonemes due to the high level of coarticulation of the consonant phonemes in the cluster. The influence of the Spanish code complexities and consonant clusters in spelling development has also been verified in Spanish children with dyslexia (Serrano & Defior, 2012, 2014).

As in other languages, it has been shown that PA is more related to spelling than reading (Defior & Tudela, 1994; Serrano, Jiménez-Fernández & Defior, 2005). Spelling development is also affected by psycholinguistic factors like word frequency and lexical value (e.g., Defior et al., 2003).

11.3.2.3 Reading and Spelling Difficulties   Despite the orthographic consistency of Spanish orthography, there are some cases of struggling in learning to read and write. Dyslexia prevalence is estimated as being between 8.6% (3.2% only reading, 5.4% both reading and spelling; Jiménez, Guzmán, Rodríguez & Artiles, 2009) and 11.8% (Carrillo, Alegria, López & Pérez, 2011).

The presence of complex graphonemes creates general difficulties in reading and spelling accuracy (Defior et al., 2009). However, dyslexia seems to be more associated with speed than in both reading and phonological processing tasks (Serrano & Defior, 2008; Suarez-Coalla, Ramos, Álvarez-Cañizo & Cuetos, 2014).

Children with dyslexia have lower spelling performance than the typically developing children (both matched in age and reading level), especially when they have to write words with consonant clusters (Serrano & Defior, 2012) and digraphs (Serrano & Defior, 2014). Moreover, the spelling errors persist into adulthood, in particular in inconsistent graphonemes (Serrano & Defior, 2014).

Beyond the difficulties in phonological segmental processing, they are struggling in suprasegmental phonology, namely prosody as detecting word stress pattern (Jiménez-Fernández et al., 2015). It is noteworthy that Spanish children with dyslexia show problems developing word orthographic representation (Suarez-Coalla et al., 2014) as well as implicit learning of sequences (Jiménez-Fernández, Vaquero, Jiménez & Defior, 2011).

Taking all these facts together, dyslexic populations in Spanish show the same difficulties (mainly in phonological and orthographic domains) as in other languages, although speed and fluency impairments could be considered the hallmark of dyslexia in Spanish.

11.3.3   Reading Comprehension

11.3.3.1 Predictors of Reading Comprehension   Studies on comprehension in Spanish, as in other languages, have validated the *simple view of reading* – the influence of word decoding and listening comprehension – and the relevance of several factors. Kim and Pallante (2012) investigated predictors of word reading and reading comprehension skills using longitudinal data in Spanish-speaking kindergartners and first graders in Chile. Both vocabulary knowledge and decoding (word recognition and nonsense word fluency) were related to the growth trajectory of reading comprehension. This has also been evidenced in fourth- and fifth-grade Peruvian children by Morales Silva, Verhoeven, and van Leeuwe (2008 and 2011, respectively). In turn, Infante (2001) found a relationship between listening and reading comprehension skills in Chilean fourth graders with and without reading comprehension difficulties. The meta-analysis of Ripoll, Aguado, and Castilla-Earls (2014) testing the simple view of reading show that decoding and linguistic comprehension are moderately correlated, and that both decoding and linguistic comprehension are highly correlated with reading comprehension, although this relationship may change with schooling (for another meta-analysis, see García & Cain, 2014).

Word recognition/decoding makes a unique contribution to reading comprehension in Spanish. There is a relationship between developmental progress in reading comprehension and both the automatization of more basic decoding processes, which release cognitive resources, and the acquisition of metacognitive control strategies (García Madruga, Gárate, Elosúa, Luque & Gutiérrez, 1997; García Madruga, Elosua, Gárate, Luque & Gutiérrez, 1999). The relationship among decoding, semantic processing, and fluency in reading comprehension in fourth, fifth, and sixth grade was examined by Balbi, Cuadro, and Trías (2009) in Spanish-speaking children in Uruguay; they also accounted for a relative and independent contribution of decoding to reading comprehension. Besides, the influence of prosodic knowledge has also been addressed in second and fourth Spanish graders (Calet, 2013; Calet et al., 2015; Gutiérrez-Palma et al., 2016).

The relationship among reading comprehension and a variety of cognitive skills, including visual and listening attention, working memory, reasoning, executive functions, and long-term memory has also been validated. Urquijo (2010) tested Spanish-speaking first-grade students (N = 127) from Argentina and found all these cognitive skills, as well as metalinguistic phonological skills, to be significant and positively correlated to sentence comprehension.

Another relevant factor, beyond word decoding and oral language role, is naming speed (RAN). Some studies (Onochie, Simpson, Caravolas & Defior, 2011; Suárez-Coalla et al., 2013) have highlighted that besides phonological awareness, rapid naming would be a predictor of reading, in general, and comprehension, in particular.

Moreover, the role of memory in reading comprehension in Spanish has been extensively studied, showing positive correlations between working memory and reading comprehension and recall (García Madruga, Carriedo & González-Labra,

2000; García Madruga, Gutiérrez, Carriedo, Luzón & Vila, 2007). Garcia Madruga and Fernández Corte (2008) argued that the complexity of the cognitive processes involved in reading comprehension implies an intact memory function. The relationship between memory and reading comprehension in the first and fourth grades of secondary education students (13 and 16 years old, respectively) was found to be 0.38 and 0.47, respectively.

Research by Gárate, Gutiérrez, Luque, García Madruga, and Elosúa (1999) and Gutiérrez-Calvo (1999) shows the role of prior knowledge in coordinating text ideas, suggesting the relevance of inference processes in establishing coherence. Canet-Juric, Urquijo, Richards, and Burin (2009) also supported the role of interference suppression and resolution inferences as well as other cognitive skills like monitoring and working memory in Argentinean children (8–9 years old, N = 89); the failure in general processing skills, such as phonological working memory, characterized individuals with low comprehension skills. Other works about inference (Borella, Carretti & Pelegrina, 2010; León & Escudero, 2002) and metacognitive skills like monitoring (e.g., Otero, Campanario & Hopkins, 1992) have been reported.

Accordingly, the importance of executive functions in text comprehension in Spanish has also been highlighted. Miranda, Soriano, and García (2006) tested Spanish children with and without ADHD in four types of reading comprehension tasks (literal comprehension, inferential comprehension, a fragment-ordering task, and recall of story content), showing that, although the two groups did not differ in respect of literal comprehension or inferential comprehension, children with ADHD performed significantly worse than children without ADHD on self-regulation abilities (fragment-ordering task and the recall of story), that is, executive functions.

Regarding text characteristics, studies show the influence of knowledge of the rhetorical text markers ("due to ...," " "in consequence ...," " etc.) on comprehension, finding a strong relationship between these markers and comprehension in expositive texts (García, Bustos & Sánchez, 2013; Sánchez & García, 2009; Sánchez & García-Rodicio, 2013).

Addressing task effects in enhancing readers' ability to integrate text elements, Cerdán and Vidal-Abarca (2008) compared essay writing with answering integration questions. They found that answering integration questions increased readers' integration and decreased their processing of isolated units of information more than did writing an essay. Later, Cerdán, Vidal-Abarca, Martínez, Gilabert, and Gil (2009) found that high-level questions facilitated deep comprehension but not immediate performance or delayed recall of text, independently of the reading condition, and that high- and low-level questions differentially affected text-inspection patterns.

Beyond the linguistic and cognitive influences, the role of other factors of an emotional nature, like motivation and anxiety (e.g., Sellers, 2000, studying

Spanish as a foreign language), and socio-cultural factors has been addressed. SES and home literacy climate substantially predict reading comprehension development, in a direct or indirect way (Morales Silva et al., 2008, 2011).

11.3.3.2 Word-Level Effects in Comprehending Text As in other languages, studies in Spanish have addressed the highly important relationship between language skills at the word level and comprehension.

Principally, vocabulary has an important role in predicting comprehension. Kim and Pallante (2012) and Morales Silva et al. (2008, 2011) showed that reading comprehension development depends on children's level of vocabulary in addition to other skills such as word decoding, nonsense word fluency, and word reading, as well as early phonological decoding skills. Similarly, Canet-Juric et al. (2009) showed that the deficit in the ability to relate concepts (vocabulary) was characteristic of individuals with low comprehension skills.

Gomes, Simpson, and Defior (2017) tested the relation of both receptive (PPVT-III) and expressive vocabulary (WISC-Subtest Vocabulary) to reading comprehension. Generally, in contrast to previous studies in English (Ouellette, 2006) in which only expressive vocabulary knowledge was significantly correlated to reading comprehension, the Spanish work shows that both receptive and expressive vocabulary knowledge are significantly correlated to reading comprehension. These results not only reinforce the role of vocabulary knowledge and the lexical quality hypothesis (Perfetti, 2007) for successful reading but also highlight the complexity of word knowledge and the relevance of considering different measures of vocabulary.

11.3.4 Conclusion

Early reading and spelling acquisition in Spanish seems to be based on the same core underlying skills that are found in other alphabetic orthographies. Thus, research has suggested the relevance of the ability to segment and manipulate the speech segments (phonemes), the ability to learn the sound–symbol mappings of the alphabet, and the ability to fluently retrieve the pronunciation associated with symbols (letter, syllable, and word reading). Phonological awareness, letter knowledge, and RAN have been found as predictors of both reading and spelling development (Caravolas et al., 2012). More particularly, RAN has been specially linked to the characteristic acceleration of reading growth in consistent orthographies once formal teaching begins (Caravolas et al., 2013); moreover, it seems to predict reading for a more extended period than phoneme awareness and letter knowledge. Other predictors, such as stress awareness and morphological awareness, have also been evidenced as indicators, the later one more related to comprehension development.

Spanish children, compared to learners in opaque orthographies, become fast and accurate readers earlier on. Typically developing children learn grapheme–phoneme correspondence (GPC) straightaway, and they achieve high levels of accuracy after a few months of teaching. The main characteristic of further development is to become fast and fluent. The growth of reading skills is slower, and it follows a different trajectory in English than in Spanish (Caravolas et al., 2013). Spelling acquisition represents a major challenge, mainly in spelling words containing inconsistent spellings and in placing correct stress markers. An overall impact of Spanish studies has been to high-light the role of orthographic mapping, which is shallow in Spanish, in literacy acquisition.

Fluency difficulties and the need of extra time to perform phonological tasks are better indicators of dyslexia than accuracy, as well as reading very complex phonological items, mainly pseudowords and non-words (Serrano & Defior, 2008). Older children with dyslexia also have problems in acquiring ortho-graphic representations needed to correctly write inconsistent or irregular words.

Regarding reading comprehension, the simple view of reading has been validated as in other languages, as well as the myriad of factors that influence comprehension development.

11.4   Discussion

The synchronic and diachronic characterization has shown that Spanish can be considered as a melting pot, the product of the fusion of several influences over its main base, the Vulgar Latin. Spanish phonology is simple, particularly the vowel subsystem, and the syllabic structure and the code transparency ultimately help in literacy acquisition and development. In contrast, complex morphology and syntax characterize the Spanish language as well, affecting literacy development.

Research in Spanish has validated the influence of universal factors in literacy acquisition in alphabetic systems. However, it also draws attention to language-specific factors that affect literacy development in alphabetic writing, including stress markers and the emergence of fluency indicators of skill when high accuracy is achieved.

11.4.1   Challenges in Learning to Read Spanish

Despite the apparent simplicity of Spanish orthographic code, some character-istics may introduce learning challenges. Thus, the code includes complex rules, graphemes that correspond to more than one grapheme, and the special feature of stress mark, which is related to prosody. Altogether, these character-istics make the process of literacy acquisition harder to accomplish, especially in spelling (Defior et al., 2009).

The learning challenges for struggling learners, of course, exceed those for typically developing children. The orthographic code complexity is multiplied for children who struggle to learn to read. This complexity challenge is seen in dealing with complex GPC rules (*gue, gui*; Serrano & Defior, 2014), consonant clusters (Serrano & Defior, 2012), and persistent problems in fluency (Serrano & Defior, 2008).

Spelling acquisition, in turn, represents more of a challenge than reading, both for typically developing learners and children with learning difficulties. This is especially due to inconsistent graphemes and the stress mark, which require extended opportunities for learning. Apart from phonology, many kinds of knowledge need to be combined in order to achieve high standards of reading and spelling: sufficient specific orthographic knowledge (including words with inconsistent spelling patterns), plus morphological, semantic, and etymological knowledge.

For typically developing children, reading comprehension seems to be the main problem. Thus, international student assessments, like PISA (Programme for International Student Assessment) and PIRLS (Progress in International Reading Literacy Study), have dramatically highlighted low scores in comprehension in 10-year-old (PIRLS) and 15-year-old (PISA) students. Although comprehension is a complex skill that depends on many factors, the scarcity of studies dealing with some of the relevant linguistic factors, such as vocabulary or oral comprehension, may undermine our understanding of these low scores. Furthermore, the lack of studies may indicate how the value of oral skills in reading acquisition is under-estimated when compared to the predominance of writing skills in the classroom.

11.4.2   Implications for Instruction

Formal literacy instruction is not part of the compulsory curriculum during the preschool period (0–6 years old). However, most schools start familiarizing children with letters (name/sound) and teaching them other metalinguistic skills at the syllabic level. In the first grade of compulsory schooling, formal and systematic teaching of literacy begins. However, there is high presence of pen and pencil – instead of oral language activities, as mentioned.

A very positive aspect to be highlighted is the widespread use of methods – or even mixed methods – which have been shown to benefit most of the learners. Consistent with the structure of Spanish, these methods also highlight syllabic units.

The importance of phonological awareness has been recognized for years in Spanish literacy education. However, the importance of other levels of language awareness now needs to be recognized – morphological (word structure) and prosodic (stress, pauses, and expression) knowledge – and become part of teachers' preparation.

Clearly, more attention is due to oral language skills, especially concerning enhancing vocabulary and grammar skills. Both lexical quality and grammatical knowledge have to be addressed, because both contribute to comprehension. Improving comprehension should become the highest objective in school.

In preparing literacy teachers, both initial and in-service training need to promote a foundation for effective education practice for classroom teachers and those responsible for special or supportive education. Schools must also implement practices that reduce the impact of social disadvantages.

Certainly, the school is not the only location for addressing learning outcomes. The larger community should be involved, and, given the research on family factors, parents' participation in their children's education is needed. For this participation, guidelines are needed and are already available in some Spanish regions. Efforts to develop adequate and evidence-based psychoeducational materials for assessment and treatment in literacy are increasing.

11.5   Final Conclusion

As one of the world's most spoken languages, the study of Spanish reading is of interest not only to Spanish-speaking researchers but also to the international research community. The chapter has reviewed the synchronic and diachronic aspects of Spanish and highlighted the results of research on the skills, factors, and processes involved in literacy acquisition in Spanish.

Since the standardization of its written language in 1844, Spanish has been a transparent orthography, characterized by a high degree of consistency between spelling and pronunciation. However, it also has some complexities, above all for spelling.

Written word recognition appears to be acquired relatively quickly. Children rapidly achieve great accuracy and speed, with errors decreasing quickly. Cross-linguistic studies suggest that learning to read Spanish is more efficient than in less transparent systems. Syllable units are prominent in this learning, probably due to the syllable-timed character of Spanish. Phonological awareness and also, as shown more recently, prosodic awareness play a crucial role in literacy acquisition. The role of PA seems to be restricted to the very beginning of the learning process, and RAN is a better predictor in later development.

The asymmetry in transparency between reading and spelling may partly account for the greater difficulty of spelling over reading in Spanish, both for typically developing children (Defior et al., 2009) and dyslexia (Serrano & Defior, 2014).

Beyond the beneficial effects of transparency, children face challenges in specific aspects of the writing system, including complex graphonemes and stress markers. Nevertheless, the main challenge is reading comprehension. Research has suggested some sources of comprehension difficulty, but more attention to linguistic factors in spoken as well as written language are needed.

Finally, research in Spanish literacy development matches the main findings universally agreed in other languages. It nevertheless reveals influences of some of the distinctive characteristics of Spanish.

Acknowledgments

The research reported here was partially funded by the MICIN Project PSI2010-21983-C02-01, and the Junta de Andalucía research group HUM 820.

References

Acevedo, M. A. (1993). Development of Spanish consonants in presUNEDchool children. *Communication Disorders Quarterly, 15*(2), 9–15.

Alarcos Llorach, E. (2007). *Gramática de la lengua española* [Spanish grammar], 22nd edn. Madrid: Espasa Calpe.

Balbi, A., Cuadro, A. & Trías, D. (2009). Comprensión lectora y reconocimiento de palabras [Reading comprehension and recognition words]. *Ciencias Psicológicas, 3*, 153–160.

Baños, H. (2000). Phonological awareness, literacy and bilingualism. Doctoral dissertation, Oxford University.

Borella, E., Carretti, C. & Pelegrina, S. L. (2010). The specific role of inhibitory efficacy in good and poor comprehenders. *Journal of Learning Disabilities, 43*, 541–552.

Calet, N. (2013). Efectos del entrenamiento en fluidez lectora sobre la competencia lectora en niños de educación primaria: El papel de la prosodia [Effects of fluency training on reading competence in primary school children: The role of the prosody]. Doctoral dissertation, University of Granada. Retrieved from http://hera .ugr.es/tesisugr/22209797.pdf.

Calet, N., Defior, S. & Gutiérrez-Palma, N. (2013). A cross-sectional study of fluency and reading comprehension in Spanish primary school children. *Journal of Research in Reading*. Advance online publication. DOI:10.1111/ 1467-9817.12019.

Calet, N., Gutiérrez-Palma, N., Simpson, I., González-Trujillo, M. C. & Defior, S. (2015). Suprasegmental phonology development and literacy acquisition: A longitudinal study. *Scientific Studies of Reading, 19*(1), 51–71. DOI:10.1080/ 10888438.2014.976342.

Canet-Juric, L., Urquijo, S., Richards, M. M. & Burin, D. (2009). Predictores cognitivos de niveles de comprensión lectora mediante análisis discriminante [Cognitive predictors of reading comprehension levels using discriminant analysis]. *International Journal of Psychological Research, 2*(2), 99–111.

Caravolas, M., Lervåg, A., Defior, S., Seidlová-Málková, G. & Hulme, C. (2013). Different patterns, but equivalent predictors, of growth in reading in consistent and inconsistent orthographies. *Psychological Science, 24,* 1398–1407. DOI:10.1177/0956797612473122.

Caravolas, M., Lervåg, A., Mousikou, P., Efrim, C., Litavský, M., Onochie-Quintanilla, E., Salas, N., Schöffelová, M., Defior, S., Mikulajová, M., Seidlová-Málková, G. & Hulme, C. (2012). Common patterns of prediction of literacy development in different alphabetic orthographies. *Psychological Science, 23,* 678–686.

Carreiras, M., Álvarez, C. J. & de Vega, M. (1993). Syllable frequency and visual word recognition in Spanish. *Journal of Memory and Language, 32,* 766–780.

Carreiras, M. & Perea, M. (2004). Naming pseudowords in Spanish: Effects of syllable frequency. *Brain and Language, 90,* 393–400.

Carrillo, M. (1994). Development of phonological awareness and reading acquisition: A study in Spanish language. *Reading and Writing, 6,* 279–298.

Carrillo, M. S., Alegria. J., López, P. M. & Pérez, N. S. (2011). Evaluación de la dislexia en la escuela primaria: Prevalencia en español [Evaluating dyslexia in primary school children: Prevalence in Spanish]. *Escritos de Psicología, 4*(2), 35–44.

Carrillo, M.S., Alegria, J. & Marin, J. (2013). On the acquisition of some basic word spelling mechanisms in a deep (French) and a shallow (Spanish) system. *Reading and Writing, 26,* 799–819. DOI:10.1007/s11145-012-9391-6.

Cerdán, R. & Vidal-Abarca, E. (2008). The effects of tasks on integrating information from multiple documents. *Journal of Educational Psychology, 100,* 209–222.

Cerdán, R., Vidal-Abarca, E., Martínez, M., Gilabert, R. & Gil, L. (2009). Impact of question-answering tasks on search processes and reading comprehension. *Learning and Instruction, 19,* 13–27.

Clahsen, H., Aveledo, F. & Roca, I. (2002). The development of regular and irregular verb inflection in Spanish child language. *Journal of Child Language, 29,* 591–622.

Comrie, B. (Ed.) (2009). *The world's major languages,* 2nd edn. New York: Routledge.

Defior, S. (2008). ¿Cómo facilitar el aprendizaje inicial de la lectoescritura? Papel de las habilidades fonológicas [Improving literacy early acquisition? Role of phonological skills]. *Infancia y Aprendizaje, 31,* 333–345.

Defior, S. & Alegría, J. (2005). Conexión entre morfosintaxis y escritura: Cuando la fonología es (casi) suficiente para escribir [Connecting morphosyntax and spelling: When phonology is (almost) enough]. *Revista de Logopedia, Foniatría y Audiología, 25*(2), 51–61.

Defior, S., Alegría, J., Titos, R. & Martos F. (2008). Using morphology when spelling in a shallow orthographic system: The case of Spanish. *Cognitive Development, 23,* 204–215.

Defior, S., Jiménez-Fernández, G. & Serrano, F. (2009). Complexity and lexicality effects on the acquisition of Spanish spelling. *Learning and Instruction, 19,* 55–65. DOI:10.1016/j.learninstruc.2008.01.005.

Defior, S., Justicia, F. & Martos, F. (1996). The influence of lexical and sublexical variables in normal and poor Spanish readers. *Reading and Writing, 8,* 487–497.

Defior, S., Martos, F. & Aguilar, E. (2003). Influence of reading level on word spelling according to the phoneme–grapheme relationship. In R. M. Joshi, C. K. Leong & B. L. J. Kaczmarek (Eds.), *Literacy acquisition: The role of phonology, morphology and orthography* (pp. 131–151). Amsterdam: IOS Press.

Defior, S., Martos, F. & Cary, L. (2002). Differences in reading acquisition development in two shallow orthographies: Portuguese and Spanish. *Applied Psycholinguistics*, *23*, 135–148.

Defior, S. & Serrano, F. (2005). The initial development of spelling in Spanish: From global to analytical. *Reading and Writing*, *18*, 81–98. DOI:10.1007/s11145-004-5893-1.

Defior, S., Serrano, F. & González Trujillo, M. C. (2004). Influencia de la complejidad lingüística de los ítems en la evolución de la conciencia fonológica [Item linguistic complexity influence on phonological awareness development]. In F. Miras, N. Yuste & F. Valls (Eds.), *Calidad Educativa* [Educational quality] (pp. 335–342) [CD-Rom]. Universidad de Almería.

Defior, S., Serrano, F. & Herrera, L. (2006). Habilidades de análisis y síntesis fonémica: Su evolución y relación con la lectoescritura [Phonemic analysis and blending: Role and relationship with literacy development]. In J. Salazar, M. Amengual & M. Juan (Eds.), *Usos sociales del lenguaje y aspectos psicolingüísticos. Perspectivas aplicadas* [Social applications of language and psycholinguistic aspects. Applied perspectives] (pp. 16–27). Palma de Mallorca: Servicio de publicaciones de la Universidad de Palma de Mallorca.

Defior, S., Serrano, F., Onochie, E. & Simpson, I. (2011, June). Early steps in Spanish literacy development. Paper presented at Eldel Conference, Prague, Czech Republic.

Defior, S. & Tudela, P. (1994). Effect of phonological training on reading and writing acquisition. *Reading and Writing*, *6*, 299–320.

Denton, C. A., Hasbrouck, J. E., Weaver, L. R. & Riccio, C. A. (2000). What do we know about phonological awareness in Spanish? *Reading Psychology*, *21*, 335–352.

de Vega, M., Carreiras, M., Gutiérrez Calvo, M. & Alonso-Quecuty, M. (1990). *Lectura y comprensión: Una perspectiva cognitiva* [Reading and comprehension: A cognitive perspective]. Madrid: Alianza Psicología.

Domínguez, A., Cuetos, F. & Segui, J. (1999). The processing of grammatical gender and number in Spanish. *Journal of Psycholinguistic Research*, *28*, 485–498.

Duncan, L. G., Castro, S. L., Defior, S., Seymour, P. H. K., Baillie, S., Leybaert, J., Mousty, P., Genard, N., Sarris, M., Porpodas, C. D., Lund, R., Sigurdsson, B. Thráinsdóttir, A. S., Sucena, A. & Serrano, F. (2013). Phonological development in relation to native language and literacy: Variations on a theme in six alphabetic orthographies. *Cognition*, *127*, 398–419. DOI:10.1016/j.cognition.2013.02.009.

Echenique Elizondo, M. T. & Martínez Alcalde, M. J. (2000). *Diacronía y gramática histórica de la lengua española* [Diacrony and historic gramar of Spanish language]. Valencia: Tirant lo Blanch.

Gárate, M., Gutiérrez, F., Luque, L., García Madruga, J. A. & Elosúa, R. (1999). Inferencias y comprensión lectora [Inferences and reading comprehension]. In J. A. García Madruga, M. R. Elosúa, F. Gutiérrez, J. L. Luque & M. Gárate (Eds.), *Comprensión lectora y memoria operativa: Aspectos evolutivos e instruccionales* [Reading comprehension and operative memory: Developmental and instructional issues]. Buenos Aires: Paidós.

García, J. R., Bustos, A. & Sánchez, E. (2013).The contribution of knowledge about anaphors, organisational signals and refutations to reading comprehension.

Journal of Research in Reading, Advance online publication. DOI:10.1111/ 1467-9817.12021.

García, J. R. & Cain, K. (2014). Decoding and reading comprehension: A meta-analysis to identify which reader and assessment characteristics influence the strength of the relationship. *Review of Educational Research*, *84*, 74–111. DOI:10.3102/ 0034654313499616.

García Madruga, J. A., Carriedo, N. & González-Labra, M. J. (Eds.) (2000). *Mental models in reasoning*. Madrid: Universidad Nacional de Educación a Distancia, UNED.

García Madruga, J. A., Elosúa, M. R., Gárate, M., Luque, J. L. & Gutiérrez, F. (1999). *Comprensión lectora y memoria operativa. Aspectos evolutivos e instruccionales* [Reading comprehension and operative memory. Developmental and instructional issues]. Barcelona: Paidós.

García Madruga, J. A. & Fernández Corte, T. (2008). Memoria operativa, comprensión lectora y razonamiento en la educación secundaria [Operative memory, reading comprehension and reasoning in secondary education]. *Anuario de Psicología, 39*, 133–157.

García Madruga, J. A., Gárate, M., Elosúa, M. R., Luque, J. L. & Gutiérrez, F. (1997). Comprensión lectora y memoria operativa: Un estudio evolutivo [Reading comprehension and operative memory: A longitudinal study]. *Cognitiva, 1*, 99–132.

García-Madruga, J. A., Gutiérrez, F., Carriedo, N., Luzón J. M. & Vila, J. O. (2007). Mental models in propositional reasoning and working memory's central executive. *Thinking & Reasoning, 13*, 370–393.

Gathercole, V. C. M., Sebastián, E. & Soto P. (1999). The early acquisition of Spanish verbal morphology: Across the-board or piecemeal knowledge? *International Journal of Bilinguism, 3*, 133–182.

(2000). The emergence of linguistic person in Spanish-speaking children. *Language Learning, 52*(4), 679–722.

Goikoetxea, E. (2005). Levels of phonological awareness in preliterate and literate Spanish-speaking children. *Reading and Writing, 18*, 51–79.

Gomes, C., Simpson, I. & Defior, S. (2017). A multivariate model of the relationship between vocabulary, decoding and comprehension skills in Spanish-speaking children. Ms. submitted for publication.

Gómez, P. C. & Pérez, R. A. (2009). Estudio cuantitativo de los afijos en español. *Bulletin of Hispanic Studies, 86*, 453–468.

González Trujillo, M. C. (2005). *Comprensión lectora en niños: Morfosintaxis y prosodia en acción* [Reading comprehension with children: Morphosyntax and prosody in action]. Doctoral dissertation, University of Granada. Retrieved from http://hera.ugr.es/tesisugr/15808932.pdf.

Guerra, R. (1983). Estudio estadístico de la sílaba en español [Statistic study about the syllable in Spanish]. In M. Esgueva & M. Cantarero (Eds.), *Estudios de fonética I* [Phonetic studies] (pp. 9–112). Madrid: Consejo Superior de Investigaciones Científicas.

Gutiérrez-Calvo, M. (1999). Inferencias en la comprensión del lenguaje [Inferences in language comprehension]. In M. de Vega & F. Cuetos (Eds.), *Psicolingüística del español* [Spanish Psycholinguistics] (pp. 231–270). Madrid: Editorial Trotta.

Gutiérrez-Palma, N., Defior, S. & Calet, S. (2016). Prosodic skills and literacy acquisition in Spanish. In J. Thompson & L. Jarmulowicz (Eds.), *Linguistic rhythm and literacy* (pp. 265–281). Amsterdam and Philadelphia: John Benjamins.

Hernandez Pina, F. (1984). *Teorías psicosociolingüísticas y su aplicación a la adquisición del español como lengua materna* [Psycholinguistic theories and applications to Spanish language acquisition]. Madrid: Siglo XXI.

Herrera, L., Defior, S. & Lorenzo, O. (2007). Intervención educativa en conciencia fonológica en niños prelectores de lengua materna española y tamazight. Comparación de dos programas de entrenamiento [Educational intervention on phonological awareness for Spanish-speaking and Tamazight-speaking prereaders]. *Infancia y Aprendizaje, 30*, 39–54.

Infante, M. D. R. (2001). Social background and reading disabilities: Variability in decoding, reading comprehension, and listening comprehension skills. Doctoral dissertation, University of Missouri, CO.

Instituto Cervantes (2014). *El español: Una lengua viva. Informe 2014* [Spanish: A living language. Report 2014]. Madrid: Departamento de Comunicación Digital del Instituto Cervantes.

Jiménez, J., Guzmán, R., Rodríguez, C. & Artiles, C. (2009). Prevalencia de las dificultades específicas de aprendizaje: La dislexia en español [Prevalence of specific learning disabilities: The case of dyslexia in Spain]. *Anales de psicología, 25*, 78–85.

Jiménez, J. E. & Haro, C. R. (1995). Effects of word linguistic properties on phonological awareness in Spanish children. *Journal of Educational Psychology, 87*, 193–201.

Jiménez-Fernández, G., Defior, S., Cantos, I. & Serrano, F. (2006). Las complejidades del lenguaje escrito: Comparación entre lectura y escritura [Written language complexities: Comparing reading and spelling]. In J. Salazar, M. Amengual & M. Juan (Eds.), *Usos sociales del lenguaje y aspectos psicolingüísticos: Perspectivas aplicadas* [Social applications of language and psycholinguistic aspects: Applied perspectives] (pp. 343–352). Palma de Mallorca: Servei de publicacions i intercanvi cientific de la UIB.

Jiménez-Fernández, G., Gutiérrez-Palma, N. & Defior, S. (2015). Impaired stress awareness in Spanish children with developmental dyslexia. *Research in Developmental Disabilities, 37*, 152–161. DOI:10.1016/j.ridd.2014.11.002.

Jiménez-Fernández, G., Vaquero, J. M. M., Jiménez, L. & Defior, S. (2011). Dyslexic children show deficits in implicit sequence learning, but not in explicit sequence learning or contextual cueing. *Annals of Dyslexia, 61*, 85–110. DOI:10.1007/s11881-010-0048-3.

Jiménez González, J. E. & Jiménez Rodríguez, R. (1999). Errores en la escritura de sílabas con grupos consonánticos: Un estudio transversal [Errors in syllable with consonant cluster writing: A cross-sectional study]. *Psicothema, 11*, 125–135.

Kieffer, M. J., Biancarosa, G. & Mancilla-Martinez, J. (2013). Roles of morphological awareness in the reading comprehension of Spanish-speaking language minority learners: Exploring partial mediation by vocabulary and reading fluency. *Applied Psycholinguistics, 34*, 697–725. DOI:10.1017/S0142716411000920.

Kieffer, M. J. & Lesaux, N. K. (2007). Breaking down words to build meaning: Morphology, vocabulary, and reading comprehension in the urban classroom. *The Reading Teacher, 61*, 134–144. DOI:10.1598/RT.61.2.3.

Kim, Y. & Pallante, D. (2012). Predictors of reading skills for kindergartners and first grade students in Spanish: A longitudinal study. *Reading and Writing, 25*, 1–22.

León, J. A. & Escudero, I. (2002). La memoria de trabajo y el procesamiento de inferencias en la comprensión del discurso [Working memory and inferential processing in reading comprehension]. In M. D. Sainz, J. Fuentes, J. Baqués & J. Sáiz (Eds.), *Psicología de la memoria: Aportaciones recientes* [Psychology of memory: Recent issues] (pp. 25–34). Barcelona: Avesta.

Miranda, A., Soriano, M. & García, R. (2006). Reading comprehension and written composition problems of children with ADHD: Discussion of research and methodological considerations. *Advances in Learning and Behavioral Disabilities, 19*, 237–256. DOI:10.1016/S0735-004X(06)19009-6.

Morales Silva, S., Verhoeven, L. & van Leeuwe, J. (2008). Socio-cultural predictors of reading literacy in fourth graders in Lima, Peru. *Written Language & Literacy, 11*, 15–34.

   (2011). Socio-cultural variation in reading comprehension development among fifth graders in Peru. *Reading and Writing, 24*, 951–969.

Onochie, E., Simpson, I., Caravolas, M. & Defior, S. (2011, July). Letter knowledge, phoneme awareness and RAN as predictors of reading fluency in Spanish. Poster presented at the Tenth International Symposium of Psycholinguistics, Donostia, San Sebastián, Spain.

Otero, J. C., Campanario, J. M. & Hopkins, K. D. (1992). The relationship between academic achievement and metacognitive comprehension monitoring ability of Spanish secondary school students. *Educational and Psychological Measurement, 52*, 419–430.

Ouellette, G. P. (2006). What's meaning got to do with it: The role of vocabulary in word reading and reading comprehension. *Journal of Educational Psychology, 98*, 554–566. DOI:10.1037/0022-0663.98.3.554.

Pérez Pereira, M. & Singer, D. (1984). Adquisición de morfemas del español [Morphemes acquisition in Spanish]. *Infancia y Aprendizaje, 7*, 205–221.

Perfetti, C. A. (2007). Reading ability: Lexical quality to comprehension. *Scientific Studies of Reading, 11*, 357–383.

Ramirez, G., Chen, X., Geva, E. & Kiefer, H. (2010). Morphological awareness in Spanish-speaking English language learners: Within and cross-language effects on word reading. *Reading and Writing, 23*, 337–358.

Real Academia Española (2010). *Ortografía de la lengua española* [Orthography of the Spanish language]. Madrid: Espasa Calpe.

Ripoll, J. C., Aguado, G. & Castilla-Earls, A. P. (2014). The simple view of reading in elementary school: A systematic review. *Revista de Logopedia, Foniatría y Audiología, 34*(1), 17–31.

Sánchez, E. & García, J. R. (2009). The relation of knowledge of textual integration devices to expository text comprehension under different assessment conditions. *Reading and Writing, 22*, 1081–1108.

Sánchez, E. & García-Rodicio, H. (2013). Using online measures to determine how learners process instructional explanations. *Learning and Instruction, 26*, 1–11.

Sellers, V. D. (2000). Anxiety and reading comprehension in Spanish as a foreign language. *Foreign Language Annals, 33*, 512–521.

Serrano, F. & Defior, S. (2005). Las habilidades de conciencia fonológica en niños disléxicos españoles: ¿déficit o retraso? [Phonological awareness and dyslexia in Spanish: Deficit vs. developmental lag?]. In M. L. Carrió Pastor (Ed.), *Perspectivas interdisciplinares de la Lingüística Aplicada* [Interdisciplinary perspectives of Applied Linguistics] (pp. 169–178). Valencia: Asociación Española de Lingüística Aplicada. Universidat Politècnica de València.

(2007). Niveles de conciencia fonológica: La tarea de "detección del extraño" [Phonological awareness levels: The oddity task]. In R. Mairal Usón et al. (Eds.), *Actas del XXIV Congreso Internacional de AESLA. Aprendizaje de lenguas, uso del lenguaje y modelación cognitiva: Perspectivas aplicadas entre disciplinas* [Annals of XXIV AESLA International Conference. Language learning and use and cognitive modeling: Applied multidisciplinary perspectives] (pp. 1117–1123). Madrid: Universidad Nacional de Educación a Distancia, UNED.

(2008). Dyslexia speed problems in a transparent orthography. *Annals of Dyslexia, 58*, 81–95. DOI:10.1007/s11881-008-0013-6.

(2012). Spanish dyslexic spelling abilities: The case of consonant clusters. *Journal of Research in Reading, 35*, 169–182. DOI:10.1111/j.1467-9817.2010.01454.x.

(2014). Written spelling in Spanish-speaking children with dyslexia. In B. Arfé, J. Dockrell & V. Berninger (Eds.), *Writing development in children with hearing loss, dyslexia, or oral language problems: Implications for assessment and instruction* (pp. 214–228). New York: Oxford University Press.

Serrano, F., Defior, S. & Martos, F. (2003). To be or not to be phonologically aware: A reflection about metalinguistic skills of student of teacher. In R. M. Joshi, C. K. Leong & B. L. J. Kaczmarek (Eds.), *Literacy acquisition: The role of phonology, morphology and orthography* (pp. 209–215). Amsterdam: IOS Press.

Serrano, F., Genard, N., Sucena, A., Defior, S., Alegria, J., Mousty, P., Leybaert, J., Castro, S. L. & Seymour, P. H. K. (2011). Variations in reading and spelling acquisition in Portuguese, French and Spanish: A cross-linguistic comparison. *Journal of Portuguese Linguistics, 10*(1), 183–204.

Serrano, F., González Trujillo, M. C., Defior, S. & Carpio, M. V. (2005). La emergencia de la conciencia fonémica en niños prelectores españoles [Emergency of phonemic awareness in Spanish prereading children]. In J. M. Oro, J. Varela Zapata & J. Anderson (Eds.), *Lingüística Aplicada al aprendizaje de lenguas* [Applied Linguistic to language learning] (pp. 371–379). Santiago de Compostela: Servizo de Publicacións da Universidade de Santiago de Compostela.

Serrano, F., Jiménez-Fernández, G. & Defior, S. (2005). Development of spelling skills in Spanish orthography: A longitudinal study. In L. Allal & J. Dolz (Eds.), *Proceedings of the Ninth International Conference of the EARLI Sig Writing 2004*. Geneva: Adcom Productions.

Seymour, P. H. K., Aro, M. & Erskine, J. M. (2003). Foundation literacy acquisition in European orthographies. *British Journal of Psychology, 94*, 143–174. DOI:10.1348/000712603321661859.

Simpson, I. & Defior, S. (2017). Are reading models developed in English applicable to Spanish? Ms. in preparation.

Singson, M., Mahoney, D. & Mann, V. (2000). The relation between reading ability and morphological skills: Evidence from derivational suffixes. *Reading and Writing, 12*, 219–252.

Suárez-Coalla, P., García-de-Castro, M. & Cuetos, F. (2013). Variables predictoras de la lectura y la escritura en castellano [Predictors of reading and writing in Spanish]. *Infancia y Aprendizaje, 36*(1), 77–89.

Suárez-Coalla, P., Ramos, S., Álvarez-Cañizo, M. & Cuetos, F. (2014). Orthographic learning in dyslexic Spanish children. *Annals of Dyslexia, 64*, 166–181.

UNESCO Institute for Statistics (2013). Education and literacy. Retrieved from www .uis.unesco.org/literacy/Pages/default.aspx.

Urquijo, S. (2010). Funcionamiento cognitivo y habilidades metalingüísticas con el aprendizaje de la lectura [Cognitive operation and metalinguistic abilities in reading learning]. *Educar em revista*, 38, 19–42. DOI:10.1590/S0104-40602010000300003.

Valle-Arroyo, F. (1989). Reading errors in Spanish. In P. G. Aaron & R. M. Joshi (Eds.), *Reading and writing disorders in different orthographic systems* (pp. 163–175). Dordrecht: Kluwer.

(1996). Dual-route models in Spanish: Developmental and neuropsychological data. In M. Carreiras, J. E. García-Albea & N. Sebastián-Gallés (Eds.), *Language Processing in Spanish* (pp. 89–118). Mahwah, NJ: Lawrence Erlbaum.

12   Learning to Read German

Karin Landerl

12.1   Introduction

12.1.1   *German and Its Orthography*

German language and orthography are in many ways similar to English. Both have a Germanic language structure, there is considerable overlap in the words used and both are written in alphabetic orthographies, using more or less the same set of letters. With respect to written language acquisition and processing, there is, however, a critical difference: While over time English has traded in the vast expansion of its vocabulary for inconsistencies and irregularities of grapheme–phoneme correspondences, German letter–sound relationships are highly consistent and reliable. This difference in phonological transparency and consistency has important implications for reading acquisition: Grapheme–phoneme based decoding provides a useful and highly reliable default reading strategy to which the reader can revert whenever more efficient reading strategies are not available or do not produce satisfactory results. The implications of this comparably high phonological transparency for reading and spelling acquisition will be discussed in this chapter.

12.1.2   *Synchronic and Diachronic Characterization*

The oldest known written German texts date back to the eighth century. In the sixteenth century, Martin Luther's translation of the Bible into an east-central (Saxonian) version of German set important early standards to written language usage. The pressure to develop a standard written language system increased with the introduction of compulsory schooling in the eighteenth and early nineteenth centuries. This was mostly achieved when Konrad Duden, a Prussian high school teacher, published the *Vollständiges Orthographisches Wörterbuch der deutschen Sprache* (Complete Orthographic Dictionary of the German Language) in 1880, which was declared authoritative by an orthographic conference in 1901 and soon after approved by the governments of the

German Empire, Austria, and Switzerland. From then on, the German spelling system was essentially determined by the editors of the Duden dictionaries. The Duden editors exercised their power in a cautious way, that is, documenting contemporary usage rather than creating new rules.

A recent spelling reform provides a vivid demonstration of how difficult it is to change a linguistically based, widely used system by introducing new official rules and regulations. From 1980 on, various expert committees discussed steps to simplify the orthography and thus to make it easier to learn, without substantially changing the system familiar to the competent user. In 1996, the governments of the German-speaking countries (Germany, Austria, Liechtenstein, and Switzerland) signed an international agreement that made the reformed orthography obligatory in schools and in public administration. However, there was controversial and occasionally emotionally charged public debate and a campaign against the reform that was supported by, amongst many others, important newspapers like the *Frankfurter Allgemeine Zeitung* and the Nobel Prize-winning writers Günther Grass and Elfriede Jelinek. The debate culminated in a German court decision stating that orthography is not subject to legal regulations and that outside the school system everybody was free to use the preferred spelling, including the traditional word form. In 2006, the Council for German Orthography agreed unanimously to remove the most controversial changes from the reform and to accept both *traditional* and *reformed* spellings for some words. This reform of the reform is now widely accepted. The main intentions of the spelling reform were to strengthen the morphological principle of the orthography, to systematize capitalization of nouns, and to simplify punctuation.

12.1.3   *Literacy and Schooling*

Standard German evolved not from a traditional dialect of a specific region but as a written language, developed over centuries, in which writers tried to write in a way that was understood by a large number of people speaking different dialects. Until about 1800, Standard German was almost entirely a written language. In some regions (such as around Hannover) the local dialect has almost completely died out and was replaced by Standard German over time. Austria and Switzerland have somewhat distinct versions of Standard German. Until today there exists a broad variety of German dialects and vernaculars (Besch, Knoop, Putschke & Wiegand, 1982) with variations on all levels of language (phonology, inflectional morphology, vocabulary, and syntax), which are not always intelligible to other German speakers. When children from such dialect communities enter school, they may be unable to speak Standard German, but will be familiar with it via book reading activities and media use

(TV and radio programs are dominantly presented in Standard German). In some regions primary school teachers will also use dialect for spoken communication while in other regions Standard German is the language of teaching. For example, Luxemburgish constitutes a dialect that is very distant from Standard German; nevertheless, children learn to read in German (although there is also a recent movement toward writing books in Luxemburgish).

In all German-speaking countries, children enter school around their sixth birthday and compulsory schooling lasts nine or ten years. Reading instruction, which is usually phonics based, mostly happens during the first four to six years of elementary school, after which students move on to different strands of secondary schools. Traditionally, the kindergarten system is distinct from the school system and is administered by different organizations (e.g., state, churches, parent organizations) which follow very different curricula, mostly focusing on playing activities and social skills. Recently, however, more and more states introduce one or two years of obligatory preschool attendance. Preschools may or may not offer phonological awareness training programs, only some of which present letters as well. Explicit training in letter–sound knowledge is unusual, and there is no formal reading instruction before Grade 1.

12.2   Description of German and Its Written Forms

German is spoken by an estimated 90 million native speakers (Lewis, 2009) and is therefore one of the major languages of the world. In the following, we will mostly concentrate on the description of Standard German as this is the language that corresponds to the written form.

12.2.1   Linguistic System

German is a West Germanic language and is linguistically very closely related to English and Dutch. In this chapter, we will make use of the relationship with English and characterize German in its similarities to and differences from English.

12.2.1.1 Phonology   Tables 12.1 and 12.2 present the German phoneme system (together with their corresponding graphemes, which will be discussed in Section 12.2.2.2). The consonant inventory (see Table 12.1) is largely overlapping with English. It has the same six plosives, three nasals and two approximants as English. A rhotic consonant can be realized in either alveolar or uvular position, depending on the dialect spoken and the phonemic context. The fricative inventory includes a voiced and a voiceless labiodental (/v/, /f/), the glottal fricative /h/, an

Table 12.1 *German consonant system together with corresponding graphemes (in square brackets)*

	Bilabial	Labio-dental	Alveolar	Post-alveolar	Palatal	Velar	Uvular	Glottal
Unvoiced stop	p [p, pp, b]		t [t, tt, th, d]			k [k, ck, g]		
Voiced stop	b [b, bb]		d [d, dd]			g [g, gg]		
Affricate		p͡f [pf]	t͡s [z, tz, ts]	t͡ʃ d͡ʒ [ch, tsch]				
Unvoiced fricative		f [f, ff, v]	s [s, ss, ß]	ʃ [sch, s]	ç [ch, g]	x [ch]		h [h]
Voiced fricative		v [w, v]	z [s]	ʒ [sch]				
Nasal	m [m, mm]		n [n, nm]			ŋ [n, ng]		
Approximant			l [l, ll]		j [j, y]			
Trill			r [r, rr, rh]				ʀ [r, rr, rh]	

Note. Secondary correspondences that occur in foreign or loan words are not represented.

Table 12.2 *German monophthong vowels together with their corresponding graphemes (in square brackets)*

	Front				Central		Back	
	Unrounded		Rounded					
	Short	Long	Short	Long	Short	Long	Short	Long
Close	ɪ [i]	i: [ie, ih, ieh]	ʏ [ü, y]	y: [ü, üh, y]			ʊ [u]	u: [u, uh]
Close-mid		e: [e, ee, eh]		ø: [ö, öh]	ə			o: [oo, oh]
Open-mid	ɛ [e, ä]	ɛ: [e, ee, eh, ä, äh]	œ [ö]		[e, er]		ɔ [o]	
Open					a [a]	a: [a, aa, ah]		

Note. Secondary correspondences that occur in foreign or loan words are not represented.

alveolar fricative (/z/, /s/) that in some (especially southern) dialects is always unvoiced, and a postalveolar fricative, which in most variants of German is realized only in a voiceless version /ʃ/. A palatal (/ç/) and a velar (/χ/) fricative constitute two allophones of one and the same phoneme. German has the affricates /pf/ and /ts/, which constitute quite typical syllable onsets. There is linguistic disagreement whether /tʃ/ and /dʒ/ (which only occurs in foreign words) are affricates or consonant clusters (Wiese, 1996).

The Standard German vowel system has eight vowels which exist in short as well as long monophthong pronunciations (see Table 12.2) and the three diphthongs /ao/, /ai/, and /ɔi/. Short vowel phonemes are all lax, while long vowels (with the exception of /ɛ:/) are tense.

Syllable structure and stress patterns are mostly comparable to English. An important difference is that in unstressed syllables, only the /ɛ/ vowel is reduced to schwa, while all other vowels are pronounced in their short versions. The phonotactic rules of German are more lenient than in English, so that complex consonant clusters are not simplified, but fully pronounced in spoken language (e.g., *Knie* 'knee', *Psychologie* 'psychology').

12.2.1.2 Inflectional Morphology An important difference between German and English (as well as Dutch) is that German has a richer inflectional morphology system. Noun phrases (including articles and any adjectives) inflect into four cases (nominative, genitive, dative, accusative), three genders (masculine, feminine, neuter), and two numbers (singular, plural) which are marked by different suffixes (e.g., nominal singular: *der große Mann* 'the big man'; genitive singular: *des großen Mannes* 'the big man'). The declension of adjectives depends on the number and case of the noun and also on whether the definite article, indefinite article, or no article is used (e.g., das *laute Kind* 'the noisy child' vs. ein *lautes Kind* 'a noisy child'; *vor* der *verschlossenen Tür* 'before the closed door' vs. *vor verschlossener Tür* 'in front of a closed door').

The verb system is in many ways similar to English, but again, verb forms (including the infinitive) receive different suffixes (e.g., *leben* 'to live': *ich lebe, du lebst, er lebt, wir leben, ihr lebt, sie leben*) and prefixes (e.g., *gelebt, Vorleben*).

Phonology of stem morphemes is usually consistent across grammatical forms, but there are numerous exceptions: Plural formation of nouns or building comparative forms of adjectives can involve fronting of back vowels (e.g., /man/ – /mɛnə/, /groːs/ – /grøːsə/. The stressed vowel also changes in a number of irregular verbs (e.g., *sehen* /seːn/ 'to see'; *er sieht* /siːt/ 'he sees'; *er sah* /saː/ 'he saw'). On the surface structure, adding a grammatical morpheme to a word stem may also alter the pronunciation of plosives due to devoicing in syllable-end and preconsonantal positions (e.g., *leben* – *lebt*).

12.2.1.3 Word Formation Processes   A feature that is of high relevance with respect to reading is that German allows complex compounds which are written as one word that can then easily have four to six syllables and more than ten letters (e.g., *Geburtstagskuchen* 'birthday cake', *Autoschlüssel* 'car key'). Morphological processes frequently induce complex consonant sequences, for example at the end of inflected verbs (e.g., *du kämpfst* 'you fight') or in the middle of compound nouns (e.g., *Wohnungsschlüssel* 'apartment key').

12.2.2   Writing System

12.2.2.1 Script and Punctuation   German is written in Latin script and uses the very same letters as English plus three umlaut letters (Ä-ä, Ö-ö, Ü-ü) and a special /s/-grapheme (‹ß›) which historically evolved as a ligature of an obsolete version of the *s*-writing ("long s") and *z* (*ʃz*) and "long s over round s" (*ʃs*) in morpheme-final position. In capitalized spellings it is replaced by ‹SS› or ‹SZ›. In Switzerland and Liechtenstein, this so-called "sharp s" is always replaced by ‹ss›. A special feature of German orthography is that all nouns (as well as verbs and adjectives in noun position) are capitalized, so capital letters at word beginnings are used more systematically than in English. The punctuation system is also similar to English, only the types of subordinate clauses that are obligatorily or optionally marked by a comma vary somewhat between the two languages.

12.2.2.2 Orthography   German uses an alphabetic orthography which is morphologically structured. Tables 12.1 and 12.2 provide an overview of the standard graphemic correspondences for each phoneme. It is obvious that most phonemes have two or three graphemic correspondences, which explains why spelling in German is difficult. Before going into detail on the (mostly morphology- and etymology-based) reasons for these inconsistencies of phoneme–grapheme correspondences, we will discuss the much simpler grapheme–phoneme correspondences.

For consonant and vowel doublings, diphthongs, and some single consonant graphemes (‹f›, ‹m›, ‹l›), there exists only one pronunciation. Two pronunciations for one and the same consonant grapheme (like /f/ and /v/ for ‹v›) are exceptional in German (apart from certain irregular foreign and loan word pronunciations which will not be discussed here). Grapheme pronunciation is often specified by context-sensitive rules, e.g., ‹s› before ‹p› and ‹t› in syllable onsets is pronounced as /ʃ/ in most German dialects. As a matter of fact, ‹sp› and ‹st› are taught as units to young learners. The graphemes ‹b›, ‹d›, and ‹g› are pronounced as /p/, /t/, and /k/ due to the phonological process of devoicing in syllable end and preconsonant position (e.g., *Dieb* 'thief', *glaubt* 'believes'). Additionally, some (northern) variants of German palatalize /g/ to /ç/ in certain positions (e.g., *lustig* 'funny') and the grapheme *g* can correspond to both phonemes.

In contrast to English, where orthographic consistency for vowels is particularly low, vowel quality is unambiguously represented in German orthography. Vowel length is coded by a complex set of context-sensitive rules (the simplified version is that short vowels are succeeded by two consonants, e.g., *beten* 'to pray' vs. *betten* 'to embed'). Interestingly, this has limited implications for word recognition as the number of minimal word pairs that differ only in vowel length is relatively small and their meaning is most often very distinct so that word identification is usually possible even if vowel length is underspecified or incorrect during the decoding process. Indeed, young learners who predominantly rely on a strategy of systematic left-to-right decoding typically produce artificially lengthened phonemes (/m:a:n:/), and this artificial pronunciation is usually sufficient to access the correct word in their lexicon (/man/ – *Mann*).

Just like English, German adheres to the principle of morpheme constancy, that is, the spelling of morphemes is preserved in different word forms (e.g., *fahren* 'to drive', *Fahrer* 'driver', *Gefährt* 'vehicle'). However, in contrast to English, the morphological principle never overrides the phonological principle. Sometimes the German umlaut graphemes can help to retain both morpheme and phonological consistency. For example, plural formation frequently involves a change of the main vowel: the plural of /man/ is /mɛnə/. The spellings of the two word forms are *Mann* and *Männer*. The grapheme *ä* corresponds consistently to the vowel phoneme /ɛ/ so that the phonological word form can unambiguously be derived from the letter sequence. At the same time, the singular and plural word forms are visually similar, thus retaining consistency at the morphemic level. The recent spelling reform has introduced more of these morphology-based umlaut spellings.

The principle of morpheme constancy is the main reason why German is clearly less consistent in the spelling than in the reading direction. Whereas in reading there is almost always only one possible translation of a grapheme into a phoneme, in spelling, one has to choose among various possible translations of a phoneme into a grapheme. This explains why German (just like English) has a considerable number of homophonic spellings, for example, *mehr – Meer* 'more – sea', *viel – fiel* 'a lot – fell', *Lied – Lid* 'song – eyelid', *Wal – Wahl* 'whale – election'.

The orthographic marking of vowel length is particularly inconsistent and tricky. Short vowels are typically marked by two following consonant letters, but there are a limited number of high-frequency words (mainly function words and prepositions) for which the short vowel is not orthographically marked. For long vowels, there are three different kinds of orthographic marking, doubling of the vowel (*Moos* 'moss', *Haar* 'hair'), a "silent h" after the vowel (e.g., *Bahn* 'train', *mehr* 'more'), or no orthographic marking at all (*baden* 'to bathe', *Regen* 'rain'). There are no clear algorithms for the particular orthographic marking (e.g., *Tal* 'valley', *Zahl* 'number', *Saal* 'hall'). Doubling of umlaut letters is orthographically illegal, therefore, some words that are spelled with a double vowel as singular word forms have a simple vowel spelling in plural and other word forms requiring vowel change (e.g., *Saal – Säle*), thus, violating the principle of morpheme consistency.

The main intention of the recent spelling reform was to further strengthen the morphological principle and to make morphological relationships between word forms more explicit. In one important case, this also improved phonological consistency: Unvoiced /s/ is written as ⟨ß⟩ after a long vowel and – according to the general short vowel rule – as ⟨ss⟩ after short vowels (*Flüsse* 'rivers' vs. *Füße* 'feet'). However, for orthotactic reasons, traditional German spelling replaced ⟨ss⟩ by ⟨ß⟩ in morpheme-final position. But this position-dependent letter substitution violated the rule that *-ß* marks a preceding long vowel and induced inconsistency at the morpheme level as, for example, singular and plural word forms had different /s/-spellings (*Fluß – Flüsse* 'river – rivers'). During the spelling reform this dated orthotactic rule was deleted. (Note that Switzerland and Liechtenstein accept phonological inconsistency in the other direction: In these orthographic variants of German, ⟨ss⟩ is consistently used instead of ⟨ß⟩, even after long vowels – violating the general rule that consonant doublets mark a preceding short vowel.)

Inconsistency on the grapheme–phoneme level also arises for plosives due to the already mentioned phonological process of devoicing in syllable-end position (e.g., *Grad* /gra:t/ 'degree'; plural: *Grade* /gra:də/ 'degrees'). Thus, the spelling retains the voiced phoneme of the deep structure although the surface pronunciation changes in voicing. Furthermore, in certain areas (e.g., in Austrian Standard German) the phonemic distinction between voiced and unvoiced labiodental, and palatal plosives is neutralized in most phonemic contexts so that two graphemes correspond to one and the same phoneme.

In order to compensate for the high flexibility of German word order, nouns are systematically spelled with a capital letter to allow the reader to identify them easily in any position. Note that in German, verbs and adjectives can take the noun position which means that words which are usually spelled with a small letter (*spielen* 'to play', *blau* 'blue') need to be capitalized when they are used as nouns (*zum Spielen* 'for playing', *das Blaue* 'the blue one'). There is no empirical evidence for whether readers indeed make use of the information provided by capital letters. On the other hand, capitalization poses particular problems for spelling acquisition, which is why abolishing the capitalization rule has often been discussed.

12.2.3   Conclusion

The grapheme–phoneme system of the alphabetic German orthography is highly consistent with only few exceptions (e.g., *Mond* 'moon' and *Papst* 'pope'; which both include a long vowel pronunciation although the postvocalic consonant structure suggests otherwise) that mostly occur for foreign words typically imported from English (*Computer, googeln, Baby*). For spelling, morphological consistency induces a good deal of inconsistency on the phoneme level with the limitation that phonologically irregular spellings are again exceptional and mostly limited to foreign words.

12.3   Acquisition of Reading and Spelling in German

Because of the high consistency of letter–sound associations in German, insight into the alphabetic principle is relatively easy. Systematic and accurate phoneme synthesis (as in decoding) and phoneme analysis (as in spelling) provide a solid scaffolding for the further development of reading and spelling competence; however, it is only a starting point for efficient written language processing.

12.3.1   Becoming Linguistically Aware

12.3.1.1 Phonological Development and Phonological Awareness   Early segmental as well as prosodic phonological development in German is in many ways similar to English. A language-specific characteristic is that closed syllables with a (C)VC-structure seem to appear relatively early. They have been observed in children's babbling productions in their first year of life and can appear in the very first spoken (proto)words. From 20 months onwards, there is a strong increase in closed syllable productions which constitute 90% of all spoken words at the end of the second year. First, coda consonants can be plosives, nasals, or liquids (Elsen, 1991; Grijzenhout & Joppen, 1998; Lleó, Kuchenbrandt, Kehoe & Trujillo, 2003). Affricates appear before consonant clusters, and cluster productions appear in syllable codas before they are produced in syllable onsets (Lleó & Prinz, 1997). Complex clusters with three constituents are pronounced early in codas, even before the second birthday (Elsen, 1991), but clearly later, during the third year, in onsets (Fox, 2006).

Caravolas and Landerl (2010) showed direct effects of the typical syllable structure on the development of phoneme awareness. German children showed higher awareness of phonemes in codas than in onsets (whereas the reverse was true for Czech children, reflecting the fact that Czech language has more onset than coda clusters). These effects were present among pre-readers and persisted to the end of Grade 1, indicating that children's experience with the syllable structure of their native language plays an important role in shaping phoneme awareness from early in development and predates influences of alphabetic reading skills.

In German, as in other languages, phonological awareness at the syllable and onset-rime level develops during the preschool years, while awareness of phonemes usually develops in the context of learning to read (e.g., Schaefer et al., 2009; Wimmer, Landerl, Linortner & Hummer, 1991; Wimmer, Landerl & Schneider, 1994). Children who receive phonological awareness training in kindergarten have been demonstrated to show significantly better reading and spelling skills in Grades 1 and 2, but only when the training involves letters as well as sounds (Schneider, Roth & Ennemoser, 2000). Still, the predictive quality of phonological awareness for reading development has been demonstrated to be lower in German than in English in studies that directly compared these languages (Landerl et al., 2013; Mann & Wimmer, 2002). Furthermore, the effect of early phonological awareness training is relatively small, which is probably due to the fact that in Grade 1 children receive systematic instruction in letter–sound knowledge and phoneme blending and analysis in the context of reading instruction, which is likely to compensate any early phonological deficits. As a matter of fact, Wimmer, Mayringer, and Landerl (2000) could show that children with poor phonological awareness at school entry did not develop any reading problems later on. Interestingly, however, these children showed marked spelling problems in Grades 3 and 4. As explained in Section 12.3.2.2, at that age even poor spellers are well able to segment spoken words into their constituent sounds and produce phonologically adequate spellings, but they have very limited knowledge of word spellings.

A plausible explanation for the association of phonological awareness with orthographic spelling is that the phonological underpinning (Perfetti, 1992) of orthographic representations might be impaired, which in turn negatively affects an amalgamation of spoken and written words in the orthographic lexicon (Ehri, 1992).

While phonological awareness predicts spelling rather than reading, the best predictor of word and nonword reading in German is rapid automatized naming (Landerl & Wimmer, 2008; Moll, Fussenegger, Willburger & Landerl, 2009; Wimmer et al., 2000). Rapid automized naming (RAN) deficits clearly dissociate from phonological awareness deficits (Wimmer & Mayringer, 2002), supporting the view that they constitute an independent cause of dyslexia (Wolf & Bowers, 1999). Moll et al. (2009) tested the assumption that RAN indicates phonological processing speed while the usually untimed phonological awareness tasks measure accuracy of phonological processing. However, the predictive pattern of RAN and phonological awareness remained unchanged when response time instead of response accuracy was used as the phonological awareness measure. It is also unlikely that RAN is an indicator of orthographic processing as it is only moderately associated with orthographic spelling and shows an equally strong relationship with word and nonword reading (Moll et al., 2009). The most likely explanation for the association of RAN with reading is that RAN is an indicator of the speed and efficiency of visual-verbal processing, or in other words of the automaticity of orthography to phonology associations at the letter and letter cluster level. However, further research is needed in order to identify the precise mechanisms explaining the RAN–reading relationship.

12.3.1.2 Morphological Development and Morphological Awareness Production of inflected word forms is exceptional before children's second birthday. Inflectional morphology is mostly acquired between the ages of 2 and 5 years. Note that plural marking is not as straightforward as in most English words because German has various different plural markers for different word stems (e.g., *Spiel* 'game' – *Spielei*; *Ball* 'ball'– *Bälle*; *Zahl* 'number' – *Zahlen*; *Kind* 'child' – *Kinder*; *Auto* 'auto' – *Autos*). Sometimes plural forms are not specifically marked (e.g., *Löffel* 'spoon(s)', *Käfer* 'bug(s)') and dialectal plural morphemes are not always identical to those of Standard German (*zwei Auto* is acceptable in colloquial language, but not in Standard German). During language acquisition, children frequently use inadequate plural markers (e.g., *Autoen*, *Löffels*). Gender marking in nominative forms is produced with high accuracy, but sometimes errors occur in other cases (e.g., Röhr-Sendlmeier, 1985). A typical overgeneralization in the context of verb morphology is that strong verbs are conjugated in analogy to weak verbs (Lindner & Kieferle, 2003). Depending on frequency of occurrence, such errors may still appear in children's writings in elementary school (e.g., *beißen* 'to bite'; past tense: *beißte* instead of correct *biss*).

Compositional as well as derivational processes are actively used from the age of about two years on to build neologisms. While compounds (e.g., *Fenstermacher* 'window maker') predominate at first, derived word forms increase continuously.

Morphological awareness is indispensable in order to spell correctly in German and is explicitly taught, though to a very variable extent. Importantly, the German capitalization rule requires children to identify any word that has a noun function. In Grades 3 and 4, they are typically expected to spell nouns correctly with a capital letter; however, capitalization of nominalized verbs and adjectives is usually acquired in Grades 4 to 6 and can even cause problems to adult spellers. Children also learn a number of explicit derivation rules that they are expected to apply to spelling. For example, they are instructed to lengthen word forms (by adding another inflectional morpheme) ending in a plosive (which is always devoiced) in order to identify whether the stem is spelled with a voiced or an unvoiced sound (e.g., *Lied – Lieder* 'song – songs' vs. *Boot – Boote* 'boat – boats', where voicing of the alveolar plosive is different in intervocalic, but not in word end position). Doubling of consonants is also not phonologically transparent in many word forms and can only be derived (e.g., *halt* 'stop' vs. *hallt* 'it echoes'). As explained in Section 12.2.2.2, many umlaut spellings result from morphological change, so children are instructed to consider the spelling of simple word forms when spelling plural words (e.g., *Bälle*, not *Belle*, as it is derived from *Ball*). Intervention programs that focus on the morphological structure of the orthography have been demonstrated to improve children's spelling competence and also to have a positive impact on word reading (Kargl, Purgstaller, Weiss & Fink, 2008).

12.3.2   Development of Word Identification

12.3.2.1 Word Decoding Development   The combination of a phonologically consistent orthography and a systematic phonics teaching approach makes the acquisition of phoneme synthesis in word recognition relatively easy for German-speaking children. Evidence consistently shows that after only a few months of formal reading instruction in school, even relatively poor readers are able to decode words as well as nonwords with high accuracy (Seymour, Aro & Erskine, 2003; Wimmer & Hummer, 1990). To illustrate, Figure 12.1 presents direct comparisons of reading accuracy for cognate words and nonwords in monolingual German and English 9-year-olds (Landerl, Rau & Moll, 2012). Even the long items were read reasonably well by these young German readers. As a matter of fact, a sample of English-speaking adults produced a similarly high number of errors for the longest nonwords. Similarly, 12-year-old

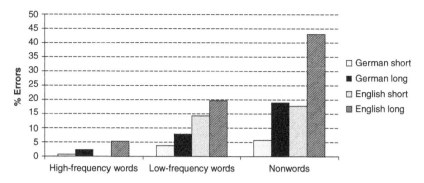

Figure 12.1 Reading accuracy: percent reading errors for high- and low-frequency words and nonwords for 9-year-old native speakers of German or English. Age group (Grade 1–6 and adults) and term (1st/2nd).

German-speaking dyslexic children were found to read three syllabic nonwords with about the same accuracy as English-speaking dyslexic children read rather simple one-syllabic high-frequency words (Frith, Wimmer & Landerl, 1998). Errors mostly occur when the reader tries to trade in reading speed for reading accuracy. Especially under speeded conditions (*read as fast as you can*), poor readers do make errors; however, when the error is pointed out to them and they get a chance to reread the word (or nonword) without time limitation, most of the time they will be able to work out the correct pronunciation. Incorrect readings are usually close to the correct pronunciation and in many cases deviate in only one or two phonemes (Landerl, Wimmer & Frith, 1997; Wimmer & Hummer, 1990). Even after only a few months of reading instruction, children typically have sufficient competence in decoding to at least attempt to sound out unfamiliar grapheme sequences, and refusals or *don't know* responses hardly ever occur (Wimmer & Hummer, 1990).

Thus, the main criterion of word and nonword reading competence in German is reading speed, which increases continuously during reading acquisition (Klicpera & Schabmann, 1993; Landerl & Wimmer, 2008; Wimmer, 1993). Reading speed is often assessed by list reading paradigms measuring the number of words or nonwords read correctly in a limited amount of time (e.g., Moll & Landerl, 2010; Torgesen, Wagner & Rashotte, 1999), but note that such paradigms are purer measures of speed in consistent orthographies like German (due to the high reading accuracy) than in English where a low number of correctly read items may result from slow but correct decoding as well as from a high number of incorrect readings. Figure 12.2 presents data from the standardization sample of such a one-minute reading test with words and

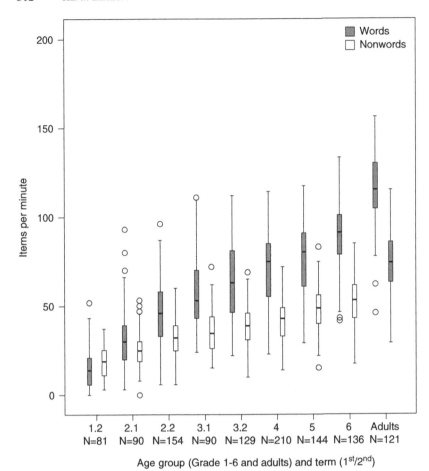

Figure 12.2 Reading speed across grade levels: number of words and nonwords read correctly in one minute. Lower end of the boxes represent 25th percentile, upper end of the box represents 75th percentile, horizontal line in the middle of the box represents the median.

nonwords (Moll & Landerl, 2010), illustrating the increase of reading speed across different age groups, ranging from end of Grade 1 to young adults. These box plots also show that variability of reading speed is high at all ages. Impressively, some of the poor readers in Grades 5 and 6 are still only reading on the level of Grade 2.

Systematic grapheme-phoneme based decoding constitutes a highly reliable default strategy in German, and it also provides input for the buildup of word-specific orthographic representations (Share, 1995). In a recent eye-tracking study, Rau, Moeller, and Landerl (2014) showed that effects of item length were largely comparable between items of differing visual familiarity (high- and low-frequency words and nonwords) for Grade 2 readers, whereas for more experienced readers (Grades 3, 4, and adults), length effects increased with decreasing visual familiarity. Thus, early word recognition appeared to be mostly based on phonological recoding, while from Grade 3 on word recognition appeared to be dominantly based on lexical access. Similarly, Moll and Landerl (2009) found significantly lower response times for real words than for visually similar pseudo-homophonic spellings of these words in a sample of primary school children (Grades 2 to 4). This response time effect indicates that children were not purely decoding words and pseudo-homophones in the same way, but relied on lexical access which worked for words but was disturbed for pseudo-homophones. Interestingly, this response time effect was also evident (and actually quite marked) in poor readers, but not in a sample of children who showed marked spelling problems in accordance with age-adequate reading. It seems that this group of poor spellers but good readers relied on a highly efficient decoding strategy and did not use lexical access, not even for words that they could spell correctly, suggesting that they had lexical knowledge available. Further research is needed to find out why these children were unable to use their efficient decoding strategy for orthographic learning.

12.3.2.2 Word Spelling Development It has been argued that the spelling of consonant clusters poses a major phonological hurdle to young children as they are particularly difficult to segment into separate phonemes (Treiman, 1993). German provides an interesting test case for this conclusion because just like in English, consonant clusters in syllable onset as well as coda position are frequent (e.g., *blau* – 'blue', *drei* – 'three', *Hand* – 'hand', *Wolf* – 'wolf'). Contrary to this prediction, Wimmer and Landerl (1997) showed that after only nine months of formal instruction, German-speaking first graders did not show particular problems with cluster spellings. Phonologically inadequate cluster spellings occurred for only four onsets and seven coda clusters among the whole sample of sixty-eight children. The relative ease of consonant-cluster spelling suggests that early segmentation difficulties are easily overcome by the combination of a consistent orthography and an instructional regime that induces children to early word recognition in reading by means of grapheme–phoneme decoding. This laborious procedure provides systematic segmentation training that makes the phonemic composition of consonant clusters transparent.

While spelling words in a phonemically acceptable way is achieved early, acquisition of orthographically correct word spellings is a long-term enterprise.

As a matter of fact, dyslexia is traditionally perceived as a spelling rather than a reading problem in German-speaking countries because the high number of spelling errors in children's writing is much more obvious than the reading fluency problems described above. The obvious reason for children's difficulties to acquire word spelling is the relatively low consistency of phoneme–grapheme correspondences. Incorrect spellings typically provide acceptable transcriptions of the phoneme sequence (sometimes representing colloquial language or dialect rather than Standard German), but orthographic markers like consonant or vowel doubling or the silent letter *h* that marks vowel length are omitted or placed incorrectly. Spelling of the umlaut *ä* is mostly morphologically motivated and often replaced by the more frequent letter *e* (which corresponds to the very same phoneme) in children's spellings. In line with certain dyslexia theories (e.g., Tallal, 1984), correct spellings of plosives poses a particular problem in German; however, it is mostly voicing ($b - p, d - t$) that is represented incorrectly, but hardly ever place of articulation (Klicpera, 2000), which is not in line with Tallal's assumption that the relevant phoneme categories are not adequately established in dyslexic individuals. As explained in Section 12.2.2.2, incorrect use of voiced vs. unvoiced plosive graphemes is most often due not to phonological misperceptions but to the fact that there is a lot of allophonic variation in the voicing of plosives inducing inconsistency in the use of the corresponding letters.

On the morphosyntactic level, capitalization of nouns (and only nouns), correct use of commas for listings and to mark certain infinitive groups and clauses are also typical sources of error not only in children's but also in adults' writings.

12.3.2.3 Reading and Spelling Difficulties   Owing to the relatively high consistency of grapheme–phoneme correspondences and the phonics teaching approach applied in most schools, even struggling readers usually acquire sufficient decoding skills to read words as well as nonwords accurately. However, their reading remains extremely slow and laborious, constituting a pervasive impairment in reading speed (Landerl, 2001; Wimmer, 1993). Spelling deficits mostly concern familiarity with orthographic patterns, while poor spellers' understanding of the alphabetic principle is usually sufficiently developed in order to produce phonologically adequate spellings. Owing to the inconsistencies of the German phoneme–grapheme system, these spellings typically deviate from the correct spellings as specified in Section 12.3.2.2.

Interestingly, deficits in reading vs. spelling can be dissociated (Moll & Landerl, 2010; Wimmer & Mayringer, 2002). Poor spelling in accordance with adequate reading skills has been observed and studied in many orthographies, including English (e.g., Frith, 1980; Holmes & Castles, 2001), and is usually explained by two facts: (1) in most orthographies, phoneme–grapheme correspondences are less consistent than grapheme–phoneme correspondences, and (2) word spelling requires retrieval of fully specified orthographic representations, while for word reading, bottom-up processes of word recognition can be complemented by top-down lexical processes. There is evidence that children with poor spelling but adequate reading skills have a phonological awareness deficit at the onset of reading acquisition (Wimmer & Mayringer, 2002), which they seem to be able to overcome later due to heavy practice in phonemic decoding (Moll & Landerl, 2010). They also manage to acquire highly accurate phonemic analysis skills allowing them to spell words in a phonologically acceptable way. However, their early phonological deficit seems to prevent them from establishing orthographic word representations that are amalgamated with the phonology of the word (Ehri, 1992).

Poor reading in correspondence with age-adequate orthographic spelling has not been reported for other orthographies, although Moll and Landerl's (2010) analysis indicated that 40% of primary school children with marked problems in reading fluency (below 10th percentile) showed spelling skills within 1 standard deviation to the age norm. A dissociation of deficits in reading and spelling was also reported by Wimmer and Mayringer (2002) who could demonstrate that at school entry, children who later on showed poor reading in association with age-adequate spelling skills did not experience any deficits in phonological awareness. They were, however, already deficient in a rapid naming paradigm. Overall, phonological awareness was found to be a less good predictor of reading disorders in German than in English (Landerl et al., 2013), indicating that problems in the phonological domain are less detrimental in the consistent German compared to the complex and often phonologically opaque English writing system.

12.3.3   Reading Comprehension

12.3.3.1 Predictors of Reading Comprehension   Apart from the international Organisation for Economic Co-operation and Development (OECD) studies on literacy in 10- and 15-year-olds (Progress in International Reading Literacy Study [PIRLS], Programme for International Student Assessment [PISA]), language-specific research on reading comprehension in German is limited. Landerl and Reiter (2002) reported a robust correlation (.64) between a test of word reading fluency and the PISA-literacy score for the Austrian sample of the first PISA study. However, Klicpera and Schabmann (1993) showed that in this age group, vocabulary was a stronger predictor of reading comprehension than decoding speed. Artelt, Schiefele, and Schneider (2001) made an interesting distinction between online processing of a text that is currently available and reading a text in order to refer to the presented information later on. Online reading comprehension was best predicted by students' metacognitive knowledge of reading strategies, followed by the number of books at home (as an indicator for literacy environment) and decoding speed. For learning from a text in order to answer questions later on, Artelt et al. (2001) assumed that the construction of a mental representation (Kintsch, 1998) would be triggered more strongly. Indeed, after controlling for decoding speed, memory-based text comprehension was most strongly predicted by students' prior knowledge about the content of the text, which they could probably use for the construction of a mental representation. Metacognitive knowledge of text comprehension strategies was again a significant predictor, as well as number of books at home and personal interest in the topic of the text. In a younger sample (Grades 3 and 4), van Kraayenoord and Schneider (1999) also identified metacognitive strategies and decoding as significant predictors of reading comprehension. Both components were in turn significantly influenced by children's reading motivation, while this component did not exert a significant direct influence on reading comprehension.

12.3.3.2 Word-Level Effects in Comprehending Text Richter, Isberner, Naumann, and Neeb (2013) recently investigated the relationship between the accuracy and efficiency of phonological, orthographic, and meaning representations in German primary school children (Grades 1 to 4). Together, these measures of lexical quality could account for 60% of the variance in text-level comprehension. Grade-level differences in reading comprehension could be fully accounted for by individual differences in lexical quality. Interestingly, measures of accuracy and efficiency of access to lexical representations contributed to reading comprehension via two largely separate paths (with only moderate correlations between accuracy and speed measures), suggesting that they constitute two different and partly independent facets of lexical quality. While the accuracy of phonologic and orthographic representations exerted direct effects on reading comprehension, it also exerted indirect effects via the accuracy of the meaning representation. Analogously, the effects of the efficiency of phonological and orthographic representations were mediated via the efficiency of the meaning representation. Unfortunately, the orthographic measure in this study only partly required orthographic processing. In this lexical decision task, children had to decide whether or not a presented letter sequence represented an existing word. In a consistent orthography, lexical decision can be mostly solved via phonological decoding. Orthographic processing is only necessary for pseudo-homophonic spellings that sound like a real word but their spelling is different from the regular word spelling. In the Richter et al. (2013) study, only some of the to-be-rejected items were pseudo-homophones. The fact that this task required both phonological and orthographic knowledge of words may explain why it showed particularly strong associations with the other components in the model. Nevertheless, this study provides further evidence for the high relevance of the quality of lexical representations for reading comprehension (Perfetti, 2003).

12.3.4   Conclusion

Research on reading and spelling acquisition in German is mostly focused on the word level, while research on reading comprehension processes is still scarce. The most likely explanation is that differences from the dominant English orthography are very obvious at the word level while specific implications of the German language and writing system with respect to reading comprehension are not very clear. One implication that might be interesting to look at is that learning new words from text should be easier in consistent orthographies like German compared to the unreliable English orthographic system. The reliable "default" strategy of phonological decoding that German-speaking children acquire relatively early allows them to read any text and therefore provides a good foundation for vocabulary expansion. This is, however, an implication that can be made for any consistent and therefore decodable writing system, not only for German.

On the word level, the most interesting finding based on German data is that good orthographic spelling in accordance with very poor reading fluency is a quite frequent phenomenon. It has so far not been reported for other orthographies, as it is generally assumed that poor spelling is an inevitable consequence of poor reading. This reading–spelling discrepancy is very interesting with respect to the relevance of the orthographic lexicon for efficient word reading. It is generally assumed that reading becomes more fluent when the reader is increasingly able to replace effortful decoding procedures by access to orthographic word representations (Share, 1995). However, it seems that children with good spelling skills who read extremely slowly have marked problems in accessing their orthographic representations even though they have them available. The finding that this reading–spelling discrepancy is associated with persistent problems in rapid naming challenges any orthographic explanations of the RAN–reading relationship (e.g., Bowers & Newby-Clark, 2002). It seems more likely that RAN indicates the efficiency of visual-verbal associations, which is an indicator of the automaticity of orthography to phonology associations at the letter and letter-cluster level.

12.4   Discussion

12.4.1   Challenges in Learning to Read German

The complexity of the German orthographic system arises mainly from the grammatical language structure. Owing to inflection, words typically have more than one syllable and may include heavy consonant sequences. Thus, while cracking the alphabetic code is not a major stumbling block due to the reliability of grapheme–phoneme correspondences, decoding long and complex words is an enormous challenge for inexperienced readers. It is mostly the efficiency with which words of variable length and variable morphological complexity can be read that differentiates between good and poor readers.

Because German orthography adheres closely to the principle of morpheme constancy, spelling requires efficient access to an extensive morphologically structured orthographic lexicon. Phonological decoding provides a useful self-teaching mechanism for the buildup of orthographic representations (Share, 1995), but note that a considerable number of children develop efficient word decoding skills but nevertheless fail to acquire adequate spelling competence (Moll & Landerl, 2009). A highly plausible assumption is that children with good morphological awareness should find it easier to understand and apply the morphological regularities inherent in the German orthographic system. However, to date there is no language-specific evidence on the relationship between morphological awareness and orthographic spelling competence in German.

12.4.2   Implications for Instruction

Early reading and spelling instruction in German-speaking countries is dominantly phonics oriented. This approach works rather well even though primary school teachers are not always aware of the complexities of letter–sound mappings that even the relatively transparent German orthographic system provides (Schabmann, Landerl, Bruneforth & Schmidt, 2012). After the first one or two years in primary school, instruction is mostly focused on spelling. There are reasons to assume that this is adequate, as spelling instruction makes frequent letter patterns and the morphological structure of German orthography explicit to the learner and therefore provides information on what typical German words look like. However, it is unclear whether this information is in fact useful for children's reading.

Reading in itself is mostly practiced as text reading after the very early stages of decoding instruction. Repeated reading of the same text is sometimes considered boring and is therefore somewhat out of fashion, although it is an evidence-based approach to improve children's word reading skills (Kuhn & Stahl, 2003). Teachers are also not always aware of the enormous variability of word reading efficiency in their classrooms. It is often assumed that children who are able to decode but have problems in text comprehension have a higher-level reading problem that is specific to comprehension processes. Perfetti's (2007) verbal efficiency theory makes very clear that effortful decoding is no sufficient basis for text comprehension.

12.5   Final Conclusion

The combination of consistent grapheme–phoneme correspondences and a systematic phonics teaching approach enables young learners of German orthography to grasp the alphabetic principle with relative ease. Applying this insight efficiently as well as storing and accessing orthographic representations for automatic and fluent reading is the central obstacle. Fortunately, reading fluency is gaining increasing attention, not only in orthographies with consistent grapheme–phoneme correspondences but also in English (e.g., Torgesen et al., 1999).

Although acquisition of any alphabetic orthography without phonological awareness is hardly conceivable, the importance of phonological awareness for reading acquisition that was derived from findings in English may have been overrated. It turns out that the predictive strength of phonological awareness measures for German children's reading development is comparably low and limited to the very early phases when children still struggle with decoding. In the long run, phonological awareness seems to be more strongly associated with orthographic spelling than with reading. Obviously, the simple and straightforward German grapheme–phoneme correspondences allow even children with poor phonological skills to grasp the alphabetic principle. Intense practice in decoding is likely to help children compensate for any early problems. However, when the mappings between spoken and written language are more complex, as is the case for German phoneme–grapheme associations, the relevance of phonological skills for reading and spelling reappears.

References

Artelt, C., Schiefele, U. & Schneider, W. (2001). Predictors of reading literacy. *European Journal of Psychology of Education*, *16*, 363–383.
Besch, W., Knoop, U., Putschke, W. & Wiegand, H. E. (1982). *Dialektologie: Ein Handbuch zur deutschen und allgemeinen Dialektforschung*. Berlin: De Gruyter.
Bowers, P. G. & Newby-Clark, E. (2002). The role of naming speed within a model of reading acquisition. *Reading and Writing*, *15*, 109–126.
Caravolas, M. & Landerl, K. (2010). The influences of syllable structure and reading ability on the development of phoneme awareness: A longitudinal, cross-linguistic study. *Scientific Studies of Reading*, *14*, 464–484.
Ehri, L. C. (1992). Reconceptualizing the development of sight word reading and its relationship to recoding. In P. B. Gough, L. C. Ehri & R. Treiman (Eds.), *Reading acquisition* (pp. 107–143). Hillsdale, NJ: Lawrence Erlbaum.
Elsen, H. (1991). *Erstspracherwerb: Der Erwerb des deutschen Lautsystems*. Wiesbaden: Deutscher Universitäts-Verlag.
Fox, A. V. (2006). Evidence from German-speaking children. In Z. Hua & B. Dodd (Eds.), *Phonological development and disorders in children: A multilingual perspective* (pp. 56–80). Clevedon: Multilingual Matters.

Frith, U. (1980). Unexpected spelling problems. In U. Frith (Ed.), *Cognitive processes in spelling* (pp. 495–515). London: Academic Press.

Frith, U., Wimmer, H. & Landerl, K. (1998). Differences in phonological recoding in German- and English-speaking children. *Scientific Studies of Reading, 2,* 31–54.

Grijzenhout, J. & Joppen, S. (1998). *First steps in the acquisition of German phonology: A case study* (SFB 282 Working Paper Nr. 110). Düsseldorf: Heinrich-Heine-Universität.

Holmes, V. M. & Castles, A. E. (2001). Unexpectedly poor spelling in university students. *Scientific Studies of Reading, 5,* 319–350.

Kargl, R., Purgstaller, C., Weiss, S. & Fink, A. (2008). Effektivitätsüberprüfung eines morphemorientierten Grundwortschatz-Segmentierungstrainings (MORPHEUS) bei Kindern und Jugendlichen. *Heilpädagogische Forschung, 34,* 147–156.

Kintsch, W. (1998). *Comprehension: A paradigm for cognition.* Cambridge University Press.

Klicpera, C. (2000). Sind Rechtschreibschwierigkeiten Ausdruck einer phonologischen Störung? Die Entwicklung des orthographischen Wissens und der phonologischen Rekodierungsfähigkeit bei Schülern der 2. bis 4. Klasse Grundschule [Are spelling difficulties the expression of a phonological deficit? The development of orthographic knowledge and phonological recoding ability in the 2nd to 4th grade of the elementary school]. *Zeitschrift für Entwicklungspsychologie und Pädagogische Psychologie, 32,* 134–142.

Klicpera, C. & Schabmann, A. (1993). Do German-speaking children have a chance to overcome reading and spelling difficulties? A longitudinal survey from the second until the eighth grade. *European Journal of Psychology of Education, 8,* 307–323.

Kuhn, M. R. & Stahl, S. A. (2003). Fluency: A review of developmental and remedial practices. *Journal of Educational Psychology, 95,* 3–21.

Landerl, K. (2001). Word recognition deficits in German: More evidence from a representative sample. *Dyslexia, 7,* 183–196.

Landerl, K., Ramus, F., Moll, K., Lyytinen, H., Leppänen, P. H. T., Lohvansuu, K., ... Schulte-Körne, G. (2013). Predictors of developmental dyslexia in European orthographies with varying complexity. *Journal of Child Psychology and Psychiatry, 54,* 686–694.

Landerl, K., Rau, A. & Moll, K. (2012, July). Development of eye-movement patterns in word and nonword reading in English and German. Paper presented at the Annual Meeting of the Society for the Scientific Study of Reading, Montreal, Canada.

Landerl, K. & Reiter, C. (2002). Lesegeschwindigkeit als Indikator für basale Lesefertigkeiten. In C. Wallner-Paschon & G. Haider (Eds.), *PISA PLUS 2000: Thematische Analysen nationaler Projekte* (S. 61–66). Innsbruck: Studien Verlag.

Landerl, K. & Wimmer, H. (2008). Development of word reading fluency and orthographic spelling in a consistent orthography: An 8-year follow-up. *Journal of Educational Psychology, 100,* 150–161.

Landerl, K., Wimmer, H. & Frith, U. (1997). The impact of orthographic consistency on dyslexia: A German-English comparison. *Cognition, 63,* 315–334.

Lewis, M. P. (Ed.) (2009). *Ethnologue: Languages of the world*, 16th edn. Dallas, TX: SIL International.

Lindner, K. & Kieferle, C. (2003, October). Ging, gehte or gang? What do children in third and fourth grade know about past tense forms of irregular verbs? International conference: Oral language of school children: Acquisition, teaching and remediation, Grenoble, France.

Lleó, C., Kuchenbrandt, I., Kehoe, M. & Trujillo, C. (2003). Syllable final consonants in Spanish and German monolingual and bilingual acquisition. In N. Müller (Ed.), *(In)vulnerable domains in multilingualism* (pp. 191–220). Amsterdam: John Benjamins.

Lleó, C. & Prinz, M. (1997). Syllable structure parameters and the acquisition of affricates. In S. J. Hannahs & M. Young-Scholten (Eds.), *Focus on phonological acquisition (Language acquisition & language disorders)* (pp. 143–163). Amsterdam: John Benjamins.

Mann, V. & Wimmer, H. (2002). Phoneme awareness and pathways into literacy: A comparison of German and American children. *Reading and Writing, 15*, 653–682.

Moll, K., Fussenegger, B., Willburger, E. & Landerl, K. (2009). RAN is not a measure of orthographic processing: Evidence from the asymmetric German orthography. *Scientific Studies of Reading, 13*, 1–25.

Moll, K. & Landerl, K. (2009). Double dissociation between reading and spelling deficits. *Scientific Studies of Reading, 13*, 359–382.

(2010). *Lese- und Rechtschreibtest (SLRT II)* [Reading and spelling test SLRT II]. Bern: Huber.

Perfetti, C. A. (1992). The representation problem in reading acquisition. In P. B. Gough, L. C. Ehri & R. Treiman (Eds.), *Reading acquisition* (pp. 145–174). Hillsdale, NJ: Lawrence Erlbaum.

(2003). The universal grammar of reading. *Scientific Studies of Reading, 7*, 3–24.

(2007). Reading ability: Lexical quality to comprehension. *Scientific Studies of Reading, 11*, 357–383.

Rau, A. K., Moeller, K. & Landerl, K. (2014). The transition from sublexical to lexical processing in a consistent orthography: An eye-tracking study. *Scientific Studies of Reading, 18*, 224–233.

Richter, T., Isberner, M.-B., Naumann, J. & Neeb, Y. (2013). Lexical quality and reading comprehension in primary school children. *Scientific Studies of Reading, 17*, 415–434.

Röhr-Sendlmeier, U. M. (1985). Zum sprachlichen Entwicklungsstand des Grundschulkindes. *Linguistische Berichte, 98*, 338–346.

Schabmann, A., Landerl, K., Bruneforth, M. & Schmidt, B. M. (2012). Lesekompetenz, Leseunterricht und Leseförderung im österreichischen Schulsystem: Analysen zur pädagogischen Förderung der Lesekompetenz. In B. Herzog-Punzenberger (Ed.), *Nationaler Bildungsbericht Österreich 2012. Band 2: Fokussierte Analysen bildungspolitischer Schwerpunktthemen* (pp. 17–70). Graz: Leykam.

Schaefer, B., Fricke, S., Szczerbinski, M., Fox-Boyer, A.V., Stackhouse, J. & Wells, B. (2009). Development of a test battery for assessing phonological awareness in German-speaking children. *Clinical Linguistics & Phonetics, 23*, 404–430.

Schneider, W., Roth, E. & Ennemoser, M. (2000). Training phonological skills and letter knowledge in children at risk for dyslexia: A comparison of three kindergarten intervention programs. *Journal of Educational Psychology, 92*, 284–295.

Seymour, P. H. K., Aro, M. & Erskine, J. M. (2003). Foundation literacy acquisition in European orthographies. *British Journal of Psychology, 94,* 143–174.

Share, D. L. (1995). Phonological recoding and self-teaching: Sine qua non of reading acquisition. *Cognition, 55,* 151–218.

Tallal, P. (1984). Temporal or phonetic processing deficit in dyslexia? That is the question. *Applied Psycholinguistics, 5,* 167–169.

Torgesen, J. K., Wagner, R. K. & Rashotte, C. A. (1999). *Test of word reading efficiency.* Austin, TX: PRO-ED Publishing.

Treiman, R. (1993). *Beginning to spell: A study of first-grade children.* Oxford University Press.

van Kraayenoord, C. E. & Schneider, W. E. (1999). Reading achievement, metacognition, reading self-concept and interest: A study of German students in grades 3 and 4. *European Journal of Psychology of Education, 14,* 305–324.

Wiese, R. (1996). *The phonology of German.* Oxford University Press.

Wimmer, H. (1993). Characteristics of developmental dyslexia in a regular writing system. *Applied Psycholinguistics, 14,* 1–33.

Wimmer, H. & Hummer, P. (1990). How German-speaking first graders read and spell: Doubts on the importance of the logographic stage. *Applied Psycholinguistics, 11,* 349–368.

Wimmer, H. & Landerl, K. (1997). How learning to spell German differs from learning to spell English. In C. A. Perfetti, L. Rieben & M. Fayol (Eds.), *Learning to spell: Research, theory, and practice across languages* (pp. 81–96). Mahwah, NJ: Lawrence Erlbaum.

Wimmer, H., Landerl, K., Linortner, R. & Hummer, P. (1991). The relationship of phonemic awareness to reading acquisition: More consequence than precondition but still important. *Cognition, 40,* 219–249.

Wimmer, H., Landerl, K. & Schneider, W. (1994). The role of rhyme awareness in learning to read a regular orthography. *British Journal of Developmental Psychology, 12,* 469–484.

Wimmer, H. & Mayringer, H. (2002). Dysfluent reading in the absence of spelling difficulties: A specific disability in regular orthographies. *Journal of Educational Psychology, 94,* 272–277.

Wimmer, H., Mayringer, H. & Landerl, K. (2000). The double-deficit hypothesis and difficulties in learning to read a regular orthography. *Journal of Educational Psychology, 92,* 668–680.

Wolf, M. & Bowers, P. G. (1999). The double-deficit hypothesis for the developmental dyslexias. *Journal of Educational Psychology, 91,* 415–438.

13   Learning to Read Dutch

Ludo Verhoeven

13.1   Introduction

13.1.1   Dutch and Its Orthography

Dutch functions as the official language of the Netherlands and part of Belgium. It is spoken in the two countries by about 23 million people. Officially, the language is called *Nederlands* (Dutch) but the language variety spoken in the Netherlands is often referred to as *Hollands* (Hollands) and the language variety spoken in Belgium is usually referred to as *Vlaams* (Flemish). Despite a variety of dialects, the vast majority of the inhabitants of these countries have a good command of the standard language. Frisian is considered a dialect by many but has an official language status. It is spoken by more than 60 percent of the inhabitants of the northern province of Friesland. For about 5 million inhabitants of the Netherlands and Belgium, Dutch is not the native language. Non-indigenous language varieties have thus been introduced as immigrant languages from abroad. Chinese, Italian, and Polish were the home languages of small ethnic communities in the Netherlands and Belgium before World War II. It is estimated that more than 15 percent of the populations of the Netherlands and Belgium is of a non-indigenous origin.

The orthography used to write the Dutch language is largely phonemic and much more consistent than that of English. The basic letter-to-phoneme correspondences in Dutch are not strictly one-to-one or invariant. The mapping of graphemes to phonemes is straightforward for most short words of Dutch origin but not always for longer words. Dutch syllable structure is quite complex because multiple consonants can occur in both onset and coda positions. Numerous deviations from a one-to-one correspondence between letters and sounds can be found in longer Dutch words, moreover.

13.1.2   Synchronic and Diachronic Characterization

Multiple interactions have occurred over the years between the oral and literate varieties of the Dutch language, sometimes producing clear register differences. Written Dutch tends to be more formal than spoken Dutch and calls upon more academic forms, such as the use of Latin-based vocabulary and nominalizations. Passive voice constructions, ellipsis, and numerous clause linking devices are widespread in written Dutch.

Historically, Dutch is considered one of the West Germanic languages, and it is, indeed, closely related to the German language. However, like English, it has lost most of its original Germanic noun morphology. The term *Dutch* comes from the Middle Dutch word *Diets*, which is the name for the low German language variety. There are only a few documents of the Old Dutch language variety, spoken before 1100. A substantial number of texts has been preserved from the Middle Dutch period up until 1500. Most of these documents originate from the southern provinces of Brabant (The Netherlands) and Flanders (Belgium).

During the Middle Dutch period, the language lost most of its inflectional morphology, including most case distinctions. This evolution toward modern standard Dutch drew mostly on the varieties spoken in the province of Holland (with Amsterdam at its center). Some striking changes occurred during this period, such as the dipthongization of /u/ to /ɑu/ and /i/ to /ɛi/. The foundation for the standardization of Dutch orthography was laid during the nineteenth century with the basic spelling rules provided by de Vries and te Winkel (1866) in their manual *Grondbeginselen der Nederlandse Spelling* (Basic principles of Dutch orthography). The official and thus standard spelling of Dutch was realized only in 1947, however.

13.1.3   Literacy and Schooling

The home environments of Dutch-speaking children have been shown to be an important predictor of later school success. Storybook reading enhances the vocabularies, phonological awareness, and early literacy development of young children (Mol, Bus & de Jong, 2009). In preschool and kindergarten, storybook reading and emergent literacy activities are part of the daily routines aimed at strengthening the oral communication skills and vocabularies of children and thereby help them discover the alphabetic principle. In keeping with this principle, the basic task of children learning to read in Dutch is to move from the sequential grapheme-to-phoneme decoding of words to the fast, parallel, and mostly phonological processing of written language.

Formal Dutch reading instruction starts in first grade and involves a large amount of phonics instruction with a focus on the decoding of regular CVC word patterns. In a period of about four months, all of the regular grapheme–phoneme correspondences are taught within the contexts of words and small bits of text. In subsequent months, this instruction is extended to include the reading of monosyllabic words containing consonant clusters and the reading of bisyllabic words.

By the end of first grade, Dutch children are expected to be able to spell and decode simple, regularly written Dutch words. In second grade, the words get longer, irregularities are increased, and specific context-sensitive rules are introduced for the conversion of sounds to letters and letters to sounds. In subsequent school years, the fluency of word decoding stands central with a variety of book reading routines used to accomplish this along with special attention to spelling difficulties.

13.2   Description of Dutch and Its Written Forms

As a West Germanic language related to both German and English, Dutch did not undergo the High German consonant shift. Dutch has also been released, by and large, from the grammatical case system of German, resulting in a relatively simple morphology. Dutch words mainly originate from Germanic but loan words from Roman languages are also numerous.

13.2.1   The Linguistic System

13.2.1.1 Phonology Dutch vowels are pronounced according to the phonological features of place of articulation (frontal, central, back) and height (high, middle, low) (See Table 13.1). At the same time, there is an opposition between long and short vowels: Long vowels tend to be tense and short vowels lax. And there are three diphthongs: frontal ɛɪ as in *hei* 'heath', central œy as in *bui* 'shower', and back ʌu as in *dauw* 'dew'.

The system of Dutch consonants is relatively simple. Place and manner of articulation in addition to voicing are the main distinctive features (see Table 13.2). The voiced–voiceless opposition is distinctive for plosives but not so much for fricatives.

The vast majority of Dutch monosyllabic words follow a CVC pattern. Consonant clusters can occur in both initial and final position, with the following distribution possible – in principle – within a single word: CCCVCCCC or *striktst* ('most strict'). When a liquid or nasal is followed by a non-homorganic consonant in postvocalic position, the word is pronounced with an unstressed schwa inserted between the two consonants. Thus *melk* 'milk' is pronounced as [mɛlək], *kalm* 'calm' as [kɑləm], but *wens* 'wish' as [wɛns].

The main stress in polysyllabic words otherwise tends to be on the prefinal syllable. And with the exception of only the schwa, all vowels in Dutch can receive stress. In nominal and verbal compounds, primary stress is on the first part and secondary stress on the second part.

Table 13.1 *Classification of Dutch vowels according to their place and height of articulation*

	High	Middle	Low
Frontal	i	ɪ / e:	ε
Central	y	ʏ / ø:	a:
Back	u	ɔ / o:	ɑ

Table 13.2 *Classification of Dutch consonants according to their place and manner of articulation*

| | Labial | | Alveolar | | Velar | | Palatal | Uvular | Glottal |
	+V	−V	+V	−V	+V	−V			
Obstruent									
– Plosive	b	p	d	t	k	-			
– Fricative	v	f	z	s	ý	x			
Nasal	m		n		ñ				
Liquid			l					R	
Glide	w						j		h

Sentence intonation in Dutch is rather flat. Unmarked Dutch declarative sentences have a low declining contour at the beginning, a high declining contour in the middle, and a final low declining contour at the end. Interrogative sentences have a high declining contour at the end.

13.2.1.2 Inflectional Morphology   The general rule for Dutch plural formation is adding *-en* to a singular word form, e.g., *deur* 'door' – *deuren* 'doors'. However, many exceptions apply, e.g., *jongen* 'boy' – *jongens* 'boys'. With respect to verbal morphology, Dutch can be characterized as a language with a restricted tense system and a very limited aspect system. Basically, there are contrasts among present, simple past, and perfect. The basic tense opposition is present versus past tense. Only the singular forms of verbs require differentiation for person (see van der Putten, 1997). The first person form of the verb is *verb stem + 0*, while the second and third person forms are *verb stem + t*. For regular verbs, the past tense is formed by adding *-de/-te* to the verb stem. For so-called strong verbs, the past is formed by a vowel change, as in *ik loop* 'I walk' vs. *ik liep* 'I walked'. The regular past participle is created with the addition of the prefix *ge-* and the suffix *-d/-t*, as in *ge-droom-d* 'dreamed' or *ge-kus-t* 'kissed'. Most strong verbs take the suffix *-en*, as in *ge-holp-en* 'helped', to form the past participle. The auxiliaries for the perfect tense are *hebben* 'have' for transitive verbs and *zijn* 'be' for intransitive verbs at times. The auxiliary for the passive voice in Dutch is *worden*. Word order is the basic marker of syntactic roles in Dutch, which does not have case inflections (Geerts, Haeseryn, de Rooij & van den Toorn, 1984).

In Dutch words lacking an internal morphological structure, the main stress is generally placed on the prefinal syllable, which leaves the vowel in the final syllable unstressed. Depending on vowel length and syllable weight, however, the main stress may be shifted to the final syllable at times (see Kooij, 1990). According to the CELEX database, approximately 74 percent of Dutch bisyllabic words are pronounced with first syllable stress (Baayen, Piepenbrock & van Rijn, 1993). Stress assignment to the first syllable can thus be seen as regular and stress assignment to the final syllable as irregular. Prefixes are quite frequent in Dutch words (cf. Schreuder & Baayen, 1995) but *never* stressed. For instance, the presence of a prefix in a bisyllabic verb form leads to a shift of stress from the first (i.e., prefinal) syllable to the second (i.e., final) syllable as in BŪKKEN ('to bend') and GEBŪKT ('bent', past participle), respectively. The unmarked case for stress assignment is thus violated by such prefixed words and therefore an interesting domain for study.

13.2.1.3 Word Formation Processes   Word formation in Dutch is primarily accomplished via affixation and compounding (cf. Booij, 1977). For affixation, the processes of declination, conjugation, and derivation can be distinguished. And for declination, there are more or less regular devices available to form the plural, possessive, comparative, and superlative.

Nominal compounds are *not* morphologically marked in Dutch. Nevertheless, additional elements not associated with the compounded words may be added and thus be considered a part of the compound structure itself. That is, a phonological element (*-e-, -s-, -en-, -er-*) is inserted between two compounded words as a sort of "morphonological glue" on many but not all occasions. And according to van den Toorn (1982), phonological, syntactic, and semantic constraints can explain the occurrence of such binding phonemes.

13.2.2   Writing System

13.2.2.1 Script and Punctuation   Dutch orthography uses the Latin alphabet. The twenty-six letters of the Roman alphabet and digraph combinations cover the thirty-five phonemes of which sixteen are vowels. Four consonants (‹c, q, x, y›) are used for only Latin-based loan words, such as *centrum* ('center'), *quasi*, *extra, yen*. Excluding these foreign consonants, most consonants have a one-to-one correspondence to speech sounds. Exceptions are the stop consonants ‹b› and ‹d›, which represent voiced stops in word-initial position and unvoiced stops in word-final position. The same used to hold for the letter ‹g›

Table 13.3 *Rules for phoneme-to-grapheme conversion of native or non-native sublexicons*

Native rule	Example	Non-native rule	Example
/i/ – ⟨ie⟩	*wieg*	/i/ – ⟨i⟩, ⟨ie⟩	*gitaar, specie*
/o/ – ⟨oo⟩	*boom*	/o/ – ⟨o⟩, ⟨oo⟩	*oncoloog*

representing the voiced velar fricative /ɣ/ in word-initial position and the voiceless sound /x/ in word-final position but, nowadays, the latter tends to be used throughout. Other exceptions are the digraph ⟨ch⟩ for the voiceless velar fricative /x/, the digraph ⟨ng⟩, and the ⟨n⟩ before ⟨k⟩ in word-final position representing the velar nasal /ŋ/ (*tong*, 'tongue'; *rank*, 'slender').

The conversion of vowel graphemes to phonemes is less straightforward than that for consonants. Table 13.3 shows the representation of Dutch vowels in simple CVC words. The single vowel graphemes ⟨a⟩, ⟨e⟩, ⟨i⟩, ⟨o⟩, and ⟨u⟩ can occur in initial or medial position representing the phonemes /a/, /e/, /i/, /o/, and /u/. In word-final position, however, these vowel graphemes represent long vowels. The ⟨e⟩ in word-final position represents the neutral schwa sound, as in *de* ('the'). The ⟨i⟩ in word-final position occurs only in loan words such as *ski*, otherwise ⟨ie⟩ is used, as in *knie* ('knee'). If the letter ⟨u⟩ occurs in penultimate position, it is followed by the letter ⟨w⟩ while the vowel pronunciation gets lengthened (*ruw*, 'rough'). And if the vowel symbols ⟨i⟩ and ⟨u⟩ occur as the last elements of trigraph vowels, they represent the consonants /j/ and /w/, respectively as in *baai* 'bay' and *dauw* 'dew'.

With regard to punctuation (cf. Donaldson, 1997), Dutch declarative sentences start with a capital letter and end with a period. Interrogative sentences end with a question mark, exclamations with an exclamation mark. A semicolon can be used instead of a period at the end of a sentence and thereby connect two sentences. A colon is used to introduce a list, a quotation, or an illustrative example. A comma is used to distinguish coordinate or subordinate clauses within a sentence; may occur between adjectives referring to the same entity; and may be placed at the end of a quote. Quotation marks are used to indicate quoted material. Compound words may sometimes be hyphenated to prevent the pronunciation of two vowels as a single unit. The repeated parts of subsequent compound words may also be preceded by a hyphen. A diaeresis is placed on the first letter of a syllable to prevent the pronunciation of two vowels as a single syllable (e.g., *kopieën* 'copies'). Finally, an apostrophe is used with the plural forms of singular roots that end with a short vowel (e.g., *foto's* 'photographs') or in the case of letter omissions/contractions (e.g., *'s avonds* 'in the evening').

13.2.2.2 Orthography   Dutch orthography is largely but not completely phonemic (Nunn, 1998). Monosyllabic words show a highly consistent mapping between letters and phonemes, but this is not always the case for longer, multisyllabic words. Dutch syllable structure is quite complex, in part because multiple consonants can occur in both onset and coda positions with specific constraints then applying. In words with postvocalic consonant clusters, for instance, the word may be pronounced with an unstressed schwa between the consonants but only when a liquid or a nasal precedes the other consonant. In longer words, numerous deviations from the one-to-one correspondence between letters and sounds occur. To start with, the vowel ‹e› can represent three different sounds in polysyllabic words: /ɛ/ in a closed stressed syllable; /e/ in an open stressed syllable; or /œ/ in an unstressed syllable. The Dutch word *weggeven* 'give away' encompasses all of these variants and is pronounced /wɛggevœn/.

Furthermore, the phonological status of the schwa when it occurs as the central vowel in polysyllabic words is quite unclear. It occurs in unstressed syllables only where it can nevertheless be alternatively represented by the letters ‹e›, ‹ij›, or ‹i› as in *bodem* 'bottom', *eerlijk* 'honest', and *handig* 'handy', respectively. A schwa can also be inserted in sonorant consonant clusters in unstressed syllables, as in *bever* 'beaver'. Yet another deviation concerns the written reduplication of vowels and consonants. Vowels that are normally spelled with reduplication (‹aa›, ‹ee›, ‹oo›, ‹uu›) are written with a single letter when occurring in an open syllable position; the plural of *poot* 'leg' is thus spelled *poten*. In contrast, a single letter consonant is reduplicated when it occurs in intervocalic position after a stressed short vowel; the plural of *pot* 'jar' is thus spelled *potten*.

With the standardization of Dutch orthography in the nineteenth century, four main principles or orthographic conventions were established (see also Bosman, de Graaff & Gijsel, 2006). The first principle is that distinctive phonemes are represented by distinctive graphemes. Non-distinctive (subphonemic) variation in pronunciation is thus neglected. The second principle is that grammatical morphemes are written invariably, or in other words, the phonetic variation occurring in morphological equivalents should not give rise to different spellings. The singular of a plural noun like *handen* 'hands' in Dutch is thus *written* with a final *-d* even though a voiceless *-t* is pronounced for *hand* 'hand'. The third principle requires that grammatical morphemes are written even when they are absent from the pronunciation of a word. By analogy to *hij denk-t* 'he think-s'– which indicates the third person, singular, present tense – the spelling of the same form for another verb is *hij bid-t* 'he pray-s' but the final *-t* is not pronounced separately from the *-d*. When the relevant grammatical morpheme is added to a verb stem that already ends with the letter *-t*, it is not doubled, which shows autonomous rules also exist.

The final principle is maintenance of etymological derivation in current spelling practices and thus differs from earlier orthographic stages with no current phonological impact. Examples of this principle are the alternative spellings of *ɛɪ*, as in *eis* 'claim' versus *ijs* 'ice'. Viewed synchronically, these spelling differences have no significance for the morphophonological basis of Dutch orthography (see Kooij,1992).

From a theoretical point of view, Dutch orthography can be classified as deep synchronic: Conversion rules apply to phonemes, which take the morpheme as their main domain. Phoneme-to-grapheme conversion rules are applied on the basis of phonological context to Dutch morphemes. But Dutch uses partly different sets of phoneme-to-grapheme conversion rules for native versus non-native sublexicons (cf. Nunn, 1998).

Dutch orthography also calls upon autonomous rules that change the sequence of letters when morphemes are combined into words. Such rules are sensitive to the orthographic context but not to sublexicon differences, which can lead to non-isomorphemic written forms. An example is the Dutch rule of *g*-deletion from such graphemic sequences as ‹ngk›, allowing *koning* 'king' to become *koninkje* 'little king'. Other such autonomous rules are as follows.

Spelling devoicing:	*poezen – poez > poes*
Prevocalic e-deletion:	*race – race+en > racen*
i-ie elternation:	*ski+de > skiede*
Diaeresis placement:	*ge-interview+d > geïnterviewd*

13.2.3   Conclusion

Dutch orthography is largely phonemic and much more consistent than, for example, English or French. However, the basic grapheme-to-phoneme correspondences in Dutch are not strictly one-to-one or invariant. Dutch syllable structure is relatively complex because multiple consonants apply in both the onset and coda positions of words. In longer words, moreover, morphological complexity may interact with rules calling for orthographic transparency and autonomous graphotactic rules. Non-isomorphemic written forms may often be the result.

13.3   Acquisition of Reading and Spelling in Dutch

The basic task for children learning to read in Dutch is to become phonologically aware and then progress from the sequential grapheme-to-phoneme decoding of words to the fast, parallel, and mostly phonology-based processing of words from different grammatical classes and simple grammatical structures. The reading and spelling of more complex words and structures will follow, accompanied by the automatization of word decoding, to produce fluent integration of word with text and reading comprehension.

13.3.1 Becoming Linguistically Aware

13.3.1.1 Phonological Development and Phonological Awareness For Dutch phonology, five manners of articulation have been identified (Rietveld & van Heuven, 1997): plosives (b, d, k, p, t), fricatives (f, g, s, v, z), liquids (l, r), nasals (m, n), and glides (h, j, w). Manner of articulation has been found to influence the difficulty of the items used to assess phonological awareness.

Position has also been found to influence phonological awareness with the isolation of initial phoneme easiest, followed by final phoneme and middle phoneme (de Graaff, Hasselman, Bosman & Verhoeven, 2008). In a follow-up study, an interaction was found between type of task and the influence of phoneme position (de Graaff, Hasselman, Verhoeven & Bosman, 2011). Children performed better on both phoneme isolation and phoneme segmentation tasks for phonemes in initial position, but better on phoneme blending for phonemes in word-final position.

In two experiments, Schreuder and van Bon (1989) examined the effects of Dutch word properties such as length, consonant-vowel structure, syllabic structure, and meaning on phonemic segmentation. This was done for a group of fifty first graders who could segment shorter words better than longer words. Phonemic segmentation was also found to be easier for them between onset and rime than within an onset constituent. The type of phoneme has also been shown to affect children's phonemic processing. Geudens and Sandra (2003) found differences in the segmentation of CV and VC syllables as a function of the sonority or vowel-likeness of the component consonants: sonorants (liquids and nasals) cohered more strongly with the preceding vowels than obstruents (plosives and fricatives) and were thus harder for the children to manipulate (i.e., segment). In a similar vein, Geudens, Sandra, and Van den Broeck (2004) indicated that the cohesion between phonemes interacts with the sonority of consonants. And in an experimental study with 5-year-old preliterate children, Wagensveld, van Alphen, Segers, and Verhoeven (2012) indeed found Dutch rhyming skill (which requires determination of the phonemic structure of words) to be influenced by global similarities between words; phonologically related pairs (*bel – bal*) were more difficult to rhyme/segment than phonologically unrelated pairs (*sok – bal*). In other research, the same effect was found for both literate children and adults (Wagensveld, Segers, van Alphen & Verhoeven, 2013).

Moreover, in two additional studies, neural evidence of a global similarity effect for rhyme processing was found in both children (Wagensveld, van Alphen, Segers, Hagoort & Verhoeven, 2013) and adults (Wagensveld, Segers, van Alphen, Hagoort & Verhoeven, 2012).

When Vloedgraven and Verhoeven (2007) examined the development of phonological awareness in relation to reading skills for 172 kindergartners and 173 first graders, they found performance on four different tasks to reflect a single underlying ability. The tasks ranged in difficulty with rhyming proving easiest; phoneme segmentation most difficult; and phoneme blending and phoneme identification occurring in between. In addition, strong growth in phonological awareness was observed between kindergarten and first grade. In a follow-up study (Vloedgraven & Verhoeven, 2009), the phonological awareness of children from kindergarten through fourth grade was examined in greater detail but again found to be unidimensional across tasks and also grades with the items measuring rhyming, phoneme identification, and phoneme blending proving easier than the items measuring phoneme segmentation and phoneme deletion.

Interestingly, de Jong and van der Leij (1999) documented changing relations between phonological awareness and the reading abilities of children over time. Children's kindergarten phonological awareness did not relate to their later reading skills, while their phonological awareness in first grade did. Phonological awareness in first grade was a strong predictor of their later reading skill, but this predictive power subsided for phonological awareness in subsequent grades. This effect was tentatively explained in terms of the transparent nature of Dutch orthography. However, a study of phonological awareness and alphanumeric naming speed as predictors of the word decoding skills of Dutch versus English school-aged children showed no differences in the prediction of word decoding speed and word decoding accuracy in the two languages (Patel, Snowling & de Jong, 2004). When de Jong and Olson (2004) explored the extent to which the emergence of letter knowledge can be predicted by children's phonological working memory and rapid automatized naming (RAN), however, phonological working memory was found to be a strong predictor and the effects of RAN much smaller. A life-span perspective on the development of continuous naming speed of numbers, letters, colors, and pictures was given by van den Bos, Zijlstra, and lutje Spelberg (2002), whereas its impact on word reading fluency was evidenced in van den Bos, Zijlstra, and Van den Broeck (2003).

13.3.1.2 Morphological Development and Morphological Awareness   When Wexler, Schaeffer, and Bol (2004) used extensive data to test cross-linguistic models of the development of verb agreement in children, they found that Dutch-speaking children produced more root infinitives than English-speaking children. They also found specific tense and agreement errors to occur in Dutch but not in English.

In other research, morphological awareness was found to be differentially related to the word recognition and spelling skills of Dutch first- and sixth-grade children (Rispens, McBride-Chang & Reitsma, 2008). In first grade, only children's awareness of nominal inflectional morphology related to their word decoding. In sixth grade, the children's awareness of derivational morphology contributed to both their word reading and spelling, while their awareness of verbal inflectional morphology related to only their spelling. Knowledge of lexical compounding did not relate to the children's reading or spelling skills in either of the two grades.

Children have been found to be sensitive to morphological segments, even in pseudowords, from an early age on. Verhoeven, Schreuder, and Baayen (2006) examined the extent of sensitivity to morphological boundaries in reading Dutch bisyllabic pseudowords and, more specifically, children's interpretation of the initial syllable as a content morpheme, a prefix, or a random string. The children's pronunciations and assignment of stress for the pseudowords were both found to depend on word type, which shows them to be able to identify morpheme boundaries and prefixes at an early age.

In a follow-up study, Verhoeven, Schreuder, and Haarman (2006) provided further evidence for children's morphological sensitivity by having both children and adults read Dutch bisyllabic words with the first syllable being either a real prefix, a phonological prefix (i.e., same sound pattern as a prefix), or a pseudo-prefix (i.e., sound pattern deviant from a prefix). The results showed that both children and adults retrieve words with phonological prefixes more quickly and more accurately than words with a pseudo-prefix. These data show that both beginning and advanced readers of Dutch successfully apply conversion rules to identify not only elementary grapheme–phoneme correspondences but also correspondences for larger orthographic units.

13.3.2 Development of Word Identification

13.3.2.1 Word Decoding Development In a longitudinal study, the acquisition of Dutch word decoding throughout the elementary school grades was examined by Verhoeven and van Leeuwe (2009, 2011) for words that varied in orthographic transparency (cf. Nunn, 1998): (1) regular CVC words, (2) complex monosyllabic words with consonant clusters in prevocalic and postvocalic positions, and (3) polysyllabic words (see Figure 13.1). The word decoding of beginning readers of Dutch started out slow and laborious with a fair number of mistakes but quickly reached a level of virtual mastery by the beginning of second grade (see Figure 13.2). The growth of word decoding skill in

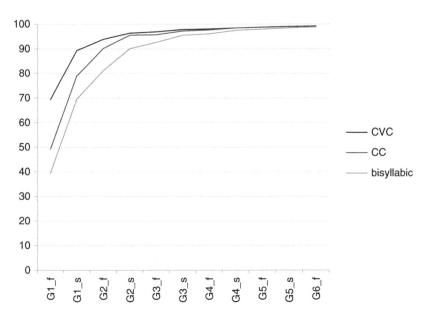

Figure 13.1 Word decoding accuracy proportions for words varying in orthographic transparency over the six primary grades. f = fall; s = summer.

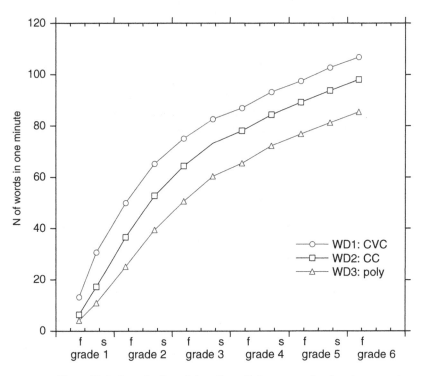

Figure 13.2 Growth of word decoding efficiency over the six primary grades. f = fall; s = summer.

Dutch appears to be largely a matter of increased speed. And the exponential increases in the learning curves that level off later parallel the logistic learning functions featured in neural networks representing the reading process under supervised learning conditions.

Furthermore, the three measures of word decoding show considerable commonalities and strong longitudinal interrelationships over the years. Some unique variance also characterized the three word decoding skills, which shows that specific orthographic complexities have to be learned over the years to become a fully proficient reader of Dutch. Further evidence for the unidimensionality of Dutch word decoding comes from the results of a study by Keuning and Verhoeven (2007) showing the means of item response theory analysis for a representative set of Dutch word decoding items administered to children throughout the elementary school grades to reflect a single underlying ability.

In other research, Verhoeven and van Leeuwe (2011) investigated the roles of gender and linguistic diversity in the development of children's word decoding. Small but significant effects were observed: Girls generally did better than boys – mainly on regular CVC word patterns – and children learning to read Dutch as a first language generally did better than children learning to read Dutch as a second language – but mainly on polysyllabic words. From a structural point of view, the development of word decoding was nevertheless highly comparable for the different subgroups.

In a range of experimental studies, the role of morphology in the development of Dutch word decoding was investigated and found to be greatly complicated by the understanding of graphotactic rules for which the reader must convert a phonological representation on the basis of spelling adaptation rules. Verhoeven, Schreuder, and Baayen (2006) examined the learning of autonomous graphotactic rules, indicating that the contrast between a long versus short vowel is expressed by the alternation between single versus double *consonant* letters in *open* syllables, but by single versus double *vowel* letters in *closed* syllables (see Section 13.2.2.2). Both children and adults were found to be significantly less accurate and slower when they had to recognize plural word forms that had undergone a vowel change as a result of the pluralization as opposed to no such change. Graphotactic rules greatly complicate early Dutch word identification and continue to do this, even in adult reading.

Verhoeven and Schreuder (2011) examined the extent to which beginning and advanced readers, including dyslexic readers of Dutch, call upon morphological access units to read polymorphemic words and found a complicated picture. In lexical decision experiments, the influence of the frequency of the singular root form of a word on the reading of the plural form of the word was investigated. For adults, both the speed and the accuracy of the lexical decision process was largely determined by the frequency of the plural word form. The frequency of the singular root form also played a role only for low-frequency plural word forms. For children, the frequencies of both the singular and the plural word forms played a role in their lexical decision making. In a related study, de Zeeuw, Schreuder, and Verhoeven (2013) investigated the extent to which the reading of compound words was determined by the frequency of the compound as a whole and the frequency of the constituent parts. For children learning Dutch as a first language but also those learning Dutch as a second language, both frequencies affected the speed and accuracy of their responding. The results of these two studies taken together make it clear that the characteristics of constituent morphemes affect the reading of polymorphemic words in conjunction with the level of reading skill and experience but also word and morpheme frequency.

13.3.2.2 Word Spelling Development   Keuning and Verhoeven (2008) examined the dimensional structure of spelling development throughout the elementary grades. Factor analysis of the results showed that spelling can be conceptualized as a unidimensional ability for second grade through to sixth grade. When the rate of developmental change was examined in conjunction with gender, ethnicity, and word reading skill, a different pattern of results presented itself. The children's spelling ability was indeed found to systematically increase from the beginning of second grade to the end of sixth grade. However, the children also showed a tendency to master specific types of spelling problems during different – partially overlapping – periods in their development. Further structural analyses showed the children's spelling ability to nevertheless be highly consistent. And while word reading skill proved an important predictor of spelling growth, neither gender nor ethnicity showed an influence.

While the spelling errors of younger or poor spellers are usually less consistent than those of older or good spellers (Bosman, 1994), there is no evidence that phonology plays a less important role for younger/poorer spellers than for older/better spellers (Bosman, Vonk & van Zwam, 2006). Formal spelling instruction has proved necessary to help children advance their spelling abilities (Cordewener, 2014), and visual dictation has been found to be an excellent device for doing this: The speller carefully studies the word to be spelled, covers the word, spells it from memory, and then checks the spelling with the original word and makes the necessary correction (van Leerdam, Bosma & van Orden, 1998). Another procedure shown to be particularly effective for the memorization of words is overpronunciation (i.e., the regularization of the spelling of words by reading the word according to prototypical grapheme-to-phoneme relationships aloud). This approach is particularly effective for the memorization of loan words (Bosman, van Hell & Verhoeven, 2006; Hilte & Reitsma, 2006). Finally, explicit rule instruction is obviously effective for the acquisition of rule-based spelling conventions. When both Hilte and Reitsma (2011) and Kemper, Verhoeven, and Bosman (2012) compared an implicit instruction condition in which spellers were asked to simply practice spelling words with an explicit instruction condition in which the spellers were presented the rule together with examples, explicit instruction was found to be more effective than implicit instruction for good as opposed to poor spellers but only for words with a clear morphological rule (Kemper et al., 2012). The finding of significant differences between the instructional conditions for good as opposed to poor spellers suggests that a fundamental threshold degree of spelling awareness may be needed to benefit from explicit spelling instruction.

13.3.2.3 Reading and Spelling Difficulties   For many children, learning to read is a process that proceeds without major difficulties. However, about 10 percent of the children experience serious difficulties with word decoding and spelling including about 4 percent who are dyslexic (Blomert, 2005). Behavioral studies have shown that dyslexic readers have no problems in processing digraphs as perceptual units (Marinus & de Jong, 2008), although their orthographic representations have been found to be less specified and less redundant as compared to typical readers (de Jong & Messbauer, 2011; van den Bos, 2008; van den Bos et al., 2002; van den Bos et al., 2003; Marinus & de Jong, 2011) and that this is especially true for reading nonwords (Van den Broeck & Geudens, 2012; Van den Broeck, Geudens & van den Bos, 2010). Furthermore, their reading and spelling problems have been found to be associated with problems in phonological awareness, phonological memory, and rapid naming (de Bree, Wijnen & Gerrits, 2010; Gijsel, Bosman & Verhoeven, 2006). In several studies of the role of phonological abilities in the development of word decoding in Dutch, de Jong and van der Leij (2003) found manifestations of phonological problems as concomitant reading problems. Poor readers, for example, also showed rapid naming impairments from kindergarten through sixth grade. Their phonological impairments manifested themselves in first grade but tended to disappear by the end of elementary school – depending on task demands, which led the authors to conclude that the different manifestations of phonological awareness and phonological deficits may lead to distinct developmental pathways.

More recently, neurocognitive studies have provided additional support for the hypothesis of a phonological deficit underlying developmental Dutch dyslexia. First, it is generally concluded that letter–speech sound pairs develop into unique audiovisual objects that need to be processed in a unique way in order to enable fluent reading (Blomert, 2011; Blomert & Froyen, 2010). Deficits in the integration of letters and speech sounds and letter processing have been demonstrated in beginning dyslexic readers (Blau et al., 2010; Blomert, 2011) and interpreted as a major cause of later problems in reading fluency (Blomert, 2011; Bonte & Blomert, 2004).

A similar orthographic-phonological deficit was also evidenced in children at familiar risk for dyslexia (Blomert & Willems, 2010). Furthermore, Noordenbos, Segers, Wagensveld, and Verhoeven (2013) showed that pre-literate children at risk for dyslexia have difficulty in distinguishing rhyming word pairs from word pairs with phonological overlap. In a parallel study (Noordenbos, Segers, Serniclaes, Mitterer & Verhoeven, 2012), it was shown that children at risk tend to have problems with categorical perception of speech sounds. They tended to make a shift in their speech perception abilities from an allophonic mode of perception in kindergarten to a phonemic mode of perception in first grade.

13.3.3   Reading Comprehension

13.3.3.1 Predictors of Reading Comprehension   In the simple view of reading, it is assumed that reading comprehension is the product of word decoding and listening comprehension (Hoover & Gough, 1990). It is further claimed that listening comprehension – or the linguistic processes involved in the comprehension of oral language – strongly constrains reading comprehension. In keeping with the simple view of reading, Droop and Verhoeven (2003) found the development of reading comprehension in the intermediate grades of elementary school to be more influenced by top-down oral language comprehension than by bottom-up word decoding for both first and second language learners. Oral language skills turned out to be more prominent in the explanation of the variation in the reading comprehension for the first language learners than for the second language learners, however.

When word decoding and listening comprehension were more recently examined in relation to the reading comprehension of children throughout elementary school (Verhoeven & van Leeuwe, 2012), the longitudinal data showed that the two components accounted for all the systematic variance in both first and second language learners. With the progression of grade, the impact of word decoding on reading comprehension decreased while the impact of listening comprehension increased to similar extents for the two groups. However, the *reciprocity* of the relationship between listening comprehension and reading comprehension tended to be less prominent for the group of second language learners: Improved reading comprehension did not correlate with improved listening comprehension to the same extent for the two groups of learners.

13.3.3.2 Word-Level Effects in Text Comprehension   When Verhoeven, van Leeuwe, and Vermeer (2011) longitudinally examined the associations between vocabulary growth and reading development for a representative sample of Dutch elementary school children, they found knowledge of word forms and word meanings to be significant predictors of reading comprehension over time.

Significant progress was seen for all measures over time: basic and advanced vocabulary, word decoding, and reading comprehension. The stability of the vocabulary measures was high, moreover, and beginning vocabulary predicted both early word decoding and reading comprehension as the so-called lexical restructuring hypothesis predicts. Starting in second grade, word decoding also predicted children's later vocabulary development, and finally a reciprocal relationship between advanced vocabulary and reading comprehension was found. The clear prediction of reading comprehension by children's knowledge of word forms and word meanings provides support for the lexical quality hypothesis and the assumption that word-level knowledge drives early text comprehension.

In an analysis of the structural relations between word decoding, vocabulary, listening comprehension, and the reading comprehension of a representative sample of Dutch children (Verhoeven & van Leeuwe, 2008), it became clear that both the *quantity* and the *quality* of word representations were important for adequate word identification and reading development to take place. The data showed that a rich vocabulary along with a high level of listening comprehension help children integrate words into text.

13.3.4   Conclusion

Word properties such as length, consonant-vowel structure, syllabic structure, and meaning significantly influence children's implicit as well as their explicit phonological processing. The position of phonemes and the division of a word into rime and coda clearly influence explicit phonological processing as well. Children's rime sensitivity was nevertheless found to be based on global similarity judgments rather than explicit rime awareness. And the associations between phonological awareness and word decoding change over the years. In addition to phonological awareness, morphological awareness is important for learning to read. At the word level, reading development is just a matter of becoming faster in word decoding. Moreover, when it comes to comprehension, vocabulary and oral language comprehension come into the picture. The data from the Dutch studies of reading comprehension reviewed here make it clear that both lexical skills and oral language comprehension are important in learning to read.

13.4   Discussion

13.4.1   Challenges in Learning to Read Dutch

The present review shows the orthographic characteristics of the Dutch language and the development of literacy to be highly interrelated. Clear evidence exists for the claim that the development of sufficient phonological skill, including phonological awareness, is crucial for gaining insight into the alphabetical principle underlying written Dutch. The development of Dutch word decoding appears to be largely a matter of increased speed. Children learning to read in a language with a relatively transparent orthography like Dutch rarely produce recognition errors after the earliest phase of acquisition; they show gains in the rate of recognition as opposed to accuracy over time. Moreover, rather than linear increases, the gains in the accuracy of word reading are very rapid at the outset of reading instruction and taper off thereafter. The steep initial rise in the accuracy of word recognition characterizes the developmental trajectories more for simple than difficult words, with continuous as opposed to discontinuous growth. The initial exponential learning curves that later taper off parallel the logistic learning functions found for neural networks related to the reading process under supervised learning conditions (cf. Seidenberg & McClelland, 1989). Beyond this, other specific orthographic factors appear to play a role in the development of Dutch children's word decoding, and the unique contributions of specific word decoding skills were found to vary as a function of the length of formal reading instruction.

Dutch word spelling has been found to be more difficult than Dutch word reading, which is in keeping with what has been found for other languages with relatively transparent orthographies like Dutch. It appears that children need considerable practice to solidify the spelling representations of words. For poor spellers, explicit teaching of the spelling rules themselves may also be needed to gain sufficient insight into rule-based patterns of spelling.

Finally, there is clear evidence that the lexical quality of children's vocabularies and their listening comprehension are highly important for the development of their reading comprehension in Dutch, just as in English (cf. Perfetti & Hart, 2001). A strong influence of vocabulary on reading comprehension has been found across grade levels, for example, with only a weak reciprocal influence of reading comprehension on vocabulary development. For listening comprehension, however, reciprocal relations with reading comprehension have been found in Dutch and related languages.

13.4.2   Implications for Instruction

The effects of different instructional guidelines for learning to read Dutch have been explicitly investigated in a small number of studies to date. The explicit training of phonological awareness and letter knowledge while in kindergarten has been examined. For example, Eleveld (2005) found an intervention program for the training of phonological awareness to promote both the phonological awareness and the letter knowledge of kindergartners at risk but no later transfer of the effects to first-grade reading abilities.

In other research, de Graaff, Verhoeven, Bosman, and Hasselman (2007) investigated the effects of a computer training program that used picture mnemonics together with a fading procedure to train the production of letter sounds. The program proved effective, independent of the children's initial level of phonological awareness. In a follow-up study, the effects of systematic versus non-systematic phonics instruction were compared for two groups of kindergartners (de Graaff, Bosman, Hasselman & Verhoeven, 2009). Similar progress was found for productive letter knowledge, but the kindergartners given systematic phonics instruction showed greater progress for phonemic awareness, word decoding, and spelling than the kindergartners given non-systematic phonics instruction.

Droop, van Elsacker, Voeten, and Verhoeven (2016) have most recently shown that sustained instruction may be needed to effectively promote reading development. In their study, they explored the long-term effects of an instructional program that focused on the explanation and modeling of a small set of reading strategies within meaningful reading contexts. The results of multilevel analyses showed clearly positive effects of the instruction on the children's knowledge of reading strategies one year following intervention at the end of third grade. There was also evidence of positive intervention effects on the children's reading comprehension skill at the end of fourth grade. No significant interaction effects were found for age, gender, SES, or ethnic/linguistic background. The intervention effects also did not depend on the level of nonverbal intelligence, vocabulary knowledge, or decoding skill. These findings show that the sustained teaching of reading comprehension strategies can help children make the step from declarative knowledge to procedural knowledge, which is needed to effectively apply reading strategies and understand text.

13.5   Final Conclusion

Dutch orthography can be considered largely phonemic and much more consistent than, for example, English or French. That is, a rather straightforward mapping of graphemes to phonemes occurs in short Dutch words, but not in longer Dutch words. Dutch syllable structure can be complex because multiple consonants may occur in both the onset and the coda positions. In longer words, moreover, numerous deviations from a one-to-one correspondence between letters and sounds can occur. The basic task for children learning to read Dutch is thus to progress from the sequential grapheme-to-phoneme decoding of words to the fast, parallel, and largely phonology-based processing of different word classes. Phonological awareness and rapid naming turn out to be the strongest predictors of word decoding. In addition, morphological awareness is important for learning to read. As soon as children have discovered the alphabetic principle, they can easily decode new words. And by seeing the same words more often in context, more stabilized word representations emerge and may become automated so that full attention can be paid to text comprehension. The data from the Dutch studies on reading comprehension highlight the importance of lexical skills and oral language comprehension in learning to read. The present findings thus lend support to both the lexical quality hypothesis and the simple view of reading.

References

Baayen, R. H., Piepenbrock, R. & van Rijn, H. (1993). The CELEX lexical data base on CD-ROM. Philadelphia, PA: Linguistic Data Consortium.

Blau, V., Reithler, J., van Atteveldt, N. M., Seitz, J. M., Gerretsen, P., Goebel, R. W. & Blomert, L. P. M. (2010). Deviant processing of letters and speech sounds as proximate cause of reading failure: A functional magnetic resonance imaging study of dyslexic children. *Brain*, *133*(3), 868–879.

Blomert, L. (2011). The neural signature of orthographic-phonological binding in successful and failing reading development. *Neuroimage*, *57*(3), 695–703.

Blomert, L. & Willems, G. (2010). Is there a causal link from a phonological awareness deficit to reading failure in children at familial risk for dyslexia. *Dyslexia*, *16*(4), 300–317.

Blomert, L. P. M. (2005). *Dyslexie in Nederland*. Amsterdam: Nieuwezijds.

Blomert, L. P. M. & Froyen, D. J. W. (2010). Multi-sensory learning and learning to read. *International Journal of Psychophysiology*, *77*(3), 195–204.

Bonte, M. & Blomert, L. (2004). Developmental changes in ERP correlates of spoken word recognition during early school years: A phonological priming study. *Clinical Neurophysiology*, *115*(2), 409–423.

Booij, G. (1977). *Dutch morphology: A study of word formation in generative grammar*. Dordrecht: Foris.

Bosman, A. M. T. (1994). Reading and spelling in children and adults: Evidence for a single-route model. Doctoral dissertation, University of Amsterdam.

Bosman, A. M. T., de Graaff, S. & Gijsel, M. A. R. (2006). Double Dutch: The Dutch spelling system and learning to spell in Dutch. In R. M. Joshi & P. G. Aron (Eds.), *Handbook of orthography and literacy* (pp. 135–150). Mahwah, NJ: Lawrence Erlbaum.

Bosman, A.M.T., van Hell, J. & Verhoeven, L. (2006). Learning the spelling of strange words in Dutch benefits from regularized reading. *Journal of Educational Psychology*, *98*, 879–890.

Bosman, A. M. T., Vonk, W. & van Zwam, M. (2006). Spelling consistency affects reading in students with and without dyslexia. *Annals of Dyslexia*, *56*, 271–300.

Cordewener, K. (2014). Variation in spelling ability in children: Acquisition and intervention. Doctoral dissertation, Radboud University Nijmegen.

de Bree, E. H., Wijnen, F. N. K. & Gerrits, P. A. M. (2010). Non-word repetition and literacy in Dutch children at-risk of dyslexia and children with SLI: Results of the follow-up study. *Dyslexia*, *16*, 36–44.

de Graaff, S., Bosman, A., Hasselman, F. & Verhoeven, L. (2009). Benefits of systematic phonics instruction. *Scientific Studies of Reading*, *13*, 318–333.

de Graaff, S., Hasselman, F., Bosman, A. & Verhoeven, L. (2008). Cognitive and linguistic constraints on phoneme isolation in Dutch kindergartners. *Learning & Instruction, 18*, 391–403.

de Graaff, S., Hasselman, F., Verhoeven, L. & Bosman, A. (2011). Phonemic awareness in Dutch kindergartners: Effects of task, phoneme position and phoneme class. *Learning & Instruction, 21*, 1634–173.

de Graaff, S., Verhoeven, L., Bosman, A. & Hasselman, F. (2007). Using integrated pictorial mnemonics and stimulus fading: Teaching kindergartners letter sounds. *British Journal of Educational Psychology, 77*, 519–539.

de Jong, P. F. & Messbauer, V. C. S. (2011). Orthographic context and the acquisition of orthographic knowledge in normal and dyslexic readers. *Dyslexia, 17*, 107–122.

de Jong, P. F. & Olson, R. K. (2004). Early predictors of letter knowledge. *Journal of Experimental Child Psychology, 8*, 254–273.

de Jong, P. F. & van der Leij, A. (1999). Specific contributions of phonological abilities to early reading acquisition: Results from a Dutch latent variable longitudinal study. *Journal of Educational Psychology, 91*, 450–476.

(2003). Developmental changes in the manifestation of a phonological deficit in dyslexic children learning to read a regular orthography. *Journal of Educational Psychology, 95*, 22–40.

deVries, M. & Winkel, L. A. te (1866). *Woordenlijst voor de spelling der Nederlandse taal met aanwijzing van de geslachten der naamwoorden en de vervoeging der werkwoorden.*'s Gravenhage-Leiden-Arnhem: Thieme.

de Zeeuw, M., Schreuder, R. & Verhoeven, L. (2013). Processing of regular and irregular past-tense verb forms in first and second language reading acquisition. *Language Learning, 63*, 740–765.

Donaldson, B. (1997). *Dutch: A comprehensive grammar.* London: Routledge.

Droop, M., van Elsacker, W., Voeten, M. & Verhoeven, L. (2016). Long-term effects of strategic reading instruction in the intermediate primary grades. *Journal of Research on Educational Effectiveness, 9*(1), 77–102.

Droop, M. & Verhoeven, L. (2003). Language proficiency and reading comprehension in first and second language learners. *Reading Research Quarterly, 38*, 78–103.

Eleveld, M. (2005). At risk for dyslexia. Doctoral dissertation, University of Amsterdam.

Geerts, G., Haeseryn, W., de Rooij, J. & van den Toorn, M. C. (1984). *Algemene Nederlandse spraakkunst.* Groningen: Wolters-Noordhoff.

Geudens, A. & Sandra, D. (2003). Beyond implicit phonological knowledge: No support for an onset-rime structure in children's explicit phonological awareness. *Journal of Memory and Language, 49*, 157–182.

Geudens, A., Sandra, D. & Van den Broeck, W. (2004). Segmenting two-phoneme syllables: Developmental differences in relation with early reading skills. *Brain and Language, 90*, 338–352.

Gijsel, M. A. R., Bosman, A. M. T. & Verhoeven, L. (2006). Kindergarten risk factors, cognitive factors, and teacher judgments as predictors of early reading in Dutch. *Journal of Learning Disabilities, 39*(6), 558–571.

Hilte, M. & Reitsma, P. (2006). Spelling pronunciation and visual preview both facilitate learning to spell irregular word. *Annals of Dyslexia, 56*, 301–318.

(2011). Effects of explicit rules in learning to spell open- and closed-syllable words. *Learning and Instruction, 21*(1), 34–45.

Hoover, W. A. & Gough, P. B. (1990). The simple view of reading. *Reading and Writing: An Interdisciplinary Journal, 2,* 127–160.

Kemper, M. J., Verhoeven, L. & Bosman, A. M. T. (2012). Implicit and explicit instruction of spelling rules. *Learning and Individual Differences, 22,* 639–649.

Keuning, J. & Verhoeven, L. (2007). Screening for word reading and spelling problems in elementary school: An item response theory approach. *Education and Child Psychology, 24,* 42–56.

(2008). Spelling development throughout the elementary grades: The Dutch case. *Learning and Individual Differences, 18,* 459–470.

Kooij, J. G. (1992). Dutch. In B. Comrie (Ed.), *The major languages of Western Europe* (pp. 129–146). London: Routledge.

Marinus, E. & de Jong, P. F. (2011). Dyslexic and typical-reading children use vowel digraphs as perceptual units in reading. *The Quarterly Journal of Experimental Psychology, 64*(3), 504–516.

Marinus, E. & de Jong, P. F. (2008). The use of sublexical clusters in normal reading and dyslexic readers. *Scientific Studies of Reading, 12*(3), 253–280.

Mol, S. E., Bus, A. G. & de Jong, M. T. (2009). Interactive book reading in early education: A tool to stimulate print knowledge as well as oral language. *Review of Educational Research, 79*(2), 979–1007.

Noordenbos, M. W., Segers, P. C. J., Serniclaes, W., Mitterer, H. A. & Verhoeven, L. T. W. (2012). Allophonic mode of speech perception in Dutch children at risk for dyslexia: A longitudinal study. *Research in Developmental Disabilities, 33*(5), 1469–1483.

Noordenbos, M. W., Segers, P. C. J., Wagensveld, B. & Verhoeven, L. T. W. (2013). Aberrant N400 responses to phonological overlap during rhyme judgements in children at risk for dyslexia. *Brain Research, 1537,* 233–243.

Nunn, A. M. (1998). *Dutch orthography.* The Hague: Holland Academic Graphics.

Patel, T. K., Snowling, M. J. & de Jong, P. F. (2004). A cross-linguistic comparison of children learning to read in English and Dutch. *Journal of Educational Psychology, 96*(4), 785–797.

Perfetti, C. A. & Hart, L. (2001). The lexical bases of comprehension skill. In D. Gorfien (Ed.), *On the onsequences of meaning selection* (pp. 67–86). Washington, DC: American Psychological Association.

Rietveld, A. C. M. & van Heuven, V. J. (1997). *Algemene Fonetiek.* Bussum: Coutinho.

Rispens, J. E., McBride-Chang, C. & Reitsma, P. (2008). Morphological awareness and early and advanced word recognition and spelling in Dutch: A Cross-sectional study. *Reading and Writing, 21,* 587–607.

Schreuder, R. & Baayen, R. H. (1995). Modeling morphological processing. In L. B. Feldman (Ed.), *Morphological aspects of language processing* (pp.131–154). Hove: Lawrence Erlbaum.

Schreuder, R. & van Bon, W. H. J. (1989). Phonemic analysis: Effects of word properties. *Journal of Research in Reading, 12,* 59–78.

Seidenberg, M. & McClelland, J. (1989). A distributed, developmental model of word recognition and naming. *Psychological Review, 96*(4), 523–568.

van den Bos, K. P. (2008). Word-reading development, the double-deficit hypothesis, and the diagnosis of dyslexia. *Educational and Child Psychology, 25,* 51–69.

van den Bos, K. P., Zijlstra, B. J. H. & lutje Spelberg, H. C. (2002). Life-span data on continuous-naming speeds of numbers, letters, colors, and pictured objects, and word-reading speed. *Scientific Studies of Reading*, *6*, 25–49.

van den Bos, K. P., Zijlstra, B. J. H. & Van den Broeck, W. (2003). Specific relations between alphanumeric-naming speed and reading speeds of monosyllabic and multisyllabic words. *Applied Psycholinguistics*, *24*, 407–430.

Van den Broeck, W. & Geudens, A. (2012). Old and new ways to study characteristics of reading disabilty: The case of the nonword-reading deficit. *Cognitive Psychology*, *65*, 414–456.

Van den Broeck, W., Geudens, A. & van den Bos, K. P. (2010). The nonword-reading deficit of disabled readers: A developmental interpretation. *Developmental Psychology*, *46*, 717–734.

van den Toorn, M. (1982). *Nederlandse taalkunde*. Utrecht: Spectrum.

van der Putten, F. (1997). Matter and mind in morphology: Syntactic and lexical deverbal morphology in Dutch. Doctoral dissertation, University of Nijmegen.

van Leerdam, M., Bosman, A. M. T. & van Orden, G. C. (1998). The ecology of spelling instruction: Effective training in first grade. In P. Reitsma & L. Verhoeven (Eds.), *Problems and interventions in literacy development* (pp. 307–320). Dordrecht: Kluwer Academic Publishers.

Verhoeven, L. T. W. & Schreuder, R. (2011). Morpheme frequency effects in Dutch complex word reading: A developmental perspective. *Applied Psycholinguistics*, *32*(3), 483–498.

Verhoeven, L., Schreuder, R. & Baayen, H. (2006). Learnability of graphotactic rules in visual word identification. *Learning and Instruction*, *16*, 538–548.

Verhoeven, L., Schreuder, R. & Haarman, V. (2006). Prefix identification in the reading of Dutch bisyllabic words. *Reading and Writing: An Interdisciplinary Journal*, *19*, 651–668.

Verhoeven, L. & van Leeuwe, J. (2008). Predictors of text comprehension development. *Applied Cognitive Psychology*, *22*, 407–423.

(2009). Modeling the growth of word decoding skills: Evidence from Dutch. *Scientific Studies of Reading*, *13*, 205–223.

(2011). Role of gender and linguistic diversity in word decoding development. *Learning and Individual Differences*, *21*(4), 359–367.

(2012). The simple view of second language reading throughout the primary grades. *Reading and Writing*, *25*(8), 1805–1818.

Verhoeven, L., van Leeuwe, J. & Vermeer, A. (2011). Vocabulary growth and reading development across the elementary school years. *Scientific Studies of Reading*, *15*, 8–25.

Vloedgraven, J. M. T. & Verhoeven, L. (2007). Screening of phonological awareness in the early elementary grades: An IRT approach. *Annals of Dyslexia*, *57*, 33–50.

(2009). The nature of phonological awareness throughout the elementary grades: An item response theory perspective. *Learning and Individual Differences*, *19*, 161–169.

Wagensveld, B., Segers, E., van Alphen, P. & Verhoeven, L. (2012). A neurocognitive perspective on rhyme awareness: The N450 rhyme effect. *Brain Research*, *1483*, 63–70.

(2013). The role of lexical representations and phonological overlap in rhyme judgments of beginning, intermediate and advanced readers. *Learning and Individual Differences, 23*, 64–71.

Wagensveld, B., van Alphen, P. M., Segers, P. C. J., Hagoort, P. & Verhoeven, L. T. W. (2013). The neural correlates of rhyme awareness in preliterate and literate children. *Clinical Neurophysiology, 124*(7), 1336–1345.

Wagensveld, B., van Alphen, P. M., Segers, P. C. J. & Verhoeven, L. T. W. (2012). The nature of rhyme processing in preliterate children. *British Journal of Educational Psychology, 82*(4), 672–689.

Wexler, K., Schaeffer, J. & Bol, G. (2004). Verbal syntax and morphology in Dutch normal and SLI children: How developmental data can play an important role in morphological theory. *Syntax, 7*, 148–198.

14   Learning to Read English

Charles Perfetti and Lindsay Harris

14.1   Introduction

14.1.1   English and Its Orthography

English is widely spoken around the world as both a first language and a second language. Although English originated in Britain, the United States has the world's largest population of first-language speakers of English. The modern varieties of spoken English constitute dialects that vary in their mutual intelligibility. British English, American English, Australian English, South African English, and Scottish English are but a few of these.

English as a second language is prevalent around the world. Although difficulties in calibrating proficiency levels across regions make it nearly impossible to identify the total number of English speakers, it is likely that the number of people who speak English as a second language exceeds the number who speak it as a first language.

Written English is fundamentally alphabetic, despite the well-known complexities of its orthography, which creates spellings that fail to have a one-to-one mapping to English phonemes. English writing contains both single-letter graphemes and multi-letter graphemes that map onto spoken English at the phoneme level; that there are multiple mappings for a given grapheme is important for reading and writing.

14.1.2   Synchronic and Diachronic Characterization

English is classified as a Germanic language, resulting from two major invasions of Celtic Britain by Germanic groups (first Anglo-Saxons from northwestern Europe and then Scandinavians) in the fifth through ninth centuries. The resulting period of Old English was disrupted by the Norman invasion, which brought dramatic changes to the language from French and Latin influences. These changes included not only additions of Latinate vocabulary but also grammatical changes, especially reductions in inflectional morphology.

This Norman period marked the beginning of modern English, which has remained largely unchanged in its basic structure since then. However, continuous change in pronunciation occurred over time. The most significant from a reading standpoint was the Great Vowel Shift during the fifteenth through eighteenth centuries, in which English lost the pure vowels that occur in continental languages (Stockwell & Minkova, 2001). Vowels that had been produced lower in the vocal cavity moved up, such that "name" came to be pronounced with the long vowel that it has today. Prior to the shift, "name" was pronounced as the vowel in the German word "name," whose first syllable rhymes with the English word "Tom." This shift occurred over several long phases with the vowel first moving to the front: [ae] as in "pan" before raising to the long [e:] in "name." Finally, in some dialects the vowel became a diphthong, [ei], a glide across two simple vowels. Similarly, prior to the shift, the vowel in "mouse" was pronounced [u:] as in "moose," moving in stages to its present raised diphthong [aʊ] vowel. These two examples illustrate slightly different orthographic mappings. In "name," the final "silent" *e* indicates the long vowel pronunciation of the vowel [e:]. In "mouse," the vowel spelling ‹ou› indicates a diphthong pronunciation but uses an *o* instead of *a*. (Compare this with the German spelling "maus," which contains a diphthong that has the same initial segment pronunciation as English. Compare it also with the unrelated French word "mousse," which retains the "moose" pronunciation that was present in fourteenth-century English (Bloomfield & Newmark, 1963)).

As with all modern alphabetic orthographies, written English is completely standardized; i.e., an English word has only one "correct" spelling. However, standardized spellings develop over long periods of time, and standardization was certainly not present in the early ascendancy of Anglo-Saxon English. The Roman alphabet was well suited for Latin and its derivative Romance languages but less so for English. When monks used Latin to write early English, they added Runic characters for some consonants that did not occur in Latin (Wagner, Outhwaite & Beinhoff, 2013). These consonants were later spelled by creating digraphs, two letters to map a single phoneme, from the set of Roman alphabet letters, specifically *th*, *sh*, and *gh*. It is worth keeping in mind that standardization arises from cognitive and social processes. Cognitively, remembering a spelling in the absence of accessible and authoritative models from writing is an error-prone memory process. The increasing availability of such models provided a social support for increasing standardization.

Meanwhile, the gradual changes in writing were outstripped by the more rapid changes in pronunciation, producing a considerable gap between orthography and phonology even before the Great Vowel Shift. Some of this gap came with the Norman dominance from the late eleventh century, when English was replaced by French as the scribal language. This is the source of the inconsistent mapping of the English letter ‹c›, for example. The English word "city" came from the French "cité," which in turn derived from Latin "civitas," where ‹c› represented only the /k/ phoneme. A similar duality emerged in the use of ‹g› to map both the hard palatal /g/ in "give" and the alveolar fricative sound of "giant" (Powell, 2009). Thus, the inconsistencies of English orthography have multiple origins in changes in spoken language, both from the blending of languages (especially French and English) and from later vowel changes in spoken English. In addition, the adaptation of the Roman alphabet was, from the beginning, inadequate for the sounds of English.

Nevertheless, the multiple linguistic influences on English resulted in a partial systematicity to modern English spelling. Specifically, many English spellings that are inconsistent in their mapping to phonology are reliable indicators of morphology. Although the digraph ‹ea› in "health" is not pronounced as it is in "real" or "meal" or "heal," its spelling connection with "heal" exposes a meaning connection. Similarly, in "judge" the letter ‹d› does not map to the phoneme /d/. (The consonant sound represented by "g" is the same as the word-initial consonant represented by "j.") However, in "judicial" the ‹d› letter does map to the consonant /d/, allowing another connection based on meaning. Whereas these examples link spelling through lexical stem morphemes, a more reliable source of morphemic linking is in the inflectional system. Thus, the long vowel in the first syllable of "nation" becomes reduced with the adjectival inflection, "national." Overall, as the study of English orthography by Venezky (1970, 1999) continues to demonstrate, English spelling variation has considerable predictability at the level of morphology and other sources of systematic variance; but it still contains much variance that, at least from the view of a reader not versed in linguistic and orthographic history, is unsystematic.

14.1.3   Literacy and Schooling

With its worldwide reach, instruction in English literacy is quite varied across regions. In addition, instructional approaches within a region also change with dominant pedagogical philosophies. The major historical division concerns the relative emphasis on teaching the alphabetic code – the mapping of letters and phonemes. In both the United States and England, shifts have occurred between a relatively strong emphasis on teaching the code and an alternative emphasis on ignoring the alphabetic code in exchange for a focus on meaning. Currently in the United States, formal literacy instruction begins when children are around 6 years as they enter first grade. In the United Kingdom, there is some variability, with England and Wales introducing reading at reception, the first year of schooling at age 5, prior to primary year 1. Scotland omits the reception grade and moves to primary school at age 5, as does Northern Ireland. In all the United Kingdom, phonics has become the primary approach to beginning reading instruction.

In the United States, a similar movement from instruction grounded on whole-word learning (Chall, 1983) and then whole language philosophy (Goodman, 1986) has been replaced gradually by instruction that includes at least some explicit teaching of phonics, often part of a "blended" approach. In contrast, New Zealand literacy instruction continues to be grounded largely on philosophies that exclude explicit phonics instruction, based instead on language and authentic literacy experience.

14.2   Description of English and Its Written Forms

English is spoken in a wide range of dialects around the world. The spoken language differences – the inventory of phonemes – is the variation that is the most relevant for reading, because all dialects are written in Standard English using the twenty-six-letter Roman alphabet. British English has many regional dialects, as does American English, including regional variations of African American Vernacular English. Written English is the standardizing agent for this wide variety, but its mapping to the sounds of specific dialects could be an obstacle to reading acquisition.

14.2.1   The Linguistic System

14.2.1.1 Phonology   Because of variations across the dialects of English, the phoneme inventory varies around forty (between thirty-seven and forty-two). This places English substantially above the average across languages of thirty phonemes (Hay & Bauer, 2007). Twenty-four consonants, more or less, serve all varieties of English, with vowels, of course, producing the largest variation in dialects. British Received (upper class) English has more vowels, including many diphthongs, than Australian English, which in turn has more than standard American English. All varieties of English, however, use diphthongs freely.

English internal syllable structure is assumed to follow a hierarchical onset + rhyme structure (Figure 14.1), with the sonorant peak (or vowel nucleus) a separate constituent from the syllable onset. So the syllable in "sat" has the internal structure /s/ + /æt/ and "spat" is /sp/ + /æt/. It is important to recognize that alternative syllable structures locate the sonorant peak with the onset or as a separate constituent. Thus, "sat" is /sæ/ + /t/ in a body + coda structure that groups the sonorant peak with the onset. These alternative structures can capture variation across English words and across languages, e.g., Korean vs. English.

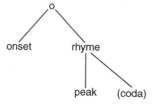

Figure 14.1 Standard analysis of English syllable structure as onset + rhyme, illustrating both open and closed syllable options. (The sonorant peak is also referred to as the nucleus.) In English, onsets are both simple (single consonants) and complex (more than one consonant). Other internal syllable structures are possible both within English and across languages, depending on the location of the sonorant peak, which can be a constituent of the head (onset + peak) or a separate constituent (onset + peak + coda). The assumption that English syllables have onset + rhyme structure has influenced the analysis of reading and recommendations for reading instruction.

English syllables vary in phonetic richness, with both simple consonant and consonant cluster onsets (and codas) and both open and closed syllables. English words are predominantly multisyllabic with a free stress pattern that allows variation in which a particular syllable receives primary stress (van Donselaar, Koster & Cutler, 2005). English stress patterns are highly predictable by grammatical form class, however. Disyllabic nouns overwhelmingly (93%) receive stress on the first syllable, whereas verbs tend to receive stress on the second syllable (around 70%; Kelly & Bock, 1988).

14.2.1.2 Inflectional Morphology   English follows the root + affix paradigm of inflectional morphology but with relatively simple grammatical paradigms. In particular, English nouns have neither gender markings nor case markings. English grammar generally relies on word order and prepositions (*in, to, of, from, with*) to indicate critical morphological and semantic relations between words. Grammatical paradigms include inflections for number on noun roots and verbs, tense on verb roots, and a case and number paradigm for pronouns, which are marked for gender (*he, she, it*).

The inflectional system for tense is only partly regular, a mix of the German model of strong verbs that undergo stem alterations with tense changes and a more straightforward affixation rule. Thus, regular English verbs (analogous to weak German verbs) add *-ed* to root spellings, representing the past tense morphophoneme [ed], which is realized as /t/, /d/, or /ed/ depending on the phonemic environment – /t/ for *kicked*; /d/ for *jogged*; and /ed/ for *surrounded*. Irregular verbs undergo stem alteration with a restricted set of phonological tense patterns. Thus, *buy/bought, catch/caught, fight/fought* reflect one pattern, and *sing/sang, swing/swung,* and *ring/rang* show another. However, these phonological patterns are highly varied and do not constitute a rule. *Sit/sat* (but *fit/fitted*), *shine/shone* (but *fine/fined*), *stand/stood* (but *land/landed*) illustrate the range of variation among irregular past tense forms.

Plural markings have this same duality, with the morphophoneme [s] added to noun roots as the regular pattern, and realized in relation to phonemic environment as /s/, /z/, /às/, /əz/. Thus, /s/ for *bits, tops,* and *bikes*; /z/ for *bids, tubs,* and *bugs*; /əs/ for *packages,* and /əz/ for *roses.* Voicing assimilation accounts for all the phonetic variations of the plural [s]. Other forms have irregular plurals. A few use *-en* (*children, oxen, brethren*) following old English (and German); a larger number of one-syllable words undergo a stem change in the vowel, e.g., *foot/feet, mouse/mice, woman/women.* Words ending in the unvoiced fricative /f/ alternate to its voiced complement /v/ (and undergo vowel lengthening) and add the regular plural marker: *loaf/ loaves, scarf/scarves.* These examples are unusual in that spelling is altered to reflect pronunciation changes. Some nouns use the same form for singular and plural: *aircraft, deer, shrimp,* and many use patterns consistent with their original Latin and Greek origins: *stimulus/stimuli, symposium/symposia, prognosis/prognoses* (Carstairs-McCarthy, 2002).

14.2.1.3 Word Formation Processes   English has a rich derivational morphology, including substantial compounding and creation of words across grammatical categories. Noun compounding abounds and creates issues for writing because of word spacing conventions: *saltwater, seawater*; but *spring water* and *sparking water.* Compounding also occurs for modifiers, as nouns and verbal participles combine with adjectives to become compound modifiers with hyphens: *high-speed chase, late-blooming flower.* If the compound modifier uses an adverb instead of an adjective, hyphens are not used: *slowly blooming flower.*

Derivational processes freely create adjectives from verbs. *Drink/drinkable, kiss/kissable, watch/watchable, live/livable.* For any transitive verb and for many intransitive verbs, an adjective can be created. Although somewhat less productively, adjectives also are created from nouns, especially abstract nouns: *hope/hopeless/hopeful, peace/peaceful, idea/ideal*; the derived adjective can also spawn its own derived attributives: *ideal/ idealistic.* Many concrete nouns also yield derived adjectives: *child/childish, vehicle/vehicular.*

The noun-based examples above illustrate denominal derivational processes. These processes are very productive in English. Many human nouns can be made by adding *-er* to a stem with inanimate semantics: *village/villager, bank/ banker, farm/farmer.* Many other human nouns are created through other alterations to a noun stem: *library/librarian, electricity/electrician*. In addition to noun-to-noun derivation, denominal processes include the creation of verbs and adjectives from nouns: *nation/national/nationalize* (Beard, 1995).

The reverse derivation has become very common in English: nominalization, the formation of a noun from a verb or adjective. For example: *stupid/stupidity, tedious/tedium, refuse/refusal; agree/agreement; vary/variance*. Nominalization is so prolific in English that its wide use has led to laments that a loss of direct expression, which is implemented through verbs linked to actors, has created a more passive, sterile form of expression.

14.2.2   Writing System

Any written language expresses forms that vary along multiple dimensions: the visual appearance (script), the dominant mapping principle for connecting writing units to linguistic units (writing system), and the detailed implementation of the writing system (orthography).

14.2.2.1 Script and Punctuation

English writing is a linear array of twenty-six Roman alphabet letters that can appear in various scripts. Standard print and computer fonts use "block letters" without connections between the letters. In contrast, writing by hand can connect the letters to create handwritten scripts termed *cursive* (United States) or *joined-up writing* (United Kingdom). These scripts also are mimicked in computer fonts. Fonts – size and letter spacing – can affect the reading experience in complex ways, which, despite a large body of research, resist easy generalization.

The conventions of English writing require spaces between words. As we described above, word compounding creates a single word without spaces, or two words separated by a space or by a hyphen. Choosing the correct option for writing compounds is systematic but somewhat complex. Whereas this can be a problem for the writer, it should pose little problem for the reader. This is also the case for clause-level English punctuation, where the correct use of commas, periods, colons, and semi-colons can be confusing for the writer but perhaps less so for the reader.

14.2.2.2 Orthography   If the alphabetic ideal is one-to-one mapping of grapheme and phoneme, as represented by Finnish or Welsh and approximated by Italian and Czech, then English is far from ideal. Its mappings are one-to-many for all vowel graphemes and also for some letters that are considered consonant graphemes (e.g., *c, g, ch*). These inconsistencies earn English a place at the opaque end of the transparency dimension or the "deep" end of the shallow–deep dimension among alphabetic orthographies. Its labeling as

orthographically "deep" is recognition that its spellings sometimes preserve meaning (morphology) instead of consistency of pronunciation (e.g., *heal*; *heal*th).

However, even when there is no gain for morphology, the chaos of English spelling has been greatly exaggerated (Kessler, 2003), as in whimsical examples of spelling options for English words ("fish" could be spelled as *ghoti*). Objective measures of inconsistencies make overly simple assumptions about mapping options – for example, that the proper measure of inconsistency is simply the context-free number of mappings a grapheme can have. This ignores both the relative frequencies of mappings and the positional constraints imposed by both phonology (phonotactics) and spelling conventions. Kessler (2003) notes this example: In American English the phoneme /a/ is usually spelled *o*, as in *lock, top, flop*, etc. However, when it precedes /r/ in the same syllable, it is spelled with the letter *a*, as in *car, start, harp*. Some degree of sensitivity to the linguistic environment reduces the mapping uncertainty substantially. Add to this context a simpler sensitivity to token frequencies – for any given phoneme or grapheme, some mappings are much more frequent than others – and English orthography becomes considerably more consistent.

14.2.3   Conclusion

Written English conforms approximately to the alphabetic principle. However, its orthography sometimes encodes morphology at the expense of grapheme–phoneme consistency. The bulk of English inconsistency is less about morphology trade-offs than about more mundane variation, which is more manageable than is sometimes acknowledged. Taking into account the position of letters (within spellings) and phonemes (within syllables) and the relative frequencies of grapheme–phoneme pairs makes the orthography–phonology mappings more predictable.

14.3   Acquisition of Reading and Spelling in English

Learning to read and spell English can be difficult because of the inconsistency of its orthography–phonology mappings, even if the extent of this problem has been exaggerated. The benefits of context-sensitivity and mapping frequencies that can reduce the effects of inconsistency must be acquired through reading experience. Struggles with learning to read at the beginning will reduce the very experience that is needed. The learning challenges have been exacerbated by questionable instructional methods that avoid teaching letter–sound correspondences and by the high variability in preliteracy skills that children have upon entering school. In fact, variability seems to be the key feature of learning to read English. Despite its orthographic challenges, many children learn to read quickly, whereas many others struggle.

14.3.1   Becoming Linguistically Aware

14.3.1.1 Phonological Development and Phonological Awareness   The course of phonological production in English-speaking children reflects the phonological structure of English as well as basic developmental factors. The dominant strong–weak stress template of English, which includes a longer and louder first syllable and a reduced second syllable, shapes babies' babbling: Infants exposed to English are much less likely to begin a syllable with a vowel than infants exposed to other European languages (Vihman & Croft, 2007). Moreover, toddlers and young children imitate nonwords more accurately and acquire new words at faster rates when they contain segment sequences with high phonotactic probabilities in English (Storkel, 2001; Zamuner, Gerken & Hammond, 2004).

English phonology also influences the development of phonological awareness. Awareness of syllables typically precedes awareness of phonemes, although English's relatively complex syllable structure and poorly marked syllable boundaries cause English-speaking children to acquire syllable awareness relatively late (Anthony & Francis, 2005). English-speaking three- and four-year-olds also show increased phonological awareness for words belonging to phonological neighborhoods that are densely populated in English (Metsala, 1999). Preliterate English-speaking children develop a sensitivity to the onset-rhyme structures that are prevalent in English syllables (as well as in Dutch, German, and Chinese). (See Figure 14.1.) Awareness of individual phonemes emerges after exposure to literacy instruction (Liberman, Shankweiler, Fischer & Carter, 1974; Pierrehumbert, 2003; Port, 2007).

Once literacy instruction has begun, a reciprocal relationship between reading and phonological awareness develops (Nation & Hulme, 2011; Perfetti, Beck, Bell & Hughes, 1987). Ziegler and Goswami (2005) demonstrated that children who speak languages with a one-to-one mapping of graphemes to phonemes acquire phonemic awareness at faster rates than English-speaking children, further suggesting that robust awareness of phonemes depends on alphabetic literacy. Many languages with alphabetic orthographies that have consistent grapheme–phoneme mappings also feature simple CV syllables, causing phonemic and syllabic boundaries to be aligned. English combines a non-transparent orthography with a complex syllable structure, and this combination might be why English-speaking children rank last among European kindergartners in their ability to identify the phonemes in words (Goswami, 2010; Table 14.1).

Table 14.1 *Illustrative data (% correct) from studies comparing phoneme counting in different languages in kindergarten or early Grade 1 (adapted from Goswami, 2010)*

Language	Phonemes counted correctly (%)
Greek	98[1]
Turkish	94[2]
Italian	97[3]
German	81[4]
Norwegian	83[5]
French	73[6]
English	70[7]

Note:
1 = Harris and Giannouli, 1999
2 = Durgunoglu and Oney, 1999
3 = Cossu et al., 1988
4 = Hoien et al., 1995
5 = Wimmer et al., 1991
6 = Demont and Gombert, 1996
7 = Liberman et al., 1974

Phonological awareness is a reliable predictor of children's reading success in English, although English-speaking children do not appear to benefit any more than children who speak other languages from strong phonological skills in learning to read. A meta-analysis examining the predictive power of phonemic awareness, rime awareness, and verbal short-term memory for reading development found phonemic awareness to correlate most strongly of the three with individual differences in word reading skill (Melby-Lervåg, Lyster & Hulme, 2012).

14.3.1.2 Morphological Development and Morphological Awareness
Brown (1973) identified fourteen grammatical morphemes in English that are acquired in a more or less set order. Typically developing children acquire these morphemes between 2 and 2.5 years of age. The rate of acquisition varies considerably, however, and few toddlers master all fourteen during this time period (Lahey, Liebergott, Chesnick, Menyuk & Adams, 1992). By the time children enter school, they have an implicit understanding of the morphological rules of English and can use them productively. For example, Berko (1958) reported that 76% of 4- and 5-year-olds and 97% of 5.5- to 7-year-olds correctly responded /wugz/ when asked for the plural of the nonsense word *wug*.

An explicit understanding of English morphology is slower to develop. Although 57% of first graders in one study could decompose words into constituent morphemes, in defining words children were unable to use grammatical and semantic information contained in suffixes until Grade 3 (Carlisle & Fleming, 2003). Whereas growth in phonological and orthographic awareness slows substantially after the primary grades (Berninger, Abbott, Nagy & Carlisle, 2010), morphological awareness continues to expand throughout elementary school and into middle school (e.g., Tyler & Nagy, 1989; Wysocki & Jenkins, 1987). This extended trajectory of morphological awareness development may be due in part to the tendency of morphological shifts in English to result in phonological shifts in the base word; children have difficulty recognizing words as morphologically related when the phonology of the base form differs between them (Carlisle, Stone & Katz, 2001; Shankweiler et al., 1995), and word reading is slowed or inaccurate when the base form within the derived form being read is phonologically opaque (Carlisle & Stone, 2005; Deacon, Whalen & Kirby, 2011). In general, awareness of derivational morphology lags behind that of inflectional morphology (e.g., Anglin, 1993; Berninger et al., 2010; Kuo & Anderson, 2006).

Morphological awareness is a reliable predictor of skill at both decoding and comprehending text (e.g., Carlisle, 2000; Deacon & Kirby, 2004; Nagy, Berninger & Abbot, 2006; Roman, Kirby, Parrila, Wade-Woolley & Deacon, 2009) and predicts unique variance in vocabulary knowledge (McBride-Chang, Wagner, Muse, Chow & Shu, 2005). Morphological awareness appears to play a greater role in children's reading development after the primary years, when the complexity of the words they encounter increases (Wolter, Wood & D'zatko, 2009).

14.3.2 Development of Word Identification

Learning to identify printed words is the hallmark achievement of learning to read in any writing system. In general terms, a high level of skill in word reading entails important overlapping knowledge: learning to discriminate among the twenty-six letters of the Roman alphabet, learning the phonemic mappings of these letters and their combinations into digraphs and letter clusters, and developing orthographic memory representations of specific words. Decoding words based on the connections between English graphemes and English phonemes is critical in allowing reading to progress so that these word-specific representations can develop.

14.3.2.1 Word Decoding Development The lack of phonological transparency in English may be responsible for the delayed and less efficient development of word decoding skills by English-speaking children, compared with the development of decoding by children learning to read other alphabetic languages, including German (Frith, Wimmer & Landerl, 1998), Spanish and

Table 14.2 *Classification of the reading errors made by Welsh and English children (adapted from Ellis & Hooper, 2001)*

Error type	Proportion of errors for Welsh-reading children (%)	Proportion of errors for English-reading children (%)
Null response	13.7	30.8
Whole-word substitution	24.3	44.8
Other attempt (nonword)	72.5	24.5

French (Goswami, Gombert & de Barrera, 1998), Greek (Goswami, Porpodas & Wheelwright, 1997), and Dutch (Patel, Snowling & de Jong, 2004).

In addition to delaying the acquisition of decoding skills, the opacity of English also leads learners to adopt decoding strategies that differ from those used by learners of more transparent orthographies. Children who learn English rely less on phonological information than children learning to read other European languages. This difference is demonstrated in a study that takes advantage of the fact that in Wales children learn both a very transparent orthography, Welsh, alongside the less transparent English. The study compared two groups of 6- and 7-year-olds in Wales, one group who began reading instruction in English and another who began reading instruction in Welsh (Ellis & Hooper, 2001). The Welsh-reading children relied on grapheme–phoneme correspondences (which are highly reliable in Welsh) in decoding, whereas the English-reading children used the alphabetic procedure inconsistently and their reading errors suggested the use of non-decoding, whole-word strategies in word identification. The English children were twice as likely as the Welsh children to give a null response during a word reading task and were nearly twice as likely to make a whole-word substitution error (e.g., "computer" for *complete*; Table 14.2).

Part of the different use of decoding in English is the grain size children use. In a transparent alphabetic orthography, readers can use single grapheme–phoneme mappings efficiently. Children learning to read in English may map written language to spoken language at a larger grain size, possibly an adaptive strategy for English orthography. Although grapheme–phoneme correspondences are inconsistent in English, grapheme string–rime correspondences are quite reliably pronounced (Kessler, 2003; Kessler & Treiman, 2001; Treiman, Mullennix, Bijeljac-Babic & Richmond-Welty, 1995). Accordingly, British 6-year-olds were able to decode unknown words (e.g., *tap*) that shared entire rimes with known words (e.g., *cap*) but were less successful at decoding words that shared only the vowel grapheme (e.g., *fat*; Goswami, 1993).

Despite the unreliability of grapheme–phoneme mapping in English, pho-nemic awareness is closely linked to the development of beginning word reading (Ehri et al., 2001), and research suggests this awareness can be supported by instructing preschoolers about the articulatory features of pho-nemes (Boyer & Ehri, 2011). There is some evidence that for older children (ages 9–12) morphological awareness is a primary mediator of the efficiency of phonological decoding (Richards et al., 2002).

Development in reading skill goes beyond decoding to establishing memory representations of written word forms. Much of skilled reading comes to rely on access to these word forms (lexical access) to retrieve their pronunciation and meaning constituents. Decoding skill, based on grapheme–phoneme con-nections, continues to be part of this process, and a rapid, automatic, phonolo-gical process is part of word reading at high levels of skill (Halderman, Ashby & Perfetti, 2012). However, the increased accessibility of fully specified orthographic representations that results from practice alters the role of these phonological processes. In beginning reading, these processes allow the reader to find a written word in his or her spoken lexicon. At high levels of skill, phonological processes allow a rapid access to a written representation of the word, one specified by its orthography as well as its phonology. Acquiring these high-quality representations is supported by decoding processes in a bootstrapping procedure that yields attention to the visual form of an unfa-miliar word as the child attempts to decode it (Share, 1995). This moves the representation of individual words toward fuller orthographic specification and more redundancy between orthographic and phonological units for a specific word (Perfetti, 1992).

As reading ability develops, the extent to which children rely on context in identifying words varies with reading skill. For example, US fifth graders with higher reading achievement are less dependent on context during word identification than are lower-skilled fifth graders (Perfetti, Goldman & Hogaboam, 1979).

14.3.2.2 Word Spelling Development Preliterate children develop some knowledge of English letters long before they attempt to spell; for example, 3-year-olds can accurately discriminate writing from pictures (Lavine, 1977). Children demonstrate an understanding that writing is linked to the sounds of words relatively early on, and their spelling errors often reveal a strong sensi-tivity to these sounds. For example, US children commonly omit the vowel preceding a syllabic /r/ (e.g., Read, 1975; Treiman, Goswami, Tincoff & Leevers, 1997) and, although English spelling does not differentiate between voiced and voiceless consonant stops following an initial /s/ (e.g., it is *sky*, not *sgy*), children sometimes do (a first grader in one study produced *sgie*; Treiman, 1993).

Once children are in school, their writing often reveals their sensitivity to statistical regularities in English letter shapes and orthographic patterns. Kindergartners are more likely to make reversals of left-facing letters, such as *d* and *j*, than of the more numerous right-facing letters, such as *k* and *f* (Treiman, Gordon, Boada, Peterson & Pennington, 2014), and kindergartners and first graders taught to spell *rug* as *rrug* later tended to shift the letter repetition to the word-final position, where it actually occurs (i.e., *rugg*; Wright & Ehri, 2007). Additionally, simple morphological relationships between words can guide children's spellings (e.g., kindergartners produce *dirty* rather than *dirdy*; Treiman, Cassar & Zukowski, 1994), although more complex morphological relationships (e.g., *sign* and *signal*) often provide little assistance in spelling, even for older children (Waters, Bruck & Malus-Abramowitz, 1988) and adults (Fischer, Shankweiler & Liberman, 1985).

14.3.2.3 Reading and Spelling Difficulties   Learning to read tends to be more difficult in English than in other European languages. Seymour, Aro, and Erskine (2003) report a comparison of children after one year of instruction. English children showed only a 40% accuracy rate in reading words and nonwords. Most other European samples were above 90%, and even the worst among the remainder, France and Denmark, were much higher on word reading. Of course, even such a careful international comparison cannot control for all the factors that are relevant across nations, languages, and schooling practices. However, the conclusion that English is more difficult for children to decode than German has been demonstrated in well-controlled comparisons of German and English (Wimmer & Goswami, 1994). In light of such comparisons, it seems natural to ask whether the prevalence of reading disabilities in English-speaking countries exceeds that of non-English-speaking countries. To that, we believe there is no clear answer, given problems of diagnostic standards, educational variations, and reporting issues. However, there are more restricted comparisons between well-matched samples of children from two language backgrounds who do meet comparable diagnostic criteria and are matched on reading levels. The question for such a comparison of German and English children by Ziegler, Perry, Ma-Wyatt, Ladner, and Schulte-Körne (2003) was whether they would show differences in markers of reading disability. In fact, the two groups showed no differences in markers of deficits in phonological decoding, nonword reading (relative to real words), and reading speed. With more research, some differences might emerge, but for now we should be slow to conclude that reading disability in English is qualitatively different from that in other alphabetic orthographies.

Spelling generally should lag behind reading in alphabetic orthographies, because phoneme-to-grapheme mappings, which are functional when one tries to spell a word from its pronunciation, are less reliable generally than grapheme-to-phoneme mappings. English, of course, already has a penalty in the grapheme-to-phoneme inconsistencies. The inconsistencies in the reversed spelling direction are even greater. Naturally, skilled readers read words easily that they have trouble spelling. This is in the nature of a recognition process that requires only discriminating one word from its neighbors, compared with a retrieval process that must either produce a string from memory in accurate detail or generate it from unreliable grapheme-to-phoneme processes. Specific difficulties in English spelling, however, go along with difficulties in reading. Young children's spelling difficulties are predicted by their reading (Wade-Woolley & Siegel, 1997) and so are the spelling difficulties of adolescents, which are strongly associated with decoding (Shankweiler, Lundquist, Dreyer & Dickinson, 1996). Thus, whereas the mapping direction is different for spelling than reading, it appears that the mapping in one direction is associated with mapping with the other.

14.3.3   Reading Comprehension

To the extent that comprehension in reading is much the same as comprehension in listening, then reading comprehension is determined by a combination of written word identification and language comprehension. The simple view of reading (Hoover & Gough, 1990) specifically argues that reading comprehension is the algebraic product of word decoding x linguistic comprehension. This compelling simplification of the complexity of reading comprehension pre-empts any attention to reading comprehension as a specific problem that affects reading success. However, reading is obviously different from listening in ways that might matter. The possibility that comprehension-by-print may place special demands on readers cannot be ruled out based on the correlational studies that show the success of word decoding and listening comprehension in predicting reading comprehension.

14.3.3.1 Predictors of Reading Comprehension   Direct evidence for the simple view requires two conditions: Appropriate measures of listening comprehension and word decoding (or word identification) should (1) reflect independent factors and (2) account for all systematic variance in an appropriate measure of reading comprehension. Evidence for the first condition is mixed. In support of independence are factor analytic studies that report that various word-level and comprehension assessments load on two separate components for children of 4–7 years (Kendeou, Savage & van den Broek, 2009) and 7–10 years (Nation & Snowling, 1997), using rather different tasks. However, as described in Section 14.3.3.2, other results suggest some complexity to this conclusion, once word meaning knowledge is considered. Moreover, there is no clear evidence on the stronger requirement to show that all systematic variance is accounted for. Such a test would require competing models that would ask whether additional variance might be captured by reading-specific measures that, on a plausible alternative model, would contribute to reading comprehension.

14.3.3.2 Word-Level Effects in Comprehending Text   Even without reading-specific assessments, the relationships among reading comprehension, word knowledge, and listening skill are a bit more complex. Is knowledge of word meanings (vocabulary) a factor that contributes to decoding or to listening comprehension? Or both? If it contributes to both, then the assumption that decoding and listening comprehension are independent is violated. Using assessments of 7-year-olds, Tunmer and Chapman (2012) found that vocabulary made a contribution to reading comprehension beyond that made by word decoding (word recognition). They further tested structural equation models that showed that a latent construct representing spoken language comprehension influenced reading comprehension indirectly through decoding as well as directly as assumed in the simple view. Wagner, Herrera, Spencer, and Quinn (2015) provide a critique of this model but conclude that a model that allows listening comprehension to influence decoding is equivalent to the simple view model.

Results with adult readers also complicate the simple view. Braze, Tabor, Shankweiler, and Mencl (2007) reported a study of 16- to 24-year-olds with a range of reading ability. Based on an extensive battery of tests, they concluded that although the simple view gave a reasonable fit to the data, it fell short of accounting for all the systematic variance in the data. Vocabulary, assessed orally, captured unique variance after accounting for listening comprehension and decoding. Braze et al. (2007) point out a rationale for an asymmetry in how word knowledge contributes to comprehension through print more than through speech. This asymmetry arises because mappings from print to word representations are less practiced than those from speech and because the speech signal is stronger than the print signal, which lacks information used by human speech production and perception mechanisms (co-articulation, prosody, nonlinguistic context).

Thus, the specific patterns of correlations across studies and the conclusions from correlation-based factor analyses and modeling differ somewhat. Moreover, it appears that knowledge of word meanings penetrates reading, both as part of comprehension and as part of word identification. This is the essence of the *lexical quality hypothesis* (Perfetti, 2007) and of a theoretical framework for reading comprehension (Perfetti & Stafura, 2014) that assumes the centrality of word knowledge. However, to the extent that this complicates the simple view of reading, it leaves intact the critical assumption that general language comprehension and written word identification are the critical components of reading comprehension.

14.3.4   Conclusion

The big picture is that reading comprehension is indeed well predicted by the combination of decoding (word identification) and listening comprehension. This conclusion is in accord with the basic dependency that reading has on spoken language. Learning to identify written words is the distinctive aspect of reading. However, the role of word meaning knowledge, perhaps especially because of the relative opaqueness of English orthography, seems to have a complex relation, being both intrinsic to spoken language skill and a specific factor in word reading beyond its role in spoken language.

14.4   Discussion

14.4.1   Challenges in Learning to Read English

Written English does present orthographic challenges to the learner, although its grapheme–phoneme inconsistencies are less severe than often implied. It does appear that learning alphabetic orthographies other than English presents less of a challenge because of their more consistent grapheme–phoneme mappings. However, learning English, as with any alphabetic orthography, entails learning phoneme mappings to graphemes. These mappings can be learned implicitly through reading practice, as apparently happens for many – but not all – children taught in the book-centered methods of New Zealand. Similarly, American and English children who learn to read without decoding instruction do so while implicitly learning that a given grapheme corresponds to some phonemes and not others.

Implicit learning is a powerful procedure available to humans in all situations that afford ample – and successful – experience. Learning one's native language occurs this way and although learning to read is quite different in its relation to culture and biology, it too can occur through implicit means. However, reliance on implicit learning for reading carries more risk, because, unlike language, children can opt out of the experience, which provides much weaker feedback from the learning environment than does language learning. Frustration from reading difficulties can lead to a child's opting out of reading experience. Implicit learning can work only when conditions support continued and successful practice. Thus, for many children learning to read requires explicit instruction aimed at supporting what is challenging in alphabetic reading – the arbitrary pairing of graphs with sounds that have no meaning. Instruction in decoding is clearly recommended by both the structure of alphabetic writing and by empirical studies of reading instruction, as reviewed in two national reports in the United States (National Institute of Child Health and Development, 2000; Snow, Burns & Griffin, 1998).

14.4.2 Implications for Instruction

The additional challenges imposed by English orthography may interact with beliefs about how best to teach reading. Although learning to read an alphabetic orthography requires learning basic grapheme–phoneme connections, the inconsistencies in English orthography may have reinforced advocacy for the meaning-based, whole-word, and whole language approaches that have been dominant in English-speaking regions at various times. In fact, teaching reading has not been uniform in English and some of the variability is systematic enough to allow some intriguing comparisons across English-speaking regions. In particular, New Zealand, which for some time has used a book-centered approach to literacy that omits letter–phoneme instruction and phonics in general, offers a contrast with Scotland, which has used a phonics-centered approach. Connelly, Thompson, Fletcher-Flinn, and McKay (2009) reviewed a number of studies comparing the Scottish and New Zealand situations. The studies collectively report an advantage to 6- to 8-year-old Scottish children over reading-level-matched New Zealand children in reading aloud nonwords and regular words. The advantage was reversed for reading exception words. The specificity of the advantage highlights the principle that what is learned is usually what is taught. Reading experience is important for reading words in general, wheras decoding instruction is important for learning generalizable grapheme–phoneme mappings. The research adds to this that decoding is foundational for experience to be useful (National Institute of Child Health and Development, 2000).

14.5   Final Conclusion

Compared with learning to read in other alphabetic orthographies, learning to read English involves challenges imposed by the inconsistencies of English spelling. The inconsistencies arise from many factors in the development of spoken English and its conventions for spelling. A significant factor in the complexity of English is its merging of linguistic influences from Germanic and Latinate languages. The phonological structure is complex with multiple syllable morphemes, changing stress patterns, consonant clusters, and a large vowel inventory, rich in diphthongs, that far outstrips the vowel letters assigned to represent their pure (monophthong) vowel ancestors. Moreover, and as a result of merging language influences, English vocabulary is large, allowing encounters with unfamiliar words. The resulting inconsistencies, however, often tend to be exaggerated. When one considers orthographic environments beyond the single letter (i.e., letter strings), the pronunciations are more predictable. When one also takes into account that some grapheme–phoneme mappings are more common than others, additional predictability emerges. Overall, however, English linguistic and orthographic factors do pose obstacles to learning to read that exceed those of other languages written alphabetically.

The facts on learning to read English are consistent with the assumption that these language and orthographic factors create difficulties for children learning to read. Cross-national comparisons (Seymour et al., 2003) show lower performance in reading both words and nonwords for English children, and such differences are confirmed in narrower comparisons between well-matched English and German readers (Landerl et al., 2013). Phonological awareness is a critical component of learning to read English, and some level of awareness prior to literacy instruction is important for initial success in learning to read. Phoneme-level awareness develops further with learning to decode. Spelling English words, which naturally lags behind reading, depends on phoneme–grapheme mappings that are even less reliable than in the grapheme-to-phoneme direction used by reading.

Beyond decoding, gaining skill in reading involves acquiring word-specific representations of written English words. This process continues throughout literacy as reading experience strengthens representations of specific words, which allow a fluent word process that is relatively context free, driven by word form knowledge. Word reading skill continues to be an important part of reading, as reading comprehension depends on it, in addition to general language comprehension mechanisms.

References

Anglin, J. M. (1993). Vocabulary development: A morphological analysis. *Monographs of the Society for Research in Child Development, 58*(10), 1–166. Serial no. 238.

Anthony, J. L. & Francis, D. J. (2005). Development of phonological awareness. *Current Directions in Psychological Science, 14*, 255–259.

Beard, R. (1995). *Lexeme-morpheme base morphology: A general theory of inflection and word formation*. Albany, NY: SUNY Press.

Berko, J. (1958). The child's learning of English morphology. *Word, 14*, 150–177.

Berninger, V. W., Abbott, R. D., Nagy, W. & Carlisle, J. (2010). Growth in phonological, orthographic, and morphological awareness in grades 1 to 6. *Journal of Psycholinguistic Research, 39*, 141–163.

Bloomfield, M. W. & Newmark, L. (1963). *A linguistic introduction to the history of English*. New York: Alfred A. Knopf.

Boyer, N. & Ehri, L. (2011). Contribution of phonemic segmentation instruction with letters and articulation pictures to word reading and spelling in beginners. *Scientific Studies of Reading, 15*, 440–470.

Braze, D., Tabor, W., Shankweiler, D. P. & Mencl, W. E. (2007). Speaking up for vocabulary: Reading skill differences in young adults. *Journal of Learning Disabilities, 40,* 226–243.

Brown, R. (1973). *A first language: The early stages.* Oxford and Cambridge, MA: Harvard University Press.

Carlisle, J. F. (2000). Awareness of the structure and meaning of morphologically complex words: Impact on reading. *Reading and Writing, 12,* 169–190.

Carlisle, J. F. & Fleming, J. (2003). Lexical processing of morphologically complex words in the elementary years. *Scientific Studies of Reading, 7,* 239–253.

Carlisle, J. F. & Stone, C. A. (2005). Exploring the role of morphemes in word reading. *Reading Research Quarterly, 40,* 428–449.

Carlisle, J. F., Stone, C. A. & Katz, L. A. (2001). The effect of phonological transparency on reading derived words. *Annals of Dyslexia, 51,* 249–274.

Carstairs-McCarthy, A. (2002). *An introduction to English morphology: Words and their structure.* Edinburgh University Press.

Chall, J. S. (1983). *Learning to read: The great debate,* updated edn. New York: McGraw-Hill.

Connelly, V., Thompson, G. B., Fletcher-Flinn, C. M. & McKay, M. F. (2009). Does the type of reading instruction have an influence on how readers process print? In C. Wood & V. Connelly (Eds.), *Contemporary perspectives on reading and spelling* (pp. 239–253). Abingdon: Routledge.

Deacon, S. H. & Kirby, J. R. (2004). Morphological awareness: Just "more phonological"? The roles of morphological and phonological awareness in reading development. *Applied Psycholinguistics, 25,* 223–238.

Deacon, S. H., Whalen, R. & Kirby, J. R. (2011). Do children see the *danger* in *dangerous*? Grade 4, 6, and 8 children's reading of morphologically complex words. *Applied Psycholinguistics, 32,* 467–481.

Ehri, L. C., Nunes, S. R., Willows, D. M., Schuster, B. V., Yghaoub-Zadeh, Z. & Shanahan, T. (2001). Phonemic awareness instruction helps children learn to read: Evidence from the National Reading Panel meta-analysis. *Reading Research Quarterly, 36,* 250–287.

Ellis, N. C. & Hooper, A. (2001). Why learning to read is easier in Welsh than in English: Orthographic transparency effects evinced with frequency-matched tests. *Applied Psycholinguistics, 22,* 571–599.

Fischer, F. W., Shankweiler, D. & Liberman, I. Y. (1985). Spelling proficiency and sensitivity to word structure. *Journal of Memory and Language, 24,* 423–441.

Frith, U., Wimmer, H. & Landerl, K. (1998). Differences in phonological recoding in German- and English-speaking children. *Scientific Studies of Reading, 2,* 31–54.

Goodman, K. (1986). *What's whole in whole language?* Portsmouth, NH: Heinemann.

Goswami, U. (1993). Toward an interactive analogy model of reading development: Decoding vowel graphemes in beginning reading. *Journal of Experimental Child Psychology, 56,* 443–475.

(2010). Phonological development across different languages. In D. Wyse, R. Andrews & J. Hoffman (Eds.), *The Routledge international handbook of English, language and literacy teaching* (pp. 98–109). Abingdon: Routledge, Taylor & Francis Group.

Goswami, U., Gombert, J. E. & de Barrera, L. F. (1998). Children's orthographic representations and linguistic transparency: Nonsense word reading in English, French and Spanish. *Applied Psycholinguistics, 19*, 19–52.

Goswami, U., Porpodas, C. & Wheelwright, S. (1997). Children's orthographic representations in English and Greek. *European Journal of Psychology of Education, 12*, 273–292.

Halderman, L. K., Ashby, J. & Perfetti, C. A. (2012). Phonology: An early and integral role in identifying words. In J. Adelman (Ed.), *Visual word recognition, Vol. I: Models and methods, orthography and phonology* (pp. 207–228). New York: Psychology Press.

Hay, J. & Bauer, L. (2007). Phoneme inventory size and population size. *Language, 83*, 388–400.

Hoover, W. A. & Gough, P. B. (1990). The simple view of reading. *Reading and Writing, 2*, 127–160.

Kelly, M. H. & Bock, J. K. (1988). Stress in time. *Journal of Experimental Psychology: Human Perception and Performance, 14*, 389–403.

Kendeou, P., Savage, R. & van den Broek, P. (2009). Revisiting the simple view of reading. *British Journal of Educational Psychology, 79*, 353–370.

Kessler, B. (2003). Is English spelling chaotic? Misconceptions concerning its irregularity. *Reading Psychology, 24*, 267–289.

Kessler, B. & Treiman, R. (2001). Relationships between sounds and letters in English monosyllables. *Journal of Memory and Language, 44*, 592–617.

Kuo, L. & Anderson, R. C. (2006). Morphological awareness and learning to read: A cross-language perspective. *Educational Psychologist, 41*, 161–180.

Lahey, M., Liebergott, J., Chesnick, M., Menyuk, P. & Adams, J. (1992). Variability in children's use of grammatical morphemes. *Applied Psycholinguistics, 13*, 373–398.

Landerl, K., Ramus, F., Moll, K., Lyytinen, H., Leppänen, P. H. T., Lohvansuu, K., ... Schulte-Körne, G. (2013). Predictors of developmental dyslexia in European orthographies with varying complexity. *Journal of Child Psychology and Psychiatry, 54*, 686–694.

Lavine, L. O. (1977). Differentiation of letterlike forms in prereading children. *Developmental Psychology, 13*, 89–94.

Liberman, I. Y., Shankweiler, D., Fischer, F. W. & Carter, B. (1974). Explicit syllable and phoneme segmentation in the young child. *Journal of Experimental Child Psychology, 18*, 201–212.

McBride-Chang, C., Wagner, R. K., Muse, A., Chow, B. W.-Y. & Shu, H. (2005). The role of morphological awareness in children's vocabulary acquisition in English. *Applied Psycholinguistics, 26*, 415–435.

Melby-Lervåg, M., Lyster, S. A. H. & Hulme, C. (2012). Phonological skills and their role in learning to read: A meta-analytic review. *Psychological Bulletin, 138*, 322–352.

Metsala, J. L. (1999). Young children's phonological awareness and nonword repetition as a function of vocabulary development. *Journal of Educational Psychology, 91*, 3–19.

Nagy, W., Berninger, V. W. & Abbott, R. D. (2006). Contributions of morphology beyond phonology to literacy outcomes of upper elementary and middle-school students. *Journal of Educational Psychology, 98*, 134–147.

Nation, K. & Hulme, C. (2011). Learning to read changes children's phonological skills: Evidence from a latent variable longitudinal study of reading and nonword repetition. *Developmental Science, 14,* 649–659.

Nation, K. & Snowling, M. (1997). Assessing reading difficulties: The validity and utility of current measures of reading skill. *British Journal of Educational Psychology, 67,* 359–370.

National Institute of Child Health and Development (2000). *Report of the National Reading Panel. Teaching children to read: An evidence-based assessment of the scientific research literature on reading and its implications for reading instruction: Reports of the subgroups* (NIH Publication No. 00–4754). Washington, DC: US Government Printing Office. Retrieved from www.nichd.nih.gov/publications/pubs/nrp/documents/report.pdf.

Patel, T. K., Snowling, M. J. & de Jong, P. (2004). A cross-linguistic comparison of children learning to read in English and Dutch. *Journal of Educational Psychology, 96,* 785–797.

Perfetti, C. A. (1992). The representation problem in reading acquisition. In P. B. Gough, L. C. Ehri & R. Treiman (Eds.), *Reading acquisition* (pp. 145–174). Hillsdale, NJ: Lawrence Erlbaum.

(2007). Reading ability: Lexical quality to comprehension. *Scientific Studies of Reading, 11,* 357–383.

Perfetti, C. A., Beck, I., Bell, L. C. & Hughes, C. (1987). Phonemic knowledge and learning to read are reciprocal: A longitudinal study of first grade children. *Merrill-Palmer Quarterly, 33,* 283–319.

Perfetti, C. A., Goldman, S. R. & Hogaboam, T. W. (1979). Reading skill and the identification of words in discourse context. *Memory & Cognition, 7,* 273–282.

Perfetti, C. A. & Stafura, J. (2014). Word knowledge in a theory of reading comprehension. *Scientific Studies of Reading, 18,* 22–37.

Pierrehumbert, J. B. (2003). Phonetic diversity, statistical learning, and acquisition of phonology. *Language and Speech, 46,* 115–154.

Port, R. (2007). How are words stored in memory? Beyond phones and phonemes. *New Ideas in Psychology, 25,* 143–170.

Powell, B. B. (2009). *Writing: Theory and history of the technology of civilization.* Malden, MA: Wiley Blackwell.

Read, C. (1975). *Children's categorization of speech sounds in English.* NCTE Research Report No. 17. Urbana, IL: National Council of Teachers of English.

Richards, T. L., Berninger, V. W., Aylward, E. H., Richards, A. L., Thomson, J. B., Nagy, W. E., Carlisle, J. F., Dager, S. R. & Abbott, R. D. (2002). Reproducibility of proton MR spectroscopic imaging (PEPSI): Comparison of dyslexic and normal-reading children and effects of treatment on brain lactate levels during language tasks. *American Journal of Neuroradiology, 23,* 1678–1685.

Roman, A. A., Kirby, J. R., Parrila, R. K., Wade-Woolley, L. & Deacon, S. H. (2009). Toward a comprehensive view of the skills involved in word reading in Grades 4, 6, and 8. *Journal of Experimental Child Psychology, 102,* 96–113.

Seymour, P. H. K., Aro, M. & Erskine, J. M. (2003). Foundation literacy acquisition in European orthographies. *British Journal of Psychology, 94,* 143–174.

Shankweiler, D., Crain, S., Katz, L., Fowler, A. E., Liberman, A. M., Brady, S. A., Thornton, R., Lundquist, E., Dreyer, L., Fletcher, J. M., Stuebing, K. K.,

Shaywitz, S. E. & Shaywitz, B. A. (1995). Cognitive profiles of reading-disabled children: Comparison of language skills in phonology, morphology, and syntax. *Psychological Science, 6*, 149–156.

Shankweiler, D., Lundquist, E., Dreyer, L. G. & Dickinson, C. C. (1996). Reading and spelling difficulties in high school students: Causes and consequences. *Reading and Writing, 8*, 267–294.

Share, D. L. (1995). Phonological recoding and self-teaching: Sine qua non of reading acquisition. *Cognition, 55*, 151–218.

Snow, C. E., Burns, M. S. & Griffin, P. (Eds.) (1998). *Preventing reading difficulties in young children*. Washington, DC: National Academy Press.

Stockwell, R. P. & Minkova, D. (2001). *English words: History and structure*. Cambridge University Press.

Storkel, H. L. (2001). Learning new words: Phonotactic probability in language development. *Journal of Speech, Language, and Hearing Research, 44*, 1321–1337.

Treiman, R. (1993). *Beginning to spell: A study of first-grade children*. New York: Oxford University Press.

Treiman, R., Cassar, M. & Zukowski, A. (1994). What types of linguistic information do children use in spelling? The case of flaps. *Child Development, 65*, 1318–1337.

Treiman, R., Gordon, J., Boada, R., Peterson, R. L. & Pennington, B. F. (2014). Statistical learning, letter reversals, and reading. *Scientific Studies of Reading, 18*, 383–394.

Treiman, R., Goswami, U., Tincoff, R. & Leevers, H. (1997). Effects of dialect on American and British children's spelling. *Child Development, 68*, 229–245.

Treiman, R., Mullennix, J., Bijeljac-Babic, R. & Richmond-Welty, E. D. (1995). The special role of rimes in the description, use, and acquisition of English orthography. *Journal of Experimental Psychology: General, 124*, 107–136.

Tunmer, W. E. & Chapman, J. W. (2012). The simple view of reading redux: Vocabulary knowledge and the independent components hypothesis. *Journal of Learning Disabilities, 45*, 453–466.

Tyler, A. & Nagy, W. (1989). The acquisition of English derivational morphology. *Journal of Memory and Language, 28*, 649–667.

van Donselaar, W., Koster, M. & Cutler, A. (2005). Exploring the role of lexical stress in lexical recognition. *Quarterly Journal of Experimental Psychology Section A: Human Experimental Psychology, 58*, 251–273.

Venezky, R. L. (1970). *The structure of English orthography*. The Hague: Mouton.

(1999). *The American way of spelling: The structure and origins of American English orthography*. New York: Guilford Press.

Vihman, M. & Croft, W. (2007). Phonological development: Toward a "radical" templatic phonology. *Linguistics, 45*, 683–725.

Wade-Woolley, L. & Siegel, L. S. (1997). The spelling performance of ESL and native speakers of English as a function of reading skill. In R. Treiman (Ed.), *Spelling* (pp.73–92). Dordrecht: Kluwer Academic Publishers.

Wagner, E.-M., Outhwaite, B. & Beinhoff, B. (2013). *Scribes as agents of language change*. Studies in Language Change [SLC], Vol. 10. Berlin: De Gruyter Mouton.

Wagner, R. K., Herrera, S. K., Spencer, M. & Quinn, J. M. (2015). Reconsidering the simple view of reading in an intriguing case of equivalent models: Commentary on Tunmer and Chapman (2012). *Journal of Learning Disabilities, 48*, 115–119.

Waters, G. S., Bruck, M. & Malus-Abramowitz, M. (1988). The role of linguistic and visual information in spelling: A developmental study. *Journal of Experimental Child Psychology, 45,* 400–421.

Wimmer, H. & Goswami, U. (1994). The influence of orthographic consistency on reading development: Word recognition in English and German children. *Cognition, 51,* 91–103.

Wolter, J. A., Wood, A. & D'zatko, K. W. (2009). The influence of morphological awareness on the literacy development of first-grade children. *Language, Speech, and Hearing Services in Schools, 40,* 286–298.

Wright, D.-M. & Ehri, L. C. (2007). Beginners remember orthography when they learn to read words: The case of doubled letters. *Applied Psycholinguistics, 28,* 115–133.

Wysocki, K. & Jenkins, J. R. (1987). Deriving word meanings through morphological generalization. *Reading Research Quarterly, 22,* 66–81.

Zamuner, T. S., Gerken, L. & Hammond, M. (2004). Phonotactic probabilities in young children's speech production. *Journal of Child Language, 31,* 515–536.

Ziegler, J. C. & Goswami, U. (2005). Reading acquisition, developmental dyslexia, and skilled reading across languages: A psycholinguistic grain size theory. *Psychological Bulletin, 131,* 3–29.

Ziegler, J. C., Perry, C., Ma-Wyatt, A., Ladner, D. & Schulte-Körne, G. (2003). Developmental dyslexia in different languages: Language-specific or universal? *Journal of Experimental Psychology, 86,* 169–193.

15 Learning to Read Czech and Slovak

Markéta Caravolas

15.1 Introduction

15.1.1 Czech and Slovak and Their Orthographies

Czech and Slovak are closely related languages and orthographies within the West Slavic sub-branch of Indo-European language varieties. Each uses the Latin alphabet to convey spoken language in a relatively consistent orthography, yet each encodes a number of unique, language-specific features. Below, we briefly outline the historical context within which the two orthographies evolved and describe the similarities and differences between the oral and written language features that are most relevant to the acquisition of reading and writing skills. Then, we review the available literature on literacy development in Czech and Slovak.

15.1.2 Synchronic and Diachronic Characterization

The Czechs and Slovaks arrived in the present-day lands of Bohemia, Moravia, and Slovakia by AD 500 as separate Slav tribes and lived jointly in what became the Slav state of Great Moravia until approximately AD 900. The first Slav orthography was introduced by the Greek brothers, Constantine (Cyril) and Methodius, who came from Thessaloniki, Byzantine Empire, in AD 863. The brothers devised the first *Glagolitic* alphabet, based on Greek letters, to transcribe the Slav literary language called Old Church Slavonic. This orthography and the advent of the Cyrillic alphabet laid the foundation for literacy and education among the Slavs of Eastern Europe. At the turn of the tenth century, the Great Moravian state crumbled under the Magyar (Hungarian) invasions and the shared history of the Czech and Slovak people underwent a thousand-year separation. Their contact with the Byzantine Empire was also disrupted and Western influences prevailed, including a transition from the Cyrillic to the Latin alphabet, around AD 950.

The Czechs migrated westward to present-day central Bohemia, and they evolved as a nation under growing German influence until 1918. The Slovaks did not escape the Magyar invasions, and over the next 300 years they were gradually assimilated or were driven into the mountains of present-day Slovakia. Their status did not change significantly until attaining statehood in 1918. During these thousand years, the Czechs and Slovaks maintained their links and written communication largely through the medium of Czech, despite the fact that Latin remained their official written language for centuries.

From the tenth century onward, the development of the Czech orthography has been characterized by five main phases, each step bringing it closer to a reflection of the phonology of Czech (rather than Latin) (e.g., Berger, 2012); by comparison, milestones of the Slovak orthography were less clearly demarcated until the eighteenth century. A pivotal development occurred with the publication of the *Orthographia Bohemica* (1406/1412), attributed to the first church (Protestant) reformer Jan Hus. It introduced the diacritic alphabet as a means of representing Czech phonemes that did not exist in Latin. This and other works provided the basis for modern codifications of the nineteenth (e.g., Dobrovský, 1809; Hanka, 1817) and early twentieth centuries (e.g., Gebauer, 1902), and in turn for the subsequent official *Rules of the Czech Orthography* (e.g., *Ústav pro jazyk český ČSAV*, 1993). The development of the Slovak orthography was delayed due to the Slovaks' minority status within the Hungarian Kingdom, with the first codified orthography, founded on Czech and later a *Slovakized Czech*, appearing in the late 1700s (Bartoš & Gagnaire, 1972).

When the two nations were finally (re)united in 1918, the Czechoslovak state recognized the two languages, their orthographies, and their respective literary traditions. During the Czechoslovak era (1918–1992), lasting seventy-four years, efforts were made to achieve harmonized educational and social provision, delivered within the official policy of Czech–Slovak bilingualism. To this day, each nation has its own Academy to promote and protect its language and culture, and each continues to publish the *official* rules of the orthography (e.g., Czech: 2005; Slovak: 2000). The Czechoslovak Republic dissolved in 1992, following the Velvet Revolution of 1989. Each Republic now exists as an independent nation, with approximately 10 million and 5 million inhabitants, respectively. The age-old connection between these two peoples and nations continues, not least in developments in education.

15.1.3   Literacy and Schooling

Reading instruction in Czech and Slovak dates back to the fifteenth century, with the publication of Jan Hus' *Orthographia Bohemica*, which included the first Czech reading primer, and within it, alliteration exercises for teaching each letter–sound association of the (new) Czech alphabet. The first formal primer for Czech pupils (B. Optát, 1547) presented a method similar to contemporary phonics approaches. These early works indicate that the orthography was designed to be as phonographically consistent as possible, lending itself naturally to teaching methods that capitalized on the alphabetic principle, namely phonics. This approach persists in Czech and Slovak reading education to this day.

Universal access to education for the Czechs (under the rule of the Austrian Kingdom) was decreed in 1744 by Empress Maria Theresia for children of 6 to 12 years of age, with subsequent reforms by Emperor Josef II enacting teaching in the *native* languages. In Hungary a similar reform was introduced in 1777, but Latin and the native Hungarian remained the languages of instruction; these developments did not promote teaching in Slovak. The field was finally leveled with the formation of the First Czechoslovak Republic, when the two nations adopted the same educational structures and practices, including methods of literacy instruction, which have changed little over the past one hundred years.

Czech and Slovak schooling currently comprises (up to) three years of kindergarten for children aged 3 – 5 years, which mainly focuses on social, motor, and cognitive (but not formal literacy) development. Most children attend at least the final, non-statutory, kindergarten year at the age of 5; however, only those who have had their sixth birthday by the start of the school year (September 1) can begin first grade. This is followed by eight or nine years of "basic" (primary) education.

Government guidelines for desirable end-of-kindergarten competencies in both countries include awareness of syllables, rhymes, and phonemes, recognition of some letters and digits, recognition of one's own name in print, and some environmental print. The traditional method of reading and spelling instruction in the primary grades is called *analytic-synthetic phonics*. Much of the first term of Grade 1 is devoted to completing and consolidating letter–sound knowledge, and phonics skills. Children are expected to know the alphabet by the middle of first grade, and to decode and write simple words according to their sounds. By the end of first grade, children are expected to read words and simple texts accurately and autonomously. From the second to fourth (Slovakia) or fifth (Czech Republic) grade, the focus turns to systematic instruction in orthography and grammar. Reading comprehension skills are trained as a means of acquiring domain-specific knowledge.

15.2 Description of Czech and Slovak and Their Written Forms

In this section we present a comparative overview of the Czech and Slovak languages and their orthographies, focusing mainly on aspects of oral and written language that are most relevant for the study of literacy development. Selected contrastive details at the level of phonology, morphology, and orthography are presented in Table 15.1.

Table 15.1 Comparison of Czech and Slovak phonological, grammatical, and orthographic features

I. Phonology

Phonemic inventory

Czech	Slovak
Total phonemes: 40 • 13 vowels: 10 monophthongs, 3 diphthongs • 27 consonants: of which 1 specific /ř/ Important allophones: • 2 syllabic consonants [l̩, r̩]	**Total phonemes: 43** • 14 vowels: 10 monophthongs, 4 diphthongs • 29 consonants: of which 2 specific /ʒ, ʎ/ Important allophones: • 4 syllabic consonants [l̩, l̩ː, r̩, r̩ː]

Syllable structure and word length

Czech	Slovak
Estimated number of syllable types: 6,500[1] Possible syllables: (C)(C)(C)(C) V (C)(C)(C) Estimated prevalence of syllable onset types:[1] • C(V+) = 80%; CC(V+) = 14%; Ø(V+.) = 4%, CCC(V+) = 1%; ll others = < 1%. Percent of word lengths:[1] • 1 syll = 4% ; 2 syll = 32%; 3 syll = 40% ; 4 syll = 19% ; 5 syll = 4% ; 6+ syll = 0.6%	Estimated number of syllable types: 5,330[2] Possible syllables: (C)(C)(C) V (C)(C)(C) Estimated prevalence of syllable onset structures:[2] • C(V+) = 79%; CC(V+) = 15%; Ø(V+.) = 5%, CCC(V+) = 1%; All others = < 1%. Percent of word lengths:[2] • 1 syll = 6% ; 2 syll = 33% ; 3 syll = 38% ; 4 syll = 19% ; 5 syll = 4% ; 6+ syll = 0.6%

II. Morphology

Inflectional morphology

Example of nominal inflection, marking gender, number, and case[3]

Example	Nominative	Genitive	Dative	Accusative	Locative	Instrumental	Vocative
Singular / Plural	*who, what*	*who, what, whose*	*to whom, to what*	*whom, what*	*about/of whom, about/of what*	*by/with whom, by/with what*	*calling*
Noun, masc.–animate (man/men)	muž / mužové, muži chlap / chlapi	muže / mužů chlapa / chlapov	mužovi, muži / mužům chlapovi / chlapom	muže / muže chlapa / chlapov	muži, mužovi / mužích chlapovi / chlapoch	mužem / muži chlapom / chlapmi	muži!/ mužži!, mužové!

Noun, masc.–inanimate (castle/s)	hrad / hrady	hradu / hradů	hradu / hradům	hrad / hrady	hradu, hradě / hradech	hradem / hrady	hrade! / hrady!
(oak/s)	dub / duby	duba / dubov	dubu / dubom	dub / duby	dube / duboch	dubom / dubmi	
Noun, fem. (woman/women)	žena / ženy	ženy / žen	ženě / ženám	ženu / ženy	ženě / ženách	ženou / ženami	ženo! / ženy!
	žena / ženy	ženy / žien	žene / ženám	ženu / ženy	žene / ženách	ženou / ženami	
Noun, neuter (city/cities)	město / města	města / měst	městu / městům	město / města	městu, městě / městech	městem / městy	město! / města!
	mesto / mestá	mesta / miest	mestu / mestám	mesto / mestá	meste / mestách	mestom / mestami	

III. Orthography

Phoneme–grapheme mappings

Czech and Slovak phoneme inventory with corresponding grapheme(s). Uniquely Slovak instances are presented in subjacent row. Uniquely Slovak instances are presented in **bold**; uniquely Czech instances are presented *italicized*. Alternative spellings for any given sound indicate phoneme–grapheme mapping inconsistency. Slash (/) brackets designate phonemes.

	/a/	/aː/	/e/	/eː/	/i/	/iː/	/o/	/oː/	/u/	/uː/	/au/ /ia/	/eu/ /ie/	/ou/ /iu/	/uo/
Vowels	a	á	e ě ä	é	i y	í ý	o	ó	u	ú ů	au ia/ja	eu ie/je	ou iu/ju	ô
Soft consonants		/ɟ/ ď, d	/c/ ť, t	/ɲ/ ň, n	/ʎ/ **ľ**	/j/ j	/ts/ c	/tʃ/ č	/ʃ/ š	/ʒ/ ž	/r̝/ **ř**	/dz/ **dz**	/dʒ/ **dž**	
Hard consonants		/d/ d	/t/ t	/n/ n	/l/ l	/r/ r	/k/ k	/x/ ch	/h/ h			/r/ r	/r/ **ŕ**	
Unmarked consonants		/b/ b	/p/ p	/m/ m	/v/ v	/f/ f	/s/ s	/z/ z			/r/ r	/r/ **ŕ**	/l/ l	/l/ **ĺ**

Notes. [1] = drawn from the Weslalex Czech corpus of 63,940 word types and 185,368 onsets; [2] = drawn from the Weslalex Slovak corpus of 35,105 word types and 99,772 onsets; [3] = Czech examples in the upper half of the cell, Slovak examples in the lower part of cell. Weslalex Czech and Slovak corpus from "Weslalex: West Slavic lexicon of child-directed printed words," by B. Kessler & M. Caravolas, 2011.

15.2.1   Linguistic System

Czech and Slovak are closely related languages whose dialects can be considered to lie on a continuum. They are distinguished, however, by certain features of phonology, morphology, grammar, and lexical stock.

15.2.1.1 Phonology   The Czech and Slovak phoneme inventories are characterized by a five-vowel system, which retains a phonemic opposition between short (/a, e, i, o, u/) and long (/aː, eː, iː, oː, uː/) vowels. In addition, each language uses several distinct diphthongs and several language-specific consonant phonemes (see Table 15.1, panel III). The consonant inventories are similar and notably contain palatalized consonants /ɟ, c, ɲ/ (which have inconsistent spellings). Both languages allow /l, r/ to be syllabic, making words composed exclusively of consonants possible (e.g., /vl̩k/ 'wolf', /kr̩p/ 'fireplace').

As inflectional languages, Czech and Slovak have a predominantly polysyllabic word structure (see Table 15.1, panel I). Their distribution of word length is virtually identical, with words of three syllables being the most prevalent (40% in Czech, 38% in Slovak), followed by those of two syllables, then four syllables, with monosyllabic words ranking only in fourth place (Kessler & Caravolas, 2011). Both languages have a predominantly open (CV, CCV, etc.) syllable structure, and the singleton onset (C) is by far the most prevalent. However, a special feature is their wide range of complex onsets (e.g., /kv, dl, zbr, fstr/, etc.) of up to four consonants, which occur relatively more frequently than in other languages, such as English and German (e.g., Kučera & Monroe, 1968).

Several phonological processes operate in both languages, which causes inconsistency in phoneme–grapheme mappings. Notably, *assimilation of voicing* operates regressively on consonant groups, such that voiced obstruents are, in certain circumstances, realized as voiceless and vice versa (e.g., *podpora* [potpora] 'support', where /p/ causes the devoicing of /d/). The underlying morphemes are represented in spelling, but the inconsistency can be readily resolved; and as we will see, children are explicitly taught specific strategies to deduce morpheme boundary spellings. Voicing assimilation can occur within words – across morpheme boundaries and within morphemes – and across word boundaries, including at word endings (Volín, 2010). In *word-final devoicing*, final voiced obstruents are realized as voiceless, although in spelling and in inflected forms they retain their underlying voiced phonemes (e.g., compare the uninflected *plod* 'fruit' → [plot] with the inflected *plodu* 'of fruit' → [plodu]). Other processes, such as elision and addition of phonemic segments are quite restricted.

Lexical stress is fixed to the first syllable of the word, or of the *prosodic word* in Czech and Slovak. Prosodic words comprise words with attached short words (clitics) that are pronounced as affixes but are written as independent words (typically prepositions). Proclitics attach to word onsets and become part of the first stressed syllable. For example, *do školy* 'to school' becomes the prosodic word ['doʃkoli]; *z masa*, 'from/of meat' becomes the prosodic word ['zmasa]. Such prosodic words produce sound–spelling inconsistency at the level of word boundaries. The learner must know, for example, that ['doʃkoli] is made up of two words, the preposition ‹do› and the noun ‹školy›, but by contrast ['doʃkolit] 'to complete schooling' is a single word, in which ‹do› is a prefix.

In sum, Czech and Slovak overlap greatly in terms of their phonemic inventories, syllable structure, and features such as use of clitics and placement of primary lexical stress. They undergo largely the same phonological processes of voicing assimilation and word-final devoicing, which impacts similarly on phoneme–grapheme inconsistency. By contrast, Slovak contains a different set of diphthongs and has, overall, a slightly higher number of phonemes than Czech.

15.2.1.2 Inflectional Morphology Czech and Slovak are inflectional languages, sharing a complex grammatical system which marks seven cases (six in Slovak), three genders, two numbers, three tenses, two voices, three moods, and two aspects. Nouns, pronouns, adjectives, and numerals undergo declension based on: gender (feminine, masculine [animate and inanimate], and neuter), number (singular, plural), and case (nominative, genitive, dative, accusative, locative, instrumental, and vocative, the last case being reserved in Slovak for some archaic words). Thus, each word may have fourteen different forms depending on its part of speech, case, gender, and number. Grammatical inflections – mainly suffixes – affect all of the major parts of speech except prepositions, adverbs, conjunctions, and interjections.

Noun phrase elements undergo declension, and their inflectional endings must agree with the subject in case, gender, and number. For example, the endings are different for feminine singular vs. plural nominative forms, as in singular: *skvělá žena* 'splendid woman' → plural: *skvělé ženy* 'splendid women'. Note that Czech and Slovak sometimes have different inflectional endings, as, for example, the neuter, plural, dative forms (e.g., '[to the] splendid cities', Czech: *skvělým městům* vs. Slovak: *skvelém mestám*). A set of examples illustrating nominal declension in each language is provided in panel II of Table 15.1. As can be seen, the same endings sometimes mark different cases, resulting in some grammatical ambiguity. Knowledge of the grammar and context, or at least of the specific prepositions that may be used with each case, is therefore required for disambiguation. In both languages, the ambiguity is compounded when the inflectional morpheme has an inconsistent spelling (e.g., the spelling of /i:/ in the adjective /skvjeli:/, *skvělý muž* 'splendid man' vs. *skvělí muži* 'splendid men').

Despite the general similarities of the Czech and Slovak declension systems, a number of differences exist, generally reflecting a lesser variability in the later-codified Slovak. For example, while Czech allows for dual inflectional endings in certain cases, Slovak permits only one. Slovak also maintains greater root morpheme invariance when undergoing inflection (e.g., compare Czech *Praha* ['praha] → *praze* ['praze] with Slovak *Praha* ['praha] →*prahe* ['prahe]), and it has fewer possible inflectional case endings across word paradigms. For example, in Slovak the locative case ending for masculine plural is restricted to -*och*, while in Czech three endings are possible depending on the paradigm -*ech*, -*ích*, and (rarely) -*ách* (see also Table 15.1, panel II).

Verb morphology is also complex in both languages, with conjugation in three main tenses (present, past, future), two voices (active, passive), three moods (indicative, imperative, conditional), and two aspects (perfective, imperfective). Verb phrases (predicates) must agree with the subject for number and person with specific inflectional suffixes. In addition, the participles expressing the past tense, conditional mood, and passive voice are inflected for gender and must, therefore, additionally agree with the gender of the subject. The subject–predicate agreement rules are particularly complex for the spelling of verbs ending in /i:/, which may be spelled as ⟨i⟩ or ⟨ý⟩ depending on their grammatical status (verb tense/mood/aspect, subject, gender, and number).

As with declension, Slovak verb conjugation is somewhat less complex than Czech. It contains fewer irregular verbs, allows for fewer doublet verb forms (e.g., the Czech 'it is pouring' *leje* = *lije*; 'I write' *píšu* = *píši*), and has a smaller set of inflectional endings across cases. For example, the first person singular always ends in -*m* (e.g., *niesem, volám, kryjem*), while Czech has more than one ending (e.g., *nesu, volám, kryji*).

15.2.1.3 Word Formation Processes   Word formation in Czech and Slovak predominantly entails affixation of prefixes and suffixes to stems. Prefixation generally preserves the stem morpheme and generates clear morpheme boundaries. However, most prefixes also exist as prepositions, and thus speakers must distinguish morpheme sequences comprising two separate words (preposition and content word) from those comprising a single polymorphemic word, as in the ['doʃkoli] *do školy* / ['doʃkolit] *doškolit* example, provided in Section 15.2.1.1. In spelling, the presenting difficulty is knowing where to place word boundaries in such cases.

Suffixation is widespread and complex in both languages. Suffixes are typically added to stems, often entailing changes to the stem morpheme. This includes dropping stem endings before adding derivational suffixes (e.g., ⟨ský⟩ in *Pražský*), morphophonological alternations (e.g., /praha/ → /praze/, as noted above), less frequently compounding of multiple suffixes, and insertion of single-letter or syllable infixes. Such processes create difficulty in determining the stem-suffix boundary. The derivation of adjectives from nouns sometimes causes consonant doubling, most often with ‹nn› (e.g., ‹výkon› + ‹ný› → ‹výkonný›; ‹telefon› + ‹ní› → ‹telefonní›); doubling is otherwise quite rare, and where it does occur it has no audible phonetic consequences (i.e., [viːkoniː], [telefoɲiː]), thus presenting sound–spelling inconsistency. Moreover, derived words may undergo normal inflectional processes. Compounding is a less common process.

In summary, although the inflectional and derivational morphology of both languages is based on the same general framework of affixation, each has a somewhat different set of inflectional paradigms and endings, as well as derivational affix forms, with Slovak having less variation than Czech (see also panel II of Table 15.1).

15.2.2 Writing System

Czech and Slovak use the Latin alphabet in a linear, left-to-right sequence. A special feature of both alphabets is the inclusion of letters with diacritics to denote non-Latin phonemes (see Section 15.1.2). The diacritic marking for long vowels is the acute accent (ˊ), which in Slovak also marks the long /l:/ and /r:/. In Czech only, the circle (°) marks long /u:/, ‹ů› in non-word-initial positions; word-initially, /u:/ is spelled ‹ú›; in Slovak the diaeresis (¨) marks the vowel ‹ä›, historically corresponding to /æ/ but currently equivalent to /e/, and the circumflex (ˆ) specific to the letter ‹o› marks the diphthong /uo/. The háček (ˇ) marks only one vowel ‹ě›, which corresponds to /je/, in Czech; otherwise it marks non-anterior coronal consonants, ‹š, ž, č, ř›, and the palatalized consonant ‹ň›. Finally, the háček, represented as a short stroke (ʼ) on the letters ‹d›, ‹t› and, in Slovak, also on ‹l›, marks the palatalized consonants ‹d'›, ‹t'› and the Slovak "soft" ‹l'› (/ʎ/). The full letter inventories, along with their orthographic groupings are provided in panel III of Table 15.1.

15.2.2.1 Script and Punctuation
Both languages use typed (printed) and cursive scripts. In literacy education, the alphabet is introduced in both script types. Beyond the primer stage, most reading books and instructional materials contain mainly printed letters. First-grade children are typically taught to write cursive lowercase, followed by uppercase letters, then syllables and small words; print writing is not usually encouraged in the primary years.

Punctuation in Czech and Slovak is similar to its use in other Latin-based alphabetic orthographies. The main punctuation marks are ‹ . ! ? , ; : – →›. Comma, semicolon, colon, and dash (also brackets) are subject to rather strict proscriptive rules. The apostrophe is the least used punctuation mark and is reserved for some abbreviations (e.g., 1989 → '89) and foreign words (e.g., *hors d'oeuvre*).

15.2.2.2 Orthography As per the current *Rules of the Czech/Slovak Orthography* (2005/2000), respectively, both systems are based on four main guiding principles: (1) the *phonological principle* states that phonemes and corresponding letters (graphemes), have one-to-one mapping relationships. The digraph ‹ch› – /x/ (both languages) and Slovak ‹dz› – /ʣ/ and ‹dž› – /ʤ/ also function as alphabetic letters (although the phonemic status of /ʤ/– ‹dž› is unclear). (2) The *morphological principle* states the rules for spellings that reflect the underlying root or base words when these are altered by phonological processes such as assimilation of voicing, and word-final devoicing; in such cases the spelling is determined by its pronunciation of the inflected form. (3) The *grammatical principle* or *syntactic principle* (sometimes grouped with the morphological principle) pertains to rules at the phrase (or multiword) level for the spellings of inflections ending in /i/ or /iː/, which may be spelled with ‹i›/‹y› or ‹í›/‹ý› depending on subject–verb/adjective agreement (see examples in Section 15.2.1.2). (4) The *etymological* (or historical) *principle* applies to spellings that reflect pronunciations that existed historically but are no longer valid. In fact, the ambiguity of the spellings of ‹i›/‹í› and ‹y›/‹ý›, which is so widespread in both orthographies, is due to the fact that historically each grapheme was associated with a different vowel. Although, as we have seen, Slovak has dealt with this inconsistency to some extent in equalizing all /iː/-endings in past participles with the spelling ‹i›, Czech has retained the historical spellings. Several other vowels underwent historical transformations resulting in inconsistent phoneme–grapheme mappings, such as the Czech spellings for /uː/ – ‹ú› and ‹ů›. The etymological principle also applies to foreign loan words – when these retain their original foreign spellings – and especially to the spelling of /i/ and /iː/, even at the cost of violating certain graphotactic rules or the morphological principle.

The phonological principle is dominant, and this is reflected in the high degree of phoneme–grapheme (approximately .90) and grapheme–phoneme (approximately .92) consistency in both languages (Kessler & Caravolas, 2011). However, the morphological, grammatical, and etymological principles create inconsistency at the phonographic mapping level, usually presenting two possible spellings or pronunciations for a particular segment or letter (e.g., /i/ spelled as ‹i› or ‹y›; ‹v› pronounced as /v/ or /f/). The rules and strategies for disambiguation are taught progressively and systematically throughout the primary language arts curriculum. Because orthographic inconsistency in Czech and Slovak manifests mainly in the direction of spelling, a great emphasis is placed on instruction of spelling and writing.

15.2.3   Conclusion

Czech and Slovak are highly inflected Slavic languages with relatively long (polysyllabic) words and complex syllable onset structure – but a simple coda system. They have fairly simple vowel systems from the point of view of both phonology and spelling. The prosodic properties of both languages and their clitic systems introduce difficulties for learning word structure and boundaries in spelling. Their morphological systems are complex both in inflectional and in derivational morphology, and the orthographic morphological principle sometimes overrides the phonological principle, causing phoneme–grapheme inconsistency. Orthographic consistency is also reduced by some preservation of historical spellings and, perhaps more importantly, of loan word spellings. Given the recent surge in English loan words, the etymological principle continues to have relevance. Below we return to these linguistic properties and their impact on learning to read and spell.

15.3   Acquisition of Reading and Spelling in Czech and Slovak

In the sections that follow, we examine literacy development in Czech and Slovak, describing the manifestations of typical as well as atypical reading and spelling development, beginning with their precursor skills, and underlying cognitive predictors. Wherever possible, we take a cross-linguistic perspective, reporting studies comparing Czech and Slovak as well as English and other languages.

15.3.1   Becoming Linguistically Aware

15.3.1.1 Phonological Development and Phonological Awareness   Phonological awareness training, often referred to as "phonemic perception," has a long tradition in Czech and Slovak education and often forms a daily part of the preschool curriculum (Caravolas et al., 2012, supplementary materials). Studies of the development of phoneme awareness in children learning in Czech relative to English (Caravolas & Bruck, 1993) and German (Caravolas & Landerl, 2010) revealed that sensitivity to the salient aspects of phonological structures of the native language already exists prior to literacy instruction. Awareness of consonants in cluster syllable onsets develops earlier in Czech (and Slovak) than in Germanic languages, reflecting the phonological structure of the input language; however, phoneme awareness emerges as a skill separate from letter knowledge (also decoding and spelling, see Section 15.3.3.1), and its *role* in literacy development appears to be similar across alphabetic languages. For example, in a comparative study of the European, longitudinal, cross-linguistic project, ELDEL (Enhancing Literacy Development in European Languages, www.eldel.eu), Czech and Slovak 6-year-old

kindergarten children were compared to Spanish 5-and-a-half-year-old kindergarteners not yet formally learning to read and write, and a group of slightly
younger, 5-year-old British-English children in the first (Reception) year of
formal instruction. The Czech and Slovak children performed similarly on all
measures. Importantly, despite knowing significantly fewer alphabet letters and
reading significantly fewer words than their Spanish and English counterparts,
they attained scores on phoneme awareness similar to the English children and
higher than Spanish children. Thus, their phoneme awareness performance was
not *contingent* on their letter knowledge or word identification skills (see
Hulme, Caravolas, Málková & Brigstocke, 2005, for a similar finding).

15.3.1.2 Morphological Development and Morphological Awareness Despite
the complexity of the morphological systems of Czech and Slovak, surprisingly
little empirical research has been carried out on morphological development
and its relationship to literacy acquisition. One study, carried out in the ELDEL
project, compared Slovak, English, French, and Spanish first-grade children's
ability to generate derivational morphemes (Salas, Caravolas, Efrim &
Schöffelová, 2010). These languages lie on a continuum of the "richness"
(and complexity) of their derivational and inflectional processes. Slovak is
the most complex, followed by Spanish, and French; English is the least
complex, being a more "isolating" language with a preference for compounding over derivational affixation. On the hypothesis that greater morphological
richness should be associated with a faster growth of morphological awareness
(e.g., Dressler, 2007), we predicted that Slovak children would attain the
highest scores and English children the lowest. The children were asked to
supply derived nouns from orally presented prompts (e.g., someone who *bakes*
is a ... [*baker*]; a place that sells *baked goods* is a ... [*bakery*]). As predicted,
Slovak children were the most accurate (71%), followed by the Spanish (63%),
French (60%), and English (53%) groups. Also, most errors involved incorrect
suffixation (e.g., *pâtisseur* instead of *pâtissier*) for all but the English children,
who predominantly made errors of compounding (e.g., *bank man* instead of
banker). Thus, children seem sensitive to the most typical morphological
processes in their spoken language from a relatively early age, and the richness
of the system may accelerate the development of derivational, morphological
awareness.

Interestingly, in Caravolas et al.'s (2012) study of kindergarten predictors of
reading and spelling ability in Grade 1, morphological skills did not play an
important role in predicting literacy development (despite moderate longitudinal correlations in both languages), over and above phonological skills.
We return to this issue in Section 15.3.2.

Table 15.2 *Longitudinal scores tracking development in reading words aloud among Czech and Slovak children*

| | Reading aloud word lists[a] | | | |
| | Czech | | Slovak | |
	Mean words correct	Mean errors	Mean words correct	Mean errors
Kindergarten	4	11	4	_[b]
Mid-Grade 1	16	9	15	8
End-Grade 1	51	2	47	2
Mid-Grade 2	66	1	63	1
End-Grade 2	78	1	78	1

Note: [a] = reading words aloud for 1 minute; [b] = analogous error data were not available for kindergarten scores.

15.3.2 Development of Word Identification

15.3.2.1 Word Decoding Development As in many relatively consistent alphabetic orthographies (e.g., Seymour, Aro & Erskine, 2003), the acquisition of word-level reading skills progresses quickly in Czech and Slovak, independent decoding and reading of simple texts typically being attained by the end of Grade 1. Accordingly, in Caravolas and Landerl's (2010) study, the Czech children progressed from knowing less than half of the alphabet and reading virtually no words at the start of Grade 1, to knowing all of the letters and decoding lists of basic words and nonwords perfectly by the end of the year.

Czech and Slovak follow similar paths of development in reading-aloud efficiency (speed and accuracy). On a matched one-minute-reading test (described in Caravolas et al., 2012), administered at five time points between kindergarten and Grade 2, both groups made gains of approximately 12–16 words per minute in each half-year, with the notable exception of a marked growth spurt during the second half of Grade 1, with gains of 32 (Slovak) and 34 (Czech) words. By the end of Grade 2, both groups were reading aloud 78 words per minute, and – as reported in Table 15.2 – produced virtually identical error rates, which declined to negligible levels by the end of Grade 1.

The same two groups, as well as their British-English peers, were assessed at the end of Grade 1 on reading aloud a list of twenty-five cognate words (e.g., English: *paper*, Czech: *papír*, Slovak: *papier*), ranging in difficulty from Grades 1 to 5. Children's reading accuracy as well as errors were analyzed. As expected, the English group attained lower scores, reading just over 50% of the items correctly; the Czech and Slovak groups exceeded 80%. The patterns of errors also differed. The English children misread almost 20% of the words as other real words (e.g., *paper* ➔ *page*), another 10% as nonwords (e.g., *paper* ➔ *parp*), and refused to attempt a further 15% of items. This pattern seems typical for English readers (see Share, 2008), but it was very rare in Czech and Slovak. Children in these two groups attempted most items, and their misreadings most frequently reflected *syllabified* reading – that is, the read-aloud syllables were not blended into word units.

In a study of the growth of silent reading efficiency between kindergarten and Grade 2, groups of Czech, Spanish, and English children were directly compared over six time points (Caravolas et al., 2013). The test comprised a graded list of approximately sixty cognate words. The Czech and Spanish groups both showed a growth profile similar to that described for the one-minute reading measure above; however, the English children's rate of growth was characterized by a slower and generally linear pattern. Thus, single-word reading, aloud or silent, seems to develop along a similar trajectory in languages with consistent alphabetic orthographies, including Czech and Slovak.

Finally, in the study of Caravolas et al. (2012), the kindergarten predictors of first-grade word reading development in Czech, Slovak, Spanish, and English were examined. The kindergarten predictors included vocabulary, nonverbal reasoning, morphological awareness, verbal short-term memory, visual attention, letter knowledge, rapid automatized naming (RAN), phoneme awareness, and reading. Structural equation modeling yielded remarkably clear results, with only three skills accounting for unique variance in Grade 1 reading, over and above the autoregressor; these were letter knowledge, RAN, and phoneme awareness. Moreover, this set of skills accounted for similar proportions of variance and had the same relative weightings across all four languages. Thus, although children learning to read Czech, Slovak, and other consistent orthographies (e.g., Spanish) acquire decoding and word recognition skills more quickly than learners of English, the foundation skills most strongly driving this development are the same, regardless of orthographic consistency. Interestingly, the absence of a unique predictive role for morphological awareness in our Czech and Slovak samples further suggests that it is the nature of the orthography and its primary mapping principle (i.e., phonological) that determines the importance of the relevant oral language skills for early literacy development.

15.3.2.2 Word Spelling Development   Although Czech and Slovak decoding skills are acquired quickly, spelling and grammatical writing take comparatively much longer to learn. The spelling/writing curriculum spans the first four (Slovakia) or five (Czech Republic) years of schooling. It covers the skill of handwriting (typically cursive), which receives intensive attention in Grade 1 and is maintained as part of the curriculum until Grade 5. Alongside this, orthographic knowledge is explicitly taught as a part of the language arts curriculum, which is focused on the complex grammatical system and its manifestations in the written language. Teaching is structured in order of complexity and follows a similar progression in both countries; the highlights are outlined below.

- Grade 1: The phonological principle is taught. Children are instructed to "write what you hear." Writing practice includes learning to form all letters of the alphabet – including the correct writing of diacritics – as well as blending skills for writing syllables and eventually short, phonologically consistent words.

- Grade 2: Two main *graphotactic rules* are taught. First, the palatalized consonants /ɟ, c, ɲ/ are spelled in their canonical form as ‹ď, ť, ň›, except when they are followed by the vowels ‹i, í› in both languages, and additionally by ‹e, ia, ie, iu› in Slovak; in the last cases, the diacritic is not used. Second, the so-called *soft, hard,* and *bivalent* (unmarked) consonant rule for writing of ‹i, í, y, ý› is taught (see the bottom panel of Table 15.1). Following the soft consonants, /i, iː/ are spelled ‹i, í› (e.g., *žirafa, bacil*); following the hard consonants, they are spelled with ‹y, ý› (e.g., *chyba, mladý*). Following the unmarked consonants, the default spelling is ‹i, í›, unless the word is a codified *selected* exception, or a loan word.

- Grade 3: The basic expressions of the morphological principle are introduced in rules regarding the *assimilation of voicing* and *word-final devoicing*. Children are taught to inflect target words to determine ambiguous spellings at morpheme boundaries (e.g., pluralize [ploti] vs. [plodi] to determine whether [plot] is spelled with a final ‹t› or ‹d›). *Word boundary* rules focus on the difference between prepositions as separate words and prefixes as parts of main words. Also, children rote-learn the codified *exception word list*; its knowledge is consolidated throughout Grade 4.

- Grades 4–5: The assimilation of voicing rule is extended to word-internal morpheme boundaries (e.g., ['natstolem] → *nad stolem,* 'above the table'). The morphosyntactic rules concerning the spelling of /i, iː/ inflectional endings in subject–adjective and subject–verb agreement are introduced, and learning/consolidation continues throughout Grade 5.

Two large-scale surveys of spelling development, published as standardized batteries of spelling assessment in Czech (Caravolas & Volín, 2005) and Slovak (Caravolas, Mikulajová & Vencelová, 2008a) investigated primary schoolchildren's acquisition of skills in basic phonological recoding as well as of inconsistent mappings arising from the various violations of the phonological principle. Both studies included cross-sectional samples of approximately one hundred children per grade (Grades 2–5 in Czech Republic; Grades 1–4 in Slovakia). Within languages, the same tests were administered across several grades to ascertain when mastery in each aspect of orthographic knowledge was reached.

Reassuringly, children's learning reflected the explicitly taught curriculum, and the sequence of development was similar in both languages. Phonological recoding skills were mastered the earliest, both groups exceeding 85% on phonologically plausible spellings by the end of Grade 2, a finding that is consistent with previous studies in other alphabetic orthographies (e.g., Alegria & Mousty, 1996; Wimmer & Landerl, 1997). Graphotactically determined spelling patterns were mastered next, between the end of Grades 2 and 3; these spellings do not necessitate linguistic analysis and can be learned simply as letter sequencing rules (e.g., /i/ is spelled ⟨y⟩ following hard consonants and ⟨i⟩ following soft consonants). Morphophonological voicing assimilation rules were mastered next between Grades 3 and 4, as were the selected exception words. Finally, both language groups showed learning of the morphosyntactic rules for spellings of inflectional endings; however, mastery was not attained by Grade 4 or 5, suggesting that this aspect of spelling requires a protracted period of learning and consolidation.

A more in-depth exploration of the Slovak data revealed several other interesting findings (Caravolas & Mikulajová, 2008). First, children rapidly mastered the appropriate use of diacritic markers in those consonant graphemes that use them consistently (e.g., /ʃ/ is always spelled ⟨š⟩). Letters with diacritic markers were spelled with over 90% accuracy already in Grade 1, and were almost as accurate as letters without diacritics (e.g., /s/ → ⟨s⟩). However, first graders omitted diacritics marking long vowels over 20% of the time (e.g., /a:/ → ⟨á⟩), even though these spellings are also completely consistent. This suggests that it is awareness of vowel duration that presents some difficulty, and not merely the addition of the diacritic. Caravolas and Mikulajová (2008) further found that Slovak children did not reach mastery in representing diacritics of the palatalized consonants /ɟ, c, ɲ/, which are subject to graphotactic conditional rules (see above), until after the rule had been explicitly taught in Grade 3. Thus, the ability to represent letters with diacritics depends in part on phonemic awareness (for vowels) and in part on the consistency in their phoneme–grapheme mappings.

Our Slovak survey further showed that explicit instruction had powerful effects on children's learning of all types of inconsistent letter–sound mappings (graphotactic, exception word, or inflectional endings). This was clearly illustrated in the spellings of the vowel /i, i:/, which in the *default* or canonical case is spelled ⟨i, í⟩, but in most conditioned contexts requires the letter ⟨y, ý⟩. Until explicitly taught the relevant disambiguating rules, children systematically produced the default ⟨i, í⟩ spellings. For example, prior to instruction on the conditional graphotactic soft/hard consonant rule (see above and Table 15.1, panel III), first graders spelled /i, í/ → ⟨i, í⟩ in *all* contexts approximately 85% of the time (i.e., they were only 15% accurate in using the ⟨y, ý⟩ spellings in the hard consonant contexts). In second grade, when the rules are taught, accuracy in the conditioned contexts increased to approximately 80%. Children spelled the consonants affected by the assimilation of voicing at morpheme boundaries, phonetically (e.g., *led*, 'ice' misspelled *let*) approximately 70% of the time, only reaching mastery in Grade 3, when the rules were explicitly taught. Moreover, the word-internal (prefix-root, root-suffix) assimilation of voicing patterns were learned more slowly than those in the word-final position. In learning the word boundary rule, children failed to mark word boundaries between prepositions (clitics) and content words, only approaching mastery in this skill in Grade 4; in contrast, they practically never erroneously inserted word boundaries between prefixes and root morphemes, or within single morpheme words. This suggests that children were relying on the prosodic rather than the morphological or grammatical information until taught about the boundaries between prepositions and root words.

We briefly turn to the issue of predictors of early spelling development in Czech and Slovak, drawing on Caravolas et al. (2012). Spelling performance was estimated from a composite of simple dictation tests given in mid-kindergarten and again in mid-Grade 1. Multigroup structural equation modeling again produced very clear results, replicating the reading analysis. Grade 1 spelling was predicted by letter knowledge, RAN, and phoneme awareness, in addition to the autoregressor, which together accounted for similar proportions of variance and had the same relative weightings across all four languages. These results demonstrate that languages can have very different phonologies, morphologies, and (alphabetic) orthographies, which present learners with different types of challenges, and yet the architecture of cognitive skills enabling learners to develop their literacy skills is the same.

15.3.2.3 Reading and Spelling Difficulties Studies of the profiles of Czech and Slovak children with dyslexia are still relatively rare. Caravolas, Volín, and Hulme (2005) compared Czech and British-English dyslexic children in Grades 3 to 7 to test the assertion (e.g., Wimmer, 1993, 1996) that, unlike in English, the easy-to-learn consistent orthographies enable learners with dyslexia to acquire adequate decoding skills, and thereby also phoneme awareness skills, by the end of Grade 2. The phoneme awareness deficit, which is a hallmark of dyslexia in English, is argued to be milder and transient in languages with relatively consistent orthographies. Caravolas et al. (2005) found that on parallel measures of phoneme awareness, reading fluency, and reading comprehension, both groups with dyslexia performed significantly worse than age-matched controls, and only similarly to or worse than younger, spelling-ability-matched controls. Although all Czech groups attained higher mean phoneme awareness (and reading fluency) scores than the English groups, as expected, neither dyslexic group showed signs of having resolved their phoneme awareness difficulties, despite being beyond Grade 2.

Caravolas and Volín (2001) further analyzed the spelling profiles of the Czech dyslexic children from the above study, focusing on phonological errors. Their dyslexic participants committed more phonological errors than age-matched peers, and the magnitude of this deficit remained stable, showing no sign of resolving still in Grade 5.

Caravolas et al. (2008b) examined the spelling profiles of Slovak third- and fourth-grade children with dyslexia across the range of spelling patterns (and rules) that are taught in the primary grades. Both age groups found all but the most basic and consistent sound–letter associations difficult to learn. Their skills lagged at least two years behind those of their age/grade peers. In addition to difficulties with inconsistent letter–sound mappings (bearing on graphotactics, morphophonology, and morphosyntax), they demonstrated a persistent problem with the correct designation of vowel length. The latter spellings are completely consistent and are mastered by non-dyslexic children by Grade 2; however, as mentioned earlier, they require sensitivity to the phonological feature of duration. Together, our studies suggest that, as in English, Czech and Slovak individuals with dyslexia experience persistent deficits in phonological processing skills and perhaps also in broader language skills.

15.3.3   Reading Comprehension

15.3.3.1 Predictors of Reading Comprehension   Research into literacy skills beyond the word level are still scarce in Czech and Slovak, although empirical studies are now under way. To our knowledge, the only study of the predictors of reading comprehension in Czech was that by Caravolas and colleagues (2005). Here 107 Czech and 71 English children from Grades 2 to 5 (Czech) / 2 to 7 (English) completed a time-limited cloze reading test that was matched across languages and graded in difficulty. Each item presented a short text with one or two missing words, to be selected from five alternatives. A multigroup structural equation model revealed that this aspect of reading comprehension was predicted by concurrent measures of nonverbal ability, vocabulary, phoneme awareness, and reading speed. After reading speed, vocabulary knowledge was the strongest predictor in both languages, suggesting that its central role in extracting meaning from text is not weaker in consistent alphabetic orthographies than in English. Still needed are detailed longitudinal studies of the development of reading comprehension in typical and poor readers, which will evaluate a variety of reading comprehension paradigms to elucidate whether models of reading comprehension developed from studies with readers of English are also valid for learners of Czech and Slovak.

15.3.3.2 Word-Level Effects in Comprehending Text The rich morphologies of the Czech and Slovak languages offer fertile ground for exploring the role of vocabulary development in reading. However, research in this aspect of reading has yet to be undertaken systematically by scholars of these languages.

15.3.4 Conclusion

The above studies indicate that the core underlying skills that launch learners into alphabetic literacy are the same in Czech and Slovak. Contrary to some claims (e.g., Wimmer, 1993, 1996), phoneme awareness is as important in predicting reading and spelling success in these as in other consistent orthographies (e.g., Spanish) and in English. Letter knowledge and rapid naming represent two further precursor skills across these languages. Compared to learners of English, Czech and Slovak children acquire basic literacy skills more quickly; learning to read single words silently or aloud presents relatively little difficulty despite the preponderance of complex, polysyllabic words encountered. In contrast, Czech and Slovak children require several years to learn the inconsistencies in spelling brought about by the complex grammatical system. The codified exceptions (selected words) are relatively few, and thus only the continually imported loan words may require additional learning. Among learners with literacy difficulties, phoneme awareness and phonological coding deficits are indicative of dyslexia in Czech and Slovak, as they are in English. These findings hold despite clear and sizable differences in performance profiles of the groups. Research on reading comprehension still awaits the development of measurement tools and further investigation. This is a potentially interesting area, in which the role of morphological awareness and vocabulary knowledge may shed new light on how lexical and semantic skills interact with orthographic consistency in these Slavic languages.

15.4   Discussion

15.4.1   Challenges in Learning to Read Czech and Slovak

The studies of Czech and Slovak literacy development highlight the differential impact of consistent alphabetic orthographies on learning to read and spell. While grapheme–phoneme consistency confers clear advantages on reading acquisition, even a relatively small amount of phoneme–grapheme inconsistency slows the process of learning to spell. Explicit instruction of highly productive spelling rules clearly helps children to learn, but inconsistency generated by morphosyntactic processes remains difficult despite instruction. However, their spelling difficulties must be put into perspective: almost all inconsistencies involve a choice of only two possible spellings, and the vast majority can be resolved with knowledge of graphotactic, morphophonological, or grammatical rules. We contrasted two highly similar languages and, thus not surprisingly, the groups' linguistic awareness and reading acquisition appeared to be indistinguishable. Interestingly, our surveys of spelling development systematically showed that the Czech children lagged somewhat behind their Slovak age and grade peers in mastering inconsistent spelling patterns. This may reflect the somewhat greater system-wide consistency of orthographic and grammatical patterns in Slovak as compared with Czech. However, this finding needs to be replicated in a study using directly comparable test materials (now under way). To date, it seems that Czech and Slovak literacy development follows largely the same trajectories and learning challenges.

15.4.2   Implications for Instruction

Already the earliest primers of the fifteenth and sixteenth centuries revealed a conceptualization of the written code of Czech as a phonetic approximation of the spoken language, lending itself to phonics approaches as the optimal methods of reading instruction. The spelling/writing curriculum entailing explicit and systematic grammar instruction that is currently taught in both countries also has a long-standing tradition. It seems that these teaching approaches are effective, as Czech and Slovak pupils have historically enjoyed very high levels of literacy. Currently, more freedom of choice in methods is permitted, and although some new approaches are being adopted, the analytic-synthetic method is reportedly still used by the vast majority (over 70%) of primary school teachers. The effectiveness of the alternative methodologies awaits evaluation.

15.5   Final Conclusion

To conclude, Czech and Slovak are very similar languages, sharing historical roots. Their thousand-year separation brought about different influences from the cultures and powers that dominated over them, and this has resulted in differences in the development of the codification of their orthographies and in certain aspects of the languages themselves. Ironically, the delay in the codification of Slovak has produced the current advantages in a somewhat greater consistency in both the grammar and the orthography relative to Czech. We found only an indirect indication that this has a benefit on spelling development for Slovak children. Further study is needed to test this hypothesis directly. To date, it is clear that the development of reading skills and their cognitive underpinnings are virtually indistinguishable in these two languages.

This is certainly largely attributable to the fact that Czech and Slovak learners experience linguistically and educationally rather similar environments; however, over and above these factors is the growing evidence that alphabetic literacy skills (and perhaps non-alphabetic ones as well) draw on a strongly constraining set of cognitive universals.

Acknowledgments

Many thanks are due to Zuzana Šlosárová-Elliott, Jean Caravolas, and Václava Caravolas for their assistance with the linguistic and historical background research for this paper. Thanks also to Brett Kessler for his most useful feedback on the manuscript.

References

Alegria, J. & Mousty, P. (1996). The development of spelling procedures in French-speaking, normal and reading-disabled children: Effects of frequency and lexicality. *Journal of Experimental Child Psychology, 63*, 312–338.

Bartoš, J. & Gagnaire, J. (1972). *Grammaire de la langue slovaque*. Bratislava: Matica Slovenská.

Berger, T. (2012). Religion and diacritics: The case of Czech orthography. In S. Baddeley & A. Voeste (Eds.), *Orthographies in early modern Europe* (pp. 255–268). Berlin: Mouton de Gruyter.

Caravolas, M. & Bruck, M. (1993). The effect of oral and written language input on children's phonological awareness: A cross-linguistic study. *Journal of Experimental Child Psychology, 55*, 1–30.

Caravolas, M. & Landerl, K. (2010). The influences of syllable structure and reading ability on the development of phoneme awareness: A longitudinal, cross-linguistic study. *Scientific Studies of Reading, 14*, 464–484.

Caravolas, M., Lervåg, A., Defior, S., Seidlová Málková, G. & Hulme, C. (2013). Different patterns, but equivalent predictors, of growth in reading in consistent and inconsistent orthographies. *Psychological Science, 24*, 1398–1407. DOI: 10.1177/0956797612473122.

Caravolas, M., Lervåg, A., Mousikou, P., Efrim, C., Litavský, M., Onochie-Quintanilla, E., Salas, N., Schöffelová, M., Defior, S., Mikulajová, M., Seidlová-Málková G. & Hulme, C. (2012). Common patterns of prediction of literacy development in different alphabetic orthographies. *Psychological Science, 23*, 678–686.

Caravolas, M. & Mikulajová, M. (2008). Effects of letter-sound consistency, letter-form complexity, and frequency in learning canonical and contextually conditioned letter spellings in Slovak. *Phonetica Pragensia, 11*, 21–30.

Caravolas, M., Mikulajová, M. & Vencelová, L. (2008a). *Súbor testov na hodnotenie pravopisných schopností* [Battery of tests for the assessment of orthographic skills]. Bratislava: SAL, s.r.o.

(2008b). Spelling of Slovak children with dyslexia. Paper presented at the International Conference of the British Dyslexia Association, Harrogate, UK.

Salas, N., Caravolas, M., Efrim. C. & Schöffelová, M. (2010). The acquisition of derivation in English, Spanish, French and Slovak. Paper presented at Barcelona Conference on Language Development.

Caravolas, M. & Volín, J. (2001). Spelling errors among dyslexic children learning a transparent orthography: The case of Czech. *Dyslexia, 7*, 229–245.

(2005). *Baterie diagnostických testů gramotnostních dovedností pro žáky 2. až 5. ročníku ZŠ* [Battery of diagnostic tests of literacy skills for pupils in 2nd to 5th grades of primary school]. Prague: IPPP.

Caravolas, M., Volín, J. & Hulme, C. (2005). Phoneme awareness is a key component of alphabetic literacy skills in consistent and inconsistent orthographies: Evidence from Czech and English children. *Journal of Experimental Child Psychology, 92*, 107–139.

Dressler, W. U. (2007). Introduction. In S. Laaha & S. Gillis (Eds.), *Typological perspectives on the acquisition of noun and verb morphology. Antwerp Papers in Linguistics* 112 (pp. 3–10). University of Antwerp.

Dobrovský, J. (1809). *Ausführliches Lehrgebäude der böhmischen Sprache* [Detailed grammar of the Czech language]. Prague: Johann Herrl.

Gebauer, J. (1902). *Krátká mluvnice česká* [Brief grammar of Czech]. Prague: Unie.

Hanka, V. (1817). *Pravopis české podle základů gramatiky Josefa Dobrovského* [Czech orthography according to Josef Dobrovský's foundations of grammar]. Prague: U Bohumila Háze.

Hulme, C., Caravolas, M., Málková, G. & Brigstocke, S. (2005). Phoneme isolation ability is not simply a consequence of letter-sound knowledge. *Cognition, 97*, B1–B11.

Kessler, B. & Caravolas, M. (2011). Weslalex: West Slavic lexicon of child-directed printed words. Retrieved from http://spell.psychology.wustl.edu/weslalex.

Kučera, H. & Monroe, G. K. (1968). *A comparative, quantitative phonology of Russian, Czech, and German*. New York: Elsevier.

Optát, B. (1547/1559). *Slabikář český* [Czech primer].

Seymour, P. H. K., Aro, M. & Erskine, J. M. (2003). Foundation literacy acquisition in European orthographies. *British Journal of Psychology, 94*, 143–174.

Share, D. L. (2008). On the Anglocentricities of current reading research and practice: The perils of overreliance on an "outlier" orthography. *Psychological Bulletin, 134*, 584–615.

Ústav pro jazyk český ČSAV (1993). *Pravidla Českého pravopisu* [Rules of the Czech orthography]. Prague: ČSAV.

Volín, J. (2010). Fonetika a fonologie [Phonetics and phonology]. In V. Cvrček (Ed.), *Mluvnice současné češtiny* [The grammar of contemporary Czech] (pp. 35–64). Prague: Karolinum.

Wimmer, H. (1993). Characteristics of developmental dyslexia in a regular writing system. *Applied Psycholinguistics, 14*, 1–33.

(1996). The nonword reading deficit in developmental dyslexia: Evidence from children learning to read German. *Journal of Experimental Child Psychology, 60*, 80–90.

Wimmer, H. & Landerl, K. (1997). How learning to spell German differs from learning to spell English. In C. Perfetti, L. Rieben & M. Fayol (Eds.), *Learning to spell: Research, theory, and practice* (pp. 81–96). Mahwah, NJ: Lawrence Erlbaum.

16 Learning to Read Russian

Natalia Rakhlin, Sergey A. Kornilov, and Elena L. Grigorenko

16.1 Introduction

16.1.1 Russian and Its Orthography

The earliest evidence of a writing culture in Russia comes from the so-called birch-bark charters first discovered in 1951 during archeological excavations in the ancient city of Novgorod. Over one thousand of such documents have since been discovered containing household records, debtor lists, tax records, notes on litigations, prayers, petitions, love letters, school exercises, and so forth, etched on the outer layer of birch bark, dating from the eleventh to the fifteenth centuries. Remarkably, these writings were not official documents written by scribes or clerks but casual notes written by laypeople. This suggests that in early medieval Russia there existed a widespread urban literacy across wide swaths of society (Franklin, 1985). In one estimate, in the mid-thirteenth century, 20% of the urban male population in Russian city-states was literate (Mironov, 1991).

Even more notable is that the language of this casual literacy was the spoken vernacular, distinct from the Old Church Slavonic, the language of the Orthodox Mass and liturgical texts, created expressly for the purpose of bringing literacy to the Slavonic world. The Slavonic writing system originated from the work of two Christian missionaries, brothers Cyril and Methodius from Thessaloniki, who, in the year 863 CE, went on a mission from Constantinople to Moravia on the orders of the Byzantine emperor Michael III to translate the Gospels into Slavonic and develop a writing system for it. What resulted was essentially a new written language, distinct from any of the existing vernacular languages (but closest to Southern Slavonic). It became known as Old Church Slavonic. The newly created script for writing was based on Greek cursive (Cubberley, 2002), but new letters were invented for those vowels that did not exist in Greek. The original alphabet later became known as the Glagolitic script. Glagolitic was gradually replaced by Cyrillic, most likely developed by disciples of Cyril and Methodius in the tenth century. It was also based on the Greek alphabet and most likely adopted the letters for the Slavonic-specific sounds from the Glagolitic script (Schenker, 1996).

Thus, although the church must be credited with the introduction of literacy and for being the source of the first exposure to written language for most people in medieval Russia, the impetus for the development of lay literacy apparently came from the urban merchants and craftsmen themselves.

[L]iteracy in medieval Russia was not stimulated by any specific needs and requirements . . . It was demanded by nobody, and it seemed to have afforded no special status. A layman could conduct his affairs as comfortably without it as with it. Why, then, did significant numbers of laymen choose to acquire it? . . . *Literacy was there to be simply acquired and it was simply acquired because it was there.* (Franklin, 1985, p. 38; emphasis added)

This observation underscores an important point about literacy. When contrasted with spoken language acquisition, it is often emphasized that the latter is acquired spontaneously, effortlessly, and naturally, while the acquisition of literacy is a process of cultural transmission that requires rigorous schooling, conscious effort, and is achieved with a less uniform degree of success. Although this is correct and mass literacy is dependent on certain cultural preconditions, such as access to schooling, nevertheless, humans, as a species, possess a capacity for using symbolic systems for converting a transient form of language into a permanent form, and the mechanisms that allow for acquisition of this skill are intimately intertwined with the human capacity for language.

16.1.2   Synchronic and Diachronic Characterization

Contemporary Standard Russian, called *literary Russian* in Russia, had been in place (although still evolving, particularly through contact with German and French) since the time of Peter the Great. It began to be formalized after the establishment, in the 1730s, of the Russian Academy and with the publication of the first grammar of Russian by Mikhail Lomonosov in 1755/1757 (Cubberley, 2002). Lomonosov differentiated between *high, middle,* and *low* styles, equating Church Slavonic (a descendant from the Old Church Slavonic) with the high style and spoken Russian with the low. The association between the low style and Russian resulted in a situation (by the early nineteenth century) where French became the spoken language of prestige used by the aristocracy, while Russian was associated with the lower social classes. Russian national poet Aleksandr

Pushkin is credited with creating modern literary Russian. Inspired by the beauty of Russian dialects spoken by the peasants and by Russian folklore, he abandoned high in favor of non-high styles and successfully blended the spoken vernacular with the existing literary language. Literary Russian became the standard in both writing and speech, while other varieties of Russian gradually became marginalized. The standardization of both spoken and written language led literary Russian to be considered "the correct Russian" and regional or social dialectal features to become stigmatized, particularly during the Soviet period, when centralized education and employment systems became enforcers of the linguistic standard. The Russian Language Institute at the Russian Academy of Sciences, to this day, issues prescriptive grammars and dictionaries of pronunciation (so-called orthoepic dictionaries) explicitly labeling various colloquial forms or usages as "unacceptable" or "not recommended." The Institute's mission is

to conduct the scientific study of the Russian language in Russia and abroad in order to evaluate linguistic innovations with respect to their consistency with language norms and to codify the norms of the literary language in dictionaries, grammars, and reference works on the culture of speech. (Russian Language Institute, 2014)

16.1.3   Literacy and Schooling

The Russian Federation (hereafter, Russia), with a territory of 17,075,400 square kilometers (6,592,800 square miles), is inhabited by approximately 144 million people, which makes Russia the largest and the ninth most populous nation in the world. Its population is highly diverse, encompassing 160 ethnic groups, who speak some 100 languages (not all have writing systems). Yet the Russian language is the only official state/federal language. It is also spoken outside of the Russian Federation, in the former Soviet republics and by expatriate Russian communities throughout the world. It is estimated that about 120 million Russian speakers reside outside of Russia.

The Russian Constitution gives its twenty-one autonomous republics the right to institute their native language co-officially next to Russian, but according to the 2010 Census data, the overwhelming majority of the population (99.4%) spoke and read Russian (with only approximately 81% of the population recorded as ethnically Russian). Thus, Russian is the language of literacy in the Russian Federation; the literacy rate is estimated by the United Nations at 99.5% for adults older than 24 years of age and at 100% for youth between 15 and 24 years, which places Russia ahead of the UK and US (99%), but somewhat behind a number of other countries (e.g., Norway).

16.2   Description of Russian and Its Written Forms

The Russian language belongs to the East Slavonic (Slavic) branch of a group of closely related languages, which also includes West (Polish, Czech, Slovak) and South (Bulgarian, Macedonian, Serbo-Croatian, and Slovene) Slavonic languages. The considerable similarity among all Slavonic languages with respect to their grammatical structure and vocabulary led scholars to believe that they had originated from a common source fairly recently. Common Slavonic is generally considered to have differentiated into major Slavonic dialects (i.e., South, West, and East Slavonic) around the sixth century AD (Cubberley, 2002). As attested in documents dating from the tenth century, East Slavonic (or Old Russian) is the parent language of Russian, Belorussian, and Ukrainian. The first written Slavonic records (and hence, the first reliable historical information concerning Slavonic tribes) date back to the ninth century (Kiparsky, 1979). At that time, Slavonic dialects still had so many similarities that they were able to use a common written language, Old (Church) Slavonic written in the Cyrillic script; thus, the early Slavonic societies maintained a form of diglossia. Eventually, as spoken languages diverged (and civil societies developed), the orthographies evolved to fit the respective spoken languages.

16.2.1   Linguistic System

16.2.1.1 Phonology   Contemporary Standard Russian (CSR) has five vowel phonemes: /a, e, i, o, u/. Some scholars also posit the sixth high mid vowel /ɨ/, treated by others as an allophonic variation of /i/, which undergoes backing after plain (non-palatalized) consonants (Halle, 1959; Trubetzkoy, 1969). The Russian consonantal inventory is moderately large (according to the *Word Atlas of Linguistic Structures* [WALS], Dryer & Haspelmath, 2013), with approximately thirty-three consonants (see Table 16.1; Padgett, 2003).

Interestingly, the phonological inventory of Old Russian contained more vowels but fewer consonants than CSR (Cubberley, 2002). Most importantly, there were two so-called "jers," short (or lax) counterparts of /i/, /u/, ubiquitous in Old Russian, which, unlike CSR, had a simple open syllable structure. These vowels, sometimes referred to as "ghost segments" (Szpyra, 1992), have since disappeared, but their historical presence is registered in contemporary Russian (and other Slavonic languages) by the existence of numerous morphologically related word pairs, with one but not the other form containing a vowel (*den^j – dn^ja*, 'day'-nominative – 'day'-genitive). In many otherwise analogous word pairs, this phenomenon of "fleeting vowels" is not found (e.g., *les – lesa*, 'forest' – 'forests'; *dom – doma*, 'house' – 'houses'). Historically, the alternating pairs contained the

Table 16.1 *The consonant inventory of Russian*

	Labial		Dental/Alveolar		Palatal		Velar	
	Hard	Soft	Hard	Soft	Hard	Soft	Hard	Soft
Plosives	p b	pʲ bʲ	t d	tʲ dʲ			k g	
Fricatives	f v	fʲ vʲ	s z	sʲ zʲ	ʃ ʒ	ʃ	x	
Affricates			t͡s			t͡ʃ		
Nasals	m	mʲ	n	nʲ				
Trills			r	rʲ				
Laterals			l	lʲ				
Glide						J		

jers. Beginning with Lightner (1972), these vowel-zero alternations have been analyzed as resulting from a synchronic presence of the jers as abstract underlying vowels, which both trigger and undergo phonological operations: The presence of a jer triggers all of the preceding jers to lower (to surface as /o/, /e/); those jers that did not undergo lowering are deleted.

As a result of the *fall of jers* and other historical changes, modern Russian has acquired complex syllable structures (e.g., *vzbryknutʲ* – 'kick with hind legs', *monstr* – 'monster') with typologically unusual phonotactics. The complex onsets and codas may violate the sonority sequencing principle, which requires the sonority of the segments preceding the peak (nucleus) to be rising and those following it falling. This principle disallows sonority plateaus and sonority reversals, which, however, occur in Russian (e.g., *tkatʲ* –'weave', *zdesʲ* – 'here'). A second consequence of the fall of jers was the emergence of contrastive palatalization, which existed in Old Russian as an allophonic alternation in the context of front vowels (Cubberley, 2002).

In CSR, most labial and alveolar consonants come in pairs of palatalized and non-palatalized counterparts, e.g., /p/ vs. /pʲ/. Some are not paired and are invariably either palatalized, e.g., /ʃ/, /t͡ʃ/, or not, /ts/, /ʃ/, /ʒ/. Palatalization is contrastive before back vowels, word-finally, and pre-consonantally (i.e., there are minimal pairs that differ solely by the palatalization feature of one consonant (*vol – vʲol*, 'ox' – 'he-led'; *ugol – ugolʲ*, 'corner' – 'coal'; *polka – polʲka*, 'shelf' – 'polka')). Before front vowels, all consonants undergo palatalization as a systematic phonological process (i.e., are predictively palatalized). The velars are thought to not contrast in palatalization (although some argue for the phonemic status of *soft* velars).

Another pervasive phonological process in Russian is voicing assimilation; that is, all members of an obstruent cluster assume the voicing feature of the last obstruent (/rybka/ → [rypka], 'fish'-diminutive, cf. [ryba], 'fish'). In addition, obstruents in the word-final position are devoiced, as in /klub/ → [klup], 'club' (cf. gen. sg. [kluba]), with a rule of *final devoicing feeding voicing assimilation*: /vizg/ → [vizk] → [visk], 'shrieking'.

Two other important features of Russian phonology are its free stress and vowel reduction. Except for compounds, Russian words contain only one stressed vowel. The position of the stress cannot be determined by the phonological properties of the word or from syllable counting and must be learned by rote. Many unrelated words are distinguishable solely by the stress (e.g., *pólka – polká*, 'shelf' – 'regiment'-genitive). Within nominal and verbal inflectional paradigms, there are various stress patterns, such that for some words the stress consistently falls either on the stem or on the inflection throughout the paradigm, but for some it alternates between the stem in some forms and the inflection in others.

The stress is related to another, pervasive characteristic of Russian phonology, vowel reduction. While in stressed syllables, Russian has five phonemes, in unstressed syllables, this five-way contrast is neutralized to a two-way contrast after palatalized consonants, and to a three-way contrast elsewhere. Note the different degree of /a/ and /o/ reduction in the first pretonic syllable versus elsewhere (Padgett, 2003).

a. Vowel reduction pattern after palatalized consonants:

/u/ → /u/

/i/, /e/, /a/, /o/ → /i/

b. Vowel reduction pattern after non-palatalized consonants:

Vowels in the first pretonic position:	Elsewhere:
/i/, /e/ → /i/	/i/, /e/ → /i/
/a/, /o/ → /ɐ/	/a/, /o/ → /ə/
/u/ → /u/	/u/ → /u/

Free functional morphemes, such as prepositions, form phonological words with the following word and vowels in them also undergoing two-level reduction (cf. [pɐ úlitse] and [pə dɐrógʲe] 'on the street' – 'on the road'). Thus, word stress is an important organizing feature of the phonological structure of Russian.

16.2.1.2 Inflectional Morphology Russian has a complex system of inflectional morphology, rich in both nominal and verbal categories. Nouns (and their dependents) are inflected for case, number, and gender. Six cases (nominative, accusative, genitive, dative, instrumental, and locative), two numbers (singular and plural), and three genders (masculine, feminine, and neuter) are normally distinguished. Because the inflectional paradigms contain intricacies not easily accommodated by these categories, some scholars posit two additional cases, second genitive and second locative (Tiberius, 2014); vestiges of a third number, dual, a feature left over from Old Russian (Rakhlin, 2003), and a sub-gender category of animacy, with masculine singular and feminine and neuter plural paradigms being different for animate and inanimate nouns (Corbett, 1982). Based on gender, as well as the phonological form (i.e., whether the word ends in a consonant or vowel), the nouns belong to one of three or four declension classes.

Pronouns and demonstratives follow their own declension, as well as adjectives (with the exception of a small number of possessive adjectives that have mixed – part adjectival/part noun – declension paradigms). Adjectives come in two forms: a full form, which follows the declension strategy of the demonstratives and establishes concord in gender/number and case with the noun it modifies; and the so-called "short" adjectives, which do not decline and can be used only as predicates, not modifiers. The relatively flexible word order in Russian, where almost any linear order between subject, verb, direct and indirect object is possible, makes case morphology important for identifying structural and semantic relations between constituents in the sentence.

Russian verbs are systematically marked as either perfective or imperfective, the distinction often expressed by a prefix or a suffix, which, in addition to the aspectual, have additional lexical meaning. As a result, a single verbal root can be modified to express a large number of subtle changes in meaning involving aspectual and other meaning elements, e.g., *chitat'* ('to read'), *procitat'* ('to read'-perfective), *perechitat'* ('to read again'), *dochitat'* ('to read to the end'), *zachitat'* ('to read out loud'), *vychitat'* ('to discover through reading'), *otchitat'* ('to reprimand'), and so forth. Russian imperfective verbs can have past and present tense, expressed synthetically (with a bound morpheme), and future, expressed analytically (using an auxiliary "to be" and the infinitival form of the verb). Perfectives can have past and future (both expressed synthetically). Verbs in the present and past tense follow different agreement patterns: In the past tense, they agree with the subject for gender and number, but in the present tense for person and number. Verbs belong to one of two conjugation classes.

The Russian inflectional system contains a number of morphological phenomena that contribute to its irregularity. One is case syncretism, i.e., homonymy between morphological case forms (e.g., dative and locative for feminine singular nouns), which leads to a reduction of forms to be memorized, but at the same time to a greater irregularity of the system. Another phenomenon is suppletion (Corbett, 2007), when different grammatical forms are formed with two morphologically unrelated roots, rather than with grammatical endings (singular and plural of 'human' – *chelovek* vs. *l'udi* or 'child' – *reb'onok* vs. *deti*). Finally, the Russian morphological system is characterized by a phenomenon sometimes referred to as *defectiveness* (Surrey Morphology Group, 2009); that is, idiosyncratic gaps in the inflectional paradigms, such that

Table 16.2 *Examples of Russian derivational suffixes*

Suffix and its semantic meaning	Base	Derivative
-ot (abstract)	*vys(okij)* 'tall'	*vys-ot(a)* 'height'
-ets,	*borʲ(ba)* 'fight',	*borʲ-ets* 'fighter'
-telʲ	*uchit-elʲ* 'teacher'	*uchitʲ* 'teach'
-ak (person)	*ryb(a)* 'fish'	*ryb-ak* 'fisherman'
-k	*artist* 'actor'	*artist-k(a)* 'actress'
-(n)its(a) (female)	*uchitelʲ* 'teacher'	*uchitelʲ-nitsa* 'teacher_fem'
	lev 'lion'	*lʲv-itsa* 'lioness'
-in (singulative)	*gorox* 'peas'	*gorosh-in(a)* 'pea'
-onok (baby animal)	*kot* 'cat'	*kotʲ-onok* 'kitten'
-chka	*mama* 'mom'	*mama-chka* 'mommy'
-ik (diminutive)	*dom* 'house'	*dom-ik* 'little house'
-ishche (augmentative)	*dom* 'house'	*dom-ishche* 'huge house'

certain morphological forms simply do not exist for certain roots (e.g., future perfective form of the verb "to win," imperative of the verb "to insist," or genitive plural for the noun "dream").

In addition to the richness and considerable irregularity of Russian inflectional paradigms, its morphological complexity comes from its being a fusional language, i.e., a language with not only a relatively high number of morphemes per word (3.33 on average, compared to 1.68 in English; Bauer, 2003) and reaching 4–5 in verbs (WALS), but also combining multiple grammatical categories in a single morpheme (e.g., case/number/gender). Consequently, very few words in Russian are mono-morphemic, and there is rarely a one-to-one correspondence between a grammatical morpheme and meaning. Furthermore, due to the fusion between formative elements, often there are no clear boundaries between morphemes, and a change in category leads not simply to an addition or change of an inflectional and/or derivational element, but to a phonological change in the stem, some conditioned phonologically and some apparently idiosyncratic.

16.2.1.3 Word Formation Processes   The most common type of word derivation in Russian is suffixation, but prefixation, compounding, and "zero affixation" are also present. Nouns represent the largest word class in Russian with the most productive word formation system. Russian derivational suffixes vary in productivity and can be characterized according to their semantic category and the type of bases they can modify (e.g., nouns, adjectives, verbs). In addition, there are expressive (or evaluative) suffixes that express diminutive, augmentative, affectionate, or pejorative shades of meaning; see Table 16.2 for examples (Hippisley, 1996).

Word derivation, like inflection, is associated with phonologically and morpho-phonologically conditioned alternations. In other words, adding a derivational suffix conditions the stem-final consonant to undergo a sound change (e.g., palatalization or mutation).

16.2.2   Writing System

16.2.2.1 Script   As discussed above, Russian, along with Ukrainian, Belorussian, Bulgarian, Macedonian, and Serbian, uses the Cyrillic script, which is also used by a number of non-Slavonic languages spoken by peoples of the former Soviet Union and Mongolia.

The Old Cyrillic alphabet contained forty-four letters, many of which were also used as numerals in the Greek tradition. Since it was adapted to Russian from Old Church Slavonic (and since the spoken language underwent certain phonological changes, including the loss of jers), the alphabet contained multiple superfluous and redundant letters and spelling rules that did not reflect the contemporary phonology. The first attempt to reform Russian orthography was made by Peter the Great in 1708–1710, and then again in 1918, when some letters were eliminated, bringing the number of letters to thirty-three (including two auxiliary signs – the "soft sign" and "hard sign"; Cubberley, 2002). Debate about the necessity of further reform has continued to the present time, with proponents arguing that Russian orthography needs to be further simplified and regularized to make it more accessible for the masses, while opponents pre-dictably call the attempts to reform the orthography an "assault on the Russian literary language." Many educators acknowledge that the time allocated to the study of Russian in secondary schools is spent disproportionately on learning the rules of spelling and memorizing "all the exceptions, justified illogical details, variants and intricate traps, which strongly smell of 'medieval scholas-tics'" (Klein, 1964).

16.2.2.2 Orthography   Russian orthography is highly transparent in the direc-tion from letters to sounds, such that every written syllable has only one pronunciation, with only a few irregularities (Grigorenko, 2005). One quirk of Russian orthography is related to the contrast between palatalized and non-palatalized consonants, reflected in writing not by the consonantal grapheme itself, but by the vowel grapheme that immediately follows it or the soft sign. Despite having only five vowel phonemes, the Russian alphabet has ten vowel letters, which come in pairs: the so-called "hard vowels" (а, о, у, ы, э; the last occurs only word initially and in foreign loan words) and their "soft" counter-parts, written after palatalized consonants (я, ё, ю, и, е). Four of the "soft" vowels (я, ё, ю, е), when they occur initially in a word or syllable, are "jotated" (i.e., pronounced as "hard" vowels with the preceding glide j). Thus, both sets

Table 16.3 *Russian vowel letters*

	"Hard" letter	Non-palatalized consonant	"Soft" letter	Palatalized consonant	Jotated vowels
/i/	ы	мыла [myla] 'she-washed'	и	Мила [mʲila] Mila (name)	-
/e/	э*	эхо [ekho] 'echo'	е	снег [snʲeg] 'snow'	ехал [jekhal] 'he-drove'
/a/	а	мал [mal] 'small'	я	мял [mʲal] 'he-crumpled'	ярко [jarko] 'brightly'
/o/	о	мода [moda] 'fashion'	ё	мёда [mʲoda] 'honey'-genitive	ёж [josh] 'hedgehog'
/u/	у	лук [luk] 'onion'	ю	люк [luʲk] 'hatch, manhole'	юг [juk] 'south'

of vowel letters represent one set of vowel phonemes, while one set of consonant letters represents both palatalized and non-palatalized members of the consonant phoneme pairs. In non-vowel contexts (e.g., word or syllable final), an auxiliary soft sign is used to indicate palatalization. Another quirk is that when a jotated vowel is preceded by a consonant that belongs to a preceding syllable (rather than being an onset of the same syllable), a soft or a hard sign is used to indicate the syllable boundary and the lack of the vowel's effect on the preceding consonant (барьер, pronounced as [barʲjer], which is the consonant contrastively palatalized, the vowel jotated; подъезд, pronounced as [podjezd], i.e., the consonant is non-palatalized, the vowel jotated) (see Table 16.3).

Russian orthography has a high degree of inconsistency and irregularity in predicting spelling from sounds. One major reason for this is the morphological principle – the spelling of morphemes remains invariant and the words containing the same morphemes have the same spelling even though, as discussed above, various phonological and morpho-phonological processes alter their sound shape in the course of derivation and inflection. This creates many words with spellings that are unpredictable from their pronunciation, including homophones distinct only in spelling. For example, unstressed vowels, as discussed above, undergo reduction, as a result of which phonemic contrast between them is neutralized. However, spelling reflects their underlying phonological and not the surface phonetic form, i.e., the spoken form a beginning reader/speller is familiar with (e.g., both /o/ and /a/ when unstressed are pronounced as [ə] but are spelled as ‹o› and ‹a›, respectively). Linking the two requires developing a high level of phonemic and morphological awareness skills.

The spelling of unstressed vowels and consonants that undergo voicing assimilation and final devoicing is one of the most difficult aspects of Russian orthography, which requires the child to become adept at verifying the correct spelling by finding a cognate word, if such exists, in which the unstressed vowel in question is stressed and hence not reduced, or the consonant in question is followed by a vowel and hence unchanged.

In addition to the morphological unity principle, spellings may be determined by the word's origin or the orthographic, phonological, or morphological context – "spelling rules" that often have numerous "exceptions." In some instances, the "rule" is too obscure, and the correct spelling appears to be arbitrary. All these phenomena make spelling skills more difficult to acquire than decoding skills, reflected in the fact that children are expected to acquire foundational reading skills by the end of Grade 4, while spelling continues to be taught through Grade 7, with spelling skills acknowledged to continue being a problem area for many high school students, even those with no reading difficulties.

16.2.3   Conclusion

Russian orthography has a high degree of transparency from letters to sounds. This transparency works at the level of syllables, not individual letters, given the quirk of the Russian alphabet to use vowels and auxiliary signs to indicate the consonant's palatalization status (in other words, one has to decode the consonant in combination with the following vowel letter to know whether it is "hard" or "soft"). Despite this idiosyncrasy, for any written syllable, there is only one way it can be pronounced. On the other hand, Russian has a low degree of transparency from sounds to letters. There are several typological properties of the Russian language that contribute to this lack of transparency. One phonological phenomenon creating distance between the sound and spelling is unstressed vowel reduction, which neutralizes contrasts between unstressed vowels, making it difficult to predict their spelling from the sound. Consonant assimilation processes and final consonant devoicing have a similar effect of contrast neutralization and homonymy. Complex inflectional morphology with a high level of irregularity and complex patterns in which phonology and morphology interact to alter word shapes is another factor that adds challenges to literacy acquisition in Russian. Finally, Russian phonotactics allowing complex consonant clusters in both syllable onset and coda positions may also complicate literacy acquisition, particularly the process of developing phonological awareness (Bruck & Treiman, 1990; Treiman, Zukowski & Richmond-Welty, 1995).

16.3   Acquisition of Reading and Spelling in Russian

There is a relative scarcity of systematic studies, particularly published in English, with regard to spoken and written language acquisition in Russian. Those that are available are primarily diary studies, case studies, or small sample studies.

16.3.1   Becoming Linguistically Aware

16.3.1.1 Phonological Development and Phonological Awareness   The ideas relating reading acquisition to phonemic awareness originate from the work of Soviet psychologists (e.g., Elkonin, 1963, 1973), who first proposed that a prerequisite for subsequent success in learning to read is to become aware of the phonemic composition of spoken words. These ideas strongly influenced the pedagogy of reading in Russia, where the approach to teaching pre-reading skills involved training the skills of rhyming, phonemic word matching, and phonemic word segmentation. The role of phonemic awareness in reading acquisition was empirically supported by numerous studies conducted in various orthographies, including Russian.

Grigorenko (2011c) followed a group of young children (mean age = 5.2, standard deviation [*SD*] = .90) for one year, observing the dynamics of their performance on Russian versions of the Rosner Test of Auditory Analysis Skills (TAAS, a test of phonemic awareness; phonological awareness [PA]; and rapid automatized naming [RAN]). The children were also asked to read single words. When the children were re-evaluated four years later, the indicators of reading in primary school were predicted not only by mean values of early indicators of language functioning but also by slopes of their maturation.

Similarly, a study of seventy-nine Russian-speaking first- and second-grade children aimed at determining the strongest predictors of reading fluency and accuracy (Pechko, 2009) reported the results of a series of multiple regression analyses, in which PA, verbal short-term memory, listening comprehension, nonverbal IQ, RAN, and vocabulary were used to explain variance in decoding accuracy, decoding rate, and reading comprehension. PA accounted for unique variance in both decoding accuracy and decoding rate, whereas RAN was a unique predictor of decoding rate only.

Likewise, a study of 502 schoolchildren (mean age = 9.63, *SD* = 1.18) from one of the regional centers of Russia investigated the differential contribution of PA and RAN to single-word reading accuracy and fluency. Whereas PA indicators predicted the accuracy of single-word reading, RAN indicators predicted its fluency (Grigorenko, 2011b).

These findings were further corroborated in a study with intermediate readers (Rakhlin, Cardoso-Martins & Grigorenko, 2014). This study investigated the contribution of PA and RAN to reading fluency, accuracy, orthographic awareness, and spelling skills in Russian. In addition to taking a test of phonemic segmentation, ninety-six Russian children and adolescents (mean age = 13.67, *SD* = .88) completed tests of word and pseudoword reading fluency, pseudoword reading accuracy, orthographic choice, and spelling accuracy. Phonemic segmentation scores were better predictors of both phonological and orthographic processing (i.e., pseudoword reading accuracy, orthographic choice, and spelling accuracy) than RAN. RAN, on the other hand, contributed more variation to word and pseudoword reading fluency than PA. Its contribution to word reading fluency was not reduced after controlling for orthographic choice or spelling, but it disappeared after controlling for pseudoword reading fluency.

These findings suggest that ability for fluent reading in Russian (and its componential skills of phonological and orthographic processing) are dependent both on the phonological awareness/phonological processing skills (as indexed by phonemic segmentation tasks) and on the mechanisms underlying fluency (i.e., timing, automaticity/efficiency of processing) that RAN taps into. Spelling skills appear to be dependent on PA but not RAN.

The independent contributions of PA and RAN to literacy were also supported by a genetically informed study (Naples, Chang, Katz & Grigorenko, 2009) which found that RAN and PA, assessed in a large sample of unselected Russian-speaking families (child-probands and their parents), had only partially overlapping genetic etiology; in other words, each skill involved both shared and unique genes, consistent with the two being non-redundant contributors to literacy ability.

16.3.1.2 Morphological Development and Morphological Awareness   Given the morphological unity principle of spelling and morphological complexity of Russian, morphological awareness is an important skill required for literacy. This hypothesis was supported in a study (Grigorenko, Bulvere-Guden & Rakhlina, 2012) that examined the relative contributions of phonological, orthographic, and morphological skills on literacy development (as measured by spelling skills) in a sample of 171 middle school children (Grades 4–8). Morphological skills in the study were measured by a task based on the work by Carlise (2000), in which children had to use a series of word-prompts to derive an appropriate grammatical form or a new cognate word to make it fit the given syntactic frame. The study evaluated two regression models: one in which the scores for morphological skills were entered as the first step (after entering grade and sex); the other in which it was entered last (after the demographic, phonological, and orthographic skills scores). In both models, morphological skills explained unique variance in spelling accuracy: approximately 8% in the former and approximately 50% in the latter model. Similarly, a study with ninety-six elementary school students by Kornilov, Rakhlin, and Grigorenko (2012) found that morphological skills accounted for 27% and 20% of children's spelling and reading comprehension scores, respectively.

16.3.2   Development of Word Identification

16.3.2.1   Word Decoding Development   There are few published studies documenting developmental trajectories of word decoding development in Russian. One study (Grigorenko, Kornev, Rakhlin & Krivulskaya, 2011) examined literacy skills in ninety-six second- and third-grade children using a literacy-skills assessment battery that incorporated both international (i.e., the traditional IQ-achievement discrepancy-based) and Russia-specific (i.e., typology-based) approaches to identifying reading difficulties in emergent readers. Children were assessed on word reading accuracy and text reading fluency. The latter included not only the score of correctly read words per minute, but also the number of errors classified as one of three types: (1) incorrect phonological decoding; (2) incorrect word stress placement; (3) dysfluent (letter-by-letter or syllable-by-syllable) reading. Children's levels of general intelligence were also measured. Although the intercorrelations between the three types of errors were found to be statistically significant and substantial in magnitude, the existence of multiple nonredundant sources of variance in performance was in evidence. Therefore, a good measure of reading skills in Russian would include multiple types of errors as a composite measure to reflect the contributions of all these error types. Another interesting finding was the lack of a consistent and substantial pattern of correlations between the indicators of word- and text-level reading performance. Likewise, single-word reading captured a correlated but different skill from single-word spelling. At the text level, reading fluency, accuracy, and comprehension also captured correlated but not interchangeable skills.

This study also investigated the two typologies used to identify reading difficulties in Russian and in the West. A traditional Russian approach includes a qualitative rating of children's reading *method*, namely whether the child reads letter-by-letter (stage 1), syllable-by-syllable (stage 2), in whole words (stage 3), and with full fluency (i.e., reading with correct phrasing; stage 4). Reading disability in Russian is manifested by reading expected at an earlier stage of reading acquisition (e.g., reading syllable-by-syllable when whole-word reading is already expected) (Kornev, Rakhlin & Grigorenko, 2010). In this sample, there were no children who were still reading at the letter-based stage, and 59% read using word-based or word-group-based techniques. However, there were quite a few children still reading at the syllable level. The study considered to what extent a classification based on the reading method typology would overlap with a more standardized and conventional

IQ-discrepancy approach. The results indicated that although a substantial overlap between these diagnostic criteria was observed, this overlap was not complete. Further research is needed to investigate the reasons for this partial overlap and understand the typology of reading difficulties that each of these two classifications taps into.

Another Russian-language study (Kerek & Niemi, 2009a) examined the pattern of acquiring foundational-level literacy skills (particularly, word and pseudoword decoding accuracy and speed) in forty-three Russian-speaking first-grade children tested at three time points throughout the year. This study focused on the role of item length and complexity on children's accuracy and speed. The results showed a clear effect of word length, as well as syllable complexity (with CV syllables being easier than VC and CVC syllables). Contrary to what is typically reported for English, the study found no lexicality effect in simple words and pseudowords (with a 1:1 relationship between all of the phonemes and letters). However, with respect to complex words and pseudowords (the number of phonemes not equal to the number of letters), a reversed lexicality effect was reported, with pseudowords read more accurately than words. As the lexicality effect (i.e., more accurate decoding of words than pseudowords) is typically interpreted as evidence that beginning readers resort to holistic visual word recognition rather than phonological recoding, these findings suggest that Russian-speaking children use phonological recoding for reading both pseudowords and words rather than holistic word recognition. Reading words via phonological assembly is more complex because it involves not only sounding them out correctly but also agglutinating the sounds into cohesive wholes and linking the resulting strings with meanings.

16.3.2.2 Word Spelling Development   Given the complexity of sound–letter correspondence in Russian, the development of spelling skills has been and remains at the center of literacy education in Russia. As mentioned earlier, Russian spelling is predominantly morphological, and it is well known that robust meta-linguistic morphological skills are good predictors of spelling (Casalis, Deacon & Pacton, 2011; Kemp, 2006; Ravid, 2012). It is of no surprise, then, that when four indicators of literacy (spelling, comprehension, teacher report, and self-report) were considered (Grigorenko, 2011a) in a sample of 1,048 schoolchildren (mean age = 12.3, *SD* = 2.26), spelling was the variable that dominated the first principle component (59% of the total variance); it was also the variable that correlated the highest with teacher evaluation of literacy level (*r* = .60 for spelling compared to *r* = .53 and .42 for student self-report and for indicators of comprehension).

16.3.2.3 Reading and Spelling Difficulties   There is a dearth of systematic quantitative studies of reading disability (RD) in Russian. Although the first case studies of RD were described in Russia in the 1930s, only a few dozen articles on writing disorder and no more than thirty on reading disability have been published (Kornev & Chirkina, 2005): these are for the most part qualitative descriptive papers. It is recognized that RD in Russian is manifested primarily as slow, effortful decoding and poor word recognition, i.e., syllabic reading, low reading rate, incorrect placement of word stress, and incorrect phrasing/sentence melody. Effortful decoding may also lead to accuracy errors, when the child makes letter/sound substitutions or omissions, which are unsystematic (i.e., the child may make different errors in the same sentence at different times) and are likely a result of guessing. These errors, however, are not qualitatively different from the types of errors made by typically developing younger children (Kornev et al., 2010). Persistent spelling errors, particularly phonetically incorrect spelling (i.e., syllable omissions, substitution errors with consonants or accented vowels), are another well-documented symptom of RD in Russian.

The patterns of reading and spelling difficulties in Russian seem to parallel those in other transparent orthographies and can be predicted by the same componential skills as have been reported for other alphabetic scripts, namely PA and RAN. Furthermore, as in English, good RAN skills in Russian appear to be a protective factor for foundational-level literacy skills in children with spoken language difficulties (Rakhlin, Cardoso-Martins, Kornilov & Grigorenko, 2013).

16.3.3   Reading Comprehension

16.3.3.1 Predictors of Reading Comprehension   A study of predictors of reading comprehension (Prikhoda, 2013) considered ninety-six children in Grades 2 to 3 with the aim of identifying major predictors of reading comprehension and spelling. The predictor variables evaluated in the study were nonverbal IQ, word reading accuracy, and text reading accuracy and fluency. The results of a hierarchical regression analysis showed that word reading accuracy explained 30% of variance in spelling and 12% in reading comprehension; however, these indicators lost significance after including reading fluency scores (i.e., number of correctly read words from a text in 1 minute) in the model, which explained an additional 5% of variance for both outcome measures. These results confirm findings from other transparent orthographies which suggest that in such orthographies fluency measures are a better predictor of literacy skills in general and reading comprehension in particular.

16.3.3.2 Word-Level Effects in Comprehending Text
The predictive power of single-word reading for text comprehension was studied in a sample of 502 school-age students (mean age = 9.63, SD = 1.18),

in the presence of indicators of TAAS and RAN and demographic character-istics (Grigorenko, 2012). Whereas the total regression explained 23% of the variance in indicators of comprehension, none of this was attributable to indicators of single-word reading.

In a different sample ($n = 1048$, mean age = 12.3, $SD = 2.26$), reading comprehension was predicted based on meta-linguistic indicators of phonolo-gical, orthographical, morphological awareness, spelling, and demographic characteristics (Grigorenko, 2012). Again, a substantial amount of variance (24.3%) was explained, but the largest contribution (20.5%) was made by indicators of morphological awareness, with all other variables' contributions being relatively small (0.5% – 1.6%), although unique.

16.3.4 Conclusion

The studies of literacy acquisition in Russian showed that this process follows a trajectory quite similar to what has been observed in other languages; it has an alphabetic script with a transparent orthography and morphological unity spelling principle. In particular, PA skills are associated with reading accuracy and spelling, while RAN speed is related to reading fluency. In addition, morphological skills have been found to be important for both spelling and reading comprehension. Interestingly, unlike in studies with children learning to read in English, a reversed lexicality effect (an accuracy advantage for reading pseudowords relative to words) has been reported for Russian begin-ning readers, contradicting the hypothesis that beginning readers rely on holistic word recognition rather than phonological assembly. The patterns of difficulty exhibited by children with reading disability are similar to what has been reported for other orthographically transparent languages, namely slow effortful decoding and spelling difficulties. Consequently, reading fluency serves as a better indicator of overall reading efficiency than accuracy errors.

16.4   Discussion

16.4.1   Challenges in Learning to Read Russian

The main challenge in learning to read Russian comes from the multi-level organization of Russian orthography. Along with the phonemic level, with its relatively regular letter–sound correspondences, other salient organizational levels are the level of syllables (to determine the palatalization status of the consonant based on the following vowel) and morphemes (to determine the word stress and the pronunciation of the vowels). Thus, a child who has mastered phonological coding skills at the level of phonemes would not automatically become a fluent reader until he or she becomes fluent in reading syllables, as the sound of the first

Table 16.4 *Grade targets for reading achievement*

Grade	Fall term targets	Spring term targets
1	Accurate syllabic decoding; oral reading rate of at least 20–25 words per minute.	Accurate whole-word decoding of words with simple syllabic structure and syllabic reading of words of complex syllabic structure; oral reading rate of at least 35–40 words per minute.
2	Accurate whole-word reading of texts with correct sentence accenting; words of complex syllabic structure may still be read syllabically; oral reading rate at least 40–50 words per minute.	Accurate whole-word reading of texts with correct accenting, phrasing, and melody; oral reading rate at least 55–60 words per minute.
3	Accurate whole-word reading of texts with correct accenting, phrasing, and melody; good text comprehension; oral reading rate at least 60–70 words per minute.	Accurate whole-word reading of texts with correct accenting, phrasing, and melody; good text comprehension; oral reading rate at least 70–75 words per minute.
4	Accurate whole-word reading of texts with correct accenting, phrasing, and melody; demonstrating good comprehension of the text meaning and its emotive significance; oral reading rate at least 75–80 words a minute.	Accurate whole-word reading of texts with correct accenting, phrasing, and melody; demonstrating good comprehension of the text meaning and its emotive significance; oral reading rate at least 85–95 words per minute, with an optimal target rate of 120–150 words per minute.

Note. Basic reading skills are not taught post-elementary school, with work on word, sentence, and literary text analysis continuing throughout middle school.

segment is often dependent on the following segment, and hence fluent reading requires syllables to be read as a unit. In Russian, children are expected to master syllabic reading by the end of Grade 1 (Kerek & Niemi, 2009b). The next reading fluency stage is to master whole-word reading, since, without recognizing the main morphological building blocks of words, it is impossible to know the stress placement, which is necessary for correctly pronouncing the vowels that depend on their position relative to the stressed syllable. Thus, one must be able to recognize morphological units in order to recognize the word and pronounce it correctly. As described by Kerek and Niemi (2009b), "It is a bit like the chicken-and- egg problem: you cannot read the word accurately unless you know the stress pattern, but you cannot know the stress pattern unless you read the word" (pp. 13–14). Finally, full fluency requires instantly recognizing not only each word but also the syntactic and semantic relationship between them, a task complicated by the flexible word order in Russian, necessitating a greater reliance on morpho-syntactic information (see Table 16.4 for reading achievement targets for elementary grades).

16.4.2   Implications for Instruction

The Russian method for teaching literacy is based on phonics (analytic-synthetic). Children are actively taught to analyze spoken words phonologically (i.e., identify the constituent syllables and phonemes) in parallel to learning letter names and shapes, to map graphemes onto phonemes by first reading single syllables and simple mono- and disyllabic words, and subsequently to blend syllables into words. Early readers are taught to pay attention to word stress and to notice the difference between stressed and unstressed vowels and palatalized and non-palatalized consonant pairs. Reading instruction is focused on reading fluency, trained through reading out loud and measured by the number of correctly read words per minute. Throughout the elementary and middle school years, children receive explicit instruction in Russian word and sentence structure and spelling rules, with their numerous exceptions. At the same time, reading and writing are taught in parallel through reading progressively more complex works of literature (poetry and prose) and writing compositions.

16.5   Final Conclusion

Reading research in Russian offers a unique perspective not only because of some of the distinct features of the Russian language and orthography discussed above but also because it is instructive to observe how certain historical factors that shaped Russian society in the last century brought seemingly non-ideological concepts of literacy, psychological testing, and the genetic basis of individual differences from the narrow and specialized domains of education and science to the domain of the political. This has led to interesting paradoxes. The country in which the phonological basis of learning to read originated, from where it was transmitted to the West (but see Chirkina & Grigorenko, 2014), for many decades was isolated from the West and consequently its psychological and education sciences developed independently. The strong ideological prohibition against psychological testing during the middle and late 1930s led to an interruption in the development of psychology (Grigorenko & Kornilova, 1997). Psychological testing was called a "pedological perversion" and was prohibited. Psychology departments were closed, experimental psychological research stopped and a number of researchers were fired, arrested, and imprisoned. The only sanctioned framework explaining behavior was Pavlov's theory and the only bases for individual differences allowed to be discussed were environmental. As a result, to this day, there is a dearth of objective standardized measures for diagnosing reading disability or language impairment. The existing classifications of developmental language disorders reflect a long-standing cultural distaste for mentalist explanations of behavioral symptoms in favor of physical, by implying specific neurological damage, particularly during pre- and perinatal development, as an etiological mechanism of various disorders, contrary to the wide recognition in the West that many cases of disorders of language development have no apparent physical cause.

Another interesting perspective is that reading research in Russian offers an opportunity to study reading acquisition outcomes before and after the dissolution of the Soviet Union. This provides an interesting glimpse into how social changes seemingly unrelated to education can have profound effects on the state of mass literacy. In the Soviet Russian culture, books and reading were afforded a high level of prestige, writers were seen as moral and spiritual leaders, a home library was considered a status symbol, and periodicals enjoyed circulations in the millions of copies, unheard of in the West. The Soviet Union prided itself as "the most well-read country in the world," a propaganda line often repeated in the Soviet media. As noted by a literary critic, "literature used to be the substitute for everything – from science to consumer goods. This became pathological – everything was concentrated in the sphere of art as there was almost no action elsewhere" (Stelmach, 1993). Because of the high prestige of reading and low book prices, Russian society enjoyed a high level of reading activity among adults, with 95% of adults reporting reading frequently or occasionally, according to a survey conducted right before the dissolution of the Soviet Union (Stelmach, 1993). After the dissolution of the Soviet Union and the development of a consumer economy, there has been a sharp drop in the prestige of reading, a steep decline in the amount of reading, and a lowering of reading proficiency among Russia's middle and high school students, as indicated by Russia's standing on international assessments of reading proficiency. This underscores the importance of cultural/societal factors in maintaining the high standards of literacy required in the modern world.

Note

Preparation of this article was supported in part by grant R21 HD070594-01 from NIH/NICHD (PI: E. L. Grigorenko). Grantees undertaking such projects are encouraged to express their professional judgment freely. Therefore, this article does not necessarily reflect the position or policies of the National Institutes of Health, and no official endorsement should be inferred. We are grateful to the editors for their comments and to Ms. Mei Tan for her editorial support.

References

Bauer, L. (2003). *Introducing Linguistic Morphology*, 2nd edn. Edinburgh University Press.
Bruck, M. & Treiman, R. (1990). Phonological awareness and spelling in normal children and dyslexics: The case of initial consonant clusters. *Journal of Experimental Child Psychology*, *50*(1), 156–178.

Carlisle, J. F. (2000). Awareness of the structure and meaning of morphologically complex words: Impact on reading. *Reading and Writing*, *12*, 169–190. DOI:10.1023/A:1008131926604.

Casalis, S., Deacon, S. H. & Pacton, S. (2011). How specific is the connection between morphological awareness and spelling? A study of French children. *Applied Psycholinguistics*, *32*, 499–511.

Chirkina, G. V. & Grigorenko, E. L. (2014). Tracking citations: A science detective story. *Journal of Learning Disabilities*, *47*, 4, 366–373.

Corbett, G. G. (1982). Gender in Russian: An account of gender specification and its relationship to declension. *Russian Linguistics*, *6*, 197–232.

(2007). Canonical typology, suppletion, and possible words. *Language*, *83*, 8–42.

Cubberley, P. (2002). *Russian: A linguistic introduction*. Cambridge, MA: Cambridge University Press.

Dryer, M. S. & Haspelmath, M. (Eds.) (2013). *The world atlas of language structures online*. Leipzig, Germany: Max Planck Institute for Evolutionary Anthropology. Retrieved from http://wals.info/languoid/lect/wals_code_grk.

Elkonin, D. B. (1963). The psychology of mastering the elements of reading. In B. Simon & J. Simon (Eds.), *Educational psychology in the U.S.S.R.* (pp. 165–179). London: Routledge & Kegan Paul.

Elkonin, D. B. (1973). Psychology in the USSR. In J. Downing (Ed.), *Comparative reading* (pp. 551–579). New York: Macmillan.

Franklin, S. (1985). Literacy and documentation in Early Medieval Russia. *Speculum*, *60*, 1–38.

Grigorenko, E. L. (2005). If John were Ivan: Would he fail in reading? In R. M. Joshi & P. G. Aaron (Eds.), *Handbook of orthography and literacy* (pp. 303–320). Mahwah, NJ: Lawrence Erlbaum.

(2011a). Грамотность школьника; её оценка учителем, самим школьником и объективными тестами [Student literacy: Its assessment by the teacher, student and objective tests]. *Мир образования*, No. 3, 119–125.

(2011b). Универсальные предикторы грамотности: Универсальны ли они и для русского языка? [Universal predictors of literacy: Are they universal and for the Russian language?]. *Новое в Психолого-педагогических Исследованиях*, No. 4, 63–68.

(2011c). Этап «дочтения», его характеристики и их роль в овладении чтением [The "dočteniâ" stage, its characteristics and their role in mastering reading]. *Вопросы психологии*, No. 6, 122–130.

(2012). Понимание прочитанного школьниками и его предикторы [Students reading comprehension and its predictors]. *Психологическая наука и образование*, No. 1, 65–74.

Grigorenko, E. L., Bulvere-Guden, R. & Rakhlina, N. V. (2012). Грамотность и морфологическое осознание [Literacy and morphological comprehension]. *Психология: Журнал высшей школы экономики*, *9*, 104–112.

Grigorenko, E. L., Kornev, A. N., Rakhlin, N. & Krivulskaya, S. (2011). Reading-related skills, reading achievement, and inattention: A correlational study. *Journal of Cognitive Education and Psychology*, *10*, 140–156.

Grigorenko, E. L. & Kornilova, T. V. (1997). The resolution of the nature-nurture controversy by Russian psychology: Culturally biased or culturally specific?

In R. J. Sternberg & E. L. Grigorenko (Eds.), *Intelligence, heredity, and environment* (pp. 393–439). New York: Cambridge University Press.

Halle, M. (1959). *The sound pattern of Russian: A linguistic and acoustical investigation*. The Hague: Mouton.

Hippisley, A. (1996). Russian expressive derivation: A network morphology account. *Slavonic and East European Review, 74*, 201–222.

Kemp, N. (2006). Children's spelling of base, inflected, and derived words: Links with morphological awareness. *Reading and Writing, 19*, 737–765.

Kerek, E. & Niemi, P. (2009a). Learning to read in Russian: Effects of orthographic complexity. *Journal of Research in Reading, 32*, 157–179.

(2009b). Russian orthography and learning to read. *Reading in a Foreign Language, 21*, 1–21.

Kiparsky, V. (1979). *Russian historical grammar: The development of the sound system*. Ann Arbor, MI: J. I. Press (Ardis).

Klein, K. (1964). Recent Soviet discussion on reform of Russian orthography. *Slavic and East European Journal, 3*, 54–61.

Kornev, A. N. & Chirkina, G. V. (2005). Современные тенденции в изучении дислексии удетей [Modern tendencies in research on dyslexia in children]. *Defectology, 1*, 89–93.

Kornev, A. N., Rakhlin, N. & Grigorenko, E. L. (2010). Dyslexia from a cross-linguistic and cross-cultural perspective: The case of Russian and Russia. *Learning Disabilities: A Contemporary Journal, 8*(1), 41–69.

Kornilov, S. A., Rakhlin, N. & Grigorenko, E. L. (2012). Morphology and developmental language disorders: New tools for Russian. *Psychology in Russia: State of the Art, 5*, 371–387.

Lightner, T. (1972). *Problems in the theory of phonology: Russian phonology and Turkish phonology*. Edmonton: Linguistic Research.

Mironov, B. (1991). The development of literacy in Russia and the USSR from the 10th to the 20th centuries. *History of Education Quarterly, 31*, 229–252.

Naples, A. J., Chang, J. T., Katz, L. & Grigorenko, E. L. (2009). Same or different? Insights into the etiology of phonological awareness and rapid naming. *Biological Psychology, 80*, 226–239.

Padgett, J. (2003). The emergence of contrastive palatalization in Russian. In E. Holt (Ed.), *Optimality theory and language change* (pp. 307–335). Dordrecht: Springer.

Pechko, K. (2009). Predicting reading achievement in a transparent orthography: Russian children learn to read. Doctoral dissertation, Temple University, PA: (3344384).

Prikhoda, N. (2013). *Факторы понимания прочитанного и правописания в русском языке* [Factors related to reading comprehension and spelling in Russian]. Paper presented at the student conference Lomonosov April 8–13, 2013, Moscow State University, Russia.

Rakhlin, N. (2003). Genitive of quantification in Russian: What morphology can tell us about syntax. Paper presented at the CONSOLE XI, University of Padua, Italy.

Rakhlin, N., Cardoso-Martins, C. & Grigorenko, E. L. (2014). Phonemic awareness is a more important predictor of orthographic coding than rapid serial naming: Evidence from Russian. *Scientific Studies of Reading, 18*(6), 395–414.

Rakhlin, N., Cardoso-Martins, C., Kornilov, S. A. & Grigorenko, E. L. (2013). Spelling well despite developmental language disorder: What makes it possible? *Annals of Dyslexia, 63*, 253–273.

Ravid, D. D. (2012). Morphological scaffolding in learning to spell: A cross-linguistic review. *Spelling morphology* (pp. 41–56). New York: Springer.

Russian Language Institute (2014). Institut russkogo iazyka im. V. V. Vinogradova RAN. Retrieved from www.ruslang.ru/agens.php.

Schenker, A. M. (1996). *The dawn of Slavic: An introduction to Slavic philology.* New Haven, CT: Yale University Press.

Stelmach, V. (1993). Reading in Russian: Findings of the Sociology of Reading and Librarianship section of the Russian State Library. *International Information and Library Review, 25*, 273–279.

Surrey Morphology Group (2009). Typology of defectiveness: Introduction. In G. Corbett, M. Baerman & D. Brown (Eds.), *Typology of defectiveness project.* Retrieved from www.defectiveness.surrey.ac.uk/index.html.

Szpyra, J. (1992). Ghost segments in nonlinear phonology – Polish Yers. *Language, 68*, 277–312. DOI:10.2307/416942.

Tiberius, C. (2014). Russian Language Report. *Surrey database of agreemement – Russian.* Retrieved from www.smg.surrey.ac.uk/Agreement/index.aspx, January 12, 2014.

Treiman, R., Zukowski, A. & Richmond-Welty, E. D. (1995). What happened to the "n" of sink? Children's spellings of final consonant clusters. *Cognition, 55*(1), 1–38.

Trubetzkoy, N. (1969). *Principles of phonology* (C. Baltaxe, Trans.). Berkeley: University of California Press.

17   Learning to Read Finnish

Mikko Aro

17.1   Introduction

17.1.1   Finnish Language and Its Orthography

From the point of view of reading acquisition, Finnish is in many respects an interesting contrast to major languages traditionally dominating reading research. It is regarded as one of the most transparent alphabetic orthographies (see Seymour, Aro & Erskine, 2003), being close to perfect in the consistency of its grapheme–phoneme (G–P) correspondences. On the other hand, the Finnish morphological system is complex, and due to the agglutinating and rich derivational system, words tend to be long. These features pose the beginning reader somewhat different challenges from those faced by readers aiming, for example, to master the challenges of English orthography.

Finnish is spoken as a first language by around 5 million speakers. Outside Finland, there are native Finnish-speaking minority groups in neighboring countries, most notably in Sweden, where Finnish has traditionally been spoken in the northeastern part of the country. Finnish does not belong to the Indo-European family. Instead, it is one of the Uralic languages, spoken by some 25 million people. The widest spoken Uralic languages are Hungarian, Finnish, and Estonian. Finnish and Estonian are major representatives of the Finno-Permic branch of Uralic languages, whereas Hungarian is more distantly related to the two, belonging to the Ugric branch of the Uralic language family.

17.1.2   Synchronic and Diachronic Characterization

The Finnish dialects are typically classified into western and eastern dialects. Western dialects have been influenced by Swedish and Estonian, whereas eastern dialects are more closely related to Carelian language and have loan words also from Russian. The first book in Finnish (*Abckiria*, a primer for reading and a catechism) was published in the 1540s by Mikael Agricola, a clergyman who is considered the founder of Finnish orthography. The work of Agricola was based on Latin, German, and Swedish influences. By that time,

Finnish was used as a spoken language mostly in colloquial contexts. Swedish was the language of administration (Finland was part of Sweden until 1809), German was relevant in commerce, and Latin was the language of religion. The early orthography was less regular than modern-day Finnish orthography, and spelling remained unestablished until the nineteenth century, when the orthography started to develop toward its modern form. The modern orthography was established by a revision of the Bible in the 1850s. The written language and its principles represent modern-day Standard Finnish, but more colloquial spoken language is used and accepted nowadays even in more formal communicative contexts.

Since its origins, the Finnish orthography has developed as a strictly phonemic system, so that present-day Finnish orthography is almost perfectly regular at the level of single phonemes/letters. As an interesting detail, the development of the orthography has also affected the spoken language. The voiced and unvoiced fricative sounds /ð/ and /θ/ were in the initial orthography marked in texts with ⟨d⟩ (or ⟨ts⟩ and ⟨tz⟩), respectively. By the nineteenth century, the fricative sounds had disappeared from spoken language, largely due to the effect of written language: People who were educated in Swedish interpreted and pronounced these graphemes as their Swedish versions (Campbell, 1998, pp. 73–74). Today, the fricative sounds can be heard only as rudiments in some rare dialects and, correspondingly, the /d/ sound is part of the phonological system of Standard Finnish, although not present in dialects.

17.1.3 Literacy and Schooling

Literacy is traditionally highly valued in Finland, and written language is ubiquitous. The foreign films in television and movies are subtitled, instead of being dubbed. The daily newspaper circulation is higher than in most industrial countries (United Nations Development Program, 2010). However, the parents typically do not instruct the children in reading before school age. The school entry age in Finland is comparatively late and takes place in the year the child turns 7 years old. Preschool year includes support for linguistic awareness and activities aimed at strengthening the motivation and readiness for literacy skills. The children are familiarized with most letters and letter names, but there is no formal literacy instruction before Grade 1. The reading instruction is based on synthetic phonics approaches and proceeds into phonemic assembly after the first letters are introduced. The phonemes and corresponding letters are taught in an order allowing reading of words, sentences, and short passages already at the early stages of instruction. During the first semester of Grade 1, practically all letters are introduced. Since phonemic assembly is practiced from the start, most children are able to decode independently at that point. The instruction methods typically explicitly emphasize the syllable as a sub-stage of decoding, and the early reading materials are syllabicated. The instruction in spelling starts at the same time as the instruction of reading; due to symmetrical regularity of the orthography, it is thought to support reading acquisition too. During Grade 2 there is still a strong instructional focus on reading and spelling skills. From Grade 3 on, the children are supposed to be able to use reading and spelling skills for independent learning, and the instructional focus shifts toward other areas. Part-time special education is offered with a low threshold for children who seem to be lagging behind their peers in the development of literacy skills. Roughly one-quarter of children from Grades 1–9 participate yearly in part-time special education, the focus being on the early grade levels. Reading problems are the most common justification for special educational support at Finnish schools.

17.2   Description of Finnish and Its Written Forms

Finnish shares some features typical for Uralic languages. It has an agglutinative morphological system with a large set of grammatical cases. There is no grammatical gender, nor articles or definite or indefinite forms. The main stress is always on the first syllable, and the secondary stress usually on odd syllables, so the speech rhythm is based on a two-syllabic foot. Although Finnish has been usually categorized as a syllable-based language, Finnish is often defined also as mora-timed, like Japanese. However, it seems that Finnish does not readily fall into any timing category, since there is no consistent isochrony and the length can vary in syllables, stresses, and morae alike.

17.2.1   Linguistic System

17.2.1.1 Phonology   There are eight vowel sounds altogether: back vowels /a/, /o/, /u/; front vowels /y/, /ä/, /ö/; and neutral vowels /i/, /e/. Finnish has front/back vowel harmony, which means that in (non-compound) words there can be either back or front vowels (+ neutral vowels) only. Vowel harmony also affects grammatical and derivational endings. Thus, the endings typically have two variants (e.g., inessive case ending *-ssa* or *-ssä*). There are thirteen native consonant sounds (/p, t, k, d, m, n, ŋ, r, l, s, h, j, v/). In addition, consonant sounds /f/, /b/, and /g/ are used in loan words, and they can be considered part of the phonological system. In colloquial spoken language, they are often replaced by corresponding unvoiced phonemes. Replacement of voiced plosives by unvoiced can be seen also in older loan words that have been adapted into Finnish (e.g., 'bank' → *pankki*). There are altogether sixteen diphthongs: *ai, au,* *ei, eu, ie, iu, oi, ou, ui, uo, yi, yö, äi, äy, öi, öy.* In Finnish the diphthongs are typically considered as combinations of two distinct vowel sounds.

All vowels have two phonemic lengths, short and long. Similarly, most consonants also have two phonemic lengths, with the exception of /v/, /d/, /h/, and /j/. The long consonant sounds occur only medially, whereas long vowel sounds can also be present in an initial or final position. The long phonemic quantity is articulated longer, or in the case of stop consonants, the explosion is held. The length distinction is lexical and grammatical, and the length of the vowel and consonant sounds is completely independent. So, words like ‹taka› [taka] 'behind', ‹takaa› [taka:] 'from behind', ‹takka› [tak:a] 'fireplace', ‹takkaa› [tak:a:] 'fireplace' + partitive case, ‹taakka› [ta:k:a] 'burden', or ‹taakkaa› [ta:k:a:] 'burden' + partitive case differ phonologically only with respect to phonemic quantity.

The syllable structure in Finnish is relatively simple. The nucleus is formed by one or two vowels, which can be preceded by an onset of one consonant, and followed by a coda of one or two consonants. Thus, there are ten different types of syllables altogether: V, VV, CV, VC, CVV, VVC, CVC, VCC, CVVC, and CVCC. Double vowel within a syllable can be either a long vowel or a diphthong. Between geminated consonants there is a syllable border. The native Finnish phonotactics do not allow initial clusters, but they do exist in recent loan words, like *traktori* or *stressi*, so loan words may have more complex syllables. Because of the foreign origin of the initial clusters, the pronunciation is often simplified in informal spoken language. In older loan words, only the last consonant of the cluster is maintained (e.g., Swedish *stall* 'a stable' – *talli*, and *frakt* 'a freight' – *rahti*).

Consonant gradation affects plosives (*p, t, k*) in Finnish. Gradation refers to alterations between *strong* and *weak* grades that are related to both morphosyntax and phonology. The gradation occurs in nouns before case suffixes, and in verbs before person agreement suffixes. The basic phonological rule covering gradation is that a closed syllable causes the weak form of the syllable-initial consonant. The consonant gradation is present as degemination in the case of double consonants (*kukka*/*kukan* 'a flower'/ + gen.); lenition in the case of single plosive consonant (*satu*/*sadut* 'a fairy tale'/ + plural); and assimilation to a preceding sonorant (*ranta*/*rannat* 'a beach'/ + plural).

17.2.1.2 Inflectional Morphology The morphology is relatively complex. Finnish is structurally considered synthetic and agglutinative. Nouns, adjectives, verbs, numerals, and pronouns are inflected depending on their grammatical role within the sentence. There are also a number of post- and prepositions, the latter being more infrequent. Words can have several agglutinated affixes, and thus the number of morphemes per word can be high (see Figure 17.1 for an example). Because grammatical relations are marked by endings, word order is less important in Finnish than, for example, Germanic languages.

istua – 'to sit'
istu**mme** – 'we sit'
istu**isimme** – 'we **would** sit'
ista**hta**isimmeko – 'Would we sit **(for a while)?'**
istahtaisimmeko**han** – '**(I wonder if)** we would sit (for a while)?'

Figure 17.1 Examples of inflectional and derivational affixation of the verb *istua* 'to sit'.

Nouns, adjectives, numerals, and pronouns can have fifteen cases expressed with inflections. With different combinations of case, plural marker, possessive suffixes, and clitics, a word can have over 2,000 different forms, of which around 150 are considered so-called core forms (Niemi, Laine & Tuominen, 1994; for an example see Karlsson, 1996). Verbs have even more, 12,000 to 18,000, word forms when the inflections for tense, mood, and person, as well as cliticisation is taken into account (Niemi et al., 1994). Affixation can also affect the stem, so there are also indications of fusionality within the morphological system. For example, the singular genitive form of the word *lammas* 'sheep' is *lampaan*.

17.2.1.3 Word Formation Processes   Finnish has a rich derivational system, and the use of various derivative suffixes is very common in word formation. As a commonly used example, a word *kirja* 'book' is a source for a number of derivatives: *kirjain* 'a letter of the alphabet', *kirje* 'a letter', *kirjoittaa* 'to write', *kirjailija* 'an author', *kirjasto* 'a library', *kirjallisuus* 'literacy', *kirjoitus* 'writing', *kirjasin* 'a font', just to name a few. Verbal suffixes are even more diverse. For example, a few derivations from the verb *istua* 'to sit' include *istuutua* 'to sit down', *istuttaa* 'to make someone sit', *istuskella* 'to sit idly', *istahtaa* 'to sit down for a short time', *istahdella* 'to sit down repeatedly', *istututtaa* 'to make some sit for a long time'. Compounding is also productive, and compounds can consist of a large number of morphemes: *mustaviinimarjamehupullo* 'a bottle of black currant juice' consists of root morphemes *musta* 'black' + *viini* 'wine' + *marja* 'berry' + *mehu* 'juice' + *pullo* 'bottle'. In sum, compound words and derivations are more common than words with just one morpheme. In vocabularies, compounds cover typically 60%–70% of all items, and derivations 20%–30% (Hakulinen et al., 2004).

17.2.2   Writing System

17.2.2.1 Script and Punctuation   The Finnish writing system uses the Swedish variant of the Latin alphabet, consisting of twenty-six letters of the Latin alphabet with the addition of ⟨å⟩, ⟨ä⟩, and ⟨ö⟩. The sound value of each letter corresponds to its value in the International Phonetic Alphabet, with minor discrepancies (for details see Karlsson, 2008). It is important to note that the dotted vowel letters ⟨ä⟩ and ⟨ö⟩ are regarded as individual letters, not umlauts as in German. Of all phonemes, only velar nasal sound /ŋ/ does not have a distinct corresponding grapheme; the short /ŋ/ sound is marked with ⟨n⟩ (it always precedes /k/ and could also be considered as an allophone). In some recent loan words, short /ŋ/ can also be marked with ⟨g⟩ (*magneetti, kognitiivinen*) or ⟨ng⟩ (*gangsteri, Englanti*). The geminated /ŋ/ is written with letter combination ⟨ng⟩. Letters ⟨c⟩, ⟨q⟩, ⟨x⟩, ⟨z⟩, ⟨w⟩, and ⟨å⟩ are used in citation loans only, and their pronunciation follows the language of the origin. Diacritics are not used in native Finnish words, and the two dots in letters ⟨ä⟩ and ⟨ö⟩ are not considered diacritic marks. The long phonemic quantity is systematically marked in written language by doubling the corresponding letter. Although long vowels and consonants are linguistically distinct phonemes, the principle of doubling the corresponding letter is an economical solution from the point of script. Correspondingly, long phonemes are typically thought of as "double sounds."

The conservative nature of the writing system is reflected in the fact that the spelling of loan words tends to adapt into the Finnish orthographic system (e.g., ⟨pizza⟩ ➔ ⟨pitsa⟩). However, the most recent loan words have maintained their original spelling (e.g., ⟨doping⟩, ⟨diesel⟩), and as the influence of foreign languages is increasing, it is plausible that such discrepancies will increase. Concerning punctuation, a couple of rules are worth mentioning. The spelling rule for consecutive same short vowel sounds in compound words is to separate them with a hyphen (e.g., ⟨ilta-aurinko⟩ 'evening sun'), and in inflected abbreviations a colon is used to separate the ending (e.g., ⟨EU:ssa⟩ 'in the EU').

17.2.2.2 Orthography   The Finnish orthography is based on a rather conservative phonemic principle: Each letter represents a single sound and each phoneme is represented with a single letter (see Table 17.1). To be more precise, this strict phonemic rule is applied within the boundaries of a single morpheme, since morphemes retain their spelling despite relatively frequent sandhi. So despite assimilation effects on morpheme boundaries (e.g., ⟨olenpa⟩ /olempa/ 'I am' + clitic), the spelling is not affected. Similarly, the gemination of morpheme-initial consonants that takes place under certain conditions (and is relatively frequent) is not marked in the written language. This gemination of morpheme-initial consonants can happen between morphemes in a single word (⟨meillekin⟩ – /meillek:in/ 'for us' + too), in compound words (⟨kaide-puu⟩ – /kaidep:uu/ 'railing'), or between words (⟨tule tänne⟩ – /tulet:änne/ 'come here').

Because of productive compounding, derivation, and agglutinative inflectional morphology, Finnish words tend to be long. Depending on the corpus, the average length of words in written language is between seven and eight letters (Pääkkönen, 1990). The number of monosyllabic words in Finnish is very low: there are only around fifty monosyllabic words altogether, and most of them are pronouns or interjections (Kyöstiö, 1980).

Table 17.1 *The basic grapheme–phoneme correspondences of Finnish*

	Phoneme	Grapheme	Phoneme
Vowels			
	/a/	a	/a/
	/o/	o	/o/
	/u/	u	/u/
	/y/	y	/y/
	/ä/	ä	/ä/
	/ö/	ö	/ö/
	/i/	i	/i/
	/e/	e	/e/
Consonants			
	/p/	p	/p/
	/t/	t	/t/
	/k/	k	/k/
	/d/	d	/d/
	/m/	m	/m/
	/n/	n	/n/
	/ŋ/	(short) n[+k]	
		(long) ng	
	/r/	r	/r/
	/l/	l	/l/
	/s/	s	/s/
	/h/	h	/h/
	/j/	j	/j/
	/v/	v	/v/
"Loan consonants"			
	/b/	b	/b/
	/f/	f	/f/
	/g/	g	/g/

Note. /ŋ/-sound is the only exception from the principle of marking the long sound with doubling the letter. In some recent loan words, the marking of ŋ-sound may vary from what is listed here (see text).

17.2.3   Conclusion

Finnish has a complex inflectional, agglutinative morphology, which is, how-ever, marked phonemically in the written text. Morphophonological variation, most notably vowel harmony and gradation, are similarly consistently repre-sented in the text. On morphemic level, Finnish orthography is almost perfectly transparent on the level of single letters and phonemes. The exceptions to this transparency are very few in native Finnish vocabulary, but some recent loan words have maintained their foreign spelling. From the point of view of reading acquisition, the bidirectionally regular G–P correspondences are easy to mas-ter, and phonemic assembly is straightforward without contextual effects.

The length of words poses a challenge for decoding, and during early reading instruction, decoding is typically instructed to be carried out syllable-by-syllable, which reduces the memory load of phonemic assembly and underlines the prosodic rhythm of the word. Another challenge of Finnish orthography is the length contrast that seems to require a second overlapping cycle of processing, especially in spelling (see Lehtonen & Bryant, 2004). In the case of stop consonants, the length might be especially difficult to discriminate for beginning spellers, since long sound is produced by holding the explosion. Thus, the length is not perceived as longer phonemic sound, but rather as longer articulatory process or longer silence before the explosion of the plosive.

17.3   Acquisition of Reading and Spelling in Finnish

During the last couple of decades, the research on reading acquisition has been the focus of many research groups in Finland. The Jyväskylä Longitudinal Study of Dyslexia (JLD; see Lyytinen et al., 2004), in particular, as a large follow-up of children at familial risk for dyslexia has increased knowledge on the development of literacy, as well as dyslexia in Finnish. In addition, a number of smaller-scale longitudinal studies have been carried out with the focus on development of linguistic awareness and literacy.

17.3.1   Becoming Linguistically Aware

17.3.1.1 Phonological Development and Phonological Awareness   Perhaps the most comprehensive study on the development of linguistic awareness in Finnish has been carried out by Silvén, Poskiparta, Niemi, and Voeten (2007). They followed the course of language acquisition from infancy to primary school with yearly assessments in order to investigate the precursors of word reading at first grade. They assessed vocabulary (1–3 years), mastery of inflectional forms (3–6 years), phonological awareness (3–7 years), and word reading (5–8 years). Their findings, based on structural modeling of continuity, showed a developmental sequence of language skills affecting successive stages of development, and reading at school age. Early vocabulary development was predictive of mastery of inflectional forms at age 3 and 4, which further predicted rhyming and alliteration skills at age 5. In sum, the early language development did not have direct effects on first-grade reading skill. Such effects were mediated by awareness of larger multiphonemic units at age 5, which in turn predicted word reading skill at first grade. Since phonemic awareness or syllabic awareness at age 5 was not predictive of later reading skill, this mediation effect was specific to rhyme and alliteration skills. In a model where phonemic awareness was assessed after 5 years of age (phoneme recognition at 6 years and phoneme blending at kindergarten) and reading skill at kindergarten were included, phoneme recognition skills at 6 years predicted emergent reading at kindergarten, which in turn was predictive of word reading skill at Grade 1 and explained 45% of variance in first-grade reading. Phoneme blending skill at kindergarten had no association with first-grade reading if emerging reading skill was controlled for. In sum, the findings showed that awareness of larger units precedes awareness of phonemes. Awareness of multiphonemic units at age 5 – before reading skills are present – is predictive of first-grade reading in Finnish, explaining 17% of the variance. On the other hand, kindergarten phonological awareness (PA) was not directly predictive of first-grade reading if concurrent reading skill – the best predictor of first-grade reading – was controlled for. As the authors note, this can be interpreted as reflecting the similarity of decoding and phonemic awareness tasks in Finnish, and the lack of a logographic reading stage in transparent orthography. Explicit phonemic awareness tasks seem to tap the same under-lying processes as reading.

In a study with the control group children of the JLD, Puolakanaho, Poikkeus, Ahonen, Tolvanen, and Lyytinen (2003) investigated early PA at the age of 3.5 years with four computerized tasks. The tasks required identifi-cation of given word- or syllable-level segments among three alternatives, blending of phonological units varying in size from words to phonemes, and ability to create a word starting with the given syllable. Structural modeling resulted in a model with two latent factors based on cognitive operations demanded by the tasks: identification skills and blending skills. The alternative models involving two factors based on the size of the units to be processed or a model with single latent factor did not receive support. However, the item-level analysis revealed a performance difference that was related to the unit size: The accuracy of performance decreased with the size of the unit, suggesting a developmental trend from larger to smaller units in the development of PA. In the blending task, the accuracy in word and syllable levels were relatively similar (74% and 68%), in contrast to the low accuracy in phoneme-level tasks (12%).

In another study comparing the JLD control group with children at familial risk for dyslexia at age 3.5 years with the same tasks, Puolakanaho, Poikkeus, Ahonen, Tolvanen, and Lyytinen (2004) showed that the proportion of children with low PA was about 2.5 times higher in the at-risk group than in the control group. The group difference was most pronounced in tasks requiring explicit phonological manipulation. The group difference remained after controlling for earlier (at 14 to 26 months of age) or concurrent language skills covering vocabulary, syntax, and morphology. In sum, the aforementioned studies by Puolakanaho and her colleagues suggest that phonological development in Finnish progresses from large units to smaller ones, and that awareness of the syllable as a sublexical unit is present early. This is understandable considering the role of syllables in prosody in Finnish. The studies also showed that early PA is specifically associated to familial risk for dyslexia. It is worthwhile to note that at the age of 3.5 years the median letter knowledge was only one letter. Hence, the findings concerning PA are not confounded with letter knowledge or precocious reading skills, which is relatively hard to achieve at later ages in a transparent orthography.

In a study by Holopainen, Ahonen, Tolvanen, and Lyytinen (2000), structural equation modeling was applied to uncover the relations of PA and emerging reading skills in preschoolers. The model where PA was a prerequisite for reading skill fitted the data slightly better than the alternative model showing the opposite direction of the effects, but both models were statistically accessible. The authors point out that the activation of orthographic forms is hard to avoid in the tasks tapping phonemic awareness in a transparent orthography. In their study, the mean letter knowledge was 16 out of 19 letters assessed, and the preschoolers consistently gave letter name responses in phoneme awareness tasks, which further underlines the issue. It should be pointed out that letter names consistently mark letter–sound values in Finnish: All letter names include the corresponding letter sound. Also, the follow-up study by Lerkkanen, Rasku-Puttonen, Aunola, and Nurmi (2004b) revealed a reciprocal relationship between phonemic awareness and reading performance during first grade.

17.3.1.2 Morphological Development and Morphological Awareness   Inflected forms are already used in the first utterances (Nieminen, 1991), but this is not considered to reflect cognitive morphological processing. According to a summary by Dasinger (1997), some frequent inflections are present in speech at the age of roughly 1.5 years. At this stage, the attention to structure of inflected words increases. Morphophonemic features like vowel harmony are rarely violated, although at this stage other inflectional errors are typical. The third year seems to mark the stage of increasing morphological awareness in Finnish children (Lyytinen & Lyytinen, 2004; Silvén, Ahtola & Niemi, 2003). After the third year, inflectional errors decrease, and the development toward full control of inflectional system continues until mid-childhood. As compared to development of phonological awareness, studies assessing the role of morphological awareness with regard to reading skills are few. In most studies morphological awareness has been measured with a test, where morphological skills are assessed as a skill of inflecting given pseudo-words according to the syntax of example sentences (Lyytinen, 1988). The inflections include elative case of nominals (from/out of), third person singular and plural inflections of past and present tense verbs, and comparative and superlative degrees of adjectives. In a study by Silvén et al. (2007), summarized earlier, these morphological skills at ages 3–4 predicted awareness of multiphonemic units at age 5, which mediated the effects on word reading later. The awareness of inflectional morphology seems to support the development of sensitivity to sound patterns within words. The findings of the JLD show also that awareness of inflectional morphology from 3 years onward predicts reading acquisition and is also related to familial risk for dyslexia (Lyytinen & Lyytinen, 2004). However, the relative roles of subcomponents of morphological skills with regard to reading acquisition remain largely unstudied, and the aforementioned relations concern inflectional morphology as a general skill, assessed with a rather limited set of inflectional types.

17.3.2 Development of Word Identification

17.3.2.1 Word Decoding Development In cross-linguistic comparisons of reading acquisition, Finnish children have performed close to ceiling level at word identification and decoding accuracy by the end of the first grade (Aro & Wimmer, 2003; Seymour et al., 2003). In Finnish studies assessing reading skills at school entry, 25%–50% of the children were found to be accurate decoders before any formal reading instruction (e.g., Aro, 2004; Lerkkanen et al., 2004b; Silvén et al., 2007). Since the knowledge of letter sounds and phonemic assembly suffice for accessing pronunciation of any written item, reading skill often seems to develop spontaneously with the support of preschool activities or siblings. Leppänen, Niemi, Aunola, and Nurmi (2004) have shown that although individual differences in reading accuracy grow larger during the preschool year, as the children with some mastery of reading develop faster in their skills, these individual differences largely disappear after reading instruction begins at Grade 1, and the nonreaders also gain decoding skills. This reflects nonlinear initial development of decoding skill in a transparent orthography and also efficacy of initial reading instruction in reducing early individual differences. In a follow-up of children entering Grade 1 (Aro, 2004), it was found that reading accuracy distribution is close to dichotomous at this stage, and nonreaders seem to make rapid developmental leaps into accurate decoding within a relatively short time period (see Figure 17.2). Typically, there is a ceiling effect in reading accuracy often by the end of Grade 1, and individual variation is manifested mostly in reading rate. The findings concerning early and rapid development toward accurate decoding are consistent in a number of follow-ups of early literacy skills (Holopainen, Ahonen & Lyytinen, 2001; Leppänen et al., 2004; Lerkkanen, Rasku-Puttonen, Aunola & Nurmi, 2004c; Silvén et al., 2007). There are no empirical indications of early whole-word processing during the development of reading acquisition. The early correlations between word and pseudoword reading accuracy are very high, close to .90 (e.g., Aro, 2004; Holopainen et al., 2000), which reflect the fact that early reading is based on decoding. At Grade

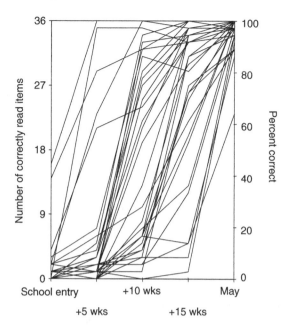

Figure 17.2 Reading accuracy development during Grade 1 in a group of children not reading at school entry. From *Learning to read: The effect of orthography* by M. Aro, 2004, Jyväskylä Studies in Education, Psychology and Social Research 237. University of Jyväskylä.

1, the lexicality effects in reading are relatively small (Seymour et al., 2003). At Grade 2, typical readers do not show reliable word length effects in word recognition, whereas poor readers do (Hautala, Aro, Eklund, Lerkkanen & Lyytinen, 2013). This implies development toward parallel processing in typical readers, although syllable structure had a small effect on naming and word recognition, suggesting presence of sublexical processing too.

In a longitudinal study of the very early phonological skills in a JLD-sample, Puolakanaho et al. (2007) found that a number of language skills (phonological awareness, rapid naming, short-term memory, expressive vocabulary, pseudoword repetition), measured at ages 3.5, 4.5, and 5.5 years, as well as familial risk for dyslexia, shared a large amount of variance and formed a common, developmentally stabile latent factor reflecting early phonological and language processing. Phonological awareness was the measure representing this latent factor most powerfully at all ages. Indeed, this factor accounted for half of the observed variation in reading and spelling accuracy at Grade 2 but was only weakly predictive of reading speed. Only with the inclusion of developing letter-naming skills was a moderate prediction of reading speed achieved in the model. In sum, these findings suggest that early language skills are strongly interrelated and seem to be predictive of reading accuracy in particular. In a study assessing the predictors of dyslexia status at Grade 2 in a JLD sample, Torppa, Lyytinen, Erskine, Eklund, and Lyytinen (2010) found that school-age dyslexia was predicted by poorer expressive speech at 1.5 years, smaller vocabulary at 2 years, shorter length of utterances at 2.5 years, and smaller vocabulary as well as poorer morphological skills at 3.5 to 5 years. In the same study, second-grade reading skills were directly predicted at 3.5 to 5 years by letter knowledge, rapid naming, morphological skills, and phonological sensitivity, the model accounting for 26% of the variance in the composite score of reading accuracy and fluency. To summarize the findings of JLD at different ages, the three most prominent predictors of reading acquisition seem to be letter knowledge, rapid naming, and phonological awareness, early letter knowledge being the most powerful predictor (Lyytinen, Erskine, Aro & Richardson, 2007).

A number of other studies have investigated the predictive value of phonological skills for later reading skills. Letter knowledge was also a strong predictor of word reading on a follow-up study by Lerkkanen et al. (2004c). Correspondingly, in a follow-up of preschool children, Lepola, Poskiparta, Laakkonen, and Niemi (2005) found that rapid naming, phonological awareness, and letter knowledge are all distinct predictors of beginning reading. Early letter knowledge predicted later phonological awareness before school age, and phonological awareness was a mediator for later reading skills. It was also found that the concurrent relationship of phonological awareness to word reading was rapidly strengthened after reading instruction. This was interpreted to reflect the close correspondence between decoding and phonemic awareness tasks in a transparent orthography. Also, Korkman, Barron-Linnankoski, and Lahti-Nuuttila (1999) observed a significant increase in phonemic awareness after the start of formal reading instruction. The same effect was not present on syllabic awareness.

Holopainen et al. (2001) applied preschool assessments of cognitive and linguistic skills in predicting the time required for reaching accuracy criteria of 90% in pseudoword reading at school age. Preschool phonological awareness reliably differentiated the group of children who reached this criterion at school entry, but it was not predictive of delayed development among the rest of the children. Again, rapid naming speed was predictive of reading speed at Grade 2. Of the longitudinal studies that have followed the development of reading skills past the early stages, Leppänen, Aunola, Niemi, and Nurmi (2008) found, again, that letter knowledge was the strongest predictor of reading skills at Grade 4. The predictive power of letter knowledge extends from the very early stages of decoding skill development to the phase where fluency of reading and reading comprehension are mastered. In Holopainen's (2002) follow-up, however, the only preschool measure still predictive for reading skills at Grade 4 was rapid naming speed, which was related to reading speed.

17.3.2.2 Word Spelling Development   At the very early stages of literacy acquisition, the development of reading and spelling seem to go hand in hand, reflecting the symmetrical transparency of the Finnish orthography. In a follow-up by Aro (2004), the intercept parameters of growth curve models of reading and writing accuracy correlated close to perfectly, showing that the emerging literacy is reflected in both reading and spelling skills. In an investigation of the developmental dynamics of these skills during the first grade, Lerkkanen, Rasku-Puttonen, Aunola, and Nurmi (2004a) concluded that both the development of reading performance and spelling is stabile, and they develop in a reciprocal manner. In a follow-up from preschool to the beginning of Grade 2, Leppänen, Niemi, Aunola, and Nurmi (2006) also found a recursive pattern of development in word and sentence reading accuracy and spelling. In their study, preschool phonological awareness predicted both reading and spelling skills at preschool but not after that, whereas early letter knowledge predicted later development in both skills. In sum, the symmetrical transparency of Finnish orthography does not seem to pose any general difficulties from the point of view of accurate spelling, and spelling accuracy typically goes hand in hand with reading accuracy.

However, one specific difficulty in spelling development seems to be the marking of long phonemic duration by doubling the corresponding letter. This is the most common type of error in early spelling (Lyytinen, Leinonen, Nikula, Aro & Leiwo, 1995). Lehtonen and Bryant (2004) investigated the spelling skills of children from Grades 1–3 in relation to awareness of phonemic quality and phonemic length assessed separately with an oddity task. They found length awareness to be more strongly related to spelling than quality awareness. It was related to spelling of long phonemes but also to general spelling skills, whereas phoneme quality awareness was not. The authors suggested that length awareness might be a partly distinct dimension of phonemic awareness that is especially relevant for developing spelling skills in Finnish. Length marking requires paying attention not only to phonemic quality (which sound?) but also to an additional phonemic feature (long or short?). Typical length-related error is to leave out one letter of the doublet. Further, there is no absolute acoustic sound duration for a long or short phoneme. Instead, the perception of long and short quantity is based also on the suprasegmental features of the word (Lehtonen, 1970). Therefore, it seems reasonable to conclude that phonemic length awareness reflects a more advanced phonological analysis skill, and thus, is more strongly related to spelling ability.

17.3.2.3 Reading and Spelling Difficulties   As has been shown in other transparent orthographies, in typical readers reading accuracy reaches a ceiling quite fast, and reading problems manifest mostly as problems in reading speed (see, e.g., Torppa et al., 2007). Therefore, reading accuracy has seldom been followed after the early stages of reading development, and the identification of reading problems is typically based on measures of reading efficiency: combined scores of reading speed and accuracy. In a recent study, Eklund, Torppa, Aro, Leppänen, and Lyytinen (2014) investigated the later reading development of children diagnosed with reading difficulties on the basis of reading speed, or reading and spelling accuracy at Grade 2 in the JLD. At Grade 2 the reading speed of reading disabled children was around 50% that of control children, and was 65% at Grade 3, and 75% at Grade 8, indicating a reading speed lag of 5 years at Grade 8. Reading accuracy also remained lower as compared to controls at all grade levels, but was still relatively high: in the word list reading task, it was 87.6% at Grade 2 (controls 94.5%), 90.0% at Grade 3 (controls 96.0%), and 97.3% (controls 99.5%) at Grade 8. According to the findings, reading speed was highly stabile over time: The correlations between reading speed scores at Grade 2 and 8 were .72. In reading and spelling accuracy, the corresponding correlations were .51 and .41, respectively. The comparisons between groups and reading tasks showed smaller performance differences between word and pseudoword reading in reading disabled children. This indicates longer developmental reliance on letter-by-letter decoding, or difficulties in using orthographic lexicon. In sum, the findings show that in this sample of children with familial dyslexia, the reading problems, especially with regard to reading speed, are persistent over time.

17.3.3   Reading Comprehension

17.3.3.1 Predictors of Reading Comprehension   Oral language comprehension (Lepola, Niemi, Kuikka & Hannula, 2005; Leppänen et al., 2008) as well as word reading skill (e.g., Lerkkanen et al., 2004c) have been shown to be strong predictors of reading comprehension. These findings are consistent with what is generally found in other orthographies. Lepola, Niemi, et al. (2005) noted that oral language comprehension skills (comprehension of spoken instructions and listening comprehension) explained 13%–24% of variance in the reading comprehension task (assessing literal and inferential comprehension of narrative and expository texts) on top of the effects of prior word reading ability, phonological awareness, and rapid naming. Further, their findings indicated that comprehension of spoken instructions and listening comprehension relate to distinct aspects of reading comprehension and suggested that comprehension of spoken instructions taps procedural working memory, and listening comprehension memory for prose. Interestingly, in the study by Leppänen et al. (2008), kindergarten letter knowledge predicted fourth-grade reading comprehension even after controlling for later reading skills (word and sentence reading accuracy, sentence comprehension) at the end of kindergarten or at Grade 1, whereas the effect of listening comprehension disappeared after taking into account the effects of later reading skills. The strong predictive role of letter knowledge could reflect the effect of the home literacy environment, or the possibility that letter knowledge in a transparent orthography taps more general linguistic ability, extending its influence more generally on literacy development.

17.3.3.2 Word-Level Effects in Comprehending Text   Whereas previous findings revealed the direct effects of word decoding and spoken language comprehension on reading comprehension, the effect of vocabulary on reading comprehension seems to be more indirect. Müller and Brady (2001) found that vocabulary knowledge shared only 3% of the variance with reading comprehension at Grade 1. However, in a study attempting to subtype the developmental paths of the JLD children during the first two school years, vocabulary skills were the most compromised early skills of the subgroup of poor comprehenders (Torppa et al., 2007).

In addition to linguistic skills, other factors such as task-focused behavior (Hirvonen, Georgiou, Lerkkanen, Aunola & Nurmi, 2010) and metacognitive awareness (Leppänen et al., 2008) have also been shown to be significant predictors of reading comprehension from preschool up to Grade 4. In their follow-up concerning the effects of motivational orientation on subsequent reading skills, Lepola, Niemi, et al. (2005) concluded that task orientation and social dependence orientation make unique contributions to reading skills from preschool onwards, even after controlling for prior linguistic skills. High social dependence orientation was especially detrimental for development of reading comprehension skills.

17.3.4   Conclusion

Phonological awareness in Finnish seems to develop from larger to smaller units. In particular, the development of small unit awareness in Finnish seems to be intertwined with letter learning and early reading skills, due to the regular orthography and one-to-one relationship between phonemes and letters. Morphological development and its relation to later reading development are yet far from clear, especially considering the complexity and versatility of Finnish morphology. Basic decoding and spelling skills develop rapidly and even children with reading disabilities reach relatively high accuracy allowing independent practice. The challenges in reading disabilities relate to persistent speed problems, which are amplified by long, inflected word items not suitable for whole-word recognition strategy.

17.4   Discussion

17.4.1   Challenges in Learning to Read Finnish

The symmetrical regularity of Finnish orthography is optimal for the beginning reader, since knowledge of basic letter–sound correspondences and the ability to assemble phonemes is sufficient for independent decoding of any written item. The early steps into reading seem relatively easy: A large proportion of children enter school as readers already, reading accuracy reaches a ceiling quite soon after reading instruction starts, and even the children developing slowest are, with very rare exceptions, able to decode independently after one or two school years. Problems in reading development manifest as problems in reading rate that can be as much of a handicap as poor accuracy for literacy development. Laborious and slow decoding skill is often detrimental to motivation in independent reading and creates challenges for school learning as well as for managing homework. The decoding problem is amplified by the long words caused by agglutinative morphology. Another specific challenge for learning Finnish orthography seems to be marking of length, which has been shown to be the single most frequent indicator of problems in spelling.

Whereas Finnish orthography is regular and easy to master, the morphological system is complex, with rich inflectional and derivational systems and productive compounding. Although spelling is phonemic, words can be multimorphemic and linguistically complex. There is relatively little data on the effects of morphological skills in reading development, and especially the specifics of morphological awareness development – perhaps partly due to the rich nature of Finnish morphology. The issue of morphology is especially interesting from the point of view of reading fluency development. The cognitive underpinnings of fluency development – or its problems – are relatively poorly understood at present. However, it seems plausible that morphological processing plays an important role in reading development after the initial skill of phonological recoding is achieved.

17.4.2   Implications for Instruction

From the point of view of reading instruction, it is interesting that letter knowledge seems to be the strongest predictor of reading development in Finnish. In the JLD, almost all the children who subsequently experienced difficulties in beginning reading had a delayed letter name learning curve, irrespective of whether they belonged to the at-risk or non-risk group (Torppa, Poikkeus, Laakso, Eklund & Lyytinen, 2006). As mentioned earlier, Finnish letter names always include the phonemic sound: Vowel names are identical to the long vowel sounds, and consonant names consist of the consonant sound and a vowel (e.g., /tee/, /koo/, /jii/, /äs/, /äm/). When orthography is transparent at the level of single letters, letter knowledge, phonemic awareness, and decoding are very closely intertwined skills. As children become familiar with letters, the letters make the phonemic structure of the words reliably visible. This is reflected in the fact that before being explicitly instructed on phonemes, children typically give letter name responses in phonemic awareness tasks and count long phonemes (marked with double letters) as two. In an orthography like Finnish, its seems that reading instruction is an especially strong intervention on phonemic awareness, which possibly explains why phonological awareness does not seem to be a very good indicator of persistent reading problems.

17.5   Final Conclusion

The Finnish orthography can perhaps be summarized as optimal for the beginning reader: Mastery of relatively few regular letter–grapheme correspondences and the ability of phonemic assembly are sufficient for independent reading. Further, the transparency of the orthography and the single letter-graphemes also support the development of basic decoding skills in children with compromised phonological skills. However, the complex morphology with long, agglutinated words in texts creates specific challenges for the efficiency of the system. The future challenges for reading research in Finnish concern especially the development of fluent reading. For this purpose there is a need for more fine-tuned knowledge of morphological development and its role in later reading development. From the practical point of view, the major challenge relates to the means for supporting reading fluency development and willingness to practice reading independently. It is probable that to reach this goal, in addition to cognitive and linguistic skills, there is a need to pay attention to a wider scope of factors, such as motivation, self-beliefs, or parenting and instructional styles (see, e.g., Kiuru et al., 2012).

References

Aro, M. (2004). *Learning to read: The effect of orthography.* Jyväskylä Studies in Education, Psychology and Social Research 237. University of Jyväskylä.

Aro, M. & Wimmer, H. (2003). Learning to read: English in comparison to six more regular orthographies. *Applied Psycholinguistics, 24,* 621–635.

Campbell, L. (1998). *Historical linguistics: An introduction.* Edinburgh University Press.

Dasinger, L. (1997). Issues in the acquisition of Estonian, Finnish, and Hungarian: A cross-linguistic comparison. In D. I. Slobin (Ed.), *The cross-linguistic study of language acquisition*, Vol. IV (pp. 1–86). Mahwah, NJ: Lawrence Erlbaum.

Eklund, K., Torppa, M., Aro, M., Leppänen, P. & Lyytinen, H. (2014). Literacy skill development of children with familial risk for dyslexia through Grades 2, 3, and 8. *Journal of Educational Psychology, 107*(1), 126–140.

Hakulinen, A., Vilkuna, M., Korhonen, R., Koivisto, V., Heinonen, T.-R. & Alho, I. (2004). *Iso Suomen kielioppi* [The extensive grammar of Finnish]. Helsinki: SKS.

Hautala, J., Aro, M., Eklund, K., Lerkkanen, M.-K. & Lyytinen, H. (2013). The role of letters and syllables in typical and dysfluent reading in a transparent orthography. *Reading and Writing, 26*, 845–864.

Hirvonen, R., Georgiou, G. K., Lerkkanen, M.-K., Aunola, K. & Nurmi, J.-E. (2010). Task-focused behaviour and literacy development: A reciprocal relationship. *Journal of Research in Reading, 33*, 302–319.

Holopainen, L. (2002). *Development in reading and reading-related skills: A follow-up study from preschool to the fourth grade*. Jyväskylä Studies in Education, Psychology and Social Research 200. University of Jyväskylä.

Holopainen, L., Ahonen, T. & Lyytinen, H. (2001). Predicting delay in reading achievement in a highly transparent language. *Journal of Learning Disabilities, 34*, 401–413.

Holopainen, L., Ahonen, T., Tolvanen, A. & Lyytinen, H. (2000). Two alternative ways to model the relation between reading accuracy and phonological awareness at preschool age. *Scientific Studies of Reading, 4*, 77–100.

Karlsson, F. (1996). *The word-forms of the Finnish noun kauppa "shop"*. Retrieved from www.ling.helsinki.fi/~fkarlsso/genkau2.html.

(2008). *Finnish: An essential grammar*, 2nd edn. London: Routledge.

Kiuru, N., Aunola, K., Torppa, M., Lerkkanen, M.-K., Poikkeus, A. M., Niemi, P., Viljaranta, J., Lyyra, A. L., Leskinen, E., Tolvanen, A. & Nurmi, J.-E. (2012). The role of parenting styles and teacher interactional styles in children's reading and spelling development. *Journal of School Psychology, 50*, 799–823.

Korkman, M., Barron-Linnankoski, S. & Lahti-Nuuttila, P. (1999). Effects of age and duration of reading instruction on the development of phonological awareness, rapid naming, and verbal memory span. *Developmental Neuropsychology, 16*, 415–431.

Kyöstiö, O. K. (1980). Is learning to read easy in a language in which the grapheme-phoneme correspondences are regular? In J. F. Kavanagh & R. I. Venezky (Eds.), *Orthography, reading and dyslexia* (pp. 35–49). Baltimore, MD: University Park Press.

Lehtonen, J. (1970). *Aspects of quantity in Standard Finnish*. University of Jyväskylä.

Lehtonen, A. & Bryant, P. (2004). Length awareness predicts spelling skills in Finnish. *Reading and Writing, 17*, 875–890.

Lepola, J., Niemi, P., Kuikka, M. & Hannula, M. M. (2005). Cognitive-linguistic skills and motivation as longitudinal predictors of reading and arithmetic achievement: A follow-up study from kindergarten to grade 2. *International Journal of Educational Research, 43*, 250–271.

Lepola, J., Poskiparta, E., Laakkonen, E. & Niemi, P. (2005). Development of and relationship between phonological and motivational processes and naming speed in predicting word recognition in grade 1. *Scientific Studies of Reading, 9*, 367–399.

Leppänen, U., Aunola, K., Niemi, P. & Nurmi, J.-E. (2008). Letter knowledge predicts grade 4 reading fluency and reading comprehension. *Learning and Instruction, 18*, 548–564.

Leppänen, U., Niemi, P., Aunola, K. & Nurmi, J.-E. (2004). Development of reading skills among preschool and primary school pupils. *Reading Research Quarterly, 39*, 72–93.

(2006). Development of reading and spelling Finnish from preschool to grade 1 and grade 2. *Scientific Studies of Reading, 10*, 3–30.

Lerkkanen, M.-K., Rasku-Puttonen, H., Aunola, K. & Nurmi, J.-E. (2004a). The developmental dynamics of literacy skills during the first grade. *Educational Psychology, 24*, 793–810.

(2004b). Developmental dynamics of phonemic awareness and reading performance during the first year of primary school. *Journal of Early Childhood Research, 2*, 139–156.

(2004c). Predicting reading performance during the first and the second year of primary school. *British Educational Research Journal, 30*, 67–92.

Lyytinen, H., Aro, M., Eklund, K., Erskine, J., Guttorm, T., Laakso, M. L., Leppänen, P. H., Lyytinen, P., Poikkeus, A. M. & Torppa, M. (2004). The development of children at familial risk for dyslexia: Birth to early school age. *Annals of Dyslexia, 54*, 184–220.

Lyytinen, H., Erskine, J., Aro, M. & Richardson, U. (2007). Reading and reading disorders. In E. Hoff & M. Shatz (Eds.), *Blackwell handbook of language development* (pp. 454–474). Oxford: Blackwell Publishing.

Lyytinen, H., Leinonen, S., Nikula, M., Aro, M. & Leiwo, M. (1995). In search of the core features of dyslexia: Observations concerning dyslexia in the highly orthographically regular Finnish language. In V. W. Berninger (Ed.), *The varieties of orthographic knowledge* (pp. 177–204). Dordrecht: Springer.

Lyytinen, P. (1988). *Morfologiatesti: Taivutusmuotojen hallinnan mittausmenetelmä lapsille* [The Morphology Test: A method for assessing children's mastery of inflectional forms]. Reports from the Department of Psychology 298. University of Jyväskylä.

Lyytinen, P. & Lyytinen, H. (2004). Growth and predictive relations of vocabulary and inflectional morphology in children with and without familial risk for dyslexia. *Applied Psycholinguistics, 25*, 397–411.

Müller, K. & Brady, S. (2001). Correlates of early reading performance in a transparent orthography. *Reading and Writing, 14*, 757–799.

Niemi, J., Laine, M. & Tuominen, J. (1994). Cognitive morphology in Finnish: Foundations of a new model. *Language and Cognitive Processes, 9*, 423–446.

Nieminen, P. (1991). *Äidin ja lapsen kommunikaatio ja lapsen kielen omaksuminen* [Communication of mother and child, and the language acquisition of the child]. Acta Universitatis Tamperensis Ser A, vol. 323. Tampere: Tampereen yliopisto.

Pääkkönen, M. (1990). *Grafeemit ja konteksti: Tilastotietoja suomen yleiskielen kirjaimistosta* [Graphemes and context: Statistical information of the Finnish alphabet]. Helsinki: SKS.

Puolakanaho, A., Ahonen, T., Aro, M., Eklund, K., Leppänen, P. H., Poikkeus, A. M., Tolvanen, A., Torppa, M. & Lyytinen, H. (2007). Very early phonological and language skills: Estimating individual risk of reading disability. *Journal of Child Psychology and Psychiatry, 48,* 923–931.

Puolakanaho, A., Poikkeus, A. M., Ahonen, T., Tolvanen, A. & Lyytinen, H. (2003). Assessment of three-and-a-half-year-old children's emerging phonological awareness in a computer animation context. *Journal of Learning Disabilities, 36,* 416–423.

—— (2004). Emerging phonological awareness differentiates children with and without familial risk for dyslexia after controlling for general language skills. *Annals of Dyslexia, 54,* 221–243.

Seymour, P. H. K., Aro, M. & Erskine, J. M. (2003). Foundation literacy acquisition in European orthographies. *British Journal of Psychology, 94,* 143–174.

Silvén, M., Ahtola, A. & Niemi, P. (2003). Early words, multiword utterances and maternal reading strategies as predictors of mastering word inflections in Finnish. *Journal of Child Language, 30,* 253–280.

Silvén, M., Poskiparta, E., Niemi, P. & Voeten, M. (2007). Precursors of reading skill from infancy to first grade in Finnish: Continuity and change in a highly inflected language. *Journal of Educational Psychology, 99,* 516–531.

Torppa, M., Lyytinen, P., Erskine, J., Eklund, K. & Lyytinen, H. (2010). Language development, literacy skills, and predictive connections to reading in Finnish children with and without familial risk for dyslexia. *Journal of Learning Disabilities, 43,* 308–321.

Torppa, M., Poikkeus, A. M., Laakso, M. L., Eklund, K. & Lyytinen, H. (2006). Predicting delayed letter knowledge development and its relation to grade 1 reading achievement among children with and without familial risk for dyslexia. *Developmental Psychology, 42,* 1128–1142.

Torppa, M., Tolvanen, A., Poikkeus, A. M., Eklund, K., Lerkkanen, M.-K., Leskinen, E. & Lyytinen, H. (2007). Reading development subtypes and their early characteristics. *Annals of Dyslexia, 57,* 3–32.

United Nations Development Program (2010). *Human development report.* New York: Author.

18 Learning to Read Turkish

Aydın Yücesan Durgunoğlu

18.1 Introduction

18.1.1 Turkish and Its Orthography

Turkish is a language spoken by about 80 million people worldwide, with about 70 million speakers in Turkey and the rest distributed in the Balkans, the Middle East, and through recent immigrations, in Europe. Turkish is classified as an Altaic language, with origins in Central Asia; hence, it is quite different from Indo-European and Semitic languages. The earliest written records are on Orkun memorials from the eighth century found in today's Mongolia. By the eleventh century, there was a westward expansion from Central Asia and tribes settling in Anatolia. Therefore, the closest relatives of Turkish are spoken in Azerbaijan and the Central Asian Republics (Turkmenistan, Uzbekistan, Kazakhstan, Kyrgyzstan, and Tajikistan).

18.1.2 Synchronic and Diachronic Characterization

A brief historical overview is useful in understanding how the language and its orthography have changed across the years. Following the adoption of Islam in the eleventh century, Turkish was influenced by Persian and Arabic, leading to the development of what is now called Ottoman Turkish. Ottoman Turkish was promoted by the Ottoman Palace during the Empire's reign between 1299 to 1918 as the language of the palace and the administration. Ottoman Turkish was written in Arabic script, and it heavily borrowed words from Arabic and Persian, though syntactically, the three languages were quite dissimilar. During this time, the rural areas and less-educated people continued to use the purer Turkish and a different body of literature developed (literally "people's literature" *halk edebiyatı*) that was distinct from the dense and opaque literature of the palace (literally "literature of the royal court" *divan edebiyatı*).

After World War I, the Ottoman Empire was dissolved and occupied. In Anatolia, under the leadership of Mustafa Kemal Atatürk, the Turkish Independence War was waged and consequently the modern Turkish Republic was founded in 1923. The creation of the new Republic was followed by a series of social reforms to establish the identity of the Republic. After considerable discussions among political leaders, journalists, writers, and educators, the Latin alphabet was adopted in 1928 (Kiliç, 1991). This was followed by the establishment of a National Language Academy in 1932, as part of the efforts to "purify" the language and reduce the impact of Persian, Arabic, and to some extent, French. It is important to mention that the reformist movements in the Ottoman Empire in the nineteenth century were influenced by the French, and borrowed their terminology.

It is not a coincidence that the new Turkish alphabet was developed to be quite systematic and transparent, mapping one sound to one letter for the most part. Although one of the goals of these language and alphabet initiatives was clearly to westernize the country, another goal was to quickly increase the literacy rates. In hindsight, current research supports the soundness of the decision to reform the alphabet, as transparent orthographies lead to rapid development of decoding and spelling, compared to opaque orthographies such as Arabic and Hebrew. The literacy rate, which was only 2.5% in 1923, reached 20.4% by 1935, according to the census. One can speculate that several factors, such as the sense of urgency to improve literacy levels across the new Republic using this new transparent alphabet and teaching reading in the regular spoken language of the people, must have contributed to the accelerated increase in literacy rates.

18.1.3   Literacy and Schooling

Turkey has a centralized policy for education. Across the country, there is a common curriculum and common textbooks for literacy instruction, as developed by the Ministry of Education, that are used in all schools. In 2005, the Ministry of Education implemented a new curriculum that progresses from sounds to syllables to words and sentences. The Ministry also identified the sequence of sounds that will be covered. Hence, there is explicit instruction to facilitate decoding.

In the Turkish educational system, there is also formal instruction on the morphological structure of the language, and building vocabulary through derivational and inflectional analysis. In language arts classes, the inflectional forms are explained thoroughly, for example the elementary education curriculum covers "five forms of nouns" (inflections of nouns) or the different conjugations of verbs. Despite the formal instruction on the morphological structure of the language and building vocabulary through derivational and inflectional analysis to facilitate comprehension, the wide variability in the home environments of the children cannot be ignored. Children come to school with highly diverse linguistic skills as a function of their home environment and early childhood experiences.

For example, Ural, Yuret, Ketrez, Koçbaş, and Küntay (2009) compiled a corpus of child-directed speech when two children were between 9 months to 2 years old. In the first family, the parents had an eighth-grade education, whereas in the other family, parents had doctoral degrees. Even though the total number of utterances were very similar in the two families, 32,362 versus 32,933, the family with the higher education and socioeconomic status (SES) had more child-directed utterances, 68% vs. 48%. In addition, the higher SES family had 170 different verbs, appearing ten or more times, whereas this number was 124 for the other family.

Aarts, Demir, and Vallen (2011) studied Turkish-speaking mothers and their 3-year-old children in the Netherlands. Mothers read a book and discussed a picture (in Turkish) with their child. Overall, factors such as lexical diversity, high-level abstraction, and complex syntactic structure in the mother–child conversations were positively correlated with maternal education and SES.

In another study, Aksu-Koç (2008) compared middle-class and working-class families in Turkey. There were significant differences between the two types of families in terms of parental education (e.g., twelve versus five years of education, for middle-class and working-class mothers, respectively). The children of the two groups of families showed significant differences in their production and comprehension of oral language. For example, children had word definition scores of 13 and 8, in middle- and working-class families, respectively.

18.2   Description of Turkish and Its Written Forms

The Turkish language has been influenced by the intermingling of cultures that occurred as the Turkic tribes moved westward from Asia, adopted Islam, and started establishing states, such as the Selçuk and later the Ottoman Empire. In addition to such historic developments, political forces and policies have shaped, and continue to shape, the oral and written language (Boeschoten, 1991).

18.2.1   Linguistic System

18.2.1.1 Phonology   The phoneme inventory of Turkish is summarized in Tables 18.1 and 18.2, in their orthographic form. In Turkish, syllables are the salient unit in phonology. They can occur in V, CV, VC, and CVC forms, but CV is the most common. Given their saliency and limited forms, it is very easy to break long words into syllables. Syllables can override morphological boundaries. For example, the word *top* 'ball' can take the dative form *topa* 'to the ball' by the addition of *-a*. It is syllabified as *to-pa*, rather than *top-a*, overriding the morphological boundaries.

Table 18.1 *The characteristics of Turkish vowels*

| | −back | | +back | |
	−round	+round	−round	+round
+high	i	ü	ı (undotted)	u
−high	e	ö	a	o

Table 18.2 *Turkish consonant inventory (using orthographic rather than phonetic symbols) (from van der Hulst and van de Weijer, 1991)*

	Labial	Labio-dental	Dental	Palato-alveolar	Palatal	Velar	Glottal
Voiceless stop	p		t	ç		k	
Voiced stop	b		d	c		g	
Voiceless fricative		f	s	ş			
Voiced fricative		v	z	j			
Nasal	m		n				
Liquid			l, r				
Approximant					y		h

Another important characteristic of the language is vowel harmony, which is a left-to-right process along syllables. Any of the eight vowels in Table 18.1 can appear in the first syllable of the word, but the vowels in the following syllables are conditioned by that first vowel, based on its front/back characteristics. For example, to make a noun plural, the inflection -*lar* or -*ler* is used. *Top* 'ball' is pluralized as *toplar*, but *tip* 'type' is pluralized as *tipler*. Likewise, the plural of *at* 'horse' is *atlar*, and the plural of *et* 'meat' is *etler*.

There are exceptions to vowel harmony that usually occur in borrowed words. For example, in the Arabic-origin word *kitap* 'book', the vowel harmony is violated. However, even if the two syllables of a word do not have vowel harmony, the suffixes that are added match the last vowel in the word, so plural of *kitap* is *kitaplar*, and not *kitapler.

18.2.1.2 Inflectional Morphology Turkish is a left-branching language (Kornfilt, 1990); i.e., governed elements precede the governors. For example, instead of prepositions, there are postpositions (*topa* – *top-a* 'to the ball'). One of the most important characteristics of Turkish is its very rich morphological system, accomplished predominantly via the use of suffixes. Borrowed words do have prefixes but in everyday language, especially among the younger generation, prefixed words appear to be used without a clear awareness of the existing prefix, e.g., *bihaber* 'non-knowledgeable', *hemfikir* 'co-idea', *hem-* and *bi-* originally being Persian prefixes.

As Hakkani-Tür, Oflazer, and Tür (2002) computed, the number of possible word formations obtained by adding three morphemes to a noun base can be as high as 4,825, whereas 11,313 formations can be derived from a single verb base when three morphemes are added.

In nouns, suffixes can mark voice, aspect, modality, mood, person, or number. For verbs, suffixes mark negation, tense, or person. The iterative loops of these suffixes can technically produce words of infinite length. For example:

> *kedi* 'cat'
> *kediler* 'cats'
> *kedilerde* 'on the cats'
> *kedilerdeki* '(that) on the cats'
> *kedilerdekiler* '(those) on the cats'
> *kedilerdekilerde* 'on (those) on the cats'

The suffixes follow a certain order of attachment: for example, in verbs the tense suffix comes before the person suffix (*gittim* 'I went' *git-ti-m* go+past tense+first person, and not **git-im-ti*). Hence, some probabilistic information on morphotactics is used by speakers to know which suffixes can follow each other, especially in iterative loops. As words get more inflected, the number of possible suffixes is considerably reduced. In a study with elementary schoolchildren, when children were asked to produce the correct suffix for nonwords, they tended to make the nonwords more complex by adding the plural and/or the possessive suffix, thus reducing the probability of possible suffixes, before they added the new suffix to the nonword. This, of course, made the word longer and orthographically more complex, but the overall length of the word did not hurt performance, since morphological complexity was reduced in these longer (non)words (Durgunoğlu, 2003).

Each suffix can have many phonological forms. In the simplest case, the plural suffix can take the form of *-ler* or *-lar*. Other suffixes, such as the past tense *-ti*, can take many forms (*ti, tı, tu, tü, di, dı, du, dü*), matching the root word in terms of both the final vowel's front/back nature and the voicing assimilation on the final consonant (Yavuz & Balcı, 2011).

The following examples illustrate both the vowel harmony and the voicing assimilation at work: git git**tim** 'I went'; gel gel**dim** 'I came'; öt öt**tüm** 'I crowed'; öl öl**düm** 'I died'; tut tut**tum** 'I caught'; ol ol**dum** 'I matured'; sat sat**tım** 'I sold'; kal kal**dım** 'I stayed'. The vowels in the past-tense suffix match the front/back nature of the root's vowel. In addition, the suffix is

Table 18.3 *Examples of derivational morphology of Turkish*

Derived	From nouns	From verbs	From adjectives
Nouns	*göz – gozlük*	*bil – bilgi*	*uzak – uzaklık*
	eye – eyeglasses	know – knowledge	distant – distance
Verbs	*toz – tozlan*	*ovmak – ovalamak*	*uzak – uzaklaş*
	dust – get dusty	scrub – scrub repeatedly	far – move afar
Adjectives	*toz – tozlu*	*bil – bilgiç*	*uzak – uzakça*
	dust – dusty	know – knowledgeable	far – somewhat far

voiceless (*-ti*) when the stem ends with an unvoiced consonant (*git*), but the suffix is voiced (*-di*) when the stem ends with a voiced consonant (*gel*). Finally, these verbs also illustrate the pro-drop nature of Turkish. The pronoun/noun can be dropped from a sentence because the verb ending includes the person information following the tense information: *git-ti-m* 'I went', whereas, *git-ti-k* 'we went'.

18.2.1.3 Word Formation Processes   Derivations are quite rich as well. Yavuz and Balcı (2011) report an example by Aksan listing a hundred derivations of a single stem *sür* 'drive'. There are suffixes creating nouns from other nouns, verbs, and adjectives; suffixes creating verbs from other verbs, nouns, adjectives, and adverbs; finally suffixes creating adjectives from nouns, verbs, and adjectives, as illustrated by some examples in Table 18.3.

In fact, during the language reforms in the early years of the Republic, the derivations were used extensively to enrich the Turkish lexicon. For example, *Uçak* 'airplane' was derived from the verb *uç* 'fly' to replace the Arabic form *tayyare*.

Some derivational suffixes also have multiple forms and they change according to the vowel of the stem For example, *-lük, -luk, -lik, -lık*, are phonological variations of the same suffix that can change a noun into a different noun. The vowel harmony applies to these derivational suffixes: *göz – gözlük* 'eye – eyeglasses'; *kitap – kitaplık* 'book – bookcase'.

Turkish has an SOV construction, but word order is flexible. Although there are five different word orders (SOV, SVO, OVS, OSV, and VSO) and the canonical SOV accounts for 48% of the cases, the least frequent (VSO) still occurs in 6% of the cases (Slobin & Bever, 1982). Contributing to the flexibility is the pro-drop, which leads to frequent subject omission, reported in 70% of transitive clauses in adult conversations (Demiral, Schlesewsky & Bornkessel-Schlesewsky, 2008). Moreover, of sentences beginning with a noun phrase (NP) in the METU-Sabancı Treebank adult corpus (Oflazer, Say, Hakkani-Tür & Tür, 2003), subject-initial

(52%) and object-initial (48%) sentences appear with approximately the same frequency. Thus, although the SOV order is very common in Turkish, the first NP can just as often be an object. Because the word order is flexible with subjects and objects in different locations, suffixes distinguish subjects and objects, as illustrated in the following example (with *adam* 'man'; *aslan* 'lion').

> *Adam aslanı yedi.* 'The man ate the lion.'
> *Adamı aslan yedi.* 'Lion ate the man.'

Rhetorically, the word immediately before the verb is the one that is stressed. In the first sentence, *Aslan adamı yedi*, Lion ate THE MAN, not another kind of food. In the second sentence, *Adamı aslan yedi*, LION ate the man, not another predator. Note that in both sentences, the subject (*aslan-Ø*) and object (*adam-ı*) are marked by the nature of the inflection, but the word order provides additional information, specifying shades of meaning. Readers and listeners need to pay close attention to word endings as well as how words are ordered, because the emphasis changes as a function of ordering of the words (Erguvanlı-Taylan, 1987) and consequently, this may place a bigger burden on memory during comprehension.

18.2.2   Writing System

18.2.2.1 Script and Punctuation   The Turkish alphabet has twenty-nine letters, eight vowels, twenty consonants; the twenty-first consonant ğ is not pronounced, but lengthens the vowel that precedes it. There are no consonant clusters at the beginning of words, with the exception of borrowed words (e.g., *tren* 'train'). However, consonant clusters such as *-nt*, *-ft*, *-rk* can occur at the ends of words (*kent* 'city'; *çift* 'pair'; *terk* 'leave').

18.2.2.2 Orthography   Because of its relatively recent history and deliberate choices made during the language reforms in 1920s, Turkish orthography is highly transparent. There is one-to-one mapping both from spelling-to-sound, as well as from sound-to-spelling. Despite this regularity, the silent letter ⟨ğ⟩, rounding of sounds in fast speech and in different dialects (*gidiyorum* pronounced as *gidiyom*), as well as voicing assimilation (*kitap – kitabı*) can be challenging and lead to spelling errors.

18.2.3   Conclusion

To summarize, there are several distinct properties in Turkish which are likely to affect how literacy development progresses. Phonologically, the syllable structure is strong and well-defined, making it easy to identify syllable boundaries. Vowel harmony and voicing assimilation in oral language necessitate even young children to notice differences among phonemes. Morphologically, it is very complex, and since the rich suffixation carries most of the meaning, listeners and readers have to pay special attention to word endings. This includes paying attention to how the suffixes can be ordered and which sequences are allowed in iterative loops.

18.3   Acquisition of Reading and Spelling in Turkish

In Turkish, several factors can be assumed to provide a challenge for beginning reading and spelling. Because of the complex morphology, long and multi-syllabic words are quite common, providing a possible obstacle for beginning readers. In addition, the phonological variation in suffixes can be expected to be difficult for spellers. However, the seemingly effortless acquisition of vowel harmony and suffixation systems in oral language may show its positive effects in written language. In addition, the transparent and systematic orthography can also be expected to make decoding and spelling easier for beginning readers.

18.3.1   Becoming Linguistically Aware

18.3.1.1 Phonological Development and Phonological Awareness   Turkish speakers need to continuously monitor and manipulate subword linguistic units in order to articulate and comprehend morphologically complex structures. Even young children do this very well, as evidenced by the lack of vowel harmony or voicing assimilation errors in their speech (Aksu-Koç & Slobin, 1985; Verhoeven, 1991). It can be predicted that phonological awareness will develop rapidly in Turkish prior to literacy, especially when tasks require the manipulation of syllables and word-final phonemes. This is expected due to the saliency of the syllables, the need to pay attention to subtle changes in word endings and to consider the phonemes of the variable suffixes when producing complex morphological structures. In fact, studies have shown these predictions to be true. On identical pseudowords, Turkish-speaking children performed better on both syllable and final phoneme manipulations compared to English-speaking children (Durgunoğlu & Öney, 1999).

Across several studies (Babayiğit & Stainthorp, 2007, 2011; Durgunoğlu & Öney, 1999; Öney & Durgunoğlu, 1997), a clear pattern emerges as to how phonological awareness develops in Turkish across grades. Since the materials are not equivalent across the studies, this discussion is for illustrative purposes rather than actual numerical comparisons. Syllable tapping is accurate even in preschoolers and reaches high levels in a year or so. Phoneme deletion is more challenging and preschoolers are not able to do that task. However, by kindergarten, final phoneme deletion shows considerable progress and reaches ceiling levels in Grades 1 and 2. Initial phoneme deletion is more difficult and grows more slowly, but that too reaches ceiling levels in early elementary years.

In a cross-sectional study, Acarlar, Ege, and Turan (2002) gave identical test items to children between the ages of 3 and 8. Children who were 7 and 8 had started school and were in Grades 1 and 2, respectively. These researchers demonstrated that isolating a syllable in a word is relatively easy for Turkish-speaking children and even 3-year-olds achieve 83% success. Older children perform at 100% accuracy. Counterintuitively, isolating meaningful words in a sentence is a more difficult task despite the help of vocabulary in that task. Young children had only about 36% accuracy, which rose to about 62% accuracy for 5- to 6-year-olds, and finally reached about 92% accuracy for children who had started school. Memory load differences cannot be the sole reason for the poorer performance in the word isolation task because although the sentences consisted of two to five words in the word isolation task, the syllable isolation task consisted of words with two to four syllables. These data further support the assertion that the syllable is a quite salient unit in Turkish.

Another interesting result is that isolating phonemes is a skill that develops after literacy instruction starts. Despite high levels of performance on other phonological tasks, phoneme isolation was a very difficult task for 3- to 6-year-olds, that is, before literacy instruction started. The performance levels were around 0%. Once children started school, their phonemic isolation skill developed rapidly, reaching 73% and 93% in Grades 1 and 2, respectively. These results replicate the previous patterns across studies reported above.

18.3.1.2 Morphological Development and Morphological Awareness In a longitudinal syntactic bootstrapping study, Ural and colleagues (2009) analyzed the speech directed at two young girls, starting when the children were about 9 months old and ending when they were about 2 years old. The two girls had parents with different educational backgrounds; one set of parents had an eighth-grade education, the other parents had doctoral degrees. Across the two speech samples, however, similar cues were present about syntactic information. For example, as is the case for English, the number of nominals surrounding a word was a reliable cue for determining verb categories such as transitive versus intransitive. However, in classifying the Turkish verb types, morphological cues were more reliable than the number of nouns. This implies that in morphologically rich languages, the role of morphology in providing clues to syntactic categories should not be overlooked. For such languages, word order is still useful, especially if the morphological cues are sparse, but word order seems to play a smaller role in morphologically rich languages such as Turkish as compared to English.

Evidence on the role of morphological information comes from an eye movement study (Candan et al., 2012). Children's eye movements were studied as they were listening to a test sentence (horse pushed a bird). The auditory stimulus was accompanied by two scenes, with one scene matching the auditory stimulus (horse pushing the bird) and the other scene mismatching the auditory stimulus (bird pushing the horse), as enacted by people in costumes. The sentences were transitive and no case markings were present on the nouns. In Turkish this leads to the object of the sentence being interpreted as a generic noun, similar to one that would have an indefinite article in English: *At kuş itti* 'Horse pushed *a* bird'. Since morphological information that usually signals the object was not provided, and only word order was available as a cue, Turkish-speaking children struggled a bit but could still use the first noun as the subject in the canonical SVO order when the important morphological cues were absent.

In short, morphological cues provide strong syntactic information even in the speech directed to very young children, and it is reasonable to expect morphological awareness to develop rapidly. Supporting this prediction, Aksu-Koç and Slobin (1985) documented that in Turkish-speaking children, by 24 months of age, noun inflections are mastered and most verb inflections are also present in their speech. The accusative is the first nominal inflection and the past tense is the first verbal inflection that appears. One complex structure that presents a problem is relativization. In Turkish, verbs change form and become nominalized while embedding one clause within another, as in the example *Çocuk top oynuyordu. Çocuk gitti.* ➔ *Top oynayan çocuk gitti.* 'The boy was playing ball. The boy left ➔ The boy who was playing ball left.' The verb *oynuyordu* is nominalized as *oynayan*.

Children also have a keen sense of morphosyntactic probabilities. For example, even young children do not make errors in the sequence of inflections (Ekmekçi, 1979, as cited in Verhoeven, 1991). As a Turkish word is more and more inflected, the number of possible suffixes that can be used at that point declines. A word in its nominal form (e.g., *kitap* 'book') can take 139 suffixes, but when it is pluralized (*kitaplar* 'books') the possible number of suffixes is reduced to 69. Finally, when a word is plural and also has the possessive suffix (*kitaplarimiz* 'our books'), the number of possibilities now drops to 9. In a study, children in Grades 2 and 4 were asked to provide the correct suffixes for an imaginary animal name in the story. Children tended to make the word more complex by first adding a plural and/or possessive suffix to the nonword before choosing the correct suffix despite the fact that the new nonword was orthographically longer (Durgunoğlu, 2003).

Babayiğit and Stainthorp (2010) measured morphological awareness by a similar nonword task where a pseudoword representing a fictional animal was used in a sentence with a wrong suffix. Grade 1 children judged the grammaticality of the sentence and in the second part, corrected the suffix. In a separate syntactic awareness task, the children were also asked to unscramble sentences. Because the SOV positions can be flexible in Turkish, the unscrambling task required children to move adverbs and adjectives to their correct position, rather than moving S, V, or O. Babayiğit and Stainthorp (2010) found both morphological and syntactic awareness were correlated with each other as well as with phonological awareness, indicating the close relationships between phonological and morphological knowledge in these Grade 1 children.

18.3.2 Development of Word Identification

18.3.2.1 Word Decoding Development
In Turkish, word and nonword recognition accuracies are very strongly correlated, providing further evidence of the regularity of the orthography, and the use of similar strategies for both types of items. In addition, there are strong autoregressor effects. The strongest predictors of Time 2 decoding accuracy levels are Time 1 decoding accuracy levels, indicating a relatively stable and consistent developmental pattern. As is true in many other languages, phonological awareness is significantly related to decoding in Turkish as well (Babayiğit & Stainthorp, 2007, 2010, 2011; Durgunoğlu & Öney, 1999; Öney & Durgunoğlu, 1997).

Because of the systematic orthography and advanced phonological awareness of words and syllables, it is expected that word identification will develop rapidly in young readers. That is precisely the pattern across several studies. Children with word and nonword accuracy levels of 15%–20% in kindergarten and beginning of first grade reach 100% accuracy by the end of first grade (Durgunoğlu & Öney, 1999; Öney & Durgunoğlu, 1997). Babayiğit and Stainthorp (2011) reported that even with morphologically complex words that may contain one to five suffixes and up to seven syllables (e.g., a single word with three suffixes and five syllables: *ormandakiler* 'those in the forest'), decoding accuracy was quite high. Because decoding accuracy reaches ceiling levels quickly, it does not correlate with reading comprehension very strongly. Therefore, fluency may be a better indicator of decoding proficiencies of Turkish readers than accuracy. Measuring the number of items read in one minute, Babayiğit and Stainthorp (2011) saw an increase from 13 to 26 words per minute from Grade 1 to Grade 2, reaching 40 words per minute by Grade 4.

In a thorough longitudinal study, Babayiğit and Stainthorp (2011) followed 109 Grade 2 and Grade 4 children for a year and gave them a battery of tests to assess the predictors of word recognition, spelling, reading comprehension, and narrative writing performance. The battery included measures of working memory, rapid automatized naming (RAN), phonological awareness, listening comprehension, and vocabulary. When predictors of decoding fluency were analyzed, the predictors observed in other languages appeared in Turkish as well.

In examining the predictors of children's Time 2 reading fluency 9 months later, age, IQ, vocabulary, RAN, and Time 1 fluency were entered in to the structural equation. The strongest predictor was fluency during Time 1. In the final equation, Time 1 fluency predicted 90% of Time 2 fluency, indicating consistent fluency levels across time. When the facilitators of this dominant predictor, Time 1 fluency, were examined, both phonological awareness and RAN together explained the outcome, although RAN was a stronger predictor.

18.3.2.2 Word Spelling Development Rapid growth in spelling, words, and nonwords are also observed in young children. Öney and Durgunoğlu (1997) noted that spelling accuracy improved from 20% to 93% from the beginning to the end of the year in Grade 1. Compared to word identification, spelling is a more difficult process as it requires production of a pattern. Babayiğit and Stainthorp (2011) used the same predictors (working memory, RAN, phonological awareness, listening comprehension, and vocabulary) to assess spelling. For Time 2 spelling performance, Time 1 spelling proficiency was a significant predictor, but the autoregressor effect of earlier spelling skills on later levels was not as strong as the effect found for word recognition. Of course, spelling requires a precise representation of the orthographic pattern, and this precision seems to be still developing and is not as heavily influenced by existing Time 1 proficiency, as was the case in word recognition. In addition to its indirect influence via Time 1 spelling, phonological awareness continued to be a predictor of Time 2 spelling. Finally RAN also predicted Time 1 spelling, but to a lesser degree than phonological awareness.

Similar patterns are found with adult beginning readers. We have developed an adult literacy program in Turkey for adults with no or minimal schooling, and low levels of literacy. The Functional Adult Literacy Program, implemented since 1995, has now reached almost 200,000 adults (Durgunoğlu, Öney & Kuşcul, 2003). In one study, we analyzed adult literacy development after 90 hours of instruction. In that study, the word recognition and spelling levels at the beginning of the course were the main predictors of later outcomes, as is the case for children. In addition, replicating the pattern with children, phonological awareness was a significant predictor of both word recognition and spelling of these adults (RAN was not assessed in that study).

18.3.2.3 Reading and Spelling Difficulties Because there is stability in reading and spelling scores across time (Babayiğit & Stainthorp, 2010; Durgunoğlu & Öney, 1999), it indicates that children who struggle with word recognition and spelling tend to remain at the same levels compared to their peers. As could be expected in a transparent orthography, studies have not found vocabulary to be a significant predictor of word recognition or spelling (Babayiğit & Stainthorp, 2010, 2011). It must be noted, however, that there is still a word frequency effect in Turkish, even with experienced adult readers (Raman & Baluch, 2001), so decoding is not purely a grapheme–phoneme conversion process. We need more studies to illustrate which other aspects of decoding, such as an understanding of phonotactic probabilities, orthographic pattern frequencies, are related to decoding proficiencies in this transparent orthography.

18.3.3   Reading Comprehension

18.3.3.1 Predictors of Reading Comprehension   In many languages, including English, the trend across grades is for decoding to lose its influence, and listening comprehension to become a stronger predictor of reading comprehension (e.g., Catts, Hogan & Adlof, 2005; Verhoeven & van Leeuwe, 2008). For example, by Grade 8, listening comprehension rather than decoding is the main predictor of English reading comprehension. One possible reason for this development is that with age and experience, decoding becomes automatic and reaches ceiling levels. Another reason is that as texts themselves become more complex over time, vocabulary skills gain importance (e.g., Cain, Oakhill & Bryant, 2004). As an example from a different population, children from diverse linguistic backgrounds tend to reach the decoding levels of their monolingual peers, but their under-developed vocabulary is more likely to compromise their reading comprehension. Indeed, several studies have found vocabulary skills to be a particularly important predictor for bilinguals' reading comprehension (Mancilla-Martinez & Lesaux, 2011; Proctor, Carlo, August & Snow, 2005).

In transparent orthographies, with rapid progress in decoding, it can be assumed that the predictive power of word recognition on reading comprehension will weaken much earlier, and listening comprehension will be the dominant factor (Joshi, Tao, Aaron & Quiroz, 2012). In fact, in Turkish, even during first grade, reading comprehension proficiency at the end of the school year is predicted by listening comprehension skills at the beginning of the year rather than decoding skills in mid-year (Öney & Durgunoğlu, 1997).

Babayiğit and Stainthorp (2011) analyzed predictors of Turkish reading comprehension at Time 2 (9 months later) as a function of age, Time 1 reading comprehension, IQ, vocabulary, listening comprehension, working memory and reading fluency. As would be expected, Time 1 reading comprehension was the strongest predictor of Time 2 reading comprehension. In addition, children's age mattered (some were in third and some were in fifth grade). More importantly, reading fluency had no impact on reading comprehension, but listening comprehension did. Even when reading comprehension at Time 1 was analyzed, it was predicted by vocabulary and listening comprehension, but not by reading fluency. Overall, listening comprehension had both a direct effect on

Time 2 reading comprehension and an indirect effect through Time 1 reading comprehension.

18.3.3.2 Word-Level Effects in Comprehending Text   There is a growing body of evidence suggesting that comprehension strategies generalize across different modalities (Kim, Wagner & Lopez, 2012; Lepola, Lynch, Laakkonen, Silvén & Niemi, 2012; Potocki, Ecalle & Magnan, 2013). For example, there is an overlap in proficiencies when children read a story, listen to it, or watch its video (Kendeou, Bohn-Gettler, White & Van den Broek, 2008; Kendeou et al., 2005). These results indicate that higher order comprehension processes such as inferencing, metacognitive control, and precise but flexible representations of word meanings (i.e., good lexical quality; Perfetti, 2007) contribute to both listening and reading comprehension. In sum, comprehension strategies used to understand materials presented in oral or written form greatly overlap, especially once the decoding hurdle that only affects reading comprehension is overcome (for a review see Durgunoğlu, 2009). In Turkish, we are missing in-depth studies of vocabulary, morphological analyses, metacognition, and reading comprehension to illustrate the increasing role of these factors in literacy development.

18.3.4   Conclusion

In transparent orthographies, including Turkish, decoding develops rapidly. Therefore, reading comprehension seems to be more affected by language comprehension skills rather than decoding fluency. However, more research is needed to understand the specific impact of linguistic knowledge and vocabulary on Turkish reading comprehension.

18.4   Discussion

18.4.1   Challenges in Learning to Read Turkish

Although more research is needed, one can speculate that linguistic comprehension and vocabulary – regardless of modality – are key factors to consider in reading comprehension in transparent orthographies, since decoding does not seem to be the bottleneck. In Turkish, another factor to consider is morphological awareness and understanding the subtle changes in meaning as a result of the suffixes. Although beginning readers can decode long words relatively rapidly, there is not much research on how these complex words are comprehended. Another understudied topic is the comprehension of complex sentential structures and embedded clauses that are found in academic texts. Since relativization is a source of difficulty in language acquisition, the comprehension of embedded clauses may prove to be challenging for Turkish readers. However, this prediction also awaits further research.

18.4.2 Implications for Instruction

The overlap between vocabulary, listening, and reading comprehension can be expected to appear earlier in a language like Turkish because comprehension strategies used to understand materials presented in oral or written form are very similar, especially once the decoding is mastered. This situation is analogous to the profile of *poor comprehenders* of English. English poor comprehenders (older readers) are proficient decoders but have difficulties with *both* listening and reading comprehension (e.g., Cain & Oakhill, 2007).

One can also speculate that these poor comprehenders may be more likely to come from disadvantaged backgrounds where the level of support for literacy in the home may be weak. We can expect to find strong effects of SES in a transparent orthography because more of the variability in children's literacy development will be predicted by their language comprehension, background knowledge, and higher-order cognitive strategies, rather than basic decoding proficiencies. This is a topic that awaits further systematic research. With such poor comprehenders, emphasis on developing language comprehension and vocabulary can be expected to have a big impact on reading comprehension. This awaits more intervention research with Turkish poor comprehenders, both at home and in school.

18.5 Final Conclusion

Literacy development in Turkish reflects the characteristics of the language quite clearly. Because of vowel harmony, consonant assimilation, and complex suffixation, from a very young age, children learn to pay attention to the phonological structure of language, especially to word endings. This focus enables phonological awareness to develop rapidly. In addition, the Turkish alphabet has very systematic spelling–sound mappings. The transparent orthography and rapidly developing phonological awareness enable decoding to progress smoothly and reach high levels of proficiency within the first year of schooling. Therefore, in Turkish literacy development, vocabulary and listening comprehension skills exert their influence on reading comprehension at an earlier stage. Instructionally, once the basics of decoding are in place, greater emphasis on vocabulary and linguistic development, especially for those from disadvantaged backgrounds, can be expected to be quite effective in improving reading comprehension.

References

Aarts, R., Demir, S. & Vallen, T. (2011). Characteristics of academic language register occurring in caretaker-child interaction: Development and validation of a coding scheme. *Language Learning, 61*, 1173–1221.

Acarlar, A., Ege, P. & Turan, F. (2002). Türk çocuklarinda üstdil becerilerinin gelişimi ve okuma ile ilişkisi [Development of metalinguistic abilities and its relationship with reading in Turkish children]. *Türk Psikoloji Dergisi, 17*(50), 63–73.

Aksu-Koç, A. (2008). Bilişsel gelişim ve dil gelişim [Cognitive and linguistic development]. Presentation at Mother Child Education Foundation, Istanbul, Turkey.

Aksu-Koç, A. A. & Slobin, D. I. (1985). The acquisition of Turkish. In D. I. Slobin (Ed.), *The crosslinguistic study of language acquisition*, Vol. I (pp. 839–880). Hillsdale, NJ: Lawrence Erlbaum.

Babayiğit, S. & Stainthorp, R. (2007). Preliterate phonological awareness and early literacy skills in Turkish. *Journal of Research in Reading, 30*, 394–413.

(2010). Component processes of early reading, spelling, and narrative writing skills in Turkish: A longitudinal study. *Reading and Writing, 23*, 539–568.

(2011). Modeling the relationships between cognitive–linguistic skills and literacy skills: New insights from a transparent orthography. *Journal of Educational Psychology, 103*, 169–189.

Boeschoten, H. (1991). Aspects of language variation. In H. Boeschoten & L. Verhoeven (Eds.), *Turkish linguistics today* (pp. 150–176). Leiden: E. J. Brill.

Cain, K. & Oakhill, J. (2007). Reading comprehension difficulties: Correlates, causes, and consequences. In K. Cain & J. Oakhill (Eds.), *Children's comprehension problems in oral and written language: A cognitive perspective* (pp. 41–75). New York: Guilford Press.

Cain, K., Oakhill, J. & Bryant, P. (2004). Children's reading comprehension ability: Concurrent prediction by working memory, verbal ability, and component skills. *Journal of Educational Psychology, 96*, 31–42.

Candan, A., Küntay, A., Yeh, Y. C., Gheung, H., Wagnerd, L. & Naigles, L. (2012). Language and age effects in children's processing of word order. *Cognitive Development, 27*, 205–221.

Catts, H. W., Hogan, T. P. & Adlof, S. M. (2005). Developmental changes in reading and reading disabilities. In H. Catts & A. Kamhi (Eds.), *The connections between language and reading disabilities* (pp. 25–40). Mahwah, NJ: Lawrence Erlbaum.

Demiral, Ş. B., Schlesewsky, M. & Bornkessel-Schlesewsky, I. (2008). On the universality of language comprehension strategies: Evidence from Turkish. *Cognition, 106*, 484–500. DOI:10.1016/j.cognition.2007.01.008.

Durgunoğlu, A. Y. (2003). Recognizing morphologically complex words in Turkish. In E. Assink & D. Sandra (Eds.), *Reading complex words: Cross-language studies* (pp. 81–92). New York: Kluwer Academic Publishers.

(2009). *The impact of L1 oral proficiency on L2 (reading) comprehension.* Commissioned paper for the US National Academy of Sciences oral language task force.

Durgunoğlu, A. Y. & Öney, B. (1999). A cross-linguistic comparison of phonological awareness and word recognition. *Reading and Writing, 11*, 281–299.

Durgunoğlu, A. Y., Öney, B. & Kuşcul, H. (2003). Development and evaluation of an adult literacy program in Turkey. *International Journal of Educational Development, 23*, 17–36.

Erguvanlı-Taylan, E. (1987). The role of semantic features in Turkish word order. *Folia Linguistica, 21*, 215–228.

Hakkani-Tür, D., Oflazer, K. & Tür, G. (2002). Statistical morphological disambiguation for agglutinative languages. *Computers and the Humanities, 36*, 381–410.

Joshi, R. M., Tao, S., Aaron, P. G. & Quiroz, B. (2012). Cognitive component of componential model of reading applied to different orthographies. *Journal of Learning Disabilities, 45*, 480–486.

Kendeou, P., Bohn-Gettler, C., White, M. J. & van den Broek, P. (2008). Children's inference generation across different media. *Journal of Research in Reading, 31*, 259–272.

Kendeou, P., Lynch, J. S., van den Broek, P., Espin, C. A., White, M. J. & Kremer, K. E. (2005). Developing successful readers: Building early comprehension skills through television viewing and listening. *Early Childhood Education Journal, 33*, 91–98.

Kiliç, S. (1991). Türkiye de latin harfleri meselesi (1908–1928). *Ankara Üniversitesi Türk İnkılap Tarihi Enstitüsü Atatürk Yolu Dergisi, 2*(7). Retrieved from http://de rgiler.ankara.edu.tr/dergiler/45/784/10087.pdf.

Kim, Y.-S., Wagner, R. K. & Lopez, D. (2012). Developmental relations between reading fluency and reading comprehension: A longitudinal study from Grade 1 to Grade 2. *Journal of Experimental Child Psychology, 113*, 93–111.

Kornfilt, J. (1990). Turkish and the Turkic languages. In B. Comrie (Ed.), *The world's major languages* (pp. 619–644). New York: Oxford University Press.

Lepola, J., Lynch, J., Laakkonen, E., Silvén, M. & Niemi, P. (2012). The role of inference making and other language skills in the development of narrative listening comprehension in 4–6-year-old children. *Reading Research Quarterly, 47*, 259–282.

Mancilla-Martinez, J. & Lesaux, N. K. (2011). The gap between Spanish speakers' word reading and word knowledge: A longitudinal study. *Child Development, 82*, 1544–1560.

Oflazer, K., Say, B., Hakkani-Tür, D. Z. & Tür, G. (2003). Building a Turkish treebank. In A. Abeillé (Ed.), *Treebanks: Building and using parsed corpora, 20*, 261–227. DOI:10.1007/978-94-010-0201-1_15.

Öney, B. & Durgunoğlu, A. Y. (1997). Beginning to read in Turkish: A phonologically transparent orthography. *Applied Psycholinguistics, 18*, 1–15.

Perfetti, C. (2007). Reading ability: Lexical quality to comprehension. *Scientific Studies of Reading, 11*, 357–383.

Potocki, A., Ecalle, J. & Magnan, A. (2013). Narrative comprehension skills in 5-year-old children: Correlational analysis and comprehender profiles. *The Journal of Educational Research, 106*, 14–26.

Proctor, C. P., Carlo, M., August, D. & Snow, C. (2005). Native Spanish-speaking children reading in English: Toward a model of comprehension. *Journal of Educational Psychology, 97*, 246–256.

Raman, I. & Baluch, B. (2001). Semantic effects as a function of reading skill in word naming of a transparent orthography. *Reading and Writing, 14*, 599–614.

Slobin, D. I. & Bever, T. G. (1982). Children use canonical sentence schemas: A crosslinguistic study of word order and inflections. *Cognition, 12,* 229–265.

van der Hulst, H. & van de Weijer, J. (1991). Topics in Turkish phonology. In H. Boeschoten & L. Verhoeven (Eds.), *Turkish linguistics today* (pp. 11–59). Leiden: E. J. Brill.

Verhoeven, L. (1991). Acquisition of Turkish in mono- and bilingual settings. In H. Boeschoten & L. Verhoeven (Eds.), *Turkish linguistics today* (pp. 113–149). Leiden: E. J. Brill.

Verhoeven, L. & van Leeuwe, J. (2008). Prediction of the development of reading comprehension: A longitudinal study. *Applied Cognitive Psychology, 22,* 407–423.

Ural, A. E., Yuret, D., Ketrez, F. N., Koçbaş, D. & Küntay, A. C. (2009). Morphological cues vs. number of nominals in learning verb types in Turkish: The syntactic bootstrapping mechanism revisited. *Language and Cognitive Processes, 24,* 1393–1405.

Yavuz, H. & Balcı, A. (2011). Turkish phonology and morphology. *T.C. Anadolu Üniversitesi yayını* (No. 2290). Retrieved from http://eogrenme.anadolu.edu.tr/e Kitap/TUR401U.pdf.

19 Epilogue: Universals and Particulars in Learning to Read across Seventeen Orthographies

Charles Perfetti and Ludo Verhoeven

In our introductory chapter, we set the stage for the cross-linguistic study of learning to read by defining potential universals and operating principles on the part of the learner. The subsequent chapters provided close-up reviews of seventeen languages, their writing systems, and the research outcomes concerned with learning to read in those languages. This final chapter discusses the universals and particulars in learning to read as evidenced by the languages under consideration and then addresses the implications of these universals and particulars for education.

19.1 Writing Systems and Languages

First, let's consider the range of languages and writing systems. The chapters do not represent many Asian and sub-Saharan African languages. Our single example of a South Asian alphasyllabary does not do justice to the number of people around the world who speak a language written in an alphasyllabary. In contrast, we have a large representation of European languages, which may be judged as over-representation because the European languages and writing systems are so similar. It is nevertheless possible that the set of seventeen languages reviewed here shows ample research to have been done to allow some generalizations about learning to read across languages and writing systems.

We think the sample of languages provides a reasonable window on the variety of languages and writing systems for which there is research on learning how to read. We are far from the era of drawing conclusions based exclusively on English – an "outlier orthography" as Share (2008) has reminded us. Research in recent years on Chinese and Japanese reading development has helped fill in the picture across writing systems. Alphasyllabaries, which are used by so many readers, have not been studied enough to allow clear-cut conclusions, but even for them some interesting observations are made.

In the light of so many alphabetic orthographies, one may wonder why pure syllabaries are so rare. Furthermore, the one language that would appear to be particularly well suited for using a syllabary has borrowed a logographic system that provides less consistent mappings. Very few pure syllabaries are still in use (Cree is one), which raises the question of whether it was even possible to have "sampled" syllabaries. This is emphatically true for what we opted to call morphosyllabic systems (and others call "logographic" systems). Chinese is in a class by itself, developed in antiquity and modified over time from pictographic to more abstract and partially componential. In principle, the design space for writing systems allows more examples than are currently active in the world.

Seeing functioning systems *blend* principles of the classic three systems reminds us that writing systems, aside from invented systems (like Korean) and purposeful adoptions of alternative writing systems (alphabetic Turkish), develop through actual use with their forms responding to both underlying information-processing principles and a variety of other pressures. Indeed, the variety of writing systems and mix of mappings possibilities reflect the universal aspects of both language and writing. Thus, the differences between abjads (called vowel-less alphabets by some) and true alphabets remind us of the special status of consonants as the fundamental articulatory units of speech and, correspondingly, units of writing. Similarly, alphasyllabaries reflect this same fact, with vowels used only to modulate consonant graphs. Both abjads and alphasyllabaries reflect a compromise between syllabic and phonemic writing.

Korean is a special case that has combined alphabetic and syllabic writing into its Hangul system. Rather than compromise between the two systems, however, Hangul has managed to incorporate an advantage from each system without sacrificing the value of the other. Hangul joins the other writing systems in demonstrating that two levels of linguistic structure, which generally compete for mapping honors, can be simultaneously mapped onto a single grapheme string. The morpheme level, so salient in the morphosyllabary of Chinese, is also competing for this honor. Indeed, the meaning level of language appears to have been the most accessible and, accordingly, the first-discovered means of communicating via writing – in both China and Mesopotamia. The low productivity of morphemes and word-level meanings nevertheless limits this system and helps explain why only Chinese has survived with this mapping principle. The abjad, in contrast, preserves morpheme meaning inside a consonant alphabet system and is thus very productive.

These observations suggest that the development and subsequent preservation of writing systems and orthographies are shaped by multiple factors as opposed to an inexorable evolution toward maximum productivity or phonemic transparency. Very few systems have remained unchanged over thousands of years. Moreoever, most systems show mixes of authoritative writing dictates and uncontrolled language changes affecting their development. A plausible claim is nevertheless that writing adapts to language rather than being the result of dictates of convention. That is, the idea that "languages get the writing systems they deserve" appears to have some merit. Frost (2012) has provided a forceful argument for this idea, while showing why a Hebrew letter order must be preserved in word reading, whether or not that is necessary in reading alphabetic languages. The argument that writing systems are adapted to specific features of language was made by Halliday (1977) and Seidenberg (2011), with the key idea being that writing systems make the trade-off between morphology and phonology in response to relevant properties of the language. Perfetti and Harris (2013) provide examples of how specific language factors (phoneme inventory, syllable inventory, morphological complexity) might have influenced writing in a sample of languages across the range of the world's writing systems.

Claims are sometimes made that a certain language would benefit from having a different writing system or orthography – for example, that English could (or should) abandon its complex spellings in favor of more "phonetic" spellings; or that Japanese should abandon its borrowed Chinese system and Kanji characters in favor of its phonologically transparent syllabaries; indeed, abandoning Chinese writing has been suggested even for the Chinese. In each case, there are answers that suggest the writing system has been adaptive in other ways, despite its apparent complexities. Keeping in mind that writing systems are at least partially adaptive for the languages that use them, we are less inclined to ask whether a different system might be better. Instead, we ask how reading works for a given writing system for the language that it encodes. And we think that the chapters in this book provide promising answers.

19.2   Reading Development across Languages and Orthographies

19.2.1   Universals in Reading

In our introductory chapter, we suggested three underlying universals of word reading. Two of the claims are mainly logical and definitional, namely that reading depends upon learning (i) how one's writing system encodes one's language and (ii) how word reading and spelling call upon phonology and morphology. The force of these universals is that writing communicates meanings through language rather than independently, which means levels of language that map onto meaning; hence, phonology and morphology. We regard these universals as noncontroversial for modern writing, provided we allow the knowledge relevant for the first to be implicit rather than explicit and the second to not imply a specific privilege for one or the other set of language units. An important aspect of the second universal is just how a writing system manages the trade-off between phonology and morphology, which depends on the properties of the language and the degree of preservation of its orthography in the face of language change.

The third claim is strictly empirical, namely that familiarity shifts word reading from computational to retrieval. Taken together, the universals generally imply that learning to read requires sensitivity to the specific mapping of linguistic forms onto meaning. Awareness of both phonology and morphology is thus needed to learn how one's writing system encodes one's language. And the writing system and its specific orthography (which are themselves influenced by language factors) influence the relative priority of morphology and phonology for reading and learning to read.

The role of visual encoding of orthographic forms needs to be emphasized. This aspect is often ignored when attention is concentrated on linear alphabetic writing with a small number of graphs. Even for such writing systems, however, building an orthographic lexicon requires establishing memory representations for graphemes that can take a variety of graphic forms. The orthographic demands of Chinese and also of alphasyllabaries draw attention to this important factor. A study by Chang (2015) of over 100 written languages highlights the range of grapheme inventories, their correlated grapheme complexity, and the challenges of this complexity for visual encoding.

Finally, we suggested in Chapter 1 that reading comprehension also has some universal properties and the two we proposed also have some evidence from cross-linguistic comparisons. Across languages, knowledge of word meanings and the ability to retrieve this knowledge from written words are critical for reading comprehension (Universal 4). In addition, cross-linguistic evidence supports the assumption that reading comprehension is a function of word identification and language comprehension (Universal 5). In this so-called simple view of reading, moreover, vocabulary has mostly been assessed as a component of language comprehension, again stressing the importance of lexical quality in reading comprehension (cf. Verhoeven & van Leeuwe, 2008).

19.2.2   Operating Principles in Learning to Read

Appended to this chapter is a table that presents a picture of relevant information across the seventeen languages, as presented in the preceding chapters.[1] Some of the information is systematic (e.g., phoneme inventory, syllable

---

[1] PhD students in a seminar taught by Charles Perfetti in 2015 made input into a similar table as part of the seminar. They included Regina Calloway, Frank Dolce, Xiaoping Fang, Rundi Guo, Rebecca Hays, Michelle Holcomb, Jaihui Huang, Echo Ke, Kelsey Mandak, Caitlin Rice, Zhaohong Wu. Some of their contributions are reflected in the table.

structure, and selected morphological features are identified for each language) and some is selective and incomplete, particularly on word reading development. In its conclusions concerning predictors of learning to read and the development of word reading, the appendix table reflects some of the operating principles (OPs) proposed in the introductory chapter of this volume. The idea is to suggest some high-level generalizations that we think can be drawn on the basis of selected empirical results. The generalizations ignore some of complexities that are brought out in the chapters and could be subject to disagreement.

Below we identify generalizations related to the OPs for developing linguistic awareness, word identification, and reading comprehension.

19.2.2.1 Becoming Linguistically Aware

i. Linguistic awareness at multiple levels supports learning to read (OP1).
Across languages and writing systems, both phonological awareness and morphological awareness were found to be predictive of early reading. What we do not know is the extent to which these two levels of linguistic knowledge make independent as opposed to joint contributions to the process of learning to read. Some languages, however, have relevant studies on this question.

ii. Syllable awareness universally emerges earlier than phoneme awareness and is predictive of early reading (OP2).
That awareness of syllables emerges earlier than awareness of phonemes is an obvious generalization, given the acoustic salience of syllables relative to phonemes, irrespective of language. It is interesting that this turns out to be true across languages that have very different syllable structures. The predictive power of syllable-level awareness across different writing systems and languages – including alphabets, which do not encode syllables – highlights the general importance of sensitivity to the sound structure of a language for learning to read.

iii. Phonemic awareness in alphabetic reading is uniformly important and does not depend on orthographic transparency (OP2).
Early reading in even the most transparent of orthographies (e.g., Czech, Spanish) is associated with phonemic awareness. It is not the case, then, that phonemic awareness is important for only English and other phonologically opaque alphabetic orthographies.

iv Evidence in alphabetic languages for the late emergence of an association between phonemic awareness and literacy suggests that phonemic awareness and learning to read alphabetically can develop reciprocally (OP3).
Some languages show direct evidence for this bidirectional relationship. This means that phonemic awareness should be taken not as a prerequisite for alphabetic reading but as an enabler.

v. Phoneme-level awareness is not a uniformly important factor in reading syllabaries and morpho-syllabaries (OP3).

Associations between phoneme-level awareness and reading are sometimes found to be related to reading in Chinese and in Japanese Kana. These associations, however, either occur late, and thus well into literacy (Japanese), or show marked variation depending on instructional practices (alphabetic reading instruction prior to character learning), spoken language factors, and specific script factors (Chinese). There is thus some convergence between the most important phonological level for reading and what the writing system requires for mapping.

vi. Morphological knowledge is variably associated with reading across languages and writing systems.

We should expect, given the assumption that writing systems manage trade-offs between exposing morphology or phonology, that reading morphosyllabic Chinese is related to morphological knowledge. Also, despite its embedding its root morphology in distributed letters, the abjad system of Arabic and Hebrew might be expected to benefit from morphological knowledge. However, even the most transparent alphabetic orthographies (Finnish, Korean) show a morphological effect in learning to read.

19.2.2.2 Development of Word Identification

i. Orthographic knowledge is foundational for reading (OP4).

The importance of orthographic knowledge, sometimes neglected for alphabetic writing, spans from initial learning to later automatized word identification. The more graphs an orthography has, the more demanding orthographic learning will be. The massive grapheme inventory of Chinese makes it an orthographic outlier and means that the learning of Chinese characters continues for years. The orthographic demands are also high for alphasyllabaries, whose graphic forms can take several years to fully master.

ii. For alphabetic literacy, spelling develops slower than reading and heavily relies on morphological knowledge (OP4).

That spelling lags behind reading is trivially true insofar as children and adults read more than they write. The larger point, however, is that reading itself does not assure that readers acquire the word-specific orthographic knowledge needed to spell in writing systems with imperfect phoneme–grapheme correspondences. Orthographies that are fully consistent in the phoneme–grapheme direction, which are rare, may not show this gap. Thus, Finnish spelling develops with Finnish reading; however, Italian, which is nearly consistent in both directions, may show some lag. French and English both have very low phoneme–grapheme correspondences and thus require the acquisition of considerable morphological knowledge in order to learn to spell.

iii. The development of word identification benefits from phonological transparency (OP5).

Although there is little new about this generalization, it is interesting to note the extent to which learning to read gets a quick start when the orthography consistently maps to its phonology. Within alphabetic orthographies, Finnish, Turkish Czech/Slovak, Greek, Spanish, Italian, Russian, and German all show rapid learning. English and French seem to be slower. And Japanese children quickly learn the Japanese syllabary, demonstrating that transparency at both syllable and phoneme levels supports learning.

iv. The role of morphology in word identification depends on the morphology of the language and the phonological transparency of the orthography (OP7).

Thus, despite its phonological transparency, Finnish reading is associated with morphology because of the rich agglutinative morphology that creates long multimorpheme words. Reading in French and English is associated with morphology because the orthographies of these languages fail to provide consistent phonological mapping.

v. Word identification shifts from computation to memory-based retrieval for words when they become familiar (OP6).

This is an empirical conclusion about the development of word reading with evidence from the present chapters that is mainly suggestive rather than direct. Generally speaking, reading speed becomes the distinguishing marker of skill once children have reached a threshold level of high accuracy for word identification and decoding. This fact does not distinguish the use of sublexical decoding procedures from lexically based retrieval procedures, however. Sublexical procedures may always be involved in word decoding even with increased word familiarity. However, the widespread frequency effect observed for word reading, quite aside from its interaction with orthographic regularity in English and other languages, is evidence that readers retrieve word-related information (pronunciation, meaning) more quickly as word forms become more familiar. Frequency effects once were believed to be absent in transparent orthographies because sublexical processes were sufficient. More recent evidence shows that although word frequency effects can vary with orthography, they are not entirely absent for any orthography. Consistent with these familiarity effects is the negative effect of vowel markings on the development of Hebrew reading as the vowel-less forms become the more familiar, standard-like form. Whether developing readers use sublexical letter strings or whole-word retrieval cues, they increasingly use a rapid "look-up" procedure rather than a computational procedure no matter what the language or writing system.

19.2.2.3 Development of Reading Comprehension

i. Reading comprehension depends on language comprehension, word identification, and vocabulary in all languages (OP8).

We might assume that the contribution of orthography is exhausted at the level of word reading and spelling. From the word identification point on, domain-general and language-specific factors should control comprehension of what is read. This is approximately correct, but the weighting of these factors might be affected by the orthography. When a transparent orthography reduces the variance in word reading so that accuracy is easily attained, reading comprehension becomes more dependent on spoken language comprehension. Thus, just as writing systems manage trade-offs between morphology and phonology, related downstream trade-off effects appear in comprehension.

ii. The importance of vocabulary for reading comprehension was reported for every language in which this was studied.

It might be convenient to subsume vocabulary under spoken language comprehension and thereby have a two-factor (as opposed to three-factor model) of reading comprehension. However, this would fail to capture the fact that vocabulary knowledge directly supports word identification in orthographies that have less phonological transparency and the general role that morphemes play in written word identification. A model that allows a more direct influence of knowledge of word meanings on reading comprehension may prove to be more correct across languages.

iii. Reading comprehension requires the reader to encode a linguistic representation of the text (OP9) and to link this representation to other knowledge to generate a more specified mental model (OP10).

Although research relevant for this generalization was not directly addressed in most of the chapters, its accuracy across languages rests on the logic of comprehension and the demonstration that language is not fully explicit in specifying referential information.

19.3   Educational Implications

Studies of learning to read across our sample of languages and writing systems have made it clear that the attainment of literacy can be stimulated and extended by offering children a learning environment of positive literacy experiences. Primary among these experiences is targeted instruction in basic decoding as a means to written word identification. Beyond this generalization are some implications concerning the components of literacy that are the basis of the operating principles we suggested.

19.3.1 Stimulating Linguistic Awareness

In preschool and kindergarten, providing opportunities for children to attend to the formal aspects of language can promote awareness of the language structures that later become important for reading. This includes multiple levels of phonology (syllable structures and phonemes) and morphology, both inflectional and derivational. Although specific strategies for promoting awareness may depend to some extent on the particular language and the writing system, enhancing phonological awareness has value universally as attested in Chinese (Ho & Bryant, 1997) as well as in languages with alphabetic writing (Mol, Bus, de Jong & Smeets, 2008). Morphological awareness can be taught effectively in both alphabetic languages (Bowers, Kirby & Deacon, 2010) and morphosyllabic languages (Nagy & Anderson, 1998).

Beyond linguistic awareness is the early stimulation of orthographic knowledge. In alphabetic writing, knowledge of letters (along with phonemic awareness and rapid naming) is among the core indicators of learning to read (Hulme & Snowling, 2013). The importance of orthographic knowledge increases for writing systems whose graphic inventories make greater demands. Visual skills relevant for reading are important in Chinese, for example, and some form of early support for orthographically relevant visual skills may be useful. Many of the reading-relevant skills can be fostered with the use of storybook reading and interactive reading/language games in education (see Scarborough, 2005).

19.3.2 Instructing Word Identification

Preschool linguistic awareness and exposure to written language are very important but do not replace the crucial role of targeted instruction in reading. Basic reading instruction supports learning the language's written code and sets the foundation for further literacy development. The continued development of word identification toward fluency or automaticity and the fluent integration of word meanings with text meanings build on this word decoding foundation.

Although there are various instructional strategies that can produce this foundational learning, the most successful strategies typically include sequentially structured activities directed by a teacher. For transparent alphabetic orthographies, this instruction can begin with the straightforward teaching of letter–phoneme correspondences. For less transparent alphabetic orthographies, the same general strategy applies, but with more attention to sequencing and how to teach irregular patterns. A variety of systematic programs centered on letter–phoneme correspondences is available (see Ehri, Nunes, Stahl & Willows, 2001). Such systematic phonics approaches have been shown to achieve the best results for the development of letter knowledge, word decoding, and word spelling (de Graaff, Bosman, Hasselman & Verhoeven, 2009).

The general value of direct instruction of orthographic-phonological mappings extends to other systems, abjads, alphasyllabaries, and syllabaries. Even learning Chinese can benefit from an initial phase of teaching alphabetic reading, as is done in the mainland and Taiwan prior to a transition to characters. Such a strategy not only allows initial success in reading but also emphasizes for children that the visual forms they see stand for language units, words, or syllables in their language. For learning to read characters, it is possible to organize instruction to take advantage of the compositional structure of most characters by teaching the function of these components and by sequencing characters that share phonology-cueing phonetics and meaning-cueing semantic radicals (McBride & Wang, 2015; McBride-Chan et al., 2008). We emphasize also that writing systems with large grapheme inventories and the attendant complexity of graphic form combinations can benefit from writing or even copying graphic forms.

19.3.3   Fostering Reading Comprehension

Although reading comprehension can be erected onto the scaffold of listening comprehension without special instruction, many children seem not to do this spontaneously. A wide variety of instructional programs for reading comprehensions has been tested in English language research with mixed results but also positive recommendations for certain interventions (National Reading Panel, 2000). The core comprehension events triggered by word reading and text memory – word-to-text integration – are likely strengthened by successful reading practice and the increased fluency of word identification. The use of incremental book series can lead to more proficient reading comprehension across languages and writing systems (McBride-Chang, 2004). In general, beyond reading practice, activities that drive deeper engagement with tests are to be recommended. Such engagement should lead the reader to use relevant knowledge and thus construct richer mental models of the text.

19.4   Final Conclusion

Like all generalizations that aim to apply over wide variation, the universals we have suggested are, indeed, highly general. Claims for empirical universals in reading do not imply that there are no specific influences of writing system, orthography, and language. Indeed, such influences are significant, and it is important to understand the particular ways that language and writing affect reading, even when they may seem minor in comparison with reading's broad universal principles.

Reading engages a reading network in the brain that increasingly shows universal properties, including high overlap with brain areas that support spoken language (Rueckl et al., 2015). This convergence of speech and reading areas in the brain across unrelated languages reflects the broad universal principles that writing encodes language and that reading engages phonology. Nevertheless, there appear to be variations in parts of the network that reflect writing system factors (e.g., Perfetti, Cao & Booth, 2013). There is no doubt that writing and language factors accompany learning to read. The incremental learning of many Chinese characters over extended years contrasts with the rapid learning of a small set of alphabetic letters that allows most words written in a transparent alphabet to be read within a few weeks of literacy instruction. On the other hand, the effect of reading experience (practice) is to allow reading in both systems to become increasingly fluent, based on retrieval of word identities from orthographic input.

The story of learning to read thus is one of universals and particulars: Universals, because writing maps onto language, no matter the details of the system; particulars, because it does matter how different levels of language – morphemes, syllables, phonemes – are engaged. And this in turn depends on the structure of the language and how its written form accommodates this structure.

The seventeen languages studied here provide examples of both the universals and the particulars in learning to read. How the study of more languages would add to the particulars (or challenge the universals) remains to be seen.

References

Bowers, P. N., Kirby, J. R. & Deacon, S. H. (2010). The effects of morphological instruction on literacy skills: A systematic review of the literature. *Review of Educational Research, 80*, 144–179.

Chang, L. (2015). Visual orthographic variation and learning to read across writing systems. Doctoral dissertation, University of Pittsburgh.

De Graaff, S., Bosman, A., Hasselman, F. & Verhoeven, L. (2009). Benefits of systematic phonics instruction. *Scientific Studies of Reading, 13*(4), 318–333.

Ehri, L. C., Nunes, S. R., Stahl, S. A. & Willows, D. M. (2001). Systematic phonics instruction helps students learn to read: Evidence from the National Reading Panels meta-analysis. *Review of Educational Research, 71*, 393–447.

Frost, R. (2012). Towards a universal model of reading. *Behavioral and Brain Sciences, 35*(5), 263–279.

Halliday, M. A. K. (1977). Ideas about language. *Aims and perspectives in linguistics: Occasional Papers 1* (pp. 32–55). Applied Linguistics Association of Australia.

Ho, C. S.-H. & Bryant, P. (1997). Learning to read Chinese beyond the logographic phase. *Reading Research Quarterly, 32*(3), 276–289.

McBride, C. & Wang, Y. (2015). Learning to read Chinese: Universal and unique cognitive cores. *Child Developmental Perspectives, 9*(3), 196–200.

McBride-Chang, C. (2004). *Children's literacy development*. London: Routledge.

McBride-Chang, C., Tong, X., Shu, H., Wong, A. M.-Y., Leung, K.-W. & Tardif, T. (2008). Syllable, phoneme, and tone: Psycholinguistic units in early Chinese and English word reading. *Scientific Studies of Reading, 12*, 171–194.

Mol, S. E., Bus, A. G., de Jong, M. T. & Smeets, D. J. H. (2008). Added value of dialogic parent–child book readings: A meta-analysis. *Early Education & Development, 19*, 7–26.

Nagy, W. & Anderson, R. C. (1998). Metalinguistic awareness and literacy acquisition in different languages. In D. Wagner, R. Venezky & B. Street (Eds.), *Literacy: An international handbook* (pp. 155–160). New York: Garland.

National Reading Panel (2000). *Teaching children to read: An evidence-based assessment of the scientific research literature on reading and its implications for reading instruction*. Washington, DC: The National Institute of Child Health and Human Development.

Perfetti, C. A. & Harris, L. N. (2013). Universal reading processes are modulated by language and writing system. *Language Learning and Development, 9*(4), 296–316.

Perfetti, C. A., Cao, F. & Booth J. (2013). Specialization and universals in the development of reading skill: How Chinese research informs a universal science of reading. *Scientific Studies of Reading, 17*(1), 5–21.

Rueckl, J. R., Paz-Alonso, P. M., Molfese, P. J., Kuo, W.-J., Bick, A., Frost, S. J., Hancock, R., Wu, D. H., Mencl, W. E., Duñabeitia, J. A., et al. (2015). Universal brain signature of proficient reading: Evidence from four contrasting languages. *Proceedings of the National Academy of Sciences of the United States of America*, 15 December 2015, *112*(50), 15510–15515.

Scarborough, H. S. (2005). Developmental relationships between language and reading: Reconciling a beautiful hypothesis with some ugly facts. In H. W. Catts & A. G. Kamhi (Eds.), *The connections between language and reading disabilities* (pp. 3–24). Mahwah, NJ: Lawrence Erlbaum.

Seidenberg, M. S. (2011). Reading in different writing systems: One architecture, multiple solutions. In P. McCardle, J. Ren, O. Tzeng & B. Miller (Eds.), *Dyslexia across languages: Orthography and the brain-gene-behavior link* (pp. 146–168). Baltimore, MD: Brookes.

Share, D. (2008). On the Anglocentricities of current reading research and practice: The perils of overreliance on an "outlier" orthography. *Psychological Bulletin, 134*, 584–615.

Verhoeven, L. & van Leeuwe, J. (2008). Prediction of the development of reading comprehension: A longitudinal study. *Applied Cognitive Psychology, 22*, 407–423.

Yin, L. & McBride, C. (2015). Chinese kindergartners learn to read characters analytically. *Psychological Science, 26*(4), 424–432.

Appendix

Comparisons of phonology and morphology, writing system and orthography, predictors of learning to read and word reading development in seventeen languages

Language	Phonology and morphology	Writing system and orthography	Predictors of learning to read	Reading development
Chinese (Mandarin) 普通話	Sino-Tibetan Several distinct languages. Mandarin has the most speakers and is the official language of China and Taiwan. Mandarin is a tonal language with 4 tones in addition to 21 initial consonants, 3 glides, and 6 vowels. Simple open syllable structure; CV, CVC, V, and VC with addition of glides in some syllables; highly constrained syllable offsets; no consonants except nasals. Both multisyllabic and monosyllabic words. Sparse inflectional morphology; substantial derivational morphology through compounding.	Morphosyllabic (also called logographic and morphemic). Large number of characters (over 6,000), each corresponding to a Chinese one-syllable morpheme. 80%–90% of characters are compounds of two components, a semantic radical and a phonetic. These are helpful as cues to meaning and pronunciation, but of modest reliability. Relatively few characters retain clear pictographic properties Characters are separated by fixed space without writing cues to word boundaries.	Syllable-level phonological awareness develops readily and predicts reading; role of phonemic awareness, which develops slowly, is less clear. Visual and orthographic skills are important given the demands of the writing system. Morphological awareness at multiple levels, especially compounding, also predicts learning to read.	Visual skills and morphological knowledge important in learning to read characters. Differences between Cantonese (Hong Kong) and Mandarin (mainland) areas probably due to use of pinyin but also script and language differences. Even within Hong Kong, results not consistent on role of phonological awareness; morphological awareness consistently found to be important. Longitudinally, morphological awareness and orthographic knowledge predict character recognition; phonological awareness for word spelling; and rapid naming for all outcomes with all other variables controlled for.

Two different scripts. Simplified used in mainland China; traditional used in Taiwan, Hong Kong, and Macau. Alphabetic systems used for beginning reading instruction on mainland (Pinyin) and in Taiwan (Zhuyin).

Language				
Japanese 日本語	Japonic	Two main writing systems: (1) the Kana syllabaries (Hiragana and Katakana); (2) Kanji, Chinese characters but not really morphosyllabic. The Kanji can have a Chinese reading (*On*), providing a single syllable and a Japanese	Kana and Kanji reading require distinct subskills. Kana reading: sensitivity to mora boundaries. Kanji reading: vocabulary knowledge and visual skills.	Children learn Kana before moving to Kanji. Hiragana mastered in Grade 1; Katakana in Grade 3; Kanji learning proceeds incrementally from Grades 2–6, by which time 1,000 characters are learned. Kanji learning different for On and Kun readings; children acquire Kun readings more readily because they map onto
	Modest phoneme inventory (19) includes 5 simple vowels. Number of short vowel syllables (mora) also small (around 110). A long vowel is two mora. CV structure dominates and only the			

(cont.)

Language	Phonology and morphology	Writing system and orthography	Predictors of learning to read	Reading development
	nasal *n* can close a syllable. Rich inflectional morphology in verb and adjective systems; productive compounding in nouns.	reading (*Kun*), providing a Japanese word. Alternative systems get used together in most writing: Kanji for the roots of content words; the two Kana syllabaries for grammatical information (Hiragana) and transcription of borrowed and foreign words (Katakana).		multisyllabic whole words; On readings yield single syllables that join with other characters in a multisyllabic word. Vocabulary in early grades shows strong relation to Kanji learning in Grade 6. Phonological memory and analysis then become powerful predictors of Kanji learning.
Korean 한국어/조선말	Koreanic Modest phoneme inventory (14 consonants, 10 vowels); no voicing contrast. Syllables have body-coda structure (not onset-rime) with single consonant onsets (CV, CVC, CVCC); a few vowel-only syllables; nuclei of one or two vowels.	Hangul alphabet of 24 letters invented for one-to-one mapping. Letters designed to suggest articulation features. Letters arranged in syllable blocks that begin with consonants, even for vowel-initial syllables. Vowels distinguished from consonants by their horizontal and vertical lines, which also	Phonological awareness associated with spelling and reading development. Visual abilities important; research needed on more specific orthographic awareness.	Orthographic skills are extremely important in literacy development. Spatial configuration poses unique processing demands. Morphological awareness important in reading because of rich inflectional system.

Kannada
ಕನ್ನಡ

A rich agglutinative morphology, both inflectional and derivational, including compounding.

Dravidian
Phoneme inventory around 30 (12 vowels, 18 consonants).
Syllable structure varies; open CV is most common. However, clusters of two and three consonants occur at both onsets and codas.
Rich inflectional morphology (suffixes). Compounding also common.

to determine their location in syllable space. Highly transparent; changes slightly reduced one-to-one mapping to preserve morphology.

Alphasyllabary
System widely used throughout South and Southeast Asia including Indo-European languages (e.g., Hindi).
Akshara are basic writing units, consisting of alphabet graphemes (12 vowels, 34 consonants) that are modified in form by syllabication: 34 consonant graphemes with inherent vowels; 34 x 11 consonants with full vowels. These 454 Akshara, with the addition of permissible consonant clusters.

Research so far is limited. However:
Literacy may have an unusually strong effect on linguistic knowledge because of the complex mappings between orthography and multiple level linguistic units.
Literacy seems to affect morphophonological and morphosyntactic knowledge as well as vice versa.
Phoneme awareness appears to develop slowly and be associated with increasing experience with writing.

Limited research suggests different profiles for reading development. Reading fluently, reading Akshara one at a time but with comprehension, and failing in Akshara decoding and in comprehension.
Writing Akshara requires resyllabification, which may increase awareness of syllable structure and boundaries.
Reading accuracy and phonological processing predict 44% of variance in comprehension; vocabulary predicts 5%.

Language	Phonology and morphology	Writing system and orthography	Predictors of learning to read	Reading development
Arabic اللغة العربية	West Semitic 34 phonemes; multisyllabic body/coda structure; single consonant onsets. Nonlinear morphology through consonantal root system with slots for vowel patterns; rich inflectional verb morphology. Diglossia issue: many local dialects.	Abjad Short vowels typically omitted; indicated by diacritics below consonants in other texts. Transparent grapheme–phoneme mapping. Cursive script; letter forms modified by position; written right to left.	Phonological awareness best predictor, especially for final consonant; stronger than rapid naming and morphological awareness. Phoneme awareness more predictive with increasing age. Syllable awareness develops early.	Poor decoding on pseudowords surprising from transparency perspective. Diglossia variations from standard Arabic are a challenge. Vowelized script important in early reading; may have negative effect with increasing skill. Relative importance of phonological decoding and morphological abilities may depend on specific language and instructional method. Sublexical processes and phonological awareness predict reading comprehension.
Hebrew עברית	West Semitic 27 consonants, 5 vowels. Multisyllabic; extensive consonant clusters. Morphology includes productive nonlinear consonant root system similar to Arabic. Highly synthetic with long multimorpheme strings.	Abjad 22 letters (5 change forms in word-final position). Transparent grapheme–phoneme mapping, but vowels usually not indicated; vowel letters and diacritics ("points") on consonants in children's and religious texts.	Phonological awareness including awareness of syllable bodies and consonants (especially final) predict early reading. Morphological awareness is powerful predictor across variations in text form (with vowels, without vowels) and reader age.	Early word reading proceeds rapidly, taking advantage of phonological transparency in the explicit vowels; vowel diacritics facilitate reading compared with vowel-less script over first two grades. With increasing reading skill, as in Arabic, reading appears to be negatively affected by vowel diacritics. Vowel-less writing comes to be preferred.

Language	Linguistic features	Orthography	Phonological development	Reading outcomes
		Squared letter shapes; unlike Arabic, never ligatured; written right to left.		Reading comprehension in first grade related to vocabulary and language (syntactic) abilities as well as phonological awareness and morphological awareness.
Greek ελληνικά Hellenic	5 vowels; consonant estimates vary from 15–31 because of disagreement about phonemic status of palatal and affricate allophones. Multisyllabic. Very few monosyllables; variable stress patterns. Extensive inflectional morphology, including case system; verbs have 48 forms. Highly productive compounding.	Greek Alphabet with 24 letters; diacritic marks used to separate successive vowels and distinguish syllables. Most vowels have more than one spelling, but reliable multi-letter strings nevertheless produce 85 graphemes with high (95%) grapheme–phoneme transparency. Stressed syllable carries vowel diacritic.	Phonological awareness develops during pre-school; syllable and phoneme awareness independently predict reading. Letter knowledge and phonological awareness predict early literacy; rapid naming predicts reading fluency in elementary grades. Alphabetic reading from beginning (no logographic stage).	Phonological recoding procedures in reading and spelling in first grade; spelling accuracy high in first grade. High correlations of reading comprehension and listening comprehension. Vocabulary strongest concurrent and longitudinal predictor of reading comprehension.
Italian italiano Romance		Latin alphabet of 21 letters.	Phonological awareness predicts reading in	Word reading rapidly acquired; 90% accuracy by end of Grade 1.

Language	Phonology and morphology	Writing system and orthography	Predictors of learning to read	Reading development
	23 consonants, 7 vowels; no long-short vowel contrast. Multisyllabic; modest number of syllables; open CV structure with a few complex onsets. Inflectional morphology; number and gender on nouns/adjectives. Phonological structure of stem morpheme unchanged in derivational morphology.	High transparency; nearly pure phonemic system.	bidirectional manner; formal instruction mediates the relationship. Letter knowledge, cognitive skills, conceptualization of written language also predict reading.	Reading speed continues to develop. Both sublexical and lexical knowledge is used. Sensitivity to morphological structure also develops quickly. Lexical and morpheme processes lead to fluency. Spelling accuracy high as a result of sublexical mapping.
French français	Romance More vowels (16) than other Romance languages, along with 3 semi-vowels and 20 consonants. Open (CV) syllable structure dominates followed by CVC. Inflectional morphology (gender, number on nouns; person, mood, aspect on verbs) typical of other Romance languages.	Latin alphabet of 26 letters and two ligatured digraphs supplemented by vowel diacritics. Multi-letter strings create 130 distinct graphemes. Phonological expression of certain letters depends on context. Pronunciation changes have resulted in less transparency, more redundancy (many graphemes with the same	Phonological awareness important, but relative effects of different levels unclear. Syllabic awareness high, phonemic awareness low relative to English. Morphological awareness is predictive over and beyond phonological awareness.	Rapid learning of single-letter grapheme mappings reflected in first regularity effects in first-grade reading and spelling, but prolonged learning for mastery of multi-letter grapheme mappings. Lexicality effect (words read better than pseudowords) emerges by end of Grade 1. Reading comprehension strongly associated with oral language comprehension in younger grades; word decoding more

		pronunciation), mute letters.		important by Grades 4 and 5. Receptive vocabulary among strongest predictors in Grade 3 and beyond.
Spanish español	Romance 5 simple vowels, 19 consonants. Open (CV) syllables most common, then CVC. Syllable-timed (cf. stress-timed) temporal structure. Inflectional morphology typical of Romance languages: number, gender for nouns; tense, aspect, person for verbs.	Latin alphabet of 27 letters; 5 digraphs; 2 diacritics. Transparent orthography with some departure from one-to-one mapping. Consonant letters participate in more than one grapheme. Three graphemes map to more than one phoneme.	Phonological awareness shows typical progression to phoneme level. Some studies find low levels of phoneme awareness. Although phonological awareness predicts reading, morphological knowledge may be an important driver of reading success.	Rapid mastery of word reading accuracy; gradual increase in speed. Syllable may function as a sublexical unit, perhaps reflecting the syllable-timed temporal structure of the language. Spelling skill higher than for other European languages. Both receptive and expressive vocabulary predict reading comprehension. So do inference making skill and working memory.
German Deutsch	Germanic 16 vowels, 3 dipthongs, 25 consonants.	Latin alphabet written in various scripts; 26 letters in modern alphabet. Also 3 umlaut vowels and the double S (Eszett).	Rapid naming predicts word reading and nonword decoding better than phonological awareness.	Word decoding mastered early; children can read words and nonwords at high levels in first grade.

(cont.)

Language	Phonology and morphology	Writing system and orthography	Predictors of learning to read	Reading development
	Varied syllable structure, simple and complex onsets and codas. Inflectional morphology includes cases as well as number and gender. Derivational morphology including productive compounding.	All letters also appear as uppercase in initial position in nouns. Relatively transparent orthography with morphology preserved; phoneme-to-grapheme, less so.	Training studies demonstrate phonological awareness is important for learning to read. Phonological awareness predicts spelling better than reading. Morphological development is rapid prior to schooling and important for reading and spelling.	Shift from decoding to lexical-level reading with increasing skill. With high levels of reading accuracy, speed deficits associated with reading problems. Spelling lags behind reading; can be improved with instruction on morphology. Vocabulary predicts reading comprehension better than decoding speed does.
Dutch Nederlands	Germanic Phonemic inventory of 35; 19 consonants and 16 vowels, including 3 diphthongs. Syllable structure primarily CVC, but consonant clusters at both onset and coda allow a maximal syllable of CCCVCCC. Inflectional morphology not as rich as German.	Latin alphabet with 27 letters. High degree of grapheme–phoneme consistency; nearly perfect for monosyllabic words but not polysyllabic words. Graphotactic rules complicate mapping consistency (e.g., changed letter sequences in plural noun formation).	Strong growth of phonological awareness between kindergarten and first grade. Phonological and morphological awareness are both predictive of early reading.	Rapid learning of decoding during second half of Grade 1. Subsequent development is in speed of decoding. Some decoding difficulty attributed to graphotactic rules. Spelling more difficult and is enhanced by direct instruction. Reading comprehension related more to oral language comprehension than decoding in first two grades.

English	Germanic Many dialects around the world. Phonemic inventory around 40, but vowels vary greatly with dialect; standard pronunciation recognizes 12 vowels and 8 diphthongs. Full range of syllable types across about 16,000 syllables; onset +rime structure. Relatively simple inflectional morphology; very productive derivational morphology.	Latin alphabet with 26 letters plus numerous digraphs. Longer multi-letter strings also form graphemes. An opaque orthography at phonological level; vowel graphemes (both single letter and diagraphs) especially are not mapped consistently onto phonemes. Morpheme identity sometimes preserved through spelling at expense of pronunciation.	As in all languages, syllable awareness precedes phoneme awareness. Phonological awareness, especially phonemic awareness, predicts early reading success. Training of phonemic awareness in combination with reading instruction produces reading gains.	Decoding less accurate in English than more transparent orthographies. Explicit instruction in decoding is helpful. Morphological knowledge can support reading and spelling. Despite low transparency, sublexical decoding procedures dominate in early word reading; with increasing skill, lexical procedures take over. Reading comprehension depends on spoken comprehension and word identification; vocabulary knowledge affects all three. Vocabulary growth and word form knowledge predict reading comprehension over time.
Czech, Slovak Čeština, slovenčina	Slavic Large phoneme inventory (40–43) includes 13–14	Latin alphabet of 26 letters with diacritics for 31 graphemes.	Awareness of consonants within onset clusters develops early (relative to Germanic languages).	Word reading develops rapidly in both languages, with parallel growth spurt in the second half of Grade 1.

Language	Phonology and morphology	Writing system and orthography	Predictors of learning to read	Reading development
	vowels, 10 of which are monophthongs. Multisyllabic words; 3 syllables most common. Open syllables dominate although onset clusters of 4 and coda clusters of 3 occur. Very rich inflectional morphology includes 7 case markers as well as gender and number for nouns and tense, mood, and aspect for verbs.	Orthography is very transparent; inconsistencies appear only in phoneme-to-spelling direction. Some spellings represent historical pronunciations that are no longer accurate. Spellings preserve underlying base morpheme when altered by phonological processes (e.g., voicing assimilation).	Letter knowledge, rapid naming and phonemic awareness in kindergarten each uniquely predict first-grade reading. Children show high level of morphological knowledge, but this does not predict reading development.	Growth rate exceeds that of children reading English. Spelling inconsistencies require longer learning period. Reading comprehension predicted by vocabulary, phonemic awareness, and reading speed, but not by nonverbal ability.
Russian Русский	Slavic Large consonant inventory (33) along with 5 vowel phonemes. Complex syllabic structure; many multi-consonant onsets; unusual phonotactics and sonority distributions. Very rich inflectional morphology with case marking that affects verb	Cyrillic alphabet of 33 letters (reduced from 44 in Old Cyrillic). A relatively transparent orthography with one-to-one mappings. Vowels occur in two versions (thus 10 graphemes) to control the soft vs. hard consonant phonemes. The spellings preserve morphemes; difficult to	Early preschool education emphasizes phonological skills, including phonemic awareness. Phonological awareness predicts word reading accuracy and rate.	For older children, phonological awareness predicts word reading accuracy; rapid naming predicts reading fluency. Morphological awareness associated with reading beyond contributions of phonological and orthographic knowledge. Reading skills precede spelling skills. By around Grade 4, children show good decoding skills; by around

Finnish suomi	agreement patterns as well as nouns. Uralic Phoneme inventory of 13 consonants, 8 vowels; 16 diphthongs. Multisyllabic; syllable nucleus of either 1 or 2 vowels; single consonant onsets with 1 or 2 consonant codas. Rich inflectional morphology with cases (but not gender). Derivational compounding is common. Combination of inflectional affixes and compounding creates long words; monomorphemic words are rare.	predict spellings from pronunciations. Swedish version of Latin alphabet with 29 letters. Strict grapheme–phoneme correspondence in both directions. Morphologically influenced phonological changes (Sandhi) are not reflected in spellings.	Phonological awareness, first at syllable level and by age 6 at phoneme level, is predictive of early reading. Morphological awareness of inflectional forms develops by age 3 and is predictive of reading. Letter knowledge in kindergarten also a strong predictor.	Grade 7, they have become skilled spellers. Literacy instruction begins at age 7; word identification is at asymptote after one year. Decoding skill develops readily from consistent mappings; sublexical procedures dominate. Reading speed continues to develop and problems with reading are related to speed more than accuracy. Spelling develops rapidly with reading. Reading comprehension highly correlates with listening comprehension, but prediction of reading comprehension in Grade 4 by kindergarten letter knowledge is better than by listening comprehension in Grade 4.

(cont.)

Language	Phonology and morphology	Writing system and orthography	Predictors of learning to read	Reading development
Turkish Türkçe	Turkic 8 vowels, 20 consonants. Salient syllables, open CV most common; CVC, VCC also occur. Rich inflectional morphological system through suffixes; phonological forms vary for each suffix.	Latin alphabet of 26 letters (replaced Arabic alphabet in 1928). Transparent orthography; one-to-one mappings.	Phonological awareness at syllable and final consonant levels develop rapidly because of salience of syllables. Morphological awareness also develops rapidly and is correlated with phonological awareness.	Complex morphology, multisyllabic words, and phonological variation in suffixes challenge learning to read. Nevertheless, word identification develops rapidly because of consistent grapheme–phoneme mappings. Decoding skill is at asymptote by end of Grade 1 – even for multisyllabic and multi-morphemic words. Because word reading is so readily attained, it does not predict comprehension, which is predicted by listening comprehension and vocabulary.

Index

Aarts, R., 439
Abdelhadi, S., 139
abjads, 2, 6, 23, 133, 156, 160, 163, 167, 173, 174, 175, 456, 464
Abu-Ahmad, H., 138, 143
abugida. *See* alphasyllabary
Abu-Rabia, S., 141
Acarlar, A., 445
African American Vernacular English, 350
Agricola, Mikael, 416
Aguado, G., 285
Ahonen, T., 424, 425
Aidinis, A., 191, 192, 197
akshara, 104–107, 110–122, 471
Aksu-Koç, A., 439, 446
Alegria, J., 221, 283
Alfonso X, King, 271
alphabetic writing, 5–7, 14–15, 16, 23, 100, 211, 364, 458, 460, 463
alphabets, 2, *See also* individual names of alphabets
alphasyllabary (abugida), 6, 16, 23, 105, 115, 156, 455–456, 458, 460, 464
Al-Rashidi, M., 143
Altaic language family, 82, 437
American English, 347, 350, 354
Anderson, R. C., 10, 42
Anglo-Saxon English, 348
Arabic, 2, 24, 437, 438
    challenges in learning to read, 145
    implications for reading instruction, 146–147
    inflectional morphology, 130
    letter connectedness, 135, 138, 139, 145, 146
    literacy and schooling, 128–129
    morphological development and awareness, 137
    morphological structure, 131, 472
    numerical system, 2
    orthographic processing, 139, 143
    orthography, 127, 132–135

phonological development and awareness, 136–137
phonology, 472
predictors of reading comprehension, 143
punctuation, 131–132
reading and spelling difficulties, 142–143
script, 131–132
spelling development, 141–142
synchronic and diachronic characterization, 128
word decoding development, 137–141, 472
word formation processes, 186
word level effects in comprehending text, 144
Arabic alphabet, 131–133, 139
Aramaic, 131, 158, 160
Aramaic alphabet, 131
Aro, M., 17, 360, 429, 430
Artelt, C., 316
articulation, place and manner of
    Dutch, 325, 331
    French, 245
    Korean, 83
assimilation of voicing. *See* voicing assimilation
Atatürk, Mustafa Kemal, 437
Aunola, K., 425, 426, 428, 429
Australian English, 347, 350
Austrian Standard German, 307
Aveledo, F., 280

Baayen, H., 333, 335
Baayen, R. H., 20
Babayiğit, S., 446–448, 449
Balbi, A., 285
Balcı, A., 442
Barbiero, C., 229
Bar-Kochva, I., 165, 171
Bar-On, A., 166, 168–169, 170
Barron-Linnankoski, S., 428
Basque, 270
Bear, D. R., 45